UNDERSTANDING MARRIAGE

This edited volume draws together a wide range of new and exciting developments in the study of marital interaction. A significant feature of the book is its focus, not only on conflict and negative interactions, but also on the processes by which couples maintain happy and constructive relationships. The chapters review and integrate the extensive literature in this area and present important new research findings. The contributors come from the disciplines of communication, social psychology, and clinical psychology and have national and international reputations for their work in this area. The findings reflect the latest developments in theory and methodology and have important implications for those working to strengthen and repair marital relationships.

Patricia Noller is Professor of Psychology at the University of Queensland. She has published twelve books and more than eighty journal articles and book chapters.

Judith A. Feeney is Senior Lecturer in Psychology at the University of Queensland. She has published three books and more than fifty journal articles and book chapters.

ADVANCES IN PERSONAL RELATIONSHIPS

HARRY T. REIS
University of Rochester

MARY ANNE FITZPATRICK
University of Wisconsin-Madison

ANITA L. VANGELISTI
University of Texas, Austin

Although scholars from a variety of disciplines have written and conversed about the importance of personal relationships for decades, the emergence of personal relationships as a field of study is relatively recent. *Advances in Personal Relationships* represents the culmination of years of multidisciplinary and interdisciplinary work on personal relationships. Sponsored by the International Society for the Study of Personal Relationships (ISSPR), the series offers readers cutting-edge research and theory in the field. Contributing authors are internationally known scholars from a variety of disciplines, including social psychology, clinical psychology, communication, history, sociology, gerontology, and family studies. Volumes include integrative reviews, conceptual pieces, summaries of research programs, and major theoretical works. *Advances in Personal Relationships* presents first-rate scholarship that is both provocative and theoretically grounded. The theoretical and empirical work described by authors will stimulate readers and advance the field by offering up new ideas and retooling old ones. The series will be of interest to upper division undergraduate students, graduate students, researchers, and practitioners.

OTHER BOOKS IN THE SERIES

Attribution, Communication Behavior, and Close Relationships
Valerie Manusov and John H. Harvey
Stability and Change in Relationships
Anita L. Vangelisti, Harry T. Reis, and Mary Anne Fitzpatrick
Personal Relationships Across the Lifespan (forthcoming)
Frieder Lang and Karen Fingerman

Understanding Marriage

*Developments in the Study of
Couple Interaction*

Edited by

PATRICIA NOLLER
University of Queensland

JUDITH A. FEENEY
University of Queensland

CAMBRIDGE
UNIVERSITY PRESS

PUBLISHED BY THE PRESS SYNDICATE OF THE UNIVERSITY OF CAMBRIDGE
The Pitt Building, Trumpington Street, Cambridge, United Kingdom

CAMBRIDGE UNIVERSITY PRESS
The Edinburgh Building, Cambridge CB2 2RU, UK
40 West 20th Street, New York, NY 10011-4211, USA
477 Williamstown Road, Port Melbourne, VIC 3207, Australia
Ruiz de Alarcón 13, 28014 Madrid, Spain
Dock House, The Waterfront, Cape Town 8001, South Africa

http://www.cambridge.org

First published 2002

Printed in the United Kingdom at the University Press, Cambridge

Typeface Palatino 10/13 pt.   *System* LATEX 2$_\varepsilon$ [TB]

A catalog record for this book is available from the British Library.

Library of Congress Cataloging in Publication Data

Understanding marriage : developments in the study of couple interaction / edited by
Patricia Noller, Judith A. Feeney.
    p.   cm. – (Advances in personal relationships)
Includes bibliographical references and index.
ISBN 0-521-80370-5
1. Marriage.   2. Interpersonal relations.   3. Marital conflict.   4. Married people –
Psychology.   5. Couples – Psychology.   I. Noller, Patricia.   II. Feeney, Judith.
III. Advances in personal relationships (Cambridge, England)
HQ728 .U54   2002
306.81–dc21   2001052759

ISBN 0 521 80370 5 hardback

Contents

Contributors

Alicia L. Alexander, University of Texas at Austin

Arthur Aron, State University of New York at Stony Brook

Elaine N. Aron, State University of New York at Stony Brook

Steven R. H. Beach, University of Georgia

Thomas N. Bradbury, University of California, Los Angeles

Lorne Campbell, Texas A&M University

Andrew Christensen, University of California, Los Angeles

Margaret S. Clark, Carnegie Mellon University

Janice Driver, University of Washington

Tim Dun, University of Iowa

Helen E. Edwards, Queensland University of Technology, Australia

Kathleen A. Eldridge, University of California, Los Angeles

Judith A. Feeney, University of Queensland, Australia

Frank D. Fincham, State University of New York at Buffalo

Eli J. Finkel, University of North Carolina at Chapel Hill

John M. Gottman, University of Washington

Steven Graham, Carnegie Mellon University

Danielle R. Greenberg, University of Wisconsin-Madison

Nancy Grote, University of Pittsburgh

W. Kim Halford, Griffith University, Australia

William Ickes, University of Texas at Arlington

Deborah Jones, University of Georgia

Benjamin R. Karney, University of Florida

Madoka Kumashiro, University of North Carolina at
Chapel Hill

Kenneth E. Leonard, Research Institute on Addictions and State
University of New York at Buffalo Medical School

Gary Lewandowski, State University of New York at
Stony Brook

Alf Lizzio, Griffith University, Australia

Valerie Manusov, University of Washington

Elizabeth Moore, Griffith University, Australia

Lisa A. Neff, University of Florida

Patricia Noller, University of Queensland, Australia

Christine C. Norman, Columbia University

Heather A. O'Mahen, University of Georgia

W. Steven Rholes, Texas A&M University

Linda J. Roberts, University of Wisconsin-Madison

Nigel D. Roberts, University of Queensland, Australia

Alexia D. Rothman, University of California,
Los Angeles

Caryl E. Rusbult, University of North Carolina at
Chapel Hill

Regina Rushe, University of Washington

William E. Schweinle, University of Texas at Arlington

Alan Sillars, University of Montana

Jeffry A. Simpson, Texas A&M University

Lisa B. Story, University of California, Los Angeles

Abraham Tesser, University of Georgia

Sisi Tran, Texas A&M University

Anita L. Vangelisti, University of Texas at Austin

Daniel Whitaker, University of Georgia

Tim Wildschut, University of Southhampton

Carol Wilson, Texas A&M University

Keithia L. Wilson, Griffith University, Australia

Dan Yoshimoto, University of Washington

Introduction

> Seldom or never does a marriage develop into an individual relationship, smoothly and without crises. There is no birth of consciousness without pain.
>
> —C. G. Jung

A great deal of publicity has been given to the fact that more adults in western societies are remaining single than in the past, and that rates of cohabitation are continuing to rise. In fact, some writers have gone so far as to extrapolate from these recent trends, and to conclude that marriage is becoming an unpopular and outdated institution. Nevertheless, studies show that most young people still see marriage and children as an important part of their future, and still view marriage as playing a crucial role in meeting their needs for companionship and emotional security.

Consistent with this viewpoint, Waite and Gallagher (2000) present empirical support for the proposition that there are several major advantages to marriage. First, married men and women tend to enjoy better mental and physical health than the unmarried. Second, married men and women are likely to have more assets and income than the unmarried, with marriage even being described as a "wealth-enhancing institution" (Hao, 1996). Third, married people have more and better sex than the unmarried. Fourth, children of married parents also enjoy a number of advantages, including better physical and mental health, and higher levels of education and career success.

Although marriage has clear implications for individuals' general sense of well-being, it is important to remember that the essence of the marital relationship lies in the day-to-day interactions in which married couples engage. Marital interactions are, of course, immensely varied,

1

sometimes dealing with the more mundane aspects of married life, and sometimes involving highly emotional issues that may be either positive or negative in tone. As the quotation from Jung suggests, however, even negative interactions can be important in promoting growth toward a healthy and satisfying marriage.

In their discussion of close relationships, Kelley and his colleagues (1983) refer to interaction as "the give and take between two persons," involving regularities and recurrent patterns of behavior. A similar but somewhat more technical definition is offered by McLintock (1983), who has defined interaction as "a sequence of causally interconnected events within the behavior chains of two people" (p. 71).

McLintock (1983) notes that, in order to systematically understand couple relationships, researchers must not only describe the interactional regularities that characterize those relationships, but also explain these patterns by identifying causal factors and processes. As this position implies, understanding interaction involves studying the *couple* as a unit. In contrast to an individual perspective on behavior, the study of couple interaction recognizes that there is an intricate system that connects the two relationship partners and that needs to be understood. This system encompasses the psychological realities of both husband and wife, and hence, issues of agreement and understanding between partners are also relevant. As these concepts of agreement and understanding imply, the emphasis on interaction does not mean that couple relationships can be understood purely in terms of observable behavior. Rather, as we shall see throughout this book, cognition and emotion are also major components of the system that connects marital partners to one another.

The earliest attempts to formally study couple relationships focused primarily on issues of attraction and mate selection, rather than on the everyday aspects of couple interaction. For example, Harris's (1912) work on assortative mating was essentially a review of statistical facts about the mating process. By the 1930s, however, a number of researchers (such as E. L. Kelly, Terman, and Burgess) were beginning to explore the notion of marital success, and to apply longitudinal methods to this area of research.

A major shift in the study of couple processes came with the early observational research, such as that of Raush, Weiss, Gottman, and their colleagues (Birchler, Weiss, & Vincent, 1975; Gottman, 1979; Raush, Barry, Hertel, & Swain, 1974). Although some of this early work involved audiotaping and coding of transcribed utterances, there is no doubt that the advent of the video recorder made this work more feasible, and promoted the development of relatively complex systems for coding couple interaction. In fact, under the impetus of these technological advances, behavioral observation became the "gold standard" for work on relationship processes, with the result that cognitive and emotional processes tended to be largely ignored.

By contrast, as the work in the present volume illustrates, many recent studies of marital interaction have incorporated measures of cognition and emotion, as well as behavior. This current trend reflects the growing recognition of several key points: that close relationships are intensely emotional in nature, that our emotions are often driven by how we perceive and interpret events, and hence, that emotion, cognition, and behavior are inextricably linked. This recognition has led to the widespread consensus that multiple methods are essential for developing a complete understanding of marital processes. For example, studies reported in this volume include such diverse methods as self-report questionnaires, structured diary records, physiological recordings, and behavioral observation.

In preparing this volume, we had three interrelated goals. The first of these was to bring together the exciting research on marital interaction being conducted in a number of key centers, focusing particularly on new trends in the area. Our second goal was to highlight the theoretical underpinnings of recent work on marriage; as we note throughout this book, recent theoretical advances enable researchers to develop and test specific predictions about marital processes and outcomes. Third, we wanted to explore the implications of recent findings for the practice of couple enrichment and therapy. As Holmes and Boon (1990) pointed out roughly a decade ago, the study of interactional processes in marriage has developed to the point where theorizing about relationships, and the research findings that follow from those theories, can provide a basis for significant progress in programs of education, counseling, and therapy.

We have organized the chapters in this volume into six sections that draw out the major themes emerging from recent research. We acknowledge that the divisions we have made are to some extent a matter of convenience, and that there are overlapping themes. It is also important to note that the introductions to each section provide additional information about each of the chapters.

The first section deals with the effect of cognitions on couple interaction patterns; the chapters in this section include work on attributions for partners' behavior, on how spouses process feedback about their own and their partner's strengths and weaknesses, and on spouses' thoughts about one another during their conflict interactions. The second section focuses on the role of positive marital interaction, including such issues as individual differences in expressions of love and intimacy, the importance of partners' adopting a communal norm for meeting each other's needs, and the effects of shared involvement in novel and challenging activities. The third section explores how partners cope with instances of disappointment, criticism, and betrayal in their relationships. In particular, the chapters in this section contrast constructive and destructive ways of responding to negative relationship events. The following section also deals with negative relationship events, but with regard to issues of power, conflict, and violence. These chapters explore the nature of the complex links among communication, emotion, and violence. The fifth section describes marital interaction patterns at important transition periods in the marital lifecycle, from first-time parenthood to caregiving for an elderly spouse. Such transition periods generally require spouses to negotiate major changes to their lifestyles and their patterns of interaction. The final section deals with interventions for strengthening marital relationships. These chapters suggest ways in which couples can be assisted in communicating more effectively and working toward achieving their relationship goals.

In brief, the chapters in this book represent some of the best scholarship in the expanding area of couple interaction. This volume is unique because we have assembled eminent researchers whose latest work reflects the enormous breadth of research on marital processes. The new procedures and findings presented in the book provide a strong case for further research that is theoretically based, rigorous in its methodology, and provides a basis for the development of programs of education and intervention.

REFERENCES

Birchler, G. R., Weiss, R. L., & Vincent, J. P. (1975). Multi-method analysis of social reinforcement exchange between maritally distressed and nondistressed spouse and stranger dyads. *Journal of Personality and Social Psychology, 31*, 349–360.
Gottman, J. M. (1979). *Marital interaction: Experimental investigations.* New York: Academic Press.

Hao, L. (1996). Family structure, private transfers, and the economic wellbeing of families with children. *Social Forces, 75*, 269–292.

Harris, J. A. (1912). Assortive mating in man. *Popular Science Monthly, 80*, 476–492.

Holmes, J. G., & Boon, S. D. (1990). Developments in the field of close relationships: Creating foundations for intervention strategies. *Personality and Social Psychology Bulletin, 16*, 23–41.

Kelley, H. H., Berscheid, E., Christensen, A., Harvey, J. H., Huston, T. L., Levinger, G., McLintock, E., Peplau, L. A., & Peterson, D. R. (1983). Analyzing close relationships. In H. H. Kelley et al. (Eds.), *Close relationships* (pp. 20–67). New York: W. H. Freeman & Co.

McLintock, E. (1983). Interaction. In H. H. Kelley et al. (Eds.), *Close relationships* (pp. 68–109). New York: W. H. Freeman & Co.

Raush, H. L., Barry, W. A., Hertel, R. K., & Swain. M. E. (1974). *Communication, conflict and marriage*. San Francisco: Jossey-Bass.

Waite, L. T., & Gallagher, M. (2000). *The case for marriage: Why married poeple are happier, healthier, and better off financially*. New York: Doubleday.

THE EFFECT OF COGNITION ON INTERACTION PATTERNS

Introduction to Section One

One feature of the study of marital relationships over the past 20 years has been a focus, not just on couple behaviors, but on the cognitive processes that may drive those behaviors. A wide range of cognitive processes have been studied including appraisals, attributions, beliefs, standards, expectations, rules, perceptions of intention, and subjective interpretations of ongoing interaction. (Some of these cognitive processes are discussed further in the section on coping with disappointment, criticism, and betrayal.) These cognitive processes can be even more powerful than observed behaviors in discriminating between satisfied and dissatisfied couples. The chapters in this section illustrate something of this diversity of cognitive processes and their impact on marital relationships.

Although attributions have been frequently studied by marital researchers, a novel aspect of Manusov's work is its exploration of couples' attributions for their partner's nonverbal behavior, and the effect of these attributions on their own nonverbal behavior. As she notes, one of the intriguing aspects of nonverbal communication is its ability to be interpreted in a myriad of ways. Spouses' interpretations of their partner's nonverbal communication are likely to be affected by many factors including their level of relationship satisfaction. An innovative feature of Manusov's work is the recruitment of one member of each couple to act as a confederate who is instructed to use particular kinds of nonverbal behavior in structured interactions with their spouse. This approach ensures that clear examples of positive and negative behavior are displayed by couples, irrespective of marital satisfaction. In earlier research, Manusov found that satisfied couples made more relationship-enhancing attributions for partners' nonverbal behavior than dissatisfied couples (for example, attributing positive communication to more internal, stable, and global factors; attributing equally positive motives to the partner as to themselves).

In the new research reported in this chapter Manusov focuses on the link between attributions for partners' nonverbal behavior and the emotion displayed by the attributor. Spouses who made relationship-enhancing attributions for their partner's behavior tended to display positive facial and vocal cues; conversely, those who made distress-maintaining attributions tended to display cues indicative of discomfort in the interaction. This study provides evidence that spouses' interpretations of their partners' behaviors have a powerful effect on their responses to those behaviors, with the links between attributional patterns and nonverbal cues being particularly strong for positive behavior.

Neff and Karney take a different approach to considering the types of feedback that spouses give to, and receive from, one another. This approach focuses on the roles and characteristics that spouses assume within the relationship, and the processes by which they come to understand and accept each other's relational identities. Neff and Karney focus on self-evaluation motives, noting that two views have emerged in the literature about the type of feedback that enhances relationship quality. On the one hand, self-enhancement theory proposes that individuals prefer positive feedback, assuring them of their partner's positive regard. On the other hand, self-verification theory argues that individuals prefer feedback that accurately mirrors their own self-perceptions, even when those perceptions are relatively negative. Although many researchers have seen these two views as in opposition to each other, Neff and Karney suggest that both enhancement and verification processes are important to successful relationships.

Central to their position is the argument that motives to be enhanced or verified operate at different levels of abstraction. Specifically, enhancement motives seem to operate at a global level; in other words, people generally want their spouses to affirm them as worthwhile people. In contrast, verification motives operate at the specific level, with spouses wanting partners to understand them and agree with their own views of their various strengths and weaknesses.

Neff and Karney report on two studies of married couples, in which they tested the prediction that the happiest spouses would be those whose partners provided them with both global affirmation and specific understanding. These studies confirmed that satisfied spouses were accurate in their perceptions at the specific level and positive at the global level. The researchers argue that this combination of feedback processes allows individuals to feel loved and understood by their partner despite any negative characteristics they may have. This combination of processes also enables the partner to make accurate predictions about their spouse's likely behavior while retaining a positive view of the overall relationship. An important area for future research is to clarify how these processes work over time. For example, in happy relationships, how are specific negative beliefs reconciled with an overall positive view? And how and why do these processes fail in relationships where global views of the partner become increasingly negative and the relationship becomes increasingly destructive?

The work of Beach and his colleagues also addresses issues concerning individual strengths and weaknesses and how they are perceived and dealt with within the relationship. These researchers test the Self-Evaluation Maintenance model, which argues that reactions to being outperformed depend on the closeness of the other, and the relevance of the particular activity to the individual's self-definition. When an individual is outperformed by a close other in a particular area, the relevance of that area to the individual's self-definition is likely to be decreased. On the other hand, when an individual performs better than a close other in a particular area, that area is likely to remain central to the individual's self-definition.

Beach and his colleagues propose that this mechanism may serve to improve the fit between the self and the partner, and reinforce the bond between them. When individuals are outperformed by their spouse, they are likely to cede that area to the spouse, and be content with playing a supportive role. In this way, certain areas come to be defined as the domain of a particular spouse, although others may continue to be shared. This process of defining patterns of leadership and expertise within the couple is likely to be highly adaptive: It should allow spouses to coordinate their efforts and work to a common purpose, and should also enable them to accept their areas of weakness and encourage their partners' superior performance.

Beach and his colleagues report three studies of dating and married couples. In all three studies, individuals who received feedback that they had been outperformed by their partner rated the task as less relevant to themselves than to their partner, suggesting that they were willing to cede this area to their partner. This divergence of ratings became somewhat stronger when the competitive nature of task performance was emphasized. In addition, for married couples, relevance ratings diverged not only for areas where the spouse was outperformed, but also for areas where they outperformed their partner. Perhaps married couples are more attuned to partner and relational outcomes than are dating couples, and more willing to work at cooperating with the partner in defining areas of expertise. Given that this process is believed to be adaptive for individuals and their relationships, more needs to be known about how the building of niches in this way impacts on ongoing interaction patterns and on relational satisfaction over time.

In comparison to the other chapters in this section, the research reported by Sillars et al. focuses more directly on the conscious thoughts and feelings that individuals experience during conflict interactions. The study combined video-assisted recall, involving a comparison of couples with aggressive and nonaggressive husbands, and an experimental manipulation of husbands' alcohol consumption. Couples took part in two conflict-related conversations. Spouses then watched a videotape of their conversations, and commented every 20 seconds on the thoughts and feelings they remembered experiencing during the original interaction. Observable behaviors were coded using the Marital Interaction Coding System (MICS), and the thoughts were coded using a scheme designed specifically for this study. The thoughts reported by the participants were very diverse, indicating the usefulness of this methodology for capturing the complex cognitive processes that drive couple interaction. This type of research, which taps observable behavior and underlying thought processes "in tandem," has the potential to greatly increase our understanding of the intricacies of couple interaction.

One interesting finding of the study was that a husband and wife could appear to be talking about the same topic, but be thinking about the interaction in very different ways. For example, one partner may have been thinking about the content of the argument, whereas the other may have been thinking about the communication process. There were several indications that wives were more "other-focused" than husbands; they tended to have more thoughts about their partner than about themselves, whereas husbands had more thoughts about themselves than about their partner. Overall, there was little evidence of spouses trying to take the perspective of the partner, and little recognition of the potential ambiguity and complexity of the communication process.

These researchers also explored the role that aggression and alcohol can play in affecting both observable behavior and cognitive processes.

They found that aggressive couples tended to have a very negative communication style marked by strong differences between individuals' descriptions of their own and their partner's roles in the interaction, and in the direction of self-serving distortions. In addition, aggressive couples were highly vigilant about their communication, suggesting defensiveness toward their partner ; they also showed a lack of objectivity and an inability to control negative emotion. All of these effects were exacerbated when the husband had been drinking alcohol. Further, aggressive husbands tended to be unrestrained in verbalizing their negative thoughts, especially when under the influence of alcohol.

The chapters in this section highlight the complexity and diversity of cognitive processes, as well as the importance of these processes to marital functioning. The findings suggest that happy couples make relationship-enhancing attributions for their partner's behavior, make fewer self-serving distortions in the way that they evaluate couple communication, and are in tune with their partner's perceptions of their own strengths and weaknesses. These results illustrate the importance of understanding the cognitive processes that are likely to drive dysfunctional relationship behavior.

CHAPTER ONE

Thought and Action: Connecting Attributions to Behaviors in Married Couples' Interactions

Valerie Manusov

Causal and responsibility attributions made by married partners are a frequent subject of study by relationship researchers (Fletcher & Fincham, 1991; Holtzworth-Munroe & Jacobson, 1988; Manusov, 1990; Miller & Bradbury, 1995). Few studies have connected couples' attributions to the behaviors they use in response to those thoughts however (see Fincham, 1994). Because overt behaviors are likely to shape the climate for a relationship (Noller, 1992), investigating how thoughts may connect with action is important for understanding the role causal attributions play within marriage.

This paper focuses particularly on nonverbal cues exhibited by married partners. Goffman (1979) refers to nonspoken cues as part of a "glimpsed" world, often unarticulated but rich in social information (Ambady & Rosenthal, 1992). According to Noller (1992), "many messages having neutral words . . . [are] changed into positive or negative messages by . . . the nonverbal channels" (p. 50). The valence of messages has been found to differentiate satisfied from unsatisfied couples consistently, and much of the affective tone of messages is relayed via nonverbal means (Gottman & Levenson, 1992; Huston & Vangelisti, 1991). Because more highly valenced (very positive or very negative) behaviors are likely to instigate greater attribution making (Wong & Weiner, 1981), they should also result in behaviors that reflect the attributions given for a spouse's actions.

Valerie Manusov is an Associate Professor in the Department of Speech Communication at the University of Washington. A previous version of this chapter was presented at the 2000 International Conference on Personal Relationships, Brisbane, Australia, June 2000. The author can be reached at the Department of Speech Communication, Box 353415, University of Washington, Seattle, WA 98195, USA.

In the following pages, I discuss the importance of investigating nonverbal behaviors as both triggers of, and reactions to, attributions by married couples. This discussion is followed by a review of some of the work on marital attributions, highlighting those focusing on nonverbal behaviors. I then discuss a recent study that looks further into attributions for nonverbal cues and how they are associated with subsequent nonverbal behaviors used by the attributors with their partners.

NONVERBAL COMMUNICATION AND ATTRIBUTIONS

The following discourse segment comes from Noller (1984) who quoted a therapy session discussed by Virginia Satir (1976, pp. 176, 194):

> **Therapist**: (to husband) I notice your brow is wrinkled, Ralph. Does that mean that you are angry at this moment?
> **Husband**: I did not know my brow was wrinkled....
> **Therapist**: Ah, then maybe that wrinkle meant that you were puzzled because your wife was hoping you would do something and you did not know that she had this hope. Do you suppose that by your wrinkled brow you were signaling that you were puzzled?
> **Husband**: Yeah, I guess so.

Later in the transcript it became clear that Alice (the wife) had assigned a different meaning to the behavior:

> **Wife**: He don't want to be here. He don't care. He never talks. Just looks at the television or he isn't home.

One of the most intriguing aspects of nonverbal communication is its ability to be interpreted in myriad ways. Depending on the context in which it occurs (that is, the verbal message, other nonverbal cues, the relationship between the interactants, or in the above case, the person who is making the interpretation), the same nonverbal behavior(s) can be given many meanings. According to Manusov (1990), "[d]eciding on the meaning for others' nonverbal messages . . . often involves choosing among alternative translations by making *attributions* as to what may have caused actors to send the message and/or enact the cues they did" (p. 104). The inherent ambiguity in many nonverbal messages makes them particularly well-suited to an attributional framework.

There are a large number of cues included in the nonverbal system (for example, body movement, gaze, touch, vocalics, and facial behavior; see Andersen, 1999; Burgoon, Buller, & Woodall, 1996). Further, the cues have been found to perform many functions for interactants (Patterson, 1991). Of greatest note for people in close relationships are two such functions: the expression of emotions and the display of relational messages. Emotional expressions show people's feelings about something or someone (for example, anger, happiness). Relational messages reflect the definition that one person holds for the type of relationship s/he has with another (for example, intimate, distant, dominant). Both of these functions reveal the *affect* people experience in relationships, and, as mentioned earlier, affective messages are a particularly important part of marital interaction and may help distinguish satisfied from dissatisfied couples.

A primary way in which affect distinguishes couples has to do with the *amount* of positively and negatively toned behaviors that occur in couples' exchanges. According to Burgoon et al. (1996), "[e]xtensive research on patterns of marital interaction has confirmed time and again that unhappy couples display disproportionately less positive emotion and exchange far more negatively toned nonverbal cues than happy couples do"(p. 298). Gottman (1996), for example, offers evidence that, whereas happy couples display a 5 : 1 ratio on average of positive to negative behaviors, unhappy couples have a much lower "positive to negative" ratio. Importantly however, distressed couples also tend to underreport by 50% the rates of pleasurable behavior used in their marriages (Robinson & Price, 1980).

In addition to overall occurrence of more positive or negative behavior, there is support for the argument that couples are more likely to *reciprocate* certain types of behaviors in accordance with their satisfaction level. Although matching or reciprocity is the most common type of nonverbal behavioral adaptation overall (Burgoon, Stern, & Dillman, 1995), the pattern appears to be moderated by satisfaction level. Gottman (1979); Gottman, Markman, & Notarius (1977); Margolin and Wampold (1981); and Pike and Sillars (1985) all found that negative behaviors were more likely to be matched by unhappy than by happy couples. Similarly, Manusov (1995) and Noller (1984) have both noted that certain positive nonverbal cues are reciprocated more often by satisfied than by dissatisfied spouses. Behaviors that are reciprocated are likely to result in behavioral spirals – both negative and positive – that can further affect the emotional tone of a marriage.

Perhaps more importantly for this paper, however, level of relational satisfaction appears to differentiate people on their ability to decode nonverbal behaviors accurately. In a series of studies, Noller and her colleagues (reported in Noller, 1992) looked at the degree of accuracy couples had in both encoding and decoding nonverbal behaviors with their spouses. They found that there were important differences in accuracy based on both adjustment level and sex. According to Noller (1992), overall, "spouses low in marital adjustment were less accurate decoders of their partner's nonverbal messages than was true for spouses high in marital adjustment. . . . Husbands in distressed marriages made more encoding errors and more decoding errors than those in non-distressed marriages" (p. 38).

Noller's (1992) work is important, especially regarding the decoding or interpretation of spouses' behaviors, because people's levels of relationship satisfaction appear to be associated with their accuracy in determining what their spouse was communicating. Given that attributions are a way to make sense of (that is, interpret, determine meaning for) another's behavior, the tie between satisfaction and decoding ability is particularly important to investigate. This paper now turns to a more specific discussion of decoding – or making attributions for – a partner's behavior.

ATTRIBUTIONS IN MARRIAGE

In 1985, Sillars lamented that personal relationships had not been the focus of most attribution research. Since that time, however, a number of researchers have changed that trend notably. Much of the research on attributions in marriage was summarized by Fincham and Bradbury (1992):

> Distressed spouses are hypothesized to make attributions for negative events that accentuate their impact (e.g., they locate the cause in their partner, see it as stable or unchanging, and see it as global or influencing many of the areas of their relationship), whereas nondistressed spouses are thought to make attributions that minimize the impact of negative events (e.g., they do not locate the cause in the partner and see it as unstable and specific). (p. 457)

According to Fincham, Beach, and Baucom (1987), distressed spouses "also tend to view positive partner behavior as being situationally determined and thus reflecting temporary, situation-specific causes" (p. 739). Camper, Jacobson, Holtzworth-Munroe, and Schmaling (1988) refer to dissatisfied couples' attributions as more likely to be distress-maintaining, and satisfied couples' causal claims are described as relationship-enhancing.

The most common behavior for which marital attributions have been assessed is conflict. Participants report on a conflict that occurred in their relationship (for example, Orvis, Kelley, & Butler, 1976), state how they believe that they might think about a hypothetical conflict with their spouse, or actually engage in conflict in the researchers' laboratories (for example, Fincham & Bradbury, 1992; Smith, Sanders, & Alexander, 1990). In other studies, couples have been asked to report on interaction behaviors that may have occurred (for example, spouse does not pay attention to partner, or spouse responds positively to partner's physical attention; Baucom, Sayers, & Duhe, 1989; Fincham & Bradbury, 1993); these events may or may not include nonverbal cues.

I and my colleagues, however, have focused our attribution research specifically on nonverbal communication and romantic relationships (married and unmarried couples in "intimate/romantic relationships"). In an initial study (Manusov, 1990), participants engaged in a neutral, game-playing situation. One of the members of each couple became a confederate in the study and changed his/her nonverbal behaviors (for example, lean, vocalics, facial pleasantness) to be positively or negatively valenced.

Based on analyses of responses, one spouse in each couple gave while watching a videotape of their previous interaction, it was clear that there were distortions in the ways both satisfied and dissatisfied couples offered attributions for their partner's behavior. As satisfaction increased, couple members were more likely to make internal, global, and stable attributions for their partners' positive behaviors; as satisfaction decreased, couples tended to offer attributions for negative behaviors that were more stable, controllable, and intentional. Similarly, in a study using a diary format (Manusov, 1996) quantitative ratings provided for nonverbal cues by the participants showed a link between greater attributions of intentionality for positive nonverbal cues and increased satisfaction.

In a follow-up study by Manusov, Floyd, and Kerssen-Griep (1997) couples were videotaped talking about upcoming, generally positive events. Again, one member of the pair was asked to change his/her nonverbal behaviors to act positively and negatively at particular points. Consistent with previous research, participants who reported higher marital quality were also more likely to notice and make attributions for positive behavior than were those who scored lower on relational quality (that is, happy couples noticed positive behaviors more often than did unhappy couples, even though the actual rate of occurrence for those behaviors was the same across couples). Interestingly, this result was due mainly to the males in the study.

We did *not* find support for relationship-enhancing or distress-maintaining attributions as they are defined in most studies, however. Instead, we noted two variations on the egocentric bias (that is, the extent to which people make attributions for behaviors that place them, the attributors, in a positive light; Baucom, 1987). First, satisfaction was negatively related to providing more distress-maintaining attributions for one's partner's behaviors than were made for one's own behaviors. That is, compared to those with lower levels of satisfaction, people who reported higher marital satisfaction tended to attribute their partners' behaviors in the same egocentric (relationship-enhancing) manner as they used for their own. Second, we found that satisfaction was negatively related to the tendency for one partner to offer more distress-maintaining attributions for the other partner's behavior than that person attributed to his or her own behaviors.

Although, as in other research (Bradbury & Fincham, 1990), these studies did not reveal an association between satisfaction and all of the attributional dimensions studied, there was ample evidence that people *do* make attributions as part of trying to understand the meaning of nonverbal behavior. Further, the form of the attributions for nonverbal cues largely mirrors that found for other interaction behaviors (that is, they take the form of relationship-enhancing or distress-maintaining attributions). Importantly, as in other attribution research, the studies ended with a call for investigating the behavioral responses that may emerge following attributions in marital interaction. This is what I turn to next.

BEHAVIORS FROM ATTRIBUTIONS

Fincham and O'Leary (1982) provided some early evidence that people *perceive*, at least, that attributions made are likely to affect the behavior of the attributor (especially positive behavior). Dealing with conflict behavior, Sillars (1980) also found that the attributions people made for their roommates' conflict correlated with how likely the respondents were to say they would use particular conflict resolution strategies. Specifically, attributions for greater stability (that the conflict was caused by something unlikely to change), for example, were correlated with reports that the respondent would use more passive strategies (avoidance). Attributions of greater responsibility to self for the conflict were associated with the use of more integrative (conflict-reducing, cooperative) strategies as well.

Both of the above studies relied on reports of what people *thought* they would do following attributions they made for another's behavior. Johnson, Rogge, Karney, and Bradbury (2001) report finding only four studies that have actually investigated the behaviors likely to follow from attributions, all of which focused on how certain types of attributions correlated with positive or negative problem-solving behavior. Two of these studies are discussed in Bradbury and Fincham (1992).

In both of their projects, married couples were asked to make attributions for, and talk with one another about, a problem area in their marriage, attempting to come up with a resolution for the problem. The discussions were then rated for the use of certain problem-solving skills. In both studies, the authors found a positive association between "maladjusted" attributions and negative problem-solving behavior (and, for wives, a negative association between maladjusted attributions and positive, problem-solving actions). This effect was moderated by satisfaction level (that is, it was stronger for those who were dissatisfied than for those who were satisfied in their relationships).

In their second study, Bradbury and Fincham (1992) noted more specifically that "the combination of lower marital satisfaction and more maladaptive attributions was associated with less avoidance and less reciprocity of wife avoidance by husbands, and fewer positive behaviors and more negative reciprocity by wives" (Johnson et al., 2001, p. 182). That is, the authors found a link between how couple members made their attributions and how much they reciprocated the behaviors that generated the attributions.

The other two studies cited by Johnson et al. (2001) showed similar associations between attributions and behaviors. In a supportive interactive context (that is, helping their partner with problems outside of the relationship), Miller and Bradbury (1995) revealed that wives' maladaptive attributions were associated with less functional problem-solving and supportive behaviors. Spouses with lower satisfaction also tended to have stronger associations between attributions and behavior. Bradbury, Beach, Fincham, and Nelson (1996) replicated the findings of previous studies. According to Johnson et al. (2001), "[n]ot only were behavior and attributions associated for distressed couples, but (in contrast to Miller & Bradbury, 1995) also nondistressed couples showed a strong association between behavior and attributions, suggesting a more pervasive role of attributions" (p. 183).

Given the robustness of the findings between attributions and problem-solving behavior, it seems clear that such a link should be common for behaviors most indicative of affect: nonverbal cues. As yet, however, little investigation has focused on nonverbal means of expressing attributions. Like in previous work, the nature of attributions made should shape the type of response made by the attributor, with more maladjusted or distress-maintaining attributions linked with more negative affect and more benign or relationship-enhancing attributions related to more positive affect. The study reported here aimed to find such evidence and was guided by two hypotheses. Our first hypothesis states that when couples make sense of their partners' positively toned behaviors with more internal, controllable, stable, intentional, and positive attributions, they are also likely to act positively or pleasantly with their partner. Our second hypothesis states that when couples make sense of their partners' negatively toned behaviors with more internal, controllable, stable, intentional, and negative attributions, they are also likely to act negatively or unpleasantly with their partner.

The Study

Fifty-one married couples were recruited via newspaper advertisements, flyers, and word of mouth. Each couple was paid $20.00 for their participation. The couples had been married for an average of 4.86 years (range = 2 months to 40 years, SD = 7.39), 16 of the couples had children (mean number of children = 1.81, SD = .98), and the spouses varied in age from 21 to 63 ($M = 31.22$, SD = 9.02). Seventy-seven of the couple members identified themselves as White/Caucasian, nine as Hispanic, eight as Asian or Asian American, and four as mixed ethnicities. The remainder did not indicate their ethnic group. The couples were generally quite satisfied in their marriages ($M = 31.25$, SD = 3.37, range = 22 to 35 on a scale that ranged from 7 to 35; Hendrick, 1988; Cronbach's *alpha* = .77).

When the couples arrived at the research laboratory, either the wife or husband was selected and assigned to the role of confederate, using random selection counterbalanced by sex. The confederate was asked to choose three topics for discussion: one that was neutral, one that was positive, and one that was negative for the couple. They were given a list of possible topics (for example, what was happening at work, something current in their relationship, what their children were doing, money/finances, sports), but they could choose anything to discuss that they wished. The confederates were also asked to "show nonverbally" the affect that they had about each topic when they talked to their partners (for example, anger or sadness with the negative topic, happiness or enjoyment with the positive topic). The order of the positive and negative topics was randomly assigned and counterbalanced to be sure that the order did not affect the likelihood of writing down the behaviors and offering attributions for them. During this time, the nonconfederate was completing several questionnaires that included demographic items and Hendrick's (1988) relational satisfaction scale.

After the members of the couple were brought back together, they discussed each topic on videotape for five minutes. Thus, the conversation with all three topics lasted fifteen minutes. Following the taping, the nonconfederates were asked to review two minutes of each topic period on the videotape. After each two-minute segment, the participants were asked "what nonverbal behaviors (for example, eye behavior, facial expressions, movements, and sounds) do you remember noticing (even very slightly) that your spouse used at this time in the interaction?"[1] They were encouraged to write "none" if they had not noticed any. If the participants did notice behaviors, they then rated the nonverbal cues on five dimensions, using seven-point scales: locus, control, stability, intent, and valence. Lower numbers indicated more external, unstable, unintentional, and negative attributions that were not controlled by a spouse.

An example of the participants' ratings can be seen in the following. One wife discussed her husband's "swiveling in chair." She interpreted this as due to his being "very anxious" and rated the behavior as a six on locus (more internal), a four on control (an "in between" response), a six on stability (due to a stable or unchangeable cause), a five on intentionality (more intentional than not), and a four on negativity (neutral). This behavior had occurred during the "neutral" topic.

Following data collection, four teams of raters assessed the videotapes. Each team comprised one graduate student and one undergraduate currently enrolled in a research methods course. The graduate students had some knowledge of the research questions but no specific information about the hypotheses; the undergraduates were uninformed about the nature of the project. The author worked with each

---

[1] In order to get a list of behaviors seen by the participants themselves, only a few example cues were mentioned in the questionnaire.

of these four pairs, training them to recognize and rate a subset of related behaviors (that is, four facial cues: facial pleasantness, head nodding, gaze, and facial orientation; four kinesic/body cues: body orientation, lean, shifting, and postural relaxation; three kinesic/gestural cues: touch, adaptor use, physical animation; and four vocal cues: vocal animation, vocal pleasantness, volume, and vocal hesitancy/fluency).

After training, each pair worked together until the members had adequate reliability (that is, they were rating the videotapes using the same standards and scoring them the same). They then rated the remaining interactions independently, coming together about half way through to ensure that their rating had remained consistent. Both members of each pair rated each interaction.

The raters watched several of each confederate's behaviors to ensure that the spouses adequately altered their behaviors to indicate positive, negative, and neutral affect. Again, assuming that the first minute of the interaction may have been somewhat altered by people's nervousness over the video camera and to be consistent with the period of time subject to judgments by the partners (nonconfederates), the confederates' behavior during the second minute of the interaction was rated. This rating was used as an assessment of the confederates' *baseline* behaviors. Then, each rater watched the confederates during the sixth minute of the interaction (the first minute of the valenced behavior and the one watched and judged/interpreted by the spouse). After rating the behaviors across this one-minute segment, the raters watched and assessed the eleventh minute of the interaction (the first minute of the second valenced period). The graduate raters were unaware of the assigned valence for that period, and the undergraduate raters were unaware of the valencing at all. Both groups were unaware of the participants' responses to the attribution questionnaires.

The means of the three periods were compared to assess what behaviors, if any, differentiated neutral from positive and negative nonverbal affect. The results of one-way Analyses of Variance (ANOVAs) with Student-Newmann-Keuls post hoc tests showed that the confederates did change a number of their behaviors to reflect their neutral, positive, or negative affect and that the behaviors reflected the valence appropriately. For instance, one husband had chosen to talk about household chores for the "negative" topic. During that discussion, he rolled his eyes, rocked in his chair, and "smirked," among other things. These behaviors meant that he was rated quite high on postural animation,

Table 1.1. Results of Manipulation Check on Confederates' Behaviors
(df = 2, 49)

| | Means for Time Period | | | | |
	Positive	Neutral	Negative	F	p
Body orientation[a]	6.11	6.24	6.31	3.06	.05
Facial animation[b]	3.68	3.64	3.39	8.42	.001
Fluency[b]	3.95	4.08	3.66	5.00	.001
Facial[c] pleasantness	4.29	4.05	3.94	8.16	.001
Head nods[c]	4.06	3.97	3.94	3.27	.05
Posture[d]	5.17	5.06	5.00	5.19	.009
Shifting[e]	2.91	2.53	2.66	3.67	.04
Vocal[f] animation	4.36	3.87	4.10	9.82	.001
Volume[c]	3.92	3.52	3.85	14.72	.001
Vocal[f] pleasantness	4.79	4.38	4.00	33.93	.001

[a] positive and negative times were significantly different
[b] negative time was significantly different from both positive and neutral
[c] positive time was significantly different from both negative and neutral
[d] negative and neutral times were significantly different
[e] positive and neutral times were significantly different
[f] all three times were significantly different from each other

facial animation, and was limited in the amount of gaze he gave to his partner (low gaze). When he talked about the "positive" topic, he showed greater comfort, which for him, was reflected in more postural relaxation and less vocal and facial animation. His "neutral" behaviors showed increased gaze from the negative time, less facial animation, and little gesturing. For the results of all of the manipulation checks, see Table 1.1.

The raters watched a two-minute segment that paralleled those viewed by the participants, and for which the participants made attributions. Previous investigations have found a number of behavioral composites that are important in distinguishing between couples (for example, Andersen, 1999; Burgoon & Newton, 1991; Guerrero & Burgoon, 1996; Manusov, 1995). Drawing from these sources, the following 15 behaviors were rated on seven-point scales. Grouped here by physical region, the head/face cues rated by one set of raters were *facial pleasantness* (facially unpleasant [1] to facially pleasant [7]);

facial orientation (face away from partner [1] to face oriented toward partner [7]); *head nods* (no head nods [1] to many head nods [7]), and *gaze* (no gaze at partner [1] to constant gaze at partner [7]). Vocal cues, rated by a second set of raters, were the following: *vocal pleasantness* (vocally unpleasant [1] to vocally pleasant [7]; volume (soft [1] to loud [7]); *vocal animation* (not vocally animated [1] to vocally animated [7]); and *fluency* (hesitant [1] to fluent [7]). The body/kinesic cues were *body orientation* (indirect [1] to direct [7]); *lean* (away from partner [1] to toward partner [7]); *adaptors* (many [1] to few [7]); *posture* (tense [1] to relaxed [7]); *shifting* (high [1)] to low [7]); *physical animation* (not physically animated [1] to physically animated [7]); and *affectionate touch* (no affectionate touch [1] to frequent affectionate touch [7]). The seven kinesic cues were divided between two sets of raters.

After rating was complete, Cronbach's *alpha* as a measure of rating consistency was run between the scores for the two raters on each of the behaviors across all 51 interactions and across three periods (neutral, positive, and negative) within the interactions. Thus, reliability was assessed based on 306 ratings of each behavior (51 participants, each rated by 2 raters at 3 different points in the interaction). The reliability for the individual behaviors ranged from .50 to .89, but most cues had adequate reliability. For a list of all alphas, see Table 1.2.

The first hypothesis predicted a positive association between more relationship-enhancing attributions and more positive nonverbal behaviors/affect. Pearson product moment correlations were conducted with the five attributions (locus, stability, controllability, intentionality, and valence) made for positive nonverbal cues offered by 50 out of the 51 participants. A relatively large number of positive, hypothesis-confirming associations were found. For *locus*, there were positive correlations ($p < .05$) between more internal attributions and vocal animation, $r = .33$, volume, $r = .33$, vocal pleasantness, $r = .29$, facial animation, $r = .26$, facial pleasantness, $r = .25$, and gaze, $r = .25$. Attributions of *stability* were associated positively with fluency, $r = .24$, and they were associated negatively with physical animation, $r = -.25$.

With *control* attributions, there were positive correlations between higher assessments of partner control over affect behavior and the attributor's own facial pleasantness, $r = .24$, increased gaze, $r = .31$, and straight posture, $r = .28$. Greater attributions of *intentionality* for behavior were correlated with more facial animation, $r = .25$, more gaze, $r = .37$, less shifting, $r = -.30$, and more touch, $r = .25$. Finally,

Table 1.2. Cronbach's Alpha for
Behavioral Ratings

Behavior	Alpha
Body orientation	.86
Lean	.89
Shifting	.68
Touch	.87
Adaptor use	.84
Postural relaxation	.58
Physical animation	.88
Vocal pleasantness	.50
Volume	.70
Vocal animation	.66
Vocal hesitance/fluency	.60
Facial pleasantness	.77
Head nodding	.80
Gaze	.67
Facial orientation	.83

more positive *valence* attributions were correlated with fewer adaptors, $r = -.31$, and more vocal pleasantness, $r = .28$. Hypothesis One was therefore confirmed, most notably in relation to facial and vocal behavior.

The second hypothesis predicted a positive association between more distress-maintaining attributions and more negative nonverbal behaviors/affect. Pearson product moment correlations were conducted with the five attributions (locus, stability, controllability, intentionality, and valence) made for negative nonverbal cues offered by 50 out of 51 participants. There were several significant associations, although these were fewer in number than for the positive cues. Attributions of greater *internality* were related to less fluency, $r = -.33$, more tense posture, $r = -.31$, and more vocal unpleasantness, $r = -.24$. Attributions of *stability* were associated only with more forward lean, $r = .32$. Attributions of greater *control* were correlated with less fluency, $r = -.33$, less facial pleasantness, $r = -.27$, more forward lean, $r = .25$, and straighter posture, $r = .26$. Attributions of *intentionality* were associated with less fluency, $r = -.33$, and more forward lean. Finally, more negative *valence* attributions were associated with more forward lean, r = .26, and more nodding, r = .27. Overall, then, Hypothesis Two received support, most notably for physical movements/lean and disfluency.

Discussion

This study was created to look more fully at some of the nonverbal behavioral patterns that may emerge alongside attributions in marital interactions. It was expected that nonverbal reactions to attributions made for partners' nonverbal behaviors would show patterns consistent with previous research: More "positive" (relationship-enhancing) attributions would be linked with more positive nonverbal behaviors, and that more "negative" (distress-maintaining, maladjusted) attributions would be tied to more negative nonverbal behaviors by the attributor. That was largely what was found.

In a study of 51 couples, analyses revealed that several nonverbal affect cues were associated with the attributions provided for both positive and negative behaviors. Interestingly, different types of behaviors were most notable, depending on the valence of the behaviors leading to the attribution. Specifically, more "adjusted" attributions (that is, those that attributed more internal, stable, controlled, intentional, and more positive causes) for a spouse's positive nonverbal cues were linked most often with the use of facial and vocal cues associated with pleasant affect. Thus, when partners attributed their spouse's positive affect cues as more internal, more purposeful, the other "rewarded" the partner by smiling and talking in a pleasant tone.

For negative behaviors, a "maladjusted" attributional pattern was more commonly linked to less vocal fluency and more forward lean, suggesting that partners' behavioral *discomfort* tended to be linked with negative attributions. Rather than a kind of reciprocity or reward when more relationship-enhancing attributions were made, the results here suggest that distress-maintaining attributions for nonverbal cues may engender behaviors that show the other person doesn't feel good about, or want to be in, the interaction.

Although not all of the nonverbal indices were correlated with the attributional dimensions, *all* of the behaviors, aside from face and body orientation, were related to at least *one* of the attributions. This finding suggests that a large range of affect cues may result from, or be associated with, the attributions made for a spouse's behavior.

Looking *across* behaviors, then, is important to future research in this area.

As is to be expected, there are limitations to this study. For instance, as in many examinations of volunteer couples, this was a relatively satisfied sample. Thus, the potential range of behaviors and the significance of the findings may have been less than what occurs across a broader range of couples. As well, the raters had some difficulty rating certain behaviors reliably, and this inconsistency may have diminished the strength of the results as well. On the other hand, a large number of statistical tests were performed, increasing the chances of Type I error. Finally, although a link was made in the literature review, the hypotheses did not test the role of satisfaction directly. Instead, the tests performed here were only on the association between attributions and behaviors.

Despite these limitations, the data nonetheless provide further evidence that people do respond to a partner based in part on how they make sense of (provide attributions for) their spouses' nonverbal actions. The responses are likely to differ for attributions made for positive and negative behavior, however. As well, in this study at least, links between nonverbal cues and attributional patterns were more evident for positive cues than for negative behavior. This result is consistent with Fincham and O'Leary's (1982) conclusions.

Behaviors resulting from attributions work to affect the climate of an interaction (Noller, 1992). Indeed, while watching the taping of the interactions the researcher and her assistants could tell without listening to the words when topic changes had occurred. The participants would laugh more, have more animation, and sound warmer when they were "acting positive." This climate change always became more obvious as the interaction period (and, potentially, the effects of the confederates' behaviors on their spouses) continued over time. Conversely, the negative topic interactions often felt cold, quiet, and distant, and this grew over the five minute period.

Given that people's satisfaction is likely to be affected by the current behavioral climate, the result of more positive affect behaviors co-occurring with attributions is good news for relationship researchers. Although negative, conflict, or problem-based interactions are often the focus of attribution research in marriage, the scholarship emphasizing nonverbal cues tends to see more effects during positive, enjoyable interactions. Future research should explore further the influence of attributions and behaviors during couples' happier moments.

REFERENCES

Ambady, N., & Rosenthal, R. (1992). Thin slices of expressive behavior as predictors of interpersonal consequences: A meta-analysis. *Psychological Bulletin, 111*, 256–274.

Andersen, P. A. (1999). *Nonverbal communication: Forms and function.* Mountain View, CA: Mayfield Publishing Company.

Baucom, D. H. (1987). Attributions in distressed relations: How can we explain them? In D. Perlman & S. Duck (Eds.), *Intimate relationships: Development, dynamics, and deterioration* (pp. 177–206). London: Sage.

Baucom, D. H., Sayers, S. L., & Duhe, A. (1989). Attributional style and attributional patterns among married couples. *Journal of Personality and Social Psychology, 56*, 596–607.

Bradbury, T. N., Beach, S. R. H., Fincham, F. D., & Nelson, G. M. (1996). Attributions and behavior in functional and dysfunctional marriages. *Journal of Consulting and Clinical Psychology, 64*, 569–576.

Bradbury, T. N., & Fincham, F. D. (1990). Attributions in marriage: Review and critique. *Psychological Bulletin, 107*, 3–33.

Bradbury, T. N., & Fincham, F. D. (1992). Attributions and behavior in marital interaction. *Journal of Personality and Social Psychology, 63*, 613–628.

Burgoon, J. K., Buller, D. B., & Woodall, W. G. (1996). *Nonverbal communication: The unspoken dialogue* (2nd ed.). New York: McGraw-Hill.

Burgoon, J. K., & Newton, D. A. (1991). Applying a social meaning model to relational message interpretations of conversational involvement: Comparing observer and participant perspectives. *The Southern Communication Journal, 56*, 96–113.

Burgoon, J. K., Stern, L. A., & Dillman, L. (1995). *Interpersonal adaptation: Dyadic interaction patterns.* Cambridge: Cambridge University Press.

Camper, P. M., Jacobson, N. S., Holtzworth-Munroe, A., & Schmaling, K. B. (1988). Causal attributions for interactional behaviors in married couples. *Cognitive Therapy and Research, 12*, 195–209.

Fincham, F. D. (1994). Cognition in marriage: Current status and future challenges. *Applied and Preventive Psychology, 3*, 185–198.

Fincham, F. D., Beach, S. R., & Baucom, D. H. (1987). Attribution processes in distressed and nondistressed couples: 4. Self-partner attribution differences. *Journal of Personality and Social Psychology, 52*, 739–748.

Fincham, F. D., & Bradbury, T. N. (1992). Assessing attributions in marriage: The Relationship Attribution Measure. *Journal of Personality and Social Psychology, 62*, 457–468.

Fincham, F. D., & Bradbury, T. N. (1993). Marital satisfaction, depression, and attributions. *Journal of Personality and Social Psychology, 64*, 442–452.

Fincham, F. D., & O'Leary, K. D. (1982). Causal inferences for spouse behavior in maritally distressed and nondistressed couples. *Journal of Social and Clinical Psychology, 1*, 42–57.

Fletcher, G. J. O., & Fincham, F. D. (1991). Attribution processes in close relationships. In G. J. O. Fletcher & F. D. Fincham (Eds.), *Cognition in close relationships* (pp. 7–35). Hillsdale, NJ: Lawrence Erlbaum Associates.

Goffman, E. (1979). *Gender advertisements.* New York: Harper & Row.

Gottman, J. (1996). Why marriages fail. In K. M. Galvin & P. Cooper (Eds.), *Making connections: Readings in relational communication* (pp. 219–227). Los Angeles: Roxbury Publishing Company.

Gottman, J. (1979). *Marital interaction: Experimental investigations.* New York: Academic Press.

Gottman, J., & Levenson, R. W. (1992). Marital processes predictive of later dissolution: Behavior, physiology, and health. *Journal of Personality and Social Psychology, 63,* 221–223.

Gottman, J., Markman, H., & Notarius, C. (1977). The topography of marital conflict: A sequential analysis of verbal and nonverbal behavior. *Journal of Marriage and the Family, 39,* 461–478.

Guerrero, L. K., & Burgoon, J. K. (1996). Attachment styles and reactions to nonverbal involvement change in romantic dyads: Patterns of reciprocity and compensation. *Human Communication Research, 22,* 335–370.

Hendrick, S. S. (1988). A generic measure of relationship satisfaction. *Journal of Marriage and the Family, 50,* 93–98.

Holtzworth-Munroe, A., & Jacobson, N. S. (1988). Toward a methodology for coding spontaneous causal attributions: Preliminary results with married couples. *Journal of Social and Clinical Psychology, 7,* 101–112.

Huston, T. L., & Vangelisti, A. L. (1991). Socioemotional behavior and satisfaction in marital relationships: A longitudinal study. *Journal of Personality and Social Psychology, 61,* 721–733.

Johnson, M. D., Karney, B. R., Rogge, R., Bradbury, T. N. (2001). The role of marital behavior in the longitudinal association between attributions and marital quality. In V. Manusov & J. H. Harvey (Eds.), *Attribution, communication, and close relationships* (pp. 173–192). Cambridge: Cambridge University Press.

Manusov, V. (1990). An application of attribution principles to nonverbal messages in romantic dyads. *Communication Monographs, 57,* 104–118.

Manusov, V. (1995). Reacting to changes in nonverbal behaviors: Relational satisfaction and adaptation patterns in romantic relationships. *Human Communication Research, 21,* 456–477.

Manusov, V. (1996). Intentionality attributions for naturally occurring nonverbal behaviors in intimate relationships. In J. E. Aitken & L. J. Shedletsky (Eds.), *Intrapersonal communication processes* (pp. 343–353). Plymouth, MI: Midnight Oil Multimedia.

Manusov, V., Floyd, K., & Kerssen-Griep, J. (1997). Yours, mine, and ours: Mutual attributions for nonverbal behaviors in couples' interactions. *Communication Research, 24,* 234–260.

Margolin, G., & Wampold, B. E. (1981). Sequential analysis of conflict and accord in distressed and nondistressed marital partners. *Journal of Consulting and Clinical Psychology, 49,* 554–567.

Miller, G. E., & Bradbury, T. N. (1995). Refining the association between attributions and behavior in marital interaction. *Journal of Family Psychology, 9,* 196–208.

Noller, P. (1984). *Nonverbal communication and marital interaction.* Oxford: Pergamon.

Noller, P. (1992). Nonverbal communication in marriage. In R. S. Feldman (Ed.), *Applications of nonverbal behavioral theories and research* (pp. 31–59). Hillsdale, NJ: Lawrence Erlbaum Associates.

Orvis, B. R., Kelley, H. H., & Butler, D. (1976). Attributional conflict in young couples. In J. H. Harvey, W. I. Ickes, & R. F. Kidd (Eds.), *New directions in attribution research* (Vol. 1. pp. 353–384). Hillsdale, NJ: Lawrence Erlbaum Associates.

Patterson, M. L. (1991). A functional approach to nonverbal exchange. In R. S. Feldman & B. Rime (Eds.), *Fundamentals of nonverbal behavior* (pp. 458–495). Cambridge: Cambridge University Press.

Pike, G. R., & Sillars, A. L. (1985). Reciprocity of marital communication. *Journal of Social and Personal Relationships, 2,* 303–324.

Robinson, E. A., & Price, M. G. (1980). Pleasurable behavior in marital interaction: An observational study. *Journal of Consulting and Clinical Psychology, 48,* 117–118.

Satir, V. (1976). Family communication and conjoint family therapy. In B. N. Ard & C. C. Ard (Eds.), *Handbook of marriage counseling* (2nd ed.) (pp. 175–185). Palo Alto, CA: Science and Behavior Books.

Sillars, A. L. (1980). Attributions and communication in roommate conflicts. *Communication Monographs, 47,* 180–200.

Sillars, A. L. (1985). Interpersonal perception in relationships. In W. Ickes (Ed.), *Compatible and incompatible relationships* (pp. 277–305). New York: Springer-Verlag.

Smith, T. W., Sanders, J. D., & Alexander, J. F. (1990). What does the Cook and Medley Hostility Scale measure? Affect, behavior, and attributions in the marital context. *Journal of Personality and Social Psychology, 58,* 699–708.

Wong, P. T. P., & Weiner, B. (1981). When people ask "why" questions, and the heuristics of the attributional search. *Journal of Personality and Social Psychology, 40,* 650–663.

CHAPTER TWO

Self-Evaluation Motives in Close Relationships: A Model of Global Enhancement and Specific Verification

Lisa A. Neff and Benjamin R. Karney

In their classic work on marriage, Berger and Kellner wrote: "The reality of the world is sustained through conversation with significant others" (1964, p. 53). Spouses, in particular, are said to provide each other with the most important source of feedback about the nature of the social world. More notably, spouses provide each other with the most important source of feedback about *themselves* (Berger & Kellner, 1964). Marriage involves an identity negotiation process in which spouses must determine the roles and characteristics each will assume within the relationship (for example, Schlenker, 1984). Marital satisfaction, then, may rest on whether spouses accept the identities each will hold in the marriage, and thus view and treat the other in the desired manner (Schlenker, 1984; Swann, 1984).

In fact, abundant evidence suggests that the feedback spouses provide one another concerning their identity within the relationship is associated with marital well-being. How intimates view one another has been linked to both the satisfaction and the stability of a relationship (for example, Murray, Holmes, & Griffin, 1996a; 1996b; Swann, De La Ronde, & Hixon, 1994). Nevertheless, researchers disagree on the *type* of feedback that is associated with positive relationship outcomes. Do spouses in satisfying relationships provide each other with favorable feedback, casting even negative qualities in a more positive light? Or do these spouses convey an accurate understanding of each other's qualities, acknowledging both strengths and weaknesses?

The answers to these questions have created a long-standing debate in the literature, as two views have emerged to explain how partners view each other in satisfying marriages. Self-enhancement theory argues that individuals prefer feedback that fosters a positive sense of self and allows one to remain confident in a partner's regard. Consequently, the enhancement position suggests that intimates should be happier in their relationships when their partners view them positively, perhaps more positively than intimates view themselves (Murray et al., 1996a; 1996b). On the other hand, self-verification theory suggests that intimates prefer feedback that confirms their self-concepts in order to foster a sense of prediction and control. Thus, intimates should be happier in their relationships when their partners accurately understand their self-perceived strengths and limitations (Swann et al., 1994).

In the case of individuals who have positive views of themselves, these two positions make similar predictions. That is, spouses will be happier when their partners view them positively. However, when individuals have predominantly negative self-views, the two theories make what appear to be competing predictions. Self-enhancement theory suggests that intimates with negative self-views will be happier when their partners enhance their self-concepts by evaluating them positively. On the contrary, self-verification theorists argue that these individuals will be happier when their partners confirm their self-concepts by evaluating them negatively.

As a result of the apparent incompatibility between these perspectives, much of the research in this area has attempted to reconcile these positions by determining whether the desire for enhancement or the desire for verification serves as the primary motive influencing marital communications. Thus, much of the current debate has focused on answering the question of whether enhancement *or* verification motives take priority within relationships. However, we will argue that the competition between these two views may be more illusory than real. Evidence suggests that both enhancement and verification motives may guide the exchange of feedback in marriage. Spouses should be happiest when both of these motives are fulfilled; that is, when they are both enhanced *and* verified by their partners. Consequently, we suggest that the appropriate question to be answered is not whether enhancement or verification is associated with satisfaction, but rather, how both of these motives may be fulfilled simultaneously within the same satisfying marriages. In particular, how might someone with predominantly negative self-views simultaneously receive enhancing and verifying feedback from their partner?

The goal of this chapter is to describe a model that attempts to answer this question. Briefly, this model comprises two premises. First, we argue that self-views vary in their level of abstraction, ranging from specific views of concrete abilities and characteristics to abstract, global feelings of worth. Second, we argue that motives to enhance or verify may vary at different levels of abstraction. Enhancement motives may operate at the level of global self-views, such that people may wish to receive feedback suggesting that they are generally worthwhile people, regardless of how they view themselves. In contrast, verification motives may operate at the level of specific views, such that people want others to agree with them about their specific strengths and weaknesses. This model, then, suggests a way that spouses in satisfying relationships may simultaneously fulfill both motives: Intimates may receive enhancement of their global worth and verification of their specific traits and abilities. In other words, though our partners may agree with our perceptions of our specific strengths and weaknesses, they may still evaluate us as more worthwhile persons overall than we consider ourselves to be.

To describe and elaborate upon the model of global enhancement and specific verification, the remainder of the chapter is organized into four sections. The first section describes theoretical perspectives on the motives that shape intimates' communications with one another and reviews current empirical research on enhancement and verification motives in relationships. The second section critiques previous attempts to reconcile the two perspectives. As will be seen, previous attempts to integrate self-enhancement and self-verification theories do not address how both motives may be satisfied in the context of a marriage, and thus, fail to account for how enhancement and verification strivings may be linked to satisfaction over the course of a continuing relationship. The third section presents a model to suggest how the apparent conflict between enhancement and verification theories may be resolved through the recognition that self-views vary along a global/specific dimension. We argue that the specificity of the evaluation may influence enhancement and verification motives. In the final section, we discuss how the model integrates existing research, and how it suggests concrete directions for future research by linking spouses' views of each other with broader relationship outcomes.

THEORETICAL PERSPECTIVES ON ENHANCEMENT AND VERIFICATION MOTIVES IN RELATIONSHIPS

Theories of self-enhancement and self-verification strivings were originally developed to describe the motives of the *recipient* of enhancing or verifying feedback. Thus, these theories initially sought to answer the question: How do individuals desire others to view them? Empirically, this question has been tested by examining the type of feedback individuals prefer to receive from strangers and hypothetical others. The application of self-enhancement and self-verification theories to close relationships, however, alters this fundamental question. Within the context of a marriage, satisfaction is influenced not only by the desires of the target, but also by the desires of the perceiver. In other words, within marriage, each individual may have two kinds of motives, a motive to be perceived in certain ways and a motive to perceive a partner in a certain way. Considering the perspective of both the target and the perceiver thus broadens the central question. Within marriage, the question becomes: How do spouses desire to be viewed by their partners *and* how do spouses tend to view their partners in return? As a result of this broader question, theory and research geared toward explaining self-evaluation motives in relationships have grown to include the perspective of both individuals in the marriage. The following brief theoretical review will address the role of both target and perceiver in theories of enhancement and verification.

Self-Enhancement in Relationships: The Desire for Favorable Feedback

The idea that individuals strive to maximize their self-esteem has served as the basis for many theories of social behavior (for example, Brown, 1986; Greenwald, 1980). Throughout this work, theorists have argued that individuals prefer and seek out favorable self-evaluations and avoid information that threatens a positive sense of self (Kunda, 1990; Sedikides, 1993; Taylor & Brown, 1988). Recent conceptions of self-enhancement motives expand on this basic idea, suggesting that the most rewarding evaluations represent exaggerations, or idealizations, of reality (Murray et al., 1996a; 1996b; Taylor & Brown, 1988). Individuals who view themselves in a more positive light than their attributes seem to warrant are argued to be happier and more productive than those with more accurate views of the self (Taylor & Brown, 1988).

Self-Enhancement and the Target's Relationship Satisfaction
From this perspective, spouses are predicted to enjoy greater marital satisfaction the more favorably they are evaluated by their partners

(Murray et al., 1996a; 1996b). Enhancing feedback from a partner should preserve spouses' self-esteem by allowing them to maintain a positive sense of self (for example, Taylor & Brown, 1988). Moreover, receiving enhancing feedback should allow spouses to feel more confident and secure in their partners' regard for them (for example, Murray et al., 1996b).

In fact, Murray et al. (1996a; 1996b) found evidence suggesting that spouses report greater relationship satisfaction when partners not only view them favorably, but also view them more positively than spouses view themselves. Moreover, in the critical case of individuals who have relatively low self-regard, individuals still reported more satisfaction with their relationships, the more positively they were evaluated by their partners (Murray et al., 1996a; 1996b), even though these evaluations may have been largely discrepant with self-views.

Self-Enhancement: The Role of the Perceiver in Relationships

Turning to the perspective of the perceiver in relationships, the enhancement position suggests that in satisfying marriages spouses desire to protect and maintain their positive views of the relationship (for example, Murray & Holmes, 1993; Van Lange & Rusbult, 1995). Enhancement theory, then, argues that perceivers should be happiest in their marriages when they are able to minimize their partners' faults and embellish their partners' virtues, thus viewing their partners more positively than partners view themselves (Murray et al., 1996a; 1996b). As long as intimates are able to depict their partners' faults in the best possible light, relationship satisfaction is likely to be maintained.

Given the desire to maintain a relationship, intimates' perceptions of a romantic partner may be shaped, not by the extent to which the impression is accurate, but rather by how well the impression supports the desired outcome of preserving positive beliefs about the relationship (for example, Kunda, 1990; Swann, 1984). For instance, evidence suggests that as an accurate inference about a partner's thoughts becomes more threatening to an existing relationship, individuals will display greater inaccuracy when asked to describe those thoughts (Simpson, Ickes, & Blackstone, 1995). In order to protect a relationship from doubt, then, individuals may be motivated to perceive their partners somewhat inaccurately. In fact, studies conducted by Murray and her colleagues (1996a; 1996b) suggest that the most satisfied spouses tend to idealize their partners, disregarding their partners' less-than-perfect qualities (Murray et al., 1996a; 1996b).

Self-Verification in Relationships: The Desire to be Understood

Proponents of self-verification theory do not deny that people desire to be evaluated favorably. However, self-verification theorists argue that the need for self-confirming feedback will outweigh the need to protect self-esteem. As a result, individuals desire to create environments that verify existing self-conceptions, even if these conceptions are negative (Swann, 1984; Swann, 1990). Though confirming feedback may not always protect self-esteem, this feedback will serve to bolster individuals' perceptions that the world is predictable and controllable. Confirming evaluations are rewarding in that they reinforce our sense of understanding about the world (Swann, 1990).

Self-Verification and the Target's Relationship Satisfaction

According to self-verification theory, then, spouses should prefer partners who confirm their self-concepts, thus increasing their feelings of prediction and control within the relationship (for example, Swann, Stein-Seroussi, & Giesler, 1992). In having their self-concepts verified, spouses should feel secure in their ability to predict how partners will respond to them. As long as spouses communicate an understanding of each other's strengths and limitations, their interactions will proceed smoothly and cooperative efforts to meet desired goals will prove successful (Swann et al., 1994).

On the other hand, a discrepancy between a spouse's self-perception and a partner's evaluation indicates that future interactions may be characterized by misunderstanding (Swann, 1984). Evaluations that challenge self-views cause discomfort, as spouses may fear that they will be unable or unwilling to honor such perceptions, or even begin to question whether they know themselves after all (Swann, 1990). Consequently, self-verification theory suggests that intimates who feel "misunderstood" will provide partners with corrective feedback, inducing partners to form more desired beliefs (Swann & Hill, 1982). This corrective feedback, then, is presumed to promote self-verification, which in turn leads to an accurate understanding of a romantic partner's qualities (Swann, 1984).

In fact, contrary to self-enhancement theory, Swann and colleagues (De La Ronde & Swann, 1998; Swann et al., 1994) found that, among married couples, relationship satisfaction was higher, the more partners verified each other's own self perceptions of their particular traits and abilities. Importantly, support for the theory was found even when verification entailed receiving unflattering feedback from a spouse: Spouses who evaluated themselves negatively on the specific attributes reported higher marital satisfaction when their partners evaluated them negatively as well (Swann et al., 1994).

Self-Verification: The Role of the Perceiver in Relationships
Self-verification theory devotes less attention to the perceiver in a relationship than to the target. However, accurately understanding a partner's qualities is presumed to result in increased feelings of prediction and control for perceivers as well as for targets. According to self-verification theory, when forming beliefs concerning a partner's qualities, the main goal of perceivers is for their evaluations to offer relatively precise predictions of a partner's behavior, thus allowing for smooth interactions (Swann, 1984). Once intimates' perceptions allow for accurate prediction, intimates will resist information that challenges these perceptions (Swann, 1984).

For instance, when presented with information that disconfirms their perceptions of their partners, intimates attempt to discredit that information (De La Ronde & Swann, 1998). Furthermore, as intimates' perceptions in this study tended to verify the self-concepts of their partners, Swann and colleagues argue that intimates are motivated to aid their partners in preserving self-views (1998). Spouses' desire to understand their partners accurately, then, mirrors their partners' desire to be understood accurately.

MULTIPLE MOTIVATIONS: PREVIOUS RECONCILIATIONS OF THE ENHANCEMENT-VERIFICATION DEBATE

In response to the growing evidence supporting both sides of the enhancement-verification debate, some researchers have suggested that individuals' feedback preferences are guided by multiple motivations (Morling & Epstein, 1997; Swann, 1990). In fact, recent research has indicated that enhancement and verification processes may independently contribute to reports of marital satisfaction (Katz, Anderson, &

Beach, 1997). In order to account for the existing literature, then, a theory is needed to describe how both processes may occur simultaneously within the same satisfying relationships. The following section will discuss two general approaches, a "hierarchy of motives" approach and a "level of cognitive processing" approach, that have been proposed to integrate the two types of motives.

Hierarchy of Motives

Previous attempts to integrate enhancement and verification motives have frequently involved establishing a hierarchy of motives, such that one motive is subsumed under the guiding principles of the other motive. For instance, self-enhancement and self-verification theorists frequently agree that both motives may be simultaneously satisfied when individuals receive feedback concerning their positive attributes. Receiving favorable feedback concerning one's positive attributes allows individuals to feel good about themselves without sacrificing self-consistency (Swann, Pelham, & Krull, 1989; Taylor & Brown, 1988). However, proponents of self-enhancement argue that enhancement motives are the *primary* motives guiding the search for self-relevant feedback (Taylor & Brown, 1988). Given that all individuals believe they possess at least one positive attribute (Swann et al., 1989), receiving favorable feedback on these attributes allows individuals to first fulfill their enhancement motives, and then to also satisfy their verification motives. Self-verification theorists, on the other hand, frame their interpretations of this positive feedback in terms of self-verification motives. These theorists argue that, although self-verification is the dominant motive, high and low self-esteem individuals may satisfy their secondary self-enhancement strivings by seeking verifying feedback of their positive self-views (Swann et al., 1989).

Critiques of a Hierarchy Approach
As indicated, one crucial problem with the "hierarchy of motives" approach is that researchers have failed to agree on the nature of the hierarchy. Enhancement theorists have used enhancement motives as the guiding principle, whereas verification theorists specify verification motives as dominating. Moreover, attempts to subsume one motive within the other are unable to address the current literature on evaluation motives in close relationships. In the case of intimates with low self-esteem, enhancement and verification motives most clearly contradict

one another. Hierarchical approaches to self-evaluation motives, then, do not explain why some studies have demonstrated that low self-esteem intimates are happier the more favorably they are evaluated while other studies indicate that low self-esteem intimates are happier the more accurately (or negatively) they are viewed.

Level of Cognitive Processing Approaches

In response to the previous criticisms, several theorists have purported to view the two motives as equally important to the self-evaluation processes. From this perspective, enhancement and verification strivings have been argued to be independent desires that operate at different levels of cognitive processing. For instance, Swann and colleagues (Swann, 1990; Swann & Schroeder, 1995) contend that, under minimal levels of processing, individuals prefer a self-enhancing evaluation. Enhancement is considered a "reflexlike" preference, as it requires only one step: determining if the evaluation is favorable or unfavorable. However, when cognitive resources are available, and one is sufficiently motivated to expend the additional effort, individuals will then compare the feedback to their self-views. This second step represents a deeper level of processing, resulting in behavior guided by self-verification strivings. Therefore, affective responses are characterized by enhancement motives, while cognitive responses lead to verification motives (Swann, 1990).

Morling and Epstein (1997) also propose a "level of processing" approach to understanding self-evaluation preferences. In their approach, enhancement and verification motives are assumed to operate simultaneously to produce a compromise between the two motives. Individuals want self-enhancement in increments that will not seriously challenge self-views. Unlike Swann (1990), Morling and Epstein (1997) assume that enhancement and verification require equal cognitive work. However, enhancement and verification strivings are discussed as being associated with two conceptually different, but interacting, cognitive systems. Enhancement operates within an experiential system, concerned primarily with short-term consequences. Thus, when short-term consequences become salient, compromises will emphasize enhancement. Conversely, verification operates within a rational system influenced by long-term consequences. Salient long-term consequences, then, will produce compromises emphasizing verification.

Critique of the Level of Cognitive Processing Approach

One problem with a "level of cognitive processing" approach to reconciling the enhancement-verification debate lies in the fact that these theories were developed to explain individuals' reactions to feedback from hypothetical others. To date, the theories adopted to account for the influence of multiple motivations have not been based on evidence derived from individuals in ongoing relationships. As a result, the generalization of these perspectives to the context of close relationships poses several unanswered questions.

For example, the circumstances under which intimates in long-term relationships engage in affect-free, deliberate processing of feedback from partners versus more automatic processing are unclear. Furthermore, level of processing theories do not provide clear predictions for how level of processing may be related to relationship satisfaction. If self-evaluation motives are associated with satisfaction, these theories would seem to suggest that satisfied intimates tend to process their partners' feedback differently than do less satisfied intimates. However, this conclusion does not account for the fact that some studies have linked enhancement, and others verification, to relationship satisfaction. Specifically, to explain the pattern of results found, a "level of processing approach" would suggest that, whereas spouses in the Murray et al. (1996a; 1996b) studies of enhancement were concerned with short-term consequences, spouses in the Swann et al. (1994) study of verification must have been concerned with long-term consequences. Yet there is no reason to suspect that spouses' concerns should have differed across these studies. Again, "level of processing" theories do not seem to account for the existing literature on evaluation motives and relationship satisfaction.

Thus far, integrative approaches to the enhancement-verification debate have relied on added assumptions concerning the cognitive structures and resources necessary to support independent enhancement and verification motives. The necessity of these added assumptions, however, remains unclear, as "level of processing" theories do not seem to account for how enhancement and verification strivings may be linked to satisfaction over the course of a continuing relationship. Moreover, these theories were developed based on feedback from hypothetical others, and fail to address the additional influence of the motives of the perceiver on the well-being of a long-term relationship. Consequently, current integrative approaches seem to leave us with the same fundamental question: How can enhancement and verification processes simultaneously be linked to the marital satisfaction of both spouses?

GLOBAL ENHANCEMENT AND SPECIFIC VERIFICATION: AN INTEGRATIVE THEORY OF EVALUATION PROCESSES IN RELATIONSHIPS

Although both enhancement and verification motives may guide the exchange of feedback within marriage, current integrative theories have not addressed clearly how both of these processes can operate concurrently within the same ongoing relationships. Based on a closer examination of the literature fueling the enhancement-verification debate, we suggest that a consideration of the nature and structure of intimates' self-concepts may provide an answer to the question of how intimates may be simultaneously enhanced and verified by their partners. Most research on how partners give and receive feedback has failed to distinguish between feedback at different levels of abstraction. For example, studies of enhancement have measured attributes such as kindness, understanding, and patience, while studies of verification have examined traits such as athletic ability, intellectual ability, and aptitude in music. Comparing these studies makes the implicit assumption that all of these traits are interchangeable. However, in the following section, we argue that attributes vary meaningfully in their level of abstraction. Acknowledging this variability suggests a possible reconciliation between the theories that account for previous research on evaluation motives in relationships. Namely, we propose a model suggesting that (1) self-views vary along a global/specific dimension and (2) self-evaluation motives vary at different levels of this dimension. The following section will review research supporting both of the premises of the model.

The Nature and Organization of Self-Views

Understanding the self-concept requires a consideration of not only the content, but also the structure, of self-views (Linville, 1985; Showers, 1992). Thus, the first premise of the model is that self-views vary in their level of abstraction. Namely, beliefs about the self have been suggested to differ in terms of a property described as breadth, generality, centrality, globality, or abstractness (Hampson, John, & Goldberg, 1986;

John, Hampson, & Goldberg, 1991). Hampson et al. (1986) argue that, regardless of the terminology used to describe this dimension, each of these labels implies a dimension that reflects the diversity of the behavioral referents of a trait. Thus, broad or global views may be described by a large number of distinct behaviors. For example, kindness can be expressed toward many different people in many different ways. Concrete or specific views, on the other hand, refer to a more limited range of behavioral instances. For example, "charitable" suggests a more specific set of behaviors expressed toward people in need (John et al., 1991).

The alignment of self-views along a global/specific dimension suggests, in turn, that self-views can be represented in a hierarchical structure (Hampson et al., 1986; John et al., 1991). Global views integrate related specific beliefs into an organized associative network (for example, Baldwin, 1992), and serve to summarize attitudes about the self. In other words, global views might include feelings of general self-worth, whereas specific beliefs refer to the particular traits that comprise the foundation on which global evaluations are based (Pelham & Swann, 1989; Rosenberg, 1979).

Given that global views serve to summarize many specific views, these two types of views are clearly related. Evaluations of the self on specific dimensions tend to be correlated with global self-esteem (Marsh, 1986; Rosenberg, 1979). Thus, individuals who believe that they possess few specific positive qualities are not likely to believe that they are highly worthwhile persons. Nevertheless, attempts to predict self-esteem by attending simply to the content of individuals' specific self-views demonstrate that global and specific perceptions of the self are conceptually and empirically distinct (Rosenberg, 1979). Examinations of the relationship between specific self-views and global self-esteem often find that specific self-views account for only about half of the variance in global self-esteem (Marsh, 1986), suggesting that self-esteem does not represent a simple summary of individuals' abilities and weaknesses. Rather, global self-esteem may arise from a more complex weighting system, in which attributes considered to be highly important to the individual contribute more to self-esteem than attributes not considered to be important (Pelham & Swann, 1989; Rosenberg, 1979). The translation of specific self-views into global self-esteem seems to represent an idiosyncratic process, as self-esteem depends, not only on the specific views one holds, but also on the "importance weightings" given to those views.

This idiosyncratic weighting process has important implications when examining intimates' perceptions of their spouses. Namely, this process suggests that two individuals may combine the same specific attributes differently to arrive at different global impressions. For instance, suppose Jane is a highly intelligent woman who is rather shy and reserved in social situations. Jane may have a somewhat negative global view of herself, as her self-esteem is based on the fact that she considers social skills to be more important than intelligence. However, *John's* evaluation of Jane's global worth may be more positive, as he considers Jane's intelligence to be more important than Jane's social skills. Thus, within a marriage, spouses may agree on each other's particular abilities, but differ in their perceptions of global worth, due to differences in the importance weightings assigned to the attributes.

How is the Structure of Self-Views Associated with Self-Evaluation Processes?

Having argued that self-views vary along a global/specific dimension, we argue that this dimension is important for self-evaluation motives for two reasons. First, some self-views may be better suited for enhancement than others. As stated previously, global attributes can be defined by a large number of distinct behaviors, whereas specific attributes can be defined by relatively few distinct behaviors (John et al., 1991). Accordingly, global views allow individuals to consider a broader range of behavioral criteria than specific views, when evaluating themselves on that attribute. When individuals have more criteria to consider, they also have more latitude to place themselves in a positive light. In other words, because fewer clear standards exist for evaluating global views, positive biases are more likely to be held about global attributes than about specific attributes (for example, Dunning, Meyerowitz, & Holzberg, 1989; Taylor, Collins, Skokan, & Aspinwall, 1989).

For example, Dunning et al. (1989) asked subjects to compare themselves to the average student in terms of athletics, artistic talent, and involvement in extracurricular activities. Some students were allowed to generate their own criteria to evaluate themselves against, while other students were provided with a list of specific criteria by which to judge themselves. Individuals allowed to construct their own definitions of the terms rated themselves more favorably than those provided with a specific, objective definition. Furthermore, the participants given a broader range of criteria to consider were more likely to claim a positive trait for themselves than those given a narrower range of criteria to consider.

Research conducted by Dunning and colleagues, then, indicates that enhancement processes in relationships are more likely to operate at higher levels of abstraction. As views of a romantic partner become more global, it should become easier for intimates to enhance their partners. Specifically, as the number of behavioral referents for an attribute increases, people are able to rely on idiosyncratic definitions of the attribute, and hence view their partners in a positive light (Dunning et al., 1989). Thus, sustaining positive biases concerning a partner's kindness should be easier than enhancing a partner's musical talent, due to the relative lack of objective standards for evaluating kindness. Beliefs about a partner's musical ability, on the other hand, could easily be challenged or disconfirmed by others (Taylor et al., 1989).

A second argument for why the global/specific dimension is important for self-evaluation motives concerns the implications of global versus specific views for relationship satisfaction. As views become more global, they will subsume a greater number of specific beliefs, and thus become increasingly evaluative in nature (John et al., 1991). For instance, whereas the specific attribute "punctual" is relatively descriptive of one's behavior, the global attribute "good" simply evaluates how positive or desirable one is. Thus, a positive association exists between the hierarchical level of a view and its evaluativeness (John et al., 1991).

As global views tend to be more evaluative than specific beliefs, global views of the self and of romantic partners have been argued to be more influential for well-being than are specific views (cf. Holmes & Murray, 1995). For instance, maintaining a belief that one's spouse is a good person should be more important to general marital satisfaction than maintaining the belief that one's spouse is artistically talented. Consequently, individuals should be more motivated to maintain positive global beliefs about themselves and their partner than positive specific beliefs. In fact, evidence suggests that when describing the disliked behaviors of a liked other, individuals tend to describe these behaviors in terms of attributes found at lower hierarchical levels (John et al., 1991; Maass, Salvi, Arcuri, & Semin, 1989), as using a specific attribute to describe negative behaviors narrows the range of behaviors that are inconsistent with the overall liking of the target. Thus, a liked other may be described as unpunctual, but never as unkind (John et al.,

1991). Overall, then, intimates may find it easier and also be more motivated, to enhance themselves and their partners on global rather than specific attributes.

In relationships, then, satisfied intimates should tend to verify their spouses at the level of specific traits, communicating an accurate understanding of their partners' positive and negative attributes. Given that specific views should have fewer implications for overall relationship well-being, confirming a spouse's negative specific self-view should pose little threat to a positive global view of the relationship. However, as views become more global, and thus have greater implications for one's evaluation of the relationship, intimates may become more likely to enhance their spouses. The most satisfied couples, then, should be those who maintain positively biased views of their partners' global qualities, while still acknowledging their partners' less-than-perfect specific traits. In fact, one could argue that enhancement at the global level may have a larger influence on marital satisfaction when coupled with specific verification. Though a husband may tell his wife that she is perfect in every way, over time the wife may become uncomfortable with such potentially unfounded praise, resulting in lowered marital satisfaction. Rather, communicating to a partner that he/she is a good, worthwhile person, while also demonstrating accurate knowledge of the partner's specific qualities, may represent "true love."

Evidence for Global Enhancement and Specific Verification in Relationships

Up to this point, we have argued that enhancement processes should operate at the level of global views, whereas verification processes should operate at the level of specific views. The following section will present evidence supporting these arguments. We will first address whether the model can account for the existing literature on the perceived (that is, the target of self-evaluation feedback), then turn to a discussion of the role of the perceiver within this framework.

Previous Research on Evaluation Motives in Relationships
A reexamination of the literature fueling the enhancement-verification debate provides initial support for the theory of global enhancement and specific verification. To determine intimates' perceptions of their partners' self-concepts, participants are frequently asked to rate their partners on a series of attributes. As mentioned, however, the nature

of attributes measured has varied across studies. Studies of self-enhancement motives tend to investigate attributes such as kind, affectionate, understanding, thoughtless, and self-assured (Murray et al., 1996a; 1996b), while the attributes measured in self-verification studies have included intellectual ability, physical attractiveness, athletic ability, social skills, and aptitude in arts and music (Swann et al., 1994). Thus, while self-enhancement measures seem to be tapping into more general perceptions of a partner's worth, self-verification research tends to focus on perceptions of particular abilities.

In fact, Swann (1998) examined the attributes used in self-enhancement and self-verification studies, and found that the attributes used in studies of enhancement tended to be more ambiguous than those used in studies of verification. Similarly, our own analysis of these attributes, using Hampson, Goldberg, and John's (1987) category-breadth rating for 573 personality terms, revealed that the attributes used in enhancement studies tend to be rated as broader than those used in verification studies. We found that the average z-score for the breadth ratings of the attributes used in enhancement studies was .85, while the average z-score for the breadth ratings of the attributes used in verification studies was −.69. In other words, research associating enhancement with relationship satisfaction has measured attributes that were relatively global, whereas research associating verification with satisfaction has measured attributes that were relatively specific. It is important to note that the attributes measured in enhancement studies have not been exclusively global, nor have the attributes measured in verification studies been exclusively specific. Rather, attributes measured in enhancement studies were more global, on average, than those measured in verification studies. Nevertheless, the relative ambiguity and breadth ratings of the various attributes do suggest that enhancement and verification motives may vary according to the level of abstraction of the evaluation. Studies of enhancement, then, suggest that Jane should be happier to the extent that John communicates highly positive evaluations of Jane's kindness and warmth. Thus, even though Jane may only consider herself slightly above average in kindness, John should describe Jane as one of the kindest individuals he has ever met. However, studies of verification argue that when Jane's awareness of her shyness leads her to express doubts concerning her social skills, she will be happiest if John tends to agree with her concerns, rather than suggesting that she is much more socially skilled than she gives herself credit for.

Research on the Feedback-Seeking Activities
of Depressed Individuals

Evidence of simultaneous motives for enhancement and verification can also be found within a single sample. Research on the feedback-seeking activities of depressed individuals provides evidence suggesting that individuals desire to be both understood and affirmed by others. Several studies have highlighted depressed individuals' simultaneous needs to be confirmed and consoled (Joiner, 1995; Joiner, Alfano, & Metalsky, 1993). In one such study, Joiner and colleagues (1993) assessed whether depressed individuals preferred to receive negative or positive feedback concerning their standing on several specific qualities, such as intelligence and social skills. In addition, individuals completed a measure designed to assess efforts to elicit positive emotional feedback from others. This inventory represented self-enhancement information seeking. Results indicated that depressed individuals preferred to receive negative feedback concerning their specific qualities. However, these individuals also reported engaging in high levels of reassurance-seeking behaviors. In other words, they sought self-verifying evaluations of their specific abilities *and* self-enhancing reassurance of others' positive regard for them (Joiner et al., 1993). Even individuals with negative self-concepts, then, appear to desire that their specific qualities be understood, while still desiring to be evaluated positively overall.

Research on Enhancement and Verification
in Newlywed Couples

To test a model of global enhancement and specific verification within a single sample of married couples, Neff and Karney (1999a) collected data from newlywed couples. Given that marital satisfaction should be associated with both enhancement and verification motives, we hypothesized that highly satisfied couples would engage in both of these processes. Thus, the happiest spouses should be those whose partners provide them with specific understanding and global affirmation.

The sample of newlyweds in this study reported being very happy with their relationships, as indicated by scores on the Quality Marriage Index (Norton, 1983), a marital satisfaction scale with a possible range of 6 to 45. The average scores of both husbands and wives were 42. To assess how these satisfied intimates viewed one another, couples were asked to rate themselves and their spouses on a measure of specific attributes and a measure of global worth. Swann's Self-Attributes

Questionnaire (SAQ) (Swann et al., 1994) was used to assess intimates' specific views, while Rosenberg's Self-Esteem Questionnaire (Rosenberg, 1965) was used to assess intimates' global views. The authors then compared the average difference between partner evaluations and self-evaluations on both the SAQ and the Rosenberg scales. Therefore, intimates were undervalued by their spouses if the difference score was negative, verified by their spouses if the score was close to zero, and enhanced by their spouses if the difference was positive.

Results indicated, on average, that both husbands and wives verified their partners on the SAQ. Single sample t-tests showed that neither average difference score differed significantly from zero, indicating that both husbands and wives tended to view their spouses as spouses viewed themselves. Results for the global evaluations on the Rosenberg Self-Esteem scale, however, revealed a different pattern. Here, both average difference scores were significantly greater than zero. Thus, on average, both husbands and wives enhanced their partners' global worth, viewing their spouses as more worthwhile than spouses viewed themselves.

These results are notable for two reasons. First, the metric of the two scales is quite different. Whereas scores on the SAQ can range from 6 to 114, scores on the Rosenberg scale can range only from 10 to 40. Nevertheless, spouses were in more agreement concerning each other's specific abilities than concerning their global worth. Second, for both husbands and wives, views on the SAQ and the Rosenberg scale were significantly correlated. Husbands' specific and global views of the self were correlated at .30, while husbands' specific and global views of their wives were correlated at .32. Likewise, wives' specific and global views of the self and of their husbands were both correlated at .37. However, though global evaluations of worth should be based on evaluations of specific attributes, and despite the fact that couples agreed on each other's specific attributes, intimates nevertheless tended to view their partners more positively overall than partners viewed themselves.

Thus, despite the fact that specific and global self-views were clearly related, different evaluation processes appeared to be operating at each level of abstraction. As mentioned in a previous section, this discrepancy between partner evaluations and self-appraisals at the global level is likely to arise from the fact that perceivers and targets assign different importance weights to the specific attributes on which the global views are based. Research on newlywed couples, then, indicates that satisfying relationships are characterized by both enhancement and verification processes. On average, these happy intimates received verification of their specific attributes and enhancement of their global worth. Thus, when discussing her shyness and felt lack of social skills, Jane should be happiest with her relationship if John verifies her beliefs, while also reminding her of what a wonderful person she is once people get to know her.

The Role of the Perceiver in Relationships

The previous evidence suggests that spouses in satisfying relationships receive global enhancement and specific verification from their partners. However, marital satisfaction is determined not only by the motives of the perceived, but also by the motives of the perceiver. Neff and Karney (1999b) applied the integrative model to perceivers, by examining the general tendency for satisfied intimates to enhance their partners across traits, while simultaneously verifying each particular trait. In other words, the authors hypothesized that, although perceivers may demonstrate relative accuracy for their partners' specific traits, they may still hold a more positive global impression of these traits than their partners do (Murray et al., 1996a; 1996b). For example, John may verify Jane's individual traits: When she believes herself to be low on a trait, such as tidiness, he also rates her as low, and when she believes herself to be high on a trait, such as intelligence, he also rates her as high. At the same time, however, John may enhance her self-concept across these traits. His aggregate view of her across traits may be higher than her aggregate self-view across the traits.

To model this process mathematically, Neff and Karney (1999b) estimated the following function for each couple:

$$y_i = \beta_0 + \beta_1(x_i) + \text{error}$$

In this equation, y_i represents an intimate's perception of a spouse's particular ability, as measured by the SAQ: x_i is a spouse's self-rating of that ability; and β_1 represents the within-couple average correlation between partner evaluations and spouses' self-ratings across the traits on the SAQ. Thus, β_1 can be interpreted as an index of relative accuracy, or the extent to which partners' views of their spouses agree with spouses' views of themselves. β_0, the intercept, is the tendency to systematically "misperceive" a spouse, regardless of the attribute. If this value is positive, this indicates a general tendency to view spouses more positively than spouses view themselves, across specific traits. If this value is negative, this indicates a general tendency to view spouses less positively than spouses view themselves. According to this equation, then, intimates' perceptions of their partners are made up of a degree of accurate understanding plus (or perhaps minus) a little extra. Significant β_1 and β_0 terms would indicate that intimates' perceptions of their spouses are characterized by a significant degree of both specific verification and general enhancement.

Using hierarchical linear modeling, the authors estimated this equation for each individual couple, then investigated the significance of the average β_1 and β_0 terms across couples. For both husbands and wives, both terms were significant and positive. On average, spouses were relatively accurate in their perceptions of their partners' specific traits. At the same time, however, spouses tended to view their partners more positively overall than partners viewed themselves. Thus, on average, perceivers verified their partners at the level of specific traits and enhanced their partners across traits.

SUMMARY: INTEGRATING THE PROPOSED MODEL WITH PRIOR THEORETICAL PERSPECTIVES

A model of global enhancement and specific verification provides several important benefits over previous theories integrating the two positions. First, the current model seems to tie together current research and theory on evaluation motives in relationships by suggesting, not only how enhancement and verification processes may occur simultaneously within the same satisfying marriages, but also how these processes may be associated with each partner's satisfaction. In line with research on self-enhancement, the current model suggests that receiving global enhancement from a partner should allow spouses to maintain a positive sense of self (for example, Taylor & Brown, 1988), and to remain confident in the partner's regard for them (for example, Murray et al., 1996b). However, being told that one is wonderful on all dimensions may not be associated with a successful marriage. Enhancing a spouse without providing evidence of specific understanding is likely to lead spouses to conclude that their partners are naïve, and to doubt the credibility of their opinions. To be effective, then, communications must be viewed as both sincere and believable (Schlenker, 1984).

Consequently, the current model suggests that spouses in satisfying marriages should not only enhance their partners globally, but also convey an accurate understanding of each other's self-perceived *specific* strengths and weaknesses. As suggested by verification theorists

(Swann et al., 1994), then, the mutual understanding of each other's particular abilities should increase the probability of harmonious interactions. A warm, loving relationship in which spouses feel understood should provide them with the reassurance that they may express their needs without fear of rejection or misunderstanding. Thus, trust in a partner's love and support should remain particularly strong over time when global enhancement is accompanied by specific verification. Satisfied spouses should be loved in spite of (or perhaps because of) their faults.

Turning to the perspective of the perceiver, providing a partner with global enhancement and specific understanding allows for intimates to predict their partners' behavior accurately (for example, Swann, 1984), while simultaneously protecting the relationship from doubt (for example, Murray & Holmes, 1994). The current model argues that spouses may recognize their partners' abilities and limitations, but enhance partners' status on global qualities central to marital satisfaction. An important implication of this model is that it may be misleading to call the global enhancement provided by the perceiver a "positive illusion." Rather, perceivers may have some latitude in the way they combine their accurate perceptions of specific traits into a global impression of the partner. In this manner, spouses' positive biases would lead to a desired outcome (that is, maintaining the general belief that a partner is the "right one") without interfering with the specific understanding of a partner's traits and abilities. Overall, then, spouses who globally enhance and specifically verify one another should provide each other with both the loving encouragement and the specific knowledge necessary to achieve relationship goals.

Moreover, a model of global enhancement and specific verification provides a way that even low self-esteem spouses can receive both enhancement and verification from their partners. Enhancement theorists suggest that low self-esteem intimates should be happier in their relationships when their partners evaluate them positively, while verification theorists argue that these intimates should be happier when their partners evaluate them negatively. The current model reconciles these positions by asserting that low self-esteem spouses in satisfying marriages may receive verification of their specific attributes, both positive and negative, and still be viewed more positively overall than they view themselves. Again, we do not assert that it is possible for spouses to believe that their partner has few good qualities, and then to view their partner as very worthwhile. Rather, though our partners may agree with our sometimes negative perceptions of our strengths and weaknesses, they may still evaluate us as more worthwhile persons overall than we consider ourselves to be. In this way, both high *and* low self-esteem individuals may simultaneously receive enhancement and verification from their spouses. Thus, the current model stresses the *discrepancy* between partner evaluations and self-appraisals, rather than the absolute value of intimates' evaluations of their partners.

DIRECTIONS FOR FUTURE RESEARCH

Based on a careful review of the literature, we have proposed a model of self-evaluation preferences designed to integrate the literature concerning enhancement and verification motives in relationships. Nevertheless, further research is needed to assess the utility of the model in accounting for intimates' relationship satisfaction. In order to expand our current understanding of how self-evaluation motives affect close relationships, future research may benefit from linking studies of self-evaluation motives to broader issues in marriage and close relationships.

Self-Evaluation Motives and Marital Interactions

A model suggesting that spouses desire their partners to provide feedback indicating that they both understand and affirm the identity they wish to hold within the marriage may provide a framework for examining studies of conflict and social support interactions. For instance, research on conflict exchanges has indicated that some negative conflict behaviors may actually be associated with higher marital satisfaction over time (Gottman & Krokoff, 1989). This counterintuitive finding may be explained by considering the level of abstraction at which spouses are communicating. From the perspective of the current model, negative communications should not be detrimental to the relationship when those communications are aimed at a specific behavior of the other, rather than at the whole person. A husband whose wife complains that he failed to take out the trash should not feel as threatened by this criticism as one whose wife points out that his neglect of the trash is a perfect indicator of his general laziness. Thus, negative communications that confine criticisms to lower levels of abstraction, leaving spouses' global worth intact, should lead to a more successful resolution of the issue.

Similarly, the current perspective may contribute to the understanding of successful support interactions. Marriage allows individuals in-
numerable opportunities to provide support to, and seek support from,
a spouse. Some spouses, nevertheless, are more effective at providing
and soliciting support than are others. Frequently, studies examining
supportive behaviors in marriage have focused on how personality
affects those behaviors, while neglecting the interpersonal context of
the marriage (Pasch, Bradbury, & Sullivan, 1997). The effective provision and solicitation of social support, however, may be influenced by
the extent to which spouses agree on each other's desired identities.
Specifically, poor support may result from a lack of understanding of
a spouse's desired identity. As mentioned earlier, although providing a
partner with unconditional positive regard may be effective in creating
a safe, loving environment for spouses to express their needs, positive
regard alone may not provide spouses with the information necessary
to achieve their goals successfully. Rather, understanding of a spouse's
specific traits and abilities is also needed to provide partners with more
accurate insight into when spouses need support as well as what support would best help them to accomplish their goals.

Longitudinal Implications for Reconciling Specific
Beliefs with a Global Impression

Given that evaluation motives may vary at different levels of abstraction, how do intimates combine their perceptions of their partners' specific attributes to form a global impression? In other words, how do
global and specific beliefs interact throughout the stages of an ongoing relationship? If different motives operate at the global and specific
levels, then specific beliefs should be responsive to daily fluctuations in
the relationship in a way that global views are not (Karney, McNulty, &
Frye, 2001). Thus, one challenge of maintaining a positive global evaluation of a partner involves reconciling that positive evaluation with
the specific negative views that inevitably arise (Karney et al., in press;
Murray & Holmes, 1999). Understanding how global and specific views
interact may involve the importance weightings perceivers place on
their partners' specific attributes. When evaluating their partners' attributes, spouses may attribute great importance to their partner's best
attributes and little importance to their worst attributes (for example,
Pelham, 1991). Moreover, as specific views no longer support the global
view, spouses may shift their ratings of the specifics in a manner that

will preserve a positive global view. Thus, the motivation to enhance at the global level may result in a strategic shifting of importance weightings over time.

Given that it has been argued that perceivers possess a strong motive to preserve and enhance global evaluations of their partner, how do global evaluations nonetheless change over time? That is, how does this process of combining specific views to form a global impression relate to the trajectory of satisfaction experienced during the course of a marriage? As specific beliefs are more likely to reflect accurate representations of a spouse, changes in global evaluations should follow from changes in specific beliefs. As specific beliefs fail to support the global evaluation, global evaluations may still deteriorate, despite the motives operating to enhance at that level. Nevertheless, it remains unclear how the timing and nature of the specific negative beliefs accumulated in a marriage predict future satisfaction or dissolution. Hence, a key future direction for this area is longitudinal research that examines how self-evaluation motives are linked to the development of marital outcomes over time.

CONCLUSIONS

Research on evaluation motives in relationships has been divided on the issue of how spouses in satisfying marriages view one another. To resolve this debate, we proposed a model focusing on the level of abstraction at which evaluation motives operate. We suggested that evaluation processes differ at the global and specific levels, such that satisfied spouses verify each other's specific traits and enhance each other's global worth. This distinction has been shown to account for the seemingly contradictory findings suggesting that both enhancement and verification are associated with greater marital satisfaction. The resolution of these issues offers an opportunity to move beyond the question of what motives drive self-evaluation processes in marriage, to the question of how these processes influence a broader range of close relationship phenomena.

REFERENCES

Baldwin, M. W. (1992). Relational schemas and the processing of social information. *Psychological Bulletin, 112*, 461–484.

Berger, P. L., & Kellner, H. (1964). Marriage and the construction of reality: An exercise in the microsociology of knowledge. *Diogenes, 46*, 1–24.

Brown, J. D. (1986). Evaluations of self and others: Self-enhancement biases in social judgments. *Social Cognition, 4*, 353–376.

De La Ronde, C., & Swann, W. B., Jr. (1998). Partner verification: Restoring images of our intimates. *Journal of Personality and Social Psychology, 75*, 374–382.

Dunning, D., Meyerowitz, J. A., & Holzberg, A. D. (1989). Ambiguity and self-evaluation: The role of idiosyncratic trait definitions in self-serving assessments of ability. *Journal of Personality and Social Psychology, 57*, 1082–1090.

Gottman, J. M., & Krokoff, L. J. (1989). Marital interaction and satisfaction: A longitudinal view. *Journal of Counseling and Clinical Psychology, 57*, 47–52.

Greenwald, A. G. (1980). The totalitarian ego: Fabrication and revision of personal history. *American Psychologist, 35*, 603–618.

Hampson, S. E., Goldberg, L. R., & John, O. P. (1987). Category-breadth and social-desirability values for 573 personality terms. *European Journal of Personality, 1*, 241–258.

Hampson, S. E., John, O. P., & Goldberg, L. R. (1986). Category breadth and hierarchical structure in personality: Studies of asymmetries in judgments of trait implications. *Journal of Personality and Social Psychology, 51*, 37–54.

Holmes. J. G., & Murray, S. L. (1995). Memory for events in close relationships: Applying Schank and Abelson's story skeleton model. In R. S. Wyer, Jr. (Ed.), *Knowledge and memory: The real story: Vol. 8. Advances in social cognition* (pp. 193–210). Mahwah, NJ: Lawrence Erlbaum Associates, Inc.

John, O. P., Hampson, S. E., & Goldberg, L. R. (1991). The basic level in personality-trait hierarchies: Studies of trait use and accessibility in different contexts. *Journal of Personality and Social Psychology, 60*, 348–361.

Joiner, T. E., Jr. (1995). The price of soliciting and receiving negative feedback: Self-verification theory as a vulnerability to depression theory. *Journal of Abnormal Psychology, 104*, 364–372.

Joiner, T. E., Jr., Alfano, M. S., & Metalsky, G. I. (1993). Caught in the crossfire: Depression, self-consistency, self-enhancement, and the response of others. *Journal of Social and Clinical Psychology, 12*, 113–134.

Karney, B. R., McNulty, J. K., & Frye, N. E. (2001). A social-cognitive model of relationship maintenance. In J. H. Harvey & A. E. Wenzel (Eds.), *Close romantic relationships: Maintenance and enhancement* (pp. 195–214). Mahwah, NJ: Lawrence Erlbaum Associates, Inc.

Katz, J., Anderson, P., & Beach, S. R. H. (1997). Dating relationship quality: Effects of global self-verification and self-enhancement. *Journal of Social and Personal Relationships, 14*, 829–842.

Kunda, M. (1990). The case for motivated reasoning. *Psychological Bulletin, 108*, 480–498.

Linville, P. W. (1985). Self-complexity and affective extremity: Don't put all of your eggs in one cognitive basket. *Social Cognition, 3*, 94–120.

Maass, A., Salvi, D., Arcuri, L., & Semin, G. (1989). Language use in intergroup contexts: The linguistic intergroup bias. *Journal of Personality and Social Psychology, 57*, 981–993.

Marsh, H. W. (1986). Global self-esteem: Its relation to specific facets of self-concept and their importance. *Journal of Personality and Social Psychology, 51,* 1224–1236.

Morling, B. & Epstein, S. (1997). Compromises produced by the dialectic between self-verification and self-enhancement. *Journal of Personality and Social Psychology, 73,* 1268–1283.

Murray, S. L. & Holmes, J. G. (1993). Seeing virtues in faults: Negativity and the transformation of interpersonal narratives in close relationships. *Journal of Personality and Social Psychology, 65,* 707–722.

Murray, S. L., & Holmes, J. G. (1994). Storytelling in close relationships: The construction of confidence. *Personality and Social Psychology Bulletin, 20,* 650–663.

Murray, S. L., & Holmes, J. G. (1999). The (mental) ties that bind: Cognitive structures that predict relationship resilience. *Journal of Personality and Social Psychology, 77,* 1228–1244.

Murray, S. L., Holmes, J. G., & Griffin, D. W. (1996a). The benefits of positive illusions: Idealization and the construction of satisfaction in close relationships. *Journal of Personality and Social Psychology, 70,* 79–98.

Murray, S. L., Holmes, J. G., & Griffin, D. W. (1996b). The self-fulfilling nature of positive illusions in romantic relationships: Love is not blind but prescient. *Journal of Personality and Social Psychology, 71,* 1155–1180.

Neff, L. A., & Karney, B. R. (1999a). To be adored and to be known: Global enhancement and specific verification in relationships. Paper presented at the meeting of the International Network of Personal Relationships, Louisville, KY.

Neff, L. A., & Karney, B. R. (1999b). Global enhancement and specific verification in newlywed marriage. Unpublished manuscript, University of Florida at Gainesville.

Norton, R. (1983). Measuring marital quality: A critical look at the dependent variable. *Journal of Marriage and the Family, 45,* 141–151.

Pasch, L. A., Bradbury, T. N., & Sullivan, K. T. (1997). Social support in marriage: An analysis of intraindividual and interpersonal consequences. In G. R. Pierce, B. Lakey, I. G. Sarason, B. R. Sarason (Eds.), *Sourcebook of social support and personality.* New York: Plenum.

Pelham, B. W. (1991). On confidence and consequence: The certainty and importance of self-knowledge. *Journal of Personality and Social Psychology, 60,* 518–530.

Pelham, B. W., & Swann, W. B. (1989). From self-conceptions to self-worth: On the sources and structure of global self-esteem. *Journal of Personality and Social Psychology, 57,* 672–680.

Rosenberg, S. (1965). *Society and the adolescent self-image.* Princeton, NJ: Princeton University Press.

Rosenberg, M. (1979). *Conceiving the self.* New York: Basic Books.

Schlenker, B. R. (1984). Identities, identifications, and relationships. In V. Derlega (Ed.), *Communication, intimacy, and close relationships* (pp. 71–104). New York: Academic Press.

Sedikides, C. (1993). Assessment, enhancement, and verification determinants of the self-evaluation process. *Journal of Personality and Social Psychology, 65,* 317–338.

Showers, C. (1992). Compartmentalization of positive and negative self-knowledge: Keeping bad apples out of the bunch. *Journal of Personality and Social Psychology, 62,* 1036–1049.

Simpson, J. A., Ickes, W., & Blackstone, T. (1995). When the head protects the heart: Empathic accuracy in dating relationships. *Journal of Personality and Social Psychology, 69,* 629–641.

Swann, W. B., Jr. (1984). Quest for accuracy in person perception: A matter of pragmatics. *Psychological Review, 91,* 457–477.

Swann, W. B., Jr. (1990). To be adored or to be known? The interplay of self-enhancement and self-verification. In E. T. Higgins & R. M. Sorrentino (Eds.), *Handbook of motivation and cognition: Foundations of social behavior* (vol. 2, pp. 408–448). New York: Guilford.

Swann, W. B., Jr. (1998). The self and interpersonal relationships. Paper presented at the meeting of the Society of Experimental Social Psychologists, Lexington, KY.

Swann, W. B., Jr., De La Ronde, C., & Hixon, J. G. (1994). Authenticity and positivity strivings in marriage and courtship. *Journal of Personality and Social Psychology, 66,* 857–869.

Swann, W.B., Jr., & Hill, C. A. (1982). When our identities are mistaken: Reaffirming self-conceptions through social interaction. *Journal of Personality and Social Psychology, 43,* 59–66.

Swann, W. B., Jr., Pelham, B. W., & Krull, D. S. (1989). Agreeable fancy or disagreeable truth? Reconciling self-enhancement and self-verification. *Journal of Personality and Social Psychology, 57,* 782–791.

Swann, W. B., Jr., & Schroeder, D. G. (1995). The search for beauty and truth: A framework for understanding reactions to evaluations. *Personality and Social Psychology Bulletin, 21,* 1307–1318.

Swann, W. B., Jr., Stein-Seroussi, A., & Giesler, R. B. (1992). Why people self-verify. *Journal of Personality and Social Psychology, 62,* 392–401.

Taylor, S. E., & Brown, J. D. (1988). Illusion and well-being: A social psychological perspective on mental health. *Psychological Bulletin, 103,* 193–210.

Taylor, S. E., Collins, R. L., Skokan, L. A., & Aspinwall, L. G. (1989). Maintaining positive illusions in the face of negative information: Getting the facts without letting them get to you. *Journal of Social and Clinical Psychology, 8,* 114–129.

Van Lange, P. A. M., & Rusbult, C. E. (1995). My relationship is better than – and not as bad as – yours is: The perception of superiority in close relationships. *Personality and Social Psychology Bulletin, 21,* 32–44.

CHAPTER THREE

Competition in Romantic Relationships: Do Partners Build Niches?

Steven R. H. Beach, Daniel Whitaker,
Heather A. O'Mahen, Deborah Jones,
Abraham Tesser, and Frank D. Fincham

Baumeister and Leary (1995) argue compellingly that human beings have a need to belong, and that this need may be deeply rooted in the experience of homo sapiens in their Environment of Evolutionary Adaptedness (EEA). For humans, the Environment of Evolutionary Adaptedness is commonly taken to be the Pleistocene environment in which the overwhelming majority of human evolution is thought to have occurred. The need to belong to a group may, however, be only the most basic of the adaptations that emerged during the EEA for humans. It seems likely that a variety of other social adaptations have developed as well, and that these serve to further the goal of maintaining or optimizing group involvement and pair bonding.

Leary and Downs (1995) note, for example, that evaluative feelings about the self may serve as a social adaptation "that (1) monitors the social environment for cues indicating disapproval, rejection, or exclusion and (2) alerts the individual via negative affective reactions when such cues are detected." (Leary & Downs, 1995, p. 129). Gilbert (1992) also hypothesizes that mechanisms to enhance smooth functioning within a group or dyadic context may have assumed increasing evolutionary importance as homo sapiens became more oriented to alliances and sharing. Gilbert (1992) highlights the emergence of strategies to gain and control others' attention through coalitions and cooperative activity, rather than exclusive reliance on strategies to attain dominance

Daniel Whitaker is now at the Centers for Disease Control, Atlanta, Georgia. Deborah Jones is now at the University of Pittsburgh Medical Center.
We are grateful to the National Institute of Health for supporting this work.
Correspondence should be directed to Steven Beach, Department of Psychology, University of Georgia, Athens, Georgia 30602-3013. Phone (706) 542-1173; fax (706) 542-8048; e-mail: sbeach@egon.psy.uga.edu.

via threat and aggression. Likewise, Kirkpatrick (1998) notes that humans may have benefited from a mechanism that helped foster commitment in newly forming couples, and so helped free partners from an otherwise potentially interminable mate selection process. As these examples suggest, a number of perspectives highlight a role for selective pressure in the emergence of mechanisms to regulate dyadic interaction. In particular, these arguments suggest selective pressure favoring social adaptations designed to regulate competition, focus efforts to better "fit" with close others, and to facilitate the formation of (at least moderately) stable pair bonds.

A Mechanism to Facilitate Cooperation, Fit, and Pair Bonding?

The Self-Evaluation Maintenance (SEM) model (Tesser, 1988) describes a mechanism that seems well designed to guide the development of a mental representation that could, in turn, help regulate competition, focus efforts to fit with a partner, and so facilitate pair bonding. According to the SEM model (Tesser, 1988), when the self performs better than close others in a given area, that area tends to remain central or "relevant" to one's self-definition. Conversely, performing relatively more poorly than close others is often associated with decreases in self-relevance (Tesser, 1988; Tesser & Campbell, 1982; Tesser & Paulhus, 1983), a process that may be reflected in rating the area as less important to the self.

How might this simple mechanism serve to construct a "self" that fits better with the partner and so facilitates pair bonding? We hypothesize that shifts in relevance provide a basis for partners in close relationships to change their views of themselves over time, and to do so in a manner that leads them to "cede" certain areas to the partner, while retaining decision-making or leadership authority in others. When one partner notices that the other consistently performs better in a certain area, this information will tend to result in that area being represented as less "self-relevant." The decrease in self-relevance should correspond to a tendency to defer to the partner and play a supportive role in the area. For example, if one partner has a better memory for directions, the partner should be more likely to defer to their suggestions about which way to go.

Indeed, because decreased relevance should also make it more likely that the individual will "bask in the reflected glory" of the other's good performance (Cialdini & Richardson, 1980), this shift should help partners feel good about deferring to the other. As partners increasingly sort out areas in which one or the other will take the lead (and areas in which it is fine for both to participate or even to compete), there should be substantial benefit in terms of coordination of effort. Rather than working at cross purposes or against one another, partners should be able to work more easily toward a common end. In addition, as partners feel increasingly good about each other's areas of strength, it should be easier to reinforce each other's strengths, and so provide encouragement and support.

Accordingly, the process of decreasing self-relevance in response to being outperformed by a close other should be particularly useful in regulating competition and increasing perceived fit with a close other, if it provides an occasion for the self to cede leadership in some areas while retaining leadership in other areas. It is important to note, however, that an area has only been ceded to the partner if it is viewed as more important to the partner than to the self. If the importance of the area is reduced both for the self and the partner, the resulting mental representation provides no additional guidance as to who should take the lead in that area or who should be expected to do better in that area. Accordingly, decreasing importance for both self and partner should not facilitate cooperation, or increase perceived fit with the partner. Rather, for relevance adjustments to have value as a social adaptation, self-relevance should *diverge* from partner-relevance when the self is outperformed. Because it has no parameter of partner-relevance, the original SEM model (Tesser, 1988) did not adequately deal with the issue of divergence of self and partner-relevance, and so did not adequately explicate the potentially adaptive implications of change in relevance for dyadic competition and cooperation. We provide a brief discussion of the potential adaptive problem posed by the attraction to similar others, as well as evidence that partners may build complementarity into their relationships in the following section. Doing so sets the stage for predictions regarding circumstances under which the relevance of an area to self and partner should diverge.

Similarity is a Potential Problem for Romantic Relationships

Similarity is well known to be attractive and to provide a foundation for assortative mating (for example, Berscheid & Walster, 1978; Byrne,

1997; O'Leary & Smith, 1991). However, similarity may also lead others to display abilities similar to one's own, creating a potential threat to self-evaluation and to cooperative interaction. In this context, an age-old cliché becomes an important question: If "birds of a feather flock together" how do they stay together? That is, if similarity brings people together, how do they deal with the problems created by their similarity? To solve the problem of similarity, couples may often revise self-relevance in relation to perceived partner-relevance, to create a "performance ecology" (Beach, Tesser, Mendolia, Anderson, Crelia, Whitaker, & Fincham, 1996) in which self and partner-relevance diverge.

A performance ecology is, simply, a cognitive-relational structure that maps out each partner's performance "niche" in the relationship. That is, a performance ecology maps out the performance areas in which the self is better and has a leadership role, areas that can be safely shared, and areas that are important to neither partner. As noted earlier, the original SEM model did not address the question of divergence of self and partner-relevance. When extended to marriage, the SEM model (Beach & Tesser, 1995) implies divergence of self and partner-relevance in response to performance feedback, due to sympathetic concern for partner outcomes. Thus, this model provides a theoretical basis for the prediction of divergence in committed dyads.

However, the extended model is silent with regard to divergence in less-committed dyads. Less-committed couples are of considerable interest, if one considers relevance adjustments to be an adaptation designed to help couples create better "fit" to a particular partner, or to foster commitment to the relationship. In this case, one might anticipate that divergence would occur relatively early in the couple formation process, and not only after couples were already committed. Likewise, if shifts in relevance have the function of ceding performance areas to others, such an activity would seem particularly important early in the process of pair bonding, when couple identity is being shaped. Accordingly, a mechanism prompting divergence in self and partner-relevance that does not depend entirely on concern for partner outcomes, would also seem to have important adaptive benefits. Of course these hypotheses assume that, under some circumstances, divergence in self and partner-relevance is helpful to couples.

Is Divergence of Self-Relevance and Perceived Partner-Relevance Helpful?

Several lines of evidence suggest the possibility that divergence in self and partner-relevance may be useful in romantic relationships. Working within the framework of the SEM model, Beach and Tesser (1993) examined differentiation in the area of decision making, and related this differentiation to marital satisfaction. Husbands and wives who made decisions in areas of greater personal importance were more satisfied with their marriages. Interestingly, this effect was not due to these spouses having more power; it was due to differentiation and the differentiated use of power. That is, relative to less-satisfied partners, satisfied husbands and wives reported a higher percentage of agreements in areas conferring potential SEM benefits. If the self made the decision about "where to live" and this issue was important to the self, or if the partner made the decision about "where to live" and this issue was not important to the self, there were high percentages of perceived agreement among the satisfied couples. In contrast, this pattern was less true for dissatisfied partners.

Similarly, satisfied husbands and wives reported a higher percentage of agreements when the self made the decision and the area was unimportant to the partner, or the partner made the decision and the area was unimportant to the self. Again, this pattern was less true for dissatisfied partners. However, when we examined overall level of perceived decision-making power in the relationship (regardless of importance to self or partner), overall decision-making power did not strongly discriminate between those in more- and less-satisfied relationships. Accordingly, it appears that satisfaction is related most strongly to the patterning of decision making, and its fit with the niches that have been created by each partner in the relationship.

Evidence that complementarity may be useful in enhancing relationship outcomes also comes from work outside the SEM tradition. For example, Fitzpatrick's work (1988) on relationship "types" suggests three types of couples: independents, separates, and traditionals. Although independents are often viewed as an ideal example of well functioning spouses (they appear to be supportive of each other, able to deal directly with conflict, and egalitarian in their orientation to marriage), they were *not* the group Fitzpatrick found to be most maritally satisfied. They were more satisfied than separates, who displayed a particularly low level of teamwork and "we-ness," but not as satisfied as traditionals, who reported having a very clear and distinct division of labor in the marriage and separate spheres of influence. Traditionals also reported the most time together, the most shared activities, and the most physical proximity over the course of the day. The traditional group was best differentiated and most complementary with regard to the performance domain, and regardless of the index of closeness one might use, they were also the group reporting the greatest degree of closeness.

Extending and expanding this line of reasoning to a younger population, the power of similarity and complementarity to predict relationship outcomes in dating relationships was examined by Houts, Robins, and Huston (1996) for 168 first-time marriages. They found evidence of assortative mating with regard to many social characteristics, but little evidence that such similarity predicted courtship evaluations. However, both similarity in leisure interests and complementarity in role preferences (that is, agreeing about who would take which roles) were related to positive evaluation of the relationship, and lower levels of conflict. Again, these data are correlational, but suggest the importance, for dating partners, of divergence with regard to role preferences.

Of equal interest, however, is the observation by Houts et al. (1996) that, even in a relatively homogeneous population, it is quite difficult to find a partner who is compatible with the self on multiple leisure and role performance domains. Accordingly, regardless of how well partners choose each other, there are likely to be many points of potential friction that await them as they attempt to create a workable division of labor. Accordingly, these data underscore the potential utility of a mechanism that could lead to greater complementarity of role preferences.

Adjustment when the Self is Outperformed

When the self is outperformed, individuals should be threatened with the possibility of negative comparison, and so be motivated to protect self-evaluation by decreasing the self-relevance of the area (especially if performance can not be distorted, and closeness is not free to change easily). This prediction follows directly from the SEM model (Tesser, 1988). Of interest in the current series of studies is what happens to self-relevance in relation to perceived partner-relevance. Do both types of relevance ratings change together, suggesting a "sour grapes" response to being outperformed? Or, as predicted by the current elaboration of the SEM model, is the reduction in self-relevance coupled with a divergence in self and partner-relevance ratings? Only the latter result is consistent with the hypothesis that SEM adjustments have the function of "ceding" the area to the partner, thereby fostering cooperation, enhanced fit, and pair bonding.

Adjustment when the Self Performs Better

When the self performs better, there is no threat to self-evaluation and hence no self-defensive motivation to adjust relevance. Accordingly, from the perspective of the original SEM model, there is little reason to expect divergence between self and partner-relevance. In contrast, the extended SEM model (Beach & Tesser, 1995) suggests that increased empathy and attention to partner reactions could motivate relevance adjustment, resulting in divergence when the self performs better. At least one earlier study supports the hypothesis that partners sometimes adjust partner-relevance to create greater divergence between self and partner-relevance. In a study of decision making among married partners, Beach et al. (1996, Study 3) found that spouses tended to overestimate partner-relevance for areas in which the spouse made the decision, but underestimate partner-relevance for areas in which the self made the decision. That is, we asked both partners in the marriage to say how important various areas of decision making were to them and to their partner. In this way, we could compare partners' perceptions with the reality of the other's stated importance of the area. We found that, when individuals had greater decision authority in the area, their spouses perceived the area as more important to them than their self-report indicated it really was. In contrast, when individuals had less decision authority in an area, spouses perceived the area as less important to them than their self-report indicated it was.

Highlighting Competition to Amplify Adjustments

If the adjustments in perceived relevance that follow differential performance feedback are made in the service of promoting cooperative interaction with the partner, the process should be intensified by highlighting potential competition with the partner. That is, one might expect potentially competitive interactions to lead to greater divergence of relevance ratings in response to differential performance feedback. This possibility contrasts with the hypothesis that competition will simply confer extra significance on performing well for both self and partner, leading to greater relevance ratings for both self and partner (particularly if the self performs better), and quite possibly blocking divergence in relevance ratings. It also contrasts with the prediction that potential competition with a close other may prompt a defensive reduction in relevance ratings for both self and partner (particularly if the partner performs better), again blocking divergence. If highlighting the competitive nature of an activity blocks the divergence of self and partner-relevance ratings by causing the ratings to move up or down together, the hypothesis that divergence is designed to defuse competition would be thrown into doubt. Accordingly, examining divergence in self and partner-relevance ratings in the context of an explicitly competitive task represents a critical test of relevance adjustments as social adaptations.

Hypotheses and Overview of Studies[1]

We conducted a series of three studies of dating and married couples, to examine the possibility that self and partner-relevance may diverge in response to performance feedback. Specifically, we tested three interrelated hypotheses.

1. In Study 1 (a study of dating couples), self-relevance will diverge from perceived partner-relevance in response to feedback that the partner has outperformed the self. In Study 1 and in both subsequent studies, this "self-defensive" effect will appear as the interaction of level of "Performance" (Self better versus Other better) with "Target" (Self versus Partner); that is, self-relevance will be significantly lower than partner-relevance in the "Other-better" performance condition.

2. In Study 2, using married couples, self-relevance will diverge from perceived partner-relevance both in response to feedback that the partner has outperformed the self and in response to feedback that the self has outperformed the partner. Adjustments will be examined by testing the significance of the simple effects of Target within level of Performance.

3. In Study 3 (again using dating couples), we predicted that divergence in relevance ratings would be amplified if the competitive

---

[1] A manipulation of cognitive load was present in each of the studies. However, it failed to interact with Performance Feedback in any of the studies, indicating that adjustments in response to self-better feedback and adjustments in response to partner-better feedback were not differentially disrupted. Accordingly, we mention briefly the cognitive load manipulation where appropriate, but avoid claims affirming the null hypothesis.

nature of the task were highlighted. Specifically, the interaction of "Performance" by "Target" should be significant, and in the direction predicted for Study 1. As in Study 1, self-relevance should be significantly lower than partner-relevance in the "Other-better" condition. A comparison of Studies 1 and 3 should indicate a greater impact of performance information on divergence in Study 3.

STUDY 1

Do persons in romantic relationships shift the relative importance of performance domains in response to differential performance feedback? Do adjustments of self-relevance result in *divergence* of self and perceived partner-relevance, or merely cause them to move in tandem? To address these questions, it was necessary to create a context in which credible performance feedback could be provided, and in which partners could be asked to rate the importance of various areas. Accordingly, we developed a paradigm that met this requirement and that was used throughout the following series of studies. Couples were recruited and asked to participate in a task that would "help psychologists refine a newly developed test that was diagnostic of several important abilities." In each case, participants found the cover story credible and seemed involved in the activities. Study 1 is therefore an initial test of the first hypothesis, as well as a test of the utility of the experimental paradigm for use in later studies.

Participants were 48 dating couples from a large southeastern university. Participants included both psychology undergraduates recruited from the subject pool and their partners, and couples recruited from signs posted around the campus. Psychology students received partial credit and a $5 payment for their partners in return for their participation, whereas the latter group, in which neither partner received credit, was given $10 for their participation. Participants had a mean age of 19.1 years (range 18–24 years) and had been dating for 12.5 months on average (range 1–61 months). Participants were randomly assigned to one of four between–subject conditions created by crossing Performance (Self-better versus Other-better) and Cognitive load (High versus Low).

Participants were introduced to the study and told that their participation would help in the development of a diagnostic task that related to various important abilities; they were informed that we were interested in whether they could discern the abilities measured by the task under various levels of cognitive "load." Couples were told that both partners would complete the same computerized task, and that, although they would be in different rooms, they would receive nearly instantaneous feedback on their performance as the computers on which they would be working were connected to the psychology department server. Ethernet connections consistent with the cover story were attached to both computers and were clearly visible to the participants. In addition, they were told they would receive a number at the end of the task to memorize and recall at a later point in time.

After being shown to their individual rooms, participants were asked to complete a 26-item, multiple-choice test that included trivia questions about "American culture." Examples of questions are as follows: "The newspaper most Americans subscribe to is the _____ "; and "After watching television, Americans spend the most of their time _____." After participants had completed the task, the computer displayed a message to all participants asking them to "Wait for your partner to finish." After a 15 second delay, a computer message indicated that the partner had finished and that scores were being tabulated. Both members of the dyad received the same type of feedback, either that they had scored higher than their partner had, or that their partner had scored higher than they did. Because partners did not interact regarding the feedback, assigning partners to the same feedback condition was possible, without compromising the believability of the feedback.

Dependent Measures

Following the feedback and the presentation of a number to recall later, the key dependent measure was presented. On a six-point scale, participants were asked to rate the following questions, "To what extent did the task relate to abilities that are important to you?" And, "To what extent did the task relate to abilities that are important to your partner?" Participants then completed a series of additional questions about the task, demographic information, and several questionnaires.

Performance and Task-relevance in Dating Couples

Due to the potential dependency in the ratings between members of a couple, the couple rather than the individual was used as the unit of analysis. Because the couple was the unit for all analyses, there were four scores for each unit: the male's self and partner-relevance ratings,

Table 3.1. Cell Means and Standard Deviations (in parentheses) for Relevance Ratings as a Function of Performance Feedback and Target for Study 1

	Target	
Performance Feedback	Self	Partner
Self better	2.92 (1.28)	2.98 (1.12)
Other better	2.56 (.824)	3.11 (1.99)
N = 47 couples		

and the female's self and partner-relevance ratings. Accordingly, the data were analyzed in a $2 \times 2 \times 2 \times 2$ repeated measures ANOVA with Performance and Memory Load as between-subject variables. Gender was treated as repeated within-couple, and target of the relevance ratings (Self or Other) was treated as repeated within-individual.

Our first hypothesis argues that the relevance ratings for self and partner should change differentially as a function of performance conditions, leading to divergence when the self is threatened with potential negative comparison. Providing initial support for this prediction, the Performance $\times$ Target interaction was significant, $F(1, 43) = 8.15$, $p < .01$, indicating that relevance ratings changed differentially for self and partner as a function of performance outcomes. The pattern of mean differences in relevance ratings for the self and partner was consistent with the hypothesized "self-defensive" process only. That is, the simple main effect of target was significant within the "Other-better" condition $F(1, 18) = 6.91, p = .01$ (Ms = 2.56 and 3.11 for self and perceived partner-relevance, respectively), but not within the "Self-better" condition (Ms = 2.92 and 2.98 for self and perceived partner-relevance, respectively). See Table 3.1.

Implications

Consistent with the first hypothesis, the current findings suggest that, when outperformed by the partner, dating partners decrease self-relevance relative to partner-relevance. It should be noted that this result is not the only possible pattern. One might have hypothesized a "sour grapes" pattern, in which relevance would be rated lower for both the self and the partner if the self were to be outperformed. Or, one might have hypothesized that couples would protect their "similarity" to the partner, eschewing the opportunity to create divergence in relevance ratings within the dyad, and leaving relevance ratings relatively high for both partners. Accordingly, these findings provide initial support for the notion that the relevance adjustments predicted by the SEM model serve to create divergence in self and partner ratings, and that the adjustments have the effect of "ceding" certain areas to the partner.

At the same time, Study 1 provided no evidence that self-relevance diverged from partner-relevance when the self did better. Of course, because outperforming the partner poses no threat of negative comparison, there was little reason to expect divergence in relevance ratings when the self did better. However, as relationships develop, partners may become more sensitive to the ways in which outperforming the partner affects the partner or the relationship. Consideration of possible partner outcomes may lead to relative decreases in perceived partner-relevance (for example, Beach et al., 1996), or norms of reciprocity and greater comfort with the partner may lead to relative increases in the assertion of self-relevance for areas in which the self performs better. In either case, one might expect more established couples to provide more evidence of divergence in response to the "self outperforms partner" condition.

STUDY 2[2]

Study 2 replicates and extends the findings from Study 1 to a married sample. Married couples have a more communal relationship with each other (Clark, Mills, & Powell, 1986), may expect greater reciprocity and fairness in their relationships, and may be more sensitive to partner and relationship outcomes. This situation may lead married couples to show adjustment of self and partner relevance in response to outperforming the partner, as well as showing the self-defensive adjustments found in Study 1.

In addition to examining self-defensive adjustments and adjustments in response to outperforming the partner, comparison of Study 2 results with those from Study 1 provides a window on differences between dating and married couples. In particular, the comparison of Study 1 and Study 2 allows us to directly examine the hypothesis that adjustments in

---

[2] Results of Study 2 are reported in more detail in: Beach, S. R. H., Whitaker, D., Jones, D., & Tesser, A. (in press). When does performance feedback prompt complementarity in romantic relationships? *Personal Relationships*.

response to outperforming the partner may differ significantly between dating and married couples. It should be noted, however, that differences between dating and married couples are potentially confounded with other factors that vary between the two studies, such as the experimenter running the study and the method of recruitment. Likewise, the two samples differ with regard to age, and age may influence degree of empathy and concern for others' outcomes. Nonetheless, comparison of the two samples using the same experimental procedure provides a basis for speculating about patterns of adjusting to differential performance feedback that may change as couples move from one stage of relationship development to another.

Participants were 43 married couples recruited from the county surrounding and including the University of Georgia. Participants were recruited through random digit dialing performed by the Survey Research Center at the Institute for Behavioral Research at the University of Georgia. Participants averaged 36.9 years of age (range 21–68 years) and had been married for 10.3 years on average (range 1–47 years). As in Study 1, couples were randomly assigned to one of the four between-subject conditions crossing Performance and Load.

The procedure was identical to that used in Study 1. Participants were randomly assigned to performance condition. They received feedback that they had either outperformed the partner or that the partner had outperformed the self. Following the feedback, participants were asked to rate task-relevance for the self and for the partner, and then completed additional measures.

Performance and Task-Relevance in Married Couples

As in Study 1, we conducted a $2 \times 2 \times 2 \times 2$ repeated measures ANOVA with Performance and Cognitive Load treated as between-subject factors, Target of the relevance rating treated as a within-subject variable, and gender treated as repeated within-couple. Replicating the findings of Study 1, the Performance $\times$ Target interaction was significant, $F(1, 39) = 24.49$, $p = .0001$, indicating that relevance ratings diverged in response to differential performance feedback. To test for "self-defensive" adjustments and adjustments in response to outperforming the partner, simple effects within level of Performance were examined. As in Study 1, there was a significant simple effect of Target when the partner outperformed the self, $F(1,21) = 19.30$, $p < .01$, showing that partner-relevance was rated as significantly greater than self-relevance in this condition. See Table 3.2. This result indicates that the

Table 3.2. Cell Means and Standard Deviations (in parentheses) for Relevance Ratings as a Function of Performance Feedback and Target for Study 2

Performance Feedback	Target of Relevance Ratings	
	Self	Partner
Self better	3.5 (1.29)	3.125 (1.07)
Other better	2.72 (.954)	3.37 (1.20)

N = 43 couples

self-defensive pattern of adjustment found in dating couples was found for married couples as well. In addition, the simple main effect of Target was significant when the self outperformed the partner, F (1,18) = 6.91, $p < .05$, indicating that ratings of self-relevance were significantly greater than ratings of partner-relevance. This finding supports Hypothesis 2 that married couples would show evidence of divergence in relevance ratings, both in response to being outperformed by the partner *and* in response to outperforming the partner.

From Dating to Marriage: Comparison of Study 1 and Study 2

Although Study 2 showed significant adjustments in response to outperforming the partner, and Study 1 did not, this finding does not ensure that this effect was significantly greater in Study 2 than in Study 1. In addition, if adjustments are greater among married couples in response to being outperformed as well as outperforming the partner, this finding would lead to a different interpretation than if only one of the processes appeared stronger. For example, if *both* processes seemed more extreme for the married couples, one might assume that they used the response scale differently. Accordingly, to directly test the hypothesis that dating and married partners differed in the magnitude of their adjustments in response to outperforming the partner, the data from Studies 1 and 2 were combined, and "Study" was added as an additional between-subject factor. Because level of Memory Load did not interact with Performance Feedback in either study, it was dropped as a factor in these analyses.

A significant main effect of Target and a significant interaction of Target and Performance were found. These findings indicate that relevance to partner was rated slightly higher than relevance to self overall, and that divergence between self and partner-relevance occurred in response to performance feedback in both studies. Because they were discussed previously, these effects are not mentioned further. In addition, there was a significant three-way interaction of Performance, Target, and Study, $F (1,86) = 3.94$, $p = .05$. To examine whether this finding resulted from between-study differences in adjustments to outperforming the partner, or differences in self-defensive adjustments, or both, simple interaction effects within level of Performance were examined. When the self outperformed the partner, there was a significant interaction of Study and Target, $F (1,43) = 4.73$, $p < .05$, indicating significantly greater divergence of self and partner-relevance in the married sample than in the dating sample. As predicted, there was no significant interaction of Target and Study within the "Partner-Better" condition.

Implications

The results of Study 2 replicate and extend the findings of Study 1 to a sample of married couples recruited from the community. In both studies, there was evidence of divergence between self-relevance and partner-relevance ratings when the partner outperformed the self. In Study 2, however, divergence in self and partner-relevance ratings *also* occurred when the self outperformed the partner. Further, although one must be cautious about cross-study comparisons, it appears that the divergence in response to doing better than the partner was greater among married couples than among dating couples. At a general level, this finding may indicate greater concern on the part of married couples regarding the reactions of the partner. Alternatively, it may suggest that married couples are more willing to divide performance domains into those that are self-relevant and those that are partner-relevant, and to "claim" as well as to "cede" areas in response to differential performance feedback. In either case, the results are consistent with a larger literature suggesting that married couples are more attuned to partner and relational outcomes (for example, Aron, Aron, Tudor, & Nelson, 1991; Mills & Clark, 1982; Rusbult, Yovetich, & Verette, 1996), and so may show patterns of adjustment to the partner that go beyond resolving direct threats to self-evaluation.

STUDY 3

Adjusting relevance in a manner that cedes an area to the partner (or claims it for the self) makes most sense when one person can or should handle the area, rather than when multiple persons might or should all engage in the same behavior regardless of skill. That is, divergence in self and partner-relevance should be more pronounced for an area perceived to be a potential source of competition within the dyad, than for an area in which competition is perceived to be unlikely (for example, joint projects). Highlighting the fact that the members of the dyad are engaged in a "competition" should therefore intensify divergence of self and partner-relevance.

Alternatively, one might expect that highlighting competition would lead both partners to invest some additional significance to the task, making it more difficult for them to adjust relevance downward for self or for partner. From this perspective, even though participants are told that the test is designed to help psychologists assess several important abilities, it is possible that participants are more willing to cede the area to their partner precisely because they are not engaged in a competition with their partner. Thus, the previously observed pattern of divergence in self and partner-relevance in response to feedback that the partner outperformed the self might be eliminated if the task were more inviting of a competitive set. If so, this finding would be strongly disconfirming of the hypothesis that relevance adjustments are adaptive because they help manage competitive tensions.

Participants were 56 dating couples recruited through the psychology department research pool. Participants received research credit and partners received payment for their participation. Couples were similar in age to those in Study 1. On average, they were 19.91 years old (range 18–26) and reported that they had been dating for an average of 19.88 months (range 3–62).

The procedure was identical to that in Study 1, with two exceptions. First, for the Cognitive Load manipulation, participants were told they would be asked to recall their assigned number on two occasions rather than on just one occasion. Second, couples were told they would be "competing" against their partner on a new diagnostic test that related to important abilities. To underscore that they were in competition with their partner, the experimenter emphasized the importance of starting at the same time, and started the task by saying "Ready, set, go."

Performance and Relevance when Competition is Highlighted

As in Study 1, we conducted a $2 \times 2 \times 2 \times 2$ repeated measures ANOVA with Performance and Load treated as between-subject variables, Target

Table 3.3. Cell Means and Standard Deviations (in parentheses) for Relevance Ratings as a Function of Performance Feedback for Study 3

Performance Feedback	Target	
	Self	Partner
Self better	3.11 (1.00)	2.98 (1.09)
Other better	2.71 (1.00)	3.50 (.91)

N = 56 couples

of the relevance rating repeated within-individual, and gender repeated within-couple. There were two significant effects. First, there was a significant main effect of Target $F (1,51) = 20.11$, $p < .001$, indicating that average ratings of relevance to self were lower than ratings of relevance to partner. However, this effect must be interpreted in the context of the predicted interaction of Target by Performance, $F (1,51) = 37.94$, $p < .001$. Follow-up analyses within level of Performance indicated that the effect of Target was not significant when the self outperformed the partner (Ms = 3.11 and 2.98 for self and perceived partner-relevance, respectively), but was significant when the partner outperformed the self, $F (1,26) = 58.53$, $p < .001$; in the latter condition, relevance to self (M = 2.71) was rated significantly lower than relevance to partner (M = 3.50). See Table 3.3.

Accordingly, Study 3 replicated Study 1 both in finding divergence in response to feedback that the self had been outperformed, and in *failing* to find divergence in response to feedback that the self performed better than the partner. This finding indicates that an emphasis on competition did not prevent divergence in self and partner ratings of relevance. Indeed, comparison of the means in Studies 1 and 3 suggests that the "self-protective" effect was larger in Study 3 than in Study 1.

Does Competition Matter?

To examine whether the "competition" manipulation significantly increased the self-defensive reaction of dating partners, data from Study 1 and Study 3 were combined, and "Study" was added as an additional between-subject factor. Memory Load did not interact with Performance in either study, and so it was dropped as a factor in the analyses.

It should be noted again that "Study" may be confounded with other potentially consequential variables, such as the time of year the study was run, the particular experimenters running the study, or the minor change in the "Load" manipulation. Accordingly, caution regarding interpretations of significant differences between the studies is suggested.

Three significant effects emerged in the $2 \times 2 \times 2 \times 2$ repeated measures ANOVA. As was true in the separate analyses of both studies, there was a main effect of Target $F (1,98) = 31.17, p < .001$, and a significant interaction of Performance by Target $F (1,99) = 38.43, p < .001$. In addition, there was a marginal interaction of Target by Performance and Study $F (1,98) = 3.62, p = .06$, indicating that the interaction of Performance and Target was marginally stronger in Study 3 ($F = 37.94$) than in Study 1 ($F = 8.15$). However, follow-up analyses within level of Performance did not indicate a significant interaction of Target with Study within either level of Performance feedback.

Implications

The results of Study 3 replicate the finding that dating couples show divergence in self and partner-relevance in response to being outperformed, but not in response to outperforming the partner. Making competition salient did not block divergence of self and partner-relevance in response to differential performance feedback. Nor did encouraging partners to view each other as competitors result in any dampening of the tendency to show divergence in relevance ratings in response to being outperformed.

A comparison of Studies 1 and 3 suggests, however, that when dating couples are instructed to view themselves as being in potential competition with one another, self and partner ratings diverge somewhat more. If one viewed the competition manipulation as simply accentuating the importance of the task, one might have predicted increased relevance ratings for both self and partner. Alternatively, if one viewed the competition manipulation as increasing relevance to the self and making it more difficult to change relevance, one might have predicted more intense affective responding, but no greater change in relevance in response to feedback.

GENERAL DISCUSSION

Interpreting Self-Evaluation Maintenance (SEM) processes as social adaptations, and not just as self-defense mechanisms, raises new issues about the exact nature of adjustments made by romantic partners in response to performance feedback. As a social adaptation, adjustments of relevance should help regulate social interactions. This function seems best served by adjustments that clarify who is the expert and should take the lead in a given area, suggesting that adjustments should lead to divergence in self-relevance and perceived partner-relevance. Following this logic, the current studies were designed to investigate the possibility that differential performance feedback may result in divergence between self-relevance and perceived partner-relevance. Divergence provides a mechanism for constructing adaptive complementarity in romantic and other close relationships (relationships that are otherwise strongly pulled toward similarity). In all three studies, evidence supporting the divergence hypothesis was obtained. In particular, in each of the studies, self-relevance diverged from perceived partner-relevance when the self was outperformed. That is, self-relevance was significantly lower than partner-relevance when the individual received feedback that the self had been outperformed.

The pattern of significantly lower self-relevance than partner-relevance in response to feedback that the partner had outperformed the self was labeled "self-defensive" because it occurred in response to feedback that had the potential to threaten self-evaluation. Importantly, this self-defensive pattern of adjustment led to divergence in both dating and married samples. This finding is important because it suggests that SEM adjustments may help dyads accommodate to each other's strengths and weaknesses, even at early stages of the relationship before more effortful and costly accommodations become common (for example, Rusbult et al., 1996; Rusbult, Bissonette, Arriaga, & Cox, 1999). That is, couples may start to adjust self-definition by decreasing self-relevance in areas in which the partner is performing better, and so create a better fit with a potential partner, even before they are highly committed to the particular partner. Such low-cost adjustments may also help newly forming dyads to view themselves as being a "good match," and so contribute to the idealization of partners early in the relationship. If so, such adjustments may be one of the commitment and relationship-enhancing mechanisms that allow partners to form a stable and satisfactory relationship (for example, Johnson & Rusbult, 1989; Kirkpatrick, 1998; Murray, Holmes, & Griffin, 1996; Van Lange & Rusbult, 1995).

Finally, Study 3 provided evidence that highlighting competition is not sufficient to disrupt divergence in response to differential performance feedback. Rather, a comparison with Study 1 suggested that highlighting competition served to intensify (marginally) self-defensive divergence among dating couples. Thus, the hypothesis that relevance adjustments may serve as a social adaptation survived a direct test.

The Development of Performance Ecologies in Romantic Relationships

The current studies provide only a preliminary foundation for understanding the development of performance ecologies in romantic relationships. That is, these studies indicate that divergence in self and partner-relevance in response to performance feedback occurs, but do not indicate how such changes are maintained or ultimately translated into an understanding of the self in relation to the partner. Although the longevity of self and partner-relevance adjustments in the absence of other maintaining events is unknown, it seems likely that, in some cases, relevance adjustments are maintained because subsequent relationship events tend to support the initial adjustment. For example, a particular pattern of performance feedback may be received repeatedly. Or, "ceding" a performance domain to a better performing partner may be reinforced by a positive reaction from the partner, or may occasion other positive relationship consequences. These additional relationship events could lead to a stable pattern of interaction and hence become self-maintaining (cf. Kelley, 1983a; 1983b). According to this perspective, the shift in self-relevance produced by performance feedback could provide a first step, or occasion, for other dyadic processes to foster a new and stable pattern of interaction and division of labor. The subsequent changes could, in turn, lead to greater cooperation, an enhanced sense of fit with the partner, and increased satisfaction and commitment to the relationship. Of course, these developmental speculations remain untested in the current investigation.

What might the process of constructing a performance ecology look like? We propose that, following the initial attraction created by overt similarities, couples may implicitly define specific niches in which each may perform better than the partner does, and so confer unique benefits to the dyad. Negative affective consequences for the self and threats to self-evaluation should diminish as certain niches are ceded to the partner, or as the partner is perceived as having ceded certain niches to the self. Adjustments in self-relevance relative to perceived partner-relevance should be the starting point for this process. In this case, one partner is likely to gradually take over the area, with the other partner taking a secondary role. In place of competition, some form of increased specialization and cooperation within the dyad will emerge. In some cases then, the establishment of a performance ecology may serve as a relationship maintenance strategy that eliminates potential competitive difficulties for the dyad. The divergence in self and partner-relevance that is the hallmark of a couple performance ecology should make it easier for partners to bask in each other's reflected glory, increase the reinforcement provided to the other for good performance, and decrease motivation to compete with the partner.

Does this process necessarily result in individuals giving something up? We do not think so. For example, consider a couple, Mary and John, who meet at a gourmet cooking class, and are both interested in gourmet cooking. Rather than searching for ways to "out cook" each other, a strategy that is sure to result in a negative self-evaluation for at least one partner, Mary and John might instead specialize in their cooking. Over time, and in response to various within-dyad comparisons, Mary may limit her self description to the domain of "Gourmet French Cook" while thinking of John as a "Gourmet Vietnamese Cook." In so doing, Mary is able to view herself as sharing similar interests and values with John, but also as having a unique performance domain within the area of cooking in which she is best. Alternatively, Mary and John may cook meals together with each taking a different role in the cooking process, thereby specializing with regard to the process of cooking and precluding competition about who cooks better (cf. Clark & Bennett, 1992). Or, after repeated instances of each being outperformed, either Mary or John may reduce the relevance of cooking to their self-definitions, rendering it an area in which it is easier to bask in the other's reflected glory. In each of these examples, the potential problem of competition has been resolved by changing the relevance of the original area.

Divergence in relevance ratings may also set the stage for dyadic interactions that increase the likelihood of ceding the area to the partner in the future, creating a self-sustaining positive feedback loop (Kelley, 1983a; 1983b). Indeed, areas of partner strength in which the self and partner diverge might come to be idealized as evidence of the good "fit" between the self and the partner, and so may feed into felt satisfaction and commitment (Murray et al., 1996; Van Lange & Rusbult, 1995). Likewise, once an area has been ceded to the partner, the general drive for identity and competence (Deci & Ryan, 1995; Ruble, 1987; Stryker & Statham, 1985) may come to be focused increasingly on the remaining areas of high self-relevance that have not been ceded to the partner. Thus, individuals may increasingly view themselves as compatible with their partners, and perhaps as less compatible with other potential partners.

In terms of relationship satisfaction, one might speculate that a well-developed performance ecology that provides both partners with clear areas of leadership and control within the relationship would be associated with relatively more satisfying interactions and relatively fewer negative interactions (cf. Houts et al., 1996). Conversely, difficulty in establishing a workable, shared performance ecology would seem to provide occasion for competitive interactions, with one of the partners winning and one losing, and both partners wondering if they really belong together. If so, successful adjustments of relevance should lead to more harmonious interaction with one's partner, and to the feeling that one's partner encourages one to do one's best. It should also lead to the belief that one is contributing things of value to the relationship, and that the relationship is compatible with one's own needs for self-expression. Accordingly, the impact of relevance adjustments on couple satisfaction could be profound.

In Study 2 we found that couples in more committed relationships (that is, married couples) showed "sympathetic" reactions to their partner's likely self-evaluation threat. In addition, the sympathetic reaction was significantly more pronounced among married couples than among dating couples. It may be that married couples are more closely attuned to possible reactions from the partner, and may treat partner outcomes in a manner similar to their treatment of their own outcomes (cf. Aron et al., 1991). At a minimum, married partners appear willing to make adjustments in partner relevance that create for themselves the perception that the partner has ceded to them the area in which they performed better. This process may help reduce concern that the partner has been distressed by the outcome.

Ecological Validity

Are adjustments in self-relevance limited to the laboratory, or might they affect important aspects of marital interaction? Earlier work inspired by the SEM model suggests there may be considerable ecological validity to the model, and that the processes highlighted in experimental laboratory studies may be observed in important aspects of couple interaction as well. For example, the study by Beach and Tesser (1993) examined differentiation in the area of decision making and related this to marital satisfaction. Husbands and wives who were more complementary with regard to the areas in which they exercised decision-making power were more satisfied. That is, husbands and wives who saw themselves as making decisions in the areas important to the self and saw the partner as making decisions in areas important to the partner were the most satisfied. Importantly, there was no association between satisfaction and simply having more decision-making power overall in the relationship. Likewise, work by Pilkington, Tesser, and Stephens (1991) found that dating couples provided considerable evidence of differentiation across 68 performance domains, with a strong tendency to view the self as doing better in areas important to the self and the partner doing better in areas not important to the self.

Also, if adjustments are central to avoiding negative feelings and conflict, one might expect to see consequences on the quality of problem-solving communication if one provided performance feedback while constraining the possibility of adjustments. We did this manipulation in a recent study (O'Mahen, Beach, & Tesser, 2000) and found results consistent with our model. That is, we gave couples feedback about performance in areas that they identified in advance as more or less important to the self and we precluded excuses and alternative explanations for poor performance relative to the partner. As predicted, those who were led to believe that they had been outperformed by their partner in an area in which they claimed expertise but their partner did not claim expertise, displayed a different and more negative pattern of communication during problem solving. Those who were outperformed by their partner in an area in which their partner had the expertise and they did not, displayed a more positive pattern of problem-solving communication. Accordingly, it appears that precluding adjustments in response to performance feedback can set the stage for less constructive verbal exchanges.

Methodological Implications and Future Directions

The current studies examined only the first component of a process that would need to be tied to other self and couple processes if it is to influence broad indices of couple functioning such as satisfaction or relationship maintenance. Our dependent variable may be characterized as "perceived fit with the partner," and the fact that we were successful in changing it through manipulations of feedback indicates that it is only loosely constrained by relationship history and agreement among dating partners. Hypothesized links to other self-processes, or to overt patterns of accommodation to the partner, were not examined. We cannot be certain, therefore, that initial patterns of divergence are maintained, or that they come to direct couple decision making and interaction. Most importantly, speculation that divergence in self and partner-relevance may serve to increase satisfaction with the partner and so facilitate couple commitment remains to be investigated.

Has the current series of studies established a new grounding for the SEM model, established a new theory that is independent of the SEM model, or simply taken a part of the SEM model and elaborated its implications?While it may be premature to claim success in any of these respects, an important hypothesis is suggested by the current elaboration of the SEM model, one that was not suggested by the original SEM model or its extension to marriage. The original SEM model provided us with a clear rationale for examining three dimensions: closeness (for example, married versus dating), performance (self or partner better), and self-relevance (high versus low). It also indicated that self-evaluation threat was an important source of motivation for divergence. In addition, the SEM model extended to marriage highlighted the potential importance of perceived partner-relevance in determining affective reactions, and suggested that concern for partner outcomes may also be motivating when the relationship is a committed one. In the current chapter we address the more fundamental question of the adaptive significance of SEM adjustments. Why do we have a tendency to respond in this way to performance feedback? To ask this question opens up the possibility of placing the model in an evolutionary context (cf. Beach & Tesser, 2000). As is illustrated by the current chapter, the exercise of considering the implications of an evolutionary framework may stimulate new directions in research on personal relationships.

REFERENCES

Aron, A., Aron, E. N., Tudor, M., & Nelson, G. (1991). Close relationships as including other in the self. *Journal of Personality and Social Psychology, 60,* 241–253.

Baumeister, R. F., & Leary, M. R. (1995). The need to belong: Desire for interpersonal attachments as a fundamental human motivation. *Psychological Bulletin, 117,* 497–529.

Beach, S. R. H., & Tesser, A. (1993). Decision-making power and marital satisfaction: A self-evaluation maintenance perspective. *Journal of Social and Clinical Psychology, 4,* 471–494.

Beach, S. R. H., & Tesser, A. (1995). Self-esteem and the extended self-evaluation maintenance model: The self in social context. In M. H. Kernis (Ed.), *Efficacy, agency, and self-esteem* (pp. 145–170). New York: Plenum.

Beach, S. R. H., & Tesser, A. (2000). Self-evaluation maintenance and evolution: Some speculative notes. In J. Suls and L. Wheeler (Eds.), *Handbook of social comparison: Theory and research* (pp. 123–140). New York: Plenum.

Beach, S. R. H., Tesser, A., Mendolia, M., Anderson, P., Crelia, R., Whitaker, D., & Fincham, F. D. (1996). Self-evaluation maintenance in marriage: Toward a performance ecology of the marital relationship. *Journal of Family Psychology, 10*, 379–396.

Beach, S. R. H., Whitaker, D. J., Jones, D. J., & Tesser, A. (2001). When does performance feedback prompt complementarity in romantic relationships? *Personal Relationships, 8*, 231–248.

Berscheid, E., & Walster, E. (1978). Interpersonal Attraction (2nd ed.). Reading, MA: Addison-Wesley.

Byrne, D. (1997). An overview (and underview) of research and theory within the attraction paradigm. *Journal of Social and Personal Relationships, 14*, 417–431.

Cialdini, R. B., & Richardson, K. D. (1980). Two indirect tactics of image management: Basking and blasting. *Journal of Personality and Social Psychology, 39*, 406–415.

Clark, M. S., & Bennett, M. E. (1992). Research on relationships: Implications for mental health. In D. N. Ruble, Philip R. Costenzo, & M. E. Oliveri (Eds.), *The social psychology of mental health*. New York: Guilford.

Clark, M. S., Mills, J., & Powell, M. C. (1986). Keeping track of needs in communal and exchange relationships. *Journal of Personality and Social Psychology, 51*, 333–338.

Deci, E. L., & Ryan, R. M. (1995). Human agency: The basis for true self-esteem. In M. Kernis (Ed.), *Efficacy, agency, and self-esteem* (pp. 31–49). New York: Plenum.

Fitzpatrick, M. A. (1988). *Between husbands and wives: Communication in marriage*. Beverly Hills, CA: Sage.

Gilbert, P. (1992). *Depression: The evolution of powerlessness*. New York: Guilford.

Houts, R. M., Robins, E., & Huston, T. L. (1996). Compatibility and the development of premarital relationships. *Journal of Marriage and the Family, 58*, 7–20.

Johnson, D. J., & Rusbult, C. E. (1989). Resisting temptation: Devaluation of alternative partners as a means of maintaining commitment in close relationships. *Journal of Personality and Social Psychology, 57*, 967–980.

Kelley, H. H. (1983a). Love and commitment. In H. H. Kelley, E. Berscheid, A. Christensen, J. H. Harvey, T. L. Huston, G. Levinger, E. McLintock, L. A. Peplau, & D. R. Peterson (Eds.), *Close relationships*. New York: Freeman.

Kelley, H. H. (1983b). The situational origins of human tendencies: A further reason for the formal analysis of structure. *Personality and Social Psychology Bulletin, 9*, 8–30.

Kirkpatrick, L. A. (1998). Evolution, pair-bonding, and reproductive strategies: A reconceptualization of adult attachment. In J. A. Simpson & W. S. Rholes

(Eds.), *Attachment theory and close relationships* (pp. 353–393). New York: Guilford.

Leary, M. R., & Downs, D. L. (1995) Interpersonal functions of the self-esteem motive: The self-esteem system as a sociometer. In M. Kernis (Ed.), *Efficacy, agency, and self-esteem.* (pp. 123–144.) New York: Plenum.

Mills, J., & Clark, M. S. (1982). Exchange and communal relationships. In L. Wheeler (Ed.), *Review of personality and social psychology.* Beverly Hills, CA: Sage.

Murray, S. L., Holmes, J. G., & Griffin, D. W. (1996). The self-fulfilling nature of positive illusions in romantic relationships: Love is not blind, but prescient. *Journal of Personality and Social Psychology, 71,* 1155–1180.

O'Leary, K. D., & Smith, D. A. (1991). Marital interactions. *Annual Review of Psychology, 42,* 191–212.

O'Mahen, H. A., Beach, S. R. H., & Tesser, A. (2000). Relationship ecology and negative communication in romantic relationships: A self-evaluation maintenance perspective. *Personality and Social Psychology Bulletin, 26,* 1343–1352.

Ruble, D. N. (1987). The acquisition of self-knowledge: A self-socialization perspective. In N. Eisenberg (Ed.), *Contemporary topics in developmental psychology* (pp. 243–270). New York: John Wiley & Sons.

Rusbult, C. E., Bissonnette, V. I., Arriaga, X. B., & Cox, C. L. (1999). Accommodation processes across the early years of marriage. In T. N. Bradbury (Ed.), *The developmental course of marital dysfunction.* (pp. 74–113). New York: Cambridge University Press.

Rusbult, C. E., Yovetich, N. A., & Verette, J. (1996). An interdependence analysis of accommodation processes. In G. J. O. Fletcher and J. Fitness (Eds.), *Knowledge structures in close relationships: A social psychological approach* (pp. 63–90). Mahwah, NJ: Lawrence Erlbaum Associates.

Stryker, S., & Statham, A. (1985). Symbolic interaction and role theory. In G. Lindzey & E. Aronson (Eds.), *Handbook of social psychology* (vol. 1, pp. 311–378). New York: Random House.

Tesser, A. (1988). Toward a self-evaluation maintenance model of social behavior. In L. Berkowitz (Ed.), *Advances in experimental social psychology* (vol. 21, pp. 181–227). San Diego, CA: Academic Press.

Tesser, A., & Campbell, J. (1982). Self-evaluation maintenance and the perception of friends and strangers. *Journal of Personality, 50,* 261–279.

Tesser, A., & Paulhus, D. (1983). The definition of self: Private and public self-evaluation maintenance strategies. *Journal of Personality and Social Psychology, 44,* 72–682.

Van Lange, P. A. M., & Rusbult, C. E. (1995). My relationship is better than – and not as bad as – yours is: The perception of superiority in close relationships. *Personality and Social Psychology Bulletin, 21,* 32–44.

CHAPTER FOUR

Cognition and Communication during Marital Conflict: How Alcohol Affects Subjective Coding of Interaction in Aggressive and Nonaggressive Couples

Alan Sillars, Kenneth E. Leonard,
Linda J. Roberts, and Tim Dun

At the base of every marital conflict there is a rupture of consensus. All conflicts involve differences in perception that increase in depth and magnitude as a dispute escalates. While couples may resolve or put aside differences by talking together, communication can also inflame matters and drive perspectives further apart. The variable effects of communication partly stem from the way communication itself is subjectively construed. In a bitter quarrel, disagreements are not confined to the surface issues and background events associated with conflict. Individuals may also perceive the stream of interaction differently (Watzlawick, Beavin, & Jackson, 1967), and this fact accounts for the explosive nature of some conflicts. To follow this reasoning a step further, communication patterns are also implicated in marital conflicts that culminate in violence (for example, Lloyd & Emery, 2000a). Further, there are strong indications that distorted perceptions of interaction, particularly by maritally violent men, contribute to the dysfunctional communication patterns of aggressive couples (Eckhardt, Barbour, & Davison, 1998). Thus, to better understand the role of communication in marital conflict and aggression, it is useful to consider not only how couples talk with each other, but also the subjective interpretations that accompany these acts.

This research was supported by National Institute on Alcohol Abuse and Alcoholism Grant R01-AA08128. We wish to thank coders Jennifer Brodsky, Michele Crepeau, Shannon Marr, and Karissa Reinke, project directors Maria Testa and Tanya Bowen, and experimenters Rachel Ley, Tom Daniels, Daria Papalia, Jennifer Livingston, John Sabino, and Bill Zywiak. We would also like to acknowledge Richard E. Heyman and Robert L. Weiss for their input and advice on the implementation of the video-assisted recall protocol.

In this chapter we look at the interpretive process connected with marital interaction, drawing upon a study of couple conflict, aggression, and alcohol. In this research the conscious thoughts and feelings that individuals experienced during couple interactions were reconstructed using video-assisted recall methods. Some of the couples had a history of husband-to-wife marital violence. Since alcohol is frequently implicated in marital violence (Leonard & Jacob, 1988; Roberts, Roberts, & Leonard, 1999), the research included an experimental manipulation designed to illuminate how alcohol impacts marital interaction and cognition. That is, some of the husbands received alcoholic drinks prior to the interactions and subsequent video-assisted recall sessions.

The causes of marital violence are complex and exist at different levels of analysis – cultural, societal, economic, legal, interpersonal, individual (see Feldman & Ridley, 1995; 2000; Lloyd & Emery, 2000b). At the interpersonal level, we are not directly concerned with the origin of violent predispositions in individuals or society, but rather, with the interaction process directly precipitating violence. It is our belief that interpersonal approaches complement, rather than compete with, other perspectives. An interpersonal or interactional approach presumes that physical aggression in marriage is sometimes an unplanned outgrowth of unregulated conflict. From this perspective, the build-up that precedes the point of violence (but not the act of violence itself) may reflect the same interaction processes that characterize destructive conflict in general. For example, physical aggression may follow mutual escalation of verbal aggression and anger, which is then carried to a further extreme. Previous research supporting this picture indicates that the interactions of aggressive men and their wives are characterized by high rates of negativity, negative reciprocity, verbal aggression, and demand-withdraw behavior, coupled with a low incidence of constructive and supportive communication, facilitating and deescalating behavior, and mutual problem solving (for example, Berns, Jacobson, & Gottman, 1999; Burman, Margolin, & John, 1993; Cordova, Jacobson, Gottman, Rushe, & Cox, 1993; Feldman & Ridley, 2000, Holtzworth-Munroe, Stuart, Sandin, Smutzler, & McLaughlin, 1997; Jacobson, Gottman, Waltz, Rushe, Babcock, & Holtzworth-Munroe, 1994; Margolin, John, & Gleberman, 1988).

It is important to be aware, however, that general conflict processes may pertain to some cases of marital aggression and not to others. There are different types of physically aggressive couples, including couples in which violence occurs as an unplanned outgrowth of unregulated conflict (that is, "expressive" violence), and couples in which violence is used by husbands in a calculated manner as an instrument of control (that is, "instrumental" violence; see Feldman & Ridley, 1995). Johnson (1995) draws a similar distinction between instances of "common couple violence" and "patriarchal terrorism." Mutual negativity and deficits in problem solving are presumably more relevant to instances of expressive (or "common") couple violence than to extreme and calculated forms of male violence toward women.

Thus far, interaction research shows that aggressive and nonaggressive couples differ in negativity, negative reciprocity, and related qualities of communication. These results still beg further explanation, since it is not necessarily apparent why aggressive individuals and couples adopt negative communication patterns. To help explain why couples react the way they do, it is useful to look below the surface of conflict. For example, why do some individuals reciprocate and escalate provocative statements, whereas others compensate or redirect them? In this spirit, Holtzworth-Munroe (1992) suggests that the social skills deficits of maritally violent men can be explained by cognitive biases in the decoding of social stimuli and subsequent decision making. For example, aggressive men are more likely than nonaggressive men to attribute conflict to the hostile intentions of wives (Holtzworth-Munroe & Hutchinson, 1993). Further, in response to staged conflict vignettes, maritally violent men articulate distorted, arbitrary, and selective perceptions (Eckhardt et al., 1998). In extending this line of investigation, we look even more directly at how the context of marital conflict is selectively interpreted and how couple communication is subjectively coded by participants.

PROCEDURES OF THE STUDY

Our observations are based on a study titled the *Buffalo Marital Interaction Project* (BMIP; see Leonard & Roberts, 1998 for details). The study combined direct observation of marital interactions with video-assisted recall. One hundred and eighteen couples from this study form the basis for most of our comments in this chapter.[1] Since the couples were first recruited from a large sample of newlyweds (Leonard & Senchak, 1996), they were relatively young, in their first marriage, and married from one to three years. None of the couples was in treatment for marital problems at the time of the study.

---

[1] There were a total of 139 couples in the study. However, we could not analyze the video-assisted recall data from 21 couples either because one spouse did not follow instructions or because of problems with the recording equipment.

Fifty-five of the husbands in these couples were classified as physically aggressive on the basis of husband and wife responses to the Conflict Tactics Scale (Straus, 1979). Husbands were classified as aggressive if they had committed multiple physically aggressive acts or at least one serious aggressive act (a "slap" or worse, as reported by either husband or wife). Couples who acknowledged frequent, severe aggression were excluded. This step was taken on ethical grounds, but it also made the sample more homogeneous, and presumably eliminated cases in which physical aggression stemmed from "instrumental" male violence (Feldman & Ridley, 1995).

While visiting the research lab, the couples held two 15-minute conversations, each focusing on an area of disagreement in the marriage, identified from questionnaires. The conversations took place in a room equipped for video recording, which was set up to resemble a living room/dining room combination. An interviewer asked the couple questions designed to "prime" them for their conversation (for example, "When was the last time you talked about this disagreement?"), and then left the couples alone to talk and try to resolve their differences on the issue.

In order to study the effects of alcohol, some husbands received three to four drinks of vodka and tonic prior to the second interaction, with the number of drinks based on the husband's body weight. Other husbands received either no beverage or a placebo which they were told contained alcohol but, in fact, consisted of pure tonic water. The placebo and alcoholic drinks were preceded by gargling with antiseptic mouthwash so that husbands could not detect the presence or absence of alcohol purely by taste. The placebo was used to distinguish pharmacological effects of alcohol from effects caused solely by expectancies.

Immediately after the second discussion, the spouses were escorted to separate rooms to watch a videotape of the conversation they had just completed. Spouses were asked to imagine going through the interaction again, and to attempt to reexperience how they felt and what they were thinking during the discussion. They were left alone while the videotape played. Every 20 seconds the tape paused automatically and individuals reported (by speaking into a microphone) what they remembered thinking or feeling at that point in the discussion. Although individuals heard the full audio recording of the interaction, the videotape only showed the partner, thus modeling the visual perspective that individuals had during the interaction.

Table 4.1. Percentages of Occurrence and Representative Examples for the ICCS Thought Codes and Categories

Category	Example
Emotion (9%)	
Positive emotions (2%)	*So I felt good.*
Dysphoria (2%)	*I was starting to feel sad and hurt.*
Anger & frustration (5%)	*Mad and frustrated.*
Issue Appraisal (19%)	
Elaboration (8%)	*I was thinking that maybe I will have one more child, but not right now.*
Agreement (3%)	*That's a good point.*
Disagreement (8%)	*It doesn't make sense to me.*
Solution (1%)	*What's a solution, good question.*
Person Appraisal (25%)	
Positive & neutral (9%)	*I'm glad that he made the effort.*
Admission (2%)	*It's probably my fault.*
Denial & justification (2%)	*I don't think that it's all my fault.*
Complaint (7%)	*I just want to be more appreciated.*
Hostile attribution (2%)	*All he cares about is himself.*
Rejection (3%)	*This guy is a real jerk.*
Negative relationship	*It's crazy . . . like a fatal attraction.*
Process (34%)	
Constructive Engagement (5%)	
Collaboration (1%)	*He's being very cooperative.*
Disclosure (2%)	*I liked knowing how open she is.*
Soliciting & attending (2%)	*I'm trying to get her to talk about it.*
Avoidance and Detachment (9%)	
Withdrawal (3%)	*She just wanted to blow the whole thing off and not argue about it anymore.*
Topic shifting (2%)	*He wanted to change the subject.*
Stonewalling (1%)	*He's just making a lot of excuses.*
Censorship (1%)	*I am just going to have to control what I say.*
Lying & insincerity (1%)	*I know he doesn't mean that.*
Giving in	*I'm giving in, just like I always do.*
Confrontation (5%)	
Dominating the floor	*He always cuts me off, which is as usual.*

(continued)

Table 4.1. *(continued)*

Category	Example
Inflexibility (1%)	*She's not going to give at all.*
Exaggeration & distortion (1%)	*He does make a bigger deal of it than it is.*
Criticism & verbal aggression (2%)	*She just wants to verbally attack me instead of talking to me like a human being.*
Negative voice & appearance (1%)	*She rolls her eyeballs.*
Other aversive strategies (1%)	*Heavy guilt trip, coming down.*
Neutral and Mixed Strategies (5%)	
Initiation & termination (1%)	*Trying to think of something to say.*
General talk	*We were recapping what we had said about Mark.*
Relationship repair (1%)	*I was trying to please her.*
Assertion (3%)	*Just trying to get my point across.*
Joking (1%)	*Trying joking with her.*
Process Appraisal (9%)	
Understanding (2%)	*I think he realizes how I feel.*
Not understanding (3%)	*He's not gonna understand where I'm coming from.*
Keeping score	*I was getting back the upper hand.*
Unexpected behavior	*I can't believe he said that.*
Repetitious behavior (1%)	*We've been through this a hundred times.*
Foreboding	*Oh I started something this time.*
Resolution (1%)	*I feel we're finally getting somewhere.*
Impasse (1%)	*We're not really resolving this problem.*
Uncodable & Off Topic (14%)	
Other people (1%)	*The baby likes to get in the plants.*
Can't remember (6%)	*I don't know what I was thinking.*
Thinking same as what was said	*I said what I was thinking then.*
Not thinking anything	*Wasn't really thinking anything.*
No response (2%)	*I have no comment.*
Unintelligible (1%)	
Intoxication (1%)	*I could tell that alcohol was starting to influence him.*
Off topic (2%)	*I was thinking of my cat.*

* In cases where no percentage is reported, the percentage of thought units coded
into the category was less than .5%.

The thoughts and discussions were transcribed and coded. The discussions were coded using the Marital Interaction Coding System (or MICS; see Weiss, Hops, & Patterson, 1973). Thoughts were coded using a new coding scheme (the Interaction Cognition Coding Scheme or ICCS) that was developed from inductive analysis of reported thoughts during a preliminary stage of the study (see Sillars, Roberts, Leonard, & Dun, 2000). The categories of the ICCS are illustrated in Table 4.1, with the percentage of occurrence of each code indicated in parentheses. The main categories in the ICCS distinguish different objects and levels of subjective analysis; that is, individuals might reflect on their own or their partner's emotions (*emotion codes*), explicit issues in the discussion (*issue appraisal*), abstract attributions and personal evaluations (*person appraisal*), or the communication taking place in the immediate situation (*process codes*).

The records of reported thoughts were quite complex and descriptively rich. These data point to several basic factors affecting intimate conflict. Before turning to the dynamics of aggressive marriages, we first describe general trends within the thought data and consider their implications (see also Sillars et al., 2000; Sillars, Roberts, Dun, & Leonard, 2001).

GENERAL TRENDS AND OBSERVATIONS

Selectivity

The first thing that stands out about the cognitive recall data is the sheer diversity of thought associated with communication. At various times, individuals reflected about feelings of love or anger, how to resolve the conflict, the partner's motives for getting married, past events that show blame, how well or poorly the discussion was proceeding, how disclosive or evasive the partner was being, or how the couple's children were getting along with the babysitter. There was also great variation with respect to the actor(s) identified (that is, thoughts about self, partner, both individuals, other people), time frame (memory of past events versus observations based in the immediate here-and-now), and level of abstractness associated with thought (for example, concrete observations and feelings versus abstract attributions or "meta perspectives" about what the partner was thinking, feeling, intending; Laing, Phillipson, & Lee, 1966).

The diversity seen in the cognitive recall data underscores the fact that attention to communication is highly selective. As Watzlawick et al. (1967, p. 95) state, during communication, . . . a drastic selection process is necessary to prevent the higher brain centers from being swamped by irrelevant information. But the decision about what is essential and what is irrelevant apparently varies from individual to individual, and seems to be determined by criteria which are largely outside individual awareness." These considerations apply to any mode of interaction; however, in the case of marital quarrels, selective attention to communication may be compounded by the presence of strong emotions and intense arousal, the disorderly nature of the stimulus field, the persuasive and defensive goals of each person, and other factors endemic to intimate conflict (Fincham, Bradbury, & Grych, 1990; Sillars, 1998).

Thus, we routinely see that two spouses, while outwardly discussing a common topic, are thinking about quite different things. For example, in one case the husband dwells on the couple's financial situation, the cost of eating out, and his wife's apparent reluctance to address these issues head on. She focuses on her own anxiety, his tone of voice, her feeling of being berated and attacked, and his apparent lack of appreciation for her efforts as wife and expectant mother. These differences in attentional focus are naturally linked to different conclusions about who is doing what to whom within the interaction sequence, otherwise referred to as "punctuation differences" in interaction (Watzlawick et al., 1967). The husband, in this case, sees himself as pressing a point in response to his wife's evasiveness, whereas she sees herself as defending and justifying her actions in response to his belittling.

Content-Process Confusion

Some of the thought codes (that is, *issue appraisal*) reflect attention to the "content" level of conflict; that is, relatively explicit and objectifiable issues that are directly discussed (for example, how much money to budget for food; whether the husband's drinking represents a problem). By contrast, *process* codes reflect attention to the nature of the interaction, including pragmatic intentions and communication strategies (for example, "Trying to get her to talk about it."; "He agrees just to make me shut up."), and other observations and reactions to the discussion (for example, "I was getting back the upper hand."; "I can't believe he said that."). While issue appraisal codes reflect attention to content issues in conflict, process codes show concern for implicit "relationship issues" in the way the conflict is enacted (Watzlawick et al., 1967; Wilmot & Hocker, 2001).

A common disparity in perceptions of communication occurs when one spouse monitors the discussion in terms of explicit content (issue appraisal), while at the same moment, the partner is thinking about the process of interaction and the implicit relationship messages contained therein. This asymmetry in perception may lead to a confusing pattern in which one spouse attributes strong relational meaning to which the partner is oblivious. For example, the following excerpt shows the transcribed thoughts of husband and wife at the same point in the discussion. In the excerpt, the husband mentally elaborates on his need for time alone, which is the explicit source of conflict and the topic of discussion. At the same point, the wife reacts with strong emotion to what she sees as his evasiveness and insensitivity.

She thinks . . .	*He thinks . . .*
I don't think he was really listening to me at all. . . . I felt like, he wasn't paying any attention. I was trying to be patient.	At this point we are talking about my band practice, and how Tuesdays and Fridays are the only days that uh, the band can get together and uh, Penny questions that maybe, maybe I should be more responsive to her.
I wanted an answer from him, but I knew he didn't have one.	Well, we're talking about how when I go to work I'm uh, on the go all the time, and when I get home, I'm just half alive.
. . . I think I was just aggravated.	At this point I was just trying to explain, why sometimes I'm just quiet at home.
I felt kind of hurt, really hurt.	At this point I'm talking about how, well, why I like to be alone, and how it gets to be too much.

Husband-Wife Differences in Perception

Other authors have suggested that wives are more attentive to relationship issues in interaction than men (Acitelli & Young, 1996; Roberts & Krokoff, 1990; Scott, Fuhrman, & Wyer, 1991). There were several signs to this effect in the BMIP results. For one thing, wives were more other directed. They had more thoughts about the partner than about the self, whereas husbands had more thoughts about the self than about the partner. Wives also had more "metaperspectives" than husbands (that is, thoughts about what the partner was thinking). Husbands had more issue appraisal codes. Thus, the husband was generally the more literal partner (as in the preceding illustration). In addition, wives were, in a certain sense, more "objective" about communication. This point is explained in the next section.

Objectivity of Communication Inference

About a third of the reported thoughts (34%) were coded into one of the process categories, indicating that individuals displayed considerable mindfulness about the process of communication. Many of the process codes refer to communicative acts (for example, disclosure, topic shifts, criticism) that were attributed to self or partner. It is interesting to consider how this subjective, "insider" coding of communication compares with observer-assigned codes.

Three process subcategories from the ICCS, *constructive engagement*, *avoidance/detachment*, and *confrontation*, closely parallel a familiar trilogy in the literature on conflict strategies and tactics (that is, the distinction between collaboration, avoidance, and competition; Gottman, 1998; Sillars, 1981; Wilmot & Hocker, 2001). For purposes of comparison, we formed similar summary categories (that is, "positive problem-solving," "withdrawal," and "negativity") from the MICS codes that trained raters applied to the videotaped discussions. In most cases, there were small but significant correlations (that is, in the range of .17 to .29) between the incidence of certain thought codes and relevant MICS codes.[2] For example, avoidance attributed to husbands by wives (based on ICCS codes) was associated with the observed withdrawal of husbands (according to MICS codes). Similarly, the constructive engagement that wives attributed to self was associated with the observed positive problem solving of wives; confrontation attributed to wives by husbands was associated with the observed negativity of wives; and so forth. However, there was one notable exception to the

---

[2] These were actually partial correlations that controlled for the total frequency of behavioral interaction codes, thus eliminating a potential confound between the overall rate of behavioral codes and the frequency of specific codes.

general pattern of positive associations. There was no correspondence between the husbands' self-described communication and the observed behavior of husbands (see Sillars et al., 2000). Thus, the husbands in our sample lacked objective validation for the way they saw their own communication. Wives' self-descriptions were somewhat more congruent with observer-assigned codes, suggesting that there may be a gender difference in the objectivity of self-directed thought.

Certainty and Complexity

Gender differences aside, few individuals showed great recognition of the complexity and ambiguity of communication. Most process codes lacked behavioral specificity but were framed with subjective certainty. While a few codes describe moderately specific communicative acts (for example, changing the topic or speaking with a negative tone of voice), most references to communication were stated in terms of broad intentions (for example, "We're compromising."; "I'm trying to make a point."; "He's attacking me."). Further, even extreme, highly inferential attributions about communication (for example, "She's lying."; "She's backed into a corner and just wants to push the blame off on me.") were typically made without qualification or any other recognition given to the possibility of error. The following excerpt from the reported thoughts of one couple illustrates this tendency. At a certain point in the discussion, the husband grew quiet, prompting the wife to think that "he knows I'm right." The husband, on the other hand, thinks that she is intentionally taunting and harassing him.

She thinks . . .	*He thinks . . .*
Yeah, he wants to stop talking about it because he knows it was the truth and he hates to be criticized when he's wrong.	I was looking at her. She was taunting me. She does that a lot. At that time I was getting a little teed off. So I just decided not to say anything.
Ah, he don't like when he's being put on the spot. Especially when he knows he's wrong.	She was taunting me. I didn't want to hear any more about it. She likes to rant and rave and go on and on. She is trying to nit-pick . . .
Yeah, he wants to change that subject quick. He just knows I'm right.	That is one of Janet's biggest problems. She bitches, but she won't admit it.

Along with the tendency to make strong inferences without qualification, there was also a minimal amount of perspective taking and
relationship-level thinking reflected in the thought data. Only 5% of all
reported thoughts were metaperspectives about what the partner was
thinking, and many of these were undifferentiated and simplistic, as in
the preceding illustration (for example, "... he knows he's wrong.").
Similarly, there was little explicit recognition of interdependent patterns of behavior. Although we looked for instances where individuals
adopted a relationship focus (for example, "We're getting more and
more irritated."; "We're both acting stubborn."), only 3% of thoughts
were phrased in this manner.

Elsewhere, we have suggested that processing demands associated
with interpersonal communication limit the opportunity for complex
reflection, thereby contributing to insensitivity to ambiguity and bias
in inferences during interaction (Sillars, 1998; Sillars et al., 2000). All
communication requires numerous coordinated decisions in real time
(Bavelas & Coates, 1992) and, given the need to keep pace with interaction, most inferences are necessarily snap judgements that go unques-
tioned (Fletcher & Fincham, 1991; Kellerman, 1992; Waldron & Cegala,
1992). Further, inferences about speaker intent are made so routinely
and automatically throughout interaction that they are largely experienced as unmediated observations. Thus, the inferential process that
accompanies interaction is characterized by a paradoxical relation between the inherent ambiguity of communication on the one hand and
the subjective certainty of most inferences on the other (Sillars, 1998).

Negativity

Whatever spouses said to one another during the discussions, they
were often thinking something much worse. Overall, negative thoughts
were more frequent than positive thoughts, and the blunt negativity
of thought was often a striking feature of these data. The discussions
were also confrontational at times, yet the observed interactions were
generally tame by comparison to what individuals reported thinking.
Presumably, individuals engaged in considerable editing of thoughts
when formulating messages, both out of concern for subsequent
consequences and because of the public nature of the setting. However,
as we note further on, both alcohol and aggressive tendencies seemed
to have a bearing on the extent to which husbands expressed negative
sentiments directly.

Not surprisingly, negative thoughts were associated with dissatisfaction in marriage. Three summary measures of negative sentiment were derived from reported thoughts, including partner *blame* (for example, "She's worse than I am in that."; "She totally stays away from my family, on purpose."), *pessimism* (for example, "It's a subject that just really goes nowhere."; "We've been through it a hundred times."), and *anger* (for example, "Mad and frustrated."; "I'm really going crazy."). All of these measures had negative correlations with marital satisfaction.

THOUGHT AND COMMUNICATION IN PHYSICALLY AGGRESSIVE MARRIAGES

Previously, we noted that communication patterns appear to play a role in precipitating some cases of physical aggression in marriage, particularly cases of "expressive" (rather than "instrumental") violence. We now look at subjective coding of interaction within physically aggressive marriages and consider the role that alcohol can play in affecting both overt communication and covert thought. Results from the BMIP research present a complex picture of the interactions of physically aggressive husbands and their wives. Essentially, the research suggests that aggressive couples have an acutely negative style of communication, which becomes even more negative when husbands drink alcohol. However, the thoughts reported by aggressive husbands and their wives were not necessarily angry or dark in a general sense. Instead, these relationships were distinguished by their perceptions of communication, which revealed strong differences between the way individuals described their own role and their partner's role in the interaction (that is, "actor-partner" differences), a heightened state of vigilance toward the process of communication, and low objectivity. Each of these effects was compounded by alcohol. In addition, there was a strong link between negative thought and negative communication among aggressive husbands, especially when inebriated. This linkage suggests that aggressive husbands showed little discretion in verbalizing negative sentiments. These effects are now considered in detail.

Negativity in Communication and Thought

In some respects, the interactions of physically aggressive husbands and their wives resemble those of distressed couples generally. As we noted earlier, the interactions of aggressive men and their wives are often characterized by high rates of negativity and negative reciprocity, as is also the case for distressed couples who do not have a history of aggression (see Canary, Cupach, & Messman, 1995; Gottman, 1998). However, marital violence is not simply an extreme manifestation of marital distress. For one thing, aggressive couples are even more negative and less constructive in conflict interactions than distressed but nonaggressive couples (for example, Feldman & Ridley, 2000; Jacobson et al., 1994). Further, aggressive couples are not necessarily angry or unhappy in a general sense. Marital violence sometimes occurs in couples who are moderately or even highly satisfied with their relationship overall, and who alternate between positive and destructive forms of interaction (Holtzworth-Munroe et al., 1997; Lloyd & Emery, 2000a; Marshall, Weston, & Honeycutt, 2000).

Consistent with other studies, the BMIP results showed that aggressive husbands and their wives had a higher rate of negative communication, and that they reciprocated the negative communication of their partner to a greater extent than couples who did not have a history of physical aggression. These differences were observed even after statistically controlling for the effects of marital satisfaction; so the greater negativity shown by aggressive couples cannot be attributed to dissatisfaction among aggressive husbands and their wives.[3] Alcohol (but not the placebo) further increased the negativity of husbands and wives beyond the level shown in the first (baseline) interaction (see Leonard & Roberts, 1998).

Given the negative communication observed among aggressive husbands and their wives, we might assume that these individuals come to an interaction with an angry, cynical, or otherwise negative outlook, and that this situation simply gets worse when the husband drinks. However, the cognitive recall data presented a more intricate picture. In fact, the thoughts reported by aggressive husbands and their wives were not especially negative overall. Predictably, negative thought was associated with marital dissatisfaction. However, after correcting for the effects of satisfaction/dissatisfaction, there was no difference between aggressive and nonaggressive couples in overall negativity of

---

[3] All differences were significant at beyond the .05 level, except for the difference between aggressive and nonaggressive husbands in overall negativity, which was very close ($p < .06$). The analysis actually controlled for several covariates (that is, marital satisfaction, conflict severity, race, employment, average alcohol consumption), so the tests were quite conservative.

thought.[4] Thus, it seems that aggressive husbands and their wives are not simply more angry or negative in a general sense. Nonetheless, these couples may be primed for escalation of negative conflict in other ways. We see this particularly with respect to perceptions of communication, most notably among aggressive men. These perceptions are discussed next.

Actor-Partner Attributions about Communication

When looking at the cognitive recall data, it is apparent that physically aggressive husbands and their wives made sharply contrasting inferences about their own communication versus the communication of their partner. There was a self-serving tone to such inferences; that is, individuals saw themselves as performing a constructive and legitimate role in the interaction (for example, "I'm trying to get her to talk about it."; "I was just saying how it really is."), whereas their partner was seen as evasive, obstructive, difficult, and so forth (for example, "He doesn't listen."; "She just wanted to blow the whole thing off."; "She's always got to have her way.").

Attributions about communication are depicted graphically in Figure 4.1, which shows actor-partner differences in subjective identification of constructive engagement and avoidance communication strategies. Actor-partner differences here refer to the disparity between self-description (that is, with oneself as the "actor") and description of the partner. More specifically, the actor-partner differences in Figure 4.1 refer to the difference between the percentage of a particular communication strategy attributed to the partner versus the percentage attributed by the partner to self (for example, the wife's attribution of avoidance to the husband versus the husband's self-attribution of avoidance). In aggressive marriages, both spouses attributed less constructive engagement and more avoidance to the partner than the partner attributed to self. Thus, both spouses in these marriages seemed to view themselves as making a frustrated effort to communicate constructively with

---

[4] We formed an overall measure of negative thought by combining all thought codes that imply negative emotions and evaluations (for example, "anger," "hostile attribution," "confrontation," "impasse"). Group differences were evaluated by means of two-way ANOVA (aggression group by alcohol condition), with marital satisfaction included as a covariate. The same design was used to test other group differences in interaction-based thoughts, except that a multivariate design (MANOVA) was used in certain cases.

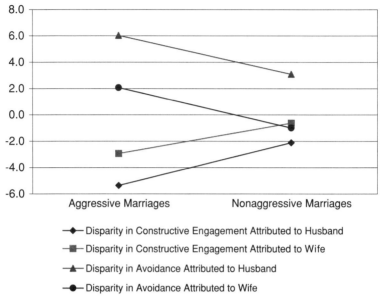

Figure 4.1. Disparity in communication strategies identified by husbands versus wives. Numbers in the figure refer to the mean difference between the percentage of a code attributed to the partner and the percentage attributed by the partner to self. Means are adjusted for the covariate, marital satisfaction.

an evasive partner. This self-perception stands in sharp contrast to the negativity and negative reciprocity that characterized the interactions of aggressive couples according to the observer-assigned codes. The perceptions of aggressive husbands seem particularly stilted and self-serving. Aggressive husbands were far more constructive and much less evasive in their own minds than in the eyes of their wives.

As one can see from Figure 4.1, there were also actor-partner differences in nonaggressive marriages; that is, nonaggressive husbands attributed more constructive engagement and less avoidance to self than was attributed to them by their wives. However, these disparities were much less extreme in nonaggressive relationships than in the aggressive marriages. The one area where aggressive and nonaggressive marriages followed a similar pattern was with respect to attributions about confrontation. Confrontation attributions are not shown in Figure 4.1, but there were actor-partner differences here as well. In both aggressive and nonaggressive marriages, husbands and wives attributed more confrontation to the partner than the partner attributed to self.[5] Regardless of the nature of the relationship, it appears that confrontation is something the partner is seen as doing, not something that individual spouses see themselves as doing. This finding further underscores the fact that communicative acts are viewed very subjectively and differently depending on one's perspective in the interaction.

Vigilance

Another difference between aggressive and nonaggressive couples was that physically aggressive husbands showed more vigilance toward the communication process. That is, a greater percentage of their thoughts fell into the "process" categories of the ICCS, by comparison to nonaggressive husbands. Considered by itself, vigilance toward communication is neither good nor bad. However, the *type* of vigilance shown by aggressive husbands seems problematic. Moderate sensitivity to the process of communication is probably helpful or even necessary for constructive conflict management because it allows one to track impending sources of misunderstanding or other difficulty, consider alternative perspectives, and make adjustments. On the other hand, preoccupation with the process of interaction may also lead to overinterpretation of implicit and ambiguous elements of communication. When combined with the self-serving bias shown by aggressive husbands, heightened vigilance toward communication presents a combustible situation. Given the self-serving inferences about communication made by aggressive husbands, we can assume that they view interaction defensively and suspiciously. This conclusion is reinforced by the biased, irrational, and hostile perceptions of conflict that aggressive husbands have displayed in other research (Eckhardt et al., 1998; Holtzworth-Munroe & Hutchinson, 1993). Thus, heightened vigilance toward communication may simply lead these men to find hidden meaning, hostile intent, or self-justification in ambiguous interaction behaviors.

As we might expect, the wives of aggressive husbands also showed special vigilance toward communication; however, this was only the

---

[5] This analysis employed a MANOVA design with marital satisfaction as a covariate and six actor-partner indices as dependent variables. There was a significant multivariate effect for the aggressive group. Constructive engagement and avoidance attributions helped to discriminate aggressive versus nonaggressive couples, but confrontation attributions did not.

case when their husbands were given alcohol or a placebo. Quite likely, these women have learned to expect trouble when their husbands are drunk, thus leading to increased monitoring of interaction behavior. For the wives in nonaggressive marriages, their husbands' drinking did not seem to create a comparable state of alert. These wives maintained a moderate focus on process, whether or not their husbands appeared to be intoxicated.

Alcohol Myopia and Communication Misattribution

So far, we have seen that the alcohol manipulation created a heightened state of vigilance among the wives of aggressive husbands. This outcome of the alcohol manipulation represents an expectancy effect associated with either alcohol or the placebo, not an effect of alcohol itself.[6] The actual state of inebriation has other important and obvious consequences for marital interaction; however, these effects are somewhat complex. Alcohol can have diverse consequences for social interaction. For example, it can, depending on personal and contextual factors, reduce or increase anxiety (Steele & Josephs, 1988), facilitate helping behavior (Steele, Critchlow, & Liu, 1985), or induce aggression (Ito, Miller, & Pollock, 1996). In an effort to untangle the variable effects of alcohol, Steele and Josephs (1990) propose that alcohol has a single, direct pharmacological effect, which is impaired information processing. Alcohol affects the ability to process multiple stimuli simultaneously, so the drinker may attend only to the most salient cues available and disregard distal cues. This state of "alcohol myopia" may have a variety of consequences depending on the set of cues and associated thoughts that come to dominate an individual's awareness (Steele & Josephs, 1990).

One implication for marital interaction is that alcohol should affect inferences about communication by further increasing selective attention to a small set of cues that are personally salient, and reducing awareness of peripheral cues that may otherwise alter the meaning of a message (also called "metacommunication"; see Watzlawick et al.,

---

[6] A primary effect of the placebo was to direct attention more toward the process of interaction. Husbands also had more process codes overall when in the placebo condition, perhaps because the placebo created ambiguity thereby increasing self-reflection. The placebo may have also caused husbands to monitor the interaction for signs of their own sobriety or drunkenness.

1967; Wilmot, 1980). Alcohol should also reduce an individual's ability to consider alternative perspectives and meanings, so messages may be interpreted rigidly and narrowly. Alcohol may enhance the influence of subjective preconceptions and prevailing mood states on communication inference. For example, Leonard and Jacob (1988, p. 402) suggest that "by impairing the individual's ability to attend and interpret cues, the inebriated husband who is hostile to begin with and is in a stressful, conflictual marriage, would be likely to perceive cues from his wife in an aggressive light." On the other hand, alcohol might reinforce a positivity bias in perception, if the dominant personal and contextual cues are positive.

Alcohol and Actor-Partner Attributions about Communication

The variable effects of alcohol can be seen when looking at attributions about communication from the BMIP research. Consumption of alcohol had relatively few effects that were consistent across the entire sample. More often, the effect of alcohol was to exaggerate differences otherwise seen between aggressive and nonaggressive husbands. This effect was apparent, for example, with respect to actor-partner differences in attributions about communication. Alcohol sharply affected the extent to which husbands saw their wives as engaging in constructive communication. However, the direction of this effect was different in aggressive versus nonaggressive marriages. Figure 4.2 graphs the relevant trends. As one can see, when husbands were sober (that is, the no alcohol and placebo conditions), they attributed slightly less constructive engagement to wives than wives attributed to self. This trend was virtually the same in aggressive and nonaggressive marriages. However, there was a sharp disparity between aggressive and nonaggressive couples when husbands were inebriated. In the alcohol condition, aggressive husbands were *partner-disparaging*; they attributed much less constructive engagement to wives than wives attributed to self. By contrast, nonaggressive husbands made *partner-enhancing* attributions to wives when under the influence of alcohol; that is, they saw wives as even more constructive and cooperative than wives saw themselves as being. For example, one inebriated, nonviolent (also highly satisfied) husband reported thinking that his wife "was listening intently," "she's the best listener in the world," and "she's just speaking it as it is, telling me the truth and that's what I love her for."

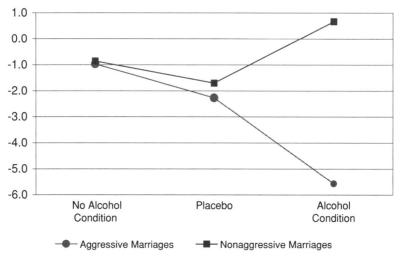

Figure 4.2. Disparity in constructive engagement attributed to the wife as a function of alcohol and marital aggression. Numbers in the figure refer to the mean difference between the percentage of a code attributed to the partner and the percentage attributed by the partner to self. Means are adjusted for the covariate, marital satisfaction.

Alcohol and the Objectivity of Communication Inference

Alcohol also appears to diminish the objectivity of inferences about communication. This finding holds true for both aggressive and nonaggressive husbands; however, aggressive husbands are especially affected. As we saw earlier, there was a small to moderate correspondence between the communication strategies that husbands attributed to wives and the observer-assigned MICS codes. However, when husbands drank alcohol, they appeared to lose objectivity, especially concerning their partner's avoidance behavior. There was no connection between avoidance attributed to wives by husbands who drank alcohol and the observed withdrawal of wives; in fact, the association was slightly negative (partial $r = -.15$; see note 2). By contrast, there was a moderate, positive association between avoidance attributed to wives by sober husbands (no alcohol or placebo conditions) and wives' observed withdrawal (partial $r = .32$). Alcohol may distort perceptions of avoidance behavior because of the way inferences about avoidance are linked to the perceived topicality or relevance of messages. For example, if the husband thinks that the wife is "changing the topic," "making excuses," or "avoiding the real issue," this suggests that her comments fail to address the crucial topic, point, or issue as he subjectively defines it. Alcohol probably narrows an individual's sense of the topic, and diminishes one's ability and inclination to track the discussion from an alternative perspective.

Not only do husbands make subjective inferences about avoidance after drinking alcohol, they seem to interpret withdrawal behavior by wives as an antagonistic form of communication. There was a surprisingly strong association in the alcohol condition between the observed withdrawal of wives and confrontation attributed to wives by husbands (partial $r = .67$). Among sober husbands, this same association was negligible, as one would normally expect (partial $r = .05$). Presumably, wives sometimes showed distancing behaviors in response to their husbands' drunken remarks. These disengagement and withdrawal behaviors may have been construed by husbands as a form of "communication disconfirmation"; that is, an aloof, impervious, or disdainful response that fails to acknowledge the original message (see Cissna & Sieburg, 1981). Significantly, aggressive husbands were especially likely to provide a negative interpretation of their wives' withdrawal behavior. Among aggressive, inebriated husbands, there was a startling association between wives' observed withdrawal and confrontation attributed to wives by these husbands (partial $r = .77$). The same association was still positive but was moderated considerably among inebriated but nonaggressive husbands (partial $r = .24$).

It appears then, that when the aggressive husbands drank alcohol, they came to view the interactions defensively. This perception created a paradoxical situation for wives in that, by attempting to disengage, they were escalating the interaction in the minds of their husbands.

Linkage between Negative Thought and Negative Communication

We have observed to this point that physically aggressive couples displayed a high degree of negativity in their interactions, and that their thoughts revealed a distorted and vigilant outlook toward communication, particularly after the husband drank alcohol. We now consider more closely how the thought processes of aggressive couples might contribute to the negativity seen in their interactions. We propose that the biased and vigilant outlook toward communication shown by aggressive husbands represents a reactive predisposition or "hair trigger" that tends to prompt a negative response to any perceived or real affront. Indeed, there was a strong link between negative thought and negative communication among aggressive husbands, suggesting that these individuals verbalized negative thoughts with little discretion. In

addition, different types of thoughts predicted the negative communication of aggressive versus nonaggressive husbands.

Not surprisingly, the degree of negativity in thought was associated
with the rate of observed negativity in the discussions. Of course, this
association does not necessarily indicate causality. Negative thoughts
may have led to negative messages or conversely, the negative tone of
some discussions may have elicited dark thoughts. To consider the possibility that negative thought was simply a reaction to what the partner
was saying or doing, we controlled for the effects of the partner's communication. There was still a moderate association between negative
thought and negative communication, after controlling for the partner's
observed negativity (partial $r = .40$ for husbands, .28 for wives). This result makes it unlikely that negative thoughts were merely a reflection
of the discussion. Instead, we will assume that negativity in the interaction was at least partly driven by cognitive recruitment of negative
memories and associations from past experience.

We are particularly interested here in the strength of the linkage between negative thought and negative communication within different
subgroups and conditions of the BMIP. To the extent that the linkage
between thought and communication is greater, it suggests a tendency
to express negative thoughts directly and (when controlling for partner
negativity) without objective provocation. There were too few couples
in the alcohol condition to make the results conclusive, but the trends
are intriguing. Notably, there was a stronger association between negative thought and negative communication (controlling for partner negative communication) among aggressive husbands versus nonaggressive
husbands. Further, this association was particularly strong among aggressive husbands who drank alcohol (partial $r = .69$). The aggressive
husbands seemed to express negative thoughts with little discretion, especially after consuming alcohol. The same association was
much smaller among nonaggressive husbands in the alcohol condition
(partial $r = .25$). Thus, the nonaggressive husbands in our sample exhibited greater restraint, whether intoxicated or not.

The wives of aggressive and nonaggressive husbands apparently
adapted to their husbands' drinking in opposite ways. Among wives of
nonaggressive husbands, there was a strong association between negative thought and negative communication when husbands drank alcohol, less so when husbands did not drink alcohol. Among wives of
aggressive husbands, there was a strong positive association between
negative thought and negative communication when husbands did not

Table 4.2. Significant Predictors of Negative Communication		
	Husbands	Wives
Aggressive Couples	Anger	Pessimism
	Blame	Partner Confrontation
	Partner Confrontation	
Nonaggressive	Blame	Partner Confrontation
Couples	Partner Avoidance	

* Based on stepwise regression of negative communication on measures of negative sentiment and perceived partner communication.

drink alcohol and an *inverse* association when their husbands were inebriated (that is, the more negative their thoughts, the less negative their communication). Thus, it appears that these wives engaged in considerable editing of negative thoughts when the husband was inebriated, perhaps in recognition of his volatility. As we have seen, the wives of aggressive husbands still expressed considerable negativity; however, they might have expressed far more if they had bluntly revealed what they were thinking.

In the final set of analyses, we identified the thoughts that best predicted negative communication. Table 4.2 shows the significant predictors of negative communication among different subgroups. Two things are notable. First, the negative communication of aggressive husbands was accompanied by explicit attention to angry emotions (for example, "Frustration . . . ."; "I was really aggravated."), which was not the case with nonaggressive husbands or wives. Although the thoughts of aggressive husbands did not reveal chronic anger overall, angry thoughts rose in proportion to the negativity of communication, suggesting that their interactions were emotionally volatile.

Second, aggressive husbands and their wives were both more negative to the extent that the partner was seen as confrontational. Both spouses may have reacted to perceived confrontation with negative messages of their own, thereby contributing to the negativity observed in the interactions of aggressive couples. We do not see quite the same indication of tit-for-tat confrontation in nonaggressive couples. Although these wives were more negative when husbands were seen as confrontational, the husbands were more negative when wives were seen as avoiding. These opposite tendencies of husbands and wives may have balanced one another to an extent, thereby reducing the likelihood of protracted negative escalation.

CONCLUSION

Differences in perception are probably an inherent feature of marital conflict. As conflicts become more profound and entrenched, spouses tend to define the issues, events, and causes of conflict in different terms. Further, when spouses talk about conflict, they selectively attend to and interpret the stream of communication. Whereas previous research has identified cognitive and communicative dynamics that underlie marital conflict and aggression, our own research examines these elements in tandem. The thoughts elicited through video-assisted recall revealed both general and specific features of cognition during communication. Some trends appear to be broadly characteristic of individuals and couples during marital conflict, whereas other perceptual phenomena are peculiar to the etiology of violent marriages and the influence of alcohol.

The most basic and widely distributed trend is simply the diversity and selectivity of thoughts associated with communication. Attention to communication is inevitably selective, often to the point of appearing scattered and idiosyncratic. One consequence is that individual spouses may define the sequence of events differently, and make contrasting inferences about the role played by each person within the interaction. Some discrepancies are linked to gender, such as the greater inclination of husbands to focus on literal content issues, and wives' tendency to focus more on the partner's thoughts and behaviors. Potentially, individuals might recognize and compensate for differences in perception; however, reported thoughts reveal little evidence of explicit perspective taking, and show limited awareness or sensitivity to sources of ambiguity and complexity in communication. Even strong inferences about communication are typically made without qualification, perhaps reflecting inherent properties and demands of communication during conflict (for example, the need to interpret a complex and involving stimulus field very quickly to keep pace with interaction; see Sillars, 1998; Sillars et al., 2000).

While differences in perspectives are to be expected in all marital conflicts, some differences reflect self-justifying distortions that may be the roots of marital violence. For example, aggressive men made particularly stilted and self-serving inferences about communication, thus contributing to strong husband-wife (or "actor-partner") disparities in aggressive relationships. Aggressive husbands also displayed a high degree of vigilance toward communication, possibly indicating a defensive and reactive disposition. The negative communication of aggressive men was accompanied by explicit rehearsal of angry emotions, suggesting a high degree of emotional volatility. Similarly, Eckhardt et al. (1998) and Holtzworth-Munroe (1992) suggest that violent husbands make selective and distorted inferences about conflicts that reinforce anger and increase the likelihood of aggression. Further, aggressive husbands may be unable to extricate themselves from escalating negativity in communication because they lack the anger-control strategies of nonaggressive husbands (Eckhardt et al., 1998).

Alcohol may affect spouses in different, even opposite, ways. An individual who feels victimized or justified in conflict, who sees the partner as provoking, distorting, and/or evading and who rehearses anger as a result, is likely to impose this scenario with increasing intensity and single-mindedness when drunk. On the other hand, alcohol may also embellish positive perceptions. We see some evidence of these disparate impacts of alcohol in the fact that aggressive husbands made partner-disparaging attributions about communication when inebriated, whereas nonaggressive husbands made partner-enhancing attributions.

Alcohol seems to diminish the objectivity of inferences about communication among all husbands, but aggressive men are particularly affected. Aggressive husbands were especially prone to see their wives as being confrontational when observer-assigned codes suggested that wives were manifesting withdrawal behavior. Aggressive men also appear to express negative thoughts very directly after drinking alcohol, as suggested by the strong association between negative thought and negative communication, controlling for the partner's negative communication. Not surprisingly, wives of aggressive men became more vigilant toward communication when given reason to think that their husbands had been drinking, and they showed evidence of considerable editing and mitigation of negative thoughts when their husbands were inebriated, presumably as a response to their husbands' volatility.

Although both husbands and wives in aggressive marriages may reciprocate negative communication, all indications here are that the distorted perceptions of violent men, along with their apparent tendency to act on negative perceptions independent of the wife's objective behavior, are key factors driving destructive conflict in aggressive marriages.

Alcohol apparently adds to an already volatile situation by increasing distortions in the way aggressive husbands interpret interaction, and by affecting their propensity to act upon these distortions.

REFERENCES

Acitelli, L. K., & Young, A. M. (1996). Gender and thought in relationships. In G. J. Fletcher & J. Fitness (Eds.), *Knowledge structures in close relationships: A social psychological approach* (pp. 147–168). Mahwah, NJ: Lawrence Erlbaum Associates.

Bavelas, J. B., & Coates, L. (1992). How do we account for the mindfulness of face-to-face dialogue? *Communication Monographs, 59*, 301–305.

Berns, S. B., Jacobson, N. S., & Gottman, J. M. (1999). Demand/withdraw interaction patterns between different types of batterers and their spouses. *Journal of Marital and Family Therapy, 25*, 337–348.

Burman, B., Margolin, G., & John, R. S. (1993). America's angriest home videos: Behavioral contingencies observed in home reenactments of marital conflict. *Journal of Consulting and Clinical Psychology, 6*, 28–39.

Canary, D. J., Cupach, W. R., & Messman, S. J. (1995). *Relationship conflict.* Thousand Oaks, CA: Sage.

Cissna, K. N. L., & Sieburg, E. (1981). Patterns of interactional confirmation and disconfirmation. In C. Wilder-Mott & J. H. Weakland (Eds.), *Rigor and imagination: Essays from the legacy of Gregory Bateson* (pp. 253–282). New York: Praeger.

Cordova, J. V., Jacobson, N. S., Gottman, J. M., Rushe, R., & Cox, G. (1993). Negative reciprocity and communication in couples with a violent husband. *Journal of Abnormal Psychology, 102*, 559–564.

Eckhardt, C. I., Barbour, K. A., & Davison, G. C. (1998). Articulated thoughts of maritally violent and nonviolent men during anger arousal. *Journal of Consulting and Clinical Psychology, 66*, 259–269.

Feldman, C. M., & Ridley, C. A. (1995). The etiology and treatment of domestic violence between adult partners. *Clinical psychology: Science and practice, 2*, 317–348.

Feldman, C. M., & Ridley, C. A. (2000). The role of conflict-based communication responses and outcomes in male domestic violence toward female partners. *Journal of Social and Personal Relationships, 17*, 552–573.

Fincham, F. D., Bradbury, T. N., & Grych, J. H. (1990). Conflict in close relationships: The role of intrapersonal phenomena. In V. Graham & S. Folkes (Eds.), *Attribution theory: Applications to achievement, mental health, and interpersonal conflict. Applied social psychology* (pp. 161–184). Hillsdale, NJ: Lawrence Erlbaum Associates.

Fletcher, G. J. O., & Fincham, F. D. (1991). Attribution process in close relationships. In G. J. O. Fletcher & F. D. Fincham (Eds.), *Cognition in close relationships* (pp. 7–35). Hillsdale, NJ: Lawrence Erlbaum Associates.

Gottman, J. M. (1998). Psychology and the study of marital processes. *Annual Review of Psychology, 49*, 169–197.

Holtzworth-Munroe, A. (1992). Social skill deficits in maritally violent men: Interpreting the data using a social information processing model. *Clinical Psychology Review, 12*, 605–618.

Holtzworth-Munroe, A., & Hutchinson, G. (1993). Attributing negative intent to wife behavior: The attributions of maritally violent versus nonviolent men. *Journal of Abnormal Psychology, 102*, 206–211.

Holtzworth-Munroe, A., Stuart, G. L., Sandin, E., Smutzler, N., & McLaughlin, W. (1997). Comparing the social support behaviors of violent and nonviolent husbands during discussions of wife personal problems. *Personal Relationships, 4*, 395–412.

Ito, T. A., Miller, N., & Pollock, V. E. (1996). Alcohol and aggression: A meta-analysis on the moderating effects of inhibitory cue, triggering events, and self-focused attention. *Psychological Bulletin, 120*, 60–82.

Jacobson, N. S., Gottman, J. M., Waltz, J., Rushe, R., Babcock, J., & Holtzworth-Munroe, A. (1994). Affect, verbal content, and psycho-physiology in the arguments of couples with a violent husband. *Journal of Consulting and Clinical Psychology, 62*, 982–988.

Johnson, M. P. (1995). Patriarchal terror and common couple violence: Two forms of violence against women. *Journal of Marriage and the Family, 57*, 283–294.

Kellerman, K. (1992). Communication: Inherently strategic and primarily automatic. *Communication Monographs, 59*, 288–300.

Laing, R. D., Phillipson, H., & Lee, A. R. (1966). *Interpersonal perception: A theory and a method of research.* New York: Springer.

Leonard, K. E., & Jacob, T. (1988). Alcohol, alcoholism, and family violence. In V. B. Van Hasselt, R. L. Morrison, A. S. Bellack, & M. Hersen (Eds.), *Handbook of family violence* (pp. 383–406). New York: Plenum Press.

Leonard, K. E., & Roberts, L. J. (1998). The effects of alcohol on the marital interactions of aggressive and nonaggressive husbands and their wives. *Journal of Abnormal Psychology, 4*, 602–615.

Leonard, K. E., & Senchak, M. (1996). The prospective prediction of marital aggression among newlywed couples. *Journal of Abnormal Psychology, 105(3)*, 369–380.

Lloyd, S. A., & Emery, B. C. (2000a). The context and dynamics of intimate aggression among women. *Journal of Social and Personal Relationships, 17*, 503–521.

Lloyd, S. A., & Emery, B. C. (2000b). *The dark side of courtship: Physical and sexual aggression.* Thousand Oaks, CA: Sage.

Margolin, G., John, R. S., & Gleberman, L. (1988). Affective responses to conflictual discussions in violent and nonviolent couples. *Journal of Consulting and Clinical Psychology, 56*, 24–33.

Marshall, L. L., Weston, R., & Honeycutt, T. C. (2000). Does men's positivity moderate or mediate the effects of their abuse on women's relationship quality? *Journal of Social and Personal Relationships, 17*, 660–675.

Roberts, L. J., & Krokoff, L. J. (1990). A time-series analysis of withdrawal, hostility, and displeasure in satisfied and dissatisfied marriages. *Journal of Marriage and the Family, 52*, 95–105.

Roberts, L. J., Roberts, C. F., & Leonard, K. E. (1999). Alcohol, drugs, and interpersonal violence. In V. B. Van Hasselt & M. Hersen (Eds.), *Handbook of psychological approaches with violent offenders: Contemporary strategies and issues* (pp. 493–519). New York: Kluwer Academic/Plenum Publishers.

Scott, C. K., Fuhrman, R. W., & Wyer, R. S. (1991). Information processing in close relationships. In G. J. O. Fletcher & F. D. Fincham (Eds.), *Cognition in close relationships* (pp. 37–67). Hillsdale, NJ: Lawrence Erlbaum Associates.

Sillars, A. L. (1981). Attributions and interpersonal conflict resolution. In J. H. Harvey, W. Ickes, & R. F. Kidd (Eds.), *New directions in attribution research* (vol. 3, pp. 279–305) Hillsdale, NJ: Lawrence Erlbaum Associates.

Sillars, A. L. (1998). (Mis)understanding. In B. H. Spitzberg & W. R. Cupach (Eds.), *The dark side of relationships* (pp. 73–102). Mahwah, NJ: Lawrence Erlbaum Associates.

Sillars, A., Roberts, L. J., Dun, T., & Leonard, K. E. (2001). Stepping into the stream of thought: Cognition during marital conflict. In V. Manusov and J. H. Harvey (Eds.), *Attribution, communication behavior, and close relationships* (pp. 193–210). Cambridge: Cambridge University Press.

Sillars, A., Roberts, L. J., Leonard, K. E., & Dun, T. (2000). Cognition during marital conflict: The relationship of thought and talk. *Journal of Social and Personal Relationships, 17*, 479–502.

Steele, C. M., Critchlow, B., & Liu, T. J. (1985). Alcohol and social behavior: II. The helpful drunkard. *Journal of Personality and Social Psychology, 48*, 35–46.

Steele, C. M., & Josephs, R. A. (1988). Drinking your troubles away: II. An attention-allocation model of alcohol's effect on psychological stress. *Journal of Abnormal Psychology, 97*, 196–205.

Steele, C. M., & Josephs, R. A. (1990). Alcohol myopia: Its prized and dangerous effects. *American Psychologist, 45*, 921–933.

Straus, M. A. (1979). Measuring intrafamily conflict and violence: The conflict tactics (CT) scales. *Journal of Marriage and the Family, 41*, 75–88.

Waldron, V. R., & Cegala, D. J. (1992). Assessing conversational cognition: Levels of cognitive theory and associated methodological requirements. *Human Communication Research, 18*, 599–622.

Watzlawick, P., Beavin, J., & Jackson, D. D. (1967). *Pragmatics of human communication: A study of interactional patterns, pathologies, and paradoxes.* New York: Norton.

Weiss, R. L., Hops, H., & Patterson, G. R. (1973). A framework for conceptualizing marital conflict: A technology for altering it, some data for evaluating it. In F. W. Clark & L. A. Hamerlynck (Eds.), *Critical issues in research and practice: Proceedings of the Fourth Banff International Conference on Behavior Modification* (pp. 309–342). Champaign, IL: Research Press.

Wilmot, W. W. (1980). Meta-communication: A re-examination and extension. *Communication Yearbook IV* (pp. 61–69). New Brunswick, NJ: Transaction Books.

Wilmot, W. W., & Hocker, J. L. (2001). Interpersonal conflict (6th ed.). New York: McGraw-Hill.

UNDERSTANDING THE IMPORTANCE OF POSITIVE INTERACTION

Introduction to Section Two

Although marital interaction has been extensively studied, much of the research has focused on conflict processes and their implications for relationship functioning. This focus was often adopted because negative processes were believed to be particularly powerful discriminators between satisfied and dissatisfied couples. More recently, however, researchers have begun to recognize the importance of positive interaction processes in maintaining relationship satisfaction.

As Roberts and Greenberg point out, the period leading up to the decision to marry is typically one of great joy, intimacy, and positivity. They contrast two radically different perspectives on the development of marital dysfunction. On the one hand, the negative affect model emphasizes the destructive role of conflict and negativity in marital breakdown. On the other hand, the intimacy process model, while recognizing the importance of responses to conflict, focuses on the role of positive interactions in maintaining relationship satisfaction. According to this latter perspective, positive exchanges serve to maintain a climate of trust, respect, and acceptance; in the absence of such a climate, relationship stress and conflict are likely to escalate.

As these authors note, there are many approaches to the observational assessment of conflict interaction. Although positive behavior can be observed in these interactions, discussion of conflict topics is unlikely to provide prototypical examples of positive couple behavior. New approaches, which are more likely to elicit positive interaction, need to be developed. In this chapter, Roberts and Greenberg describe two such paradigms: the vulnerability paradigm, which is designed to elicit caregiving responses from the partner, and the love paradigm, which is designed to elicit reciprocal expressions of affection.

Although both these paradigms were successful in eliciting emotionally charged interactions, spouses differed widely in their responses to these situations. Some spouses were intensely warm and loving, whereas others, even when faced with their partner's positive disclosures, were indifferent or rejecting. Roberts and Greenberg describe a system for coding the interaction behavior observed using these paradigms. This coding system is likely to be useful in redirecting researchers' attention toward positive interaction as an equally important way of understanding marital processes.

As we have seen, Roberts and Greenberg emphasize the importance of intimacy processes in marriage. Similarly, Clark and her colleagues focus on the norms that govern the giving and receiving of benefits in marriage and how these norms are linked to the development and maintenance of intimacy.

In particular, these researchers propose that a communal norm, involving noncontingent responsiveness to partners' needs as they arise, is the ideal norm for spouses to follow. Communal norms are contrasted with a range of other norms for relationship behavior, including equality, equity, and self-interest.

The communal norm is considered as preferable because spouses who are confident that their partners will be attentive and responsive to their needs develop a sense of trust and security, and are more willing to disclose their thoughts, needs, and feelings to one another. Consistent with this view, Clark and her colleagues present evidence that engaged and married partners generally see the communal norm as the norm of choice.

At the same time, consistently following a communal norm is not always easy in practice. When spouses are feeling particularly stressed, and when they see their needs as being neglected, they may respond by switching to one of the alternative norms. Importantly, this switch may be either temporary or permanent, depending on such factors as chronic differences in trust and attachment security. For example, a spouse who sees others as generally unpredictable and untrustworthy is more likely to interpret temporary departures from a communal norm as indicative of the partner's lack of love. A couple's ability to deal successfully with these departures from a communal style of interaction is likely to be crucial for the future of the relationship.

A very different approach to positive processes in marriage is taken by Aron and his colleagues, based on the self-expansion model.

According to this perspective, the exhilaration associated with falling in love is due largely to the rapid "expansion of self"; that is, coming to know the partner's resources and perspectives, and incorporating these into the self. Conversely, the typical decline in relationship quality over time may be explained in terms of a type of habituation, whereby there are few novel aspects of the partner remaining to be discovered. If this perspective is valid, then declines in relationship quality may be countered, at least to some extent, by partners' shared involvement in self-expanding activities; that is, activities that are novel, challenging, and arousing.

Aron and his colleagues describe a series of six studies designed to explore this proposition. The first two studies were survey studies that linked reports of shared participation in self-expanding activities with greater relationship satisfaction. Three experimental studies are also reported, in which random assignment to conditions allowed the researchers to test directly the link between involvement in such activities and increases in reports of relationship quality. The descriptions of the self-expanding activities used in these studies make fascinating reading! The three experimental studies demonstrated the importance of novelty/challenge and the salience of the partner as essential for the increase in relationship quality to occur.

The final study was a field experiment in which couples were randomly assigned to participate in either self-expanding activities, pleasant activities, or no activities, over a 10-week period. Data from this study indicate that the positive effect of self-expanding activities seems to apply, not only in the laboratory, but in real-world settings. The authors maintain that these activities have the advantages of being accessible to most couples, and of requiring little, if any, professional intervention.

The chapters in this section help to redress the imbalance that has characterized much marital interaction research by exploring the positive aspects of couple interaction. The chapters address a range of important issues including the development of paradigms for assessing positive behavior in marriage, the identification of factors that promote the development and maintenance of communal norms, and the creation of positive experiences through partners' involvement in self-expanding activities. Hopefully, this work will provide an impetus for further research exploring how couples can maintain positive interactions that enhance their relationships and sustain them over time.

CHAPTER FIVE

Observational "Windows" to Intimacy Processes in Marriage

Linda J. Roberts and Danielle R. Greenberg

Wife (W): There's lots of things I love about you . . . the way you laugh.
Husband (H): The whole package.
W: You look at me and you know what I'm thinking. The way you smile. The way your clothes are all over the house.
H: You don't love that. Don't lie.
W: No, but that's you, and I love you.

In the past two decades, researchers using behavioral observation methods to study marital functioning have focused almost exclusively on interaction processes related to conflict. As Fincham and Beach (1999) have noted, conflict processes have enjoyed a "privileged status" in marital interaction research. Negative affect and negative affect reciprocity have been established as robust correlates of marital discord (Gottman, 1998; Karney & Bradbury, 1995; Weiss & Heyman, 1990; for reviews). Distressed husbands and wives are more likely than their happily married counterparts to engage in hostile, blaming, and attacking behaviors, and further, they are more likely to reciprocate their partner's negative behavior. Although early behavioral theories of marital discord (for example, Birchler, Weiss, & Vincent, 1975; Jacobson & Margolin, 1979) explicitly acknowledged the functional role of positive behavioral transactions in successful marriages, the emphasis in

Preparation of this chapter was supported in part by a grant awarded to the first author by The Graduate School, University of Wisconsin/Madison.

Direct correspondence to Linda J. Roberts, Department of Human Development and Family Studies, 1430 Linden Drive, Madison, Wisconsin 53706. Phone (608) 263-2290; fax (608) 265-1172; e-mail: ljrober1@facstaff.wisc.edu.

recent years has been on the corrosive role of conflictual interactions in the development of marital dysfunction.

One reason for the current emphasis on negativity and conflict behavior may be the tremendous success of the problem-solving or "conflict" discussion task as a "window" to marital behavior. In the standard conflict interaction paradigm, couples are asked to discuss and resolve a current marital conflict or "disagreement," while being video-taped in a naturalistic laboratory context. The videotapes are then systematically coded by trained observers, and the couples' interactions can be described in terms of both the frequencies and the sequential structure of the behavioral codes.

The problem-solving paradigm has been enormously successful in eliciting naturalistic, emotionally charged interactions between spouses, despite the laboratory context and the presence of videocameras. Our basic knowledge of the behavioral landscape of marriage is derived primarily from observations of couples in this single interactional context. However, the problem-solving discussion task may maximize the likelihood of observing negative interactional processes and truncate opportunities for observing positive processes (Cutrona, 1996; Melby, Ge, Conger, & Warner, 1995). Melby and colleagues (1995) have recently demonstrated that different conversational tasks have a direct effect on the effective elicitation and reliable assessment of positive behavior. After two decades of careful analyses of problem-solving interactions, far more valid information is known about negative behavioral processes in marriage than about positive behavioral processes.

An Intimacy Process Model of Marital Distress

It is possible that the almost universal reliance on the problem-solving discussion task has led not only to an underestimation of the frequency of positive behaviors in naturally occurring marital interactions, but also to a premature dismissal of their importance for marital outcomes. Although a couple's ability to successfully resolve disagreements and conflicts is undoubtedly an important aspect of marital functioning, it is only one of the interactional tasks couples confront in their daily lives. To fully understand the determinants of marital quality, we need to be able to describe not only how couples handle conflict, but also how they maintain intimate connection and positive regard for one another. It is our contention that relational harmony may depend on the successful enactment of *positive behavioral interchanges in the context of intimate marital interactions.*

Since the process leading up to the decision to marry is one of building intimate connection (Altman & Taylor, 1973; Huesmann & Levinger, 1976), a natural question is how these positive, intimate interchanges between partners become replaced with negative, conflictual ones after the honeymoon. In current behavioral models of marital interaction, what triggers the cascade to marital distress and divorce are negative and conflictual interchanges that emerge after marriage and gradually erode positive sentiments. Love, respect, and affection may draw partners together, but it is the inability to handle effectively the inevitable conflicts that arise in marriage that is seen as leading to marital unhappiness.

Some longitudinal studies support the notion that these negative processes play a causal role in the erosion of marital satisfaction over time, and in eventual marital dissolution (for example, Julien, Markman, & Lindahl, 1989; Matthews, Wickrama, & Conger, 1996). However, despite the current popularity of this "negative affect model" of the development of distress, empirical support remains rather limited. Further, as Fincham and Beach (1999) have noted, there is very little explicit *theory* supporting the role of conflict in the development of marital dysfunction. In contrast, positive processes such as intimacy, expressions of positive regard, emotional responsiveness, and attachment have figured prominently in major theoretical perspectives on interpersonal functioning (see for example, Bowlby, 1969; 1973; Erickson, 1959; Rogers, 1951; Sullivan, 1953). From Bowlby's attachment theory to Sullivan's interpersonal theory, deleterious effects for relational functioning are predicted in the absence of *responsive, intimate interactions.* Given the consensus on the importance of intimate interactions in theories of human development, an *intimacy process model* of marital distress may represent a viable alternative to the negative affect model.

Although negative, conflictual interactions may be a "final common pathway" for couples in an ailing marriage, the negative affect model suggests a cascade beginning with unresolved conflict and negative interchanges sparking a corresponding decrease in positive exchanges as the explanation for the development of marital dysfunction. An intimacy process model of marital dysfunction reframes the causal process as beginning with the absence of positive, intimate interchanges, which eventually leads to negative conflictual interactions as individual needs are left unsatisfied. The regular enactment of behavioral exchanges that lead to experiences of relational intimacy will serve to maintain the climate of security, trust, and acceptance that characterize well-functioning relationships. Operating within this climate of security, partners are able to resolve conflicts without defensiveness and animosity. Conversely, neglect or inattention to the task of maintaining intimate connection with a marital partner may create fertile ground for hostile exchanges whenever sparked by stress or disagreement. Thus, it may be the absence of security and trust in the dyad due to failures in the intimacy process that lead to negative, conflictual processes, rather than negative processes invariably leading to the erosion of positive sentiments.

Recently published results of a prospective study (Huston, Caughlin, Houts, Smith, & George, 2001) examining the marital outcomes of a large cohort of newlyweds support this hypothesized central role for positive behavioral processes. Ted Huston and colleagues collected partner and self-report data on both affectional expression and negativity (including daily diary reports of marital behavior) early in marriage and used these data to predict marital outcomes 13 years later. There was little evidence to support the popular negative affect model; increases in negativity were not found to lead to marital failure. Instead, decreases in *affectional expression* and *partner responsiveness* were found to distinguish couples who would later divorce from those who would remain married. As the researchers conclude, "it appears that the well-documented deleterious effects of negativity on marriage may occur *after* marital enchantment gives way" (italics added, p. 250). As this research and the intimacy process model suggest, the neglect of intimate and affectional interaction with a partner may have significant repercussions for relational harmony.

Although not based on behavioral observations, a number of studies have shown that spouses who report more self-disclosure, partner disclosure, partner responsiveness, or intimacy are more maritally satisfied (for example, Carnelley, Pietromonaco, & Jaffe, 1996; Feeney, Noller, & Ward, 1997; Langhinrichsen-Rohling, Schlee, Monson, Ehrensaft, & Heyman, 1998; Matthews & Clark, 1982; Tolstedt & Stokes, 1983; Veroff, Douvan, Orbuch, & Acitelli, 1998). Clinical studies of distressed couples also suggest the importance of intimacy processes. Problems regarding intimacy are common in clinic couples (for example, Christensen & Shenk, 1991) and successful interventions for marital distress (for example, Greenberg & Johnson, 1988) specifically target changes in the pattern and style of partners' expressions of vulnerability and emotional responsiveness.

Using partner reports of behavioral responses, Roberts (2000) has demonstrated that partner withdrawal in response to confiding behavior ("intimacy avoidance") is related to marital dissatisfaction independently of withdrawal responses in the context of conflict. Thus, although conflict and negativity may represent a "final common pathway" for distressed couples, theory, clinical evidence, and an array of research findings suggest an acute need for further investigation of the role of positive, intimate, behavioral processes in marriage. However, to enable marital interaction researchers to effectively explore this new territory, intimate conversational tasks that elicit naturalistic positive behavioral processes are needed.

The Importance of Observing Marital Interaction

In their decade review paper, John Gottman and Cliff Notarius (2000) made a persuasive argument for the value of observing marriages:

Observational research plays a major role in research on marriage, both for purposes of description and for building theories of the mechanisms underlying central phenomena occurring within families. It is the main roadway available for the precise study of family process ... (its success) stem(s), in part, from the power of observational data to reveal a replicable portrait of complex social interaction that lies beyond the natural awareness of even the most keenly sensitive spouse or partner, and thus lies beyond assessment with self-report instruments. (p. 927)

For intimacy processes to take center stage in the marital field they must be observed and described. After two decades of observational work, the topography of conflict is now relatively well articulated. However, there are no roadmaps for positive, intimate behavioral processes. Little is known about the behavioral processes that characterize loving, tender, affectionate, caring, or intimate marital interactions. Direct observation of these intimate interactions will allow precise description of behavioral patterns that might distinguish maritally satisfied and dissatisfied couples and eventually provide information useful in the development of effective methods for preventing marital discord.

The standard problem-solving conversational task does not provide a context conducive for assessing positive, intimate behavioral processes. The task has been highly successful in eliciting naturalistic interactions between partners that include displays of strong negative and contemptuous emotions from married partners, despite the laboratory setting. The challenge is to create a procedure that elicits naturalistic expressions of strong positive emotions in the same way that the conflict discussion task elicits strong expressions of negative emotions. In what follows, we will first describe the process we undertook to develop procedures that would allow us to observe and map this new territory of intimate marital interactions. Then, we will provide initial views or "snapshots" of the landscape of marital intimacy as seen from this new vantage point.

Facilitating Naturalistic Intimate Interactions in the Lab

Reis and Shaver (1988) have specified the essential components of the intimacy process in their "interpersonal process model of intimacy" (see also elaboration of the model by Reis & Patrick, 1996). According to their model, intimacy develops through behavioral interactions in which disclosures of *personally revealing feelings* are met with *emotional responsiveness* by the partner. Intimacy is "an interactive process in which, as a result of a partner's response, individuals come to feel understood, validated, and cared for" (Reis & Patrick, 1996, p. 536). Using this model as the conceptual framework for our work, we sought to create conversational tasks that would enable partners to engage in a natural process of emotional self-disclosure and emotional responsiveness.

To assess the intimacy process in a behavioral interaction paradigm requires a procedure to elicit a "naturalistic" intimate conversation. Systematic observation procedures are predicated on the assumption that behavior is observed in a naturally occurring interactional context (Weick, 1985). Although we videotaped our conversations in an "artificial" environment – a video laboratory setting – the assumption is that the lack of experimenter-imposed control on the conversational flow produces an interactional context that reflects the couple's naturally occurring exchanges. The priming and instructional procedures for the tasks we introduce here are designed to minimize the artificiality of the interaction. A lab setting has distinct advantages; it allows for videotaping of high quality, close-up, split screen images of husband and wife interacting under controlled but unobtrusive conditions. However, in our research procedures, we make concerted efforts to minimize the artificiality of the physical environment. Remote-controlled cameras are placed in a room furnished and decorated to look like a living room/dining room, and partners sit across from one another at a dining room table to talk. Cameras are unobtrusively housed in bookshelf units behind smoked glass to minimize participants' awareness of their presence.

Since researchers have been very successful in eliciting naturalistic problem-solving/conflict conversations in the lab, we developed our intimate conversational tasks by carefully designing our procedures to incorporate key elements of the standard paradigm. In our view, the success of the problem-solving discussion task may be attributed to at least three factors. First, problem solving is a naturally occurring interactional task; couples know how to engage in this task and, in the lab setting, rely on their habitual response patterns to perform the task. Second, the conversational topic – a "current unresolved disagreement" – usually has high emotional salience for partners, rendering the artificial laboratory surroundings less salient. Third, the partners are naturally "primed" for this discussion; once a current, real, unresolved topic is identified, the partners are clear about what needs to be discussed and there is ample content to keep them talking.

Focusing on maximizing these same features, we developed procedures for eliciting two intimate interactions – a *vulnerability paradigm* and a *love paradigm*. The purpose of both paradigms is to elicit naturalistic intimate interactions involving open disclosure of personally revealing feelings and spontaneous responsiveness of the partner. Although both discussion tasks involve the core components of the intimacy process (Reis & Shaver, 1988), they differ with respect to the nature of the revealing disclosures and the type of responses naturally elicited from the partner. The vulnerability paradigm is designed to elicit disclosures of vulnerability, or threats to self-esteem, that directly or indirectly imply the need for caregiving responses from the partner. The love paradigm, on the other hand, is designed to elicit disclosures directly related to positive feelings toward the partner that implicitly invite reciprocity from the partner. Thus, the targeted disclosures in both paradigms are *personally revealing disclosures that invite the partner to be emotionally responsive.*

Development of the Vulnerability Paradigm

Working with married couples recruited from the community, we tested a variety of protocols for eliciting intimate interactions, gradually modifying our procedures to optimize the naturalness and emotional depth of the facilitated interactions. Our first attempt to elicit a caregiving interaction was based on an adaptation of the social support conversational task that researchers have used to assess "social support" in the marital context (Cutrona & Suhr, 1994; Holtzworth-Munroe, Stuart, Sandin, Smutzler, & McLaughlin, 1997; Pasch & Bradbury, 1998; Saitzyk, Floyd, & Kroll, 1997).

Although specific instructions for the social support task have varied across research labs,[1] participants are generally asked to discuss a personal problem while their partner is instructed to respond "as they normally would." Thus, each partner is assigned the role of either the support receiver or the support provider, and, in a second conversation, the partners are instructed to reverse the roles. We modified these procedures to approximate the conditions of naturally occurring intimate interactions more closely. We asked partners to disclose to their partner a personal problem or stress; however, rather than assigning "roles" to the partners, the partners were each prompted to have a particular problem in mind, and then simply told to "discuss their issues with their partner" without any instructions on how to negotiate the discussion task. Importantly, asking the partners themselves to negotiate the roles of "discloser" and "responder" more closely approximates a natural interactional context than the assignment of distinct interactional roles. Partners negotiate this turn-taking terrain naturally and regularly in their daily lives. For example, on being reunited after the workday, each partner may have a "personal problem or stress" that occurred at work to share with their partner. No structure is imposed on their interaction – they must mutually negotiate the ebb and flow of disclosing and responding.

However, using the disclosure instructions adopted from the social support interactional task was found to be problematic with respect to our goal of creating intimate interactions that involved emotional disclosure and opportunities for emotional responsiveness, or "caregiving." Participants in our pilot study brought up issues ranging from, "I need to lose five pounds to fit into my dress before my sister's wedding" to "I wish I had told my father how much I loved him before he died." Partners' responsive behaviors in these conversations were largely a function of the nature of the personal issue disclosed. Further, only some of the participants' disclosures elicited conversations with notable emotional intensity. As a result, we altered our instructions so

[1] Depending on the study, participants are asked to discuss a "current life stressor" (Cutrona & Suhr, 1994), "something you would like to change about yourself" (Holtzworth-Munroe et al., 1997; Pasch & Bradbury, 1998), or a personal problem area (Saitzyk, Floyd, & Kroll, 1997).

that all participants were instructed to talk about an issue similar to the latter example – a personal "vulnerability." Vulnerabilities are conceptualized as disclosures about the "inner-most self " – disclosures that, by definition, make the discloser feel "less safe." An expression of vulnerability directly or indirectly implies a need for reassurance, validation, support, understanding, or help. We described the conversational task to participants as follows:

> We'll be asking you to share with each other what we call 'vulnerabilities' – things that we feel insecure about, things we don't like about ourselves, things we've done that we feel badly about – any kind of feeling or experience we've had that has caused us some pain or hurt.

A further refinement was necessary so that memories, thoughts, and feelings about personal vulnerabilities would be more accessible during the conversation. First, we developed a procedure in which the lab assistants interviewed each participant about vulnerabilities prior to the conversation in an attempt to "prime" them for the subsequent conversation. However, using this procedure, the couple interactions became stilted and were reported to feel "repetitive," presumably because each partner had already engaged in an intimate dialogue with an interviewer on the subject of their vulnerability. The final version of the protocol instead introduces a writing task which, in sharp contrast to the interview-based priming, seems to function to create a readiness for sharing and facilitates the subsequent couple interaction. Not unlike the natural process of opening up to a loved one, our procedures had partners "alone with their thoughts" prior to engaging in a conversation with their partner. The lab assistant introduced the priming procedure with the following script:

> What I'd like you each to do right now is to take about 10 minutes to try to focus on these feelings, writing down some of your thoughts as a way of helping you focus on them. You may want to try to remember what it was that brought on the feeling of vulnerability, what situations bring it up for you, how you feel, why you feel that way, and so on. What you write down is not important, we just want to make sure you are ready to talk to each other. We've found that it is a good idea for you to focus on one or two things rather than to try to make a list of things. Choose one that is most important in your life now and write out your feelings.

Spouses were then left in separate rooms with a list of "common feelings" (for example, shame, guilt, dissatisfaction with self, hurt, incompetence) related to personal vulnerabilities. The lab assistant offered the following qualification on the task before leaving the participant to write:

You don't have to restrict yourself to the feelings on this list. This is only to help remind you of feelings you may have. You may very well have feelings of vulnerability that are not on this list.

After the priming period, spouses were reunited in the "living room," seated across from one another at a table, and given the following instructions:

For the next 10 minutes we'd like you to talk with each other about your vulner-abilities. Don't feel pressured to share everything you wrote down, just let the conversation flow as it might at home if you were talking about these feelings by yourselves.

The partners were thus left to work out the process of mutually bringing their feelings out in the open and responding to the other's expressed needs and feelings for a 10-minute period. No instructions or preparation was provided related to the task of responding to a partner's disclosures. The disclosure of material related to a personal vulnerability was expected to naturally elicit the opportunity for expressions of care, validation, and understanding by the responding partner (see Petronio, 1991). Partners were left to choose whether and how to respond to their partner's disclosures, with the assumption that their choices would closely mirror those they make in their daily interactions with their partner. As Guthrie and Noller (1988) have advised, ". . . to study emotional expression in marriage, we need to create an interaction situation where subjects will experience a particular emotion in relation to the partner, and then we must leave the couple free to deal with those feelings (both verbally and nonverbally) in the way that they normally would" (p. 154).

Development of the Love Paradigm

To elicit a discussion of affectional feelings in the lab, we utilized a written priming task similar to the one we had found to be successful in helping partners access a personal vulnerability. Our first attempt piloting the task involved instructing partners to think about, and then discuss, "why I love my partner." However, we found it necessary to broaden the instructions to reference "positive feelings" to make the task more comfortable and relevant for distressed couples. Thus, we introduce the task to partners as follows:

In this conversation, we'd like you to talk about feelings of love or other positive feelings you have for one another. To help you get ready for this conversation, we'd like you each to take 10 minutes and try to remember times when you've felt a strong positive feeling toward your partner – a feeling of love, respect, desire, warmth, any positive feeling. Then we'd like you to think about the reasons you had this feeling – what brought the feeling on, maybe something your partner did, or just some way your partner is. To help you do this we are going to ask you to write your thoughts and feelings down. When you each have finished, we will ask you to have a 10 minute conversation in which you each talk about your positive feelings toward one another and why you feel that way. To give you a better idea of the types of feelings we're talking about, take a few moments to look over this list. These are some positive feelings married partners report feeling for each other. You don't have to restrict yourselves to the feelings on this list. The list is only to help remind you of feelings you may have. You may very well have positive or loving feelings about each other that are NOT on this list. Think about your positive or loving feelings for your partner, try to reexperience these feelings here, and write about them.

Partners were then separated and left with a list of positive feelings to serve as a prompt while they engaged in the writing task. The list included feelings such as love, admiration, respect, desire, warmth, trust, security, and so on. The partners were then reunited and given instructions for the conversation:

For the next 10 minutes we'd like you to talk about your feelings for each other – what you feel, when you feel it, and why you feel that way. Don't feel pressured to share everything you wrote down, just let the conversation flow as it might at home if you were talking about your feelings for each other.

Emotional Realism and Naturalness of the Facilitated Intimate Interactions

Our first goal was to evaluate the success of these newly developed conversational tasks in eliciting naturalistic intimate behavior in marital dyads. Did partners make revealing, emotionally genuine disclosures despite the lab setting? Did the conversations have emotional salience and depth for the partners? Did the facilitated conversations mirror couples' natural interaction patterns? According to data collected from the participants as well as our observations and analyses of the taped interactions, we believe we can answer these questions in the affirmative. Data for our analyses come from a sample of 27 couples, with spouses ranging in age from 21 to 50. Couples were recruited from a large metropolitan area in the Northeast, and had been married an average of six years. Approximately half of the couples scored in the "distressed" range on the Locke-Wallace Marital Adjustment Test (Locke & Wallace, 1959).

Exit interviews with participants indicated that the elicitation procedures resulted in interactions that were experienced as natural and "real." Questionnaire data corroborated these qualitative data; most participants rated the task as feeling natural, indicated that their awareness of the video cameras was not inhibiting, and rated the discussion as being similar to interactions at home. For example, with respect to the vulnerability interaction, in response to the item "This discussion was similar to discussions we have at home," 75% of wives and 70% of husbands selected a response above the midpoint on a scale ranging from "not at all" to "very much." Based on careful observations of both the nonverbal and verbal elements of the discussion, coders also rated the naturalness of the couples' discussions highly. On a rating scale ranging from "very artificial and constrained" to "completely natural," coders rated no participant as less natural than "somewhat natural" and 63% of participants were rated as appearing "completely natural." Importantly, neither self nor observer reports of either husbands' or wives' naturalness differed as a function of marital adjustment (t's ranged from .06 to 1.16, all ns). Thus, from the perspective of both participants and observers, the facilitated interactions were approximate analogs of naturally occurring interpersonal interactions.

Further, strong displays of affect – both positive and negative – were common in the two discussion tasks. As in the problem-solving conversation, some couples showed intensely hostile and contemptuous behavior. For example, one husband hesitantly shared a vulnerability, beginning, "well my sensitivity . . ." to which his wife rolled her eyes and, with obvious and open disgust interrupted him with "You're not sensitive!" He then sheepishly corrected himself, "Well, yeah, I mean my *in*sensitivity." Another couple bickered intensely during the love conversation, both partners expressing strong contempt toward the other:

H: So am I still as attractive to you as you were to me, and still are?
W: Yeah, why?
H: Why, can't you say anything nice?
W: I did.
H: No you don't. You only say nice things when I ask you to say 'em. Say something on your own. I won't say anything now. You say something.
W: (sighs and rolls eyes) Say something on my own. (silence)
H: Yeah. Express your feelings.
W: I told you I love you. Why would I put up with you all this time if I didn't?

As anticipated, however, the intimate interaction tasks also elicited emotional expressions that are not typically observed in the standard marital conflict task. There were poignant, tender, seductive, caring, and loving moments observed on the videotapes. Several participants were moved to tears – either in pain or compassion – during the vulnerability interaction. For example, this couple shared a painful, but bittersweet and tender moment:

> H: I'm remembering my childhood with my aunt. Hurt. Being the "Cinderella." And my cousins got to go out and play and I had to take care of the household.
> W: I don't know . . . I guess I want to take that away from you (eyes glisten, softly smiles).
> H: What, that pain?
> W: Yeah . . . (brings her hand to her face, touches her cheek, begins to cry). So much pain.
> H: (soft and reassuringly) Well, you do. You do.

In this example, each partner was emotionally vulnerable and each was emotionally responsive to the other's pain.

Other interactions evidenced strong positive emotions, including what Shaver, Morgan, and Wu (1996) have termed "surge love"[2] – brief, unbidden experiences of "in the moment" love for the partner. The love conversation task elicited these surges of love for many couples, indicating that the task was effective in creating a context conducive to spontaneous and genuine expressions of love and care. Since the identification of surge love in the interactions relies heavily on nonverbal indicators, for example glistening eyes, soft voice, a warm smile (Shaver, Morgan, & Wu, 1996), the affective quality of these interactions is difficult to convey here in words. Although the following example was not as "intense" as some of the "surges" of love on the videotapes, the verbal and nonverbal cues for the husband's emotional expressions of love are relatively easy to describe. He is telling his wife why he loves her, and as he speaks, he becomes giddy and excited and somewhat "childish" in his demeanor. Grinning, his tone of voice like "baby talk," he says, "I really admire you." His wife's eyes open wide as she lights

---

[2] We coded instances of "surge love" according to the behavioral descriptors provided by Shaver, Morgan, and Wu (1996), as part of our care code; as we defined it, care consists of these direct emotional experiences of love that are manifest nonverbally, as well as explicit statements of care, concern, or love.

up at his emotional display, and responds in a tone much higher than normal, "You do?" In a shy and giddy tone, he continues," Yes, as a person. For your achievements, your accomplishments." As he talks his shoulder raises all the way up to his cheek and he grins from ear to ear. "I always do, I always did. And I respect you. I wish I could be more like you." Both partners were visibly moved during this short exchange.

Not all partners experienced strong positive affect or moments of felt intimacy during the interactions, but all couples talked directly about their relationship and their feelings as they were instructed to. In the vulnerability interaction, only one wife failed to emit a disclosure that qualified as a vulnerable disclosure in our coding of the behaviors. Although the disclosures elicited by the vulnerability task varied in quantity, depth, and elaboration, they were typically of a very personal nature despite the laboratory context. In the love conversation, all of the husbands and all of the wives shared some version of a "positive feeling" toward their spouse, although, again, affectional expressions varied considerably in depth, elaboration, and emotional honesty. Thus, both the love and the vulnerability paradigms appeared to be successful in eliciting naturalistic, emotionally rich interactions between married partners.

INTIMATE INTERACTIONS OBSERVED: THE BEHAVIORAL TOPOGRAPHY OF MARITAL INTIMACY

Although it will be important to link variations in couples' intimate behaviors to marital outcomes (see Roberts & Linney, 2001), an important first step is to provide a descriptive account of the behaviors that characterize this new marital terrain. How do partners seek and give care to one another? How do they express their positive feelings toward one another? In the remainder of this chapter, we will describe the behavioral processes observed in couples' intimate interactions. To document these behavioral processes, we developed the Intimate Interaction Coding System (IICS; Roberts, 1999). Frequencies of IICS codes and illustrative examples from the couple interactions are used to describe the process of vulnerable disclosure and responsive caregiving. Since microanalytic coding of the love conversation is not yet complete, we instead provide a thematic analysis relying on qualitative examples to illustrate our observations of the process of affectional disclosure.

The View from the Vulnerability Paradigm: Natural Careseeking and Caregiving Processes

As Gottman (1994) has argued, "knowing what to observe in marital interaction is neither trivial nor obvious" (p. 17). There is general consensus on the importance of examining *emotional* communication in marriage (see Gottman, 1994; Noller & Fitzpatrick, 1990), and most marital researchers routinely examine "positive affect" in addition to negative affect. However, our theoretical model suggests a somewhat different approach to the important question of "what to look for" in marital interactions; an intimacy process model is not synonymous with a positive affect model. In developing our coding scheme, we drew heavily on attachment theory and the interpersonal process model of intimacy. These theoretical frameworks, as well as a wide range of empirical work on the nature and behavioral indicators of emotional supportiveness (for example, Barbee 1990; Burleson, 1982; 1984; Cutrona, Suhr, & McFarlane, 1990; Pasch & Bradbury, 1998; Roberts et al., 1999) and caregiving (for example, Ainsworth, Blehar, Waters, & Wall, 1978; Kunce & Shaver, 1994), provided initial guidance on the important question of "what to look for" in the vulnerability conversation.

Using a "microanalytic" approach to coding, the IICS records the frequency and sequencing of 14 interpersonal behaviors (see Table 5.1). The IICS includes behaviors that either directly (*request for care*) or indirectly (*vulnerable disclosure*) signal the need for care, and a range of caregiving responses. Consistent with the interpersonal process model of intimacy (Reis & Shaver, 1988), three codes – *care, validation,* and *active understanding* – represent emotional responsiveness to the partner's needs and concerns. Three other codes – *interpretation, guidance,* and *intrusive advice* – reflect caregiving behaviors that do not directly convey emotional responsiveness to the partner, but instead guide or advise the partner. *Undermine* reflects overtly negative or hostile responses to the partner's disclosures, while *insensitive to emotion* reflects a caregiving response that clearly "misses the boat" or falls short in terms of a response to the emotion in the message. *Open questions* seek greater understanding of the partner and were expected to elicit deeper exploration and further disclosure from the partner. The IICS also includes three codes not directly related to the process of giving and receiving care. *General sharing* captures factual disclosures and affectively neutral dialogue on topics both relevant and tangential to emotional disclosures. Additionally, two codes, *contempt* and *defensive* assess

Table 5.1. Intimacy Interaction Coding System (IICS) Behavior Codes

Code	Definition
Intimacy Process Codes	
Vulnerable	Behavior that is emotionally disclosive, makes the self vulnerable, and implies the need for care or support.
Care	Direct expressions (verbal or nonverbal) of love, care, affection, or deep concern for the partner.
Validation	Behaviors that raise the partner's status, enhance the partner's self-esteem, validate the partner's worth, praise the partner's behaviors or qualities, demonstrate acceptance of the partner, or show faith or confidence in the partner.
Active understanding	Behaviors that communicate availability and understanding of the partner or the partner's feelings; behaviors range from direct statements of understanding to simple paraphrasing and restatements of the partner's disclosure to behaviors that convey a deep understanding of the partner's feelings (for example, empathy).
Insensitive to emotion	Behaviors that indicate a lack of acknowledgment, sensitivity to, or understanding of the partner's feelings; behavior is insensitive or irrelevant to partner's emotional communication but without malice, hostility, or other negative affect; includes change of topic and silence (longer than five seconds) in response to partner emotional disclosure.
Other Disclosure Codes	
Contempt	Behaviors that deflate the partner's status or worth, or indicate contempt, hostility, disdain, scorn, malice, or rejection of the partner, *not* delivered in response to a vulnerable disclosure.
Defensive	Behaviors that indicate the actor feels the need to defend him/herself; includes denials, justifications, excuse-giving, and minimizations delivered with neutral or mild negative affect.
Request for care	Direct requests for help, information, advice, opinion, or support from partner.

(continued)

Table 5.1. (*continued*)

Code	Definition
General sharing	Disclosure of facts and information, factual questions, humorous comments, tangential comments; any behavior that does not meet criteria for another code.
Other Response Codes	
Interpretation	Behaviors that challenge, confront, counter, or give a new meaning to partner's disclosures; any advice or guidance that is cognitive (as opposed to behavioral) delivered with positive or neutral affect.
Guidance	Offers of solutions, suggestions, or advice to take a specific, concrete action delivered with neutral or positive affect.
Intrusive advice	Advice or guidance that is "shoved" on the partner rather than "offered"; behaviors delivered in an authoritarian, condescending, domineering, or presumptive manner that undermines partner autonomy.
Undermine	Behaviors that deflate the partner's status or worth, or indicate contempt, hostility, disdain, or rejection of the partner delivered in the context of a partner's vulnerable disclosure.
Open question	Behaviors that probe for more and deeper information about the partner's feelings, thoughts, and perceptions; the probes are open and honest and delivered with positive or neutral affect.

negative behaviors that are not directly related to the caregiving process. While *undermine* refers to negative or rejecting behaviors in the context of a partner's vulnerable disclosure, contempt refers to rejecting and hostile behaviors that are not directly related to a disclosure. *Defensive* signals self-protection in response to a real or perceived threat, and is conceptualized as antithetical to the process of being open and vulnerable.

To accurately capture the shared interpersonal meaning of observed interaction behavior, high thresholds were set for coding care, validation, and active understanding – expressions of these behaviors were required to be *direct* and *explicit*. This approach was necessary to achieve high reliability, but also to identify and document the occurrence of behaviors that are relatively universal signals of responsiveness and not dependent on idiosyncratic personal "filters." Ambiguous and neutral behaviors are more susceptible to biased interpretations. For example, agreements and assents (for example, "Yeah, I know." "I agree with you.") may or may not be experienced as "validating," while a direct compliment ("You have great ideas here.") can be considered more directly and explicitly validating.[3] Similarly, interest and attention may or may not be experienced as "caring" while a statement such as this from one of the spouses in our study directly and explicitly communicates care: ". . . that got me to thinking about how much I like, really care, and love you, . . . and like you've become my good best friend, somebody that I can laugh with and talk to, and be myself with, and I didn't have that before, with anybody." Although more subtle and ambiguous expressions of care, validation, and understanding may be missed with this approach to coding, our goal was to establish whether there are specific behavioral determinants of the experience of responsive caregiving and intimate connection.

A "cultural informants" approach to coding (Gottman, 1996)[4] is employed in the IICS – coders are trained to integrate all available information, and to assign a code that captures the interpersonal

---

[3] Our coding of validation, then, represents a significant departure from other operationalizations of "validation" in the marital literature (see for example, Gottman, 1979; 1994; Weiss & Summers, 1993). Other validation codes typically include behaviors that may carry a range of interpersonal meanings such as agreements, open questions, and behaviors that signal listening. We are able to define validation in a less ambiguous and more explicitly positive fashion in part because we are not coding behaviors exhibited in the conflict task, but in a task that effectively elicits more direct expressions of positive behavior. Gottman and colleagues (Gottman et al., 1998) have recently noted that, in their coding of conflict interactions, the SPAFF validation code was in fact being used by observers exclusively for behaviors that indicated listening and tracking; explicit and direct validations of the partner were *not* occurring in the context of problem-solving conversations. The SPAFF validation code includes both "low intensity" expressions (acknowledgements of listening and tracking) and "high intensity" expressions that include direct statements of understanding. Thus, SPAFF low intensity validations are considered "general sharing" in the IICS and high intensity validations are included in the IICS active understanding code. The IICS validation and care codes have not been previously assessed as such in marital interaction coding schemes.

[4] A physical features approach describes communication by recording the observable behavior in each communication "channel"– the voice, face, gestures, and so on, while a cultural informant's approach asks a sensitive, trained observer to make interpretations of the meaning of communicative behaviors based on his/her cultural and interpersonal knowledge.

meaning of the target behavior. Consistent with the notion that non-verbal communication channels carry most of the emotional and relational information conveyed in an interaction (Argyle, 1975; Mehrabian, 1972), the IICS requires careful scrutiny of facial, paralinguistic, and other nonverbal cues. Coders receive extensive training in the recognition of these cues prior to coding. Reliability assessments based on coding of the vulnerability conversations indicated that coders were able to apply the system reliably (Cohen's kappa[5] for the system overall was .76).

Frequencies of IICS behaviors were highly variable across participants. For example, frequencies of contempt and active understanding each ranged from 0 to over 20 utterances. Despite a large popular literature (for example, Tannen, 1990) proclaiming strong gender differences in expressive and caring behaviors, only one significant husband-wife difference was found in rates of behavior. Wives were more likely than husbands to directly validate, compliment, or otherwise raise the status of their partners. There were no differences in rates of vulnerable disclosure or any of the other IICS behaviors. Most of the claims about gender differences in intimate relating are based on work done outside the context of close intimate relationships, and a lack of husband-wife differences in the rates of behavior should not be surprising. Although gender stereotypes and empirical studies (see Dindia & Allen, 1992 for metaanalysis) suggest differences in the extent to which males and females openly share vulnerabilities, findings from a number of studies focusing specifically on *couples* (for example, Dindia, Fitzpatrick, & Kenny, 1997; Sprecher & Sedikides, 1993) are consistent with our findings of no significant differences between husbands and wives in emotional disclosure. For example, based on their analysis of discrete social interactions, Reis, Senchak, and Solomon (1985) found that, within the context of a romantic relationship, men and women did not differ in degree of disclosure.

Although participants were primed to experience awareness of a personal vulnerability, direct requests for care or help from their partner were virtually absent. On the other hand, open disclosures related to the vulnerability were relatively frequent; 13% of all coded comments were vulnerable disclosures. When Cutrona (Cutrona et al., 1990) asked

---

[5] The kappa coefficient (Cohen, 1960) was employed to measure observer accuracy since it provides a more conservative estimate of reliability than simple percent agreement by controlling for chance agreement.

married partners about their support activation strategies, she found a similar pattern. Although partners did not report directly requesting care or help from their spouses, disclosing an emotional state was one of the most frequently mentioned strategies. These married partners indicated that the disclosure itself communicated the request for help. However, the lack of direct requests for help between married partners means that partners must be attuned to the indirect message accompanying a vulnerable disclosure, and further, must make an appropriate inference about the kind of help or care that is needed.

In response to their partners' vulnerable disclosures, all participants engaged in some form of caregiving behavior, ranging from heartfelt expressions of care and understanding, to advice and guidance. Across couples, care behavior was less frequent than either validation or active understanding; care was observed in only 25% of the couples' interactions, while validation was evident in 74%, and active understanding in 93% of the interactions. Some form of advice or guidance also characterized the majority (73%) of the interactions, with intrusive offers of advice being as frequent as open, suggestive forms (guidance). Interpretation occurred in all of the interactions. The most frequently enacted caregiving behaviors were interpretation and active understanding, suggesting that partners' responses to their spouses' needs commonly involve active attempts to "make sense" of the partner's feelings and communicate this understanding. Consider this husband's "active understanding" responses to his wife's disclosures:

W: I'm just afraid I'll fail at everything I do – just because how I was treated as a child, you know, 'you can't do this, you can't do that.' And now I feel that everybody is judging me on my relationship with you, and just waits and holds their breath to say 'see, see what you did wrong?'
H: Watching for the failure.
W: Mmm-hmm. And I feel that way with my children. And my life...I just don't do anything. I become an amoeba. I'm just like dividing cells, you know? And that's all I am doing, I'm waiting. I'm waiting for ...
H: Waiting for the crash?
W: Yeah, I've been doing that a lot, I've been sitting and waiting, it's more like a nuclear explosion I'm waiting for ...I feel like throwing up right now.
H: (softly) Painful?
W: Mm-hmm.

At each speech turn, the husband actively signals more than conversational interest and tracking, he directly communicates an understanding of his wife's *feelings*, particularly in the last instance when he supplies an accurate emotional label for her bodily sensation (see Rogers, 1951). The high frequency of active understanding behaviors observed in the vulnerability interaction stands in sharp contrast to findings from observations of conflict interactions. Gottman and colleagues (Gottman, Coan, Carrere, & Swanson, 1998) have challenged therapeutic interventions that are based on teaching couples "active listening" and "empathy" responses, arguing that there is no evidence that married partners – even those in highly satisfied marriages – engage in these "active listening" behaviors (for example, paraphrase, summarize, validate, or indicate understanding of the partner's feelings). However, it is clear that, in the context of these intimate, caregiving marital interactions, many partners do engage in active attempts to communicate an understanding of the partner's feelings.

The importance of active understanding for the outcome of the interaction is made evident by its absence. Vulnerable disclosures signal the need for care and understanding and the absence of emotionally sensitive responses often led to negativity in the interaction. In the following example, the wife reveals the emotional pain she feels because she is overweight. Although her husband maintains eye contact and stays pleasantly engaged, he "misses the boat," that is, he does not respond to her *emotional* message, which eventually leads her to angrily challenge him:

> W: Mine is my weight, you know that. I'm very insecure. . . . Every time I walk into a room I know they're talking about me. I know those people are talking about me because I'm fat.
> H: (no response, 12 seconds, but looks at her, kindly). So . . .
> W: I wonder, you know, if the people really like me, personally.
> H: Are you talking about your friends?
> W: So called.
> H: (no response, 10 seconds)
> W: (challenging, flicking a pencil at him) Even you.

Active listening and emotional validation may be irrelevant to adaptive marital functioning when expressed in the context of conflict interactions as Gottman and colleagues (Gottman et al., 1998) have argued, but these responses may be critical to marital functioning when expressed in the context of a partner's disclosure of emotional distress, need, or vulnerability.

The View from the Love Paradigm: Expressions of Enjoyment, Admiration, Desire, and Security

Although all spouses in our study were able to express positive feelings toward their partner, there were marked differences in the specific content, degree of elaboration, emotional tenor, and coherence of their affectional expressions. We identified four primary themes discussed in the interactions: (1) shared enjoyable memories, (2) feelings of respect or admiration for the partner, (3) feelings of security, comfort, and trust in the relationship, and (4) feelings of attraction and desire for the partner. Couples in highly satisfied marriages were likely to touch on many (if not all) of these themes in their 10-minute interaction, while couples who were maritally dissatisfied were more constricted in their range of topics and relied more heavily on positive feelings evoked by enjoyable memories.

Positive reminiscences were highly varied with respect to the communication of fondness and closeness. In the following exchange, the partners discuss a shared positive memory, but with little elaboration and with a focus on enjoyment rather than closeness or other relational elements of the memory:

> W: You know where we had a good time, was on that Miss Buffalo thing. Remember that?
> H: Yeah.
> W: We went on that for the summer picnic.
> H: Yeah. That was at Mountain Inn.
> W: Yeah.
> H: The Mountain Inn.
> W: We had a good time then.
> H: Yeah. That was, that was fun.

This couple, and other distressed couples, tended to focus their conversation on "fun" times in their relationship rather than being openly vulnerable and sharing more intimate feelings. In contrast, this maritally satisfied wife shared a positive memory that she immediately linked to feelings of closeness with her partner:

Another memory I have about us that made me feel really, really good was when we were sitting together over dinner in Toronto. I just felt so close to you because we had done so many great things, and had such a wonderful time, and there we were sitting there talking about all of the fun things we did. (smiling and nodding) I felt a real closeness.

Similarly, although almost all spouses shared at least one statement of admiration or love for their partner, the affective quality and depth of these statements varied greatly. Some declarations involved emotional vulnerability, others did not. For example, one wife told her husband in a banal and unconvincing tone, "I suppose I admire you for your computer knowledge," and this was her only statement of love or admiration for her partner. Her statement stands in stark relief to the many heartfelt declarations of love and admiration that other partners shared, as this husband's statement illustrates:

I walk in and see in your eyes – you have that inner beauty in addition to being good looking on the outside – and that's what I see in you. And how I feel being with you, like that's where I'm supposed to be, with you. I'm very lucky that you're my partner, I feel so blessed and lucky.

Consistent with an adult attachment perspective (for example, Feeney & Noller, 1996; Hazan & Shaver, 1987; Hazan & Zeifman, 1997), feelings of security were discussed frequently in the love interactions. Attachment theorists have suggested that, in both infant-caregiver and adult-intimate relationships, there are four components or functions of the attachment relationship: *proximity seeking*, the tendency to seek and maintain close proximity with the attachment figure; *safe haven*, the tendency to seek out an attachment figure for safety and reassurance when threatened; *separation anxiety*, the tendency to resist separation and be distressed by separations or loss; and *secure base*, the ability to engage in nonattachment behavior by virtue of deriving a sense of security and trust from the attachment figure. All of the partners in marriages in which both partners reported high marital satisfaction shared feelings related to at least one of these attachment functions, and many highly satisfied partners made reference to three or four of the components. More than one partner evoked the image of a "security blanket" in referring to their positive feelings for their spouse. Table 5.2 presents examples taken from the transcripts to illustrate the types of disclosures partners made in relation to each of the four attachment functions. As can be seen from the table, the ability of marital partners to articulate feelings predicted by the attachment theoretical perspective is striking.

Table 5.2. Partner Disclosures Related to the Four Attachment Functions

Proximity Seeking	Safe Haven	Separation Anxiety	Secure Base
Even when I'm mad, it's just good to be near you. You can be in one place reading, and I can be in another place reading, and I don't feel like I'm alone, and I love that about you.	That's what's so wonderful about being married – no matter how bad things are, you know you can come home and everything will be okay there.	I am concerned about your health and the baby's health... I hope the birth is all right. I hope you both make it through okay. I worry about that.	I just feel like I can trust you and feel that you're faithful to me. That puts me at ease. I don't have to worry about anything when I go to work. It makes me, you know, feel good inside.
When we go to bed at night we fit together perfectly and get all snuggly and cuddly. It just feels so safe and warm, I never want to leave there.	You are so supportive of me and you're there for me all the time... I can count on you.	I don't want to think about if I ever didn't have you 'cause it would be really awful.	I don't know, you just make me happy. You make me comfortable, make me feel like I matter... and it makes me feel good.
I love you. Even like when I'm on the road, I drive faster because I know I can come home to you.	I always know that no matter how bad things are, that you're going be there for me. I know no matter what that I could cry on your shoulder and you would be there for me.	I get so nervous when you smoke and drink because I'm so afraid I'm going to lose my security blanket.	You make me feel secure... Just with everything that I've been through lately, you made me feel like you're going to be there. Like I don't have to worry. It's going to be all right. I'm not so scared.
I miss you when you're at work and I'm home.	When I feel my worst, I just can't wait to be in the same room with you, so I can tell you everything, and then you will make it all better... That's a real good feeling to have – to know you can go home and be safe and secure.	Do you ever think, "what if something happened to her"? I know it's not a good thing to think, but I sometimes think like that about you.	It was the warmth that I got from you, and the feeling of security, like a security blanket, although I don't mean it like a little kid.
I love to come home from work right, right when, I can get out early, half an hour early, I'm usually racin' home.		That got me to thinking about like, how much like I really care and love you, and how I wouldn't want you to die.	

Finally, both husbands and wives shared feelings of sexual desire and physical attraction. Some partners were able to discuss only sexual themes, whereas other partners mentioned desire as one of many positive feelings they have for their spouse. For some couples, sharing their positive feelings about their sex life was accompanied by strong nonverbal signals of "surge love" (Shaver, Morgan, & Wu, 1996). For example, this couple's exchange had an undercurrent of soft, playful passion:

H: (shoulders raised, shakes his head back and forth, sheepish smile) And you are great in bed!
W: (intensely watching him, smiling softly) Yeah, our sex life is great. Sometimes I think you are better to me than I am to you.
H: (smiling) Noooo!
W: You're so patient with me. You're so good with me.
H: (smiling) I know.
W: (smiling) I know you know.

Expressions of desire were not always warmly accepted by the partner, however, as this exchange illustrates:

H: I always desire to be close to you. . . . when you're around I just want to hold you, cuddle you.
W: I hate bein' hugged.
H: I know, I know it. I know it. But I just desire to be close to you, and, and you know, it just makes me feel great. And if you . . .
W: Besides, you don't do that anyways.

Although numerous studies have used interview and self-report techniques to document the ways partners experience and talk about their positive feelings toward their partner and relationship (for example, Wallerstein & Blakeslee, 1995), the observation techniques used here are distinguished from this previous body of work by an emphasis on the assessment of natural interaction patterns between partners. The themes we have described thus far reflect differences at the level of "content" of love disclosures while the *process* of communication between husband and wife may be the locus of our most important discoveries about the nature of attachment, affection, and intimacy in relationships. How does the partner respond to a spouses' declaration of security or closeness? In the example above, the wife indicates a clear rejection of her husband's desire to be close to her. And further, she challenges his interpretation of his behavior. Other spouses also evidenced a lack of trust in their partners' declarations. Consider this wife's response to her husband's disclosures:

H: Yeah, you know. I look, I look forward to seeing you when I come home for lunch. It's just natural feelings.

W: That's 'cause you're used to me.

H: …Well, I don't know. I just get the feeling of a, you give me something to look forward to all the time, you know.

W: Well, so could a dog, Scott.

H: Nooo. No. Not that way, it's different. You're a human being. You're – it goes much deeper than that. Um, I don't know, that's how I feel. It's natural.

The husband's responses to his wife also need to be considered; he makes little eye contact and his statements are "matter of fact" with little emotional expressiveness and no content indicating what it is about his wife that he appreciates. His wife communicates a distrust of her husband's affection that he does little to address. She becomes both more visibly hurt and angry over the course of their interaction. In contrast, in the next example, the husband's emotionally open statement is met with an emotionally open response from his wife, and their intimate exchange continues throughout their conversation:

H: You just make me happy. You make me comfortable, make me feel like I matter.

W: Really? I hope so, because I think so!

H: I can't understand why you feel that way about me (chuckle), but it's nice that you do. And it makes me feel good.

W: Awwwwh (puts cheek to shoulder). Thanks. (smiles)

Not all partners responded with satisfaction to their partner's expressions of security and comfort. Although attachment theory may provide important insights into the nature of feelings of warmth, closeness, and security in adult intimate relationships, adult intimacy may involve more than the attachment system (see for example, Reis & Patrick, 1996). For example, in the following interaction, the wife indicates her desire to know more about her husband's love for her than his feelings of trust and security:

H: … I feel like I can trust you and feel that you're faithful to me and that puts me at ease you know. I don't have to worry about anything when I go to work … It makes me, you know, feel good inside.

W: So why do you love me?

H: What? That's one of the reasons why.

Many spouses directly or indirectly expressed this desire to be recognized and understood for their uniqueness, not for the love and comfort they provided to the other. Like Scott's wife above, they wanted to be known as a unique person and explicitly differentiated from "a dog" or another "human being" – even another sensitive, responsive human being. However, some partners more easily focused on feeling love for their partner as a result of their own feelings of being loved or cared for. Other partners expressed strong feelings of respect and admiration for their spouse based on the partner's qualities and not on the partner's fulfillment of their own attachment needs. In other words, in these interactions, some partners focused more on the experience of "being loved" than "giving love." How these different types of affectional expressions are related to relational functioning and marital satisfaction is an important question that our microanalytic coding of these interactions will address in the future.

As in the vulnerability interactions, an important feature of the interactions in the love conversational task appears to be the extent to which the partners are communicating an accurate understanding of the other. As this final interaction segment suggests, each partner's ability to recognize and honor the feelings and needs of the other – even when they are different than their own – may be particularly critical in the maintenance of an intimate relationship:

H: . . . you make me smile though.

W: I try hon'. It's very important. But sometimes, I realize you don't want to be cheered up, you want to be left alone. I'm beginning – I'm understanding that now more, too. Sometimes you just want to be left alone and then you'll get out of your funk.

H: Yeah.

W: In your own due time. Hmm. So I just leave you alone.

H: I appreciate that.

W: Well, I appreciate being in tune with each other's feelings. Last night when I rolled over and you just rubbed my back, that was, that was a long back rub for you!

H: Mmm mm. (smiling)

W: (laughs) 'Cause you knew I was uncomfortable. That was nice. (smiles)

CONCLUSION

Gaining a complete picture of the behavioral underpinnings of marital discord and harmony is constrained by the limited views we have of the marital interaction "territory." Current behaviorally based models of marital adjustment emphasize the absence of negative behaviors, with little specification of the positive behaviors that characterize a well-functioning marriage. Although intimacy and attachment behaviors are theorized to be important in marital functioning, behavioral processes directly related to the establishment and maintenance of intimacy have not been previously investigated with naturalistic observational methods. The procedures for eliciting and coding intimate marital interactions described in this chapter make it possible to directly observe naturalistic, intimate behavior, thus providing the opportunity to test linkages between theoretically important, positive behavioral processes and marital quality.

The "windows" to intimate behavior provided by these new procedures allow us to describe naturally occurring care seeking, caregiving, and affectional processes in marital relationships. As expected, the views of the marital landscape from these "windows" are not identical to the view obtained with the conflict discussion task. In the new conversation tasks, in varying ways and with varying responses from partners, spouses expressed feelings of vulnerability, desire, admiration, security, and attachment. Hostile and contemptuous behaviors were observed, but warm, tender "surges" of love and concern were also observed. Taken together, our preliminary analyses of couples' behaviors in the love and the vulnerability conversations highlights the potential importance of *both understanding and responding to the indirectly expressed needs of the other*. Couples differ not only in their abilities to resolve conflict and in their tendencies to express negative affect, but in their experiences and expressions of responsive caregiving, security, and love. Future observational studies of intimate interactions between spouses will be critical in providing much needed insights into the roles of love and intimacy in successful marriages.

REFERENCES

Ainsworth, M. S., Blehar, M. C., Waters, E., & Wall, S. (1978). *Patterns of attachment: A psychological study of the strange situation*. Hillsdale, NJ: Lawrence Erlbaum Associates.

Altman, I., & Taylor, D. A. (1973). *Social penetration: The development of interpersonal relationships*. New York: Holt, Rinehart, & Winston.

Argyle, M. (1975). *Bodily communication*. New York: International Universities Press.

Barbee, A. P. (1990). Interactive coping: The cheering-up process in close relationships. In S. Duck (Ed.), *Personal relationships and social support* (pp. 46–65). London: Sage Publications.

Birchler, G., Weiss, R., & Vincent, J. (1975). Multimethod analysis of social reinforcement exchange between maritally distressed and nondistressed spouse and stranger dyads. *Journal of Personality and Social Psychology, 31,* 349–360.

Bowlby, J. (1969). *Attachment and loss: vol. 1. Attachment.* New York: Basic Books.

Bowlby, J. (1973). *Attachment and loss: vol. 2. Separation: Anxiety and anger.* New York: Basic Books.

Burleson, B. R. (1982). The development of comforting communication skills in childhood and adolescence. *Child Development, 53,* 1578–1588.

Burleson, B. R. (1984). Age, social-cognitive development, and the use of comforting strategies. *Communication Monographs, 51* (2), 140–153.

Carnelley, K. B., Pietromonaco, P. R., & Jaffe, K. (1996). Attachment, caregiving, and relationship functioning in couples: Effects of self and partner. *Personal Relationships, 3,* 257–277.

Christensen, A., & Schenk, J. L. (1991). Communication, conflict, and psychological distance in nondistressed, clinic, and divorcing couples. *Journal of Consulting and Clinical Psychology, 59* (3), 458–463.

Cohen, J. (1960), A coefficient of agreement for nominal scales. *Educational and Psychological Measurement, 20,* 37–46.

Cutrona, C. E. (1996). Social support as a determinant of marital quality: The interplay of negative and supportive behaviors. In G. R. Pierce, B. R. Sarason, & I. G. Sarason (Eds.), *Handbook of social support and the family* (pp. 173–194). New York: Plenum Press.

Cutrona, C. E., & Suhr, J. A. (1994). Social support communication in the context of marriage: An analysis of couples' supportive interactions. In B. R. Burleson, T. L. Albrecht, & I. G. Sarason (Eds.), *Communication of social support* (pp. 113–135). Thousand Oaks, CA: Sage Publications.

Cutrona, C. E., Suhr, J. A., & McFarlane, R. (1990). Interpersonal transactions and the psychological sense of support. In S. Duck (Ed.), *Personal relationships and social support* (pp. 30–45). London: Sage Publications.

Dindia, K., & Allen, M. (1992). Sex differences in self-disclosure: A metaanalysis. *Psychological Bulletin, 112,* 106–124.

Dindia, K., Fitzpatrick, M. A., & Kenny, D. A. (1997). Self-disclosure in spouse and stranger interaction: A social relations analysis. *Human Communication Research, 23,* 388–412.

Erikson, E. H. (1959). Identity and the life cycle: Selected papers. *Psychological Issues, 1,* 1–71.

Feeney, J. A., & Noller, P. (1996). *Adult attachment.* Thousand Oaks, CA: Sage Publications.

Feeney, J. A., Noller, P., & Ward, C. (1997). Marital satisfaction and spousal interaction. In R. J. Sternberg & M. Hojjat (Eds.), *Satisfaction in close relationships* (pp. 160–189). New York: Guilford.

Fincham, F. D., & Beach, S. R. (1999). Conflict in marriage: Implications for working with couples. *Annual Review of Psychology, 50,* 47–77.

Gottman, J. M. (1979). *Marital interaction: Experimental investigations.* New York: Academic Press.

Gottman, J. M. (1994). *What predicts divorce? The relationship between marital processes and marital outcomes.* Hillsdale, NJ: Lawrence Erlbaum Associates.

Gottman, J. M. (1996). *What predicts divorce? The measures.* Hillsdale, NJ: Lawrence Erlbaum Associates.

Gottman, J. M. (1998). Psychology and the study of the marital processes. *Annual Review of Psychology, 49,* 169–197.

Gottman, J. M., Coan, J., Carrere, S., & Swanson, C. (1998). Predicting marital happiness and stability from newlywed interactions. *Journal of Marriage and the Family, 60,* 5–22.

Gottman, J. M., & Notarius, C. I. (2000). Decade review: Observing marital interaction. *Journal of Marriage and the Family, 62,* 927–948.

Greenberg, L. S., & Johnson, S. M. (1988). *Emotionally focused therapy for couples.* New York: Guilford.

Guthrie, D. M., & Noller, P. (1988). Spouses' perceptions of one another in emotional situations. In P. Noller & M. A. Fitzpatrick (Eds.), *Perspectives on marital interaction. Monographs in social psychology of language, No. 1* (pp. 153–181). Clevedon, England: Multilingual Matters.

Hazan C., & Zeifman, D. (1997). Attachment: The bond in pair-bonds. In J. A. Simpson & D. T. Kenrick (Eds.), *Evolutionary social psychology* (pp. 237–263). Hillsdale, NJ: Lawrence Erlbaum Associates.

Hazan, C., & Shaver, P. (1987). Romantic love conceptualized as an attachment process. *Journal of Consulting and Clinical Psychology, 57,* 47–52.

Holtzworth-Munroe, A., Stuart, G. L., Sandin, E., Smutzler, N., & McLaughlin, W. (1997). Comparing the social support behaviors of violent and nonviolent husbands during discussions of wife personal problems. *Personal Relationships, 4,* 395–412.

Huesmann, L. R., & Levinger, G. (1976). Incremental exchange theory: A formal model for progression in dyadic social interaction. In L. Berkowitz and E. Walster (Eds.), *Advances in experimental social psychology, vol. 9* (pp. 191–229). New York: Academic Press.

Huston, T. L., Caughlin, J. P., Houts, R. M., Smith, S. E., & George, L. J. (2001). The connubial crucible: Newlywed years as predictors of marital delight, distress and divorce. *Journal of Personality and Social Psychology, 80,* 237–252.

Jacobson, N. S., & Margolin, G. (1979). *Marital therapy: Strategies based on social learning and behavior exchange principles.* New York: Bruner/Mazel.

Julien, D., Markman, H. J., & Lindahl, K. M. (1989). A comparison of a global and a microanalytic coding system: Implications for future trends in studying interactions. *Behavioral Assessment, 11,* 81–100.

Karney, B. R., & Bradbury, T. N. (1995). The longitudinal course of marital quality and stability: A review of theory, methods, and research. *Psychological Bulletin, 118,* 3–34.

Kunce, L. J., & Shaver, P. R. (1994). An attachment-theoretical approach to caregiving in romantic relationships. In K. Bartholomew & D. Perlman (Eds.), *Attachment processes in adulthood. Advances in personal relationships, vol. 5* (pp. 205–237). London: Jessica Kingsley Publishers.

Langhinrichsen-Rohling, J., Schlee, K. A., Monson, C. M., Ehrensaft, M., & Heyman, R. (1998). What's love got to do with it? Perceptions of marital positivity in H-to-W aggressive, distressed, and happy marriages. *Journal of Family Violence, 13,* 197–212.

Locke, H. J., & Wallace, K. M. (1959). Short marital-adjustment and prediction tests: Their reliability and validity. *Marriage and Family Living, 21*, 251–255.

Matthews, C., & Clark, R. D. (1982). Marital satisfaction: A validation approach. *Basic and Applied Social Psychology, 3* (3), 169–186.

Matthews, L. S., Wickrama, K. A. S., & Conger, R. D. (1996). Predicting marital instability from spouse and observer reports of marital interaction. *Journal of Marriage and the Family, 58*, 641–655.

Mehrabian, A. (1972). *Nonverbal communication.* Chicago: Aldine-Atherton.

Melby, J. N., Ge, X., Conger, R. D., & Warner, T. D. (1995). The importance of task in evaluating positive marital interactions. *Journal of Marriage and the Family, 57*, 981–994.

Noller, P., & Fitzpatrick, M. A. (1990). Marital communication in the eighties. *Journal of Marriage and the Family, 52*, 832–843.

Pasch, L. A., & Bradbury, T. N. (1998). Social support, conflict, and the development of marital dysfunction. *Journal of Consulting and Clinical Psychology, 66*, 219–230.

Petronio, S. (1991). Communication boundary management: A theoretical model of managing disclosure of private information between married couples. *Communication Theory, 1*, 311–335.

Reis, H. T., & Patrick, B. C. (1996). Attachment and intimacy: Component processes. In E. T. Higgins & A. W. Kruglanski (Eds.), *Social psychology: Handbook of basic principles* (pp. 523–563). New York: Guilford.

Reis, H. T., Senchak, M., & Solomon, B. (1985). Sex differences in the intimacy of social interaction: Further examination of potential explanations. *Journal of Personality and Social Psychology, 48*, 1204–1217.

Reis, H. T., & Shaver, P. (1988). Intimacy as an interpersonal process. In S. W. Duck (Ed.), *Handbook of personal relationships* (pp. 367–389). Chichester, England: Wiley.

Roberts, L. J. (2000). Fire and ice in marital communication: Hostile and distancing behaviors as predictors of marital distress. *Journal of Marriage and the Family, 62*, 693–707.

Roberts, L. J., & Linney, K. (2001). Observing intimacy process behavior: Vulnerability and partner responsiveness in marital interactions. Unpublished manuscript, University of Wisconsin, Madison.

Roberts, L. J. with Linney, K. D., Lord, S. E., & Lindenfelser, K. (1999). Intimate Interaction Coding System (IICS): Manual for Observers, unpublished coding manual.

Roberts, L. J., Salem, D., Rappaport, J., Luke, D. A., Toro, P. A., & Seidman, E. (1999). Giving and receiving help: Interpersonal transactions in mutual-help meetings and psychosocial adjustment of members. *American Journal of Community Psychology, 27*, 841–869.

Rogers, C. R. (1951). *Client-centered therapy: Its current practice, implications, and theory.* Boston, MA: Houghton Mifflin.

Saitzyk, A. R., Floyd, F. J., & Kroll, A. B. (1997). Sequential analysis of autonomy-interdependence and affiliation-disaffiliation in couples' social support interactions. *Personal Relationships, 4*, 341–360.

Shaver, P. R., Morgan, H. J., & Wu, S. (1996). Is love a "basic" emotion? *Personal Relationships, 3*, 81–96.

Sprecher, S., & Sedikides, C. (1993). Gender differences in perceptions of emotionality: The case of close heterosexual relationships. *Sex Roles, 28*, 511–530.

Sullivan, H. S. (1953). *The interpersonal theory of psychiatry*. New York: Norton.

Tannen, D. (1990). *You just don't understand: Women and men in conversation*. New York: William Morrow.

Tolstedt, B. E., & Stokes, J. P. (1983). Relation of verbal, affective, and physical intimacy to marital satisfaction. *Journal of Counseling Psychology, 30*, 573–580.

Veroff, J., Douvan, E., Orbuch, T. L., & Acitelli, L. K. (1998). Happiness in stable marriages: The early years. In T. N. Bradbury (Ed.), *The developmental course of marital dysfunction* (pp. 152–179). New York: Cambridge University Press.

Wallerstein, J. S., & Blakeslee, S. (1995). *The good marriage: How and why love lasts*. New York: Houghton-Mifflin.

Weick, K. E. (1985). Systematic observational methods. In G. Lindzey & E. Aronson (Eds.), *The handbook of social psychology vol. 2* (3rd ed., pp. 567–634). New York: Random House.

Weiss, R. L., & Heyman, R. E. (1990). Observation of marital interaction. In F. D. Fincham & T. N. Bradbury (Eds.), *The psychology of marriage* (pp. 150–171). New York: Guilford.

Weiss, R., & Summers, K. J. (1983). Marital interaction coding system III. In E. Filsinger (Ed.), *Marriage and family assessment* (pp. 35–115). Beverly Hills, CA: Sage.

CHAPTER SIX

Bases for Giving Benefits in Marriage: What Is Ideal? What Is Realistic? What Really Happens?

Margaret S. Clark, Steven Graham, and Nancy Grote

Many, many benefits are given and received within marriages. Such benefits include, among other things, routine services (for example, doing a load of laundry), other services (for example, buying a birthday card for a mother-in-law), goods (for example, a watch), verbal affection (for example, saying, "I love you."), physical affection (for example, a backrub), emotional support (for example, reassurance that all is OK following a spouse's bad dream), and giving instructions (for example, how to use a new computer). Most people would agree that the everyday giving and acceptance of such benefits is central to the well-being of relationships. Yet, surprisingly little is known about the patterning of the giving and receiving of benefits in relationships. What drives this patterning? What are the consequences of different modes of giving and receiving benefits within marriage?

In this chapter we address these issues. We discuss what we consider to be the ideal norm for giving and accepting benefits (a communal norm) and we discuss just why we consider this norm to be ideal. We also present evidence that members of couples who are about to be married as well as couples who have been married for years agree with us. We then discuss alternative norms that may, and often are, followed in place of a communal norm – norms such as equity and equality. In particular, we discuss when and why people may replace a communal norm with one of these norms. We also discuss the possibility of people abandoning such "just" norms altogether and simply behaving in self-interested ways. As we do this, we will be presenting a model of

Preparation of this chapter was supported by National Science Foundation Grant BCS-9983417. We thank Kristin Boyd and Patricia Jennings for comments on earlier versions of this manuscript.

how, when, and why various implicit (and sometimes explicit) rules for giving and receiving benefits come into play in marriages and what the consequences of each approach may be.

It is important to note that in exploring this topic we are not so interested in distributive justice per se, as we are in what constitutes optimal functioning in terms of care giving and care receiving in marriages. We are convinced that coming to understand the normative basis for giving and receiving benefits will prove to be of considerable value in this endeavor. Care giving, after all, consists in large part in benefiting one's partner in tangible and intangible ways.

A BRIEF HISTORY OF RESEARCH ON DISTRIBUTIVE JUSTICE NORMS IN INTIMATE RELATIONSHIPS

Many different researchers have searched for the rule or norm that governs the giving and acceptance of benefits in dating relationships and in marriage, and that is associated with satisfaction and/or stability in such relationships. Some researchers have advocated that an equality rule is the rule for such relationships (Deutsch, 1975; 1985) and there is evidence consistent with the use and value of such a rule in intimate relationships (Austin, 1980; Greenberg, 1983; Lerner, 1974, study 3). That is, benefits (and sometimes costs) ought to be divided evenly between partners in a relationship. If partners, say, share a home office, each should be given equal space. If they go out to eat they should split the bill evenly (cf. Austin, 1980).

Others have advocated an equity rule as the rule (Walster, Walster, & Berscheid, 1978) and have come up with evidence for the use and value of that rule in intimate relationships (Desmarais & Lerner, 1989; Lloyd, Cate, & Henton, 1982; Sabatelli & Cecil-Pigo, 1895; Sprecher, 1986; Utne, Hatfied, Traupmann & Greenberger, 1984). That is, the ratio of one person's inputs into the relationship relative to his or her outcomes ought to equal the ratio of the partner's inputs relative to his or her outcomes. Often, in close relationships research, this is calculated globally with respondents judging their own and their partner's overall contributions to and outcomes from a relationship and then calculating equity using those subjective, and generally, retrospective, estimates. A wife may make the judgment that she brings in half the family income, does half the housework, makes all social arrangements, does three quarters of the childcare, and all the bill paying. She may further judge that these contributions make up roughly 60% of the contributions to their relationship. At the same time she may judge her husband, who makes half the income, does half the housework, does a quarter of the child-care, and does all routine car maintenance to be making 40% of the total contributions to the relationship. It's not equal. However, if she further perceives that in terms of outcomes from the relationship (satisfaction, ability to make decisions, personal purchases) that she also derives 60% of the outcomes whereas her husband derives 40%, it is equitable. According to equity theorists, both partners ought to be happy and the relationship stable.

Others have found evidence for the use and value of a "responsiveness to needs" rule (Clark & Mills, 1993; Deustch, 1975, 1985 for family relationships; Lamm & Schwinger, 1980; 1983; Mills & Clark, 1982). The idea is that people in relationships ought to be responsive to their partner's needs if and when such needs arise to the best of their ability. In the case of marriage this responsiveness is expected to be mutual. When the person has a need, he or she can expect the partner to be responsive to that need to the best of the partner's ability as well. If one partner's car is in the shop and he needs a ride to work that his wife can reasonably provide, she should give it. If he has a setback at work, his wife ought to comfort him. If she is exhausted after work and he is not, he ought to make or purchase dinner and so forth. So too should members of the relationship provide benefits, on occasion, simply as signs that they care for one another. These signs may take the form of cards, flowers, and birthday presents, hugs, or affectionate notes. Satisfaction from such a relationship should come from nurturing one's partner (cf. Grote & Clark, 1998) as well as from being nurtured by one's partner.

Still others have argued that all that really matters to people in such relationships is receiving rewards and avoiding costs (Cate et al. 1985; Huston & Burgess, 1979). Supporting this view are studies in which simple measures of the total amount of rewards received in a relationship predicted relationship satisfaction better than measures indicating the use of norms such as equality or equity (Cate, Lloyd, Henton, & Larson, 1982; Desmarais & Lerner, 1989; Hansen, 1987; Martin, 1985; Michaels, Edwards, & Acock 1984). As long as a person gets what he or she needs and wants from a relationship and as long as the costs to being in that relationship are not too high, all should be well.

What these researchers have not achieved is agreement. Instead, different researchers have tended to hold fast to their own viewpoints accumulating more and more evidence for those views. Simultaneously, they have ignored growing evidence for the use and value of different norms.

Some time ago, Clark and Chrisman (1994) reviewed the literature in this area and suggested avenues that might be taken toward resolving its seeming conflicts. Two suggestions made then were: (a) to draw clear distinctions between what norm people feel is ideal for distributing benefits in intimate relationships (such as marriages) and how they actually behave, and (b) to think about the process of changing norm use as it may unfold over time during the course of intimate relationships. In the present chapter, we take these suggestions to heart. We start by distinguishing what people judge to be ideal from how they actually behave in their relationships. Then we set forth a model of norm use over time in marriages that are ultimately happy and stable versus marriages that are ultimately less happy and, at times, unstable.

WHAT IS THE IDEAL BASIS FOR BENEFITING ONE'S PARTNER IN MARRIAGE? WHAT IS NOT?

Theoretical Argument

We begin by postulating that the ideal basis for giving and accepting benefits within marriage is a communal one. That is, we believe that following a norm of mutual, noncontingent responsiveness to the needs of the partner is ideal in marriages. Spouses should respond to partner needs if and when such needs arise. They should not require any particular benefit in return. They should not keep careful track of what each partner has done for or received from the other.

The next question, naturally, is why do we consider this rule to be the ideal for the giving and receiving of benefits in marriage? It is, perhaps, easiest to explain this by explaining what is wrong with following any of a number of alternative approaches to giving and receiving benefits. First, consider the possibility of each person simply acting in a self-interested manner, deriving as many benefits as possible from the marriage while simultaneously avoiding as many costs as possible. That is, each member could try to get the best deal for him or herself while ignoring his or her spouse's costs and benefits. Few people would consider this to be the ideal basis for giving and receiving benefits in marriage. However, it is worthwhile to raise it as the first possibility, and to comment upon why it is not the best choice.

Answers come readily to mind: Pure self-interest provides no sense of solidarity and cooperation. It individuates persons. Importantly, following such a rule indicates no caring for each other. A person who needs help is responsible for finding it because the spouse is not assumed to care about the partner's well-being, independent of what the partner can do for him or her. Thus, felt security should be low. Furthermore, a spouse who gives help only for self-interested reasons (perhaps because it is necessary to give help to elicit something in return), is not afforded a sense of nurturing his or her partner. Without having a sense of mutual love and caring, feelings of intimacy, as Reis and Shaver (1988) define that term, should be low.

To make matters worse, adherence to a self-interest rule allows for exploitation of one's partner. Persons with more power (perhaps because they have more attractive alternatives to the relationship) are in a position to demand that their partners be more responsive to their needs than they are to the partners' needs. Such exploitation could easily squash any hope of attaining a sense of intimacy in the relationship.

Of course, one may ask why achieving a sense of ongoing caring, nurturance, intimacy, and security within a relationship is, itself, important. To us, the answer is straightforward. It is precisely these things that make a relationship a *safe haven* to use a term borrowed from attachment theory (cf. Collins & Feeney, 2000). It is also precisely these things that, we suspect, provide individuals with an ongoing, perceived sense of what is widely termed *social support* (Cohen & Hoberman, 1983; Cohen & Syme, 1985; Cutrona, Suhr, & MacFarlane, 1990). Furthermore, having a trusting, caring relationship with another frees a person from being too self-occupied and self-concerned because there is at least one other person who will pick up that task and be concerned for you. In good times this allows each partner to focus on the other, and also to reach out and strive toward new goals. In bad times it allows each partner to retreat to the safe haven of the relationship for comfort and care. In both situations, a communally based relationship should be calming and should promote mental and physical health. (See, for instance, Gump, Polk, Kamarck, & Shiffman, 2001, who recently found that interactions with intimate partners are associated with lower blood pressure. The authors speculate this may be due to interactions with an established intimate partner being safe and predictable or perhaps due to a partner's presence acting, "as a classically conditioned safety signal," p. 431.) A relationship consisting of two self-interested, independent persons, we would guess, cannot provide such benefits. Rather, it adds the threat of exploitation by one's partner to one's everyday, individual stresses and strains.

So, what other possible rules exist as a basis for giving and receiving benefits within marriage? Many have been suggested, including a set of rules that involve giving benefits with contingencies or strings attached. One could, for instance, give benefits with the expectation of receiving comparable benefits as repayment, and accept benefits with the expectation of repaying the other with comparable benefits. Clark and Mills (1979; 1993) have called this an *exchange rule*. One could follow an *equity rule*, which dictates that one should keep the ratio of each person's inputs relative to that person's outcomes from the relationship equal to the ratio of the other person's inputs relative to their outcomes. Or, one could ignore inputs, and simply endeavor to keep all outcomes from the relationship exactly equal.

We can understand why such norms are considered to be superior to pure self-interest. They are superior in that, if carefully followed, and if each member trusts the other to follow the rules, these rules assure that no one partner can be exploited. However, we still would argue that none of these contingent norms is ideal for marriage.

They are not ideal because giving benefits contingently calls into question the assumption that the other person truly, and noncontingently, cares about his or her partner's welfare. If a benefit is given with the clear expectation of receiving something comparable in return, to keep partners' individual ratios of benefits given to benefits received equivalent, or to maintain equality of benefits, the giving of a benefit does not clearly convey to the recipient that the giver cares about his or her welfare. Neither will it convey to the giver (through self-perception) that that giver cares for the recipient. Unfortunately, as social psychologists have long pointed out, if there are multiple explanations for a behavior, each will be discounted to some extent (Cheng & Novick, 1990; Kelley, 1972). Thus, we would argue that, by their very nature, use of these "contingent" rules undermines both the recipient's sense that the partner truly cares for him or her and, in addition, the partner's own sense that he or she cares for the recipient. Hence, the recipients' sense of personal security may decrease. So too the donors' self-esteem (to the extent to which it is based on being a caring person) decreases. Together, decreases in a sense of being cared for and a sense of nurturing one's partner should produce overall drops in the sense of relationship intimacy. (Note that even the suspicion that a benefit is given on a contingent basis may produce these effects.)

Now that we have said what is wrong with other rules, we return to our postulate that a communal norm is ideal. It is superior to behaving in a purely self-interested fashion because it provides assurance that each partner will receive benefits from the other person, even if those benefits cannot be reciprocated. It provides much beyond that as well.

It is also superior to the contingent norms in that it should be more efficient in securing benefits when one does have a need, as well as in securing benefits matched to the particular need. This is because the typical trigger to providing benefits is the existence of the need, not the existence of a debt on the partner's part, or a desire on the partner's part to get something back from the person. Beyond that, a partner demonstrating that he or she is following this norm or, indeed, merely stating that this is the norm that he or she wishes to follow, can provide a sense (to both members of the couple) that the partner is truly caring. This, too, ought to benefit the relationship and each of its participants.

Does this mean that following a need-based or communal norm is completely unselfish (and, as a result, perhaps hopelessly unrealistic in many people's eyes)? We think not. Once a need-based or communal norm has been adopted, it does dictate that benefits should be given in response to needs on a noncontingent basis and when benefits are given on this basis the positive consequences to the relationship just discussed should ensue. However, it is important to realize that the motives that lead people to adopt a need-based or communal norm in the first place may be either selfish and/or unselfish (Clark & Mills, 1993).

Let us explain with some examples. Consider first a selfish motivation for following a communal norm. Imagine a person who has recently moved to a new city. This person is lonely and wants to form friendships and possibly a romantic relationship. The person implicitly knows that adopting a communal norm when interacting with others is a means to forming such relationships. Thus, the newcomer might ask questions about others' welfare and offer help on a noncontingent basis (for instance, help carrying boxes into a new apartment). In other words, the newcomer may behave communally hoping (but not requiring) that the other will follow a communal norm as well and that a mutual friendship or romantic relationship will ensue. The newcomer has a selfish motive for adopting a communal norm, but the norm still dictates that any given benefit is given noncontingently, in response to a need. The other may not want to accept gestures of concern or offers of help. The other may not respond to the newcomer's needs. In such a case, past investments cannot be recouped; nor does either party expect that they have to be. The newcomer simply moves on to pursue other potentially communal relationships. However, if the relationship does "take," it is likely to "take" on a communal basis. Eventually, it can afford both members a sense of security that the other really does care about them and does value the relationship.

In contrast, the motivation to follow a communal norm may often be unselfish. For instance, a person may see another in need and feel empathic concern. That empathic concern may, in turn, elicit the noncontingent giving of help (cf. Batson, Duncan, Ackerman, Buckley, & Birch, 1981; Batson, Batson, Slingsby, Harrell, Peekna, & Todd, 1991). Thus, for instance, a wife's exhausted and sad demeanor may elicit feelings of empathic concern from her husband who may respond by putting an arm around her shoulders, speak encouraging and supportive words, and perform some chores that she had been planning to do.

Empirical Evidence for a Communal Norm Being Considered to be Ideal

What evidence do we have that a communal norm really is considered ideal for marriages? To test this proposition, we did something straightforward. We asked people. Specifically, in one study we presented members of about 100 young couples with prototypes of equity, equality, exchange, and communal norms (see Table 6.1). We did this a few weeks prior to their marriages; then again about two years into their marriages. We also presented these prototypes to a group of about 70 alumni from a small private college in New England and their spouses. These couples had been married an average of 20 years.

The results were clear. Our participants rated the need-based (communal) norm on the "ideal" side of the scale in each case and they rated it as being more ideal than the other norms. Exchange and equity norms were rated on the "not ideal" side of the scale in each case and as being clearly less ideal than the need-based norm. The same held true for the equality norm among our older sample. Interestingly, among our younger couples, both before and after marriage, the equality norm fell on the "ideal" side of the scale and as being more ideal than equity or exchange norms but less ideal than a communal norm.

Table 6.1. Prototypes of Communal, Equality, Equity, and Exchange Norms

Communal: The way marital relationships ideally should operate is that each person should pay attention to the other's needs. Each person should give a benefit to the other in response to the other's needs, when the other has a real need that he or she cannot meet him or herself. Each person should do this to the best of his or her ability so long as the personal costs are reasonable. When one person does something for the other, the other should not owe the giver anything.

Equality: The way marital relationships ideally should operate is that each person should get the same number of benefits from the relationship. If one member starts receiving more benefits than the other, both members should work to get the relationship back into balance. When giving and accepting benefits, the overall level of equality of benefits should be kept in mind.

Equity: The way marital relationships ideally should operate is that members should keep track of the benefits each person gives to the relationship and gets from the relationship. If one member contributes more benefits, that person ought to get more benefits. The amount of benefit contributed to and gained from a relationship should be kept equitable. That is, what you get compared to what you give should equal what your spouse gets compared to what he or she gives.

Exchange: The way marital relationships ideally should operate is that each person should benefit the other with the expectation of receiving a benefit of similar value in return. After receiving a benefit, members should feel obligated to give the other a benefit of comparable value. Members of the relationship ought to keep track of benefits given and received in order to keep them in balance.

Why might the equality norm have fallen in the middle and not have been rated as significantly different from either a communal norm or equity or exchange norms for the young couples? We think the reason for this is that the meaning of following an equality norm is somewhat ambiguous. Following such a norm can be seen as consistent with a communal norm but it also can be seen as being more consistent with the contingent, record keeping norms such as exchange or equity. Let us explain. From our perspective, dividing benefits equally or dividing responsibilities equally cannot, on the face of it, be categorized as having been motivated by a focus on needs or a focus on fairness and what can be gotten back for what one has given. Neither do we see equality as a standard that constitutes a clear alternative to the other standards we have discussed. Rather, we believe that use of a standard of equality can be consistent with either sort of norm depending upon what motivated the use of an equality standard in the first place.

Consider situations in which an equality standard is consistent with a communal norm. Dividing benefits or responsibilities equally is consistent with a communal norm when spouses have equal needs for a benefit or equal needs to avoid and/or ability to take on a responsibility. For instance, a husband and wife might perceive that they have an equal desire and need to visit their respective families of origin. Given limited time and resources and a desire to travel together, they might work out a system in which they, as a couple, visit each family an equal number of times each year. Such an agreement, when motivated by a consideration of each spouse's needs and an implicit judgment that those needs are equal, is consistent with a communal norm. Alternatively, spouses may perceive that they have equal needs to avoid dish washing. Therefore they may split the chore equally. Again, such an agreement, when motivated by a consideration of each spouse's needs and an implicit judgment that those needs are equal, is consistent with a communal norm.

How does our view of equality fit with Deutsch's (1975; 1985) theoretical view that dividing benefits and responsibilities equally is something done when one's goal is to demonstrate the solidarity of a relationship? Although we are in agreement with Deutsch that dividing benefits and responsibilities equally often does increase solidarity in marriage, our view differs from his in that we think this is true only when dividing benefits or costs equally is consistent with an overriding communal norm. In other words, we believe that use of an equality norm promotes solidarity only when the two peoples' needs to obtain the benefits or to avoid the costs also are seen as equal. If needs are unequal, following a communal norm should promote greater cohesion than will following an equality norm. Indeed, in such a situation, insistence on following an equality norm ought to be seen as violating the communal norm and as quite consistent with (and equally undesirable) exchange or equity norms.

This sort of situation may occur when needs for benefits or needs to avoid responsibilities are unequal. Consider a situation in which the members of a marriage are equally close to their families of origin and the wife's mother is facing a life-threatening illness. All members of the husband's family are perfectly healthy. In such a circumstance, the wife would seem to have a legitimately greater need to visit her family than the husband would to visit his. Given limited family resources, for the husband to insist on an equal number of visits to each family of origin would violate a communal norm. We would predict that in such a circumstance most people would consider adhering to a communal norm and violating an equality standard to be more ideal.

Our explanation for ratings of the equality norm by our young couples falling in between ratings of a communal norm and ratings of equity or exchange norms is, therefore, that it is sometimes compatible with a communal norm but sometimes not.

Our older couples, of course, did not rate equality as positively as did our younger couples. Instead they rated it, on average, on the nonideal side of the scale and their ratings of the equality norm were very similar to their ratings of the equity and exchange norms. We cannot be sure why this occurred. One possibility is that, having been raised during times when gender roles were more differentiated and rigid, our older couples may simply do less equal splitting of tasks such as grocery shopping, dish washing, and car maintenance (to meet needs) than did our younger couple. Thus, they may have less of a tendency to view an equality norm as compatible with an overall communal norm.

WHAT IS REALISTIC IN TERMS OF BENEFITING ONE'S PARTNER IN MARRIAGE?

Clark and Chrisman (1994) have made the point that, in disentangling the rules that govern the giving and receiving of benefits in intimate relationships such as marriages, it may be useful to distinguish what is ideal from what is realistic.

A communal rule requires certain skills, fortitudes, and knowledge and thus is less realistic than it is ideal. Members of marriages (or members of engaged couples) clearly believe that a communal norm is ideal. However, they may simultaneously believe that following such a norm is not simple. There are many reasons why the norm may not be followed in marriage. First, as noted below, following a communal rule requires both a certain set of skills and certain sorts of emotional fortitudes. There are individual differences in these skills that suggest that not all people will be able to actualize a communal ideal effectively. These skills and fortitudes also vary over time within any given person or couple, depending upon their moods and outside stresses. Second, obligations in other relationships and to the self may sometimes interfere with meeting one's partner's needs. Third, even when one does possess considerable interpersonal skills and fortitudes, and has no conflicting obligations, there may still be situational barriers to perceiving and meeting another's needs.

Interpersonal Skills and Fortitudes

There are two distinct sets of social skills and fortitudes necessary for following a communal norm effectively. The set that comes to mind most easily includes skills and fortitudes necessary to respond effectively to a partner's needs. This set includes having the ability to draw out one's partner (Miller, Berg, & Archer, 1983; Purvis, Dabbs, & Hopper, 1984) and have that partner disclose worries, fears, and emotional states. The more a person is able to do this, the more that person will be aware of the partner's needs and, hence, be able to meet those needs. Empathic accuracy (Ickes, 1993) also should be important to meeting a partner's needs. Indeed, many studies do support the idea that understanding a spouse's thoughts, beliefs, and feelings is linked with good marital adjustment (for example, Christensen & Wallace, 1976 ; Gottman & Porterfield, 1981; Guthrie & Noller, 1988; Noller, 1980; 1981). One more skill that is clearly important to following a communal norm is knowing how to offer help in such a manner that it will be accepted.

Some of these skills require learning, practice, and intelligence (for example, the ability to draw a partner out, empathic accuracy, provision of emotional support). One may wish to express empathy but fail to do so out of fear of appearing awkward. Others may seem easy (for example, offering help, giving simple kinds of help), but a lack of emotional fortitude to follow through may get in the way. For instance, one may not offer help for fear it will be refused. One's history of personal relationships and the particular relationship in question may provide keys to a lack of emotional fortitude in providing help. A lack of fortitude may also stem from temporary factors such as feeling particularly stressed or being in a particularly bad mood.

The second set of skills and fortitudes necessary for effectively following a communal norm in marriages is that set required to elicit help and support from one's partner when such aid is needed. In this regard, the complement to being an opener (eliciting information about the partner's needs) is freely expressing one's own need states to the partner through self-disclosure and emotional expression. The more one does this, the more the partner will know about one's needs and the more help that can be given. Not only that but self-disclosure has also been found to increase positive affect (Vittengl & Holt, 2000) and liking (Collins & Miller, 1994) in relationships as well as satisfaction in dating relationships (Fitzpatrick & Sollie, 1999), marriages (Meeks, Hendrick, & Hendrick, 1998) and sibling relationships (Howe, Aquan-Assee, Bukowski, Rinaldi, & Lehoux, 2000). Of course, one ought also to be able to ask for help and accept it when it is offered. Perhaps less obviously, possessing the ability to say "no" to requests that interfere with one's needs ought also to be crucial to the partner meeting one's needs. It may also be important that, over time, one demonstrates that one will not exaggerate needs or constantly seek help when it is not needed. This ought to increase a partner's sense that one is appropriately, and not overly, dependent upon him or her.

Although the second set of skills might seem easy at first glance, they also require certain emotional fortitudes to enact. In particular, all these skills require having the sense that one's partner truly cares for one and will, indeed, meet one's needs to the best of his or her ability. Without this sense, self-disclosure, emotional expression, and asking for help are likely to all seem inadvisable, even frightening. Under such circumstances, one risks being rebuffed or rejected, or evaluated more negatively. The partner may even use information about one's vulnerabilities exploitatively or mockingly. Negative assertion on one's own behalf may also be quite frightening, as it too may provide a basis for rejection. Thus, it may seem safest not to express these thoughts and feelings. However, if one does not do so, keeping a marriage on a communal basis becomes very difficult. It is for just these reasons that we believe a sense of trust and security in marriage is key to following a communal norm.

Although many skills are required to effectively follow a communal norm, this norm should still seem more realistic than many of the contingent norms. Given the potential barriers to following a communal norm within marriage, one might guess that following a different rule (for example, an exchange, an equity, or an equality rule) would be perceived by people as being more realistic than striving to adhere to a communal norm. We do not think this is the case for a variety of reasons.

First, although in theory such rules, if followed precisely, will yield a "just" division of benefits in relationships, there are many reasons why this is extremely unlikely to happen in practice. Perhaps most importantly, it is likely impossible to follow these norms perfectly in a marriage, even with both members making their best efforts to do so. In a marriage, after all, many, many benefits are given and received every day. Moreover, many benefits given are not visible to the recipient (who may be physically absent or attending to something else when they are given). For instance, this might happen when one spouse spots something the other inadvertently dropped on the garage floor and puts it back where it belongs or when one spouses notices that some household supply is running low and goes to the store to replace it. Finally, a wide variety of benefits are given – physical and verbal affection, services and goods of many kinds – and they are of differing value to their recipients. The mental effort that would be required to compute whether these contingent norms have or have not been met is staggering. People implicitly know this.

Not only do we suspect that people know it is impossible to do an accurate job in tracking equal exchanges, equity, or equality of outcomes, we also suspect that when people are not stressed and not feeling particularly needy, they are not even motivated to try. After all, why bother to do all that work when there is nothing to be gained by so doing?

In contrast to the daunting task of doing a good job following contingent rules, following the communal rule is likely to seem simpler. There is no long-term or complex record keeping necessary. One merely must express ones' needs when they arise and attend to one's partner's needs and be responsive when those needs arise. Although, as we have already noted, there are possible skill and emotional barriers to doing this effectively, it nonetheless seemed to us that people would judge following a communal norm to be more realistic than following an contingent norm such as equity or exchange. (We did, however, expect it to be judged as being less realistic than it is ideal.)

Empirical Evidence that a Communal Rule Is Perceived as More Realistic for Marriage than Are Contingent or Self-Interest Norms

In addition to asking men and women who were about to be married (and then again about two years into their marriage) what rules they thought were ideal for their marriage, we also asked them what rules they actually followed. Both before marriage and after two years of marriage they reported that they were striving to follow a communal norm more than the other, contingent norms.

We asked our older, college alumni group a different question about these norms to get at how realistic these norms seem to them. That is, after asking them what norms seemed to be ideal to them, we also asked them what norms seemed *reasonable* to use. This group indicated that the communal norm was more reasonable than the other norms.

A Model of What May Happen over Time in Practice

Having said that marital partners, ideally, will follow a communal norm for giving and receiving benefits and also that there are lots of reasons to suspect that they will often fall short of this norm, we now present a preliminary model of distributive justice norm use in marriages. First, we believe that people entering romantic relationships (and later marriage) start off with high desire and motivation to follow communal norms – not with a tendency or desire to follow equity or exchange norms (cf. Berg & Clark, 1986). Not only do people believe this is the ideal norm to follow in such a relationship, but, we suspect, they implicitly know that following communal rules signals to one's partner that they desire this kind of relationship. Thus, they may choose to behave communally in an effort to start (or strengthen) a relationship. They may, for instance, offer to help another when help is needed and make it clear that no compensation is desired. So too may they encourage the other's expressions of emotion or self-disclosures in an effort to start or strengthen a communal relationship.

Another, complementary, way of initiating a relationship would be to make it clear to the other that one trusts the other with information about one's own needs and would like that other to respond to those own needs. One can do so by appropriately expressing emotion (Clark, Fitness, & Brissette, 2000), self-disclosing or asking for help. Thus, seemingly paradoxically, adherence to communal norms may be closest at the beginning of an intimate relationship (Berg & Clark, 1986). Adherence to communal norms may also be especially high at times preceding jumps in levels of commitment (for example, right before marriage), perhaps as a way to justify the commitment (that is, to reduce dissonance).

Perfect or even near-perfect adherence to communal norms, however, is impossible. Marital partners will neglect one another's needs and it is such instances of neglect, we postulate, that trigger switches to other implicit rules for distributing benefits. When one believes one's needs have been neglected, the response may be to address the neglect constructively and to come up with a solution. However, not all spouses may have the skills and fortitude to do this. Moreover, many spouses who usually do have those skills and fortitudes may, at times, be unable to use them due to stress or fatigue. In such cases the result may be to question the communal basis of the relationship and one's assumptions that the other will meet one's needs in the future. Consequently one may switch, temporarily or permanently, to another basis – a basis that allows one more control over receiving benefits from the other, and does not require the kind of trust in the other that following a communal norm requires.

An exchange rule is an example of such an alternative rule. One can say to one's spouse that one will only continue to benefit him or her if he or she provides certain benefits. Imagine, for example, two spouses who both work. Both are stressed from the combination of career, household duties, and childcare. One, typically the wife, may feel that the burden of household chores is falling unfairly upon her. She raises this issue with her husband, but receives little in the way of additional help. Eventually, probably after a particularly stressful day, she lays down an ultimatum saying, "Look, I'm only going to do all the laundry if you do the dishes." Alternatively, the switch may be an appeal to equality. "Our budget is tight. I'm tired of being the only one to make sacrifices. We're each going to spend exactly the same amount on clothes this year." Or, it may be an appeal that sounds like equity. "Look I make twice as much money as you do so I deserve the more expensive car." No matter which contingent norm a person appeals to, the result is the person having a greater sense of being in control of what he or she will get from the other without having to have high trust in the other's inherent concern for his or her welfare. Of course, a person still must trust that the other will live up to his or her end of the equity, equality, or exchange agreement. However, whether that will be the case can be more easily and quickly assessed than can the other's continuing commitment to the person's general welfare be assessed. Pay backs or equalizing of benefits must occur quickly and consistently or the agreement has been broken. The requirements for meeting the standard are clear, often can be assessed within a short period of time, and often are explicitly stated.

An alternative strategy may be a switch to self-interest. Rather than trying to extract something from a spouse by an appeal to one of the contingent norms, one may instead decide to simply watch out for oneself (and perhaps cease to watch out for the other, on a temporary basis). "Well, if you don't want to go visit my family, I'll just go by myself." And, perhaps, "Don't expect me to go visit yours."

We suspect that this sort of switch also occurs frequently in marriages. Spouses may switch from a communal norm directly to this approach or they may switch from a communal norm to an exchange norm and, if exchange rules are violated, to self-interest.

Switches to noncommunal norms do not necessarily indicate that norms of equality, equity, or exchange are the norms people really want to characterize their relationships. Neither, in the case of acting in purely self-interested ways, does the action necessarily mean that self-interest seems ideal. Indeed, very often, we suspect, the switch to such norms or to self-interest is a temporary and aversive one. When stress drops, and neglect of past needs is no longer salient, we propose, people often revert back to their desire to follow (and faith in) communal norms. As a result, they will return to behaving in ways consistent with that norm. A pattern of falling away from a communal norm when needs are not being adequately met but fairly quickly returning to the communal norm, may characterize many, relatively happy, stable marriages.

Although we postulate that temporarily falling away from adherence to a communal norm is a common pattern, we postulate that a pattern of more permanently falling away from adherence to a communal norm also may occur. In the face of stresses and neglected needs, spouses may switch to contingent norms such as equity, exchange, or equality and continue with those norms over long periods of time in the marriage. Following these norms does allow for a just division of benefits. However, following such norms may also likely be associated with lower overall marital satisfaction (cf. Buunk & VanYperen, 1991; Murstein, Cerreto, & MacDonald, 1977) because following contingent, record-keeping norms for giving and accepting benefits simply cannot afford the sense of intimacy, security, and nurturance that we postulate is essential for high quality, highly satisfying marriages. Spouses nevertheless may stay together for a whole host of reasons, many of which have been amply described by interdependence theorists. They may, for instance, stay together because they perceive their alternatives (for example, being single, entering into another possible relationship) to be poor (Bui, Peplau, & Hill, 1996; Drigotas & Rusbult, 1992; Felmlee, Sprecher, & Bassin, 1990; Thibaut & Kelley, 1959.) They may stay together because their investments in the relationship are high (for example, joint memories, financial investments, children, housing) (Rusbult, 1983), or they may stay together because they (or others important to them) hold strong moral values that divorce is wrong (Cox, Wesler, Rusbult, & Gaines, 1997).

Of course, it is also possible that people switch more permanently to a norm of self-interest, but stay together for similar reasons. They are likely to be very unhappy. However, paradoxically, they may well experience less unhappiness than will those who follow contingent rules. The reason is that simply watching out for one's own self-interests allows spouses to lead lives that are largely independent of one another and thereby avoids one spouse interrupting the other's routines and causing distress (cf. Berscheid & Ammazzalorso, 2000). Attempting to follow norms of equity, equality, or exchange, in contrast, requires considerable interdependence and, along with it, considerable opportunity for one spouse interrupting the other's plans and routines and thus, considerable negative emotion.

Some Broad Patterns that Giving and Receiving Benefits in Marriages May Take

So far we have described some very broad patterns of norm use, each of which we suspect is fairly common. Below we describe some of them in more detail.

One is a pattern characterized by partners beginning with sincere efforts to live up to a communal norm in their relationship and succeeding much of the time. However, when members' needs are not met or when members are feeling stressed, they may temporarily fall away from such a norm. They temporarily fall away because they believe their needs are not being met. Thus, they may believe that, in order to get anything from the partner, they must either insist on getting something back or simply watch out for their own interests. However, the deviance from a communal norm is temporary. We suspect that time and time again, members of many couples will return to the communal norm. We suspect that they return largely because they and their partner firmly do believe that following a communal norm is realistic and is the best way to achieve a sense of security, a sense of nurturing one's partner, and a sense of intimacy. Thus, the urge to use contingent or self-interest norms passes, along with the stress or feeling of neglect that caused it in the first place.

A different but also common pattern, we suspect, also begins with sincere efforts to live up to a communal norm. It also is characterized by people falling away from such a norm under stressful conditions. However, for these couples, the falling away becomes more permanent at some point. The couple may switch to a contingent norm and stick with that norm for a long time. Alternatively, the couple may switch to largely watching out for their own interests and stick with that mode of operating for a long time. Still another possibility is that couples will follow a contingent norm and then, if that does not seem to be working (and we believe it will not for many people), may switch to simply watching out for their own interests. Ultimately, if strong barriers to leaving the relationship are not present, the partners may terminate the relationship. If strong barriers to leaving the relationship are present, the partners may stay together, albeit unhappily.

Who Will Follow Which Pattern?

Predicting which pattern a particular couple will follow is a tricky business. Here we speculate on a number of factors that may put couples at risk for abandoning a communal norm.

One category of factors undoubtedly has to do with how well one's partner actually does, objectively, meet one's needs. In particular, the most straightforward factor putting couples at risk for abandoning adherence to a communal norm is actual and chronic neglect of needs on the part of at least one partner. Marital relationships are expected to be mutual ones. Each person should respond to the other's needs as those needs arise. Each person expects his or her partner to respond to his or her needs as those needs arise. Should a partner not live up to this norm, the other has good, objective reasons not to trust the partner, and may switch to contingent norms or to watching out for the self. Actual and chronic neglect of needs should be especially likely to produce this result when there are few apparent barriers to the partner meeting those needs. This would be the case when, for instance, the other does not have clear conflicting needs of his or her own and does not appear to lack the ability to meet one's needs.

Another category of factors likely to put couples at risk for switching norms includes temporary factors that make the potential recipient of benefits more likely than normal to feel needy and neglected. Being under high stress might fall into this category. Spouses juggling two new careers, the arrival of a new baby, and/or a move to a new location simultaneously, for instance, are very likely to be more needy than others. Consequently, they may be especially prone to believe that their needs are not being met and to believe that a switch to noncommunal means of giving and receiving benefits is in order.

A third set of factors, and the ones that are, perhaps, most interesting, are individual personality traits (and the interaction thereof) that people bring to the relationship. As we have already emphasized, neglect of needs is likely to be frequent in relationships. Yet, we predict, some people will react to neglect of needs with temporary switches to alternative norms whereas others will react with more permanent switches to alternative norms. Given the same sort of neglect of needs, we suspect that there are personality factors that will predict which path is more likely. Chronic differences in interpersonal trust ought to be crucial in this regard. Those who trust that other people are good and have their needs at heart ought to be far more comfortable adopting a communal norm in a relationship such as marriage. The reason for this is straightforward. Believing that a communal rule really will work in the long run requires one to believe that one's partner fundamentally cares for one's welfare.

Those who generally believe that others are trustworthy ought to be predisposed toward believing this about their own partner. When faced with a neglected need, someone low in this sort of trust, we predict, will be more likely to switch to using a contingent norm. After all, such a norm does not require the assumption that one's partner cares for one. It only requires faith that the partner will follow an explicitly agreed upon norm, adherence to which can be easily and repeatedly checked. Not only would we expect such a person to be especially likely to switch to such norms in the short run, that person should also be especially reluctant to switch back to a communal norm. Thus, the person should be especially likely to be following a contingent norm or merely watching out for him or herself over the long term. Although it is the case that they will miss out on the sense of security and mutuality resulting from following a communal norm, it may simply be very difficult for the person to derive this sense even when the partner is fairly responsive to their needs. This is because, even under the best of circumstances, some needs will be neglected, and, because these sorts of people may feel especially needy chronically. These individuals may find it easier to regulate their anxiety by following contingent norms for giving and accepting benefits, or by watching out for their own interests.

The concept of interpersonal trust is incorporated in the currently popular concept of attachment styles (Hazan and Shaver, 1987; Simpson & Rholes, 1998). Those said to be secure are high in such trust, whereas those said to be avoidant are low in such trust. We would, therefore, predict that secure people ought to be especially adept at following communal norms and at returning to the use of such norms when they have been abandoned. People who are avoidant, in contrast, may be likely to switch to some other rule for allocating benefits more readily, and more likely to stick with that rule over time.

Although we suspect that trust in close others is the central characteristic underlying resilience to departures from communal norms, recent literature suggests a number of specific interpersonal processes that may characterize those high in trust and self-esteem. These processes, including such things as derogating one's alternatives (Johnson & Rusbult, 1989), relating one's partner's faults to virtues (Murray & Holmes, 1993; 1999), and holding positive illusions about one's partner (Murray & Holmes, 1997; Murray, Holmes, & Griffin, 1996), when routinely utilized, undoubtedly buffer individuals from abandoning communal norms.

Some Empirical Evidence for Our Model

We have now presented a broad overview of patterns that the giving and receiving of benefits within marriages may take. This model breaks with prior theorizing in the area in a number of ways. First, we do not suggest that a single distributive justice rule is the rule governing the giving and receiving of benefits within marriages. Rather we suggest that one norm, a communal norm, is considered ideal and that most intimate relationships, including dating relationships, will start off with members striving to follow the rule. We explicitly do not think that members of intimate relationships start out by tracking just who contributes what to the relationship. We do not think they track adherence to a norm such as equity over time, remaining happy when the equity is maintained and becoming unhappy when it is not as has often been suggested in the past (Walster et al., 1978). Instead we believe it is feeling needy and neglected that leads people to conflict, to tracking of inputs and outcomes, and to (often biased) calculations of equity or equality.

We are just beginning to analyze data to test these views. However, at least one completed study does support our model (Grote & Clark, 2001). In this study, members of married couples expecting their first child filled out our surveys at three points in time: once during the wife's pregnancy, once following the birth when the child was about six months of age, and a third time when the child was about one year of age. At all three points in time we collected measures of the division of household labor, conflicts, and perceptions of fairness. Notably, both husbands and wives agreed that, when forced to consider it, the division of household labor was inequitable with the wives performing more of it than the husbands. According to our model, though, inequity (and judgments of unfairness in the division of household labor made

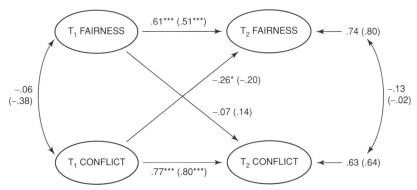

Figure 6.1. Standardized parameters for the structural model predicting husbands' and wives' Time 2 perceptions of the fairness of housework and Time 2
marital conflict. Bidirectional arrows show the correlation between the Time 1
predictors or the correlation between the error terms of the Time 2 criterion variables. These data represent 178 wives and 176 husbands (for whom complete
data were available). Values not in parentheses are for wives. Values in parentheses are for husbands. T = time. *p < .05. ***p < .001.

when individuals were forced to make them) will not necessarily lead to
conflicts (as they do not necessarily indicate a wife's needs are not being
met). On the other hand, our model does suggest that distress/conflict
(which we took as an index of needs not being met) should trigger
record keeping, a focus on inequities or inequalities and, therefore, increased judgments of unfairness. Supporting these ideas, a path analysis
of the Time 1 and Time 2 data did indicate that conflict at Time 1 predicted significant increases in perceived unfairness at Time 2 (controlling for perceived unfairness at Time 1). Also fitting with our ideas, perceived fairness at Time 1 did not predict increases in conflict at Time 2
(controlling for conflict at Time 1). The results of the path analysis are
shown in Figure 6.1.

Interestingly, and also fitting with our model, analyses of changes,
from Time 2 to Time 3 indicated that once conflict had led to perceived
unfairness (that is, by Time 2) then perceived unfairness did become a
significant predictor of later conflict (at Time 3). We suggest that this
occurred because at least a portion of our couples did switch to noncommunal, contingent, record-keeping standards of household chores
(in the face of the stress of caring for a newborn and keeping up all
other duties). In turn, unfairness was uncovered and focusing on that
unfairness (which now we assume is being driven by natural dynamics in the relationship rather than by the experimenter asking for a

judgment of how fair or unfair division of labor in the household is) did increase conflict.

SUMMARY

We have presented evidence that people believe that the ideal norm for giving and receiving benefits in marriage is a communal one. That is, each member should be concerned about the welfare of his or her spouse. Thus, to the best of a person's ability, benefits should be given in response to needs, as needs arise, with no strings attached, and with the provision that it is desirable to simultaneously consider one's own needs. This norm, we postulate, is considered more ideal than other possible norms, and than simply watching out for one's own interests, because it provides members with a sense of security and nurturance, and is consistent with the development of intimacy. We have presented further evidence that this norm is generally considered realistic, and more realistic than other possible norms.

Moving beyond the data we have presented, we have also postulated that people start their dating lives and marriages with strong desires and efforts to follow communal norms but that, over time, most couples will fall away from such norms at least temporarily. They will fall away when needs have not been met, and when they lose faith in their partners' desire to meet their needs. Finally, we have suggested that those especially likely to fall away from use of communal norms are those whose needs really have been chronically neglected, those who, perhaps temporarily, have especially high and chronic needs that their spouses cannot meet (perhaps because the spouse is stressed and needy at the same time), and, those who have least trust in people truly caring for one another's needs. Members of couples who are temporarily stressed may be most likely to bounce back to communal norms. Members of couples in which at least one spouse really does chronically neglect the other's needs and/or in which at least one spouse is insecure may be at greatest risk for more permanently falling away from adherence to communal norms.

REFERENCES

Austin, W. (1980). Friendship and fairness: Effects of type of relationship and task performance on choice of distribution rules. *Personality and Social Psychology Bulletin, 6,* 402–408.

Batson, C. D., Batson, J. G., Slingsby, J. K., Harrell, K. L., Peekna, H. M., & Todd, R. M. (1991). Empathic joy and the empathy-altruism hypothesis. *Journal of Personality and Social Psychology, 61*, 413–426.

Batson, C. D., Duncan, B. D., Ackerman, P., Buckley, T., & Birch, K. (1981). Is empathic emotion a source of altruistic motivation? *Journal of Personality and Social Psychology, 40*, 290–302.

Berg, J., & Clark, M. S. (1986). Differences in social exchange between intimate and other relationships: Gradually evolving or quickly apparent? In V. J. Derlega and B. A. Winstead (Eds.), *Friendship and social interaction* (pp. 101–128). New York: Springer.

Berscheid, E., & Ammazzalorso, H. (2000). Emotional experience in close relationships. In G. J. O. Fletcher & M. S. Clark (Eds.), *Blackwell handbook of social psychology: Interpersonal processes* (pp. 308–330). Oxford: Blackwell Publishers.

Bui, K. T., Peplau, L. A., & Hill, C. T. (1996). Testing the Rusbult model of relationship commitment and stability in a 15-year study of heterosexual couples. *Personality and Social Psychology Bulletin, 22*, 1244–1257.

Buunk, B. P., & VanYperen, N. W. (1991). Referential comparisons, relational comparisons, and exchange orientation: Their relation to marital satisfaction. *Personality and Social Psychology Bulletin, 17*, 709–717.

Cate, R. M., Lloyd, S. A., & Henton, J. M. (1985). The effect of equity, equality and reward level on the stability of students' premarital relationships. *Journal of Social Psychology, 125*, 715–725.

Cate, R. M., Lloyd, S. A., Henton, J. M., & Larson, J. H. (1982). Fairness and reward level as predictors of relationship satisfaction. *Social Psychology Quarterly, 45*, 177–181.

Cheng, P. W., & Novick, L. E. (1990). A probabilistic contrast model of casual induction. *Journal of Personality and Social Psychology, 58*, 545–567.

Christensen, L., & Wallace, L. (1976). Perceptual accuracy as a variable in marital adjustment. *Journal of Sex & Marital Therapy, 2*, 130–136.

Clark, M. S., & Chrisman, K. (1994). Resource allocation in intimate relationships: Trying to make sense of a confusing literature. In M. J. Lerner & G. Mikula (Eds.), *Entitlement and the affectional bond: Justice in close relationships* (pp. 65–88). New York: Plenum Press.

Clark, M. S., Fitness, J., & Brissette, I. (2000). Understanding people's perceptions of relationships is crucial to understanding their emotional lives. In G. J. O. Fletcher & M. S. Clark (Eds.), *Blackwell handbook of social psychology: Interpersonal processes* (pp. 253–270). Oxford: Blackwell Publishers.

Clark, M. S., & Mills, J. (1979). Interpersonal attraction in exchange and communal relationships. *Journal of Personality and Social Psychology, 37*, 12–24.

Clark, M. S., & Mills, J. (1993). The difference between communal and exchange relationships: What it is and is not. *Personality and Social Psychology Bulletin, 19*, 684–691.

Cohen, S., & Hoberman, H. M. (1983). Positive events and social supports as buffers of life change. *Journal of Applied Social Psychology, 13*, 99–125.

Cohen, S., & Syme, S. L. (Eds.). (1985). *Social support and health*. Orlando, FL: Academic Press.

Collins, N. L., & Feeney, B. C. (2000). A safe haven: An attachment theory perspective on support seeking and caregiving in intimate relationships. *Journal of Personality and Social Psychology, 78*, 1053–1073.

Collins, N. L., & Miller, L. C. (1994). Self-disclosure and liking: A metaanalytic review. *Psychological Bulletin, 116*, 457–475.

Cox, C. L., Wesler, M. O., Rusbult, C. E., & Gaines, S. O. (1997). Prescriptive support and commitment processes in close relationships. *Social Psychology Quarterly, 60*, 79–90.

Cutrona, C. E., Suhr, J. A., & MacFarlane, R. (1990). Interpersonal transactions and the psychological sense of support. In S. Duck & R. C. Silver (Eds.), *Personal relationships and social support* (pp. 30–45). Newbury Park, CA: Sage.

Desmarais, S., & Lerner, M. J. (1989). A new look at equity and outcomes as determinants of satisfaction in close relationships. *Social Justice Research, 3*, 105–109.

Deutsch, M. (1975). Equity, equality and need: What determines which value will be used as the basis of distributive justice? *Journal of Social Issues, 31*, 137–148.

Deutsch, M. (1985). *Distributive justice: A socio-psychological perspective.* New Haven, CT: Yale University Press.

Drigotas, S. M., & Rusbult, C. E. (1992). Should I stay or should I go?: A dependence model of breakups. *Journal of Personality and Social Psychology, 62*, 62–87.

Felmlee, D., Sprecher, S., & Bassin, E. (1990). The dissolution of intimate relationships: A hazard model. *Social Psychology Quarterly, 53*, 13–30.

Fitzpatrick, J., & Sollie, D. L. (1999). Influence of individual and interpersonal factors on satisfaction and stability in romantic relationships. *Personal Relationships, 6*, 337–350

Gottman, J. M., & Porterfield, A. L. (1981). Communicative competence in the nonverbal behavior of married couples. *Journal of Marriage and the Family, 43*, 817–824.

Greenberg, J. (1983). Equity and equality as clues to the relationship between exchange participants. *European Journal of Social Psychology, 133*, 195–196.

Grote, N. K., & Clark, M. S. (1998). Distributive justice norms and family work: What is perceived as ideal, what is applied, and what predicts perceived fairness? *Social Justice Research, 11*, 243–269.

Grote, N. K., & Clark, M. S. (2001). Perceiving unfairness in the family: Cause or consequence of marital distress? *Journal of Personality and Social Psychology, 80*, 281–293. Erratum, *Journal of Personality and Social Psychology, 80*, 362.

Gump, B. B., Polk, D. E., Kamarck, T. W., & Schiffman, S. M. (2001). Partner interactions are associated with reduced blood pressure in the natural environment: Ambulatory monitoring evidence from a healthy, multiethnic adult sample. *Psychosomatic Medicine, 63*, 4423–4433.

Guthrie, D. M., & Noller, P. (1988). Married couples' perceptions of one another in emotional situations. In P. Noller & M. A. Fitzpatrick (Eds.), *Perspectives on marital interaction* (pp. 153–181). Cleveland, OH: Multilingual Matters.

Hansen, G. L. (1987). Reward level and marital adjustment: The effect of weighing rewards. *Journal of Social Psychology, 27*, 549–551.

Hatfield, E., Traupmann, J., Sprecher, S., Utne, M., & Hay, J. (1985). Equity and intimate relations: Recent research. In W. Ickes (Ed.), *Compatible and incompatible relationships*. New York: Springer.

Hazan, C., & Shaver, P. (1987). Romantic love conceptualized as an attachment process. *Journal of Personality and Social Psychology, 52*, 511–534.

Howe, N., Aquan-Assee, J., Bukowski, W. M., Rinaldi, C. M., & Lehoux, P. M. (2000). Sibling self-disclosure in early adolescence. *Merrill-Palmer Quarterly, 46*, 653–671.

Huston, T. L., & Burgess, R. L. (1979). Social exchange in developing relations: An overview. In R. Burgess & T. Huston (Eds.), *Social exchange in developing relations* (pp. 3–60). New York: Academic Press.

Ickes, W. (1993). Empathic accuracy. *Journal of Personality, 61*, 587–610.

Johnson, D. J., & Rusbult, C. E. (1989). Resisting temptation: Devaluation of alternative partners as a means of maintaining commitment in close relationships. *Journal of Personality and Social Psychology, 57*, 967–980.

Kelley, H. H. (1972). Attribution I social interaction. In E. E. Jones et al. (Eds.), *Attribution: Perceiving the causes of behavior*. Morristown, NJ: General Learning Press.

Lamm, H., & Schwinger, T. (1980). Norms concerning distributive justice. Are needs taken into consideration in allocation decisions? *Social Psychology Quarterly, 43*, 425–429.

Lamm, H., & Schwinger, T. (1983). Need consideration in allocation decisions: Is it just? *Journal of Social Psychology, 119*, 205–209.

Lerner, M. (1974). The justice motive: Equity and parity among children. *Journal of Personality and Social Psychology, 29*, 539–550.

Lloyd, S., Cate, R. M., & Henton, J. (1982). Equity and rewards as predictors of satisfaction in casual and intimate relationships. *Journal of Psychology, 110*, 43–48.

Lujansky, H., & Mikula, G. (1983). Can equity explain the quality and stability of romantic relationships? *British Journal of Social Psychology, 22*, 101–112.

Martin, M. W. (1985). Satisfaction with intimate exchange: Gender-role differences and impact of equity, equality, and rewards. *Sex Roles, 13*, 597–605.

Meeks, B. S., Hendrick, S. S., & Hendrick, C. (1998). Communication, love and relationship satisfaction. *Journal of Social & Personal Relationships, 15*, 755–773.

Michaels, J. W., Edwards, J. N., & Acock, A. C. (1984). Satisfaction in intimate relationships as a function of inequality, inequity, and outcomes. *Social Psychology Quarterly, 47*, 347–357.

Miller, L. C., Berg, J. H., & Archer, R. L. (1983). Openers: Individuals who elicit intimate self-disclosure. *Journal of Personality and Social Psychology, 44*, 1234–1244.

Mills, J., & Clark, M. S. (1982). Exchange and communal relationships. In L. Wheeler (Ed.), *Review of personality and social psychology* (pp. 121–144). Beverly Hills, CA: Sage.

Murray, S. L., & Holmes, J. G. (1993). Seeing virtues in faults: Negativity and the transformation of interpersonal narratives in close relationships. *Journal of Personality and Social Psychology, 65*, 707–722.

Murray, S. L., & Holmes, J. G. (1997). A leap of faith? Positive illusions in romantic relationships. *Personality and Social Psychology Bulletin, 23*, 586–604.

Murray, S. L., & Holmes, J. G. (1999). The mental ties that bind: Cognitive structures that predict relationship resilience. *Journal of Personality and Social Psychology, 77*, 1228–1244.

Murray, S. L., Holmes, J. G., & Griffin, D. (1996). The benefits of positive illusions: Idealization and the construction of satisfaction in close relationships. *Journal of Personality and Social Psychology, 70*, 79–98.

Murstein, B. I., Cerreto, M., & MacDonald, M. G. (1977). A theory and investigation of the effect of exchange-orientation on marriage and friendships. *Journal of Marriage and the Family, 39*, 543–548.

Noller, P. (1980). Misunderstandings in marital communication: A study of couples nonverbal communication. *Journal of Personality and Social Psychology, 39*, 1135–1148.

Noller, P. (1981). Gender and marital adjustment level differences in decoding messages from spouses and strangers. *Journal of Personality and Social Psychology, 41*, 272–278.

Purvis, J. A., Dabbs, J. M., & Hopper, C. H. (1984). The "opener": Skilled user of facial expression and speech pattern. *Personality and Social Psychology Bulletin, 10*, 61–66.

Reis, H. T., & Shaver, P. (1988). Intimacy as an interpersonal process. In S. W. Duck (Ed.), *Handbook of personal relationships* (pp. 367–389). New York: Wiley.

Rusbult, C. E. (1983). A longitudinal test of the investment model: The development (and deterioration) of satisfaction and commitment in heterosexual involvements. *Journal of Personality and Social Psychology, 45*, 101–117.

Sabatelli, R. M., & Cecil-Pigo, E. F. (1985). Relational interdependence and commitment in marriage. *Journal of Marriage and the Family, 47*, 931–937.

Simpson, J. A., & Rholes, W. S. (1998). Attachment theory and close relationships. New York: Guilford Press.

Sprecher, S. (1986). The relationship between inequity and emotions in close relationships. *Social Psychology Quarterly, 49*, 309–321.

Thibaut, J. W., & Kelley, H. H. (1959). *The social psychology of groups*. New York: Wiley.

Utne, M. K., Hatfield, E., Traupman, J., & Greenberger, D. (1984). Equity, marital satisfaction, and stability. *Journal of Social and Personal Relationships, 1*, 323–332.

Walster, E., Walster, G. W., & Berscheid, E. (1978). *Equity: Theory and research.* Boston: Allyn & Bacon.

CHAPTER SEVEN

Shared Participation in Self-Expanding Activities: Positive Effects on Experienced Marital Quality

Arthur Aron, Christine C. Norman,
Elaine N. Aron, and Gary Lewandowski

Uncertainty and mystery are energies of life. Don't let them scare you unduly, for they keep boredom at bay and spark creativity.

—R. I. Fitzhenry

The period when two people first fall in love often seems to be characterized by energized and intense emotions, preoccupation with each other
and the relationship, and great optimism. Yet over time, as the partners
get to know each other, there is a typical decline in this exhilaration,
often even a sense of apathy and boredom, a reduced interest in each
other and the relationship, and a less idealized vision of the future.
Indeed, a typical decline in love and satisfaction after the initial
relationship period is one of the most well-documented findings in the
study of marriage in Western cultures (for example, Blood & Wolfe,
1960; Glenn, 1990; Locke & Wallace, 1959; Rollins & Feldman, 1970;
Tucker & Aron, 1993).

However, there is considerable variation in the rate of this decline
(Tucker & Aron, 1993). One longitudinal study that followed newlyweds for four years found that as many as 10% showed an *increase* in
marital quality over this period (Karney & Bradbury, 1997). In addition,
studies of individuals who have been married 30 years or longer have
found small but significant numbers who report high levels of passionate love (Traupmann & Hatfield, 1981; Tucker & Aron, 1993), including high scores on Hatfield and Sprecher's (1986) Passionate Love Scale

Most of the research reported here was funded by a grant to the first author from the
National Science Foundation (No. 9514417). Correspondence regarding this chapter
should be addressed to Arthur Aron, Psychology Department, State University of New York, Stony Brook, NY 11794-2500; or send electronic mail to
aron@psych1.psy.sunysb.edu.

with items such as "I would rather be with ___ than anyone else." and "I melt when I look into ___'s eyes."

Surprisingly, however, there has been very little analysis of the mechanisms behind this typical honeymoon-then-years-of-blandness pattern, of the reasons why a few lucky couples manage to avoid this pattern, or, most important, of what can be done so that more couples could be among the lucky few. In this chapter we begin by reviewing briefly the self-expansion model (and relevant supporting research), a conceptual framework that we believe offers a comprehensive perspective on the underlying mechanisms driving the honeymoon-then-blandness pattern. As part of this analysis, we offer a specific hypothesis as to why some couples manage to avoid this pattern and maintain or reestablish high levels of relationship quality many years into marriage. We suggest concrete steps any married couple could take to maintain or reestablish such high levels of quality in their own marriage. Specifically, we hypothesize that in long-term marriages, couples can enhance their relationship quality substantially by participating together in what we call "self-expanding" (novel, challenging, arousing) activities. After laying this foundation, in the remainder of this chapter we summarize a series of studies we have conducted to test this hypothesis, including two survey studies, five laboratory experiments, and a field experiment.

THE SELF-EXPANSION MODEL

Key Propositions and Some Supporting Data

The self-expansion model (Aron & Aron, 1996; 1997; Aron, Aron, & Norman, 2001) is an overarching conceptual framework for understanding cognition and motivation in close relationships. It has two key propositions. The first proposition is that a fundamental and central human motivation is to expand one's potential efficacy – that is, to increase one's resources (physical, social, and knowledge), perspectives, and identities (Aron, Norman, & Aron, 1998). The second proposition is that one common way that people attempt to bring about such an expansion is by forming close relationships, because in a close relationship the other is "included in the self" in the sense that in a close relationship, the partner's resources, perspectives, and identities are to some extent treated as one's own (Aron & Aron, 1996; Aron, Aron, Tudor, & Nelson, 1991; Aron & Fraley, 1999).

This model has generated a number of studies in the close-relationship area that lend support to key aspects of the model. For example, Aron, Paris, and Aron (1995; study 1) administered to approximately 300 U.S. college students open-ended measures of spontaneous self-concept ("who are you today?") every two weeks, for a total of five times over a one-term period. The questionnaires also asked about their various experiences over the last two weeks, and among these items was one about whether they had "fallen in love." About a third reported having fallen in love during the term. As predicted by the model, these participants showed a substantial increase from before to after falling in love in the number of different domains included in their spontaneous self-concept. That is, after falling in love, they included in their responses to "Who are you today?," a greater variety of roles, emotions, and descriptors of various kinds. In contrast (and as expected), they did not show any consistent pattern of change from before to after other testing periods (when they did not fall in love); nor was there any reliable pattern of testing-to-testing change for those who did not fall in love at all during the term.

A follow-up study (Aron et al., 1995, study 2) employed a similar design with approximately 500 students followed over a term. However, instead of measuring spontaneous self-concept, this study employed measures of perceived self-efficacy. This study also supported the expected pattern based on the self-expansion model: For those who fell in love, there was a significant increase in self-efficacy from before to after falling in love, but no consistent pattern of change from before to after other testing periods (when they did not fall in love); nor was there any reliable pattern of testing-to-testing change in self-efficacy for those who did not fall in love at all during the term.

Other studies have examined the proposition of the self-expansion model that, in a close relationship, each partner "includes the other in the self." Much of this work has focused on the specific prediction that, to some extent, individuals in a close relationship actually confuse themselves with the close others. Put more precisely, this hypothesis is that there is an overlap in cognitive representations (or activation potentials) of self and close others.

For example, participants in one study (Aron et al., 1991, study 3a) first rated themselves and their spouse on a series of trait adjectives. Later each trait was presented on a computer screen in a task in which participants were to indicate as rapidly as possible whether the trait described themselves. The prediction was that they would be slower at rating a trait as true for self when the trait was not also true for their partner. (And similarly, they would be slower at rating a trait as false for themselves when the trait was not also false for the spouse.)

Consider an example. A man is doing this task and the word "energetic" appears on the screen to which he is to respond by pressing a key marked "me" or a key marked "not me." Suppose he sees himself as energetic and also sees his wife as energetic. (We know how he sees himself and how he sees his wife on "energetic" and various other traits based on a questionnaire he completed at another time.) In this case, he will respond "me," and he will do so fairly quickly. Now suppose the trait "anxious" comes up, and he sees himself as anxious but does not see his wife as anxious. He will still respond "me" – he does see himself as anxious. But according to our model, in this case, he will make this "me" response more slowly. That is, he is only responding about himself and nothing is being asked about his wife. However, because his wife is in a sense part of who he is, there is some interference in saying something is true of him when it is in fact not true of part of him – the part that is his wife! To put this more precisely, to the extent the two representations overlap or are interconnected, accessing elements of one will be facilitated by like elements of the other and inhibited by unlike elements of the other.

The predicted facilitation/interference effects were in fact found. Traits that differed between self and spouse (true of self but false of spouse, or vice versa) were consistently rated more slowly for self than were traits that were true of both (or false of both). Aron et al. (1991, study 3b) replicated this finding with a second sample of married couples. It has also been replicated with dating couples in two independent studies (Aron & Fraley, 1999; Smith, Coats, & Walling, 1999). Perhaps most interestingly, in these more recent studies the *degree* of the effect (the amount of slow-down when the partner was not the same as self) correlated strongly with self-reported closeness and love for the partner.

Another set of studies that support this idea has used a different approach. Participants in a study by Mashek, Aron, and Boncimino (2001, study 1) rated some traits for themselves, other traits for their partner, and still other traits for a media celebrity. Later, participants were shown each trait and asked to indicate for whom they had initially rated it. The predictions here focused on the cases in which participants misremembered for which person they had originally rated the trait. Based on the self-expansion model's inclusion of other in the self idea (and specifically the notion of overlapping cognitive representations), we predicted that there would be significantly more cases of confusing self and partner than of confusing either self or partner with the media celebrity.

Again, consider an example. A woman is doing this task and rates the trait "artistic" and a number of other traits for how true they are for herself. She rates a different set of traits, such as "outgoing," for how true each is of her husband. And she rates yet another set of traits for a famous movie star. Later she is shown each trait on a computer screen and asked for whom she initially rated it. Thus, when "artistic" comes up, the correct answer would be "self." But what if she gets it wrong? The prediction of our model is that if she gets it wrong, she will be more likely to think she rated "artistic" for her husband than that she rated "artistic" for the movie star. Similarly, when the trait "outgoing" comes up, the correct answer would be husband. But if she gets it wrong, our model is that she will be more likely to think she had rated it for herself than for the movie star.

The predicted confusion effects were found. When participants made mistakes in indicating for whom they had initially rated the applicability of a trait, they were much more likely to confuse traits rated for self as having been rated for their romantic partner than for the celebrity. Similarly, when they made mistakes in indicating for whom they had initially rated a trait that was originally rated for the romantic partner, they were more likely to think they had rated the trait for the self than for the celebrity.

Further, the *degree* to which participants made this kind of confusion with their partner was significantly correlated with the quality of their relationship with their partner. In addition, a series of follow-up studies also demonstrated that this effect could not be explained by familiarity with, or similarity to, the partner, or to something special about a media celebrity as opposed to other individuals with whom one is not close (Mashek et al., 2001, study 2 and discussion).

In sum, several lines of work support key propositions of the self-expansion model that people seek to expand their potential self-efficacy, and that one way they seek to do so is by including others in the self in a close relationship. In particular, research to date supports the ideas that the formation of a close relationship expands the salient domains of self and increases perceived self-efficacy, and that in a close relationship individuals do indeed seem to include the other in the self, even to the extent of confusing self and other (and the closer they are, the more they do this).

Implications for Understanding (and Reversing) the Typical Honeymoon-then-Years-of-Blandness Pattern

The self-expansion model suggests that the exhilaration of falling in love during initial relationship formation is due to each partner's rapid expansion of self. That is, it is during this period that each comes to know and incorporate into the self, at a rapid rate, the other's resources, perspectives, and identities. Indeed, we have spelled out at some length elsewhere (Aron et al., 1998) that a major source of positive affect of any kind is rapid self-expansion – a position consistent in a general way with similar notions in Carver and Scheier's (1990) self-regulation model, and the general motivational aspect of Pyszczynski, Greenberg, and Solomon's (1997) Terror Management Theory.

Once a couple has come to know each other, however, the opportunities for further rapid expansion by including the other in the self inevitably decrease. Partners continue to change and we continue to discover previously unappreciated aspects of our partners to include in the self. However, the rate of expansion when going from an unknown to a beloved partner (as when first falling in love) is likely to be much greater than the rate of expansion when going from a known partner to a better known partner (as in a long-term marriage). This is in a sense a basic problem of habituation. Indeed, the little previous research and theorizing that has attempted to address the typical decline in relationship quality over time have mainly focused on habituation-type approaches (Aronson & Linder, 1965; Berger, 1988; Huesmann, 1980; Jacobson & Margolin, 1979; Livingston, 1980; Plutchik, 1967).

Why then should there be variation in the pattern of relationship quality over time? And what could be done to ameliorate or reverse the typical decline? One idea we proposed in our initial analysis of the situation (Aron & Aron, 1986) is that, once the partners know each other fairly well so that substantial rapid expansion is no longer available through relationship formation, an alternative would be for the couple to engage in other rapidly self-expanding activities together. In this way, the experience of rapid self-expansion is associated with their relationship (even if not directly due to the relationship). That is, initially, relationship formation provided rapid self-expansion that was inherently linked to the relationship – and thus, the relationship was experienced as being passionate and of very high quality. Once this period is over, we are proposing that some of the same effect might be obtained by other self-expanding activities (that is, other than forming the relationship), providing the self-expanding activities are done in a way that associates them with the relationship (such as by doing them together).[1] Specifically, the kinds of activities that should create this exhilarating experience of rapid self-expansion should be those that are highly novel or challenging (at least if success is also anticipated or expected). Also, because novelty and challenge are typically arousing (Berlyne, 1960), people probably come to associate self-expanding experiences with arousal. Such an association would also seem likely since many arousing activities (such as athletic games and demanding physical feats) are self-expanding. Thus, by association, arousing activities probably tend to create the exhilaration of rapid self-expansion, even over and above any novel or challenging aspects they may have. Thus, in terms of our hypothesis about shared self-expanding activities, the specific kinds of shared activities that should provide the most impact on the quality of married life are those that are novel and challenging, and also arousing.

There are a number of survey studies showing strong correlations between shared activities of any kind and marital quality (Kilbourne, Howell, & England, 1990; Kingston & Nock, 1987; Orden & Bradburn, 1968; Orthner, 1975; White, 1983). More important, in those studies that have provided a more fine-grained analysis, it has been mainly shared participation in the kinds of activities most likely to provide a sense of self-expansion that has been most strongly linked to relationship quality. For example, the strongest correlations are found for activities that are intensely interactive (Holman & Jacquart, 1988; Kingston & Nock, 1987; Orden & Bradburn, 1968; Orthner, 1975) or that involve recreational activities that are at least somewhat active and arousing (Hill, 1988).

However, there have been no previous studies directly relevant to our hypothesis that shared participation in self-expanding activities enhances relationship quality. Further, even to the extent that previous studies provide some indirect support for our hypothesis, they are entirely correlational and leave open the possibility that the causal direction is from marital quality to engaging in such activities.

[1] Other possibilities are also suggested by the model. For example, couples who live apart for long periods and then reunite might get the benefit of rapid self-expansion on each reunion, particularly if there was great change in either partner during the separations. Or one member could continually withhold a great deal of his or her self, as in cases of unrequited love, which tends to help keep love intense for years. However, these "solutions" have obvious limitations.

STUDIES TESTING THE HYPOTHESIZED POSITIVE
EFFECTS ON MARITAL QUALITY OF SHARED
PARTICIPATION IN SELF-EXPANDING ACTIVITIES

Again, based on the self-expansion model, we hypothesize that participating together in novel, challenging, and arousing activities can enhance marital quality. As we have also just indicated, prior to our undertaking the line of studies described here, there was virtually no research – and only minimal theoretical speculation – on the reasons for the typical decline in relationship quality over time, or on relationship boredom or habituation more generally. As we discussed, there *have* been studies linking time spent with partner and relationship quality, but these studies have been almost entirely atheoretical, purely correlational, and have had little to say about what specific *kinds* of shared activities might be particularly impactful.

With regard to theory, the other major relationship models contribute little to an understanding of the early decline in satisfaction and love – let alone of ways to avoid it. Instead, they seem to assume that a relationship will be at least adequately satisfying so long as, for example, one sees one's own outcomes as interdependent on the other's, or the partners have secure attachment styles and low neuroticism. These factors have been demonstrated to have significant associations with relationship quality – but they do not appear able to explain the standard pattern of decline in relationship quality over time.

Survey Studies

As our first attempt to test our hypothesis, we conducted two surveys. The first (Aron, Norman, Aron, McKenna, & Heyman, 2000, study 1) was a newspaper survey. In this survey, respondents completed a mail-in questionnaire that included the key item "How exciting are the things you do together with your partner?" (The word "exciting" served as an ordinary-language operationalization suitable for self-report that corresponds to our concept of the experience of self-expansion.) The questionnaire also included a standard marital satisfaction scale, a standard measure of relationship-related socially desirable response tendencies, plus some items we developed about overall boredom and excitement with the relationship.

The results were entirely consistent with predictions of the self-expansion model: There was a strong and significant association between reported shared participation in self-expanding activities and relationship satisfaction. That is, the more respondents reported engaging in exciting activities with their partner, the more satisfied they reported they were with their relationship. Further, this association held up after controlling statistically for social desirability response bias. This is particularly important because this result makes unlikely the possibility that the activities-satisfaction association is due to people just rating everything about their relationship with the same degree of positivity.

In addition, and especially interesting in light of our theorizing, we conducted analyses to test the prediction that the association of self-expanding activities with relationship satisfaction was mediated by relationship boredom. These analyses supported the prediction. That is, when reported relationship boredom was included in the regression equation, the size of the direct path from self-expanding activities to relationship quality was substantially (and statistically significantly) reduced. Thus, these results are consistent with the interpretation that self-expanding activities reduce relationship boredom, which in turn increases relationship satisfaction. (These mediation results also held up nicely after controlling statistically for relationship-relevant social desirability response tendencies.)

We conducted the second survey (Aron et al., 2000, study 2) to replicate these results with a new sample and to overcome possible methodological limitations of the newspaper survey approach. This was a door-to-door survey conducted in a small U.S. seaside university town. Respondents in this study completed exactly the same questionnaires used in the newspaper survey. Results again supported our hypotheses from the self-expansion model, and were virtually identical to those in the newspaper survey. That is, there was a strong and significant association between self-expanding activities and marital satisfaction, this association was significantly mediated by relationship boredom, and all of the results held up after controlling statistically for social desirability response tendencies.

Laboratory Studies of the Basic Effect

Encouraged by these initial survey results, we next conducted a series of true experiments (Aron et al., 2000, studies 3–5), where random assignment to conditions allowed us to draw unambiguous conclusions about the direction of causality. That is, these studies allowed us to test directly the extent to which couple's shared participation in self-expanding activities can cause an increase in relationship quality.

In each of these experiments, couples were recruited to participate in what they believed was a relationship evaluation session, in which they would complete some questionnaires, be videotaped participating together in a physical activity, and then complete additional questionnaires. What was really going on was that the first set of questionnaires included baseline, pretest measures of experienced relationship quality; the physical activity was experimentally manipulated to be either self-expanding (novel, challenging, and arousing) versus mundane (pleasant, but less novel and not arousing or challenging); and the final set of questionnaires included the posttest measures of experienced relationship quality.

In each of these three experiments, in the self-expanding condition, the couple was tied together on one side at the wrists and ankles and then had to crawl together on gym mats across a 10-meter distance, climbing over a barrier at the center, while pushing a foam cylinder with their heads. This was a timed task and the couple won a prize if they beat a time limit. The situation was set up so that couples almost finished within the prize-winning time the first two tries and then just barely finished within the time on the third try. The mundane task was designed to be as similar as possible, but much less novel and not at all challenging or arousing. It mainly involved the couple just crawling back and forth at the same time and at a slow pace for about seven minutes.

In each study using these procedures, manipulation checks showed that the self-expanding activity was clearly experienced as much more exciting, interesting, and so forth, as compared to the mundane activity. That is, we did seem to be manipulating something like our concept of experienced self-expansion. Of course we realize that these tasks are far removed from what couples might do in everyday life. We later present some data with more obvious external validity. However, our purpose here was to create a laboratory operationalization of our concept of experienced self-expansion that genuinely engaged the partners and permitted high levels of experimental control.

The measures of relationship quality given before and after the physical activity in these experiments included standard marital satisfaction scales and standard measures of passionate love. These two kinds of measures were substantially correlated. Thus, the results we describe below for change in reported relationship quality are based on pretest and posttest composites, each comprised of measures of both satisfaction and passionate love.

The first of these experiments tested the basic effect with a sample of mainly dating or living-together undergraduate couples. The results supported our hypothesis. There was substantially and significantly greater before-to-after change in relationship quality for couples in the self-expanding task condition than for couples in the mundane task condition.

This result was very important in providing an initial demonstration that the association between self-expanding activities and relationship quality is due, at least in part, to a causal effect from involvement in the activities to relationship quality. However, the results of our initial experiment were ambiguous in that the difference in effect between the two conditions, which we hypothesized was due to an increase in relationship quality from doing the novel/arousing activity, could instead have resulted from something about the mundane condition somehow decreasing relationship quality.[2]

Thus, in addition to the two experimental conditions used in the initial experiment, in our second experiment we randomly assigned a third of our couples to a no-activity control condition. Also, in this experiment (and all of the others described below), our participants were married couples recruited from the mainly working-class, Long Island, New York area.

The results of this three-condition study replicated our basic finding from the previous experiment. Once again, we found the predicted greater increase in marital quality for the couples doing the self-expanding task compared to the couples doing the mundane task. Most important, consistent with our hypothesis, when comparing these changes to the change for the couples in the no-activity control condition, the effect was clearly due to an increase in the self-expanding condition and not to a decrease in the mundane condition.

Still, even with this result, another concern remained regarding the basic effect: Could these results somehow be due to social desirability

---

[2] We could not test this directly from the data in this study because the pretest and posttest composites consisted of different items. (This was done so that participants would not realize that the study was a pretest-posttest design and so that they would not just give the same answers at the posttest as recalled from the pretest.) Thus, the results we report for differences in "change" between conditions are based on differences between conditions in posttest scores controlling for pretest scores. It is not possible to determine from such residualized change scores whether the absolute level of change was an increase or decrease. Further, even if we had identical pretest and posttest measures, an absolute increase or decrease could well be confounded with effects of repeated testing.

response biases, or in some other way be an artifact of our self-report measures of relationship quality? As one check on this possibility, in both of the experiments we just described (as we had also in the survey studies), we included measures of relationship-relevant social desirability response bias. And in each case, when we statistically controlled for scores on these social desirability measures, the pattern of results was unchanged.

Nevertheless, we also thought it important to test the basic effect using a measure of marital quality that did not depend at all on participants' self-reports. Thus, in our next experiment we added a standardized discussion task both before and after the experimentally manipulated physical activity. In one of these tasks, participants spent five minutes discussing how they would use $15,000 to make home improvements; in the other they were to plan a vacation together. The videotapes of these discussions were analyzed later with a standard coding scheme by trained raters who did not know which experimental condition the participants were in – or anything at all about the experiment.

Once again, our usual *questionnaire* measures showed the now-standard pattern of greater increases in relationship quality for the self-expanding condition couples than for the mundane condition couples. However, what was new here is that we *also* found the same pattern for the ratings of the discussion. That is, from before to after the physical activity, the discussions of couples doing the self-expanding activity, compared to those doing the mundane activity, showed a pattern of less hostility and negativity and more acceptance and support. Thus, not only was self-reported marital quality impacted by participation in self-expanding activities, but so also was the actual quality of a married couple's interaction as rated by outside observers.

Laboratory Experiments to Clarify Mechanisms

Having found the basic effect in the surveys and these three laboratory experiments, we turned to a further examination of the mechanisms involved, and of potential alternative explanations. We also assessed whether the key ingredient in the effect was the novelty and challenge aspect or the arousal aspect of our tasks.

Regarding alternative explanations, it was possible that the effects in the initial experiments do not depend on sharing the activities, but simply on each partner feeling good from doing the self-expanding task. Yet another possibility was that the effect might arise entirely from the couple's cooperation in doing a complex task together and not specifically from the task being self-expanding. Our theoretical model, on the other hand, holds that the effect depends importantly on the partner being salient at the time of experiencing the rapid self-expansion, and that the effect of the sense of expansion is over and above any benefit of experienced cooperation.

Thus, we next conducted an experiment in which participants did a version of the standard self-expanding activity *individually*, but we manipulated whether or not the partner was salient while doing the activity (Aron, Norman, & Aron, 2001). In this experiment, the participant did the task alone across the mat, but the task required him or her to look at a directional arrow that was just below a TV screen. That is, as they were going across the mat they needed to look at the arrow to know which side to take the foam cylinder. This was done to be sure that participants would have reason to notice anything that might be on the TV screen. For half the participants, the screen was showing the participant's partner filling out a questionnaire in the next room. For the other half, the TV was turned off. Thus, in one condition, the partner was salient to the participant at the time he or she was doing the self-expanding task; in the other condition, the partner was not particularly salient. (We should note that the experiment was designed so that the TV aspect seemed entirely incidental.)

The results were as predicted: A clearly greater increase in experienced relationship quality for those who did the activity while their partner was shown on the screen, compared to those in the control condition. This result is not easily explained by participants rating their relationship quality higher just because they were in a good mood at the moment of doing the ratings. The procedure was entirely the same in both conditions at the time of doing the ratings. The only thing that differed was the salience of the partner *during the task*. These results also can not be easily explained as due to a cooperation effect, since the activity was carried out alone.

Another question raised by these studies is how much of the effect is due to self-expanding activities being novel and challenging versus being arousing. This issue is particularly important theoretically since there is a long tradition of work in the area of initial romantic attraction suggesting that arousal by itself may create attraction (for example, Dutton & Aron, 1974; for a review, see Foster, Witcher, Campbell, & Green, 1998). Thus, we wanted to test our theory's prediction that the effect is primarily due to the self-expansion aspect, and not merely an effect of arousal, such as misattribution of arousal.

This experiment (Lewandowski & Aron, 2001, study 1) employed a 2 × 2 design, with novelty challenge and arousal being independently manipulated. That is, couples were randomly assigned to one of four groups: novel challenging/aroused, novel challenging/nonaroused, mundane/aroused, and mundane/nonaroused. In all conditions, couples began the task on opposite corners of a 2.5 × 3.5 meter rectangle. In the novel-challenging conditions, they had to bounce an unevenly balanced ball inside a hula-hoop target and across the rectangle to their partner, then each went along the long side of the rectangle to the other two corners and repeated the task. It was a timed task with rewards for number of completed catches; the ball was difficult to bounce accurately. In the mundane conditions, participants simply went back and forth from corner to corner, with no ball involved at all. Manipulation check measures of experienced self-expanding showed a very strong difference between the two conditions.

To manipulate arousal, when doing the above tasks, participants in the high arousal conditions ran back and forth from corner to corner wearing three-pound ankle weights. In the low-arousal condition, they walked slowly back and forth with no weights. The effect was that in the arousing conditions, by the end of the task period they were huffing and puffing; in the nonarousing conditions they were quite rested and unaroused.

The results were clear: There was little if any effect for arousal. However, as predicted by the self-expansion model, there was a strong effect for novelty challenge.[3]

In sum, these two experiments support the specific predictions of the self-expansion model. For the enhancement of marital quality, the partner must be salient (as the partner is when the activity is shared). Cooperation is not necessary. Nor is arousal necessary for the effect.

----

[3] We also conducted this same experiment, but using stranger pairs and measuring initial attraction (Lewandowski & Aron, 2001, study 2). Consistent with the earlier work on arousal and initial attraction, and unlike the study we just described with married couples, we found a clear effect of greater attraction in the arousing than the nonarousing conditions. At the same time, and also unlike our finding for married couples, there was little or no effect of novelty-challenge on initial attraction. In other words, these two studies suggest that shared participation in self-expanding activities enhances relationship quality for married couples because these activities are directly self-expanding (novel and challenging) and that arousal has little to do with it. But when it comes to initial attraction, the key factor seems to be arousal – perhaps due to a misattribution of arousal mechanism that would be less likely with a long-term partner.

Field Experiment

Does all this work in the real world? That is, the survey studies demonstrated that under real-world conditions, self-expanding activities are *associated* with relationship quality. The laboratory studies untangled the *causal direction* of this association under highly controlled conditions (as well as helping sort out the underlying mechanisms). However, none of the studies we've described so far address the question of whether, under real-world conditions, there is a causal direction from self-expanding activities to relationship quality.

Actually, this study was one of the first we had done (Reissman, Aron, & Bergen, 1993). In this experiment, volunteer married couples completed standard marital satisfaction scales at the start and end of a 10-week period. Participants were randomly assigned to participate in one of three kinds of activities during these 10 weeks: Couples assigned to a self-expanding activities group were instructed to spend an hour and a half each week doing one of a set of activities we listed for them. These were all activities that were selected because, on prestudy questionnaires, both partners had independently rated them as "exciting" (as noted earlier, this is the lay language term we have found that best corresponds to novel, challenging, and arousing and to what we mean by self-expanding). Examples of exciting activities on these lists that participants actually carried out included attending musical concerts, plays, and lectures; skiing; hiking; and going dancing. Couples in a pleasant activities group were assigned activities that both had rated as "pleasant," but not as particularly exciting (for example, going out to dinner or a movie, attending church). A third group of couples served as a waiting-list, no-activity control group.

The results of this field experiment clearly supported our hypothesis. The self-expanding-activity group, compared to both of the other two groups, showed a significantly greater increase in relationship quality over the 10 weeks. What is most important about this study is that it demonstrates the basic effect experimentally in a real-world setting with couples engaging in real-world self-expanding activities.

CONCLUSION

In this chapter we have focused on what we believe is a key problem in Western-style marriage, the typical tendency after the initial "honeymoon period" for there to be a steep and lasting decline in relationship quality. We next summarized the self-expansion model and some supporting research, and then put forward a hypothesis developed from this model, that long-term couples can ameliorate or even reverse this typical decline by engaging in shared activities that are novel and challenging. On this foundation, we presented a series of surveys and laboratory and field experiments that lend support to this hypothesis.

On the one hand, we are very aware that the work we have presented here has a number of important limitations. Most important, we have not tested our hypothesis with clinical samples or even as a systematic educational intervention with normal couples, and there has also been no long-term follow-up. Further, there are aspects of the effect that remain to be clarified (such as the specific role of experiencing success).

On the other hand, we are very encouraged by the present results. They provide strong initial support for a theoretical model that appears to be useful to an increasing number of relationship researchers. These results also provide strong initial support for the practical potential of an apparently straightforward procedure (doing self-expanding activities together). Indeed, this is a procedure that would seem to be capable of being implemented by virtually any couple, even those who would resist or be otherwise unsuitable for the usual verbal counseling methods, and that would appear to require minimal professional resources.

REFERENCES

Aron, A., & Aron, E. N. (1996). Self and self-expansion in relationships. In G. J. O. Fletcher & J. Fitness (Eds.), *Knowledge structures in close relationships: A social psychological approach* (pp. 325–344). Mahwah, NJ: Lawrence Erlbaum Associates.

Aron, A., & Aron, E. N. (1997). Self-expansion motivation and including other in the self. In W. Ickes (Section Ed.) & S. Duck (Ed.), *Handbook of personal relationships* (vol. 1, pp. 251–270). London: Wiley.

Aron, A., Aron, E. N., & Norman, C. (2001). Self-expansion model of motivation and cognition in close relationships and beyond. In M. Clark & G. Fletcher (Eds.), *Blackwell's handbook of social psychology, vol. 2: Interpersonal processes* (pp. 478–501). Oxford: Blackwell Publishers.

Aron, A., Aron, E. N., Tudor, M., & Nelson, G. (1991). Close relationships as including other in the self. *Journal of Personality and Social Psychology, 60,* 241–253.

Aron, A., & Fraley, B. (1999). Relationship closeness as including other in the self: Cognitive underpinnings and measures. *Social Cognition, 17,* 140–160.

Aron, A., Norman, C. C., & Aron, E. N. (1998). The self-expansion model and motivation. *Representative Research in Social Psychology, 22,* 1–13.

Aron, A., Norman, C. C., & Aron, E. N. (2001). *The effect of self-expanding activities on relationship quality: Is sharing the activities or cooperation necessary?* Manuscript in preparation.

Aron, A., Norman, C. C., & Aron, E. N., McKenna, C., & Heyman, R. (2000). Couples' shared participation in novel and arousing activities and experienced relationship quality. *Journal of Personality and Social Psychology, 78,* 273–284.

Aron, A., Paris, M., & Aron, E. N. (1995). Falling in love: Prospective studies of self-concept change. *Journal of Personality and Social Psychology, 69,* 1102–1112.

Aronson, E., & Linder, D. (1965). Gain and loss of esteem as determinants of interpersonal attraction. *Journal of Experimental Social Psychology, 1,* 156–171.

Berger, C. R. (1988). Uncertainty and information exchange in developing relationships. In S. Duck (Ed.), *Handbook of personal relationships: Theory, research and interventions* (pp. 367–389). Chichester, England: Wiley.

Berlyne, D. E. (1960). *Conflict, arousal, and curiosity.* New York: McGraw-Hill.

Blood, R., & Wolfe, D. W. (1960). *Husbands and wives.* Glencoe, IL: The Free Press.

Carver, C., & Scheier, M. (1990). Principles of self-regulation, action, and emotion. In E. T. Higgins & R. M. Sorrentino (Eds.), *Handbook of motivation and cognition: Foundations of social behavior* (vol. 2) (pp. 3–52). New York: Guilford.

Dutton, D. G., & Aron, A. (1974). Some evidence for heightened sexual attraction under conditions of high anxiety. *Journal of Personality and Social Psychology, 30,* 510–517.

Foster, C. A., Witcher, B. S., Campbell, W. K., & Green, J. D. (1998). Arousal and attraction: Evidence for automatic and controlled processes. *Journal of Personality and Social Psychology, 74,* 86–101.

Glenn, N. D. (1990). Quantitative research on marital quality in the 1980s: A critical review. *Journal of Marriage and the Family, 52,* 818–831.

Hatfield, E., & Sprecher, S. (1986). Measuring passionate love in intimate relationships. *Journal of Adolescence, 9,* 383–410.

Hill, M. S. (1988). Marital stability and spouses' shared time: A multidisciplinary hypothesis. *Journal of Family Issues, 9,* 427–451.

Holman, T. B., & Jacquart, M. (1988). Leisure-activity patterns and marital satisfaction: A further test. *Journal of Marriage and the Family, 50,* 69–77.

Huesmann, L. (1980). Toward a predictive model of romantic behavior. In K. Pope (Ed.), *On love and loving* (pp. 152–171). San Francisco: Jossey-Bass.

Jacobson, N. S., & Margolin, G. (1979). *Marital therapy: Strategies based on social learning and behavior exchange principles.* New York: Brunner/Mazel.

Karney, B. R., & Bradbury, T. N. (1997). Neuroticism, marital interaction, and the trajectory of marital satisfaction. *Journal of Personality and Social Psychology, 72,* 1075–1092.

Kilbourne, B. S., Howell, F., & England, P. (1990). A measurement model for subjective marital solidarity: Invariance across time, gender, and life cycle stage. *Social Science Research, 19,* 62–81.

Kingston, P. W., & Nock, S. L. (1987). Time together among dual-earner couples. *American Sociological Review, 52*, 391–400.

Lewandowski, G., & Aron, A. (2001). *Shared participation in self-expanding activities and relationship quality: Novelty/challenge versus arousal.* Manuscript in preparation.

Livingston, K. R. (1980). Love as a process of reducing uncertainty – Cognitive theory. In K. S. Pope et al. (Eds.), *On love and loving* (pp. 133–151). San Francisco: Jossey-Bass.

Locke, H. J., & Wallace, K. M. (1959). Short marital adjustment and prediction tests: Their reliability and validity. *Marriage and Family Living, 21*, 251–255.

Mashek, D. J., Aron, A., & Boncimino, M. (2001). *Confusions of self and close others.* Manuscript in preparation.

Orden, S. R., & Bradburn, N. M. (1968). Dimensions of marriage happiness. *American Journal of Sociology, 73*, 715–731.

Orthner, D. K. (1975). Leisure activity patterns and marital satisfaction over the marital career. *Journal of Marriage and the Family, 37*, 91–101.

Plutchik, R. (1967). Marriage as dynamic equilibrium: Implications for research. In H. L. Silverman (Ed.), *Marital counseling: Psychology, ideology, science* (pp. 347–367). Springfield, IL: Charles C. Thomas.

Pyszczynski, T. A., Greenberg, J., & Solomon, S. (1997). Why do we need what we need? A terror management perspective on the roots of human social motivation. *Psychological Inquiry, 8*, 1–20.

Reissman, C., Aron, A., & Bergen, M. R. (1993). Shared activities and marital satisfaction: Causal direction and self-expansion versus boredom. *Journal of Social and Personal Relationships, 10*, 243–254.

Rollins, B., & Feldman, H. (1970). Marriage satisfaction over the family life cycle. *Journal of Marriage and the Family, 32*, 20–28.

Smith, E., Coats, S., & Walling, D. (1999). Overlapping mental representations of self, in-group, and partner: Further response time evidence and a connectionist model. *Personality and Social Psychology Bulletin, 25*, 873–882.

Traupmann, J., & Hatfield, E. (1981). Love and its effects on mental and physical health. In J. March, S. Kiesler, R. Fogel, E. Hatfield, & E. Shana (Eds.), *Aging: Stability and change in the family* (pp. 253–274). New York: Academic.

Tucker, P., & Aron, A. (1993). Passionate love and marital satisfaction at key transition points in the family life cycle. *Journal of Social and Clinical Psychology, 12*, 135–147.

White, L. K. (1983). Determinants of spousal interaction: Marital structure or marital happiness. *Journal of Marriage and the Family, 45*, 511–519.

COPING WITH DISAPPOINTMENT, CRITICISM, AND BETRAYAL

Introduction to Section Three

Although there has been a long history of researchers focusing on conflict in marital relationships, the area of study known as the "dark side of relationships" has been a more recent development. This area tends to focus on a number of relatively neglected behaviors and emotions, such as disappointment, rejection, neglect, betrayal, and infidelity. The dynamics associated with these kinds of relationship events are likely to be very complex; different kinds of responses from one partner may have very different effects on the emotions experienced by the other partner, and on the future of the relationship.

We all enter relationships with expectations about how partners should treat us, and about how we should benefit from being in the relationship. These expectations and standards guide our evaluations of our relationships. In all relationships, however, there are occasions when these standards are not met. How we respond to such occasions will inevitably have an impact on our satisfaction with our relationships.

Vangelisti and Alexander present an inductive analysis of responses to disappointment in marriage. This analysis highlights the wide variety of possible responses to unmet standards, including such diverse coping strategies as anger, self-disparagement, getting even, ignoring the event, trying to revitalize the relationship, believing the partner will change, and seeking intervention from a third party. The authors describe how these strategies differ in terms of five important dimensions: expression versus suppression of distress, focusing on the self versus the partner, recognition of the unmet standard versus rationalization, relationship versus network as the locus for action, and constructive versus destructive outcomes.

This analysis extends the traditional literature on stress and coping, by considering the features that are unique to ongoing relationships.

Specifically, the impact of a given coping strategy is likely to depend on the response of the partner: For example, Mary might try to revitalize her relationship with Michael by increasing her efforts to please him, but this strategy can only work if he appreciates those efforts and responds appropriately to them. Similarly, the impact of a particular strategy will be affected by the history of the relationship: Michael's belief that his partner will change (and hence, not disappoint him again) may be constructive in the event of a single disappointment, but seems less appropriate if Mary has repeatedly engaged in the negative behavior. Hence, it may not be possible to make generalizations about whether particular strategies are inherently positive or negative, effective or ineffective. In short, it is crucial to remember that coping strategies are embedded within relationships, and to consider relationship dynamics in exploring instances of unmet standards.

Although many relationship behaviors are neither inherently positive or negative, some have negative consequences in almost any context. For example, the tendency to react aggressively to real or imagined criticism or rejection can have very negative consequences for relationships.

In their chapter, Schweinle and Ickes explore the issue of husband-to-wife abuse, comparing two alternative hypotheses: first, that abusive men overattribute criticism and rejection to women's thoughts and feelings, and second, that abusive men are particularly sensitive to, and vigilant for, actual signs of criticism and rejection. According to the former hypothesis, abusive men tend to perceive criticism and rejection in women's communications, even when none was intended. In contrast, the latter hypothesis suggests that men's abuse is a response to their accurately inferring that women are harboring critical thoughts and feelings about them. Evaluating these hypotheses is important, because it has implications for the design of interventions likely to reduce abusive behavior.

A noteworthy feature of the work reported by these researchers is their use of an experimental method. This method involved a community-based sample of married men viewing a series of stimulus tapes depicting therapy sessions with female clients. The men were asked to describe the thoughts and feelings of these women at various points throughout the tape, and to indicate whether the women were being critical or rejecting of their male partners. The data were analyzed using signal detection theory, a method borrowed from cognitive psychology. In this way, the researchers could control for actual levels of criticism and rejection, and show that abusive and insecure men displayed a bias to infer negative intentions, even when decoding the thoughts and feelings of female strangers. In other words, these men tend to see women's intentions negatively, even in the absence of any previous interaction on which to base those judgments. This finding is important in illustrating how individual characteristics shape the dynamics of couple relationships.

Whereas Schweinle and Ickes focus on biased perceptions of negativity, Rusbult and her colleagues discuss responses to actual instances of betrayal. Such topics as betrayal and forgiveness have only recently been studied by psychologists, having previously been mainly the province of philosophers and theologians. Psychologists are now trying to explore these issues, focusing particularly on the patterns of cognition, affect, and interaction that accompany instances of betrayal, and the factors that influence the level of forgiveness achieved.

Rusbult and her colleagues analyze these issues from the perspective of interdependence theory, which emphasizes the ways in which relationship partners manage the complex interactions that characterize their ongoing relationship. The central role of cognitive processes is evident throughout their analysis. For example, they define betrayal in terms of the violation of norms and relationship rules, and discuss the systematic differences between victims' and perpetrators' perceptions and explanations of instances of betrayal.

The authors make important distinctions between the concepts of forgiveness, reconciliation, and renegotiation. Again, cognitive processes such as attributions of responsibility are central to these distinctions. Another important distinction is between self-centered response preferences, which focus on maximizing one's own immediate self-interest, and broader preferences, which take account of long-term relationship goals. Rusbult and colleagues present data suggesting that relationship partners often modify their initial impulse to retaliate, by arriving at less negative emotional reactions and cognitive understandings of acts of betrayal. This reframing process enables them to respond more constructively to situations that might otherwise destroy the relationship. All of these issues are amply illustrated using examples from the well-known film *The War of the Roses*, which portrays a failing marriage that is marked by repeated instances of betrayal and ongoing failures to forgive.

The over-arching theme of these chapters is that responses to disappointment, criticism, and betrayal range from the constructive (for example, forgiveness) to the destructive (for example, retaliation). The studies provide a framework for classifying the variety of responses, for understanding the biases that may give rise to destructive reactions, and for identifying the antecedents of forgiveness. These chapters also highlight the links between emotion and cognition in predicting responses to negative behavior.

CHAPTER EIGHT

Coping with Disappointment in Marriage: When Partners' Standards Are Unmet

Anita L. Vangelisti and Alicia L. Alexander

When we were first married, we agreed that we would have a partner-ship – that we would both have jobs, that we would share the housework, and that we would both be active in caring for our children. Well, now that we've had a baby, all that has changed. Sure, we both have jobs, but I do almost all of the childcare. He acts like he's doing me a big favor when he holds the baby while I make dinner. It's not that he doesn't like the baby – he loves her and he really enjoys playing with her. I just thought he'd want to be more involved in feeding, diaper-changing, and stuff like that. He'll sit and watch TV or read the paper while I do all the work. I hinted around to him about this a couple of times, but he really got mad. He thought I was saying that he wasn't a good father. So now I just do everything myself. It's hard, but I'd rather keep our marriage happy and I want him to enjoy the time that he spends with the baby.

Why is it that some spouses stay relatively satisfied with their marriage even though the standards they hold for their relationship are not being fulfilled? What do people do when their relational standards are not met? Some individuals may dwell on the disappointment they feel and, as a consequence, may become disillusioned with their relationship. But others may devise ways to cope with their disappointment that enable them to experience less dissatisfaction. In short, people may have a variety of coping strategies that buffer the effects of unfulfilled standards on their relationships.

The purpose of this chapter is fivefold. First, a rationale for exploring the strategies partners use to cope with unfulfilled standards will be provided. Second, prior research examining the ways people respond to

Correspondence regarding this chapter may be addressed to the authors at Depart-ment of Communication Studies, University of Texas at Austin, Austin, TX 78712; a.vangelisti@mail.utexas.edu.

disappointments and stress in their relationships will be synthesized. Third, a study that was conducted to develop an initial typology of coping strategies will be presented. Fourth, several dimensions that underlie the categories that comprise the typology will be discussed. Fifth, and finally, implications for investigating the way people cope with unmet relational standards will be offered. The basic question put forth in the chapter is how people cope with the disappointment they experience when their standards for a "good" relationship go unmet. Understanding how partners develop and use strategies to cope with their unfulfilled standards should inform both theory and practice.

WHY LOOK AT THE STRATEGIES PEOPLE USE TO COPE WITH UNMET STANDARDS?

People enter their romantic relationships with standards – beliefs or criteria about the qualities relationships *should* have (Baucom, Epstein, Sayers, & Sher, 1989). These standards reflect individuals' goals for their relationships. They provide a way for people to evaluate the quality of their associations with others and, as such, serve as a foundation for many of the feelings individuals have toward their relational partner (Beck, 1988; Epstein & Eidelson, 1981; Lederer & Jackson, 1968).

A number of theories suggest that there is a positive link between people's standards being fulfilled and relational satisfaction (Hatfield, Traupman, Sprecher, Utne, & Hay, 1985; Homans, 1961; Huston & Burgess, 1979; Kelley & Thibaut, 1978; Rusbult, 1980; Walster, Walster, & Berscheid, 1978). Empirical research has provided evidence to support this proposition. Studies show that when individuals' relational standards are met or exceeded, partners tend to be relatively satisfied with their relationships; when their standards are not fulfilled, they are likely to be somewhat dissatisfied (Baucom, Epstein, Daiuto, Carels, Rankin, & Burnett, 1996; Fletcher, Simpson, Thomas, & Giles, 1999; Vangelisti & Daly, 1997).

Although backed by prior research, the association between the fulfillment of partners' standards and their relational happiness is not invariant: There are cases when partners remain relatively satisfied with their relationship even though their standards are not met. In spite of feeling disappointed that their partner failed to live up to their standards, these individuals develop coping strategies that help them deal with their negative feelings and that decrease the likelihood they will become dissatisfied with their relationship.

Exploring the strategies individuals use to cope with unmet relational standards offers researchers and theorists a means by which to expand upon and refine current understandings of a number of relational phenomena. For instance, a clear description of coping strategies and an explanation of how those strategies function would help researchers to explain how partners in happy, long-term relationships successfully deal with the disappointments they experience. Even people in satisfying, long-term relationships are bound to have their standards violated at one time or another. Some individuals cope with unfulfilled standards by going to their relational partner, discussing their feelings, and trying to "work things out." Others, like the woman in the example provided at the beginning of this chapter, suppress their feelings in hopes of keeping the peace. Understanding the ways coping strategies function would provide researchers with information about how couples in happy, long-term relationships maintain a certain level of stability and satisfaction.

It also would shed light on why some individuals remain in relationships that consistently fail to meet their standards. A number of theorists argue that people often stay in unhappy relationships because they believe they have few, if any relational alternatives (Kelley & Thibaut, 1978; Rusbult, Martz, & Agnew, 1998). Yet, researchers know surprisingly little about the social and cognitive processes that individuals engage in to convince themselves, and others, that the quality of their current relationship is better than the quality of any alternatives they have. When people's standards are unmet, they are forced to evaluate the extent to which their current relationship "measures up" to other, alternative relationships. The strategies individuals employ to deal with unmet standards likely affect the evaluations they make as well as the way they respond to those evaluations.

Prior research further suggests that the coping strategies people use affect individuals' psychological and physical well-being. For instance, individuals who cope with stress by seeking out support from their social network are more likely to receive support and, on average, are likely to experience greater well-being than are their counterparts who do not solicit support from friends or family (Conn & Peterson, 1989; Dunkel-Schetter, Feinstein, Taylor, & Falke, 1992). Similarly, there is evidence that people who cope with upsetting events by expressing their feelings and thoughts in writing have fewer visits to health centers and exhibit better immune function than do others (Pennebaker & Beall, 1986; Pennebaker, Kiecolt-Glaser, & Glaser, 1988; Petrie, Booth,

& Pennebaker, 1998). By contrast, individuals who have a tendency to respond to stressful situations with hostility report experiencing more interpersonal conflict and receiving less social support than do those who do not respond with hostility (Houston & Vavak, 1991; Smith, 1992). Not surprisingly, people who have a tendency to be hostile are at greater risk for health problems (for example, Adams, 1994). Exploring the techniques individuals use to cope with their unmet relational standards would help researchers and theorists further distinguish strategies that are associated with partners' well-being from those that are not.

PREVIOUS RESEARCH: COPING WITH DISAPPOINTMENT AND STRESS IN RELATIONSHIPS

A great deal of research has been conducted to examine coping strategies. Sifting through the findings of previous work and gleaning those that are relevant to personal relationships is a challenge for several reasons. First, most scholars suggest that coping is not a unidimensional phenomenon (Fleishman, 1984; Folkman & Lazarus, 1980). Instead, it is thought to be a multifaceted process that changes over time (Lazarus, 1991). The coping strategies that individuals employ at one point in their relationship may not be the same as those they use at another point. Second, a number of researchers have argued that coping strategies can vary greatly from one situation to another (Lazarus & Folkman, 1984). For instance, Thoits (1995) found that coping with chronic, ongoing strains is very different than dealing with stressors that are more limited in scope. The wide variety of stressful situations that people in close relationships encounter likely demands a number of different coping strategies. Third, and relatedly, strategies that are employed to manage stress in romantic relationships may differ from those used in other relational contexts (Bowman, 1990; Pollina & Snell, 1999). Individuals bring a unique set of vulnerabilities to their romantic relationships that may shape the strategies they employ as well as the way they interpret and respond to coping strategies used by their partner.

In spite of the complex nature of this literature, most researchers and theorists who work in the area agree that coping strategies involve "cognitive and behavioral efforts to manage specific external and/or internal demands that are appraised as taxing or exceeding the resources of the person" (Lazarus & Folkman, 1984, p. 141; also see Fleishman, 1984; Thoits, 1995). Using this definition as a foundation, coping strategies can be discussed in terms of several different factors. These include the (a) source of the strategy, (b) type of strategy, (c) outcome associated with the strategy, and (d) stimulus event.

Source of the Strategy

The coping strategies employed in romantic relationships differ in terms of the person or persons who initiates them. In many cases, efforts to cope with relational stressors may be initiated by the individual who first experienced the stress. For instance, the woman in the example at the beginning of this chapter dealt with the relational stress and the disappointments she experienced by holding back her feelings. She avoided talking with her husband because she believed that talking might be detrimental to her marriage.

The definition that most scholars use to describe coping strategies suggests that the person who initially experiences stress or disappointment is typically viewed as the source of the strategy. However, in the context of romantic relationships, a partner who observes a loved one under stress also may initiate coping strategies. For example, a husband who notices that his wife is strained by the demands of caring for a new baby may encourage her to tell him about her feelings. Because individuals involved in romantic relationships are interdependent, stress or disappointment experienced by one person may be felt by the other. Even if individuals do not feel the same stress or disappointment that their partner experiences, they may initiate coping strategies because they care about their partner and want to help him or her.

It is also important to note that the person who initiates the coping strategy and the individual(s) who enacts the strategy may differ. In a romantic relationship, one individual may initiate a coping process that requires the participation of both partners. Lyons, Mickelson, Sullivan, and Coyne (1998) note that stressful events may be both "appraised and acted upon in the context of close relationships" (p. 583). These researchers argue that "communal coping" occurs when stress is perceived by one or more individuals as a joint or relational problem. This is a collaborative process in which partners experience a stressor together and share responsibility for dealing with it. Thus, in the case of communal coping, one relational partner may initiate (serve as the source of) the coping process, but both partners act together to deal with the stress they experience.

Type of Strategy

One aspect of the literature on coping that is particularly complex involves the myriad of different coping strategies researchers have uncovered. Many of the various typologies of coping strategies can be traced
back to the theoretical work of Lazarus and his colleagues (Lazarus,
1966; 1991; Lazarus & Folkman, 1984). Lazarus noted that stress is a
three-part process involving primary appraisal, secondary appraisal,
and coping. Primary appraisals occur when individuals perceive an
event that interrupts their goals and their current course of action.
Secondary appraisals, then, focus on people's abilities to deal with the
event and any consequences that may be associated with it. Coping
is the process that individuals engage in as they address the stressful event. Folkman and Lazarus (1980) further distinguished two general types of coping. They noted that some coping strategies involve
behaviors that are enacted in an attempt to decrease feelings of stress.
These "problem-focused" strategies may actually change the relationship between individuals and their environment. By contrast, "emotion-
focused" strategies involve either behavioral or cognitive responses that
are enacted in an effort to manage the emotional consequences of stressors. These strategies do not actually change the relationship between
individuals and their environment. Instead they change the way people
interpret or attend to this relationship.

While many researchers use the distinction between problem-
focused and emotion-focused coping strategies as a conceptual foundation for their work, most – including Folkman and Lazarus (1985) –
have developed more specific typologies. The need for more detailed
typologies emerged for at least two reasons. First, the distinction between problem-focused and emotion-focused strategies is too general
(Carver, Scheier, & Weintraub, 1989). For instance, people may engage
in a variety of coping strategies that could be termed as problem-
focused (that is, strategies aimed at doing something to decrease stress).
Those strategies may or may not be related to each other – and they may
be associated with very different outcomes. Indeed, a number of researchers found that responses to the measure originally developed to assess problem-focused and emotion-focused strategies (see Folkman &
Lazarus, 1980; 1985) form several different factors (for example, Aldwin
& Revenson, 1987; Folkman & Lazarus, 1985; Folkman, Lazarus,
Dunkel-Schetter, DeLongis, & Gruen, 1986).

A second reason why a number of typologies has emerged is that
coping appears to be domain specific (for example, Bowman, 1990;

Pollina & Snell, 1999). That is, strategies that are relevant in one context (for example, the workplace) may be completely irrelevant in another (for example, marriage). Even within a given domain, such as marriage, there appear to be wide variations in the nature of the strategies people employ. Researchers have found that both problem-focused and emotion-focused strategies are used by husbands and wives, but the relevance of those strategies to partners depends on factors such as the type and severity of the stressor that is examined, the quality of the partners' relationship, and whether the husband or the wife employs the strategy. Thus, for example, Bowman's work indicated that strategies involving introspective self-blame and self-interest were positively linked to the severity of marital problems. Whiffen and Gotlib (1989) found that when husbands were distressed, both they and their wives had a tendency to use maladaptive coping strategies such as escape-avoidance and self-control. Wives' marital distress, by contrast, was associated only with their own coping strategies (not those of their husbands). Further, Pearlin and Schooler (1978) reported that women used selective ignoring more than men in dealing with marital problems (also see Billings & Moos, 1981). The range of coping strategies that emerged from these and other studies, and the different circumstances in which they are employed, helps to explain the proliferation of different typologies in the literature.

Outcome Associated with the Strategy

Studies on coping strategies also have emphasized different outcomes. Much of the literature focuses on outcomes for the individual. Scholars have examined the association between various coping strategies and individuals' psychological well-being (for example, Dunkel-Schetter et al., 1992) as well as their physical well-being (for example, Pennebaker & Beall, 1986; Petrie et al., 1998).

As researchers and theorists have begun to examine coping strategies in the context of romantic relationships and marriage, more attention has been devoted to outcomes linked to those relationships. A number of studies, for example, have examined the association between various coping strategies and relational satisfaction (for example, Bowman, 1990; Whiffen & Gotlib, 1989). Similarly, some researchers have focused on the degree to which coping behaviors are constructive or destructive to relationships. For instance, Rusbult and her colleagues (for example, Rusbult, 1980; Rusbult, Verett, Whitney, Slovik, & Lipkus, 1991; Rusbult & Zembrodt, 1983) have studied the ways in which partners respond to relationship problems. Although this line of research does not focus specifically on coping strategies, it does offer a template for conceptualizing coping behaviors as constructive (those "intended to maintain or revise the relationship") or destructive (those that are "destructive to the future of the relationship") (Rusbult, Johnson, & Morrow, 1986, p. 47).

While researchers have examined the links between various coping strategies and both individual and relational outcomes, relatively few scholars have studied possible associations between coping strategies and societal outcomes. The strategies individuals employ to deal with stress can influence society as a whole. Theorists have acknowledged that coping behaviors can affect groups or collectives (for example, Lyons et al., 1998). For example, some scholars suggest that society benefits from marriage and that, in order to maintain or strengthen the institution of marriage, couples need to develop more effective strategies for dealing with relationship stressors (Popenoe, 1993). Others argue that society is better off when the individuals within a marriage are emotionally and physically healthy – and that, at times, maintaining individual partners' well-being may come at the cost of the marital relationship (Stacey, 1993). Clearly, these two arguments place differential value on individual and relational outcomes. Both, however, place an emphasis on societal outcomes that is currently missing from the empirical literature on coping strategies.

Stimulus Event

The outcomes associated with coping strategies likely depend, in part, on the nature of the event that initially stimulated the need for coping. The problems individuals deal with differ in terms of severity: Some problems are relatively minor and require little effort (for example, a glass of spilled milk), whereas others are major and demand a great deal of effort (for example, a death in the family). Thoits (1995) suggests that, in addition to severity, stressful events vary with regard to the frequency with which they occur and the amount of time available to individuals as they make adjustments in response to the events. Thus, people have to cope with what Thoits calls "daily hassles," or small trials that require some degree of adjustment on a day-to-day basis. By contrast, individuals also may have to deal with chronic strains, or ongoing burdens that demand attention over relatively long periods of time.

The events that stimulate coping strategies also differ in terms of the degree to which they are perceived as internal or external to a relationship. If a husband experiences stress because of financial problems, he may attribute those problems to a down-turn in the economy (external), or to his wife's excessive spending habits (internal). In the example presented at the beginning of this chapter, the woman may perceive the inequity in the way she and her husband handle childcare as caused by her husband's busy schedule at work (external), or by a lack of concern on his part for her and for their new baby (internal).

The current chapter focuses on unmet standards as relationship events that stimulate the need for coping. Because standards involve partners' beliefs about what should occur in their marriage, they necessarily center around factors that are internal to a couple's relationship. However, it is important to note that partners may see the cause of unfulfilled standards as external to their relationship – that is, one way individuals may cope with their standards being unmet is to attribute the cause of the unmet standard to external factors. It also is important to be aware that relational standards vary in terms of their perceived importance (Vangelisti & Daly, 1997). On average, people believe that fidelity (being emotionally and physically faithful to each other) is an extremely important standard to uphold in their relationship. As a consequence, when that standard goes unmet, partners are likely to be particularly distressed. The coping strategies individuals employ when their standards for fidelity are unmet probably are quite different than those they use when a less important standard is violated. Furthermore, the way people cope with unmet standards is likely to differ depending on whether the standard goes unfulfilled once or twice, or whether it is repeatedly violated. In the example described at the beginning of this chapter, the wife initially coped with her unmet standards by hinting to her husband that she would like him to participate more in the care of their newborn. When her husband did not respond to her hints and her standard for sharing childcare was repeatedly unmet, she began to cope by suppressing her feelings.

GENERATING COPING STRATEGIES

To begin to explore the nature of the strategies partners use to cope with unmet relational standards, a two-part study was conducted. In the first phase of the investigation, a list of coping strategies was generated. In the second phase, partners' perceptions of the frequency with which they employed each of the strategies was assessed (Vangelisti & Alexander, in progress).

Respondents in the first phase of the study were a sample of 50 adults involved in long-term romantic relationships. Approximately one half of the participants were female ($N = 28$) and approximately one half were male ($N = 22$). The age of the respondents ranged from 22 to 63 years, with a median age of 34 years.

A trained interviewer conducted face-to-face interviews with each of the participants. The interviewer opened discussion with the respondents by introducing the concept of relationship standards. He/she noted that romantic partners have a number of beliefs or criteria about the qualities relationships should have and that, at one time or another, those relationship standards may be unmet. After the interviewer was sure that participants understood the idea that relationship standards sometimes are unfulfilled, he/she asked participants to describe the coping strategies they used when the standards they held for their relationship were unmet. A series of prompts were employed, when necessary, to generate a comprehensive understanding of each of the coping strategies described by respondents. The interviewer took notes defining each strategy during the interviews. Directly following every interview, he/she filled in the details of the definitions.

The data collected from the interviews were coded using inductive analysis (Bulmer, 1979). Two coders read the interviewer's notes and independently generated a list of coping strategies. Then, the coders met and discussed their lists. Some categories were combined and others were eliminated. Twenty-seven coping strategies emerged from this process (see Table 8.1). As can be seen in the table, a wide array of strategies were described by participants. Some focused on the expression of emotions (for example, Self-hurt, Anger); others emphasized behaviors (for example, Hurt Other, Reciprocation). Some involved seeking information or support (for example, Comparison, Third Party Intervention); others centered around denying or avoiding any problems (for example, Imagining, Ignoring). Some emphasized the self (for example, Self-referent, Self-disparagement); others focused on the partner or the relationship (for example, Person, Revitalization).

Although these findings provide a preliminary glimpse of the types of coping strategies partners may employ when they see their relational standards not being met, they do not give any indication of how likely partners are to use the strategies. Spouses may have a broad range of strategies at their disposal but, for any number of reasons, they may

Table 8.1. Descriptions of Coping Strategies

Coping Strategy	Description
Postponement	The individual postpones any action in hopes that it will not reoccur. The person might say, "It will be better later.... if it doesn't then...."
Replacement	The individual decides not to do anything because the other is meeting so many other valued standards. The other standards essentially replace the violated one.
Volition	The individual copes by believing that it was not intentional ("She didn't mean to....").
Person	The individual copes by making a special effort to understand the other person as being different from others ("You just have to understand Bob's background....").
Context	The individual copes by explaining to self that the situation occurred because her/his partner was in a setting or position where she/he "couldn't help doing it."
Habituation	The individual decides that it is something she/he is "used to." The standard has been unfulfilled before and it will happen again, so what's the use of getting concerned?
Consequences	The individual copes by understanding that she/he would be unwilling to accept the consequences of being too concerned about it ("If I got upset, she might leave me.").
Salience	The individual copes by telling her/himself that the standard wasn't that important in the first place.
Imagining	The individual copes by imagining that it never happened.
Changing	The individual copes by believing that her/his partner is going to change and, with work, will not fail to meet the standard again.
Self-referent	The individual copes by deciding that she/he is wrong to hold the standard in the first place ("Maybe I should have never expected him to....").
Ignore	The individual copes by simply ignoring it.
Right	The individual copes by deciding that she/he has no right/justification to hold the standard in the first place.
Exit	The individual leaves the relationship.
Warning	The individual threatens dire consequences if it were to reoccur.

(continued)

Table 8.1 (*continued*)

Coping Strategy	Description
Self-disparagement	The individual comes to believe that were she/he different, the other would never have failed to meet the standard. She/he caused the other to violate the standards by not doing or being something.
Self-hurt	The individual feels terrible hurt and anguish.
Reciprocation	The individual attempts to violate the same standard to "get even."
Clarity	The individual copes by deciding that the other didn't understand she/he had the expectancy. Talking about it and increasing her/his awareness should fulfill the standard.
Modification	The two people renegotiate their understanding of the standard, resulting in some modification. They "talk over" their standards and change to meet each other's.
Hurt other	The individual intentionally attempts to punish her/his partner in some way.
Hurt causal agent	The individual attempts to punish the third party who led the other to violate the standard.
Third party intervention	The individual seeks out the aid of a third party for counseling, modification, or aid.
Comparison	The individual copes by comparing her/his standards with the standards of friends/family. She/he checks their standards in the context of her/his own.
Anger	The individual displays anger and dismay.
Revitalization	The individual copes by increasing her/his efforts to please and attract her/his partner, hoping that a revitalized relationship will prevent a reoccurrence.
Guilt	The individual attempts to make his/her partner feel guilty.

opt to employ only a select few. To begin to explore the frequency with which partners report using these coping strategies, the second phase of the investigation was conducted. In this phase, data were collected from 117 married adults. Eighty-four of the respondents were female and 26 were male. Participants' age ranged from 23 to 61 years, with a median age of 35 years. The length of respondents' relationships ranged from 1 to 36 years (median length was 13.50 years).

Participants completed a questionnaire designed to assess the frequency with which they used the coping strategies generated in the first phase of the study. Respondents were provided with a series of relational standards,[1] each followed by a checklist of the 27 coping strategies (a separate page with definitions of each of the strategies accompanied the questionnaire). Participants first were asked to consider each standard and to report whether it had ever gone unfulfilled in their relationship. Then, if the standard had ever been unmet, respondents were asked to indicate which of the 27 coping strategies they had used by placing a check mark in a space provided next to each strategy.

To determine the relative frequency with which spouses perceived they employed the different coping strategies, the percentage of people who reported using each strategy when a standard was unmet was calculated. These percentages then were averaged across the various standards. The most commonly used strategies were Anger (37%), Clarity (27%), Self-hurt (27%), Modification (26%), and Ignore (24%). The coping strategies used least frequently were Salience (6%), Right (6%), and Hurt Causal Agent (3%). Table 8.2 summarizes the means, standard deviations, and rankings of all of the strategies.

Perhaps what is most striking about these findings is that, even among the most commonly reported strategies, there is a great deal of variation. People noted that they would respond to unmet standards in very different ways. Quite a few individuals said they would try to renegotiate an understanding with their partner (Modification) or that they would talk with their partner to increase his/her awareness of the issue (Clarity), but almost an equal number of respondents reported that they would disregard the entire situation (Ignore). A number of people noted that they would express their anger (Anger), but some participants said that they would feel terrible hurt and anguish (Self-hurt).

While frequency counts such as these provide important information about the range of strategies people say they use to cope with unmet standards in marriage, the counts give only limited information about the nature of the strategies or the impact that different strategies

---

[1] For a complete listing of the relational standards and details about how they were generated, see Vangelisti & Daly, 1997.

Table 8.2. Means, Standard Deviations, and Rankings of
Coping Strategies

Coping Strategy	Mean	SD	Ranking
Postponement	1.95	4.05	7
Replacement	1.57	3.50	10
Volition	.85	2.33	18
Person	1.84	3.57	8
Context	1.14	2.65	14
Habituation	1.11	2.47	15
Consequences	.79	1.99	21
Salience	.64	1.58	23
Imagining	.93	2.57	17
Changing	2.65	3.81	6
Self-referent	.85	2.25	18
Ignore	2.68	4.11	5
Right	.68	1.77	22
Exit	1.23	3.23	13
Warning	1.81	3.62	9
Self-disparagement	.83	2.21	20
Self-hurt	2.99	4.58	2
Reciprocation	1.23	2.75	13
Clarity	2.96	4.33	3
Modification	2.88	4.15	4
Hurt other	1.43	2.81	11
Hurt causal agent	.26	.78	25
Third party intervention	.84	2.22	19
Comparison	1.08	2.33	16
Anger	4.31	5.56	1
Revitalization	1.31	3.24	12
Guilt	.60	.49	24

may have on individuals' relationships. Indeed, there may be an in-
finite number of coping strategies available to participants, but those
strategies likely have similarities and differences that affect the way
they influence relationships such as marriage. In the following section, we explore the qualities of the coping strategies generated in this

study by discussing several dimensions along which the strategies vary. In brief, the strategies may be characterized as differing in terms of (a) expression versus suppression, (b) self versus other focus, (c) recognition versus rationalization, (d) relationship versus network involvement, and (e) constructive versus destructive outcomes. Discussing these characteristics helps to clarify some of the similarities and differences among coping strategies and raises a number of implications for how the strategies may influence relational outcomes.

DIMENSIONS THAT UNDERLIE COPING STRATEGIES

Expression versus Suppression

Some of the strategies that individuals reported using to cope with unmet relational standards emphasized active expression of emotional distress or dissatisfaction, whereas others involved the suppression of negative feelings that may occur as a consequence of the unmet standard. For instance, as previously noted, a number of participants said they would respond to unfulfilled standards by displaying anger. One woman reported that she would "get mad" ("I would show him that I was really angry about what he did."). Behavioral expressions of individuals' distress were apparent in a number of coping strategies. People reported that they would try to punish their partner in some way (Hurt Other), that they would threaten their partner with serious consequences if the standard went unmet again (Warning), and that they would violate the standard themselves to "get even" with their partner (Reciprocation).

Although many of the coping strategies that stressed expression centered around negative or even hostile communication, there were those that involved what appear to be more positive or relationship-centered forms of expression. For instance, some people said that they would respond to an unfulfilled standard by "talking things over" with their partner (Modification). Others, having decided that their partner did not understand that they held certain standards, noted that they would raise their concerns with their partner to increase his/her awareness (Clarity).

By contrast, a number of the coping strategies emphasized individuals suppressing their feelings about having their standards unmet. People noted that one way they coped was to come to believe that they were wrong to hold the standard in the first place (Self-referent). They reasoned that the standard was not that important (Salience). They also said that having the standard unfulfilled was something they were "used to" and that, as a result, they tended not to get upset about it (Habituation). Some individuals went so far as not only to suppress their feelings, but also to suppress the notion that they had any right to exert influence on their relationship by maintaining certain standards. These individuals reported using coping strategies that involved convincing themselves that they did not have any justification for holding the standard (Right).

Self versus other Focus

The strategies people reported using also varied in the degree to which they focused on the self or the partner. Several of the strategies involved individuals turning inward, toward themselves, to cope with their unmet standards. For instance, some people felt that they caused their partner to violate the standard – that if they were a different person or if they had behaved differently, the standard would have been fulfilled (Self-disparagement). Others similarly noted that they, not their partner, were wrong because they should never have held the standard (Self-referent). It is interesting, and potentially important, to note that the coping strategies that focused on the self tended to reflect the self as unworthy. When these participants turned inward to deal with unfulfilled standards, they did so in a way that portrayed the self as the cause of the unmet standard and the source of any distress.

When individuals' coping strategies emphasized the other, a more mixed picture emerged. For example, some strategies involved an effort to exonerate the other. Individuals noted that they coped with unmet standards by making a special effort to understand their partner (Person). They said that they realized their partner was in a setting where failing to meet their standards was unavoidable (Context). While these strategies appeared to provide individuals (and, perhaps their partners) with "good reasons" for the partner failing to meet certain standards, other strategies did not offer the other such an "easy out." In fact, a number of coping strategies tended to assume some degree of culpability on the part of the other. People noted that they coped with their unmet standards by trying to punish their partner (Hurt Other) and that they tried to make their partner feel guilty (Guilt) for what he/she did or failed to do.

Recognition versus Rationalization

Participants' coping strategies varied in the extent to which they acknowledged that relational standards had been unmet. Some of the strategies involved recognizing that a standard was unfulfilled and accepting the disappointment and distress that accompanied that situation. Others emphasized an effort to rationalize or justify the fact that the standard was unmet. People who noted that they coped with unfulfilled standards by showing their anger (Anger), by intentionally punishing their partner (Hurt Other), or by doing something to "get back" at their partner (Reciprocation) clearly recognized that their standards had been unmet. They were distressed and were willing to acknowledge that distress. By contrast, a number of individuals essentially said that they coped with unmet standards by acting as if the standards had never gone unfulfilled. These people reported postponing any action in hopes that the violation would not reoccur (Postponement), pretending that it never happened (Imagine), or ignoring it (Ignore).

Some individuals noted that they used coping strategies that might be characterized as falling in the midrange of a dimension that involves the recognition versus rationalization of unfulfilled standards. These people acknowledged their standards had been unmet, but also tried to justify the situation. They rationalized their partner's behavior (or the lack thereof) by believing that it was unintentional (Volition), by making a special effort to understand their partner (Person), or by explaining to themselves that their partner "couldn't help" what happened (Context).

Relationship versus Network as Locus for Action

In cases when individuals recognized that their standards had been unmet, the coping strategies they reported using differed in terms of whether they treated the relationship or the social network as the locus for action. Some of the strategies focused on the relationship as the "place" where change should occur. People who reported using these strategies noted that they would turn to their relational partner to discuss their standards. They said that they would talk things over with their partner and that both they, and their partner, would change to accommodate each other (Modification). Others who noted using relationship-centered coping strategies said that they would respond to unmet standards by increasing their efforts to please and attract their partner. These individuals said they would engage in such efforts in hopes of encouraging their partner to fulfill their standards in the future (Revitalization).

Rather than focus on the relationship, some people reported coping with unmet standards by turning to their social network. These individuals noted that they used strategies that treated the network as a source of information or a place to resolve distress about unmet standards. For instance, some people noted that they checked their standards up against the standards held by their friends and family (Comparison). Others sought out the help of a third party (Third Party Intervention). In a few cases, people tried to punish the individual who they felt lead their partner to violate the standard (Hurt Causal Agent).

Constructive versus Destructive

People's descriptions of their coping strategies also can be distinguished based on the extent to which they involved behaviors that most would view as constructive or destructive for the relationship. Some of the strategies centered around efforts to improve the relationship or to reward the partner. For instance, a number of people said that they talked about the unmet standard with their partner to increase his/her understanding (Clarity). Some noted that they tried to negotiate with their partner, and that they were willing to change to adapt to their partner's feelings (Modification). Others said they increased their efforts to engage in behaviors that would please and attract their partner (Revitalization).

While strategies such as these involve prosocial attempts to improve or repair the relationship, others do quite the opposite. Indeed, a number of coping strategies discussed by participants involved efforts to terminate the relationship or to punish the partner. Some individuals stated explicitly that they coped with unmet standards by intentionally punishing their partner in some way (Hurt Other). Others said that they made an attempt to violate the same standard in an effort to "get even" with their partner (Reciprocation). Finally, a number of people reported that they coped with unmet standards by leaving the relationship (Exit).

It is important to note that this dimension involves individuals' *perceptions* of their coping strategies. It is not intended to address the partner's responses to those strategies, nor does it provide any indication of the relational outcomes that might be associated with the strategies. Thus, while people may report engaging in behaviors to re-vitalize their relationship, we have no evidence that their partner will respond in positive ways to those behaviors. Indeed, if the partner re-jects individuals' efforts to revitalize the relationship, the relationship may be in trouble. In such instances, what appears to be a construc-tive coping strategy may end up being associated with destructive re-lational outcomes. Individuals' "constructive" efforts, in short, do not take place in a relational vacuum. The outcomes associated with those efforts likely depend on the responses they receive as well as the nature of the relational context in which they are embedded.

SOME IMPLICATIONS: THE INFLUENCES OF COPING STRATEGIES ON RELATIONSHIPS

There is little doubt that the strategies people employ to cope with their unmet standards affect their relationships. On average, individuals who cope by trying to calmly talk things over with their partner probably have a better chance at a satisfying relationship than do those who seek revenge as a means of coping. Yet, as noted above, the influence of any given coping strategy on relationships may be affected by the way the partner responds to the strategy, the quality of the relationship before the strategy was employed, and even the social circumstances in which the strategy was implemented.

Although empirical evidence concerning the impact of these, and other intervening variables, is lacking, previous research and theory pro-vides a backdrop against which careful speculations can be made about the influence coping strategies may have on marriage. In some cases, these speculations run contrary to popular notions about what is "good" or "healthy" for individuals and their relationships. For instance, after reading the example provided at the beginning of this chapter, it might be tempting for some to conclude that the woman in the example would be more satisfied with her relationship if she employed coping strate-gies that involved expression rather than suppression of her feelings. More communication, in short, would help her to resolve her problems (Katriel & Philipsen, 1981). Expression, however, comes in a variety of forms. Some of those forms are much more likely to result in positive re-lational outcomes than others. For instance, studies by Gottman (1979; 1991) show that communication characterized by criticism, contempt, and blaming predicts decreases, not increases, in relational satisfaction. These findings suggest that coping strategies involving expression may not always be beneficial for relationships. The ways in which people express their disappointment concerning an unmet standard is likely to have more influence on satisfaction than the expression, per se.

Research further suggests that the benefits of expression may attenuate when the expression is repeated over and over again. Greenberg and Stone (1990) found that people who disclosed their feelings about a negative event experienced some positive outcomes – but those positive effects only showed up for individuals who expressed their feelings for the first time. People who already had disclosed their feelings did not reap the same benefits. It is possible that a similar pattern of findings occurs when relational partners express their feelings about an unmet standard: The first (few) times they express their disappointment about an unfulfilled standard, they may feel better. However, repeated expressions may do little, if anything, to improve their feelings. In fact, repeatedly talking about their disappointment may serve as a sort of "verbal rumination": It may encourage people to focus on the negative aspects of their relationship. That negative focus, in turn, may have a detrimental influence on their relational satisfaction.

Of course, one reason individuals may cope with unmet standards by repeatedly expressing their disappointment is that their expressions are met with little or no response from their relational partner. Gottman and his colleagues (Gottman, Notarius, Gonso, & Markman, 1976) note that, during conflict episodes, some people engage in self-summarizing – that is, they repeatedly state their own point of view. Individuals who self-summarize may do so, in part, because they do not believe their partner has "heard" what they have to say. A similar case can be made for those who employ coping strategies that involve the repeated expression of disappointment. These individuals may feel the need to express themselves again and again because they do not believe their relational partner is responding to their concerns.

As an alternative to repeatedly expressing distress about an unfulfilled standard, a number of people opt to suppress their feelings about not having their standards met. Some of these individuals may select coping strategies that involve suppression because their previous efforts to express themselves have been ineffective. They may have "given up" after repeated attempts to engage their partner. The data reported in this chapter further suggest that many individuals who employ coping strategies involving suppression do not just "hold in" their feelings. These people also tend to focus on themselves as the source of the unmet standard or they reason that they never should have held the standard in the first place. By turning inward and, in essence, blaming themselves for the unfulfilled standard, they may reduce any negative feelings they have toward their partner. Individuals who employ this sort of coping strategy may be able to maintain a certain level of satisfaction in their relationship, in spite of their unmet standards, because they are willing to take responsibility for the disappointments they experience in their relationship.

While a number of people reported using coping strategies that (directly or indirectly) placed responsibility for the unmet standard on either the self (Self-disparagement) or the partner (Hurt Other), very few focused on the dyad or the relationship. Respondents reported only one strategy that could be described as what Lyons et al. (1998) define as a "communal" coping strategy (Modification). Part of the reason for this may be an artifact of the methods employed to generate the strategies: Participants were asked to describe the coping strategies they used when their standards were unmet. They were not explicitly told that they could include strategies that they and their partner employed together. Excluding respondents' partners from the instructions may have discouraged some participants from describing strategies that focused on the dyad or the relationship. Yet, it is important to note that the instructions did not *preclude* respondents from describing communal coping strategies or from defining their unmet standard as a relational issue as opposed to an issue that focused on the self or the partner. Furthermore, some participants did report that they (and their partner) coped with unmet standards by renegotiating their perceptions of the standard and changing to meet each other's needs (Modification). Lyons et al. note that communal coping "occurs when one or more individuals perceive a stressor as 'our' problem (a social appraisal) versus 'my' or 'your' problem (an individualistic appraisal)" (p. 583). It appears that many of the participants in the current study defined unmet standards as an individualistic ("my" or "your") problem. Exploring factors that encourage people to conceptualize unmet standards as a relational problem – that is, examining the antecedents of adopting a "communal coping orientation" – would be an interesting avenue for future study. Similarly, understanding the conditions under which communal coping strategies provide individuals with a particularly effective means for dealing with unmet standards is an issue that merits researchers' attention.

The study described in this chapter also suggests that distinguishing the focus of people's coping strategies (for example, self, partner, or relationship) from the perceived source of blame for an unmet standard may be quite important. Individuals may focus their coping strategies on their partner without blaming him or her for the unmet standard. Indeed, several of the strategies described by respondents involve what appear to be excuses or justifications for the partner failing to meet a standard. Participants noted that they made special efforts to understand their partner (Person), that they convinced themselves that their partner was in a situation where he or she "couldn't help" violating the standard (Context), and they chose to believe that their partner's behavior was unintentional (Volition). These strategies center on the partner, but they do not portray the partner as responsible for his or her own behavior. Prior research and theory suggests that individuals may be willing to justify, or even overlook, their partner's negative behavior as long as they are happy with their relationship (for example, Fincham, 1985; Fincham, Beach, & Baucom, 1987). People who are unhappy with their relationship are less likely to provide such relationship-enhancing attributions for their partner's behavior (Holtzworth-Munroe & Jacobson, 1985). Preliminary evidence from a pilot study suggests that a similar pattern may emerge when individuals' coping strategies are examined: Those who are satisfied with their relationship may be more likely to excuse any involvement their partner had with an unmet standard than are those who are relatively dissatisfied (Vangelisti & Alexander, in progress).

Using coping strategies that excuse or justify a partner's behavior may not only be a reflection of people's relational happiness. It also may be an indication of the degree to which individuals are dependent on their relationship. Rusbult and her colleagues (Rusbult et al., 1998) argue that dependence is high when individuals are highly satisfied with their relationship, when they have invested a great deal in the relationship, and when they have a relatively low comparison level for alternatives. People who are dependent may be less willing than others to employ coping strategies that acknowledge their partner's culpability. Recognizing their partner's negative behavior as intentional or controllable may come with a price that these individuals are unwilling to pay: It may require them to reassess their feelings about their relationship, to reconsider the payoffs they have received for their investments, and to acknowledge that they feel tied to their partner because they do not have any attractive alternatives.

When people engage in this sort of reassessment as a consequence of an unmet standard, one thing they may do is turn to their social network for counsel. Some participants in the current study reported that they coped with unmet standards by seeking aid from a third party (Third Party Intervention) or by comparing their standards to those of friends and family (Comparison). By and large, the literature presents a very positive outlook for those who seek support from their social network. People are more likely to receive social support when they seek it (Conn & Peterson, 1989) and those who seek and receive social support experience greater physical and psychological well-being than their counterparts who do not (see Albrecht & Adelman, 1987; Burleson, Albrecht, & Sarason, 1994). Yet, there also are costs to receiving support (Rook, 1984; Rook & Pietromonaco, 1987). For instance, individuals who cope with unmet standards by turning to their social network for aid may not receive the type of aid they desire. Or, after asking for advice, they may receive "too much" counsel from overzealous friends or family members. In addition, when people go to a third party to cope with unmet standards – rather than to their relational partner – they may miss an important opportunity to convey their feelings to their partner. By resolving their disappointment outside the context of their relationship, individuals reduce the extent to which they rely on their partner for emotional support. They may even begin to go to their social network as a way to avoid dealing with their partner and/or their relationship. In short, some of the costs associated with receiving social support may reduce the likelihood that certain coping strategies will buffer the negative influence of unmet standards on relational satisfaction.

Although the findings of the study reported in this chapter are clearly exploratory, they offer a number of potentially interesting avenues for future research. Our careful speculations about the various roads researchers and theorists might take as they continue to examine the strategies individuals use to cope with unmet standards lead us to at least one conclusion. Coping strategies, themselves, do not appear to be inherently positive or negative. As a consequence, researchers probably are not going to be able to generate simple lists of "effective" and "ineffective" strategies. Indeed, we would urge those who are interested in studying relational coping strategies to approach any prescriptive statements with caution. Strategies that involve prosocial behaviors (for example, "turning the other cheek") may be employed with malevolent intentions. Those that initially seem negative (for example, inciting conflict) may encourage some partners to confront issues they had been avoiding. Strategies that look like they are harmful to individuals (for example, self-blame) may serve an important function in maintaining relational stability. Coping strategies, in short, are enacted and

embedded within relationships. Whether they are associated with positive or negative relational outcomes very likely depends on a myriad
of issues, including the history shared by relational partners, the investments both partners have made in the relationship, the way partners enact and respond to the strategies, and the social circumstances in which
the strategies are employed.

REFERENCES

Adams, S. H. (1994). Role of hostility in women's health during midlife: A
longitudinal study. *Health Psychology, 13,* 488–495.
Albrecht, T. L., & Adelman, M. B. (1987). *Communicating social support.* Newbury
Park, CA: Sage.
Aldwin, C., & Revenson, T. A. (1987). Does coping help? A reexamination of the
relation between coping and mental health. *Journal of Personality and Social
Psychology, 35,* 337–348.
Baucom, D. H., Epstein, N., Daiuto, A. D., Carels, R. A., Rankin, L. A., & Burnett,
C. K. (1996). Cognitions in marriage: The relationship between standards and
attributions. *Journal of Family Psychology, 10,* 209–222.
Baucom, D. H., Epstein, N., Sayers, S., & Sher, T. G. (1989). The role of cognitions
in marital relationships: Definitional, methodological, and conceptual issues.
Journal of Consulting and Clinical Psychology, 57, 31–38.
Beck, A. T. (1988). *Love is never enough: How couples can overcome misunderstand-
ings, resolve conflicts, and solve relationship problems through cognitive therapy.*
New York: Harper & Row.
Berkman, L., & Syme, S. (1979). Social networks, host resistance, and mortality:
A nine year followup study of Alameda County residents. *American Journal
of Epidemiology, 109,* 186–204.
Billings, A. G., & Moos, R. (1981). The role of coping processes and social re-
sources among adults with unipolar depression. *Journal of Behavioral Medicine,
4,* 139–157.
Bowman, M. L. (1990). Coping efforts and marital satisfaction: Measuring mar-
ital coping and its correlates. *Journal of Marriage and the Family, 52,* 463–474.
Bulmer, M. (1979). Concepts in the analysis of qualitative data. *Sociological
Review, 27,* 651–677.
Burleson, B. R., Albrecht, T. L., & Sarason, I. G. (1994) (Eds.). *Communication
of social support: Messages, interaction, relationships, and community.* Thousand
Oaks, CA: Sage.
Carver, C. S., Scheier, M. F., & Weintraub, J. K. (1989). Assessing coping strate-
gies: A theoretically based approach. *Journal of Personality and Social Psychol-
ogy, 56,* 267–283.
Conn, M. K., & Peterson, C. (1989). Social support: Seek and ye shall find. *Journal
of Social and Personal Relationships, 6,* 345–358.
Dunkel-Schetter, C., Feinstein, L. G., Taylor, S. E., & Falke, R. L. (1992). Patterns
of coping with cancer. *Health Psychology, 11,* 79–87.

Epstein, N., & Eidelson, R. J. (1981). Unrealistic beliefs of clinical couples: Their relationship to expectations, goals, and satisfaction. *The American Journal of Family Therapy, 9*, 13–22.

Fincham, F. D. (1985). Attributions in close relationships. In J. Harvey & G. Weary (Eds.), *Attribution: Basic issues and applications* (pp. 203–234). New York: Academic Press.

Fincham, F. D., Beach, S. R., & Baucom, D. H. (1987). Attribution processes in distressed and nondistressed couples: 4. Self–partner attribution differences. *Journal of Personality and Social Psychology, 52*, 739–748.

Fleishman, J. (1984). Personality characteristics and coping patterns. *Journal of Health and Social Behavior, 25*, 229–244.

Fletcher, G. J. O., Simpson, J. A., Thomas, G., & Giles, L. (1999). Ideals in intimate relationships. *Journal of Personality and Social Psychology, 76*, 72–89.

Folkman, S., & Lazarus, R. S. (1980). An analysis of coping in a middle-aged community sample. *Journal of Health and Social Behavior, 21*, 219–239.

Folkman, S., & Lazarus, R. S. (1985). If it changes it must be a process: Study of emotion and coping during three stages of a college examination. *Journal of Personality and Social Psychology, 48*, 150–170.

Folkman, S., Lazarus, R. S., Dunkel-Schetter, C., DeLongis, A., & Gruen, R. J. (1986). Dynamics of a stressful encounter: Cognitive appraisal, coping, and encounter outcomes. *Journal of Personality and Social Psychology, 50*, 992–1003.

Gottman, J. M. (1979). *Marital interaction: Experimental investigation.* New York: Academic Press.

Gottman, J. M. (1991). *What predicts divorce?: The relationship between marital processes and marital outcomes.* Hillsdale, NJ: Lawrence Erlbaum Associates.

Gottman, J. M., Notarius, C., Gonso, J., & Markman, H. (1976). *A couple's guide to communication.* Champaign, IL: Research Press.

Greenberg, M. A., & Stone, A. A. (1990). Writing about disclosed versus undisclosed traumas: *Health and mood effects.* Health Psychology, 9, 114–115.

Hatfield, E., Traupman, J., Sprecher, S., Utne, M., & Hay, J. (1985). Equity and intimate relations: Recent research. In W. Ickes (Ed.), *Compatible and incompatible relationships* (pp. 91–117). New York: Springer-Verlag.

Holtzworth-Munroe, A., & Jacobson, N. S. (1985). Causal attributions of married couples: When do they search for causes? What do they conclude when they do? *Journal of Personality and Social Psychology, 48*, 1398–1412.

Homans, G. (1961). *Social behavior: Its elementary forms.* New York: Harcourt Brace Jovanovich.

Houston, B. K., & Vavak, C. R. (1991). Cynical hostility: Developmental factors, psychosocial correlates, and health behaviors. *Health Psychology, 10*, 9–17.

Huston, T. L., & Burgess, R. L. (1979). Social exchange in developing relationships: An overview. In R. L. Burgess & T. L. Huston (Eds.), *Social exchange in developing relationships* (pp. 3–28). New York: Academic Press.

Katriel, T., & Philipsen, G. (1981). "What we need is communication": Communication as a cultural category in some American speech. *Communication Monographs, 48*, 301–317.

Kelley, H. H., & Thibaut, J. W. (1978). *Interpersonal relations: A theory of interdependence.* New York: Wiley.

Lazarus, R. S. (1966). *Psychological stress and the coping process.* New York: McGraw-Hill.

Lazarus, R. S. (1991). *Emotion and adaptation.* New York: Oxford University Press.

Lazarus R. S., & Folkman, S. (1984). *Stress, appraisal, and coping.* New York: Springer-Verlag.

Lederer, W., & Jackson, D. O. (1968). *The mirages of marriage.* New York: Norton.

Lyons, R. F., Mickelson, K. D., Sullivan, M. J. L., & Coyne J. C. (1998). Coping as a communal process. *Journal of Social and Personal Relationships, 15,* 579–605.

Pearlin, L. I., & Schooler, C. (1978). The structure of coping. *Journal of Health and Social Behavior, 22,* 337–356.

Pennebaker, J. W., & Beall, S. K. (1986). Confronting a traumatic event: Toward an understanding of inhibition and disease. *Journal of Abnormal Psychology, 95,* 274–281.

Pennebaker, J. W., Kiecolt-Glaser, J., & Glaser, R. (1988). Disclosure of traumas and immune function: Health implications for psychotherapy. *Journal of Consulting and Clinical Psychology, 56,* 239–245.

Petrie, K. J., Booth, R. J., & Pennebaker, J. W. (1998). The immunological effects of thought suppression. *Journal of Personality and Social Psychology, 75,* 1264–1272.

Pollina, L. K., & Snell, W. E. (1999). Coping in intimate relationships: Development of the multidimensional intimate coping questionnaire. *Journal of Social and Personal Relationships, 16,* 133–144.

Popenoe, D. (1993). American family decline, 1960–1990: A review and appraisal. *Journal of Marriage and the Family, 55,* 527–542, 553–555.

Rook, K. S. (1984). The negative side of social interaction: Impact on psychological well-being. *Journal of Personality and Social Psychology, 46,* 1097–1108.

Rook, K. S., & Pietromonaco, P. (1987). Close relationships: Ties that heal or ties that bind? In W. H. Jones & D. Perlman (Eds.), *Advances in personal relationships* (vol. 1, pp. 1–35). Greenwich, CT: JAI Press.

Rusbult, C. E. (1980). Commitment and satisfaction in romantic associations: A test of the investment model. *Journal of Experimental Social Psychology, 16,* 172–186.

Rusbult, C. E., Johnson, D. J., & Morrow, G. D. (1986). Determinants and consequences of exit, voice, loyalty, and neglect: Responses to dissatisfaction in adult romantic involvements. *Human Relations, 39,* 45–63.

Rusbult, C. E., Martz, J. M., & Agnew, C. R. (1998). The investment model scale: Measuring commitment level, satisfaction level, quality of alternatives, and investment size. *Personal Relationships, 5,* 357–391.

Rusbult, C. E., Verett, J., Whitney, G. A., Slovik, L. F., & Lipkus, I. (1991). Accommodation processes in close relationships: Theory and preliminary empirical evidence. *Journal of Personality and Social Psychology, 60,* 53–78.

Rusbult, C. E., & Zembrodt, I. M. (1983). Responses to dissatisfaction in romantic involvements: A multidimensional scaling analysis. *Journal of Experimental Social Psychology, 19,* 274–293.

Smith, T. W. (1992). Hostility and health: Current status of a psychosomatic hypothesis. *Health Psychology, 11,* 139–150.

Stacey, J. (1993). Good riddance to "the family": A response to David Popenoe. *Journal of Marriage and the Family, 55*, 545–547.

Thoits, P. A. (1995). Stress, coping, and social support. Where are we? What is next? *Journal of Health and Social Behavior (extra issue)*, 53–79.

Vangelisti, A. L., & Alexander, A. L. (in progress). Coping with unmet standards for romantic relationships. Unpublished manuscript.

Vangelisti, A. L., & Daly, J. A. (1997). Gender differences in standards for romantic relationships. *Personal Relationships, 4*, 203–219.

Walster, E., Walster, E. W., & Berscheid, E. (1978). *Equity: Theory and research.* Boston: Allyn & Bacon.

Whiffen, V. E., & Gotlib, I. H. (1989). Stress and coping in maritally distressed and nondistressed couples. *Journal of Social and Personal Relationships, 6*, 327–344.

CHAPTER NINE

On Empathic Accuracy and Husbands' Abusiveness: The "Overattribution Bias"

William E. Schweinle and William Ickes

The following scene is excerpted from Ernest Hemingway's book *Men Without Women* (Hemingway, 1927, pp. 81–82). Max and Al are professional hit men. They are dining in a restaurant while menacing the owner, George, and another diner, Nick.

Both men ate with their gloves on. George watched them eat.
"What are *you* looking at?" Max looked at George.
"Nothing."
"The hell you were. You were looking at me."
"Maybe the boy meant it for a joke, Max," Al said. George laughed.
"*You* don't have to laugh," Max said to him. "*You* don't have to laugh at all, see?"
"All right," said George.
"So he thinks it's all right." Max turned to Al. "He thinks it's all right. That's a good one."
"Oh, he's a thinker," Al said. They went on eating.

Toch (1969) used this example to illustrate that the likelihood of a potential aggressor becoming violent depends upon how that person interprets what other people say and do. In Hemingway's scenario, the killers evoke their own violent tendencies through a twisted interpretation of what George and Nick say or do. George's stare meant nothing – nothing at all. But both killers inferred that George was thinking or feeling contempt for them and that George's stare was direct evidence of that contempt. Once this inference had been made, anything George said or did from that point on only made the situation worse. Indeed, the escalating events within this scenario could have ultimately resulted in George's fictional death, just as a similar real-life scenario resulted in the actual death of a New York waiter named Richard Adan at the hands of an exconvict named Jack Henry Abbot.

Now let's consider a similar scenario with different participants. This time the potential aggressor is a husband, Max, and the potential victim is his wife, Georgette.

Max ate the dinner that Georgette had prepared. Georgette watched him eat. "What are *you* looking at?" Max looked at Georgette.
"Nothing."
"The hell you were. You were looking at me. Maybe you meant it for a joke," Max said. Georgette laughed. "How could that be a joke?" she said.
"*You* don't have to laugh," Max said to her. "*You* don't have to laugh at all, see?"
"All right," said Georgette.
"So she thinks it's all right," Max said to no one in particular. "She's such a thinker."
"Think about *this*," he said, sweeping the plate off the table with one hand while reaching over to slap her hard in the face with the other.

This scenario, like the first, is also played out in everyday life, with consequences that devastate countless family relationships. In this chapter, we will argue that the men who are most at risk of abusing their wives are those who have strong negative reactions to any sign of rejection from women, even women whom they do not know (Dutton & Browning, 1988; Holtzworth-Munroe & Smutzler, 1996). Like the husband Max in our second scenario, these men are particularly likely to find evidence of criticism or rejection in women's ambiguous words and actions (Holtzworth-Munroe & Hutchison, 1993).

It is possible that abusive men are predisposed to take offense where none is intended, somehow managing to "find" criticism or rejection in the thoughts and feelings of women even where there is none. Why, for example, when Max asked Georgette what she was looking at, did he infer that her stare was one of contempt? Perhaps he thought that he was holding his fork incorrectly and that she was catching him in his mistake. Perhaps he thought that she had adulterated the food in some way, trying to get back at him for something, and that now she was enjoying watching him eat it. If so, he was reading a lot more into Georgette's behavior than was objectively there to be read. Perhaps Georgette was pleasantly musing about the man she had married. Or perhaps she was simply staring the stare of a person who has had a long day and is tired. If so, then Max completely *mis*inferred what was actually on her mind, leaving us to wonder if the type of inferential inaccuracy that he displayed might be typical of most, if not all, abusive men.

There is an alternative possibility, however. Perhaps abusive men like Max are not uniformly insensitive and inaccurate in inferring women's thoughts and feelings. Perhaps, instead, they are *selectively accurate* with respect to a specific category of women's thoughts and feelings – the thoughts and feelings that women have about their male partners that really *are* critical and rejecting. Suppose, for example, that Georgette really had seen that Max was holding his fork overhand, like a rube. Suppose that she was tired of all the mockery, the "walking on eggshells," the verbal and physical abuse. Suppose that she had been thinking Max was a poor excuse for a husband, even a poor excuse for a man. In this case, Max would have been correct in assuming that she was harboring critical or rejecting thoughts and feelings about him.

But what, we may ask, are real-life abusers like? Are they more likely to resemble the fictional husband who inaccurately infers criticism and rejection where it doesn't really exist? Or are they more likely to resemble the fictional husband who accurately infers criticism and rejection where it *does* really exist? Finding empirically based answers to these questions is important because, in real life, roughly one in eight husbands physically abuse their wives each year (Straus & Gelles, 1988).

Finding such answers was the major goal of the study that we report in this chapter. This study was based on an innovative method for measuring how accurately or inaccurately the men in our study could infer women's potentially critical and rejecting thoughts and feelings. By using this method, we were able to examine how the men's perceptions of women's potentially critical and rejecting thoughts and feelings were related to the men's self-reported abuse of their own female partners. Our study enabled us to test between these two possible interpretations of the Max and Georgette story. Would we find that abusive, as opposed to nonabusive, men are particularly inaccurate and biased to overattribute criticism and rejection to women's thoughts and feelings? Or would we find that abusive men are particularly sensitive to, and vigilant for, those cues in women's behavior that signify that their thoughts and feelings really are critical or rejecting of their male partners?

By the end of this chapter, it should be clear which of these two alternatives more aptly describes how abusive men are likely to "read" women's minds. With the benefit of the insights we have gained, we will suggest how our findings might be applied to help reduce the incidence of husband-to-wife abuse. We will also suggest some promising directions that future research might take to further clarify these important issues. It is our hope that research such as ours will provide useful information for treating the abusive husband.

SOCIAL SKILL DEFICITS IN ABUSIVE MEN:
A FOCUS ON EMPATHIC ACCURACY

Holtzworth-Munroe (1992), adopting the framework of McFall's (1982) social information processing model, has made a strong argument that abusive men are deficient in one or more social skills. According to McFall's model, social skills enable a person to competently perform a set of sequential tasks for responding to incoming social information: *decoding, decision making,* and *enactment*. Each task in the sequence may or may not be performed competently, depending on the skill of the person involved.

The entire sequence ultimately leads to a social response, or enactment, that can be judged as either competent, incompetent, or perhaps somewhere in between. Each step in the sequence must be performed competently in order to culminate in a competent social response. So, for instance, being able to accurately decode incoming information does not alone ensure a competent response. Nor does competent decision making by itself guarantee a competent response. It is also possible for social skill deficiencies to be more general or more specific with respect to the situation (for example, home versus office), type of interaction (for example, friendly versus work-related), and interaction partner (for example, spouse versus friend). For example, a person may behave quite competently with friends, but be unable to behave competently with his or her spouse.

Abusive husbands tend to respond less competently than nonabusive husbands to problematic marital and nonmarital situations depicted on audiotape, especially to the marital situations (Anglin & Holtzworth-Munroe, 1997). According to the social information processing model, it seems likely that abusive men are deficient in one or more of the skills leading to a competent response (see Holtzworth-Munroe, 1992). An important advantage of the model is that it provides a theoretical framework from which researchers might look for, and more clearly define, the nature of these deficits.

Our research focuses specifically on the decoding skills of abusive men. Most of the research conducted in our lab during the last 12 years has centered on the study of *empathic accuracy* – the accuracy with which people are able to infer the specific content of other people's thoughts and feelings (see Ickes, 1993; 1997). We are interested in the possibility that abusive men do not decode (that is, receive, perceive, or interpret) women's thoughts and feelings with the same level of accuracy that nonabusive men do. But are abusive men uniformly less accurate than nonabusive men? Or is there at least one respect in which abusive men are actually *more* accurate than nonabusive men – in detecting and accurately decoding the critical and rejecting thoughts and feelings that women really do have about their male partners?

The Argument for Inaccuracy and Bias

Let us first consider the argument that abusive men might be exceptionally biased and insensitive in their inferences about women's thoughts and feelings. We must say, at the outset, that this argument is intuitively appealing. Men who abuse their wives certainly *appear* to be insensitive to their partners' actual thoughts and feelings.

It is not surprising, then, that theoretical and empirical support for this argument already exists. For example, Nelson (1997) proposed that some abuse occurs because certain men are insensitive to the pain and suffering caused by their abusive behavior. Indeed, women in relationships with abusive men report less emotional and intellectual intimacy (Margolin, 1988), suggesting that these couples do not understand one another as well as nonabusive couples do. In a similar vein, perspective taking, a critical component of interpersonal understanding and empathy (Wallbott, 1995), appears to inhibit aggression in both men and women (Richardson, Hammock, Smith, & Gardner, 1994). These findings are consistent with the argument that husbands who abuse their wives are generally less empathic – that is, they are less likely to accurately infer the actual content of their wives' thoughts and feelings.

We might further argue that this deficit in understanding could stem, at least in part, from certain preexisting biases in the way that abusive men perceive women. For instance, compared to their nonabusive counterparts, abusive men tend to report having stronger sex-role stereotypes about women (Stith & Farley, 1993; Willis, Hallinan & Melby, 1996). They also tend to become more angry and react more aggressively to video depictions of a male/female couple in conflict over the woman's need for greater independence (Dutton & Browning, 1988). In addition, abusive men attribute criticism, rejection, or negative intent to women depicted in standardized videotapes or in audiotaped narratives more often than nonabusive men do (Dutton, Saunders,

Starzomski, & Bartholomew, 1994; Dutton, Starzomski, & Ryan, 1996; Holtzworth-Munroe & Hutchinson, 1993). These men are also more likely to see women as being untrustworthy and disloyal (Dutton, 1995). In fact, among a sample of men who had murdered their wives, the precipitating event most often reported was the husband's perception of rejection by his wife (Barnard, Vera, Vera, & Newman, 1982).

Given these findings, we might readily conclude that abuse-prone men infer criticism and/or rejection from women in an exceptionally *biased* way, rather than in an accurate and sensitive way. Interestingly, research on children's aggression suggests that it can be triggered by the child's biased inferences of being rejected by his or her playmates (Dodge, 1980; Dodge & Somberg, 1987). Perhaps the same type of bias is evident in many abusive men, and is responsible for impairing their ability to understand and interact appropriately with women. This preexisting bias to infer criticism and rejection where it does not really exist could systematically distort the men's empathic inferences to such an extent that an overall deficit in their empathic accuracy might be evident.

The Argument for Enhanced Accuracy for Actual Criticism and Rejection

A second, alternative argument also deserves to be considered. This argument centers on the possibility that there is at least one respect in which abusive men are actually *more* accurate than nonabusive men – in detecting and accurately decoding the critical and rejecting thoughts and feelings that women really do have about their male partners. As in the case of the first argument, there is a body of theory and research evidence that supports this alternative possibility.

This alternative argument suggests that, although abusive men might cognitively withdraw in some situations (for example, in day-to-day or intimate interactions), they are actually more vigilant than nonabusive men in other situations (for example, at times when the relationship is threatened; see Sillars, 1998). Indeed, Downey, Feldman, and Ayduk (2000) found that abusive men were particularly sensitive to, and hypervigilant for, signs of rejection from people. This hypervigilance for criticism or rejection may enable abusive men to more accurately detect those instances in which the theme and content of a woman's thought or feeling really *is* critical or rejecting. In other words, an abusive man may not pay an exceptional amount of attention to his wife, unless she is in some way expressing rejection of him. When she does, he may become hyperattentive to her verbal and nonverbal behavior and, in consequence, may more accurately infer the theme and content of her critical and rejecting thoughts and feelings.

Two additional lines of research might be viewed as supporting the possibility that abusive men can more accurately infer the theme and/ or content of women's critical or rejecting thoughts and feelings. The first pertains to the frequency with which the female partners of abusive men actually experience such thoughts and feelings, whereas the second pertains to the association between a perceiver's anxious attachment style and his or her empathic accuracy in relationship-threatening situations. Let's consider each of these lines of research in turn.

First, it seems likely that the abusive, suspicious, intimidating, overbearing behavior of abusive men (Dutton, 1995; 1998; Jacobson & Gottman, 1998), along with their more conflict-oriented interaction style (Bersani, Chen, Pendleton, & Denton, 1992), would actually *evoke* more critical and rejecting thoughts and feelings from women. If this is the case, then abusive men's more frequent attribution of criticism and rejection to women in standardized vignettes (Dutton, Saunders, Starzomski, & Bartholomew, 1994; Dutton, Starzomski, & Ryan, 1996; Holtzworth-Munroe & Hutchinson, 1993) might not represent a perceptual/inferential bias at all. Instead, it may accurately reflect the degree to which these men experience covert criticism and rejection in their own relationships or day-to-day interactions with women. At worst, then, the outcome of the vignette studies would constitute a case of overgeneralization rather than one of outright bias.

Second, abusive men appear to be hypervigilant for signs of abandonment, criticism, or rejection from women (Berry, 1998; Deschner, 1984; Dutton, 1995; 1998; Jacobson & Gottman, 1998; Nelson, 1997; Walker, 1979). These men also tend to have fearful/anxious attachment styles (Downey et al., 2000; Dutton, 1995; 1998). In a recent study, people with fearful/anxious attachment styles were more accurate than others when they inferred the content of their partner's thoughts or feelings in a relationship-threatening situation – that is, a situation in which the partners are likely to be having critical or rejecting thoughts and feelings about each other (Simpson, Ickes, & Grich, 1999). These findings suggest that a syndrome of hypervigilance or "rejection sensitivity," combined with a fearful/anxious attachment style, may be characteristic of men who abuse their domestic partners (Downey et al., 2000). If so, then we might expect that abusive men would more accurately infer the theme and content of women's thoughts and feelings when those thoughts and feelings are threatening to the relationship, or to the man's self-esteem (in other words, when they are critical and/or rejecting).

Summary

We must choose between two rather different arguments, each of which is plausible, and each of which appears to have both theoretical and empirical support. On the one hand is the argument that abusive men tend to "overattribute" criticism and rejection to women's thoughts and feelings. This "overattribution effect" should systematically bias the men's inferences and thereby impair both their "thematic accuracy" (their ability to accurately infer whether women's thoughts and feelings are critical/rejecting or not critical/rejecting) and their overall empathic accuracy (their ability to accurately infer the actual content of the women's thoughts and feelings).

On the other hand is the argument that abusive men are selectively accurate, in that they are more likely than nonabusive men to discern the theme of women's thoughts and feelings when those thoughts and feelings actually are critical or rejecting. If this argument is correct, then abusive men may exhibit an overall level of empathic accuracy that is similar to that of nonabusive men, who may be more thematically accurate in other areas.

OUR EMPATHIC ACCURACY STUDY

Arguing important issues is relatively easy; resolving such issues on the basis of fact is generally more difficult. As a step toward resolving the important issue of whether abusive men tend to be exceptionally biased or exceptionally accurate when they infer that women are having critical and rejecting thoughts and feelings about their male partners, we conducted the empathic accuracy study that is described as follows.

In this study, we used newspaper advertisements to recruit 86 married men from the Arlington, Texas metropolitan area. These men ranged in age from 19 to 72, and their marriages ranged in length from 3 months to 43 years. In all, they appeared to be a fairly representative sample of husbands from the local community. Because abusive men tend to experience nontrivial levels of distress in their marriages, we screened all potential volunteers to ensure that our sample would include only men who reported a nontrivial level of marital distress, as assessed by a telephone-administered version of the Revised Dyadic Adjustment Scale (RDAS; Busby, Christensen, Crane, & Larson, 1995). When each of these prescreened participants arrived at the lab, he was asked to complete a questionnaire packet that included the Propensity for Abusiveness Scale (PAS; Dutton, 1995) and several demographic questions. The PAS is a 39-item scale that nonreactively assesses the likelihood that a man will abuse his wife. The construct measured by the PAS is not obvious, because none of its items pertain directly to the respondent's abusiveness or current relationship conflict.

Each of our male participants then viewed in succession three highly edited stimulus tapes originally developed by Marangoni, Garcia, Ickes, and Teng (1995). Each tape depicts a different female client in a simulated psychology therapy session with a male, client-centered therapist. Each psychotherapy session was "simulated" only in the sense that the client and the therapist knew that the session was being filmed for use in subsequent research. Each of the female clients discussed with the therapist the actual relationship problems she experienced with her husband or exhusband, and the genuineness and spontaneity of the feelings she expressed were evident throughout each session (one client wept openly while discussing her divorce). Although the clients did not know before their therapy session was taped that we would ask them to view the tape immediately afterwards and make a record of all of their thoughts and feelings at the points when they actually occurred, they all consented to help us by providing these data. Through this procedure, we were able to obtain the clients' actual thoughts and feelings and to use them as the standard against which the empathic inferences of our male research participants (the husbands in our study) could be compared.

When we showed the stimulus tapes to the participants, we paused the tapes at the exact points at which the client had reported having had a specific thought or feeling. The tapes had been edited so that there were 30 of these pauses on each of the three tapes, or 90 such "tape stops" in all. At each of the tape stops, the male participant in a given session wrote down what he thought the actual content of the thought or feeling was, and then checked a box to indicate whether he thought its theme was critical/rejecting of the stimulus female's male partner, ambiguous, or noncritical/nonrejecting.

After the participant had completed the empathic inference stage of the procedure, we asked him to fill out the Conflict Tactics Scale (CTS; Straus, 1979) – a measure that assesses men's own self-reported abusiveness. Because the CTS distinctly asks about the participants' own abusive behavior, some of the husbands in our study may have been reluctant to respond with complete truthfulness about how abusive they really are/were. To help control for this problem, we adjusted the participants' self-reported abusiveness scores by statistically controlling for their scores on a brief measure of socially desirable response tendency (MC1-(10), Strahan & Gerbasi, 1972, see Saunders, 1991 for computational details).

Previous research in the area of spousal (wife) abuse has compared "violent" men to "nonviolent" men. Applying this "violent versus nonviolent" distinction in our study was not appropriate for several reasons. First, verbal and psychological abuse in a marriage often occur along with physical abuse (Tolman, 1999). Second, verbal aggression or psychological abuse alone can adversely affect women, perhaps as much as physical abuse can (Tolman, 1992; Walker, 1979; 1984). Third, although the law may clearly distinguish between them, the hypothetical line separating physical abuse from verbal or psychological abuse is not clear in a psychometric sense (Barling, O'Leary, Jouriles, Vivian, & MacEwen, 1987). For these reasons, we combined verbal and physical abuse scores into a single score, CT-Coercive, that ideally assesses "marital abusiveness" as a larger and more inclusive construct than physical assault alone.

The empathic inferences made by the male participants in our study were individually compared to each actual thought or feeling reported by the video clients, and rated for their similarity by eight independent raters. Scores were then averaged across the set of raters to yield an empathic accuracy score for each inference. (For more specific information about the stimulus tapes and our method for assessing empathic accuracy, see Gesn & Ickes, 1999, and Marangoni et al., 1995.)

The Thematic Accuracy Data

The participants' inferences about the *theme* of each thought or feeling (Critical/Rejecting, Ambiguous, Noncritical/Nonrejecting) were compared to those provided by three female raters who viewed the unedited, full-length videotapes, read the actual thought/feeling content reported by the client, and decided whether the thought or feeling was in fact critical/rejecting, ambiguous, or noncritical/nonrejecting with respect to the client's male partner. In the end, 36 of the 90 thoughts and feelings were rated as critical/rejecting or ambiguous. These

36 thoughts and feelings were combined into a single category of thoughts and feelings that were potentially critical or rejecting, in contrast to the remaining 54 thoughts and feelings, which were more obviously noncritical/nonrejecting.

We used signal detection methods to analyze the data for the men's *thematic accuracy* (their accuracy in inferring the correct "theme" – critical/rejecting versus noncritical/nonrejecting – of each thought or feeling). One signal detection measure (B''_D, Donaldson, 1992) was used to determine the strength and direction of any inferential *bias* on the part of each participant. A second signal detection measure (d', see Green & Swets, 1966) was used to provide a separate estimate of each participant's *discrimination* – how accurately each participant could discern or discriminate the actual theme of the video clients' thoughts and feelings. Signal detection theory makes an important distinction between bias and poor discrimination ability. They are distinctly different concepts, but confusion arises because they are not entirely independent either. To better appreciate the difference, assume that two individuals are shown the same set of 50 stimuli in which half the stimuli are critical/rejecting and half are not. One individual may infer criticism or rejection in 10% of the cases in which the thought or feeling is actually not critical or rejecting, and may infer criticism or rejection in 80% of the cases in which the thought or feeling really is critical or rejecting. In contrast, the other individual may infer criticism or rejection in 80% of the cases in which the thought or feeling is actually not critical or rejecting, and infer criticism or rejection in 10% of the cases in which the thought or feeling actually is critical or rejecting.

Both of these hypothetical participants inferred criticism or rejection an equal number of times across equally distributed stimuli (that is, half were critical/rejecting, and half were not). Therefore, both participants are exhibiting an equivalent degree of bias toward inferring criticism or rejection. However, determining each hypothetical participant's individual level of bias becomes more complicated as the ratio of critical/ rejecting stimuli to noncritical/nonrejecting stimuli diverges from a 50/50 split. Fortunately, signal detection theory was developed to accommodate differing stimulus (that is, signal) to nonstimulus (that is, noise) ratios, yielding accurate numerical indices of bias for almost any pattern of responses to almost any stimulus distribution.

When the first hypothetical participant inferred criticism or rejection, the stimulus was more likely to actually be critical or rejecting than when the second participant inferred criticism or rejection. In other words, the first participant more accurately inferred when the break was indeed critical or rejecting versus when it was not; that is, he discriminated between the two stimulus types with greater accuracy. The second hypothetical participant was equally biased but substantially less accurate. It is important to bear in mind that signal detection indices of bias and accuracy are not independent of one another. They do, however, characterize a set of responses in very different ways.

After we had obtained the empathic accuracy and thematic accuracy measures, we then computed partial correlations between the accuracy-related measures and the abuse-related measures, controlling for the participants' own dyadic adjustment (RDAS; Busby et al., 1995), their own relationship stability (see Schweinle, Ickes, & Bernstein, in press, for details), and how long each participant had been married. We controlled for these three variables because we assumed that they would reflect most directly how much criticism or rejection each husband actually encountered in his own wife's thoughts and feelings. In other words, our intent was to control for the base rate of actual criticism and rejection that our male participants experienced in their own marriages.

Our findings for the *thematic accuracy measure* revealed that the more that husbands reported abusing their own wives (as assessed by their CT-Coercive scores), the more biased they were to inappropriately infer that the women in the psychotherapy tapes had experienced critical or rejecting thoughts or feelings about their husbands ($r = .23$, $p < .05$; see Table 9.1). Further, scores on the Propensity to Abuse Scale (Dutton, 1995) tended to correlate positively with the overattribution bias when controlling for marital stability, adjustment, and duration ($r = .19$, $p < .085$).

It is possible that, compared to nonabusive men, abusive men may actually experience more criticism or rejection from their own female partners. If so, they may simply attribute criticism or rejection to other women's thoughts and feelings to an extent that matches what these men normally experience in their own relationship(s). Countering this interpretation, however, is the fact that the correlation between abuse and bias was computed after controlling for the influence of marital satisfaction, stability, and duration – factors that collectively should reflect, at least to some extent, the frequency of criticism or rejection these participants receive from their own marital partners. Our conclusion, though still somewhat tentative, is that the abusive men in our sample displayed a genuine inferential bias – a bias that was more pronounced among the men who were more abusive.

Table 9.1. Wife Abuse and Measures of Husbands' Inferential Accuracy or Bias on our Laboratory Task

	Theme Detection		Empathic or "Content" Accuracy		
	Bias to infer criticism or rejection (B''_D)	Ability to accurately detect when women are actually having critical/rejecting thoughts & feelings (d')	Critical/ Rejecting	Noncritical/ Nonrejecting	Overall Content Accuracy
Abuse propensity (PAS) ($M = 61.4$, $sd = 15.1$)	.19†	−.05	−.08	−.09	−.09
Anxious attachment (PAS-RSQ) ($M = 7.06$, $sd = 3.0$)	.24*	.04	−.08	.01	−.03
Use of reasoning to resolve conflict (CT-Reasoning) ($M = 11.4$, $sd = 3.9$)	−.15	.22*	.10	.11	.11
Use of abuse/aggression to resolve conflict (CT-Coercive) ($M = 11.9$, $sd = 5.12$)	.23*	.00	−.13	−.19†	−.17

Note: PAS = Propensity for Abusiveness Scale (Dutton, 1995); PAS-RSQ = Relationship Style Questionnaire in PAS (Dutton, 1995); CT = Conflict Tactics Scale (Straus, 1979). The CT Scalescores ($M = 23.3$, $sd = 7.5$) were adjusted for social desirability. All correlations statistically controlled for reported levels of relationship satisfaction, stability, and duration.
†p < .085; *p < .05.

Such evidence for an "overattribution bias" on the part of abusive men is important in at least two respects. First, it supports the position that abusive men are biased, rather than accurate, in their inferences about women's potentially critical or rejecting thoughts and feelings. Second, and perhaps even more important, it discourages the conclusion that abusive men are uniquely provoked by their own female partners, and instead suggests that they are biased to overattribute criticism and rejection to women in general. If abusive men display an inferential bias that applies to women in general, it is inappropriate to "blame the victim" (the abusive man's female partner) by attributing the man's abusive behavior to her criticism or rejection of him.

In contrast to this finding for our signal detection measure of *inferential bias* in thematic accuracy, the data for our signal detection measure of discrimination revealed that the men's ability to accurately determine when women had critical/rejecting thoughts or feelings did not relate at all to the men's reported abuse of their own wives (the relevant rs – zero-order and controlling for the marital adjustment variables – were $-.07$ and $.00$, respectively; see Table 9.1). Thus, the men's ability to detect the actual presence of women's criticism and rejection was not associated with their abuse, whereas the biased overattribution of women's criticism and rejection was.

In fact, the ability to accurately discern when the women really did have critical or rejecting thoughts and feelings was positively associated with the use of reasoning to resolve marital conflict ($r = .22$, $p < .05$). Further, the men who were able to accurately detect when the women were having unambiguously critical or rejecting thoughts and feelings reported that they were significantly more satisfied with their own marriages ($r = .22$, $p < .05$). Overall, these findings are consistent with Ickes and Simpson's (1997) theoretical speculation that inferential accuracy is generally good for relationships, whereas inaccuracy, perhaps in the form of bias, can be bad for relationships. This pattern of results has some interesting implications for future research that we will discuss later in this chapter.

Interestingly, the strength of the men's "overattribution bias" was found to be positively related ($r = .24$, $p < .05$) to one of the personality measures obtained in our study: the men's insecure attachment measured by the three relevant items that Dutton included in the PAS. These scale items originally appeared in the Relationship Styles Questionnaire developed by Griffin and Bartholomew (1992, as cited in Dutton, 1995), and men's responses to these items predicted their self-reported abusiveness (Dutton, 1995; 1998). Our finding fits well with similar reports by Dutton (1998) and Downey et al. (2000) regarding the relationship between abusiveness and fearful/anxious attachment. It should be noted, however, that in our sample there was not a significant correlation between the men's fearful/anxious attachment and their self-reported abusiveness. Therefore, it remains to be determined whether the relationship between the men's insecure attachment and their abusive behavior is a direct one, or whether it is mediated by the strength and/or direction of the men's bias in inferring that women are harboring critical and rejecting thoughts and feelings.

The Content Accuracy Data

When our measure of the men's "overattribution bias" from the thematic accuracy data was used to predict the men's overall accuracy in inferring the specific content of the video clients' thoughts and feelings, we found that the more biased the men were, the less accurately they inferred the actual content of the women's thoughts and feelings ($r = -.36$, $p < .01$). We also found that the more the men reported abusing their own wives, the less accurately they inferred the content of the video clients' noncritical/nonrejecting thoughts and feelings ($r = -.19$, $p < .085$; see Table 9.1). The first of these results indicates that the overattribution bias is a significant source of the overall impairment in empathic accuracy that was evident when the men attempted to infer the specific content of the female clients' thoughts and feelings. The second result further suggests that men's abuse of their own wives might be associated with a more general deficit in their ability to accurately "read" or decode the contents of women's noncritical/nonrejecting thoughts and feelings.

If we look at the partial correlations reported in Table 9.1, we can see that the more husbands reported abusing their own wives (CT-Coercive), the more biased they were to infer criticism or rejection in the thoughts and feelings of the three female clients when there actually was none. On the other hand, this measure of self-reported abusiveness did not relate at all to the husbands' ability to accurately infer when women do or do not have critical or rejecting thoughts and feelings about their partner. Finally, the more abusive men were less likely to correctly infer the actual content of the female clients' thoughts and feelings, particularly those thoughts and feelings that were not critical or rejecting.

FUTURE RESEARCH IMPLICATIONS

A plausible argument can be made that when abusive men attribute criticism or rejection to their partners, they become both angry and highly aroused. If this is indeed the case, then the biased overattribution of criticism or rejection may actually trigger abusive behavior in certain men. To explore this idea in greater detail, we will now consider some proposed research that is intended to validate and extend our reasoning.

In our future research, we hope to focus more specifically on four issues that are potentially relevant to men's abuse of their spouses: the emotional trigger for the abusive act, the men's attachment style and "rejection sensitivity," the different subtypes of male batterers that might exist, and the possibility that a clinical intervention could be used to reduce the strength of the overattribution bias.

The Emotional Trigger

The next step in this line of research involves studies designed to investigate the possibility that the overattribution bias displayed by many abusive men might in some way trigger their abusive behavior. We have already found evidence that abusive men tend to overattribute criticism and rejection to women they have never met. In a similar vein, previous studies have revealed that violent men are more likely to experience anger or irritation and to perceive more relationship threat in standardized presentations of relationship-threatening conflicts between couples (Dutton & Browning, 1988; Holtzworth-Munroe & Smutzler, 1996). What remains to be studied, however, is whether and how the overattribution of criticism or rejection to women might evoke this increased anger.

To begin to address this issue, we are currently planning another empathic accuracy study involving standardized stimuli and the real-time recording of husbands' attributions and emotional reactions to the events depicted on our videotapes. One goal of this study is to determine whether men's anger tends to accumulate over a succession of critical/rejecting attributions. Our tentative model of the process is one in which the men's biased overattribution of criticism or rejection evokes the men's anger, which can build up over time and eventually erupt in an abusive episode. If men's anger proves to be "additive" in this way, such a finding might help explain the repetitive cyclic pattern of build-up, abuse, and conciliation in the behavior of some abusive men (see Dutton, 1995; 1998).

Attachment and Rejection Sensitivity

Another promising avenue for future research will involve a more thorough investigation of the personality characteristics of abusive men – characteristics that could potentially relate to both the strength of their overattribution bias and the level of their abusive behavior.

From a conceptual standpoint, the overattribution bias bears an obvious resemblance to *rejection sensitivity*, another construct that has been used to characterize abusive men. Rejection sensitivity is the tendency to "anxiously expect, readily perceive, and overreact to social rejection" (Downey & Feldman, 1996, p. 1). Although the overattribution bias might sound very much like rejection sensitivity, the latter construct is presumed to be more general in scope and is assessed by self-report rather than by analyzing men's inferences about women's actual thoughts and feelings.

Both constructs have been empirically related to men's abusiveness (Downey et al., 2000; Schweinle, Ickes, & Bernstein, 2000). Downey et al. (2000) found that the relationship between men's rejection sensitivity and abusiveness was mediated by attachment style. Their data indicated that anxiously attached men (who want, but at the same time fear, close relationships) and avoidantly attached men (who fear and shun close relationships) were equally high in rejection sensitivity. However, the anxiously attached men were more likely to abuse their relationship partners, presumably because they were more likely than avoidant men to be involved in a psychologically close – as opposed to a psychologically distant – relationship (Downey et al., 2000).

At the time of this writing we are collecting data for a study that will further test the Downey et al. (2000) model by using a measure of men's rejection sensitivity (Downey & Feldman, 1996), our measure of attributional bias, and multiple measures of abusiveness. The results should provide important new information about the role of men's rejection sensitivity in wife abuse. It should also provide theoretically useful information about the relationships among this set of constructs.

Abuser Subtypes

Men who abuse their partners are often referred to as batterers. The classic stereotype of a battering husband is of a man who physically assaults his partner. Unfortunately, however, there does not appear to be a clear definition of battering behavior in the literature. Clearly, men's coercive behavior is not limited to physical assault and can take the form of sexual assault, verbal abuse, and emotional abuse (Engel 1990; Walker, 1979). Future research should investigate the possibility that abuser subtypes exist. If there is a typology that applies to all abusive men, it should be possible to investigate differences in decoding styles among the different subtypes.

Currently, there are several typological descriptions of physically abusive husbands (see Dutton, 1998) that might be used to guide such investigations. For example, Gottman, Jacobson, Rushe, Shortt, Babcock, LaTillade, and Waltz (1995) found that assaultive husbands could be grouped into two categories: Type I and Type II. The heart rates of the Type I husbands tended to decrease when they were confronted with a relationship conflict, whereas the heart rates of the Type II husbands tended to increase. If a similar Type I–Type II distinction generalizes to men who abuse their partners in ways other than physical assault (for example, psychological abuse, sexual abuse, verbal abuse, economic abuse, and so on), then future research on the inferential styles of Type I and Type II abusers might yield important information about decoding deficits that are specific to each abuser subtype.

Dutton and Browning (1988) used a standard stimulus paradigm similar to ours and found that assaultive men perceived more threat and experienced more anger than nonassaultive men while watching a videotape of a couple conflict. Interestingly, Dutton and Browning did not find any mean differences in physiological arousal between abusive and nonabusive men. However, it is possible that, compared to nonabusive men, some abusive men (Type II) become *more* physiologically aroused, whereas other abusive men (Type I) become *less* physiologically aroused when viewing such stimulus material. If so, then the true difference between abusive and nonabusive men may lie in the variability of their physiological response rather than in the average magnitude of this response.

It is also possible that Type I and Type II abusers will differ with respect to their rejection sensitivity and/or the strength of their overattribution bias. According to Jacobson and Gottman (1998), Type I abusers, or "cobras," tend to encourage their partners to be more independent, whereas Type II abusers, or "pit bulls," are more dependent and fearful of abandonment. These findings suggest that rejection sensitivity and a strong overattribution bias might be most evident in the Type II abusers.

Interestingly, Gottman et al.'s Type I and Type II abusers appear to correspond to types found in the taxonomy of abusive men proposed by Holtzworth-Munroe, Meehan, Herron, Rehman, and Stuart (2000). These authors speculated that two categories – *antisocial* and *dysphoric/borderline* – may be sufficient to categorize all abusive men. If Type I batterers prove to be the antisocial type whereas Type II batterers prove to be the dysphoric/borderline type, we might anticipate that rapid progress will be made in research designed to test for links between abusers' personality traits, their inferences about their partners' thoughts and feelings, and their preferred mode and level of abusive behavior.

Clinical Intervention

With regard to intervention, treatment programs for domestically violent men have not been very successful (Dobash & Dobash, 2000). Our findings suggest that social skills training that specifically targets abusive men's overattribution bias might be more likely to succeed than the more general social skills training that is typically employed. Unless we are dealing with the type of abusive man who is physiologically incapable of impulse control under any circumstances, we might be able to integrate anger management and social skills training into a therapeutic program that focuses on decreasing the occurrence and magnitude of angry episodes, by decreasing the men's inferential bias and increasing their empathic accuracy.

Another important application of our findings derives from their generality. In our study we did not compare a group of known batterers to a group of known nonbatterers. Instead, we treated wife abuse as a continuous variable that tapped both verbal and physical abuse. Because we used this approach, our findings have implications for the treatment of couples with an emotionally or psychologically abusive man. Many men are psychologically or emotionally abusive of their partners without ever "crossing the line" into physical abuse (Tolman, 1992). Our findings suggest that such men are more likely to display the "overattribution bias" that we have described. If this is indeed the case, then our findings suggest the utility of a therapeutic approach designed to decrease the men's bias to infer criticism or rejection where none exists. Such an approach could not only help to improve the men's empathic accuracy, but could also increase both partners' satisfaction as well as the women's feelings of being understood.

SUMMARY

In this chapter, we have examined recent evidence about the differences in the ways that abusive and nonabusive men perceive women and infer their thoughts and feelings. From this evidence, it appears that men who abuse their wives tend to display an "overattribution bias." That is, abusive men are likely to infer that women have critical or rejecting thoughts or feelings about their male partners more often than is actually the case. Further, these men are especially sensitive and reactive to signs of rejection from women.

On the other hand, it appears that men who are able to accurately discern when women have critical/rejecting thoughts or feelings about their partners are more satisfied with their own marriages and are more likely to use nonabusive methods for dealing with relationship conflict. It may be that husbands who do not overattribute critical or rejecting thoughts and feelings to women, also do not experience as much "additive" negative affect, and therefore do not abuse. Finally, our data suggest that men who have greater thematic and content accuracy for women's thoughts and feelings are able to use this information to adjust their behavior in a manner that results in less abusive, less conflicted, and more satisfying marital interactions. Future investigations should explore these possibilities.

Another important question for future research is whether the overattribution bias is a social skill deficiency that could be treated effectively in at least some abusive men. Some authors have proposed that judicial intervention is the only reasonable approach to dealing with abusive men (Jacobson & Gottman, 1998). This may indeed be the case – at least at the present time. However, as more is learned about the clinically treatable deficiencies or characteristics of abusive men, there is room for hope that more effective treatment programs can be designed and implemented. Ideally, these treatment programs could be incorporated into a more broad-based approach for dealing with domestic violence, such as the Coordinated Community Response program (Pence & Paymar, 1993).

REFERENCES

Anglin, K., & Holtzworth-Munroe, A. (1997). Comparing responses of maritally violent and nonviolent spouses to problematic marital and nonmarital situations: Are the skill deficits of physically aggressive husbands and wives global? *Journal of Family Psychology, 11*(3), 301–313.

Barling, J., O'Leary, K. D., Jouriles, E. N., Vivian, D., & MacEwen, K. E. (1987). Factor similarity of the Conflict Tactics Scales across sample, spouses and sites: Issues and implications. *Journal of Family Violence, 2*(1), 37–54.

Barnard, G., Vera, H., Vera, M., & Newman, G. (1982). Till death do us part: A study of spouse murder. *Bulletin of the American Academy of Psychiatry and the Law, 10*(4), 271–280.

Berry, D. (1998). *The domestic violence sourcebook*. Los Angeles: Lowell House.

Bersani, C., Chen, H., Pendleton, B., & Denton, R. (1992). Personality traits of convicted male batterers. *Journal of Family Violence, 7*(2), 123–134.

Busby, D. M., Christensen, C., Crane, D. R., & Larson, J. H. (1995). A revision of the Dyadic Adjustment Scales for use with distressed and nondistressed couples: Construct hierarchy and multidimensional scales. *Journal of Marital and Family Therapy, 21*(3), 289–308.

Deschner, J. P. (1984). *The hitting habit*. New York: The Free Press.

Dobash, R. E., & Dobash, R. P. (2000). Evaluating criminal justice interventions for domestic violence. *Crime and Delinquency, 46*(2), 252–270.

Dodge, K. (1980). Social cognition and children's aggressive behavior. *Child Development, 51*, 162–170.

Dodge, K., & Somberg, D. (1987). Hostile attributional biases among aggressive boys are exacerbated under conditions of threats to the self. *Child Development, 58*, 213–224.

Donaldson, W. (1992). Measuring recognition memory. *Journal of Experimental Psychology: General, 121*(3), 275–277.

Downey, G., & Feldman, S. (1996). Implications of rejection sensitivity for intimate relationships. *Journal of Personality and Social Psychology, 70*, 1327–1343.

Downey, G., Feldman, S., & Ayduk, O. (2000). Rejection sensitivity and male violence in romantic relationships. *Personal Relationships, 7*, 54–61.

Dutton, D. G. (1995). A scale for measuring propensity for abusiveness. *Journal of Family Violence, 10*(2), 203–221.

Dutton, D. G. (1998). *The abusive personality*. New York: Guilford Press.

Dutton, D. G., & Browning, J. J. (1988). Concern for power, fear and intimacy, and aversive stimuli for wife assault. In G. T. Hotaling, D. Finkelhor, J. T. Kirkpatrick, & M. A. Straus (Eds.), *Family abuse and its consequences: New directions in research* (pp. 163–175). Newbury Park, CA: Sage.

Dutton, D. G., Saunders, K., Starzomski, A., & Bartholomew, K. (1994). Intimacy-anger and insecure attachment as precursors of abuse in intimate relationships. *Journal of Applied Social Psychology, 24*, 1367–1386.

Dutton, D., Starzomski, A., & Ryan, L. (1996). Antecedents of abusive personality and abusive behavior in wife assaulters. *Journal of Family Violence, 11*(2), 113–132.

Engel, B. (1990). *The emotionally abused woman*. Chicago: Contemporary Books.

Gesn, P. R., & Ickes, W. (1999). The development of meaning contexts for empathic accuracy: Channel and sequence effects. *Journal of Personality and Social Psychology, 77*(4), 746–761.

Gottman, J., Jacobson, N., Rushe, R., Shortt, J., Babcock, J., LaTillade, J., & Waltz, J. (1995). The relationship between heart rate activity, emotionally aggressive behavior, and general violence in batterers. *Journal of Family Violence, 9*(3), 227–248.

Green, D., & Swets, J. (1966). *Signal detection theory and psychophysics.* (Reprint.) New York: Krieger, 1974.

Griffin, D., & Bartholomew, K. (1992). *Testing a two dimensional model of adult attachment: A latent variable approach.* Department of Psychology, University of Waterloo, as cited in Dutton, D. G. (1995). A scale for measuring propensity for abusiveness. *Journal of Family Violence, 10*(2), 203–221.

Hemingway, E. (1927). *Men without women.* New York: Charles Scribner's Sons.

Holtzworth-Munroe, A. (1992). Social skill deficits in maritally violent men: Interpreting the data using a social information processing model. *Clinical Psychology Review, 12*, 605–617.

Holtzworth-Munroe, A., & Hutchinson, G. (1993). Attributing negative intent to wife behavior: The attributions of maritally violent men versus nonviolent men. *Journal of Abnormal Psychology, 102*, 206–211.

Holtzworth-Munroe, A., Meehan, J., Herron, K., Rehman, U., & Stuart, G. (2000). Testing the Holtzworth-Munroe and Stuart (1994) batterer typology. *Journal of Consulting and Clinical Psychology, 68*, 1000–1019.

Holtzworth-Munroe, A., & Smutzler, N. (1996). Comparing the emotional reactions and behavioral intentions of violent and nonviolent husbands to aggressive, distressed, and other wife behaviors. *Violence and Victims, 11*(4), 319–339.

Ickes, W. (1993). Empathic accuracy. *Journal of Personality, 61*, 587–610.

Ickes, W. (1997). *Empathic accuracy.* New York: Guilford.

Ickes, W., & Simpson, J. (1997). Managing empathic accuracy in close relationships. In W. Ickes (Ed.), *Empathic accuracy* (pp. 218–250). New York: Guilford.

Jacobson, N., & Gottman, J. (1998). *When men batter women.* New York: Simon and Schuster.

Marangoni, C., Garcia, S., Ickes, W., & Teng, G. (1995). Empathic accuracy in a clinically relevant setting. *Journal of Personality and Social Psychology, 68*, 854–869.

Margolin, G. (1988). Interpersonal and intrapersonal factors associated with marital violence. In G. T. Hotaling, D. Finkelhor, J. T. Kirkpatrick, & M. A. Straus (Eds.), *Family abuse and its consequences: New directions in research* (pp. 163–175). Newbury Park, CA: Sage.

McFall, R. (1982). A review and reformulation of the concept of social skills. *Behavioral Assessment, 4*, 1–33.

Nelson, N. (1997). *Dangerous relationships.* New York: Plenum.

Pence, E., & Paymar, M. (1993). *Education Groups for Men Who Batter.* New York: Springer-Verlag.

Richardson, D., Hammock, G., Smith, S., & Gardner, W. (1994). Empathy as a cognitive inhibitor of interpersonal aggression. *Aggressive Behavior, 20*(4), 275–289.

Saunders, D. G. (1991). Procedures for adjusting self-reports of violence for social desirability bias. *Journal of Interpersonal Violence, 6*(3), 336–344.

Schweinle, W. E., Ickes, W., & Bernstein, I. H. (in press). Empathic inaccuracy in husband to wife aggression: The overattribution bias. *Personal Relationships.*

Sillars, A. (1998). (Mis)understanding. In B. Spitzberg & W. Cupach (Eds.), *The dark side of close relationships* (pp. 73–102). Mahwah, NJ: Lawrence Erlbaum Associates.

Simpson, J., Ickes, W., & Grich, J. (1999). When accuracy hurts: Reactions of anxious-ambivalent dating partners to a relationship threatening situation. *Journal of Personality and Social Psychology, 76*(5), 754–769.

Stith, S., & Farley, S. (1993). A predictive model of male spousal violence. *Journal of Family Violence, 8*(2), 183–201.

Strahan, R., & Gerbasi, K. C. (1972). Short homogeneous versions of the Marlowe-Crowne social desirability scale. *Journal of Clinical Psychology, 28*, 191–193.

Straus, M. A. (1979). Measuring intrafamily conflict and violence: The conflict tactics (CT) scales. *Journal of Marriage and the Family, 41*(1), 75–88.

Straus, M., & Gelles, R. (1988). How violent are American families? Estimates from the National Family Violence Resurvey and other studies. In G. T. Hotaling, D. Finkelhor, J. T. Kirkpatrick, & M. A. Shaw (Eds.), *Family abuse and its consequences: New directions in research* (pp. 14–36). Newbury Park, CA: Sage.

Toch, H. (1969). *Violent men.* Chicago: Aldine Publishing Company.

Tolman, R. (1992). Psychological abuse of women. In R. Ammerman & M. Hersen (Eds.), *Assessment of family violence: A clinical and legal sourcebook* (pp. 291–310). New York: Wiley.

Tolman, R. (1999). The validation of the psychological maltreatment of women inventory. *Violence and Victims, 14*(1), 25–35.

Wallbott, H. G. (1995). Congruence, contagion and motor mimicry: Mutualities in nonverbal exchange. In I. Markova and C. Graumann (Eds.), *Mutualities in dialogue* (pp. 82–98) Cambridge: Cambridge University Press.

Walker, L. E. (1979). *The battered woman.* New York: Harper & Row.

Walker, L. E. (1984). *The battered woman syndrome.* New York: Harper & Row.

Willis, C., Hallinan, M., & Melby, J. (1996). Effects of sex role stereotyping among European American students on domestic violence culpability attributions. *Sex Roles, 34*(7–8), 475–491.

CHAPTER TEN

The War of the Roses: An Interdependence Analysis of Betrayal and Forgiveness

Caryl E. Rusbult, Madoka Kumashiro,
Eli J. Finkel, and Tim Wildschut

Barbara and Oliver Rose – I think you should hear their story . . . I won't start the clock yet. My fee is $450 an hour. When a man who makes $450 an hour wants to tell you something for free, you should listen.
– Gavin D'Amata, *The War of the Roses*

Gavin D'Amata is a divorce lawyer. With the preceding words to a prospective client, Gavin begins to recount *The War of the Roses*, a (sometimes hilarious) marital cautionary tale. The unfolding narrative reveals the troubled marriage of Barbara and Oliver Rose: Oliver belittles Barbara's career; Barbara neglects Oliver during a frightening health crisis; each humiliates the other, delivering impossible-to-forget attacks on the other's tastes and habits. During their marital Armageddon, Barbara and Oliver become entangled in a chandelier suspended above a hallway. The mechanism supporting the chandelier gives way, and – embraced in the arms of the chandelier – the two crash to the unyielding terazzo floor 30 feet below. With his dying breath, Oliver reaches out to touch Barbara's shoulder, offering amends and seeking forgiveness. Barbara's hand slowly rises to meet Oliver's . . . (perhaps, one imagines, to reciprocate Oliver's act) . . . and with her dying breath, Barbara flings Oliver's hand away from her.

Why is the Rose marriage interesting, from a scientific point of view? The Roses are interesting because their marital woes do not stem from the sorts of faulty communication patterns traditionally emphasized in marital research – patterns involving negative reciprocity,

Correspondence regarding this work should be addressed to Caryl Rusbult, Department of Psychology, University of North Carolina at Chapel Hill, Chapel Hill, North Carolina 27599-3270 (rusbult@unc.edu). Preparation of this chapter was supported in part by a grant from the Templeton Foundation (No. 5158).

demand-withdraw, or coercive interaction (cf. Gottman, Coan, Carrere, & Swanson, 1998). And the Roses are interesting because their marital woes do not originate in the sorts of interdependence dilemmas traditionally emphasized in marital research – dilemmas involving incompatible preferences, external sources of stress, or extrarelationship temptation (cf. Rusbult, Olsen, Davis, & Hannon, 2001). Granted, the Roses do not communicate well, and their marital problems are exacerbated by everyday sorts of marital dilemmas. However, the Roses are interesting primarily because their marital woes rest on repeated betrayal, and a rather thoroughgoing inability to forgive. We suggest that, to date, these phenomena have received insufficient theoretical and empirical attention.

Until quite recently, the concepts of betrayal and forgiveness were addressed primarily in the fields of philosophy and theology (for example, Dorff, 1992; Marty, 1998; North, 1987). It is only during the past decade that social scientists have begun to explore the process by which individuals achieve forgiveness of betrayal (for a review, see McCullough, Sandage, & Worthington, 1997). Recent empirical studies have examined the manner in which individuals perceive and explain betrayal incidents (for example, Baumeister, Stillwell, & Wotman, 1990; Boon & Sulsky, 1997; Gonzales, Haugen, & Manning, 1994), the emotional reactions that accompany betrayal incidents (for example, Ohbuchi, Kameda, & Agarie, 1989; Tangney, Wagner, Hill-Barlow, Marschall, & Gramzow, 1996), and the role of interaction processes in promoting the resolution of betrayal incidents (for example, McCullough, Worthington, & Rachal, 1997; Weiner, Graham, Peter, & Zmuidinas, 1991). Also, some empirical work has examined the efficacy of clinical interventions designed to encourage forgiveness of betrayal (for example, Freedman & Enright, 1996; McCullough & Worthington, 1995).

Thus, recent empirical work begins to shed light on the forgiveness process by examining the cognitive, affective, and interactional concomitants of this phenomenon. Unfortunately, there have been few attempts to analyze forgiveness and related phenomena using well-established, comprehensive theories of interpersonal processes. Also, very few empirical studies have sought to examine the motivational underpinnings of this phenomenon, seeking to explain why forgiveness may be difficult, and identifying what makes individuals want to forgive others. In short, thus far we have learned somewhat more about *how* individuals forgive than *why* they forgive.

The present work uses the principles of interdependence theory to analyze betrayal and forgiveness (Kelley & Thibaut, 1978; Thibaut & Kelley, 1959). We begin by characterizing betrayal in terms of norm violations, describing characteristic profiles of response to betrayal, and discussing the concepts of victim forgiveness and perpetrator atonement. Then we turn to the concept of reconciliation, discussing renegotiation processes and reviewing distinctions among renegotiation, forgiveness, and reconciliation. Next we address transformation of motivation, advocating a motivational analysis of forgiveness and outlining the character of the transformation process. Finally, we consider the roles of several personal dispositions and relationship-specific variables in the forgiveness process, with particular attention to the concepts of commitment and trust.

BETRAYAL AND FORGIVENESS

Over the past several decades we have studied a variety of *relationship maintenance acts*, studying behaviors that are costly to the individual, yet beneficial to relationships. For example, we have examined: accommodation, or the tendency to react to a partner's rude or inconsiderate behavior by inhibiting destructive impulses and instead reacting in a constructive manner (for example, Rusbult, Verette, Whitney, Slovik, & Lipkus, 1991); willingness to sacrifice, or the tendency to forego otherwise desirable behaviors (or enact otherwise undesirable behaviors) when partners' interests conflict (for example, Van Lange, Rusbult, Drigotas, Arriaga, Witcher, & Cox, 1997); and derogation of alternatives, or the inclination to cognitively disparage attractive alternative partners (for example, Johnson & Rusbult, 1989). All of these acts (a) arise in response to interdependence situations involving the potential for harm, (b) entail some effort or cost on the part of the individual, and (c) typically are beneficial to relationships. What differentiates forgiveness from the sorts of phenomena we have examined in previous work?

Norms and Norm Violations

Unlike other sorts of maintenance acts, betrayal incidents involve norm violations. Indeed, betrayal typically is defined as "being unfaithful or disloyal," "revealing something meant to be hidden," or "seducing and deserting." In the context of close relationships, we define *betrayal* as the perceived violation of an implicit or explicit relationship-relevant norm. Betrayal may be said to have occurred when the victim believes that the perpetrator has knowingly departed from the rules that govern their relationship, thereby causing harm to the victim. Betrayal may involve minor or major normative infractions. Toward the mild end of the betrayal continuum, Oliver might embarrass Barbara during a dinner party, telling a story that makes her appear ignorant. Toward the more serious end of the continuum, Barbara might attempt to seduce Oliver's best friend.

Norms are rule-based inclinations to respond to particular interdependence situations in a specified manner – that is, partners implicitly or explicitly agree that some courses of action are forbidden, whereas other courses of action are mandated. As such, norms specify the rules by which a relationship will be governed (cf. Rusbult & Van Lange, 1996). For example, Barbara and Oliver may agree that some interaction sequences are not to be initiated (or must be initiated; for example, never humiliate the partner), that some interaction contingencies are not to transpire (or must transpire; for example, always support the partner the night before important work-related events), and that some interaction sequences are not to take place (or must take place) with particular sorts of partners (for example, never become sexually intimate with an extrarelationship partner).

Interdependence theory identifies several important properties of norms (Thibaut & Kelley, 1959): (a) norms regulate interaction behavior, making interaction orderly and predictable; (b) in situations where such regularity is interrupted, the victim frequently attempts to regain control by appealing to the norm; and (c) the norm breaker frequently feels guilty about violating the norm. Norms may initially be established as a matter of convenience – as a means of coordinating potentially complex interdependence situations. For example, to regulate their finances during the early years of marriage, Barbara and Oliver may agree to discuss all purchases exceeding $50. However, over time such rules frequently "take on the characteristics of a moral obligation" (Thibaut & Kelley, 1959, p. 128). Thus, although the Roses later become quite wealthy, and although the "$50 rule" was established in circumstances quite different from those they now confront, when Barbara fails to discuss a purchase with Oliver, Oliver experiences moral outrage and Barbara feels guilty.

The Experience of Betrayal

Consistent with this normative account, the empirical literature reveals characteristic constellations of reactions to betrayal on the part of both victim and perpetrator. Following betrayal, the victim may find it difficult to depart from the negative affect associated with the incident – Oliver may experience persistent and debilitating sadness or anger (for example, Ohbuchi et al., 1989; Rosenzweig-Smith, 1988). The victim may also develop negative patterns of cognition – Oliver may feel confused by the event and its implications, may obsessively review events surrounding the betrayal, or may reinterpret prebetrayal behavior, questioning whether earlier construals of Barbara's behavior were correct (for example, Baumeister et al., 1990; Boon & Sulsky, 1997). And the victim may adopt negative behavioral tendencies in interactions with the perpetrator – Oliver may persistently seek vengeance or demand retribution and atonement (for example, Fagenson & Cooper, 1987; Kremer & Stephens, 1983).

The perpetrator, too, may exhibit persistent negative affect – Barbara may experience sadness, shame, or guilt (for example, Baumeister, Stillwell, & Heatherton, 1995; Tangney et al., 1996). Further, the victim's negative cognitive tendencies may be mirrored by the perpetrator – Oliver's negative attributions may be met with defensive cognition on the part of Barbara, who may feel the need to absolve herself of blame, justifying the betrayal to herself and to others (for example, Gonzales, Manning, & Haugen, 1992; Stillwell & Baumeister, 1997). And the victim's negative behavioral tendencies may yield negative perpetrator behavior – Oliver's desire for revenge and demands for atonement may be met with matching negativity on the part of Barbara, in that few perpetrators will suffer endless blame and offer bottomless amends (for example, Hodgins, Liebeskind, & Schwartz, 1996; Ohbuchi et al., 1989).

Why do norm violations rather automatically yield such negativity? Over the course of extended involvement, interaction partners develop characteristic patterns of response to recognizable interdependence situations, including habitual emotional, cognitive, and behavioral impulses (cf. Rusbult & Van Lange, 1996). Humans count on adherence to rules, so adaptation to betrayal incidents is likely to include the impulse to punish transgressors – an impulse embodied in reactions such as righteous indignation and hostile behavioral tendencies. Because betrayal incidents cause the victim harm, violate moral obligations, and

challenge the "proper order of things," such incidents instigate a sig-
nature constellation of victim and perpetrator cognition, affect, and behavior. Thus, the victim's impulse toward vengeance and other forms
of "debt reduction" can be seen to be functionally adaptive – at least
in the short run – in that the inclination to punish transgressors is a
mechanism for enforcing relationship-relevant norms.

In parallel manner, the perpetrator's impulse toward guilt and behavioral "debt reduction" can be seen to be functionally adaptive, in
that such inclinations provide reassurance that betrayal incidents will
not recur. Indeed, it has been argued that reactions such as victim
vengeance and perpetrator guilt may have an evolutionary basis, rest-
ing on the functional value to social animals of mutual cooperation and
rule-adherence (cf. Ridley, 1996).

Victim Forgiveness of Betrayal

How can victim and perpetrator move beyond this constellation of
negativity? Proceeding in a positive manner rests on victim forgiveness. Forgiveness is typically defined in terms of "granting pardon" or
"cancelling a debt." Previous research has adopted related definitions,
including: "a willingness to abandon one's right to resentment, con-
demnation, and subtle revenge toward an offender who acts unjustly,
while fostering the undeserved qualities of compassion, generosity, and
even love toward him/her" (Enright & the Human Development Study
Group, 1996, p. 108); and "the set of motivational changes whereby
one becomes decreasingly motivated to retaliate against an offend-
ing partner, decreasingly motivated to maintain estrangement from
the offender, and increasingly motivated by conciliation and goodwill
for the offender, despite the offender's hurtful actions" (McCullough,
Worthington, & Rachal, 1997, pp. 321–322). Distinguishing between intrapsychic and interpersonal events, forgiveness has also been defined
in terms of: "(a) the inner, intrapsychic dimension involving the victim's
emotional state (and the cognitive and behavioral accompaniments),
and (b) the interpersonal dimension involving the ongoing relationship within which forgiveness takes place or fails to do so" (Baumeister,
Exline, & Sommer, 1998, p. 80).

The above-noted definitions differ in the degree to which they characterize forgiveness as *intra*personal versus *inter*personal. Indeed, lay
construals of this construct would seem to be rather multifaceted,
including both internal qualities (for example, mentally "forgiving"

another's transgression) and interpersonal qualities (for example, "forgiving" another by resuming prebetrayal patterns of behavior). We suggest that, from a purely logical point of view, an *inter*personal definition of forgiveness is compelling. Consider (a) intrapersonal forgiveness in the absence of interpersonal forgiveness, along with its converse, (b) interpersonal forgiveness in the absence of intrapersonal forgiveness. For example, imagine that a victim develops compassion for a transgressor who has committed a heinous act, yet condemns the transgressor to death; or imagine that Barbara understands why Oliver betrayed her, yet insists on divorcing him. Intrapersonal "forgiveness" in the absence of interpersonal "forgiveness" seems a bit hollow (the perpetrator's likely reaction might be "thank you very much for 'forgiving' me; now why won't you forgive me?"). In contrast, imagine that a victim feels nothing but contempt for a transgressor who has committed a heinous act, yet does not condemn the transgressor to death; or imagine that Barbara believes that Oliver is fully responsible for his hurtful act and feels terribly unhappy about his behavior, yet is willing to resume normal behavior in their marriage. This line of reasoning suggests that *inter*personal "forgiveness" in the absence of *intra*personal "forgiveness" is considerably more meaningful than its converse.

Our work concerns forgiveness in ongoing close relationships. In light of logical arguments favoring an interpersonal definition of the forgiveness construct, we emphasize the interpersonal character of this phenomenon, and define *forgiveness* as the victim's resumption of prebetrayal behavioral tendencies – that is, as the tendency to forego vengeance and other destructive patterns of interaction, instead behaving toward the perpetrator in a positive and constructive manner. Indeed, we suggest that *inter*personal forgiveness captures the essence of forgiveness, in that the victim effectively cancels the debt created by the perpetrator's act of betrayal.

Perpetrator Behavior and Forgiveness

Of course, forgiveness is not necessarily an immediate, unilateral response on the part of victims. In the aftermath of betrayal, perpetrators, too, may play a role in bringing about victim forgiveness. Interdependence theory uses transition list representations to characterize temporally extended interactions (Kelley, 1984). The transition list representation is predicated on the assumption that, in addition to selecting specific behaviors, interacting individuals also select, consciously or

unconsciously, future interaction possibilities. That is, in a given interaction, each partner's choice of one course of action rather than another
not only yields immediate outcomes for the two individuals, but also
creates new interaction opportunities for the dyad (and eliminates other
opportunities).

An example best illustrates the concept of the transition list: As their
marriage begins to deteriorate, Oliver accidentally runs over Barbara's
cat with his car. In revenge, Barbara locks him in his sauna to die of heat
prostration, but later repents and suggests that they talk things over. To
create a congenial environment for their "peace talk," Oliver brings a
good bottle of wine and Barbara brings a delicious paté. During their
"peace talk" Oliver risks rejection by saying that he still loves Barbara
and wants to reconcile. Barbara silently considers whether to respond
with conciliation (telling Oliver that she loves him), but instead chooses
retaliation (telling Oliver that her paté is made from his dog). Barbara's
choice of response not only degrades the outcomes for both partners in
the immediate interaction, but also enhances the negativity of the future
interactions available to the pair: Her response not only makes it difficult for Oliver to apologize for killing her cat, but also takes the spouses
down a fork in the "interaction road" on which mutual forgiveness is not
a viable possibility. Had Barbara instead chosen a conciliatory response,
she would have made available a domain of interactions in which Oliver
might apologize and offer atonement – a domain in which mutual forgiveness continued to be a viable possibility.

Given that betrayal creates an interpersonal debt, the perpetrator's
postbetrayal behavior presumably exerts some impact on the victim's
decision to forgive (for example, has the perpetrator "paid off the
debt?"; Exline & Baumeister, 2000; Gonzales et al., 1994). Forgiveness
on the part of Barbara becomes unlikely to the extent that Oliver denies
responsibility for his actions or offers an insincere apology. In contrast,
victim forgiveness is promoted by perpetrator behaviors that communicate acceptance of responsibility, such as confession, apology, or postbetrayal cooperation (Darby & Schlenker, 1982; Komorita, Hilty, & Parks,
1991; Weiner et al., 1991).

By engaging in acts of atonement, Oliver "humbles himself," acknowledging the existence of a debt and working to reduce it. Moreover, by accepting personal responsibility, Oliver provides reassurance
that the transgression will not recur. As noted earlier, in the aftermath
of betrayal the victim may question whether the rules that were seen
to govern a relationship can be trusted, and may question whether the

perpetrator values the self or relationship. Concerns such as these are likely to be exacerbated to the extent that a perpetrator denies responsibility for his or her actions, minimizes the severity of a betrayal incident, or engages in self-justification (Darby & Schlenker, 1982). In contrast, feelings of victim insecurity and concerns about possible recurrence of betrayal should be assuaged by perpetrators who provide clear assurance to the victim that trust can be restored. Indeed, recent work regarding betrayal in ongoing relationships has revealed that the probability of victim forgiveness and couple reconciliation is enhanced by perpetrator acts of atonement (Hannon, 2001).

Unfortunately, although perpetrator behaviors such as apology or confession are likely to increase the probability of victim forgiveness, perpetrators may not reliably enact such behaviors. To begin with, victims and perpetrators have differing perspectives on the issue at hand. Barbara may believe that relationship-relevant rules are clear to both parties, and may be convinced that it is Oliver's responsibility to make amends for the betrayal. In contrast, Oliver may not recognize that he has violated the rules, particularly when such rules are implicit rather than explicit. In a related vein, victims and perpetrators may perceive postbetrayal events somewhat differently: Narrative accounts of betrayal incidents reveal that whereas perpetrators frequently believe that they have fully atoned for their sins and have received forgiveness (or at the very least, "earned" forgiveness), victims frequently believe that additional atonement is "owed" (Couch, Jones, & Moore, 1999).

Even when perpetrators know that they have violated the rules, they may find it difficult to accept responsibility for their actions. Admitting guilt may imply that the perpetrator is obligated to make extensive reparations, or may imply that the perpetrator's future actions will be restricted (Exline & Baumeister, 2000). Given that acts of betrayal that are seen to be intentional and blameworthy are less readily forgiven (Boon & Sulsky, 1997; Gonzales et al., 1994), to the extent that admitting guilt enhances perceptions of perpetrator intent and blame, perpetrators may be less likely to confess, offer atonement, or otherwise accept responsibility for betrayal. Instead, they may seek to convince the victim that the betrayal was unintentional, or that there were extenuating circumstances.

Indeed, defensive accounts of betrayal may constitute more than an impression management strategy intended to maximize the probability of forgiveness. Given that acts of betrayal violate moral obligations, Oliver may feel the need to justify his actions not only to Barbara, but

also to himself (Gonzales et al., 1992). Narrative accounts of betrayal incidents reveal relatively clear evidence of self-serving bias (Baumeister
et al., 1990; Couch et al., 1999). Whereas perpetrators are likely to perceive that their acts of atonement led to improvements in the relationship, victims are somewhat more likely to perceive a net decrease in
relationship functioning. Even when presented with hypothetical betrayal descriptions, individuals who are randomly assigned to victim
versus perpetrator roles recall such descriptions differently, with those
in the perpetrator role exhibiting greater denial of responsibility for the
betrayal (Stillwell & Baumeister, 1997).

The victim's own postbetrayal behavior may also influence whether
a perpetrator is willing to offer amends. Although both Barbara and
Oliver may perceive that a given act constituted betrayal, they may differ in their beliefs about the amount of reparation that is sufficient to
constitute amends (Exline & Baumeister, 2000). Victims often induce
guilt in an effort to enhance the amount or duration of perpetrator
amends (Baumeister et al., 1995), but too much guilt induction may
yield the opposite effect. For example, if Oliver believes that he has re-
paid the debt and therefore perceives that punishment by Barbara is
excessive, the motivation to make amends may decline; as noted earlier, few perpetrators will endure endless payback and offer bottomless
amends (for example, Hodgins et al., 1996; Ohbuchi et al., 1989). Thus,
although victims may induce guilt to promote perpetrator amends, the
opposite course of action may sometimes be more effective. Specifically, abandoning guilt induction may sometimes yield superior outcomes, in that such behavior communicates that (a) the perpetrator's
reparative actions are not unrecognized, and (b) trust may eventually
be recovered.

RENEGOTIATION AND RECONCILIATION

Renegotiation of Norms

As is true for other sorts of interpersonal dilemmas, dealing with betrayal can be construed in terms of conflict resolution. Forgiveness is
not only difficult, but frequently may be antithetical to the victim's interests, in that forgiveness may leave the victim vulnerable to future betrayal. For example, imagine that Oliver humiliates Barbara at a dinner
party by telling a story that embarrasses her, and that Barbara readily
forgives Oliver's actions, perhaps without calling attention to the fact

that she feels betrayed. Oliver may continue to engage in parallel humiliating acts, not recognizing that such acts are experienced as betrayal. To avoid future problems, the partners must resolve their conflicting views of what constitutes betrayal, as well as how such incidents should be resolved.

Renegotiation may entail redefining the norms that govern a relationship ("don't tell stories that diminish me in others' eyes"), explicitly outlining the terms of forgiveness ("at our next dinner party you must tell stories that make me look good"), or specifying the consequences of future, parallel acts of betrayal ("I'll forgive you this time, but if it ever happens again..."). Peterson (1983) suggests that differences of opinion can be resolved via: (a) separation (for example, Barbara may state that she wants a divorce); (b) domination, whereby one partner specifies the operative norm and the other agrees to that norm (for example, Barbara may insist that Oliver adhere to her preferred norm); (c) compromise, whereby the partners state their opinions and then "split the difference," adjusting their preferred positions until a mutually acceptable norm is identified (for example, stories can be told if they are embarrassing but not humiliating); and (d) developing an integrative agreement, or a solution that satisfies both partners' original goals and aspirations (for example, Oliver may tell funny stories that involve both partners, so that he is allowed to be funny but she is protected from humiliation).

Especially in cases involving severe betrayal – for which forgiveness may be quite difficult – renegotiation may be an integral component of the forgiveness process. Indeed, victims may find it possible to cancel the debt incurred by betrayal, only by clarifying the new terms of their relationship. Once working rules are reestablished, the victim may more readily forego vengeance and other relationship-threatening behaviors (for example, scrupulous monitoring of the perpetrator's actions).

Thus, renegotiation may reintroduce the sense of predictability that was shattered by betrayal, enhancing the victim's sense of control and capacity to forgive. Indeed, renegotiation may promote benevolent betrayal-relevant cognition and emotion. For example, Barbara may shift attribution of responsibility away from Oliver by acknowledging his ignorance of the norm (for example, "I guess he didn't know such actions were humiliating"). Specifying the consequences of future parallel betrayals may also lessen negative affect in that the new rules can serve as guidelines for judging behavior, rendering future transgressions simpler to detect (Holmes & Murray, 1996). If an act of betrayal does not recur, the victim can cease monitoring and quit reminding the perpetrator of the consequences of such actions.

Moreover, when couples do not see eye-to-eye regarding the norms that govern their relationship, renegotiation may yield rules that protect *both* partners' interests. Indeed, renegotiation may be reassuring to perpetrators, who might otherwise believe that vengeful victims are making too many demands and restrictions on their freedom, seeking to dominate the rules governing their relationship (Exline & Baumeister, 2000). If the renegotiation process yields either compromise or an integrative agreement, the perpetrator may believe that at least some aspects of his or her interests have been protected, thereby making it easier for perpetrators to offer amends. Interestingly, the very process of renegotiation may itself reassure the victim, providing evidence that the perpetrator accepts responsibility for the betrayal and offers amends.

It should be clear that, although renegotiation arguably facilitates forgiveness, renegotiation is not essential for forgiveness to transpire. Barbara may perceive that the operative norm (and the consequences of norm violation) are clearly evident, and may simply decide that the debt incurred by the betrayal has been adequately cancelled by Oliver's acts of amends. We suspect that renegotiation may be more critical to the forgiveness process for more severe betrayal incidents (for which forgiveness arguably is more difficult), for highly idiosyncratic acts of betrayal (for which victim and perpetrator may not agree about the operative norm), and for betrayals that come about due to changing life circumstances (the birth of a child, changes in professional status).

Reconciliation

How do acts of betrayal influence the partners' broader relationship? Earlier, we defined interpersonal forgiveness as the victim's resumption of prebetrayal behavioral tendencies. Does forgiveness automatically restore a relationship to its prebetrayal state? Are forgiveness and reconciliation one and the same? In short, not necessarily.

Reconciliation is typically defined as "settling a quarrel or dispute" or "causing to become friendly again." Previous researchers have offered related definitions, describing reconciliation as "the restoration of violated trust," and arguing that this process "requires the good will of both partners" (Fincham, 2000, p. 7). We define reconciliation as the resumption by *both* partners of prebetrayal relationship status. Thus, forgiveness and reconciliation can be seen to differ in important ways. Whereas interpersonal forgiveness is rather specific to the betrayal in question, reconciliation involves the broader relationship. Although the forgiveness process is influenced by the behavior of both victim *and* perpetrator, in the final analysis, forgiveness is a unilateral act that ultimately is rendered by the victim. Accordingly, interpersonal forgiveness is not synonymous with reconciliation. Forgiveness provides the opportunity for reconciliation, but does not guarantee this outcome.

It is important to highlight the fact that reconciliation involves *both* partners and their *broader* relationship – for example, both victim and perpetrator recover their prebetrayal levels and trajectories of commitment and trust. Complete reconciliation entails fully restoring a relationship to its prebetrayal state: Oliver trusts Barbara as much as he did prior to the incident, Barbara is as willing to become dependent and committed as she was prior to the incident, and neither partner is any more inclined to scrupulously monitor the other's actions than he or she was prior to the betrayal. In short, Oliver and Barbara relate to one another fully on the basis of current (and future) interdependence opportunities, such that their relationship is virtually uncolored by the betrayal. In the case of complete reconciliation, it is as though the betrayal incident never transpired.

In order for reconciliation to come about, both victim *and* perpetrator must revert to their prebetrayal states. The fact that a victim is willing to forgive does not guarantee that the *perpetrator* can resume prebetrayal interaction tendencies (for example, guilt may interfere with normal interaction). For example, if Oliver has enjoyed an extramarital sexual involvement, he may feel compelled to telephone Barbara 10 times a day to inform her of his whereabouts. Such behavior may serve as a constant reminder of his debt, interfering with Barbara's attempts to leave the betrayal behind, and producing a somewhat artificial pretense that life is back to normal. In extreme instances, the victim may be entirely willing to forgive, yet the perpetrator may decide to terminate the relationship, denying the victim the opportunity to resume prebetrayal patterns of interaction.

Also, if interpersonal forgiveness comes about in the absence of intrapersonal forgiveness – without an accompanying shift in cognition and emotion – the victim's ongoing negative mental state may shape the broader relationship, despite the occurrence of forgiveness.

For example, Oliver may exhibit interpersonal forgiveness, cancelling Barbara's debt and resuming prebetrayal patterns of interaction, yet may have formed attributions about Barbara that cannot be "undone" (for example, "she's capable of more fundamentally self-centered behavior than I imagined"), or may have experienced erosions of trust that cannot be repaired (for example, "she's not as concerned with my well-being as I previously thought"). Such cognitive and affective shifts may continue to shape the broader relationship, irrespective of the occurrence of interpersonal forgiveness.

Moreover, when betrayal inspires renegotiation of relationship-relevant rules, the relationship may be modified despite the fact that a specific betrayal has been forgiven: The renegotiation process may yield such specific contingencies that the partners' postbetrayal behavior is necessarily altered. For example, the postbetrayal relationship may be characterized by higher levels of monitoring – Barbara may too frequently remind Oliver not to tell humiliating stories at dinner parties, and Oliver may too frequently remind Barbara that she has agreed to stand by him during health crises. Also, the introduction of new rules may result in more frequent detection of rule violations, or may yield excessively harsh consequences for such violations (cf. Holmes & Murray, 1996).

Finally, to the extent that key properties of relationships (for example, commitment, trust) are governed by both conscious *and* preconscious events (for example, events that accumulate via automatic associations; cf. Smith & DeCoster, 2000), the relationship may be modified by betrayal despite the occurrence of forgiveness. Presumably, under normal circumstances, relationships are governed by relatively automatic and preconscious processes. However, following an act of betrayal, partners may find it necessary to engage in effortful conscious attempts to ensure debt repayment, renegotiate relationship-relevant rules, and bring about victim forgiveness. Thus, even if both partners are willing to work toward restoring their relationship to its prebetrayal state, the very act of exerting such effort suggests that complete reconciliation has yet to take place. Of course, this is not to say that reconciliation can never come about. Assuming that forgiveness and reconciliation are not all-or-nothing propositions – and assuming that each phenomenon may be attained over the course of extended interaction – moving *toward* prebetrayal states is a key to attaining some degree of success on both fronts. Therefore, we need to ask how movement toward forgiveness comes about.

PRORELATIONSHIP TRANSFORMATION AND FORGIVENESS

Over the course of an ongoing relationship, partners inevitably encounter situations involving conflict of interest – situations in which the course of action yielding good outcomes for one person yields poor outcomes for the other. In such situations, one or both partners may be tempted to behave in ways that cause harm to the partner and the relationship. The empirical evidence rather consistently reveals that when an individual engages in behavior that is potentially harmful to the partner (for example, betrays the partner), couple functioning is enhanced to the extent that the partner responds constructively, rather than reciprocating (for example, Gottman, 1998; Gottman et al., 1998). Responding constructively to a partner's destructive act requires effort and may entail negative outcomes.

At the same time, such conciliatory behavior allows both partners to avoid the costs of prolonged conflict, enhances the long-term viability of the relationship, and communicates to the partner that the individual is trustworthy and motivated to continue the relationship. For example, when Barbara betrays Oliver, Oliver may feel tempted to seek vengeance. However, knowing that such behavior will prolong the conflict, Oliver may choose to swallow his pride and forgive Barbara instead of "settling the debt" by reciprocating her destructive behavior. Oliver's consideration of the future consequences of his behavior indicates his benevolent feelings for Barbara and his constructive goals for their relationship.

Given Preferences, Effective Preferences, and the Transformation Process

Following betrayal, why might some individuals (on some occasions) depart from their direct, gut-level impulses and exert considerable effort to ensure the continued viability of their relationship? Interdependence theory provides a compelling answer to this question in its distinction between "given preferences" and "effective preferences." Given preferences describe each partner's self-centered preferences – preferences that follow from a concern with maximizing immediate self-interest, or pursuing one's direct, gut-level inclinations. During the course of betrayal incidents, the victim's immediate, self-oriented impulse is generally self-protective, and favors retribution and the expectation of atonement. Under these circumstances, Oliver may find that reacting constructively seems more humiliating and less satisfying than some form of retaliation (Baumeister et al., 1998; McCullough, Rachal, Sandage, Worthington, Brown, & Hight, 1998). Of course, the degree to which Oliver feels tempted to retaliate will vary across interactions, and may be qualified by the severity of the betrayal, the centrality or importance of the domain in which the betrayal occurs, and the emotions and cognitions that accompany a specific act of betrayal (that is, some betrayals inspire greater grudge than others; for example, Boon & Sulsky, 1997; Darby & Schlenker, 1982; McCullough et al., 1998). But given the pervasiveness of reciprocity and the contingent nature of inclinations to behave in a positive and cooperative manner (cf. Gouldner, 1960; Kelley & Stahelski, 1970) – and given that betrayals violate relationship-relevant norms and arouse intense negative affect and cognition – we suggest that betrayal on the part of one person frequently engenders impulses toward retaliation on the part of the partner.

According to interdependence theory, however, impulsive "given preferences" do not necessarily guide behavior. In deciding how to react in a specific situation, Oliver may explicitly or implicitly take account of broader considerations such as long-term goals for the relationship, social norms, or knowledge of and concern for Barbara's well-being. This process of "taking broader considerations into account" is termed *transformation of motivation*. The preferences that result from the transformation process are referred to as effective preferences, in that these preferences directly guide behavior. Transformation of motivation may lead Oliver to depart from his direct self-interest (as defined by the *given* pattern of interdependence), and instead act on the basis of broader interaction goals (as defined by the *effective* pattern of interdependence) – for example, by taking into account the future implications of his behavior for the marriage. In ongoing relationships, the broader considerations that guide transformation frequently favor reacting constructively to a partner's destructive behavior. For example, taking "time out" to contemplate his long-term goals for their marriage may lessen Oliver's immediate inclination to retaliate.

Prorelationship Motives: Habit versus Meaning Analysis

Over the course of an extended relationship, some conflicts of interest may be encountered regularly. Through adaptation to repeatedly experienced situations, stable transformation tendencies may emerge that are tailored to these recurrent situations (or classes of situation;

Kelley, 1983). Once established, these habitual transformations may occur rapidly, with little or no conscious thought. For example, despite the fact that both Barbara's and Oliver's immediate self-interest is best served by leaving household chores to the other, over time the partners may develop the habit of dividing chores. However, in many situations, transformation of motivation is an effortful, time-consuming process, in that it involves reviewing possible joint behaviors and their consequences, taking account of broader considerations governing the relationship, and deciding which of several possible actions would yield the most desirable outcomes (as defined by these broader considerations).

Two recent findings are consistent with the assumption that in betrayal incidents, transformation of motivation rests on effortful processing (Rusbult, Davis, Finkel, Hannon, & Olsen, 2001). In an initial set of experiments, individuals from dating relationships and marital relationships recounted a recent act of partner betrayal, reporting on their reactions to the incident at two points in time, describing (a) the responses they considered enacting (that is, "what went through your mind?") as well as (b) the responses they actually enacted (that is, "what did you actually do?"). Consistent with expectations, the responses participants actually enacted were considerably more constructive and forgiving than the responses they considered enacting. Presumably, the destructive immediate impulses reflect given preferences, whereas the more constructive delayed responses reflect effective preferences. Thus, individuals' gut-level given reactions to betrayal appear to be relatively destructive and vengeful; their transformed, effective reactions are more constructive and forgiving.

In a second set of experiments, individuals from dating relationships and marital relationships listened to an audio recording of hypothetical partner behaviors, half of which were nonbetrayal incidents (for example, "your partner proudly tells friends about one of your accomplishments") and half of which were betrayal incidents (for example, "your partner flirts with a coworker"). Participants worked through the audio recording, and selected, using response booklets, one of two possible ways of reacting to each incident: a constructive or a destructive reaction. They were given either plentiful or limited reaction time to select a response (14 versus 7 seconds).

Consistent with expectations, for betrayal incidents, participants were more likely to select constructive reactions given plentiful reaction time than limited reaction time; the effect of reaction time was nonsignificant for nonbetrayal incidents. The fact that the reaction time effect was significant only for betrayal incidents supports the claim that, in negative interactions, prorelationship behavior rests on transformation of motivation (such behavior is controlled and effortful), whereas in positive interactions, prorelationship behavior requires no transformation of motivation (such behavior is automatic and "easy").

Together, the results of these experiments suggest that reactions to novel conflicts of interest may be guided by two distinct processes: Impulsive actions dictated by given preferences may reflect the operation of automatic, or associative processes; delayed actions dictated by effective preferences may reflect the operation of controlled, or rule-based processes (cf. Smith & DeCoster, 2000).

Mediation by Mental Events

Precisely how does the transformation process come about? We have argued that whereas this process is sometimes automatic and habit driven, it is sometimes controlled and systematic. When transformation of motivation involves controlled processes, this phenomenon arguably rests on the emergence of relatively less blameful, more benevolent emotional reactions or cognitive interpretations (cf. Rusbult & Van Lange, 1996). For example, when Oliver takes broader considerations into account – including his long-term goals and his concern for Barbara's well-being – he may come to experience reduced anger with respect to Barbara's act of betrayal, and may develop more benevolent cognitive interpretations of Barbara's actions (for example, he may identify extenuating circumstances and discount the role of internal causes).

Interestingly, there is controversy regarding the role of mental events in the forgiveness process, with some authors arguing that forgiveness does not involve mediation by mental events. Why so? First, the philosophical literature tends to characterize both intrapersonal and interpersonal events as dichotomous, all-or-nothing propositions – Barbara either absolves Oliver of blame or does not, she either forgives him or does not (cf. North, 1987). Second, the Christian theological literature tends to regard interpersonal change in the absence of intrapersonal change as the prototype of forgiveness (cf. Marty, 1998). Authors in this tradition place a high value on "saintly" forgiveness, whereby the victim recognizes the full extent of a perpetrator's sin and in *no* way absolves the perpetrator of blame, yet nevertheless forgives.

As a result of these traditions, there is a tendency to assume that forgiveness will not – or even *should* not – be accompanied by changes in betrayal-relevant mental events. The logic runs as follows: If Barbara achieves forgiveness because she comes to understand Oliver's act of betrayal – for example, if she identifies extenuating circumstances – such forgiveness does not "count." She has nullified the betrayal or reinterpreted the incident in nonbetrayal terms; given that no real transgression is perceived to have transpired, there is nothing to forgive.

We suggest that neither of the aforementioned assumptions is entirely valid. First, neither mental construal nor interpersonal forgiveness is an all-or-nothing proposition. Barbara may come to partially understand the circumstances surrounding Oliver's act of betrayal; indeed, given that there may be some disparity between victim and perpetrator construals (Stillwell & Baumeister, 1997), increased understanding may simply entail achieving a relatively "balanced" interpretation of the event. Also, Barbara may partially forgive Oliver – a possibility that becomes particularly plausible when one recognizes that forgiveness may unfold over the course of extended interaction (for example, a bit of forgiveness now, more later).

Second, we acknowledge that victims may sometimes exhibit saintly behavior, achieving interpersonal forgiveness without modifying their mental construals (for example, "I cannot find my way to anything short of full and complete blame, yet I forgive you"). At the same time, we suspect that among mere mortals – and in the absence of divine intervention – *some degree* of mental understanding may well facilitate *some degree* of interpersonal forgiveness. Accordingly, we have argued that coming to mentally understand a betrayal incident – as evidenced by reduced negative affect and cognition – *partially* mediates interpersonal forgiveness.

We conducted two studies to examine the role of emotion and cognition in mediating the association between commitment and interpersonal forgiveness (Rusbult, Finkel, Hannon, Kumashiro, & Childs, in press). One study was a cross-sectional survey study in which participants recounted previous betrayal incidents in their dating relationships, describing their emotions, cognitions, and behaviors in response to the incident. A second study was an interaction record study in which participants provided "in the moment" reports of everyday betrayals in their dating relationships over a two-week period, describing their emotions, cognitions, and behaviors in response to each incident.

Both studies revealed that the association of commitment with "forgiving" behavioral tendencies is mediated by positive cognitive interpretations – by discounting internal causes, identifying extenuating circumstances, and forming more positive, external explanations for partner betrayal (situational variables, rather than disposition or intent). In contrast, we obtained inconsistent evidence for mediation by emotion. Thus, individuals *are* capable of forgiving their partners despite persistent negative affect, but are not so "saintly" that achieving some degree of "understanding" is irrelevant to the forgiveness process. Commitment promotes forgiveness because strong commitment promotes benevolent (or less malevolent) betrayal-relevant cognition. For example, Oliver may exhibit systematic processing, carefully attending to the circumstances surrounding Barbara's betrayal, giving her the benefit of the doubt, or accepting some personal responsibility for the betrayal. In turn, the benevolent "understanding" he develops helps him find his way to forgiving Barbara.

Following betrayal, the transformation process may not be immediate. Given that this process may require effortful and systematic processing, and given that it may sometimes be difficult for victims to develop less blameful, more benevolent understandings of the reasons for betrayal, it becomes clear that individuals may rather persistently act on the basis of self-interested, vengeful preferences (cf. Enright et al., 1996; Gordon & Baucom, 1998). Therefore, it becomes important to ask: What inspires positive mental events, prorelationship motives, and interpersonal forgiveness?

PREDICTING PRORELATIONSHIP TRANSFORMATION AND FORGIVENESS

Most empirical work regarding forgiveness has examined the cognitive, affective, and interactional concomitants of this phenomenon. Fewer studies have sought to examine the motivational underpinnings of forgiveness, seeking to explain not only *how* individuals forgive, but also *why* they forgive. The interdependence theoretic concept of transformation of motivation highlights the need for research regarding the motivation to forgive. In conceptualizing the predictors of prorelationship transformation and forgiveness, it is useful to distinguish between relationship-specific and dispositional predictors. *Relationship-specific predictors* are variables that are specific to a given relationship – these variables presumably do not reflect either victim's or perpetrator's tendencies across partners and relationships. In contrast, *dispositional predictors* are argued to predict behavior in general, across partners and relationships. The following (highly selective and nonexhaustive) discussion provides a review of results from our own and others' research regarding both relationship-specific and dispositional predictors of forgiveness.

Relationship-Specific Predictors

Commitment

A good deal of empirical evidence suggests that commitment promotes prorelationship motivation and behavior (for example, Rusbult et al., 1991; Van Lange et al., 1997; Wieselquist, Rusbult, Foster, & Agnew, 1999). *Commitment level* describes the degree to which an individual experiences long-term orientation toward a relationship, including intent to persist and feelings of psychological attachment (Rusbult, Drigotas, & Verette, 1994). Following interdependence theory (Thibaut & Kelley, 1959), Rusbult's (1983) investment model suggests that commitment emerges out of the specific circumstances of interdependence characterizing a relationship. Specifically, commitment develops as a consequence of increasing dependence – Barbara becomes increasingly committed as a result of (a) increasing satisfaction with her relationship (that is, the marriage gratifies important needs, such as her needs for intimacy or sexuality); (b) declining quality of alternatives to the relationship (that is, specific alternative partners, the general field of eligibles, and noninvolvement, are seen as undesirable); and (c) increasing investments in the relationship (that is, resources such as personal identity, effort, or material possessions become linked to the relationship).

Commitment has been shown to promote a variety of prorelationship acts other than forgiveness. For example, commitment promotes persistence in close relationships, such that the relationships of highly committed individuals are more likely to "stand the test of time" than are those of less-committed individuals (for example, Bui, Peplau, & Hill, 1996; Drigotas & Rusbult, 1992; Rusbult, 1983). In addition, strong commitment yields a variety of relationship-maintenance acts that tend to enhance couple well-being. Specifically, commitment promotes (a) derogation of alternatives, or the tendency to drive away or disparage tempting alternative partners (for example, Johnson & Rusbult, 1989; Miller, 1997), (b) willingness to sacrifice, or the tendency to forego desired activities for the good of the relationship (for example, Van Lange et al., 1997), (c) positive illusion, or the tendency toward excessively favorable evaluations of one's partner and relationship (for example, Rusbult, Van Lange, Wildschut, Yovetich, & Verette, 2000), and (d) accommodative behavior, or the tendency to accommodate rather than retaliate when a partner behaves poorly (for example, Rusbult et al., 1991).

Recent evidence suggests that commitment is also a critical predictor of forgiveness, in both dating relationships and marital relationships (Rusbult et al., in press; Rusbult, Finkel, Kumashiro, Davis, Hannon, Clarke, & Kirchner, 2001). In this work, we have employed a variety of methods, using both experimental and nonexperimental procedures (for example, priming techniques, examination of real betrayal incidents in ongoing relationships), and examining both self-report and behavioral measures of forgiveness (for example, structured measures and open-ended descriptions, coding of videotaped betrayal-relevant conversations). This work reveals consistent evidence that tendencies toward interpersonal forgiveness are greater in more highly committed relationships than in less-committed relationships.

Why does commitment promote forgiveness? Prior research has highlighted four features of commitment that may explain why this variable is an important predictor of prorelationship motivation and behavior (cf. Wieselquist et al., 1999). First, highly committed individuals *need* their relationships. The more Oliver stands to lose should his marriage dissolve, the more effort he is likely to exert to keep his marriage alive and well (cf. Holmes, 1981). Second, commitment involves long-term orientation, which enhances the likelihood that individuals will consider the future consequences of their actions. In such a context, Oliver's maintenance acts are especially likely to promote reciprocal acts by Barbara, thereby maximizing the long-term viability of their marriage (cf. Axelrod, 1984). Third, commitment involves psychological attachment. To the degree that such attachment causes Oliver to feel "linked" to Barbara, behavior that departs from his self-interest, yet benefits Barbara, may not be experienced as personally costly (cf. Aron & Aron, 1997). And fourth, commitment may induce communal orientation, characterized by tendencies to respond to a partner's needs in a relatively unconditional manner (cf. Clark & Mills, 1979). In a committed, communally oriented marriage, Oliver may endure costs without calculating what he receives in return.

Trust

What role does trust play in the forgiveness process? We examine trust as an emergent property of ongoing relationships, not as a stable personal disposition. As such, trust includes three facets: (a) predictability – belief that the partner's behavior is consistent over time; (b) dependability – belief that one can count on the partner to be honest, reliable, and benevolent; and (c) faith – conviction that the partner is intrinsically motivated to be responsive and caring (Holmes & Rempel, 1989). Trust evolves over the course of extended involvement to the degree that a partner exhibits prorelationship motives, behaving in a selfless manner when his or her self-interest and the partner's interests conflict.

Why should trust promote forgiveness? First, to the degree that Barbara experiences all three facets of trust, she should be especially likely to interpret Oliver's hurtful behavior as unintentional or situationally caused. If she believes that Oliver is predictable, dependable, and worthy of faith, his acts of betrayal take on a less painful character and yield more benevolent emotion and cognition. Oliver's betrayal is less likely to be interpreted as representing disrespect or lack of consideration because – based on a history of prorelationship behavior and benevolence on the part of Oliver – Barbara more readily recognizes (or is inclined to believe) that he did not intend her any harm.

Second, trust and commitment exert mutual causal effects on one another. In characterizing these phenomena, we have advanced a model of "mutual cyclical growth," suggesting that trust in a partner is essentially the mirror-image of the partner's commitment (Wieselquist et al., 1999). How so? As Oliver becomes increasingly dependent he develops strong commitment, which in turn yields increased tendencies toward prorelationship acts such as accommodation and sacrifice. When Barbara perceives such acts she develops enhanced trust, which leads her to become increasingly dependent – more satisfied, inclined to drive away or derogate alternatives, and willing to invest in her marriage in material and nonmaterial ways. This brings us full circle, in that Barbara's enhanced dependence yields increased commitment, along with increased prorelationship motivation and behavior. We have obtained support for such a model in longitudinal studies of both dating relationships and marital relationships (Wieselquist et al., 1999).

In recent work we have also found that trust is associated with forgiveness, in both dating relationships and marital relationships (Kumashiro, Finkel, & Rusbult, 2001; Rusbult et al., 2001). In our early work regarding marital relations, we have found that (a) the individual's self-reported trust in the partner is positively associated with perceptions of the partner's forgiveness, as well as with the *partner's* self-reported commitment level and tendencies toward forgiveness, and (b) the individual's self-reported forgiveness is positively associated with the *partner's* perception of the individual's forgiveness, as well as with trust level and perceived dyadic adjustment. Thus, relationships are internally regulated: Via adaptation to evolving interdependence, changes in each person's actions and motives trigger complementary changes in the partner. Accordingly, it becomes evident that forgiveness may be both a cause and a consequence of strong trust: Trust may cause forgiveness, in that strong trust may yield benevolent, schema-congruent interpretations of a partner's betrayal. Moreover, forgiveness may cause trust, in that earlier acts of benevolence – such as forgiveness of betrayal – may yield increased trust, along with enhanced commitment and increased inclinations toward prorelationship motives and behaviors.

Personal Dispositions

In adopting an interdependence theoretic analysis, we do not wish to imply that forgiveness can be characterized solely in terms of relationship-specific variables. In addition to variables such as commitment and trust, several personal dispositions appear to affect the forgiveness process. Indeed, many researchers have followed in the footsteps of philosophers and theologians in suggesting that individuals differ in their generalized disposition to forgive. In his summary of research regarding personality and forgiveness, Emmons suggested that "a forgiving person has a chronic concern to be in benevolent, harmonious relationships with others, the ability to take the viewpoint of sufferers and to detach [the self] from the personal experience of having been harmed" (Emmons, 2000, p. 159).

Dispositional Forgiveness

To date, the most systematic attempt to measure trait-based forgiveness has resulted in a self-report instrument designed to assess dispositional forgiveness (Mauger, Perry, Freeman, Grove, McBride, & McKinney, 1992). (Although this scale was designed to measure dispositional forgiveness, an examination of its face validity suggests that it might also be characterized in terms of disinclination toward vengeance.) Preliminary evidence from our laboratory suggests that there may be variability across individuals in generalized tendencies to forgive, and that these generalized tendencies are useful in predicting whether an individual will forgive a specific betrayal incident with a specific partner (Hannon, 2001). Thus, to the extent that Barbara is a generally forgiving person, it becomes more likely that she will forgive specific acts of betrayal on the part of Oliver. If Barbara believes that vengeance is a suitable – perhaps even an obligatory – means of responding to betrayal incidents, she is less likely to forgive Oliver's acts of betrayal.

Empathy and Perspective Taking

Several other traits are likely to be associated with inclinations toward forgiveness, some of which are implicit in Emmons's (2000) description of the dispositionally forgiving individual. For example, empathy has been shown to promote the forgiveness process (McCullough, Sandage, & Worthington, 1997; McCullough et al., 1998); our own work suggests that perspective taking yields parallel effects. We suspect that the empathy-forgiveness association may rest on the fact that empathetic victims are more likely to understand the circumstances surrounding a perpetrator's norm violation (for example, empathy may promote recognition of extenuating circumstances).

Rumination

In addition, rumination has been shown to predict the degree to which individuals experience vengeful motivation in response to betrayal (McCullough et al., 1997). For example, to the extent that Barbara is inclined to ruminate about interpersonal events – to the degree that she obsessively reviews betrayal incidents, considering the many possible implications of Oliver's behavior – she is likely to find it difficult to find her way to forgiveness. Presumably, because she cannot stop thinking about Oliver's act of betrayal, she becomes especially prone to hold grudges and desire retaliation.

Narcissism

Finally, we believe that narcissism may play a role in the forgiveness process. It may be useful to construe narcissism as the "ultimate self-orientation." Narcissistic individuals have been characterized as self-admiring and inclined toward grandiose thinking, and have been shown to exhibit a sense of entitlement and a general lack of empathy toward others (Emmons, 2000; Millon, 1998). To the degree that Oliver is narcissistic, he may be especially unlikely to forgive Barbara's betrayal because he finds it difficult to "cancel the debt," and because he finds it

difficult to empathize with her, and acknowledge situational contributors to betrayal.

DIRECTIONS FOR FUTURE RESEARCH

At present, we are extending our forgiveness research program in several respects. First, we are examining forgiving behavioral tendencies
on the part of both partners in ongoing marital relationships, exploring whether commitment promotes each person's inclinations toward
forgiveness, and exploring whether forgiveness modifies each person's
feelings of trust in the partner. Second, we are videotaping married
partners' betrayal-relevant interactions, obtaining "on-line" reports of
(a) each person's emotional reactions, cognitive interpretations, and
behavioral tendencies, along with (b) each person's perception of the
partner's emotions, cognitions, and behavior. These data will allow us
to further examine whether mental events – including mutual understanding – indeed mediate perpetrator amends and victim forgiveness.
And third, we are examining a variety of specific issues regarding the
predictors and consequences of forgiveness. For example, can we characterize relationships in terms of "optimal distinctiveness," such that
ideally, both partners exhibit a balance of concern between self-interest
and marital-interests? And can forgiveness tendencies be characterized
in terms of adaptation, such that over time, partners increasingly exhibit
a workable balance of norm enforcement in relation to forgiveness? We
are eager to uncover the answers to these and other important questions
regarding the nature of interpersonal forgiveness.

CONCLUSIONS

Earlier, we noted that social scientists have only recently turned their attention to the phenomena of betrayal and forgiveness, noting that most
work to date has examined *how* individuals forgive, largely ignoring the
question of *why* individuals forgive. In this chapter, we outlined a model
of betrayal and forgiveness using a relatively comprehensive theory of
interpersonal processes. Our interdependence theoretic account helps
explain why betrayal incidents are problematic for couples, and why
perpetrator amends and victim forgiveness accordingly are not easy.
We also introduced the possibility of renegotiation following betrayal,
reviewing important distinctions among the concepts of renegotiation,
forgiveness, and reconciliation. Finally, we discussed transformation of

motivation, considering the role of mental events in mediating the forgiveness process, and identifying several personal dispositions and relationship-specific variables that play a role in motivating interpersonal forgiveness. We hope that this review may highlight the utility of interdependence theory in understanding complex interpersonal phenomena – not only betrayal and forgiveness, but also other important processes in ongoing marital relationships.

REFERENCES

Aron, A., & Aron, E. N. (1997). Self-expansion motivation and including other in the self. In S. Duck (Ed.), *Handbook of personal relationships: Theory, research, and interventions* (2nd ed., pp. 251–270). Chichester, England: Wiley.

Axelrod, R. (1984). *The evolution of cooperation*. New York: Basic Books.

Baumeister, R. F., Exline, J. J., & Sommer, K. L. (1998). The victim role, grudge theory, and two dimensions of forgiveness. In E. L. Worthington, Jr. (Ed.), *Dimensions of forgiveness* (pp. 79–104). Philadelphia: Templeton Foundation Press.

Baumeister, R. F., Stillwell, A. M., & Heatherton, T. F. (1995). Personal narratives about guilt: Role in action control and interpersonal relationships. *Basic and Applied Social Psychology, 17*, 173–198.

Baumeister, R. F., Stillwell, A., & Wotman, S. R. (1990). Victim and perpetrator accounts of interpersonal conflict: Autobiographical narratives about anger. *Journal of Personality and Social Psychology, 59*, 994–1005.

Boon, S. D., & Sulsky, L. M. (1997). Attributions of blame and forgiveness in romantic relationships: A policy-capturing study. *Journal of Social Behavior and Personality, 12*, 19–44.

Bui, K. T., Peplau, L. A., & Hill, C. T. (1996). Testing the Rusbult model of relationship commitment and stability in a 15-year study of heterosexual couples. *Personality and Social Psychology Bulletin, 22*, 1244–1257.

Clark, M. S., & Mills, J. (1979). Interpersonal attraction in exchange and communal relationships. *Journal of Personality and Social Psychology, 37*, 12–24.

Couch, L. L., Jones, W. H., & Moore, D. S. (1999). Buffering the effects of betrayal: The role of apology, forgiveness, and commitment. In J. M. Adams & W. J. Jones (Eds.), *Handbook of interpersonal commitment and relationship stability* (pp. 451–469). New York: Plenum.

Darby, B. W., & Schlenker, B. R. (1982). Children's reactions to apologies. *Journal of Personality and Social Psychology, 43*, 742–753.

Dorff, E. N. (1992). Individual and communal forgiveness. In D. H. Frank (Ed.), *Autonomy and Judaism* (pp. 193–218). Albany, NY: State University of New York Press.

Drigotas, S. M., & Rusbult, C. E. (1992). Should I stay or should I go?: A dependence model of breakups. *Journal of Personality and Social Psychology, 62*, 62–87.

Emmons, R. A. (2000). Personality and forgiveness. In M. E. McCullough, K. I. Pargament, & C. E. Thorsen (Eds.), *Forgiveness* (pp. 156–175). New York: Guilford.

Enright, R. D., & the Human Development Study Group (1996). Counseling within the forgiveness triad: On forgiving, receiving forgiveness, and self-forgiveness. *Counseling and Values, 40*, 107–122.

Exline, J. J., & Baumeister, R. F. (2000). Expressing forgiveness and repentance. In M. E. McCullough, K. I. Pargament, & C. E. Thorsen (Eds.), *Forgiveness* (pp. 133–155). New York: Guilford.

Fagenson, E. A., & Cooper, J. (1987). When push comes to power: A test of power restoration theory's explanation for aggressive conflict escalation. *Basic and Applied Social Psychology, 8*, 273–293.

Fincham, F. D. (2000). The kiss of the porcupines: From attributing responsibility to forgiving. *Personal Relationships, 7*, 1–23.

Finkel, E. J., Rusbult, C. E., Kumashird, M., & Hannon, P. A. (in press). Dealing with betrayal in close relationships: Does commitment promote forgiveness? *Journal of Personality and Social Psychology.*

Freedman, S. R., & Enright, R. D. (1996). Forgiveness as an intervention goal with incest survivors. *Journal of Consulting and Clinical Psychology, 64*, 983–992.

Gonzales, M. H., Haugen, J. A., & Manning, D. J. (1994). Victims as "narrative critics": Factors influencing rejoinders and evaluative responses to offenders' accounts. *Personality and Social Psychology Bulletin, 20*, 691–704.

Gonzales, M. H., Manning, D. J., & Haugen, J. A. (1992). Explaining our sins: Factors influencing offender accounts and anticipated victim responses. *Journal of Personality and Social Psychology, 62*, 958–971.

Gordon, K. C., & Baucom, D. H. (1998). Understanding betrayals in marriage: A synthesized model of forgiveness. *Family Process, 37*, 425–449.

Gottman, J. M. (1998). Psychology and the study of marital processes. *Annual Review of Psychology, 49*, 169–197.

Gottman, J. M., Coan, J., Carrere, S., & Swanson, C. (1998). Predicting marital happiness and stability from newlywed interactions. *Journal of Marriage and the Family, 60*, 5–22.

Gouldner, A. W. (1960). The norm of reciprocity: A preliminary statement. *American Sociological Review, 25*, 161–178.

Hannon, P. (2001). *Perpetrator amends and victim forgiveness.* Unpublished manuscript, University of North Carolina, Chapel Hill, NC.

Hodgins, H. S., Liebeskind, E., & Schwartz, W. (1996). Getting out of hot water: Facework in social predicaments. *Journal of Personality and Social Psychology, 71*, 300–314.

Holmes, J. G. (1981). The exchange process in close relationships: Microbehavior and macromotives. In M. J. Lerner and S. C. Lerner (Eds.), *The justice motive in social behavior* (pp. 261–284). New York: Plenum.

Holmes, J. G., & Murray, S. L. (1996). Conflict in close relationships. In E. T. Higgins & A. W. Kruglanski (Eds.), *Social psychology: Handbook of basic principles* (pp. 622–645). New York: Guilford.

Holmes, J. G., & Rempel, J. K. (1989). Trust in close relationships. In C. Hendrick (Ed.), *Review of personality and social psychology* (vol. 10, pp. 187–220). London: Sage.

Johnson, D. J., & Rusbult, C. E. (1989). Resisting temptation: Devaluation of alternative partners as a means of maintaining commitment in close relationships. *Journal of Personality and Social Psychology, 57*, 967–980.

Kelley, H. H. (1983). The situational origins of human tendencies: A further reason for the formal analysis of structures. *Personality and Social Psychology Bulletin, 9*, 8–30.

Kelley, H. H. (1984). The theoretical description of interdependence by means of transition lists. *Journal of Personality and Social Psychology, 47*, 956–982.

Kelley, H. H., & Stahelski, A. J. (1970). Social interaction basis of cooperators' and competitors' beliefs about others. *Journal of Personality and Social Psychology, 16*, 66–91.

Kelley, H. H., & Thibaut, J. W. (1978). *Interpersonal relations: A theory of interdependence.* New York: Wiley.

Komorita, S. S., Hilty, J. A., & Parks, C. D. (1991). Reciprocity and cooperation in social dilemmas. *Journal of Conflict Resolution, 35*, 494–518.

Kremer, J. F., & Stephens, L. (1983). Attributions and arousal as mediators of mitigation's effect on retaliation. *Journal of Personality and Social Psychology, 45*, 335–343.

Kumashiro, M., Finkel, E. J., & Rusbult, C. E. (2001). *Commitment, forgiveness, and trust.* Unpublished manuscript, University of North Carolina, Chapel Hill, NC.

Marty, M. E. (1998). The ethos of Christian forgiveness. In E. L. Worthington, Jr. (Ed.), *Dimensions of forgiveness* (pp. 9–28). Philadelphia: Templeton Foundation Press.

Mauger, P. A., Perry, J. E., Freeman, T., Grove, D. C., McBride, A. G., & McKinney, K. E. (1992). The measurement of forgiveness: Preliminary research. *Journal of Psychology and Christianity, 11*, 170–180.

McCullough, M. E., Rachal, K. C., Sandage, S. J., Worthington, E. L., Jr., Brown, S. W., & Hight, T. L. (1998). Interpersonal forgiving in close relationships: II. Theoretical elaboration and measurement. *Journal of Personality and Social Psychology, 75*, 1586–1603.

McCullough, M. E., Sandage, S. J., & Worthington, E. L., Jr. (1997). *To forgive is human.* Downers Grove, IL: Inter Varsity.

McCullough, M. E., & Worthington, E. L., Jr. (1995). Promoting forgiveness: A comparison of two brief psychoeducational group interventions with a waiting-list control. *Counseling and Values, 40*, 55–68.

McCullough, M. E., Worthington, E. L., Jr., & Rachal, K. C. (1997). Interpersonal forgiving in close relationships. *Journal of Personality and Social Psychology, 73*, 321–336.

Miller, R. S. (1997). Inattentive and contented: Relationship commitment and attention to alternatives. *Journal of Personality and Social Psychology, 73*, 758–766.

Millon, T. M. (1998). DSM narcissistic personality disorder. In E. F. Ronningstam (Ed.), *Disorders of narcissism: Diagnostic, clinical, and empirical implications* (pp. 75–101). Washington, DC: American Psychiatric Association.

North, J. (1987). Wrongdoing and forgiveness. *Philosophy, 62,* 499–508.

Ohbuchi, K., Kameda, M., & Agarie, N. (1989). Apology as aggression control: Its role in mediating appraisal of and response to harm. *Journal of Personality and Social Psychology, 56,* 219–227.

Peterson, D. R. (1983). Conflict. In H. H. Kelley, E. Berscheid, A. Christensen, J. H. Harvey, T. L. Huston, G. Levinger, E. McClintock, L. A. Peplau, & D. R. Peterson (Eds.), *Close relationships* (pp. 360–396). New York: W. H. Freeman.

Ridley, M. (1996). *The origins of virtue: Human instincts and the evolution of cooperation.* New York: Penguin Books.

Rosenzweig-Smith, J. (1988). Factors associated with successful reunions of adult adoptees and biological parents. *Child Welfare, 67,* 411–422.

Rusbult, C. E. (1983). A longitudinal test of the investment model: The development (and deterioration) of satisfaction and commitment in heterosexual involvements. *Journal of Personality and Social Psychology, 45,* 101–117.

Rusbult, C. E., Davis, J. L., Finkel, E. J., Hannon, P. A., & Olsen, N. (2001). *Forgiveness of betrayal in close relationships: Does it rest on transformation of motivation?* Unpublished manuscript, University of North Carolina, Chapel Hill, NC.

Rusbult, C. E., Drigotas, S. M., & Verette, J. (1994). The investment model: An interdependence analysis of commitment processes and relationship maintenance phenomena. In D. Canary & L. Stafford (Eds.), *Communication and relational maintenance* (pp. 115–139). New York: Academic Press.

Rusbult, C. E., Finkel, E. J., Kumashiro, M., Davis, J. L., Hannon, P., Clarke, J., & Kirchner, J. (2001). *Forgiveness of betrayal in marital relationships.* Unpublished manuscript, University of North Carolina, Chapel Hill, NC.

Rusbult, C. E., Olsen, N., Davis, J. L., & Hannon, P. (2001). Commitment and relationship maintenance mechanisms. In J. H. Harvey & A. E. Wenzel (Eds.), *Close romantic relationships: Maintenance and enhancement.* Mahwah, NJ: Lawrence Erlbaum Associates.

Rusbult, C. E., & Van Lange, P. A. M. (1996). Interdependence processes. In E. T. Higgins & A. Kruglanski (Eds.), *Social psychology: Handbook of basic principles* (pp. 564–596). New York: Guilford.

Rusbult, C. E., Van Lange, P. A. M., Wildschut, T., Yovetich, N. A., & Verette, J. (2000). Perceived superiority in close relationships: Why it exists and persists. *Journal of Personality and Social Psychology, 79,* 521–545.

Rusbult, C. E., Verette, J., Whitney, G. A., Slovik, L. F., & Lipkus, I. (1991). Accommodation processes in close relationships: Theory and preliminary empirical evidence. *Journal of Personality and Social Psychology, 60,* 53–78.

Smith, E. R., & DeCoster, J. (2000). Dual process models in social and cognitive psychology: Conceptual integration and links to underlying memory systems. *Personality and Social Psychology Review, 4,* 108–131.

Stillwell, A. M., & Baumeister, R. F. (1997). The construction of victim and perpetrator memories: Accuracy and distortion in role-based accounts. *Personality and Social Psychology Bulletin, 23,* 1157–1172.

Tangney, J. P., Wagner, P. E., Hill-Barlow, D., Marschall, D. E., & Gramzow, R. (1996). Relation of shame and guilt to constructive versus destructive responses to anger across the lifespan. *Journal of Personality and Social Psychology, 70*, 797–809.

Thibaut, J. W., & Kelley, H. H. (1959). *The social psychology of groups.* New York: Wiley.

Van Lange, P. A. M., Rusbult, C. E., Drigotas, S. M., Arriaga, X. B., Witcher, B. S., & Cox, C. L. (1997). Willingness to sacrifice in close relationships. *Journal of Personality and Social Psychology, 72*, 1373–1395.

Weiner, B., Graham, S., Peter, O., & Zmuidinas, M. (1991). Public confession and forgiveness. *Journal of Personality, 59*, 281–312.

Wieselquist, J., Rusbult, C. E., Foster, C. A., & Agnew, C. R. (1999). Commitment, prorelationship behavior, and trust in close relationships. *Journal of Personality and Social Psychology, 77*, 942–966.

POWER, CONFLICT, AND VIOLENCE IN MARITAL INTERACTION

Introduction to Section Four

Power is a critical concept in marital relationships, relevant to issues such as decision making, task allocation, and conflict resolution. Although some marriages are relatively equal in terms of power (Schwartz, 1995), other marriages can be ongoing struggles for power and dominance. Power can be expressed in a variety of ways and many arguments in marriage are really about who has the power to exert influence and make decisions. Power can also be expressed in more indirect ways such as refusing to discuss an issue or engaging in manipulative behavior. Withdrawing from conflict, in particular, may stem from a desire to exert control by maintaining the status quo.

Although the demand/withdraw pattern of conflict interaction has recently come to prominence in the work of Christensen and his colleagues, it actually has a long history. For example, Watzlawick, Beavin, and Jackson (1967) discussed a pattern of marital interaction involving a conflict-avoidant person (usually the male), and his partner who is frustrated by the avoidance and demands that the problem be confronted. Consistent with this focus in the therapy literature, Eldridge and Christensen present evidence that the demand/withdraw pattern is associated with relationship dissatisfaction, although the direction of causality is still not fully understood.

As Christensen and Eldridge discuss, a number of explanations for the demand/withdraw pattern have been proposed. These explanations focus on gender differences in the experience and expression of emotion, individual differences in personality and in desires for intimacy, discrepancies in power and status favoring men, and the specific structure of the conflict topic (that is, which partner is seeking change). In response to conflicting findings about the utility of the various explanations, Christensen and colleagues have recently emphasized the importance of taking a broader perspective when studying this pattern of interaction. For example, it may be crucial to consider the history of marital conflict; if couples have more difficulty in resolving wives' issues than husbands' issues, then wife demand/husband withdrawal is likely to become the dominant pattern. It may also be important to assess the conflict patterns of the couple across a range of topics, to ascertain whether distressed couples adhere more rigidly to gender stereotyped conflict roles than do nondistressed couples.

The most extreme expression of power is violence, when one partner attempts to control the behavior of the other by threat or physical abuse. Although "common couple violence" (Johnson, 1995) often involves physical abuse by both husband and wife, serious violence (battering) is usually perpetrated by males. Interestingly, Eldridge and Christensen discuss the possibility, supported by empirical data, that the less common male demand/female withdraw pattern may be associated with couple violence, particularly the more severe forms of violence. They suggest that an important aspect of the dynamic in these marriages may be that the male lacks power in the relationship, or sees himself as lacking power, and hence resorts to violence to enforce his will on his partner.

Issues concerning gender and relational hierarchy are also addressed by Gottman and his colleagues, who outline some recent developments in the study of power in marriage, including the observation of couples' influence patterns. The new research reported in this chapter is based on a variety of relationship types, including violent and nonviolent marriages, and committed relationships between gay males and lesbians. This research involves the mathematical modeling of couple interaction, based on the observational coding of specific affects expressed during structured conversations. In this approach, power is defined as one partner's ability to influence the subsequent emotion of the other, and separate influence functions are computed for each partner's influence on the other.

A key focus of this chapter is on the relative effects of positive and negative affect on couple interaction. As Gottman et al. note, data from heterosexual couples consistently show that reciprocity is much stronger for negative affect than for positive affect; in other words, negative affect has a more profound effect on couple interaction than does positive affect. However, this "rule" may not apply to all relationships. In fact, in gay male and lesbian couples, there is some suggestion that the relative effects may be reversed, and that partners may often find a way to maintain positive interactions when discussing conflict topics. These findings highlight the importance of partners avoiding the escalation of negative affect that so often leads to destructive outcomes. Other analyses reported in this chapter focus on violent marriages and the power struggle that is involved when spouses systematically use violence to intimidate and control.

Noller and Roberts also compare the communication patterns of couples in violent and nonviolent relationships, focusing particularly on the temporal associations between anxiety/arousal and specific emotions and behaviors. The study is multimethod, involving the assessment of physiological measures, insider ratings of anxiety, and outsider ratings of communication behavior. A unique feature of the study is the possibility of matching the behavior/affective displays of couples with their anxiety/arousal at the same point in time. Using this approach allows the researchers to determine the extent to which the anxiety/arousal of violent individuals drives their later behavior, and also the extent to which the behavior of one partner affects the anxiety/arousal of the other.

Four sets of temporal linkage are considered: the association between partners' levels of anxiety/arousal, the association between partners' observed behavior, the effect of one partner's behavior on the subsequent anxiety/arousal of the other, and the association between one partner's anxiety/arousal and his or her own later behavior. The analyses focus on comparing the patterns of violent and nonviolent couples, but the role of relationship satisfaction was also examined in a factorial design, as suggested by Lloyd (1990).

The findings show that couples in violent relationships differ from those in nonviolent relationships in terms of the temporal linkages between a number of important variables. The authors discuss the theoretical implications of their findings for three aspects of conflict interaction: negative reciprocity, mutual withdrawal, and the demand/withdraw pattern of interaction. For example, in terms of the demand/withdraw pattern, females in violent relationships tended to show more linkage between their own withdrawal and their partner's earlier displays of hostility than did females in nonviolent relationships. The techniques used in this study allowed the researchers to demonstrate the role of emotion in generating communication patterns, particularly in violent relationships.

Power in marital relationships may be particularly expressed in the ways in which spouses deal with conflict issues. Avoidance and withdrawal can be expressions of power, especially where the goal of the withdrawer is to maintain the status quo and avoid having to change. Another destructive response to conflict is negative reciprocity, which can lead to an escalation of coercive behaviors and an increase in the expression of intense negative emotion. In extreme cases, these behaviors lead to violence and abuse.

REFERENCES

Johnson, M. P. (1995). Patriarchal terrorism and common couple violence: Two forms of violence against women. *Journal of Marriage and the Family, 57,* 283–294.

Lloyd, S. (1990). Conflict types and strategies in violent marriages. *Journal of Family Violence, 5,* 269–284.

Schwartz, P. (1995). *Love between equals: How peer marriage really works.* New York: The Free Press.

Watzlawick, P., Beavin, J., & Jackson, D. D. (1967). *Pragmatics of human communication: A study of interactional patterns, pathologies, and paradoxes.* New York: W. W. Norton.

CHAPTER ELEVEN

Demand-Withdraw Communication during Couple Conflict: A Review and Analysis

Kathleen A. Eldridge and Andrew Christensen

The behavioral model of marriage has led to numerous investigations of communication in close relationships. This research indicates that specific aspects of couples' communication around conflict-laden topics are associated with, and predictive of, relationship satisfaction and stability (for example, Weiss & Heyman, 1997). As might be expected, positive behaviors are generally associated with satisfaction and negative behaviors with dissatisfaction. One pattern of interaction that has become salient in the marital interaction literature is the demand-withdraw pattern, in which one member (the demander) criticizes, nags, and makes demands of the other, while the partner (the withdrawer) avoids confrontation, withdraws, and becomes defensive. The following case example illustrates this common pattern:

Jeff and Linda have been married for 10 years and have grown increasingly unhappy in their marriage. Their conflicts have taken on a repetitive nature, often falling into the same pattern time after time. A typical argument for them takes place on a weeknight, toward the end of the week, as they are discussing their plans for the weekend:

Linda: Have you thought about plans for the weekend?
Jeff: Yeah . . . a little bit . . . I was thinking about going to the game on Saturday if tickets are still available.
Linda: Again? Can't you skip a game for once? Why do you always have to go to every game? I feel like I never see you, unless I watch for you and your friends in the stands during the sportscast.
Jeff: (sighs)
Linda: I was hoping we could spend some quality time together this weekend. The kids are going fishing with my brother on Saturday, and I wanted us to do something together. The weather has been so

nice, I thought we could take a walk to that diner down the street, have a nice lunch together, then maybe go to a matinee.

Jeff: (walks into the kitchen and looks in the refrigerator) What's for dinner?

Linda: Jeff, I was talking to you, don't you ever listen to me?

Jeff: I heard you.

Linda: So, what do you think? What about Saturday? Can we spend the afternoon together?

Jeff: Whatever, can't we discuss it later? I'm really hungry.

Linda: Later never comes, and we hardly ever spend time together anymore. It's like we live separate lives. I feel like I hardly know you anymore.

Jeff: Linda, you're overreacting. I'm going to get something to eat. (grabs his jacket and leaves)

Although systematic, empirical investigations of demand-withdraw began fairly recently, authors have written anecdotally about this pattern for several decades. It has been variously referred to as the nag-withdraw pattern (Watzlawick, Beavin, & Jackson, 1967), pursuer-distancer pattern (Fogarty, 1976), rejection-intrusion pattern (Napier, 1978), and demand-withdraw pattern (Wile, 1981). These authors wrote about this pattern in the context of couples therapy, indicating that it is destructive in relationships. In addition, as in the example above, Wile (1981) implied that wives tend to be the naggers, pursuers, intruders, and demanders while husbands tend to be the withdrawers, distancers, and rejectors.

Studying the demand-withdraw pattern is informative because it goes beyond the investigation of global positive or negative communication to an analysis of more specific behaviors. In addition, demand-withdraw interaction is important because it refers to a pattern of behaviors, rather than to isolated or unrelated behaviors. Therefore, it provides information on demanding behavior in the context of partner withdrawal, and withdrawing behavior in the context of partner demands. Further, demand-withdraw communication has been linked to central aspects of intimate relationships, such as power, gender, and violence. By studying demand-withdraw, we can learn about these related and significant facets of relationships.

Researchers have attempted to understand this pattern by investigating the concurrent and longitudinal associations between demand-withdraw interaction and relationship satisfaction, and by exploring the gender linkage in demanding and withdrawing roles. This research has led to interesting findings about the potential destructiveness of demand-withdraw interaction, and about gender differences in this pattern. However, many questions remain to be answered by further research. This chapter will provide a review of the literature on this interaction pattern, with particular emphasis on (1) assessment of demand-withdraw, (2) concurrent and longitudinal associations between demand-withdraw and relationship satisfaction, (3) demand-withdraw and domestic violence, and (4) explanations for demand-withdraw behavior. It will conclude with suggestions for future avenues of demand-withdraw research.

ASSESSMENT OF DEMAND-WITHDRAW INTERACTION

Several authors have written about the relative utility of the various methods of obtaining marital communication data, such as self-report, interview, and behavior observation (for example, Baucom & Adams, 1987). Research to date on demand-withdraw has relied largely on self-report questionnaires and observation of behavior. In this section, we will review the key assessment tools used thus far.

Self-Report Assessment

The most widely used self-report measure of demand-withdraw is the Communication Patterns Questionnaire (CPQ; Christensen & Sullaway, 1984), developed through a series of investigations (Christensen 1987; Christensen, Sullaway, & King, 1982 cited in Christensen, 1988; Sullaway & Christensen, 1983).

The CPQ asks couples to rate on a 9-point scale the extent to which 35 symmetrical and asymmetrical interaction patterns occur in their relationship during 3 phases of conflict: when the conflict arises (4 items), during discussion of the conflict (18 items), and after discussion of the conflict (13 items). The items focus on distinct behaviors and reactions to those behaviors, excluding reference to the content or topic of the discussion. The CPQ utilizes a dimensional scale from 1 (*very unlikely*) to 9 (*very likely*), which allows for greater variance in responses and higher reliability than dichotomous responses. Many investigators have used a shorter version of the CPQ, the CPQ-Short Form, or CPQ-SF (Christensen & Heavey, 1990; Heavey, Layne, & Christensen, 1993; Holtzworth-Munroe, Smutzler, & Stuart, 1998; Klinetob & Smith, 1996).

The demand-withdraw subscales on the CPQ are (1) woman-demand/man-withdraw, (2) man-demand/woman-withdraw, and (3) total demand-withdraw, which is the sum of the previous two subscales. The woman-demand/man-withdraw subscale consists of the following three items: (a) woman tries to start a discussion while man tries to avoid a discussion, (b) woman nags and demands while man withdraws, becomes silent, or refuses to discuss the matter further, and (c) woman criticizes while man defends himself. The items for the man-demand/woman-withdraw subscale are identical except that male and female roles are reversed. Although these subscales were formed based on conceptual and face valid criteria of what clinicians had written about the pattern of interaction, a factor analysis by Noller and White (1990) showed that all of the demand/withdraw items loaded onto one factor, which they labeled Destructive Process.

Recent data indicate that across several investigations using either the CPQ or CPQ-SF, the mean alpha reliability for the subscales ranges from .50 to .85, with a mean of .75 for the woman-demand/man-withdraw subscale and .66 for the man-demand/woman-withdraw subscale (Kluwer, Heesink, & Van De Vliert, 1997). The CPQ has also demonstrated moderate interpartner agreement, with significant correlations between spouses' reports of husband-demand/wife-withdraw ($r = .39$, $p < .001$) and wife-demand/husband-withdraw ($r = .54$, $p < .001$) (Babcock, Waltz, Jacobson, & Gottman, 1993). Further, in studies that include a reporter factor (man or woman) in the ANOVAs, there has been no significant difference between partners' reports on the CPQ subscales (Christensen & Shenk, 1991; Heavey et al., 1993; Noller, Feeney, Bonnell, & Callan, 1994).

Behavior Observation

Although the CPQ showed promise in assessing the insider's perspective on demand-withdraw, Christensen and his colleagues acknowledged that insiders and outsiders hold different perspectives on marital interaction (Christensen & Heavey, 1993), and therefore they developed an observational coding system to assess demand-withdraw. Based on earlier coding systems (Christensen & Heavey, 1990; Gill, Fincham, & Christensen, 1999; Heavey et al., 1993), this observational system, now called the Couples Interaction Ratings System (CIRS; Heavey, Gill, & Christensen, 1996) has several salient features: (1) It differs from the CPQ in that observers do not code patterns of interaction per se, but rate individual husband and wife behaviors; the demand ratings of one partner are then added to the withdraw ratings of the other to obtain data on the demand-withdraw pattern; (2) Observers rate behaviors that might be indicative of avoidance, since complete avoidance of discussion is not likely in a laboratory situation where partners are instructed by experimenters to discuss a specific topic; and (3) It is a global rating system, so observers watch an entire interaction before assigning ratings on a 9-point scale to indicate the extent to which demand and withdraw occurred (Christensen & Heavey, 1990; Christensen & Heavey, 1993; Heavey et al., 1993). Interobserver alphas for the CIRS subscales have averaged above .80, and interitem alphas have averaged above .70 (Christensen & Heavey, 1993).

Assessment of demand-withdraw using observer ratings of videotaped interactions is not expected to correlate highly with self-report assessment, not just because of method and error variance, but because the two types of assessment are measuring different phenomena. Videotaped interactions are based on a specific topic in the relationship, whereas the CPQ asks about conflict in general. Yet, even though correlations between the CPQ and CIRS have not been high, research findings obtained from these assessments have been largely similar. Also, correlations between the CPQ and observer ratings from a microanalytic coding system were high when the CPQ was completed based on the specific topic discussed (Klinetob & Smith, 1996). In addition, Klinetob and Smith (1996) report that Holtzworth-Munroe, Smutzler, Bates, and Vogel (1995) found a high correspondence between this microanalytic coding system, used globally, and the global CIRS codes.

In a recent investigation of German couples (Hahlweg, Kaiser, Christensen, Fehm-Wolfsdorf, & Groth, 2000), the CPQ was compared to another microanalytic coding system, the *Kategoriensystem fuer Partnerschaftliche Interaktion* (KPI; Coding System for Marital/Family Interaction; Hahlweg, Reisner, Kohli, Vollmer, Schindler, & Revenstorf, 1984). The KPI is designed to code couples' verbal and nonverbal behavior during problem-solving interactions. This investigation examined the correlation between the subscales of the CPQ and the summary codes of the KPI. As expected, wife-demand/husband-withdraw and total amount of demand-withdraw on the CPQ were correlated in meaningful ways with verbal and nonverbal summary codes of the KPI. Interestingly, the husband-demand/wife-withdraw CPQ subscale had lower correlations with the KPI summary codes than the other two demand-withdraw subscales, and these correlations were not always in the expected direction. The authors propose that the husband-demand/wife-withdraw CPQ subscale may produce lower and less consistent correlations with KPI summary codes simply because it is statistically less common than wife-demand/husband-withdraw. Based on their results, these investigators suggest that the CPQ cannot replace observational measures of demand-withdraw, but that the CPQ, a brief and inexpensive measure, may provide a reasonably accurate marker of communication (Hahlweg et al., 2000) .

Summary

Demand-withdraw communication has been assessed via self-report on the CPQ and with various observational rating systems. Although these two methods have produced highly concordant results across studies, it is most appropriate to consider them complementary but not equivalent. Hence, it is best to include both methods in research investigating the demand-withdraw pattern.

DEMAND-WITHDRAW AND RELATIONSHIP SATISFACTION

The clinical literature cited earlier suggests that the demand-withdraw pattern is a marker of couples in conflict and distress. Empirical research has consistently demonstrated that demand-withdraw is indeed associated with marital dissatisfaction.

Self-Report Associations

Using self-report of demand-withdraw on the CPQ, or an earlier version of the CPQ (the Interaction Patterns Questionnaire), diverse samples of couples have demonstrated that greater demand-withdraw communication is associated with lower relationship satisfaction. This correlation has been found among undergraduate dating couples (Sullaway & Christensen, 1983), cohabiting couples (Christensen, 1987), engaged and newlywed couples (Noller et al., 1994), and several diverse samples of married couples recruited from various sources (Christensen, 1987; Christensen et al., 1982; Noller & White, 1990). In addition, Christensen and Shenk (1991) recruited three samples: divorcing couples in custody litigation, clinic couples seeking treatment, and nondistressed couples. Results indicated that the two distressed groups (clinic and divorcing) reported significantly more demand-withdraw communication on the

CPQ than the nondistressed group. Finally, Eldridge (2000) recruited samples of high-distress couples seeking therapy, moderate-distress couples seeking therapy, and nondistressed couples, and similarly found that the two distressed groups reported significantly greater demand-withdraw than the nondistressed couples.

Observational Associations

Several studies have collected behavioral data in an attempt to provide a more stringent test of the relationship between demand-withdraw and satisfaction. An additional benefit to collecting behavioral data is that observers rate demand and withdraw separately, so that the combination of demand and withdraw can also be broken down into its component parts.

Four studies of demand-withdraw and relationship satisfaction have collected both self-report and behavioral data from participants (Christensen & Heavey, 1990; Eldridge, 2000; Heavey et al., 1993; Noller et al., 1994). Results have been consistent across both assessment methods and suggest a negative association between satisfaction and demand-withdraw communication. Various results have been reported when separating out the demand and withdraw behaviors from behavioral data. Eldridge (2000) found that greater distress was significantly associated with greater demanding and withdrawing. Other studies analyzed data for husbands and wives separately and some found different associations across genders. Heavey et al. (1993) reported that the extent to which each spouse was demanding, but not withdrawing, was significantly negatively associated with his or her marital satisfaction. Christensen and Heavey (1990) found that mothers' demanding behavior and fathers' withdrawing behavior were significantly negatively correlated with marital satisfaction, while mothers' withdrawing and fathers' demanding behavior were not significantly correlated with satisfaction. Using a coding system based on conflict resolution and compliance-gaining conflict strategies, in which participants rated their own videotaped discussions, Noller et al. (1994) found that, among engaged couples, women's avoidance was negatively associated with their own satisfaction. About two years later, among these same couples, husbands' satisfaction was negatively correlated with wives' use of coercion (a measure of intense demanding). The comparative importance of demand and withdraw is unclear based on these inconsistent findings, but they highlight the utility of behavioral data that can separate the components of demand-withdraw.

Longitudinal Associations

The aforementioned research clearly indicates a cross-sectional associa-tion between marital satisfaction and demand-withdraw, measured via questionnaires or behavioral observation. However, longitudinal and cross-sectional associations between communication and marital satis-faction may differ (Gottman & Krokoff, 1989). Longitudinal studies of marital interaction have produced inconsistent results about the associ-ation between communication and marital satisfaction over time. This inconsistency has often been attributed to methodological and statisti-cal differences across longitudinal studies (Bradbury & Karney, 1993; Gottman & Krokoff, 1990; Smith, Vivian & O'Leary, 1991; Woody & Costanzo, 1990).

There have also been inconsistent findings regarding the longitudinal association between demand-withdraw and relationship satisfaction. The main question is whether demanding and withdrawing in response to conflict lead to increases or decreases in marital satisfaction over time. In most studies (Weiss & Heyman, 1997), these behaviors lead to detrimental effects longitudinally. However, there are some ex-ceptions. For example, Heavey et al. (1993) found that husbands' demanding behavior at Time 1 led to increases in wives' marital satisfaction from Time 1 to Time 2 (a year later), but wives' demanding-ness predicted deterioration in their own satisfaction over time. More specifically, wife-demand/husband-withdraw predicted decline or no change in marital satisfaction for husbands and wives, but husband-demand/wife-withdraw predicted longitudinal increases in marital sat-isfaction. These results applied to both self-report and observer ratings of demand-withdraw. Although demanding behavior is considered negative and is assumed to be detrimental, wives reacting positively to husbands' demanding behavior may not be so counterintuitive or sur-prising; it is consistent with the notion that wives react positively to husbands' willingness to discuss their marriage (Acitelli, 1992).

Gottman and Krokoff (1989) found that men's withdrawal during conflict interactions predicted declines in marital satisfaction longi-tudinally. Although this study has been criticized on methodolog-ical grounds (Bradbury & Karney, 1993; Smith, Vivian & O'Leary, 1991; Woody & Costanzo, 1990), this finding has been replicated in several studies. Heavey, Christensen, and Malamuth (1995) conducted a longitudinal investigation in which married and dating couples were assessed at two time intervals, two and a half years apart. Two observer ratings predicted change in satisfaction, using both partial correlation and change score methods: Man-withdraw and woman-demand/man-withdraw during discussions of women's issues predicted significant declines in women's satisfaction and nonsignificant declines in men's satisfaction. Other significant associations existed, but were not consistent across methods of assessing change. Two additional published studies have provided support for the detrimental effects of the wife-demand/husband-withdraw pattern over time (Kurdek, 1995; Levenson & Gottman, 1985). In fact, Kurdek (1995) found that the wife-demand/husband-withdraw pattern accounted for more variance in concurrent satisfaction and longitudinal decreases in satisfaction than any other conflict resolution pattern.

Looking more specifically at withdraw, Smith, Vivian, and O'Leary (1991) also demonstrated that withdrawal in premarital communication was negatively correlated with marital satisfaction at 18 and 30 months of marriage, but their study highlighted the importance of the context of withdrawal. If withdrawal was accompanied by high levels of positivity, marital satisfaction improved by 30 months of marriage, indicating that withdrawal may be detrimental only when accompanied by a context of negativity (Weiss & Heyman, 1997). Roberts (2000) also asserts that the context of withdrawal is important. In contrast to previous studies, she found that husbands' withdrawal did not contribute to the prediction of wives' marital distress over and above husbands' hostility. Yet wives' withdrawal, not hostility, predicted decreased satisfaction among husbands. Consistent with this finding, Sayers, Baucom, Sher, Weiss, and Heyman (1991) found that decreases in wife withdrawal over the course of marital therapy and among control couples led to increases in husbands' satisfaction, yet there was no effect of decreases in husband withdrawal on wives' satisfaction. Roberts (2000) suggests that the gender-stereotyped presumption, that wife demanding and husband withdrawing behavior are particularly harmful to marriage, requires further investigation.

These studies all looked at the effect of communication patterns on later satisfaction. However, it is possible that earlier levels of satisfaction lead to changes in demand-withdraw communication as well. A few studies have attempted to determine how demand-withdraw communication and relationship satisfaction influence one another over time (Klinetob, Smith, & House, 1994; Kurdek, 1995; Noller et al., 1994).

Noller et al. (1994) assessed couples just prior to marriage and twice during the first two years of marriage. At all three assessment points, couples independently completed self-report measures of communication and satisfaction and engaged in videotaped discussions. This design is valuable because it assesses problem-solving behavior and satisfaction at several points and does not assume that communication unidirectionally influences satisfaction. Unfortunately, the small sample of newlyweds completing all three assessments resulted in limited power, and the stability of relationship satisfaction across the three time points left little variance to be explained by partial correlations controlling for earlier satisfaction. Therefore, correlations of demand and withdraw with satisfaction were small and inconsistent. However, results indicated that communication and relationship satisfaction were associated concurrently, that earlier communication predicted later satisfaction for wives only, and that earlier satisfaction predicted later communication for both husbands and wives.

Weiss and Heyman (1997) report on a six-month longitudinal study by Klinetob et al. (1994), which also suggested that marital dissatisfaction was a precursor of demand-withdraw communication six months later, but found that the reverse was not true. However, using self-report among a large sample of couples in their fourth year of marriage, Kurdek (1995) found no support for earlier satisfaction predicting conflict resolution styles over the course of two years.

Summary

There is clearly a strong cross-sectional association between demand-withdraw and marital dissatisfaction. Longitudinal associations are less consistent, but most studies support the conclusion that wives' tendency to be demanding and husbands' tendency to withdraw during conflict are detrimental to marital satisfaction. It is also likely that marital dissatisfaction exacerbates demanding and withdrawing behaviors in the context of conflict.

DEMAND-WITHDRAW AND DOMESTIC VIOLENCE

Julie and Ed have been married for five years and have two young children. Their marriage has become increasingly distressed, and Ed has become physically aggressive toward Julie. For the last six months, he has shoved her and thrown things at her (including a glass vase) during arguments. Julie stays home with the children and Ed works full-time to provide income for the family. On this particular Friday, Julie has been with her two children, plus the neighbor's two young boys, for the entire day. She feels exhausted by children and in need of adult companionship. She wants to visit with her girlfriends who are also in need of support and a break from their kids. Ed, also tired from a long work week, is looking forward to an evening with his wife, after putting the children to bed early. However, when he returns home from work, after a brief exchange of hellos, they have the following dispute:

Julie: I was thinking about getting together with Susan and Laura tonight, is that OK?

Ed: Well I thought we would spend the night together, it's Friday night.

Julie: I know, but I've been around the kids all day and I'd like to see my friends.

Ed: What about me? What about spending the evening with me? We'll put the kids to bed early and have the rest of the night together. You just saw your friends last week, and you talk to them on the phone all the time. And why do you have to go out with them on a Friday night? You know that there will be lots of single men out on a Friday night, and you and your friends are just a target for them.

Julie: Ed, there's no reason to be jealous, I just want to see my girlfriends.

Ed: (raising his voice) I'm not jealous; I am concerned about our marriage. You see your friends often enough, can't you just stay home for once with your husband? How are we supposed to make this marriage work? The weekends are our time together, and should be for us and our family, not your friends.

Julie: Okay, fine, I'll stay home. (walks away)

Although much research has supported the view that women tend to be the demanders and men the withdrawers in relationship conflict, investigations suggest that in domestically violent relationships (particularly husband-to-wife violence), as in the example above, the pattern may be reversed. A series of four studies has examined the relationship between demand-withdraw communication and domestic violence. Issues of power are germane to both constructs, and these studies are beginning to shed light on the ways in which power and control are exhibited in communication and in violent behavior.

Investigating a sample of maritally distressed/violent, maritally distressed/nonviolent, and maritally happy/nonviolent couples, Babcock et al. (1993) used self-report to assess demand-withdraw and marital satisfaction. In comparing the violent and nonviolent distressed groups, they found that the violent distressed couples reported significantly greater husband-demand/wife-withdraw than the nonviolent distressed couples, but the two groups did not differ in the amount of wife-demand/husband-withdraw reported. In contrast, when comparing distressed (violent and nonviolent) and nondistressed groups, the distressed couples reported significantly greater wife-demand/husband-withdraw *and* husband-demand/wife-withdraw than the nondistressed couples. These results indicate that husband demand, illustrated by Ed in the example, is particularly salient in husband-to-wife domestically violent marriages. Drawing on previous work (Christensen & Heavey, 1990; Jacobson, 1989), the authors propose that withdrawing behavior during conflict is associated with greater power in the relationship, since those who demand something of their partner are in a less powerful position than those who want to maintain the status quo in the relationship. Babcock et al. (1993) suggest that the high rates of husband demand provide evidence that domestically violent men may have less power than their female partners, and may try to compensate for their lack of power in the relationship via physical aggression.

A second study examined this same sample of couples, but used behavior observation to assess demand-withdraw behavior, allowing demand and withdraw to be analyzed separately (Berns, Jacobson, & Gottman, 1999a). Again, distressed/violent husbands engaged in more demanding behavior than distressed/nonviolent men. The authors propose that, although power and control are inherent in battering, batterers may not perceive themselves as having the power they seek, and therefore may engage in demanding behavior to seek such control. In contrast to the Babcock et al. self-report findings, battered wives exhibited greater demanding behavior than nonbattered wives, and the authors hypothesize that this demanding stems from a desire to reduce or eliminate the abusive behavior. Findings regarding withdraw in male batterers were also different from those of the Babcock et al. self-report study. Berns et al. (1999a) found that batterers did exhibit greater withdrawal behavior than nonviolent husbands, but battered wives demonstrated less withdrawal than wives in nonviolent marriages. These researchers theorized that wives in abusive relationships exhibited less withdrawal due to the potential increase in violence if they withdrew from their husbands' demands.

Among a different sample of couples, Holtzworth-Munroe et al. (1998) also used behavior observation to assess demand-withdraw, and the results of her study replicated the Babcock et al. (1993) study described previously. Interestingly, in an attempt to more effectively separate the effects of violence and distress, Holtzworth-Munroe et al. (1998) included a nondistressed/violent subsample in her study, and found that these couples did not demonstrate high levels of husband-demand/wife-withdraw. Since the distressed/violent couples in all three of these domestic violence studies were characterized by greater husband violence than the nondistressed/violent couples included in the Holtzworth-Munroe et al. (1998) study, they suggest that the findings that high levels of husband-demand/wife-withdraw may be unique to more severe domestic violence. Discrepancies between the Berns et al. (1999a) study and the studies by Holtzworth-Munroe et al. and Babcock et al. in terms of the demanding behavior of battered wives and the withdrawing behavior of batterers, may be due to methodological differences in the assessment of demand-withdraw (Berns et al., 1999a).

Although these findings require replication, they demonstrate that demand-withdraw may be structurally and contextually different among domestically violent relationships than among nonviolent or low-level violent relationships. Based on the evidence thus far, it seems that husband-demand/wife-withdraw is particularly common among more "severely violent" couples (O'Leary, 1993), but not among couples who engage in "common couple violence" (Johnson, 1995).

Looking more closely at the demand-withdraw communication of specific subtypes of batterers, Berns, Jacobson, and Gottman (1999b) attempted to determine whether two subtypes of batterers, Type I or "Cobras" and Type II or "Pit Bulls" (Jacobson & Gottman, 1998), and their wives, differed on levels of demand and withdraw communication during conflict. Their study offered preliminary evidence for greater levels of demand-withdraw among Type I batterers and their wives, than among Type II batterers and their wives. Continued research on the relationship between demand-withdraw and domestic violence, and particularly specific subtypes of violence, can help us understand, predict, and work toward better prevention and treatment of domestic violence.

EXPLANATIONS FOR DEMAND-WITHDRAW

Perhaps one of the most interesting aspects of the demand-withdraw pattern is the question of whether demanding and withdrawing behaviors are gender linked. That is, do gender differences cause the demand-withdraw pattern to arise in heterosexual relationships? It has long been speculated that women tend to be demanders in relationships, while men tend to withdraw. Authors often cite the work of Terman, Buttenweiser, Ferguson, Johnson, and Wilson (1938) as the earliest study to demonstrate this empirically. These researchers found that distressed wives complained of their husbands' withdrawal, while distressed husbands complained of their wives' nagging, criticism, and emotionality. A number of studies have supported this gender difference, finding that women were more emotionally expressive and conflict-engaging while men were more conflict-avoiding (Kelley, Conningham, Grisham, Lefebvre, Sink, & Yablon, 1978; Komarovsky, 1962; 1976; Rubin 1976; 1983; Rugel, 1997). In early studies specifically on the demand-withdraw pattern, women were more often the demanders in relationships, and men more often the withdrawers. This was true among undergraduate dating couples (Sullaway & Christensen, 1983) and a large heterogeneous sample of married and cohabiting couples of varying levels of distress (Christensen, 1987; 1988). Although there is much consistency among these findings, more recent studies have challenged this apparent gender difference. In this section, the proposed explanations for demand-withdraw, which include (a) gender differences, (b) individual differences, (c) the structure of society or of traditional marriage, and (d) the structure of the conflict topic will be presented along with the related research.

Gender Differences Perspective

The gender differences view suggests that different socialization experiences and/or different physiological characteristics between men and women account for this gendered demand-withdraw pattern. The socialization perspective notes that women are encouraged to be affiliative and expressive, and their identity is developed in the context of relationships; in contrast, men are encouraged to be independent and inexpressive, and their identity is developed in the context of separation (Chodorow, 1978; Gilligan, 1982; Rubin, 1983). Differences in how men and women are socialized to express emotion, to value emotional connections with others, and to experience intimacy, lead to misunderstandings between heterosexual partners (Brody, 1993; Markman & Kraft, 1989; Tannen, 1990). Conflicts about emotional intimacy in marriage inevitably arise, and these conflicts are likely to consist of the wife seeking closeness and the husband seeking autonomy (Christensen, 1987; 1988; Jacobson, 1989; Jacobson & Margolin, 1979). These different desires for closeness and distance are evident in the cyclical interactions between men and women, in which women respond to men's withdrawal with pressures for more intimacy via complaints, criticisms, and demands, and men withdraw from women's pressure in order to maintain their autonomy.

Gottman and Levenson (1986; 1988) proposed that a gender difference in physiology explains the demand-withdraw gender linkage. They reported that, in response to stress, men react with greater physiological arousal than do women, and may take longer to return to baseline levels of arousal. Consequently, they suggest that men's withdrawal from relationship conflict is due to their greater arousal (which creates greater discomfort) in response to the stressful, conflictual interactions. Women, on the other hand, are less physiologically reactive to stress, and thus are more likely to engage in demanding behaviors that escalate a conflictual interaction. Evidence for this physiological difference perspective is mixed, since some studies have demonstrated either no difference between genders in physiological reactivity, or greater physiological reactivity among women than men, and no studies have yet demonstrated that physiological arousal is temporally linked to behavioral withdrawal during conflict resolution (Julien, Arellano, & Turgeon, 1997).

In sum, the gender difference perspective asserts that differences in the enduring characteristics of men and women determine the roles they typically take in relationship conflict. In the two gender difference views outlined here, women's characteristics lead them to be in the demanding role, whereas the characteristics of men cause them to be in the withdrawing role during conflict.

Individual Differences Perspective

A broader perspective asserts that demand-withdraw is caused not strictly by gender differences, but by individual characteristics that may often be associated with gender. For example, the partner who desires greater closeness in the relationship, regardless of gender, may be more demanding, while the partner desiring greater independence may be more withdrawing.

Recent research (Walczynski, 1997) has supported the individual difference view, and has specifically implicated personality dimensions such as femininity as moderating or causal mechanisms in demand-withdraw interaction. Walczynski (1997) examined gay and lesbian relationships in an attempt to disassociate gender from the personality characteristics often associated with it. She reported that same-sex couples demonstrate as much demand-withdraw communication as opposite-sex couples, and that same-sex couples are similarly characterized by one partner tending to be consistently in the demanding role and the other tending to be consistently in the withdrawing role during conflict. Walczynski's (1997) results indicated that, among cross-sex and same-sex couples, demanding and withdrawing roles were predicted by sex role-related personality factors such as femininity. Specifically, possessing more feminine traits than one's partner was associated with greater likelihood of demanding behavior during conflict, whereas possessing less femininity than one's partner was associated with greater likelihood of withdrawing behavior during conflict.

Walczynski also replicated previous findings (Christensen & Shenk, 1991) that the partner desiring more closeness in the relationship tends to be more demanding during conflict, whereas the partner wanting more distance tends to be more withdrawing during conflict. She extended these findings to same-sex couples and also demonstrated that in same-sex couples, the more committed partner is perceived as more demanding during conflict, and the less committed partner is perceived as more withdrawing.

Walczynski's findings are inconsistent with a strictly gender-based difference view of demand-withdraw roles, but do indicate that personality factors, regardless of gender, may be important determinants of demand-withdraw role assignment. In addition, these results support the notion that characteristics of the relationship, such as discrepant desires for closeness and commitment, provide a fertile breeding ground for demand-withdraw communication: The partner who is more committed and/or desires more closeness exhibits demanding behavior during conflict, whereas the partner who is less committed and/or desires more independence exhibits withdrawing behavior. Julien et al. (1997), in a review of studies that compare same-sex and cross-sex relationships, also conclude that characteristics of the relationship, particularly level of distress and socialization differences between partners, are more central to determining demanding and withdrawing behavior than gender alone.

Social and Marital Structure Perspective

The third perspective on the causal mechanism for demand-withdraw is the social structure view, which focuses on the different positions of men and women in the social structure. The broadest social structure view implicates large societal-level explanations, such as discrepancies in power and status favoring men, in accounting for the gender pattern in demand-withdraw communication (Murphy & Meyer, 1991; Noller, 1993). Noller (1993) asserts that men maintain their greater status and power in society relative to women, by resisting women's requests for change. Similarly, Peplau and Gordon (1985) indicate that, if this difference in power characterizes a heterosexual relationship, men have a lot to lose but nothing to gain by discussing relationship problems, whereas women may need to use confrontation to improve their position in the relationship. Consequently, women pressure for changes in the relationship, and men avoid or withdraw from discussing those changes.

A second version of the social structure view focuses on the structure of traditional marriage specifically. This perspective asserts that, since men benefit more from traditional marriage than women in several ways (Jacobson, 1983), women are more often seeking change in the marriage (Margolin, Talovic, & Weinstein, 1983), whereas men want to preserve the status quo that places them in a "better" position than women (Jacobson, 1990). Consequently, women's requests or demands for change are met with resistance or withdrawal from men, because direct confrontation might force changes in the traditional marital structure (Christensen, 1987; 1988; Christensen & Heavey, 1990; Jacobson, 1989).

Kluwer (1998) has begun a program of research that supports the importance of the gender role beliefs associated with traditional marital structure in demand-withdraw communication. She examines communication about the division of labor among parents experiencing the transition to parenthood. In conflicts about the division of labor, wives are typically the partners who desire change while husbands are content with, and want to maintain, the status quo. Consistent with other research examining interactions in which wives desire change, she demonstrates that demand-withdraw is prevalent in these discussions. However, wives' discontent with the division of labor was associated, not only with wife-demand/husband-withdraw interaction, but also with husband-demand/wife-withdraw interaction and mutual avoidance. Kluwer (1998) proposes that husbands' and wives' gender role ideologies may moderate the relationship between discontent and conflict engagement or withdrawal. Specifically, she suggests that traditional wives, and wives with a traditional husband, may find it more difficult to engage in conflict over the division of labor because of these strongly-held gender role ideologies (DeVault, 1990). Opposing the traditional marital roles is considered inappropriate in such marriages. Therefore, regardless of how discontented wives are, they may not overtly pressure for change in the relationship if they or their husbands hold traditional gender role beliefs.

Kluwer et al. (1997) investigated the moderating role of husbands' and wives' gender role ideology on the relationship between wives' discontent and wives' conflict avoidance. This study demonstrated, that when husbands and wives held more traditional gender role ideologies, the wives exhibited more avoidance and withdrawal during their conflict discussions. The positive associations between wife discontent and husband-demand/wife-withdraw, and between wife discontent and mutual avoidance, were significantly stronger among traditional wives and wives with a traditional husband. In sum, traditional wives and wives with a traditional husband were more likely to avoid conflict about the division of labor than were egalitarian wives and wives with an egalitarian husband, *despite* their discontent. Importantly, these findings suggest that, just as certain conflict structures may exacerbate or facilitate the gender-stereotyped pattern of wife-demand/husband-withdraw (for example, when the topic is one in which the wife wants change, discussed as follows), there are moderating variables related to the relationship structure, such as traditional gender roles that may reduce or even reverse this gender-stereotyped pattern.

A recent study found that, although holding traditional gender role beliefs did not reverse or diminish the gender-stereotyped pattern of wife-demand/husband-withdraw, it was associated with greater amounts of the reverse pattern of husband-demand/wife-withdraw (Eldridge, 2000). However, this study indicated that wives in traditional relationships did not necessarily withdraw from conflict. Instead, wives with traditional husbands engaged in greater demand and greater withdraw than wives with egalitarian husbands. Further, traditional husbands and husbands with traditional wives demonstrated greater demanding behavior than egalitarian husbands and husbands with egalitarian wives. Eldridge (2000) suggests that, in a traditional marital structure, husbands may be more likely to demand that wives adapt to the status quo in the relationship, while wives may either counterdemand or withdraw as a way of expressing their discontent.

Conflict Structure Perspective

Christensen and Heavey and colleagues (Christensen & Heavey, 1990; Christensen & Heavey, 1993; Heavey et al., 1993) proposed a third structural view that focuses on the structure of the discussion topic instead of the social or marital structure. They suggested that the roles adopted by men and women during conflict depend on the specific structure of the conflict topic (Heavey et al., 1993). If the conflict topic is one in which the wife desires change from the husband, wife-demand/husband-withdraw is more likely than the reverse. However, if the conflict topic is one in which the husband wants change in the wife, husband-demand/wife-withdraw is more likely than the reverse. These patterns arise because the person who desires change must rely on the partner's compliance to induce change, and therefore must engage in behaviors to elicit change from the partner, such as complaints, demands, and pressures. Conversely, the status quo can be preserved unilaterally without the partner's cooperation, but may be lost if active problem solving occurs.

For example, if a wife wants her husband to be more affectionate toward her, she needs him to make a concession and become more affectionate. She may engage in several behaviors, such as requesting more affection, complaining about the current level of affection, or pressuring her husband to be more affectionate to try to get him to make that concession. On the other hand, the husband can continue being as affectionate as he always has been without his wife making any concession. Hence, he may avoid discussing the problem of affection in the relationship because such discussion may either lead to an argument or result in a change in the status quo (namely, having to be more affectionate). Therefore, the member seeking change demands, and the partner withdraws from problem-solving efforts. Since women are more often seeking change in marriage (Margolin et al., 1983), women are more often in the demanding role and men more often in the withdrawing role.

Assessing the Gender Difference and Conflict Structure Explanations for Demand-Withdraw

With the conflict structure explanation in mind, Christensen and Heavey (1990) introduced an innovative methodology for investigating the impact of conflict structure on conflict behavior. They

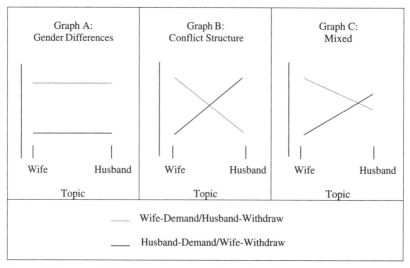

Figure 11.1. Graphical representations of gender roles in demand-withdraw communications.

experimentally manipulated which spouse wanted change in a discussion by asking married couples to have two discussions, one focused on an area in which the wife wanted change, and one focused on an area in which the husband wanted change. The investigators reasoned that a gender difference explanation would predict that wives would be more demanding and husbands more withdrawing, regardless of who chose the topic of discussion (graph A of Figure 11.1), but the conflict structure perspective would predict changes in demand and withdraw roles depending on who wanted more change in behavior (graph B of Figure 11.1). Specifically, the conflict structure view would assert that wives will be more demanding and husbands more withdrawing when discussing the wife's issue (change desired in husband), and husbands will be more demanding and wives more withdrawing during discussion of the husband's topic (change desired in wife).

Christensen and Heavey (1990) found that, on both self-report and observational data, wife-demand/husband-withdraw was significantly more likely to occur than husband-demand/wife-withdraw. However, the magnitude of this difference depended on the topic being discussed. When discussing the wife's issue, wife-demand/husband-withdraw was significantly more likely than husband-demand/wife-withdraw, but when discussing the husband's issue, there was no significant difference in the likelihood of the patterns – husband-demand/

wife-withdraw was as likely as wife-demand/husband-withdraw (graph C of Figure 11.1). These findings were replicated in four subsequent studies with varied samples, across self-report and observer ratings (Eldridge, 2000; Heavey et al., 1993; Monarch, 1998; Walczynski, 1997).

Christensen and his colleagues suggest that these results support both the gender difference perspective (wife-demand/husband-withdraw was more likely overall) *and* the conflict structure perspective (the gender roles of the pattern depended on who desired change). Heavey et al. (1993) concluded that:

... in general, women are more likely to be demanding and men are more likely to be withdrawing during conflictual discussions. When the structure of the conflict supports this gender linkage (i.e., when women's greater propensity to engage in conflict is combined with the opportunity to pursue a desired change in the relationship), the roles tend to become highly stereotyped. When the conflict is inconsistent with this gender typing (i.e., during discussion of the men's issues) there is no clear gender breakdown in demand/withdraw roles. In other words, the structure of the conflict plays an important role in terms of interacting with gender differences to move spouses either toward, or away from, their typical roles (p. 24).

Christensen and Heavey (1990) assert that previous research demonstrating that wives express more negative affect and husbands more withdrawal during conflict could be an artifact of the methodology for choosing which conflict topic to discuss: Perhaps the topics chosen for conflict discussions more often reflect the women's desire for change than the men's.

These findings, which support both the gender difference and conflict structure explanations, have not gone unchallenged. Two recent studies (Holtzworth-Munroe et al., 1998; Klinetob & Smith, 1996) have demonstrated a complete reversal of demand-withdraw roles, depending solely on who wanted change in the topic under discussion (as in graph B of Figure 11.1). These results would support only a conflict structure view of demand-withdraw interaction. Specifically, Klinetob and Smith (1996) found that during discussions of wives' issues, wife-demand/husband-withdraw was significantly more likely than the reverse, and when discussing husbands' issues, husband-demand/wife-withdraw was significantly more likely than the reverse. Similarly, Holtzworth-Munroe et al. (1998) found evidence among their sample of violent and nonviolent couples that husband-demand/wife-withdraw was more common during discussions of husbands' topics than during discussions of wives' topics, while wife-demand/husband-withdraw was more common when discussing wives' topics than when discussing husbands' topics. The authors suggested that their results supported a conflict structure explanation in which gender roles in demanding and withdrawing behavior depended on who wanted change, instead of a gender differences perspective that women are more demanding and men more withdrawing across discussions. In response to these two recent studies, two additional explanations for demand-withdraw have been presented that also account for the discrepancy in findings: history of conflict and flexibility of communication patterns.

History of Marital Conflict

Christensen and colleagues suggest that a symmetrical pattern of demand-withdraw communication develops over time into an asymmetrical pattern when couples have greater success resolving husbands' than wives' issues (Christensen & Heavey, 1993). Consequently, the discussions of his issues (which do not carry a long history of conflict) are likely to contain less demand-withdraw and less conflict than discussions of her issues. After many years of marriage, demand-withdraw would occur during discussions of wives' issues (which have continuously gone unresolved), and wives would become increasingly demanding and men increasingly withdrawing during these discussions.

In support of this view, Christensen noted that the couples investigated by Klinetob and Smith (1996) had not been married as long as the couples investigated by Christensen and Heavey (1990) and Heavey et al. (1993). Further, a recent investigation of demand-withdraw roles (Eldridge, 2000) demonstrated the importance of marriage length, particularly when couples are distressed. Couples who were highly distressed and had been together longer (over 8.5 years) were more locked into their demanding and withdrawing roles, regardless of topic. Couples who were highly distressed but had not been together as long demonstrated some role reversal, depending on the topic. In sum, among highly distressed couples, as marriages increased in length, the gender-stereotyped difference in roles was greater when discussing wives' issues, and demonstrated less crossover during discussions of husbands' issues.

Flexibility of Communication Patterns

Another explanation, based on differences in marital satisfaction, suggests that marital distress is associated with an inflexibility that makes it difficult for the couple to reverse demand-withdraw roles during conflict; in contrast, satisfied couples are able to break out of the gender-stereotyped demand-withdraw roles because their communication is more flexible, and therefore more influenced by the topic of the conflict (Klinetob & Smith, 1996). This view places primary importance on the rigidity of gender-stereotyped demand-withdraw communication patterns. Klinetob and Smith hypothesize that rigid application of demand-withdraw communication across conflicts may be more destructive to marital satisfaction than the mere presence of the pattern. Therefore, the couples in their study, being less distressed, exhibited higher flexibility in conflict style by being able to reverse roles, depending on who wanted change in the discussion, whereas the more distressed couples in the Christensen studies were unable to demonstrate this flexibility. Similarly, Heavey et al. (1993) suggested that distressed couples become locked in gender-stereotyped conflict roles that are rigidly applied across interactions and become increasingly polarized and inflexible, whereas nondistressed couples are more flexible in their communication and therefore less polarized in their roles.

Consistent with this idea, Burman, Margolin, and John (1993), using naturalistic in-home assessments of conflict, found that nondistressed couples exhibit some of the same destructive conflict patterns as distressed couples, but are able to exit them more quickly. Specific to demand-withdraw, Eldridge (2000) found that there was greater rigidity in gender-stereotyped demand-withdraw roles across both conflictual and supportive discussions among highly distressed couples than among low distress and nondistressed couples. This gender-stereotyped difference was particularly salient whenever the discussion focused on change in the husband, whether this change was sought by the wife (conflictual discussion) or by the husband (supportive discussion). Hence, nondistressed couples also exhibit demand-withdraw during conflict, but are able to move away from these roles more quickly and easily than distressed couples, who become rigidly locked in gender-stereotyped demand-withdraw roles.

Summary

Thus far, the evidence suggests that women are more likely to be demanding and men withdrawing, but not in all situations. In those situations in which men want change, they are likely to be at least as demanding as women. Similarly, in those situations, women are likely to be at least as withdrawing as men. Furthermore, it appears that distress is associated, not only with demand-withdraw, but also with the gender-stereotyped polarization in demand-withdraw roles. Conflict structure does seem to exacerbate or reduce gender-stereotyped demand-withdraw roles, but only among nondistressed or low-level distressed couples. Highly distressed couples remain in gender-stereotyped demand-withdraw roles, regardless of conflict structure. In addition, more recent findings suggest that distress alone does not determine couples' responses to the structure of conflict; how long couples have been married (or their history of conflict with a particular topic), and perhaps the marital structure (traditional or egalitarian), interact with distress level in determining demand-withdraw roles.

FUTURE AVENUES FOR DEMAND-WITHDRAW RESEARCH

Methodological and Statistical Strategies

We began this chapter with a review of the assessment of demand-withdraw, which has consisted of self-report and behavioral observation. Interview-based assessment of marital interaction in general, and demand-withdraw specifically, is underused, and provides an opportunity for enhanced assessment (Christensen, 1987). Further, observation of videotaped interactions may not provide the best indication of withdrawal or avoidance, as participants are not likely to engage in many of those behaviors, when they are instructed by an experimenter to discuss a topic for a specified amount of time. Conflict avoidance may occur in different ways naturalistically; for example, looking at the TV or reading the paper while one's partner is speaking, walking out of the room, or remaining completely silent. Even though more subtle forms of withdrawal and avoidance, such as changing the topic or giving vague responses, can be discerned in videotaped interactions, the more obvious forms may not be captured in a laboratory setting. Therefore, studies of naturalistic conflicts occurring in the home, and perhaps over lengthy sequences of time, may provide us with more accurate information (Burman, Margolin, & John, 1993; Daylen, 1994; Monarch, 1998).

Although we have used the term *demand-withdraw* throughout this chapter, we conceptualize the demand-withdraw pattern as cyclical, not necessarily starting with demand and ending with withdraw. Micro-analytic coding of videotaped interactions provides the opportunity to determine the sequencing of demand and withdraw over the course of marital interaction, and their temporal relationship to each other. In an investigation of conflict engagement and withdrawal among happy and unhappy couples, Roberts and Krokoff (1990) used micro-analytic coding of videotaped conflicts and bivariate time-series analysis to determine the temporal linkage of hostility and withdrawal. They found that one temporal pattern characterized distressed couples: husbands' withdrawal predicting wives' hostility. This temporal pattern accounted for an additional 20% of the variance in marital satisfaction, beyond the 50% of variance that was due to the overall positivity/negativity of the interaction. Interestingly, the reverse pattern (wives' hostility predicting husbands' withdrawal) occurred much less often, and did not distinguish distressed from nondistressed couples. Another investigation using a microanalytic coding system (Klinetob & Smith, 1996) found that demand and withdraw were contingent upon one another at the utterance level, and that this contingency can be either wife dominated (the wife's behavior predicts subsequent husband behavior, but the husband's behavior does not predict subsequent wife behavior), husband dominated (the reverse of the former), bidirectional (each partner's behavior predicts the subsequent behavior of the other), or nondependent (neither partner's behavior predicts the subsequent behavior of the other). Supporting a cyclical view of demand-withdraw, bidirectional contingency was the most commonly observed classification. Additional research using this methodology will make a valuable contribution to the demand-withdraw literature.

Two other methodological and statistical advances will enhance our understanding of marital communication: (1) longitudinal research designs using more than two time points, which allows data analysis using hierarchical linear modeling, and (2) as Roberts (2000) suggests, determining the unique effects of demand-withdraw over and above the effects of other communication patterns such as mutual hostile engagement.

Substantive Areas of Inquiry

Although there are many avenues for future research on demand-withdraw, four themes have begun to emerge in recent research. One of these is the impact of demand-withdraw marital interaction on children. There are some data to suggest that children respond emotionally and behaviorally to parental demand-withdraw communication (Allen, 1996; Noller, Feeney, Sheehan, & Peterson, 2000; Wilder, 1999), particularly during times of higher stress (Poleshuck, 1998). And as adults, spouses tend to model the demand-withdraw communication they observed as children between their parents (Phelps, 1995).

Second, the overwhelming majority of research on marital interaction has focused on communication during conflict. However, recent work has begun to highlight the importance of social support among spouses (Cutrona, Hessling, & Suhr, 1997; Cutrona & Suhr, 1994; Pasch & Bradbury, 1998; Pasch, Bradbury, & Davila, 1997). For example, Pasch and Bradbury (1998) observed spouses when they were discussing a personal problem of one spouse. They assessed the supportive behavior of the other spouse, as well as the support-seeking behavior of the spouse with the personal problem. Similarly, it will be important to investigate demand-withdraw in contexts other than conflict. To date, one observational study (Eldridge, 2000) has found that demand-withdraw is also present in social support interactions, although in lesser amounts than in conflict interactions. Following Pasch and Bradbury (1998), Eldridge (2000) had each spouse identify a personal problem, as well as a relationship problem, to discuss. For example, the husband might choose "dealing with his boss more effectively" as his personal topic, and "wife saving more money" as his relationship topic. Interestingly, her coding of demand-withdraw interaction during these discussions revealed that the association between topic and demand-withdraw roles (graph C in Figure 11.1) was reversed during support discussions. Wife-demand/husband-withdraw was greater than husband-demand/wife-withdraw during husbands' topics, and there was no significant difference in roles during wives' topics (the opposite of what is usually found in problem-solving interactions). However, this apparent difference between the findings from conflict and supportive interactions may mask a more substantive similarity. In both designs, wife-demand/husband-withdraw interaction is likely when the focus is on a change in husband behavior, whether that desired change is introduced by the wife (problem solving) or by the husband (social support); however, when the focus is on a change in wife behavior, there is no asymmetry in demand-withdraw interaction. Exploring these differences in communication between conflictual and supportive discussions will be an important area for continued research on demand-withdraw.

Third, the effects of marital therapy on demand-withdraw are unknown. We know that the demand-withdraw interaction pattern is associated with distress, and has been linked specifically to conflicts over closeness and independence (Christensen, 1987; Walczynski, 1997). Differences in partners' preferences for closeness and independence in their relationships are very common among distressed couples seeking therapy (Greenberg & Johnson, 1986). Yet, Jacobson and Margolin (1979) noted that couples exhibiting conflicts over affiliation and independence may be difficult to treat in couple therapy, particularly if these conflicts have been present in the relationship for an extended period. One investigation (Jacobson, Follette, & Pagel, 1986) has confirmed this assertion empirically. The possibility of reducing demand-withdraw communication through couple therapy needs to be explored. Preliminary evidence does suggest that demand-withdraw communication during conflict is significantly reduced by marital therapy (Eldridge, 2000). Other treatment-related studies have investigated demand-withdraw as a predictor of marital therapy outcome (Cain, 1996), demand-withdraw as a predictor of response to alcohol treatment (Shoham, Rohrbaugh, Stickle, & Jacob, 1998), and marital therapists' clinical judgment of couples demonstrating demand-withdraw (Pace, 1999). Further research on these topics is needed.

Fourth, a promising area of research brings together demand-withdraw communication and health psychology. For example, Ellis (1997) explored individual and marital adjustment to a diagnosis of prostate cancer, using demand-withdraw communication at time of diagnosis as a predictor of adjustment three months later. He demonstrated that demand-withdraw communication interacted with initial adjustment to predict later adjustment to the diagnosis. In addition, Pasch (1994) found that, in couples struggling with fertility problems, demand-withdraw roles were predicted by the desire to have children. Specifically, wife-demand/husband-withdraw was more likely when the importance of having children was greater for the wife than for the husband. These studies are examples of research that can help us understand, and eventually improve, couples' responses to health problems. Such research can lead to enhanced ability to cope, and thus preservation of the satisfying and supportive elements of the marriage, in the face of significant health stressors.

Finally, there are several recent studies that have investigated other important facets of demand-withdraw, and deserve further exploration. These topics include the association between intimacy and demand-withdraw (Laurenceau, 1999), femininity and gender-stereotyped demand-withdraw communication (McKelvie, 1999), depression and demand-withdraw communication (Mullin, 1999), asymmetrical power and gender roles in demand-withdraw (Calhoun, 1998), and attachment style and demand-withdraw (Klinetob, 1997).

CONCLUSIONS

This chapter has described research on what may be a fundamental interaction pattern: the demand-withdraw pattern. Both self-report and observational measures have been used to assess this pattern, and have yielded considerable correspondence in findings. Research has documented the negative association between this pattern and relationship satisfaction, both concurrently and over time. There is a clear gender difference in this pattern, with women more likely to be demanding and men withdrawing, but both theory and research have demonstrated particular conditions when this gender asymmetry may be modified or reversed. Recent studies, some employing newer methodological strategies, have begun to investigate (1) the ubiquity of this pattern throughout the family (for example, in parent-child as well as in adult relationships), in nontraditional relationships (for example, in gay and lesbian couples), and in nonconflict situations, (2) its link to other important relationship issues such as health problems and depression, and (3) its amenability to treatment and its possible function as a predictor of response to treatment.

REFERENCES

Acitelli, L. K. (1992). Gender differences in relationship awareness and marital satisfaction among young married couples. *Personality and Social Psychology Bulletin, 18*, 102–110.

Allen, M. (1996). Children's perceptions and comparisons of two marital conflict patterns: Mutually hostile and demand-withdraw. Unpublished doctoral dissertation, Texas A&M University.

Babcock, J. C., Waltz, J., Jacobson, N.S., & Gottman, J. M. (1993). Power and violence: The relation between communication patterns, power discrepancies, and domestic violence. *Journal of Consulting and Clinical Psychology, 61*, 40–50.

Baucom, D. H., & Adams, A. N. (1987). Assessing communication in marital interaction. In K. D. O'Leary (Ed.), *Assessment of marital discord* (pp. 139–181). Hillsdale, NJ: Lawrence Erlbaum Associates.

Belle, D. (1987). Gender differences in the social moderators of stress. In R. C. Barnett, L. Biener, & G. K. Baruch (Eds.), *Gender and stress* (pp. 257–277). New York: Free Press.

Berns, S. B., Jacobson, N. S., & Gottman, J. M. (1999a). Demand-withdraw interaction in couples with a violent husband. *Journal of Consulting & Clinical Psychology, 67*(5), 666–674.

Berns, S. B., Jacobson, N. S., & Gottman, J. M. (1999b). Demand/withdraw interaction patterns between different types of batterers and their spouses. *Journal of Marital and Family Therapy, 25*(3), 337–348.

Bradbury, T. N., & Karney, B. R. (1993). Longitudinal study of marital interaction and dysfunction: Review and analysis. *Clinical Psychology Review, 13*, 15–27.

Brody, L. R. (1993). On understanding gender differences in the expression of emotion: Gender roles, socialization, and language. In S. J. Ablon, D. Brown, E. L. Khantzian, & J. E. Mack (Eds.), *Human feelings* (pp. 87–121). Hillsdale, NJ: Analytic Press.

Burman, B., Margolin, G., & John, R. S. (1993). America's angriest home videos: Behavioral contingencies observed in home reenactments of marital conflict. *Journal of Consulting and Clinical Psychology, 61*(1), 28–39.

Cain, J. A. (1996). The investigation of predictor variables for successful behaviorally based marital therapy. Unpublished doctoral dissertation, Washington State University.

Calhoun, P. S. (1998). The demand-withdraw interaction pattern in close relationships: An interdependence analysis. Unpublished doctoral dissertation, Vanderbilt University.

Chodorow, N. (1978). *The reproduction of mothering: Psychoanalysis and the sociology of gender.* Berkeley: University of California Press.

Christensen, A. (1987). Detection of conflict patterns in couples. In K. Hahlweg & M. J. Goldstein (Eds.), *Understanding major mental disorder: The contribution of family interaction research* (pp. 250–265). New York: Family Process Press.

Christensen, A. (1988). Dysfunctional interaction patterns in couples. In P. Noller & M. A. Fitzpatrick (Eds.), *Perspectives on marital interaction* (pp. 31–52). Philadelphia: Multilingual Matters Ltd.

Christensen, A., & Heavey, C. L. (1990). Gender and social structure in the demand/withdraw pattern of marital conflict. *Journal of Personality and Social Psychology, 59*, 73–81.

Christensen, A., & Heavey, C. L. (1993). Gender differences in marital conflict: The demand/withdraw interaction pattern. In S. Oskamp & M. Costanzo (Eds.), *Gender issues in contemporary society* (pp. 113–141). Newbury Park, CA: Sage.

Christensen, A., & Shenk, J. L. (1991). Communication, conflict, and psychological distance in nondistressed, clinic, and divorcing couples. *Journal of Consulting and Clinical Psychology, 59*, 458–463.

Christensen, A., & Sullaway, M. (1984). Communication patterns questionnaire. Unpublished questionnaire, University of California, Los Angeles.

Christensen, A., Sullaway, M., & King, C. E. (1982, November). *Dysfunctional interaction patterns and marital happiness.* Los Angeles: Association for Advancement of Behavior Therapy.

Cutrona, C. E., Hessling, R. M., & Suhr, J. A. (1997). The influence of husband and wife personality on marital social support interactions. *Personal Relationships, 4,* 379–393.

Cutrona, C. E., & Suhr, J. A. (1994). Social support communication in the context of marriage: An analysis of couples' supportive interactions. In B. R. Burleson, T. L Albrecht, & I. G. Sarason (Eds.), *Communication of social support: Messages, interactions, relationships, and community* (pp. 113–135). Thousand Oaks, CA: Sage.

Daylen, J. L. (1994). Gender differences in spouses' coping with marital tension. Unpublished doctoral dissertation, University of British Columbia (Canada).

DeVault, M. L. (1990). Conflict over housework: The problem that (still) has no name. In L. Kriesberg (Ed.), *Research in social movements, conflict, and change* (pp. 189–202). Greenwood, CT: JAI.

Eldridge, K. A. (2000). Demand-withdraw communication during marital conflict: Relationship satisfaction and gender role considerations. Unpublished doctoral dissertation, University of California, Los Angeles.

Ellis, A. P. (1997). The effects of coping strategies and interactional patterns on individual and dyadic adjustment to prostate cancer. Unpublished doctoral dissertation, University of Kansas.

Fogarty, T. F. (1976). Marital crisis. In P. J. Guerin (Ed.), *Family therapy: Theory and practice* (pp. 325–334). New York: Gardner Press.

Gill, D. S., Fincham, F. D., & Christensen, A. (1999). Predicting marital satisfaction from behavior: Do all roads really lead to Rome? *Personal Relationships, 6,* 369–387.

Gilligan, C. (1982). *In a different voice: Psychological theory and women's development.* Cambridge, MA: Harvard University Press.

Gottman, J. M., & Krokoff, L. J. (1989). Marital interaction and satisfaction: A longitudinal view. *Journal of Consulting and Clinical Psychology, 57,* 47–52.

Gottman, J. M., & Krokoff, L. J. (1990). Complex statistics are not always clearer than simple statistics: A reply to Woody and Costanzo. *Journal of Consulting and Clinical Psychology, 58,* 502–505.

Gottman, J. M., & Levenson, R. W. (1986). Assessing the role of emotion in marriage. *Behavioral Assessment, 8,* 31–48.

Gottman, J. M., & Levenson, R. W. (1988). The social psychophysiology of marriage. In P. Noller & M. A. Fitzpatrick (Eds.), *Perspectives on marital interaction* (pp. 182–202). Philadelphia: Multilingual Matters Ltd.

Greenberg, L. S., & Johnson, S. M. (1986). Emotionally focused couples therapy. In N. S. Jacobson & A. S. Gurman (Eds.), *Clinical handbook of marital therapy* (pp. 253–276). New York: Guilford Press.

Hahlweg, K., Kaiser, A., Christensen, A., Fehm-Wolfsdorf, G., & Groth, T. (2000). Self-report and observational assessment of couples' conflict: The concordance between the Communication Patterns Questionnaire and the KPI observation system. *Journal of Marriage and the Family, 62,* 61–67.

Hahlweg, K., Reisner, L., Kohli, G., Vollmer, M., Schindler, L., & Revenstorf, D. (1984). Development and validity of a new system to analyze interpersonal communication: Kategoriensystem fuer Partnerschaftliche Interaktion (KPI). In K. Hahlweg & N. S. Jacobson (Eds.), *Marital interaction: Analysis and modification* (pp. 182–198). New York: Guilford Press.

Heavey, C. L., Christensen, A., & Malamuth, N. M. (1995) The longitudinal impact of demand and withdrawal during marital conflict. *Journal of Consulting and Clinical Psychology, 63*, 797–801.

Heavey, C. L., Gill, D. S., & Christensen, A. (1996). The couples interaction rating system. Unpublished manuscript, University of California, Los Angeles.

Heavey, C. L., Layne, C., & Christensen, A. (1993). Gender and conflict structure in marital interaction: A replication and extension. *Journal of Consulting and Clinical Psychology, 61*, 16–27.

Holtzworth-Munroe, A., Smutzler, N., Bates, L., & Vogel, D. (1995). Withdraw-demand communication behaviors: Comparing two observational coding systems. In A. Holtzworth-Munroe (Chair), *Withdraw/demand behavior in marital interaction: Methodological and conceptual issues.* Symposium conducted at the annual meeting of the Association for Advancement of Behavior Therapy, Washington, DC.

Holtzworth-Munroe, A., Smutzler, N., & Stuart, G. L. (1998). Demand and withdraw communication among couples experiencing husband violence. *Journal of Consulting and Clinical Psychology, 66*, 731–743.

Jacobson, N. S. (1983). Beyond empiricism: The politics of marital therapy. *American Journal of Family Therapy, 11*, 11–24.

Jacobson, N. S. (1989). The politics of intimacy. *Behavior Therapist, 12*, 29–32.

Jacobson, N. S. (1990). Commentary: Contributions from psychology to an understanding of marriage. In F. D. Fincham & T. N. Bradbury (Eds.), *The psychology of marriage* (pp. 258–275). New York: Guilford Press.

Jacobson, N. S., Follette, W. C., & Pagel, M. (1986). Predicting who will benefit from behavioral marital therapy. *Journal of Consulting and Clinical Psychology, 54*, 518–522.

Jacobson, N. S., & Gottman, J. M. (1998) When men batter women: New insights into ending abusive relationships. New York: Simon & Schuster.

Jacobson, N. S., & Margolin, G. (1979). *Marital therapy: Strategies based on social learning and behavior exchange principles.* New York: Brunner/Mazel.

Johnson, M. P. (1995). Patriarchal terrorism and common couple violence: Two forms of violence against women. *Journal of Marriage and the Family, 57*, 283–294.

Julien, D., Arellano, C., & Turgeon, L. (1997). Gender issues in heterosexual, gay and lesbian couples. In W. K. Halford & H. J. Markman (Eds.) *Clinical handbook of marriage and couples intervention.* Chichester, England: John Wiley & Sons.

Kelley, H. H., Cunningham, J. D., Grisham, J. A., Lefebvre, L. M., Sink, R. S., & Yablon, G. (1978). Sex differences in comments made during conflict within close heterosexual pairs. *Sex Roles, 4*, 473–492.

Klinetob, N. A. (1997). *An investigation of demand-withdraw communication in anxious, avoidant, and securely attached married couples.* Unpublished doctoral dissertation, Ohio State University.

Klinetob, N. A., & Smith, D. A. (1996). Demand-withdraw communication in marital interaction: Tests of interspousal contingency and gender role hypotheses. *Journal of Marriage and the Family, 58*, 945–957.

Klinetob, N. A., Smith, D. A., & House, V. L. (1994, November). *Longitudinal association between demand/withdraw and marital adjustment.* Poster presented to 28th Annual Convention of the Association for Advancement of Behavior Therapy, San Diego, CA.

Kluwer, E. S. (1998). *Marital conflict over the division of labor: When partners become parents.* Unpublished doctoral dissertation. Kurt Lewin Institute Dissertation Series, University of Groningen.

Kluwer, E. S., Heesink, J. A., & Van De Vliert, E. (1997). The marital dynamics of conflict over the division of labor. *Journal of Marriage and the Family, 59,* 635–653.

Komarovsky, M. (1962). *Blue collar marriage.* New York: Random House.

Komarovsky, M. (1976). *Dilemmas of masculinity.* New York: Norton.

Kurdek, L. A. (1995). Predicting change in marital satisfaction from husbands' and wives' conflict resolution styles. *Journal of Marriage and the Family, 57*(1), 153–164.

Laurenceau, J. (1999). *The interpersonal process model of intimacy and marriage: A daily-diary approach.* Unpublished doctoral dissertation, Pennsylvania State University.

Levenson, R. W., & Gottman, J. M. (1985). Physiological and affective predictors of change in relationship satisfaction. *Journal of Personality and Social Psychology, 49*, 85–94.

Margolin, G., Talovic, S., & Weinstein, C. D. (1983). Areas of change questionnaire: A practical approach to marital assessment. *Journal of Consulting and Clinical Psychology, 51*, 920–931.

Markman, H. J., & Kraft, S. A. (1989). Men and women in marriage: Dealing with gender differences in marital therapy. *Behavior Therapist, 12*, 51–56.

McKelvie, M. M. (1999). The effect of hyperfemininity on communication patterns in dating couples. Unpublished doctoral dissertation, Northern Illinois University.

Monarch, N. D. (1998). An examination of the demand-withdraw pattern in naturalistic conflicts among couples. Unpublished master's thesis, University of California, Los Angeles.

Mullin, W. J. (1999). The impact of depression on marital beliefs and marital communication. Unpublished doctoral dissertation, Boston College.

Murphy, C. M., & Meyer, S. L. (1991). Gender, power, and violence in marriage. *Behavior Therapist, 14*, 95–100.

Napier, A. Y. (1978). The rejection-intrusion pattern: A central family dynamic. *Journal of Marriage and Family Counseling, 4*, 5–12.

Noller, P. (1993). Gender and emotional communication in marriage: Different cultures or differential social power? *Journal of Language and Social Psychology, 12*, 132–152.

Noller, P., Feeney, J. A., Bonnell, D. & Callan, V. J. (1994). A longitudinal study of conflict in early marriage. *Journal of Social and Personal Relationships, 11*, 233–252.

Noller, P., Feeney, J. A., Sheehan, G., & Peterson, C. (2000). Marital conflict patterns: Links with family conflict and family members' perceptions of one another. *Personal Relationships, 7*(1), 79–94.

Noller, P., & White, A. (1990). The validity of the Communication Patterns Questionnaire. *Psychological Assessment, 2*, 478–482.

O'Leary, K. D. (1993). Through a psychological lens: Personality traits, personality disorders, and levels of violence. In R. J. Gelles & D. Loeske (Eds.), *Current controversies regarding psychological explanations of family violence* (pp. 7–30). Newbury Park, CA: Sage.

Pace, J. F. (1999). The effects of gender, race, and client interpersonal style on therapists' clinical judgments in marital therapy. Unpublished doctoral dissertation, University of Virginia.

Pasch, L. A. (1994). Fertility problems and marital relationships: The effects of appraisal and coping differences on communication. Unpublished doctoral dissertation, University of California, Los Angeles.

Pasch, L. A., & Bradbury, T. N. (1998). Social support, conflict, and the development of marital dysfunction. *Journal of Consulting and Clinical Psychology, 66*, 219–230.

Pasch, L. A., Bradbury, T. N., & Davila, J. (1997). Gender, negative affectivity, and observed social support in marital interaction. *Personal Relationships, 4*, 361–378.

Peplau, L. A., & Gordon, S. (1985). Women and men in love: Gender differences in close heterosexual relationships. In V. E. O'Leary, R. K. Unger, & B. S. Wallston (Eds.), *Women, gender, and social psychology* (pp. 257–291). Hillsdale, NJ: Lawrence Erlbaum Associates.

Phelps, J. S. (1995). The relationship between interparental and marital communication, conflict, and power: The difference between husbands and wives. Unpublished doctoral dissertation, University of Colorado at Boulder.

Poleshuck, E. L. (1998). Couple conflict, life stress, and their interactions: Links to the development of child behavior problems. Unpublished doctoral dissertation, Kent State University.

Roberts, L. J., (2000). Fire and ice in marital communication: Hostile and distancing behaviors as predictors of marital distress. *Journal of Marriage and the Family, 63*, 693–707.

Roberts, L. J. & Krokoff, L. J. (1990). A time-series analysis of withdrawal, hostility, and displeasure in satisfied and dissatisfied marriages. *Journal of Marriage and the Family, 52*, 95–105.

Rubin, L. B. (1976). *Worlds of pain: Life in the working class family.* New York: Basic Books.

Rubin, L. B. (1983). *Intimate strangers: Men and women together.* New York: Harper & Row.

Rugel. R. P. (1997). *Husband-focused marital therapy: An approach to dealing with marital distress.* Springfield, IL: Charles C. Thomas Publisher.

Sayers, S. L., Baucom, D. H., Sher, T. G., Weiss, R. L., & Heyman, R. E. (1991). Constructive engagement, behavioral marital therapy, and changes in marital satisfaction. *Behavioral Assessment, 13*, 25–49.

Shoham, V., Rohrbaugh, M. J., Stickle, T. R., & Jacob, T. (1998). Demand-withdraw couple interaction moderates retention in cognitive-behavioral versus family-systems treatments for alcoholism. *Journal of Family Psychology, 12,* 557–577.

Smith, D. A., Vivian, D., & O'Leary, K. D. (1991). The misnomer proposition: A critical reappraisal of the longitudinal status of "negativity" in marital communication. *Behavioral Assessment, 13,* 7–24.

Sullaway, M., & Christensen, A. (1983). Assessment of dysfunctional interaction patterns in couples. *Journal of Marriage and the Family, 45,* 653–660.

Tannen, D. (1990). *You Just Don't Understand.* New York: Morrow.

Terman, L. M., Buttenweiser, P., Ferguson, L. W., Johnson, W. B., & Wilson, D. P. (1938). *Psychological factors in marital happiness.* New York: McGraw-Hill.

Walczynski, P. T. (1997). Power, personality, and conflictual interaction: An exploration of demand/withdraw interaction in same-sex and cross-sex couples. Unpublished doctoral dissertation, University of California, Los Angeles.

Watzlawick, P., Beavin, J. H., & Jackson, D. D. (1967). *Pragmatics of human communication: A study of interactional patterns, pathologies, and paradoxes.* New York: Norton.

Weiss, R. L., & Heyman, R. E. (1997). A clinical-research overview of couples interactions. In W. K. Halford & H. J. Markman (Eds.), *Clinical handbook of marriage and couples intervention.* Chichester, England: John Wiley & Sons.

Wilder, J. A. (1999). The relationship between patterns of marital conflict and child behavior: Linking parental interaction and child responses to conflict. Unpublished doctoral dissertation, Syracuse University.

Wile, D. B. (1981). *Couples therapy: A non-traditional approach.* New York: Wiley.

Woody, E. Z., & Costanzo, P. R. (1990). Does marital agony precede marital ecstasy? A comment on Gottman and Krokoff's "Marital interaction and satisfaction: A longitudinal view." *Journal of Consulting & Clinical Psychology, 58,* 499–501.

CHAPTER TWELVE

Approaches to the Study of Power in Violent and Nonviolent Marriages, and in Gay Male and Lesbian Cohabiting Relationships

*John M. Gottman, Janice Driver,
Dan Yoshimoto, and Regina Rushe*

To the outsider, mathematics is a strange, abstract world of horrendous technicality, full of symbols and complicated procedures, an impenetrable language and a black art. To the scientist, mathematics is the guarantor of precision and objectivity. It is also, astonishingly, the language of nature itself. No one who is closed off from mathematics can ever grasp the full significance of the natural order that is woven so deeply into the fabric of physical reality.

—Paul Davies, *The Mind of God*, 1992, p. 93

THE STUDY OF POWER

In the 1950s Fred Strodtbeck's research on marriages in three cultures made the study of power look easy (Strodtbeck, 1951). He drove a van through the Western United States and asked Mormon (patriarchal), Navajo (matriarchal), and Anglo Texan (supposedly egalitarian) married couples to go into the back of his van, and gossip about families the couple thought were raising their kids poorly or well (something that couples in all three cultures found it easy and natural to discuss) and have some structured marital disputes. The marital disputes involved having each spouse fill out a questionnaire indicating personal preferences (like what kind of car to buy, what to order for dinner), and then the couple doing this task again by discussion. The more powerful person was defined as the person who was closer to the joint decision on his or her personal preferences. He found that women won most of the disputes in the Navajo culture, men won most in the Mormon culture, and men and women were fairly equal in the Anglo Texan culture. Around the same time, Bales (1950) suggested that power in marriage could be defined in terms of leadership, and that men and women played instrumental and affective leadership roles, respectively (a view that was not subsequently confirmed by research on marriage, for example, Raush, Barry, Hertel, & Swain, 1974). But in the 1950s, it appeared that the study of power and the study of affect would be quite straightforward.

However, that was not to be the case. While the study of affect in marriages became clearer and clearer as basic research on emotion developed and was applied, the study of power became more and more elusive. As Rushe (1995) wrote, "Ultimately, the narrow sociological measurement of power (inequities in resource utilization) did not correlate with general observations of power as process" (Raven, 1992; Szinovacz, 1987). "The concept of power turned out to be most elusive to define" (Gray-Little & Burks, 1983).

As Broderick (1993) also summarized: "Literally hundreds of studies have been done on family power, who wields it and at whose expense. The matter has turned out to be complicated and elusive. As a result, the scholarly literature on power is voluminous, complex, and often contradictory. The great majority of these studies are based on questionnaires that ask the respondent to report on who wins the most contested decisions in his or her family. Critics have noted several problems with this approach" (see Szinovacz, 1987, p. 164). Among these problems are that questionnaires filled out by independent observers do not correlate very well, nor are different measures well correlated (see Gray-Little & Burks, 1983); nor have patterns of domination proven stable over time (see Babcock, Waltz, Jacobson, & Gottman, 1993). An older paper by Gray-Little (1982) is noteworthy because it combined the observational assessment of talk time during a six-minute marital conflict discussion, and power during a marital game (the SIMFAM game, Straus & Tallman, 1971). Results were complex, but included the finding that balance in husband-wife power was related to marital quality; however, self-report and observational measures did not show a high level of agreement in classifying couples.

Several approaches have been taken to the problem of studying power. Since our interest in this chapter is in power processes, we will review three approaches toward clarifying the power concept: (1) using more precise observations; (2) power explored within the context of gender and relational hierarchy; and (3) power studied using the mathematical modeling of interaction. Then we will explore the use of these three approaches in different types of relationships: gay and lesbian relationships, nonviolent and violent marriages. Research has shown that gay and lesbian relationships are more egalitarian than heterosexual marital relationships (for example, Blumstein & Schwartz, 1983). Research has also shown that violent marriages, in turn, are even more hierarchically structured than nonviolent marriages (for example, Jacobson & Gottman, 1998).

Power Studied with More Precise Observations

Power was observed directly in a recent study by Gray-Little, Baucom, and Hamby (1996). These researchers assessed power more precisely, using a coding of the couple's influence patterns during a discussion of the Inventory of Marital Conflicts (IMC; Olson & Ryder, 1970). They found that egalitarian couples had the highest Time-1 marital satisfaction, and fewer negative Marital Interaction Coding System (MICS) behaviors (Weiss, Hops, & Patterson, 1973); also, wife-dominant couples improved the most in a 12-week marital therapy study. Later in this chapter we will briefly review the doctoral dissertation work of Rushe, who developed an observational coding system for the study of power in violent marriages.

Power Explored in the Context of Gender and Relational Hierarchy

Feminist writers have pointed to the central role that power must play in understanding marriages. Quantitative observational research has now begun to explore these ideas. We now know that women typically start most of the marital conflict discussions in laboratories that use observational methods (Ball, Cowan, & Cowan, 1995; Oggins, Veroff, & Leber, 1993). The degree of negative affect and the amount of criticism with which a conflict discussion starts is also critical in determining its outcome. In one study, for example, the way a marital conflict interaction began determined its subsequent course 96% of the time (Gottman, 1994; Gottman, Coan, Carrere, & Swanson, 1998, p. 7). White (1989), in a sequential analysis using the Raush, Barry, Hertel, and Swain (1974) coding system, found evidence for the contention that men display a more coercive style in resolving marital conflict, while women display a more affiliative style.

Coan, Gottman, Babcock, and Jacobson (1997) used sequential analysis to investigate the propensity of two types of physically violent men to reject influence from their wives during a marital conflict discussion.

The sequence of escalation of the negativity (from complaining to hostility, for example) was used to operationalize the pattern of rejecting influence. As hypothesized, abusive husbands whose heart rates decreased from baseline to the marital conflict discussion (labeled as Type I abusers in the study), rejected any influence from their wives. These men were also generally violent outside the marriage, and were more likely to have used a knife or gun to threaten their wives than abusive husbands whose heart rates accelerated from baseline to the conflict discussion (labeled as Type II abusers in the study). Recently Meehan, Holtzworth-Munroe, and Herron (in press) failed to replicate this typology.

These analyses about influence were repeated for a representative sample of nonviolent newlywed couples in the first few months of marriage; the escalation sequence of men rejecting influence from their wives predicted subsequent divorce (Gottman, Coan, Carrere, & Swanson, 1998), but the sequence of women rejecting influence from their husbands did not predict divorce. This paper was the first time that negative affect reciprocity was broken down into responding negatively in kind (for example, anger is met with anger) or escalation (for example, anger is met with contempt). Gottman et al. (1998) found that negative reciprocity in kind was characteristic of all marriages; only the escalation sequence was characteristic of marriages that were later to end in divorce. These findings suggest the need to reconceptualize the escalation of negative affect as the rejection of influence.

Power Studied with the Mathematical Modeling of Marital Interaction

An alternative definition of power has emerged from our laboratory in our mathematical modeling of marital interaction. This alternative definition defines power quantitatively as the ability of one partner's affect to influence the other's subsequent affect. In this modeling (Cook, Tyson, White, Rushe, Gottman, & Murray, 1995; Gottman, Swanson, & Murray, 1999), two influence functions are computed across the affective range of a conversation, one for the husband's influence on the wife, and one for the wife's influence on the husband. This approach to modeling is based on writing down two interlocking nonlinear difference equations for husband and wife, with influence functions computed after controlling for autocorrelation.

The method of using differential or difference equations to model marital interaction actually has a venerable history in the marital field. Long ago, Anatol Rapoport (1960; 1972) proposed two *linear* differential equations for husband and wife interaction that could describe a marital system as escalating out of control, or being self-regulated. He never operationalized these variables or applied the equations to real data, and, unfortunately, his equations were linear, and linear equations are quite unstable.

However, Cook et al. (1995) applied the new mathematics of nonlinear dynamic modeling (for example, Murray, 1989). These researchers showed that, depending on the shape of the influence functions, couples can have several stable steady states or "attractors," which are self-regulating homeostatic set points for the marital system. A stable steady state (or homeostatic attractor) is a point in husband-wife phase space toward which the interaction is repeatedly drawn, and if the system is slightly perturbed, it will move back to the attractor.

The influence functions describe the average impact of one person's affect on the partner's subsequent affect, averaging over time. This determination is made across the range of affects in the husband-wife dialogue. The influence functions make the study of power more detailed and much more specific. Power may be specific to a particular affect or set of affects. Asymmetries in influence reflect a power imbalance, and Cook et al. (1995) reported data showing that these asymmetries were predictive of divorce.

Mathematical Modeling of Marital Interaction

Before presenting our methods and findings, we will provide some background on mathematical modeling, intended to set the stage for what follows. For the past seven years, our laboratory has been constructing mathematical models of marital interaction with the applied mathematician James Murray, and his students (Cook et al., 1995; Gottman et al., 1998; in press). This modeling involves estimating two linked nonlinear difference equations, one for the husband and one for the wife (described as follows).

The desire to create these mathematical models was inspired by General System Theory (von Bertalanffy, 1968). This book inspired many major thinkers of family systems and family therapy, including Gregory Bateson, Don Jackson, and Paul Watzlawick. Unfortunately, the *mathematics* of General System Theory was not utilized by most of the social scientists who were influenced by von Bertalanffy's work. Bateson and colleagues originally envisaged making their family systems theory mathematical (for a historical review see Gottman, 1979), but did not do so. Hence, the nonmathematical work of these theorists of family interaction kept their systems concepts at the level of metaphor. Even at the level of metaphor, these concepts were tremendously influential in the field of family therapy (see Rosenblatt, 1994). However, they were never quantified or subjected to experimental processes.

Von Bertalanffy clearly viewed his theory as mathematical. He believed that the interaction of complex systems with many units could be characterized by a set of values that change over time, denoted Q_1, Q_2, Q_3, and so on. Each of these Qs were variables that indexed something about a particular unit in the system, such as mother, father, and child. He thought that the system could be best described by a set of ordinary differential equations of the form:

$$dQ_1/dt = f_1(Q_1, Q_2, Q_3, \ldots)$$
$$dQ_2/dt = f_2(Q_1, Q_2, Q_3, \ldots)$$

and so on.

The terms on the left of the equal sign are time derivatives; that is, rates of change of the quantitative sets of values Q_1, Q_2, and so on. The terms on the right of the equal sign are functions, $f_1, f_2, \ldots$, of the Qs. Von Bertalanffy thought that these functions, the fs, needed to be linear in order to be tractable. The equations von Bertalanffy selected also have a particular form, called "autonomous," meaning that the fs have no explicit function of time in them, except through the Qs, which are functions of time. Von Bertalanffy had no suggestions for what the Qs ought to measure, nor what the fs ought to be. So his vision remained a metaphorical one without a quantitative science to back it up. This has all now changed.

We obtained the Qs for our modeling from our ability to predict the longitudinal course of marriages. Gottman and Levenson (1992) reported that a variable that describes specific interaction patterns in terms of the balance between negativity and positivity was predictive of marital dissolution. In this work, we used a methodology for obtaining synchronized physiological, behavioral, and self-report data in a sample of 73 couples who were followed longitudinally during a four-year period. Applying observational coding of interactive behavior with the Rapid Couples Interaction Scoring System (RCISS; Krokoff, Gottman, &

Hass, 1989), couples were divided into two groups, a low-risk group and a high-risk group. This classification was based on a graphical method originally proposed by Gottman (1979) for use with the Couples Interaction Scoring System, a predecessor of the RCISS. On each conversational turn, the total number of positive RCISS speaker codes minus the total number of negative speaker codes was computed for each spouse. Then the cumulative total of these points was plotted for each spouse. This creates a kind of "Dow-Jones" industrial average for a marital conversation. The slopes of these plots, which were thought to provide a stable estimate of the difference between positive and negative codes over time, were determined using linear regression analysis.

The decision to utilize the slopes in this way was guided by *a balance theory of marriage*; namely that those processes most important in predicting dissolution would involve a balance, or a regulation, of positive and negative interaction. Low-risk couples were those for whom both husband and wife speaker slopes were significantly positive; high-risk couples had at least one of the speaker slopes that was either negative, or not significantly positive. We found that the high/low risk distinction was able to predict the "cascade" toward divorce, which consisted of: (a) marital dissatisfaction, (b) persistent thoughts about divorce and separation, and (c) actual separation and divorce. The ability to predict the longitudinal course of marital relationships in this manner has now been found in our laboratories in four separate longitudinal studies (see Gottman, 1993; 1994; Gottman, Coan, Swanson, & Carrere, 1998; Jacobson, Gottman, Gortner, Berns, & Shortt, 1996).

In our first paper using mathematical modeling (Cook et al., 1995), we made use of these speaker slopes as the Qs in our equations and used them to develop a mathematical model that might explain the Gottman-Levenson findings. Our own equations were very similar to the ones that von Bertalanffy had envisioned, except that we used discrete difference equations rather than differential equations.

There is one additional difference. As we noted, von Bertalanffy thought that the equations had to be linear. He presented a table in which these nonlinear equations were classified as "impossible" (von Bertalanffy, 1968, p. 20), referring to the very popular mathematical method of approximating nonlinear functions with a linear approximation. Unfortunately linear equations are generally unstable, so they tend to give erroneous solutions, except as approximations under very local conditions near a steady state. Von Bertalanffy was not aware of the mathematics Poincaré and others had developed in the last quarter of the nineteenth century for the study of nonlinear systems. It was actually no longer the case that these nonlinear systems were "impossible," even in von Bertalanffy's day. This is even more true today, when the modeling of complex deterministic (and stochastic) systems with a set of nonlinear difference or differential equations has become a productive enterprise across a wide set of phenomena in a wide range of sciences. Thus, the use of nonlinear equations formed the basis of our first attempts at modeling marital interaction (these methods are described in detail in Cook et al., 1995).

This general method of mathematical modeling with nonlinear equations has been employed with great success in the biological sciences, and many departments of applied mathematics now have a mathematical biology program (Murray, 1989). It is a quantitative approach that allows the modeler to write down, in mathematical form and on the basis of some theory, the causes of change in the dependent variables. For example, in mathematical ecology, in the classic predator-prey problem, one writes down the rate of change in the population densities of the prey and of the predator as some function of their current densities (for example, Murray, 1989). While this is a simple representation of the predator-prey phenomenon, it has served well as an initial exploratory model.

An advantage of nonlinear equations (in addition to the possibility of stability) is that by employing nonlinear terms in the equations of change, some very complex processes can be represented with very few parameters. Unfortunately, unlike many linear equations, these nonlinear equations are generally not solvable in closed functional mathematical form. For this reason, the methods are often called "qualitative," and visual graphical methods and numerical approximation must be relied upon. For this purpose, numerical and graphical methods have been developed such as "phase space plots."

These visual approaches to mathematical modeling can be very appealing in engaging the intuition of a scientist working in a field that has no mathematically stated theory. If the scientist has an intuitive familiarity with the data of the field, our approach may suggest a way of building theory using mathematics in an initially qualitative manner. The use of these graphical solutions to nonlinear differential equations makes it possible to talk about "qualitative" mathematical modeling. In qualitative mathematical modeling, one searches for solutions that have similarly shaped phase space plots, which provide a good qualitative description of the solution and how it varies with the parameters.

Another advantage of this kind of modeling is that it permits the *simulation* of the couple's interaction under new conditions, with different parameter values, such as when a partner begins the interaction much more positively than has ever been observed. This possibility leads to natural experiments.

Our modeling of marital interaction using the mathematical methods of nonlinear difference equations is an attempt to integrate the mathematical insights of von Bertalanffy with the general systems theory of family systems (Bateson, Jackson, Haley, & Weakland, 1956), using nonlinear equations. A basic concept in this modeling is that every system of equations has one or more stable or unstable "steady states" or "attractors." These stable attractors are like the old family systems notion of homeostatic set points of the system. These are values toward which the system is drawn, and, if perturbed from the stable attractor, return the system back toward it. However, in our models there are both uninfluenced attractors and influenced attractors. Uninfluenced attractors are what each person brings to the interaction, assuming there are times of zero or near-zero influence. Influenced attractors are what happens as each person begins influencing the other in particular ways. The difference between influenced and uninfluenced attractors gives one an estimate of power, or how the interactive system pushes each person.

The Concepts of Repair and Damping

In theorizing about mother-infant interaction, Brazelton (for example, Brazelton, Koslowski, & Main, 1974) suggested that mother-infant interaction could be the sine qua non of human interaction, and that the healthy norm was a cyclic shared rhythmicity and coordination of interaction. However, Gianino and Tronick (1988), in observing mother-infant interaction, reported that 70% of mother-infant interaction was actually miscoordinated. Hence *miscoordination* is the norm, not coordination. What these researchers found was that some mothers noticed the miscoordination and tried to repair the interaction, while others did not. The mother's use of repair later predicted the infant's attachment security. Gianino and Tronick built a theory of interactive regulation and repair based on their findings. Hence, repair is a down-regulation of negative affect.

In our own modeling, we also studied couples' repair of negativity. We hypothesize that, in married couples, repair is the one central theoretical construct that will consistently discriminate couples whose marriages are dissatisfied and headed for divorce from those whose marriages are satisfied and stable (for example, see Gottman, 1999). The concept of "damping" is the analogue of repair for positive affect: It is a down-regulation of positive affect. At first, we thought that damping would not be a helpful event in interaction, but our mathematical work has shown that there are many examples when down-regulating positive affect will produce a stable steady state in the positive-positive quadrant of phase space, whereas none would exist without damping. Hence, the down-regulation of positive affect can be a good thing.

Parameters of Our Modeling

Our initial modeling (Cook et al., 1995) produced the following parameters. First there was the uninfluenced steady state for each partner, which represented the attractors reflecting what that partner brought into the interaction before influence began. This uninfluenced state turned out to be a function both of that partner's personality and the immediate past history of the relationship (Gottman et al., 1998). Second were the emotional inertia parameters, which assessed the tendency of each person's behavior to be predictable from that person's immediate past behavior. Third were the influenced steady states, which were where each partner was drawn to following the social influence process. Fourth were the influence functions, which, for each spouse's affect value, describe the average effect of that affect value on the partner (over the entire interaction). These influence functions provide a more detailed description of interpersonal influence or power. The power function is thus defined in our modeling as the ability of one person's affect to change the other partner's affect. Fifth, our initial model has now been modified to include a Repair term for each partner, which is repair of negative interaction that is potentially triggered at a particular threshold of a partner's negativity and is effective at pushing the data in a more positive direction. The two Repair terms have two parameters, the threshold of the repair and its effectiveness.

Observational Coding

The Specific Affect Coding System (SPAFF; Gottman, McCoy, Coan, & Collier, 1996) was used to code the events of the day and conflict conversations of all couples. The SPAFF focuses solely on the specific affects expressed. The system draws on facial expression (based on Ekman and Friesen's system of facial action coding; Ekman & Friesen, 1978), vocal tone, and speech content, to characterize the emotions displayed. Coders categorized the affects displayed using five positive affect codes (interest, validation, affection, humor, excitement/joy), ten negative affect codes (disgust, contempt, belligerence, domineering, anger, fear/ tension, defensiveness, whining, sadness, stonewalling), and a neutral affect code. The dependent variables created were the total number of seconds duration of each SPAFF code out of the 900 seconds of the conflict discussion. Every videotape was coded in its entirety by two independent observers using a computer-assisted coding system that automated the collection of timing information; each coder noted only the onset of each code.

For the mathematical modeling, we used a weighting scheme derived from previous prediction research (Gottman, 1994). A numerical value was calculated for the SPAFF codes for each six-second time block separately for each partner by taking the sum of positive codes minus the sum of negative codes using the following weights: Disgust $= -3$, Contempt $= -4$, Belligerence $= -2$, Domineering $= -1$, Anger $= -1$, Fear $= 0$, Defensiveness $= -2$, Whining $= -1$, Sadness $= -1$, Stonewalling $= -2$, Neutral $= 0.1$, Interest $= +2$, Validation $= +4$, Affection $= +4$, Humor $= +4$, and Excitement/Joy $= +4$. This weighting yields a potential score range of -24 to $+24$. For each couple, this procedure created two time series, each with 150 data points, one series for the "initiator" and one for the "partner." In the married-couple/gay-and-lesbian study, for married couples, combined across partners, the correlation for the two observers of total weighted SPAFF over the conflict interaction was .90 ($p < .001$). For the gays and lesbians, combined across partners, the correlation for the two observers was .52 ($p < .01$).

A mathematical model using nonlinear difference equations was fit to the weighted SPAFF data during the conflict discussion for all couples. This model has been developed and tested with a number of samples of married couples (Cook et al., 1995; Gottman, Swanson, & Murray, 1999; Gottman, Murray, Swanson, Tyson, & Swanson, in press). For the study comparing gay and lesbian couples with married couples, there were two time series, the initiator's and the partner's. The initiator was the person raising the issue and the partner the person receiving the issue.

HOW THE MATHEMATICAL MODELING CHANGES THE CONCEPT OF POWER

Theory enters into the mathematical modeling by the researcher selecting what he/she believes to be the correct functional form of the influence function. This idea of an "influence function" dramatically

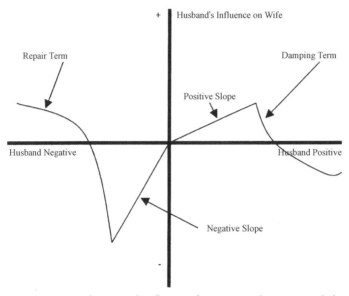

Figure 12.1. A theoretical influence function with repair and damping terms added. On the abcissa is the husband's affect, ranging from negative on the left to positive on the right. On the ordinate is the husband's influence on the wife, ranging from negative below to positive above. The influence function consists of four parts, the positive slope for positive affect, the negative slope for negative affect, and the repair and damping terms. Repair cuts in at a threshold when negativity becomes too negative and damping cuts in at a threshold when positivity becomes too positive.

changes the idea of power, because one can now speak of how much *influence* each partner has, on average, for specific levels of affect (from positive to negative). Differential amounts of influence between partners can be seen as a power asymmetry. However, it is possible that one partner is more powerful in positive affect ranges, while another is more powerful with negative affect; or one partner may be more effective than the other in repairing the interaction when it becomes too negative, or repairing at an earlier threshold of negativity, and so on. The concept of power asymmetries thus becomes much more specific.

The functional form of the influence function we have found to best fit our data is the bilinear form (Figure 12.1), with repair and damping terms. Figure 12.1 is a graph of one theoretical influence function with repair and damping terms. In the bilinear part of the function there are two slopes, the influence of positive and negative affect ranges on the partner. There are, of course, two influence functions, one for the husband and one for the wife, or, in the gay/lesbian study, one for the initiator and one for the partner. Differences in slopes are our operational definition of power imbalances in the relationship, which are defined separately for positive and negative affect. Details of the algorithms for estimating each model parameter and the influence functions are available from our laboratory's web site (see also Gottman, Murray, Swanson, Tyson, & Swanson, in press).

A replicated finding in the observational literature on marriages could be expressed as follows: The steepness of the slope is far less in the positive region than in the negative region. Translated into English, this means that negative affect has far more power to hurt the interaction than positive affect has power to help; negative affect reciprocity is far greater than positive affect reciprocity. This finding has been observed fairly consistently in marital interaction research. Is this a general law of close relationships? As we shall see, it may not be. Gay male and lesbian relationships may have the opposite principle operating: It may be the case that positive affect has far more power to help the interaction than negative affect has power to hurt; positive affect reciprocity may be far greater than negative affect reciprocity in gay male and lesbian relationships.

Power and Marital Typologies

In a monograph on the marital processes predicting divorce, Gottman (1994) also presented a marital typology with three types, looking at interaction and influence, and his types appear to be somewhat similar to Fitzpatrick's (1988) types. On a conflict task, Gottman's types were: validating couples, who are high on conflict but wait a while in the discussion and ask questions before engaging in persuasion attempts; volatile couples, who are high in conflict and engage in persuasion attempts immediately; and, conflict avoiding couples, who are low in conflict and do not engage in persuasion attempts at all. All three types were equally likely to have stable or unstable marriages. However, the validators, volatiles, and avoiders had influence functions of distinctly different shapes. The slopes were near zero in the positive affect ranges for volatile couples, but negative in the negative affect ranges. Conversely, the slopes were near zero in the negative affect ranges for avoider couples, and positive in the positive affect ranges. For validating couples, the slopes were positive in the positive affect ranges and negative in the negative affect ranges.

For stable couples, the husband and wife influence functions had the same general shapes. However, Cook et al. (1995) discovered that mismatches in influence functions between Gottman's types predicted divorce within each type. Hence, it was power differences that predicted divorce. Gottman (1994) also suggested that the demand-withdraw pattern (for example, Christensen and Heavey, 1990) may be an artifact of differences in influence functions. For example, in a couple where a validator is paired with a volatile, the volatile would demand and the validator would withdraw.

Power in Gay Male and Lesbian Committed Cohabiting Relationships

Groundbreaking longitudinal research on gay male, lesbian, and heterosexual married couples by Kurdek and his associates (for example, Kurdek, 1998) has generally concluded that gay and lesbian relationships operate on essentially the same principles as heterosexual relationships. However, some important differences were found in relation to power and autonomy. Compared to married spouses, gay partners reported more autonomy, fewer barriers to leaving, and more frequent relationship dissolution. Compared to married spouses, lesbian partners reported more intimacy, more autonomy, more equality, and more frequent relationship dissolution. Hence, gay and lesbian relationships may be ideal contexts, when compared to heterosexual relationships, for studying power and affect where there is clearly more equality than in heterosexual relationships.

The existing quantitative research on gay and lesbian relationships has revealed important information about the nature of these relationships. However, it has relied entirely on self-reports using questionnaires (for example, Kurdek, 1992), or questionnaires and interviews (for example, Blumstein & Schwartz, 1983). While these forms of data produce valuable "insider" information, they are limited to people's perceptions about their own relationships. There is considerable evidence that people's perception of their relationships may diverge markedly from their actual interaction. For example, in an observational study of positive interaction at home, Robinson and Price (1980) found that, compared to observers, distressed couples underestimated their own positive interaction by 50%.

In an observational study conducted by Levenson and Gottman, two samples of committed gay and lesbian cohabiting couples and two samples of married couples (couples in which the woman presented the conflict issue to the man, and couples in which the man presented the conflict issue to the woman) engaged in three conversations: (1) an Events of the Day conversation (after being apart for at least eight hours), (2) a Conflict Resolution conversation, and (3) a Pleasant Topic conversation.*

The observational data were coded using the SPAFF, and the data were weighted and two time series created, one for each partner, or one for the initiator and the other for the partner. The time series were then modeled with nonlinear difference equations, and parameters were estimated that indexed uninfluenced steady state, influenced steady state, emotional inertia, repair effectiveness and threshold, and the power of positive and negative affect of one partner to affect the other partner.

Some Results of the Modeling with Gay Male, Lesbian, and Married Couples

Using our 2×2 experimental design (sexual orientation by initiator), we were able to determine, from an examination of the uninfluenced steady states, that in homosexual relationships the initiator of the conflict started positively, while in heterosexual relationships the initiator started negatively. Other research suggests that women presenting conflict issues to men is the most common pattern in heterosexual couples (Ball, Cowan, & Cowan, 1995; Oggins, Veroff, & Leber, 1993). This gender pattern fits with the well-known female-demand/male-withdraw pattern identified by Christensen and colleagues (for example, Christensen and Heavey, 1990). However, in our design we were able to include male as well as female heterosexual initiators.

For the uninfluenced steady state of the initiator of the issue, there was a significant effect only for sexual orientation, with homosexuals being much more positive than heterosexuals. There was no significant

---

* There was no unmarried cohabiting group included in the study, because, while it may seem to control for being married (and yet involve heterosexuals), in the United States, it is a complicated group. This may not be the case in other countries (like Sweden). Blumstein and Schwartz (1983) found that their sample of cohabiting, unmarried, American couples were very different from all other couples in their study, and that the overwhelming majority were not committed to the relationship. Further, Waite (2000) has shown that cohabiting American couples do not receive the benefits of marriage, such as higher wealth, better health, and increased longevity. Hence, commitment seems to be a critical ingredient to include when comparing relationships, and in the United States, for heterosexuals, this means primarily sampling married couples.

difference between gay and lesbian relationships. For the uninfluenced steady state of the partner, there was again only a significant
effect for sexual orientation. This means that the way the conflict issue was presented and received was positive for homosexual couples
and negative for heterosexual couples. These results suggest that, when
observational data are analyzed, homosexual relationships seem to be
fundamentally different from heterosexual relationships. Subsequent
analyses of specific SPAFF codes showed that homosexual initiators
of the conflict issue, compared to heterosexual initiators, were characterized by less negative affect: less belligerence, less domineering, less
fear/tension, less sadness, and less whining. The homosexual initiators
of the conflict also demonstrated more positive emotions when compared with the heterosexual initiators: more affection, more humor, and
more joy/excitement. For the partner (that is, the recipient of the conflict issue), the results showed a similar pattern. These findings suggest
that homosexual relationships may be distinguished from heterosexual
relationships in the expression of specific positive and negative affects
during a conflict interaction.

Influenced Steady States
For the influenced steady states, we computed the number of stable
steady states in each of the four quadrants of phase space. The only significant difference was in the quadrant where both partners' behavior
is positive, and again there was a sexual orientation effect. The mean
number of influenced stable steady states in this quadrant was nearly
one (.86) for the homosexual couples versus nearly zero (.32) for the
heterosexual couples.

There was also a marginally significant interaction between sexual
orientation and the gender of the initiator. Subsequent tests showed
that the mean stable steady states in the positive-positive quadrant was
significantly higher for lesbians (1.14) than for the other three types of
couples. Once again, these results suggest that influence processes in
homosexual committed relationships may be dissimilar to those in heterosexual couples. These findings imply that lesbian couples, when
compared with gay and heterosexual couples, are more likely to remain
stable in their behavioral interactions when both partners are positive
in their communication content.

Gender Effects
In addition to the gender threshold effect for the repair trigger previously noted, several other significant main effects for gender were

found. Regardless of sexual orientation, men were more angry than women when presenting an issue, and women were more excited/joyful than men. For the partner, regardless of sexual orientation, women were more sad when receiving a conflict issue than were men.

Differences between Gay Men and Lesbians
The SPAFF coding revealed that, for the initiator of the issue, lesbians were more angry than gays, used more humor, and showed more excitement/joy. For the partner, lesbians showed more humor and more interest. These results suggest that lesbians are more emotionally expressive than gay men.

Slope of Influence Functions in Negative and Positive Ranges
Perhaps most exciting in the results is a suggestive, rather than a definitive, result. As we noted, in every study we have conducted with heterosexual couples using mathematical modeling, the slope of the influence functions in the negative affect range is steeper than the slope in the positive affect range. This can be referred to as "the triumph of negative over positive affect" (Gottman, 1994), meaning that it is easier to hurt one's partner with negative affect than it is to have a positive influence with positive affect.

When we compared homosexual relationships with heterosexual relationships, we found some indication that for homosexuals, where power is more equal than in heterosexual couples, there was a reversal of the pattern. The variable used in this analysis was the slope for positive affect minus the slope for negative affect, so a negative value indicates that the negative affect slope is steeper (that is, the usual finding). For the partner's influence function there was a marginally significant effect for sexual orientation, and we speculated that with increased power we may find a lessening of the effect of the triumph of negative over positive affect in homosexual couples.

Summarizing the Findings for Gay Male, Lesbian,
and Married Couples
Previous questionnaire and interview studies have suggested that committed gay and lesbian relationships are not fundamentally different than committed married heterosexual relationships, in terms of such factors as the association between costs/benefits and relationship satisfaction, and the determinants of the progress toward commitment. However, when we employed a 2×2 factorial study to compare the means of observed interaction between homosexual and heterosexual

groups, accounting for who initiates the conflict issue, a different picture emerged. The mathematical modeling revealed interesting differences between heterosexual and homosexual couples in interactional dynamics, when couples discussed areas of conflict in their relationships. In analyses of the uninfluenced steady states, we found that homosexual couples began far more positively and far less negatively in the way they presented an issue than did heterosexual couples. Homosexual couples were also more positive in the way they received an issue from their partner than were heterosexual couples. Then, after the social influence process proceeded, homosexual couples were more likely to maintain a positive influenced steady state than were heterosexual couples. Finally, homosexual couples were more likely to have influenced states in the positive-positive quadrant of phase space than heterosexual relationships.

This observational approach to studying gay and lesbian relationships is important in its own right, for determining the correlates (and eventually, the causes) of successful maintenance of satisfying long-term committed homosexual relationships. Other research has shown that the uninfluenced steady state, in and of itself, is a significant predictor of divorce in heterosexual married couples (Cook et al., 1995; Gottman et al., 1998). Thus, based on our results, heterosexual relationships may have a great deal to learn from homosexual relationships, insofar as homosexual partners seem to have found a way to begin conflict discussions in a more positive and less negative manner, and to continue to have a positive rather than a negative influence on one another. Additional observational research is clearly called for to study the correlates of successful gay and lesbian relationships, and the parameters of interaction that are indicative of long-term stability and happiness in these relationships.

Violent Marriages as Power Struggles

Violent marriages clearly anchor the scale at the other end of the power-inequity dimension than gay and lesbian relationships, with married heterosexual couples in between the two. The research on violence in marriages has focused attention on dysregulated anger, but not on the power aspects of marriage. To deal with this limitation, in an unpublished dissertation, Rushe (1995) analyzed marital transactions in terms of power and control strategies, using her Spouse Manipulation and Control (SMAC) coding system. The data base came from a larger study conducted by Jacobson and Gottman (1998). In Rushe's dissertation, she selected three groups of couples: 60 violent couples, 30 distressed nonviolent couples, and 17 nondistressed nonviolent couples. Couples were categorized as violent if, on the Conflict Tactics Scale (CTS; Straus, 1979), any of the following conditions were met: (1) six or more episodes of low-level violence (push, slap, try to hit, or hit); (2) two or more episodes of higher-level violence (kick, bite, hit with fist); (3) one or more episodes of high-level violence (beat up, threaten or use a gun or knife). Couples were categorized as distressed if the wife scored less than 90 on the Short Marital Adjustment Test (SMAT; Locke & Wallace, 1959).

In creating the SMAC, Rushe reviewed many literatures on persuasion, including sales, advertising, changing political opinions, group decision making, assertiveness, cognitive dissonance, obedience to authority, attention getting and compliance, and brainwashing prisoners of the Korean War. The SMAC consists of 32 mutually exclusive and exhaustive behaviors coded in real time. We will not review all these codes in this chapter. However, the on-line coding of interaction with the SMAC seemed a lot to Gottman like analyzing a conflict conversation in terms of a chess game, with maneuvers for control, and countermaneuvers. It was a fascinating analysis that seemed very different from an analysis based solely upon affect.

Some of these SMAC behaviors are: Assertive, High Balling, Low Balling, Hanging On, Humiliate, Patronize, Obey Authority, Threat of Withdrawal, and Watershed Complaining. There were direct and positive persuasion codes (for example, agreement, assertive behavior). Then there were indirect positive codes (for example, seeking validation, laughing with, validating the other's feelings). Direct negative codes included criticizing, disagreeing, and humiliating, and indirect negative codes included defensiveness, patronizing, high balling, and low balling. ** Kappa across all codes was .67 for the husband's behavior and .60 for the wife's. Rushe reported her data by both frequency and duration of behavior.

We will summarize some of Rushe's significant results here. She hypothesized and found that: (1) Violent couples were the least likely

---

** Low balling was any understatement that is expected to be accepted; these were often innocent-seeming understatements or questions that set a back wall for the discussion; this was a very low frequency code. High balling, which occurred much more frequently than low balling, was an overstated assertion that is expected to be rejected, increasing the probability of later compromise or compliance.

to display assertive behaviors in their conflict discussions. Distressed couples were intermediate between happy and violent couples in assertion. (2) Wives were less assertive than husbands. (3) Husbands in violent marriages exhibited more high balling than their wives, and more high balling than any other partner in any other group. High balling may result in compliance but not in actual persuasion. (4) Violent couples begin persuasion at the very beginning of an argument; nonviolent couples, on the other hand, begin by expressing feelings or ideas and delay persuasion until the middle phase of an argument. (5) In the beginning third of the discussion, violent couples had far more speech turns than distressed nonviolent couples did. This suggests a much more rapid-fire, staccato type of interaction for violent couples when they first start the discussion. (6) Both violent and happy couples had high levels of mutual visual gaze, whereas distressed couples spent one third less time in mutual visual gaze. However, it appears that violent couples are maintaining gaze with different affect (and perhaps for different reasons?) than happy couples. Happy couples also increased mutual gaze from the first to the second third of the discussion, whereas distressed and violent couples decreased mutual gaze over the same time period. Mutual gaze decreased in the final third for all couples. (7) There was much more mutual laughter in happy couples than in either distressed or violent couples. (8) There was much more blaming, criticism, defensiveness, patronizing, and obey authority in violent marriages than in either distressed or happy marriages. (9) In the video recall procedure, violent couples made less positive ratings than distressed or happy couples. Hence, there is a lowered subjective positivity in affective perception in violent couples. (10) Wives in violent marriages showed evidence of greater cardiovascular arousal (finger pulse transit time) than their husbands, whereas wives in nonviolent marriages showed less cardiovascular arousal than their husbands. As Brown and Smith (1992) found, intense persuasion and resisting persuasion increase cardiovascular arousal and reactivity.

Rushe concluded that the violent marriage is basically a power struggle, a finding that is reminiscent of the analyses carried out by Coan, Gottman, Babcock, and Jacobson (1997) on violent men rejecting influence from women. This notion of violence as a form of power struggle is distinctly different from the emphasis on anger management for batterers in the therapy literature. The power dimension of violence suggests a systematic use of violence to intimidate and control the abused wife, instead of periodic uncontrolled outbursts (see Jacobson & Gottman,

1998). In a study by Babcock, Waltz, Jacobson, and Gottman (1993), power was measured by communication skill using a structured interview about previous arguments, and assessing marital power outcomes with the Who Does What scale (Cowan, Cowan, Coie, & Coie, 1978). Babcock et al. reported that violent couples were more likely than nonviolent distressed and happily married couples to engage in the husband-demand/wife-withdraw pattern. Also, within the domestically violent group, husbands who had less power were more physically abusive toward their wives

The absence of mutual laughter in Rushe's data is interesting, and is supported by other research. Positive affect and social support in violent couples have been studied by Holtzworth-Munroe, Stuart, Sandin, Smutzler, and McLaughlin (1997). They found that violent husbands offered less social support in the Bradbury social support task (Pasch & Bradbury, 1998) than nonviolent husbands. Instead, they were more belligerent/domineering, more contemptuous/disgusted, showed more anger and tension, and were more upset by the wife's problem.

Perhaps it is the case that marriages characterized by a power struggle are necessarily higher in negative affect and lower in positive affect. Hence, it may not be a power imbalance, but a struggle for control, that impacts affect. The complete picture, as in Rushe's dissertation, involves a description of power tactics as well as affect.

CONCLUDING REMARKS

In our research, we designed a paradigm that time-synchronizes three domains of measurement: observational coding, perception (video recall ratings), and physiology, embedded within longitudinal designs. We have learned that mathematical modeling of interaction, as well as studies of perception and physiology, have all produced some insights into power and affective processes in relationships, and into the predictors of relationship outcomes. We realize that making our field mathematical will be new to many researchers and clinicians, and there will be some resistance to this. However, other fields, such as physics, have made rapid progress in the development of theory, once mathematics was employed to model phenomena. Our models have created a language for describing processes that integrate affect and power.

We have now entered an experimental phase in which we are conducting brief proximal change experiments (designed only to change subsequent interaction), and clinical trials designed to create more distal changes. In this chapter, we demonstrated that we are much closer to an integration of affect and power processes now than we were in the 1950s. We have also demonstrated the validity of this integration for understanding relationship outcomes in violent and nonviolent marriages, and in committed homosexual relationships. This integration must come from new analytic tools for modeling interaction in terms of affect and social influence processes as well as from new observational methods that examine interaction both strategically and affectively.

REFERENCES

Babcock, J. C., Waltz, J., Jacobson, N. S., & Gottman, J. M. (1993). Power and violence: The relation between communication patterns power discrepancies and domestic violence. *Journal of Consulting and Clinical Psychology, 61*, 40–50.

Bales, R. F. (1950). *Interaction process analysis: A method for the study of small groups.* Cambridge, MA: Addison-Wesley Press.

Ball, F. L. J., Cowan, P., & Cowan, C. P. (1995). Who's got the power? Gender differences in partner's perception of influence during marital problem-solving discussions. *Family Process, 34*, 303–321.

Bateson, G., Jackson, D. D., Haley, J., & Weakland, J. (1956). Toward a theory of schizophrenia. *Behavioural Science, 1*, 251–264.

Bertalanffy, L. von (1968). *General systems theory.* New York: Braziller.

Blumstein, P., & Schwartz, P. (1983). *American couples: Money, work, sex.* New York: William Morrow and Co.

Brazelton, T. B., Koslowski, B., & Main, M. (1974). The origins of reciprocity: The early mother-infant interaction. In M. Lewis & L. Rosenbum (Eds.), *The effect of the infant on its caregiver* (pp. 49–76). New York: Wiley.

Broderick, C. (1993). *Understanding family process: Basics of family systems theory.* Thousand Oaks, CA: Sage.

Brown, P. C., & Smith, T. W. (1992). Social influence, marriage, and the heart: Cardiovascular consequences of interpersonal control in husbands and wives. *Health Psychology, 11*, 88–96.

Christensen, A., & Heavey, C. L. (1990). Gender and social structure in the demand/withdraw pattern of marital conflict. *Journal of Personality and Social Psychology, 59*, 73–81.

Coan, J., Gottman, J. M., Babcock, J., & Jacobson, N. S. (1997). Battering and the male rejection of influence from women. *Aggressive Behavior, 23*, 375–388.

Cook, J., Tyson, R., White, J., Rushe, R., Gottman, J. M., & Murray, J. (1995). Mathematics of marital conflict: Qualitative dynamic modeling of marital interaction. *Journal of Family Psychology, 9*, 110–130.

Cowan, C. P., Cowan, P. A., Coie, L., & Coie, J. D. (1978). Becoming a family: The impact of the first child's birth on the couple's relationship. In W. B. Miller & L. F. Newman (Eds.), *The first child and family formation.* Chapel Hill, NC: Carolina Population Center.

Ekman, P., & Friesen, W. V. (1978). *Facial action coding system*. Palo Alto, CA: Consulting Psychologist Press.

Fitzpatrick, M. A. (1988). *Between husbands and wives*. Newbury Park, CA: Sage.

Gianino, A., & Tronick, E. Z. (1988). The mutual regulation model: The infant's self and interactive regulation and coping and defensive capacities. In T. M. Field, P. M. McCabe, & N. Schneiderman (Eds.), *Stress and coping across development* (pp. 47–70). Hillsdale, NJ: Lawrence Erlbaum Associates.

Gottman, J. (1979). *Marital interaction: Experimental investigations*. New York: Academic Press.

Gottman, J., Murray, J., Swanson, C., Tyson, R., & Swanson, K. (in press). *The mathematics of marriage: Formal models*. Cambridge, MA: MIT Press.

Gottman, J. M. (1993). The roles of conflict engagement, escalation, or avoidance in marital interaction: A longitudinal view of five types of couples. *Journal of Consulting and Clinical Psychology, 61*, 6–15.

Gottman, J. M. (1994). *What predicts divorce: The relationship between marital processes and marital outcomes*. Hillsdale, NJ: Lawrence Erlbaum Associates.

Gottman, J. M. (1999). *The marriage clinic*. New York: W. W. Norton.

Gottman, J. M., Coan, J., Carrere, S., & Swanson, C. (1998). Predicting marital happiness and stability from newlywed interactions. *Journal of Marriage and the Family, 60*, 5–22.

Gottman, J. M., Levenson, R. W. (1992). Marital processes predictive of later dissolution: Behavior, physiology, and health. *Journal of Personality and Social Psychology, 63*, 221–233.

Gottman, J. M., McCoy, K., Coan, J., & Collier, H. (1996). The specific affect coding system (SPAFF) for observing emotional communication in marital and family interaction. In J. M. Gottman (Ed.), *What predicts divorce? The measures*. Mahwah, NJ: Lawrence Erlbaum Associates.

Gottman, J. M., Swanson, C., & Murray, J. (1999). The mathematics of marital conflict: Dynamic mathematical nonlinear modeling of newlywed marital interaction. *Journal of Family Psychology, 13*, 3–19.

Gray-Little, B. (1982). Marital quality and power processes among black couples. *Journal of Marriage and the Family, 44*, 633–646.

Gray-Little, B., Baucom, D. H., & Hamby, S. L. (1996). Marital power, marital adjustment, and therapy outcome. *Journal of Family Psychology, 10*, 292–303.

Gray-Little, B., & Burks, N. (1983). Power and satisfaction in marriage: A review and critique. *Psychological Bulletin, 93*, 513–538.

Holtzworth-Munroe, A., Stuart, G. L., Sandin, E., Smutzler, N., & McLaughlin, W. (1997). Comparing the social support behaviors of violent and nonviolent husbands during discussions of wife personal problems. *Personal Relationships, 4*, 395–412.

Jacobson, N. S., & Gottman, J. M. (1998). *When men batter women*. New York: Simon & Schuster.

Jacobson, N. S., Gottman, J. M., Gortner, E., Berns, S., & Shortt, J. W. (1996). Psychological factors in the longitudinal course of battering: When do the couples split up? When does the abuse decrease? *Violence and Victims, 11*, 371–392.

Krokoff, L. J., Gottman, J. M., & Haas, S. D. (1989). Validation of a rapid couples interaction scoring system. *Behavioral Assessment, 11*, 65–79.

Kurdek, L. A. (1992). Relationship stability and relationship satisfaction in cohabiting gay and lesbian couples: A prospective longitudinal test of the contextual and interdependence models. *Journal of Social and Personal Relationships, 9*, 125–142.

Kurdek, L. A. (1998). Relationship outcomes and their predictors: Longitudinal evidence from heterosexual married, gay cohabiting, and lesbian cohabiting couples. *Journal of Marriage and the Family, 60*, 553–568.

Locke, H. J., & Wallace, K. M. (1959). Short marital adjustment and prediction tests: Their reliability and validity. *Marriage and Family Living, 21*, 251–255.

Meehan, J. C., Holtzworth-Munoroe, A., & Herron, K. (2001). Maritally violent men's heart rate reactivity to marital interactions: A failure to replicate the Gottman et al. (1995) typology. *Journal of Family Psychology, 15*, 394–408.

Murray, J. D. (1989). *Mathematical biology*. Berlin: Springer-Verlag.

Oggins, J., Veroff, J., & Leber, D. (1993). Perceptions of marital interactions among black and white newlyweds. *Journal of Personality and Social Psychology, 65*, 494–511.

Olson, D. H., & Ryder, R. G. (1970). Inventory of marital conflicts (IMC): And experimental interaction procedure. *Journal of Marriage and the Family, 32*, 443–448.

Pasch, L. A., & Bradbury, T. N. (1998). Social support, conflict, and the development of marital dysfunction. *Journal of Consulting and Clinical Psychology, 66*, 219–230.

Rapoport, A. (1960). *Fights, games, and debates*. Ann Arbor: University of Michigan Press.

Rapoport, A. (1972). The uses of mathematical isomorphism in general systems theory. In G. J. Klir (Ed.), *Trends in general systems theory* (pp. 42–77). New York: Wiley Interscience.

Raush, H. L., Barry, W. A., Hertel, R. K., & Swain, M. A. (1974). *Communication, conflict, and marriage*. San Francisco: Jossey-Bass.

Raven, B. (1992) A power/interactional model of interpersonal influence: French and Raven thirty years later. *Journal of Social Behavior and Personality, 7*, 217–244.

Robinson, E. A., & Price, M. G. (1980). Pleasurable behavior in marital interaction: An observational study. *Journal of Consulting and Clinical Psychology, 48*, 117–118.

Rosenblatt, P. C. (1994). *Metaphors of family systems theory*. New York: Guilford.

Rushe, R. H. (1995). Tactics of power and influence in violent marriages. Unpublished doctoral dissertation, University of Washington.

Straus, M. (1979). Measuring interfamily conflict and violence: The Conflict Tactics (CT) Scales. *Journal of Marriage and the Family, 41*, 75–88.

Straus, M., & Tallman, I. (1971). SIMFAM: A technique for observational measurement and experimental study of families. In J. Aldous, T. Condon, R. Hill, M. Straus, & I. Tallman (Eds.), *Family problem solving* (pp. 379–438). Himsdale, IL: Dryden.

Strodtbeck, F. L. (1951). Husband-wife interaction over revealed differences. *American Sociological Review, 16*, 468–473.

Szinovacz, M. E. (1987). Family power. In M. B. Sussman & S. K. Steinmetz (Eds.), *Handbook of marriage and the family* (pp. 651–694). New York: Plenum.

Waite, L. (2000). *The case for marriage*. New York: Doubleday.

Weiss, R. L., Hops, H., & Patterson, G. R. (1973). A framework for conceptualizing marital conflict. In L. A. Hamerlynck, L. C. Handy, & E. J. Marsh (Eds.), *Behavior change: Methodology, concepts, and practice* (pp. 309–342). Champaign, IL: Research Press.

White, B. B. (1989). Gender differences in marital communication patterns. *Family Process, 28,* 89–106.

CHAPTER THIRTEEN

The Communication of Couples in Violent and Nonviolent Relationships: Temporal Associations with Own and Partners' Anxiety/Arousal and Behavior

Patricia Noller and Nigel D. Roberts

> Interaction is the sine qua non of relationships; it is through communication that persons initiate, define, maintain, and terminate their social bonds.
>
> —Baxter, 1985, p. 245

> Once violence occurs, the threat of further violence is always present, which may be viewed as a powerful form of psychological abuse.
>
> —Cahn, 1996, p. 11

When researchers merely count the overall levels of communication behaviors, they may not capture the intricacies of couple interaction (Hooley & Hahlweg, 1989; Sayers & Baucom, 1991; Weiss 1989). To study the complexity of couple interaction, it is necessary to examine how an action by partner A affects partner B, how B consequently acts, and how partner B's actions then affect partner A, and so on (Margolin, 1988b). Subtle differences in the communication patterns of couples in violent compared with nonviolent relationships may only emerge when behaviors or emotions are analyzed in terms of their sequencing, rather than in terms of their overall levels or frequencies.

In this study, the communication patterns of couples in violent and nonviolent relationships are compared. However, rather than investigating the overall levels of anxiety/arousal experienced by couples, or the overall levels of behaviors and emotions displayed by couples, the temporal associations between these various aspects of couple communication are examined. The study is clearly multimethod, and involves the assessment of physiological measures, insider ratings of anxiety, and outsider ratings of communication behavior.

Couples engaged in four videotaped interactions during which their physiological reactions were assessed; they then viewed the videotape of the interactions, reporting on their moment-by-moment levels of anxiety. Finally, the videotapes were coded by outsiders for the presence of particular communication behaviors, and the expression of particular emotions.

THE ANALYSIS OF TEMPORAL ASSOCIATIONS

Examining sequence may be particularly important when studying the communication patterns of couples in violent relationships. There is evidence that, during conflict interaction, the behaviors of couples in violent relationships are connected temporally more than are the behaviors of couples in nonviolent relationships, particularly with regard to the reciprocation of negativity (Burman, John, & Margolin, 1992; Burman, Margolin, & John, 1993; Margolin, John, & O'Brien, 1989). These findings have been interpreted as indicating that partners in violent relationships may be more reactive to one another's immediate behavior (Margolin, John, & O'Brien, 1989), or that they may be hypersensitive to each other's actions during conflict (Lloyd, 1990).

However, these studies may have seriously overestimated the temporal connections between the behaviors and emotional displays of partners in violent relationships. Spurious associations can be obtained between two time series simply because both time series can be predicted from their own past (Griffin & Gottman, 1990; Levenson & Gottman, 1983). The current study provides a more rigorous investigation of the temporal associations between partners' behaviors and affective displays, by controlling for autocorrelation.

A key focus of the current research study is the role of anxiety/arousal in influencing the communication patterns of couples in violent relationships. However, anxiety/arousal and observable behavior during conflict interaction may also be seen as being related over time *within* an individual, as well as related *across* individuals. Thus, the role that anxiety/arousal plays in driving the observable communication patterns of individuals and couples may only be uncovered by analyzing the sequencing of emotions and behaviors for each individual, along with the sequencing of emotions and behaviors between partners.

The results of relating partners' anxiety/arousal and their behavioral responses in a temporal manner are likely to be escalating displays of dysfunctional reactions by both partners, driven by their feelings of anxiety/arousal. According to this model, couples in violent relationships will rely on negative responses (for example, hostility, invalidation, coercion, and withdrawal), when they experience heightened levels of anxiety/arousal during conflict interaction. Furthermore, they are likely to respond to the partner's negative behavior with heightened anxiety/arousal. These two anxiety/arousal-related associations may account for the high temporal linkage between the observable behavior and affective displays of violent partners during conflict that has been identified by previous researchers (Burman et al., 1992; 1993; Margolin et al., 1989).

Several general patterns of observable behavior are likely to result: firstly, a pattern in which partners respond to one another's negative behaviors or emotions with negative behavior or emotions of their own (negative reciprocity); secondly, a pattern in which, as one individual expresses negativity, the other partner withdraws from the interaction (demand/withdraw); and thirdly, a pattern in which partners respond to one another's withdrawal with withdrawal of their own (mutual withdrawal). Given these cycles of the expression of negative and destructive behaviors, which are hypothesized to be driven by high levels of anxiety/arousal, partners' levels of anxiety/arousal in violent relationships should show higher levels of temporal association, relative to those in nonviolent relationships. In addition, these individuals' levels of arousal should be more linked to their own and their partner's negative emotion and behaviors than is true for those in nonviolent relationships.

In the present study, because of the techniques used to measure the behaviors of couples, and their emotion as expressed and experienced, it is possible to match the behavior/affective displays of couples with their anxiety/arousal at the time. Therefore, we will be able to determine whether the anxiety/arousal of violent individuals drives their consequent behavior or emotional displays, as well as whether the behavior or emotional displays of one partner drive the anxiety/arousal of the other partner. Addressing these theoretically important issues is only possible because there is careful synchronization of individuals' behavior and physiology in this study, an important methodological step that has not been made in previous research (Gottman, 1994).

We expected greater linkage between one individual's anxiety/ arousal and the partner's subsequent anxiety/arousal in violent rather than in nonviolent relationships. We also expected greater linkage between one individual's behavioral/affective displays and the other partner's subsequent anxiety/arousal in violent rather than in nonviolent relationships. Another expectation was for greater linkage between individuals' anxiety/arousal and their own subsequent behavior/affective displays for those in violent as compared with nonviolent relationships. Finally, we expected that the temporal linkage between one person's behavior and affective displays and the partner's subsequent behavior and affective displays would be greater in violent than in nonviolent relationships.

THE STUDY

Participants were 33 married and 15 cohabiting couples all of whom had been married or living together in a de facto relationship for at least 12 months. For females, ages ranged from 18 to 51 years, and for males, ages ranged from 19 to 67 years. However, the majority of participants were around 30 years of age (median age of females: 27.5 years; median age of males: 31 years). Although participants had been living together in a married or de facto relationship for an average of seven years, the majority of participants had been living together for fewer than four years. Most of the sample were yet to have children and had not had children in previous relationships. Finally, the majority of participants had not been married previously. The majority of females in the sample described their current occupation as students, with the next highest category being professionals. A relatively high proportion of male participants described themselves as professionals, tradespersons, or students.

Quality Marriage Index

Relationship satisfaction was assessed using a modified version of the Quality Marriage Index (QMI; Norton, 1983). The QMI is a six-item unidimensional measure of relationship satisfaction that provides a measure of the overall "goodness of the relationship" (Norton, 1983, p. 144). The QMI contains only evaluative items (for example, Do you have a good marriage?) as opposed to descriptive items, which *assume* an association between particular behaviors and good/happy marriages (Norton, 1983). Thus, independent investigation of whether couple communication impacts on relationship quality is possible with the QMI, because marital behaviors are not measured (Norton, 1983). The measure of relationship satisfaction was included, although the focus was primarily on violence, because Lloyd (1990) has argued that it is important to use a factorial design involving both satisfaction and violence, since some couples in relationships where violence has occurred are, nevertheless, satisfied with their relationships.

Conflict Tactics Scales

The Conflict Tactics Scales (CTS; Straus 1990) is the most widely used measure of intimate violence (Arias & Beach, 1987; Babcock, Waltz, Jacobson, & Gottman, 1993; Rosenbaum, 1988). Because of the highly skewed nature of couple violence data, violence was measured using a dichotomous split of the presence or absence of violence. Individuals were categorized as violent or nonviolent based on any report of violence in the last 12 months by either partner.

Insider Ratings

Individuals were also required to review their interactions on videotape, and provide moment-to-moment ratings of their subjective feelings of "anxiety," using dials acting as calibrated potentiometers (cf., Gottman & Levenson, 1985; Levenson & Gottman, 1983). The dials were handheld and the pointer could be turned to any position on an 11-point scale fixed on the dials. By moving the pointer, participants were able to provide continuous ratings of their anxiety, ranging from 0 (absence of anxiety) to 10 (complete overwhelming anxiety) throughout their couple interactions. The dials were connected directly to the MacLab analog-to-digital converter. Anxiety was chosen as the focal emotion of interest because anxiety is rated as both negative in valence and high in arousal (Izard, 1991), and consequently captures both of these important aspects of emotion.

Physiological Measures

Participants' physiological arousal was monitored by recording their skin conductance levels (a tonic measure of electrodermal activity) and heart rate (using an electrocardiogram), which was converted off-line into interbeat interval. These two measures were used because they represent the activity of both branches of the autonomic nervous system, and because, in the work of Levenson and Gottman (Gottman & Levenson, 1985; Levenson & Gottman, 1983), skin conductance level and interbeat interval were the most powerful predictors of declines in marital satisfaction.

Large individual differences exist in the stability and level of individuals' physiological activity (Cacioppo, Marshall-Goodell, & Gormezano, 1983). To partially control for these individual differences, it is possible to take baseline measures of physiological activity and either partial out their effects or standardize physiological activity with reference to baseline activity levels (Wagner & Calam, 1988). Many researchers use rest as the state from which to measure baseline levels of autonomic activity (for example, Gottman, 1994; Levenson & Gottman, 1983; 1985). To assist in direct comparison with the findings of these researchers, a similar procedure was used in the current study.

Upon their arrival at the laboratory, a couple was shown the physiological equipment and control room. The physiological measures were then fully explained, and an example recording was displayed. Following this brief introduction, partners completed the Quality Marriage Index and the Conflict Tactics Scales in separate parts of the laboratory, and with the researcher present. Participants were then prepared for the physiological recordings that were taken during each of the interaction tasks.

Couples engaged in four interaction tasks: They discussed a critical issue of conflict chosen by the woman, a critical issue of conflict chosen by the man, a trivial issue of conflict, and an issue of sadness or disappointment not directly involving the partner. Two different critical issues of conflict were used, in line with Christensen and Heavey's (1990) finding that couples behave differently depending on whose issue is being discussed. The trivial conflict was used because of Lloyd's (1990) suggestion that couples in violent relationships may have particular problems letting go of trivial issues of conflict, and may be more likely to engage in "squabbling" than other couples. In this chapter, we will present the results only for the comparison between the two critical issues of conflict, because most of the significant effects were related to these comparisons.

Each of the four couple interactions was preceded by a five-minute rest period during which couples sat quietly with their eyes shut. At the end of each rest period, couples were asked to talk for 10 minutes about one of the issues that they had previously identified. The order of interactions was counterbalanced.

Following the interaction tasks, couples engaged in a video-assisted recall session. Participants viewed their four 10-minute interactions on videotape and provided ratings of their anxiety as they remembered experiencing it during the actual interactions. As participants viewed their interactions on videotape, a large wooden screen was used to separate them, in order to minimize their monitoring of one another, and of one another's affect ratings.

Outsider Ratings

A cultural informants' approach (Gottman & Levenson, 1986; 1988) to the outsider measurement of affect and behavior was utilized. That is, raters considered skillful in decoding the nonverbal messages of people within their culture provided ratings of interactants' behavior and emotions (Roberts & Krokoff, 1990). Using a specially designed coding system (Couple Conflict Scales; CCS), partners were rated separately on seven conflict behaviors shown to be important in the literature on couple conflict (problem solving, problem-focused description, facilitation, invalidation, coercion, withdrawal, and defensiveness) and five negative emotions (fear/anxiety, anger, contempt/disgust, shame, and sadness) every 10 seconds, on a five-point scale (0–4) throughout each 10-minute interaction. A team of two coders was used to code the videotaped interactions in the present study, with approximately one-third of the interactions being double-coded as a reliability check. The topic of discussion was counterbalanced across raters.

Moderate inter-rater reliabilities were obtained, ranging from a low of .44 for sadness to a high of .83 for problem-focused description. To increase the reliabilities of the affect scales, it was considered necessary to collapse the anger and contempt/disgust scales into a summary scale labeled "hostility," and to collapse the sadness and shame scales into a summary scale labeled "despair." Collapsing the codes in the manner described was successful in improving the reliability of the affect scales.

INTERPRETATIVE CAUTIONS

Before presenting the results and our interpretations, it is necessary to acknowledge that only the magnitude, and not the direction, of the temporal associations between particular emotions and behaviors is provided by the Gottman-Ringland procedure for conducting bivariate time-series analysis (Wagner & Calam, 1988). That is, although the z-scores used as the dependent variables in the present study indicate the strength of association between two data streams, they do not indicate the direction of the association. An increase in the predictability of one time-series from knowledge of another time-series may result from either positive or negative correlations between the two data streams.

Nevertheless, there are two major advantages of time-series analysis over the lag-sequential techniques used by previous researchers to investigate the temporal associations between the behaviors of partners who are in violent relationships. The first is that the time-series analysis used here automatically controls for auto-correlation effects. Secondly, time-series analysis, by using continuous rather than categorical data, allows for the investigation of the temporal associations between physiological processes and observable behavior. It is for these two reasons that time-series analysis, rather than lag-sequential analysis, was used in the current study.

However, as noted earlier, the disadvantage of using time-series analysis is the difficulty of determining, with any certainty, the exact meaning of the temporal associations whose strength differentiates between violent and nonviolent relationships. For instance, although the links between partners' use of withdrawal was stronger in violent as compared with nonviolent relationships, strictly speaking it is unclear whether this was because individuals in violent relationships were more likely to *decrease* their use of withdrawal in response to a partner's use of withdrawal, or because they were more likely to *increase* their use of withdrawal in response to a partner's use of withdrawal. The validity of the interpretations that are offered in the present chapter need to be judged, therefore, in light of the findings of previous researchers regarding the temporal associations between the behaviors of partners in violent relationships, as well as in terms of the broader literature on marital communication.

OUR FINDINGS

In the present study, the degree of temporal linkage between various streams of data (time-series) constitutes the dependent variables. Four "sets" of temporal linkage are considered:

a. the association between one individual's anxiety/arousal and the partner's anxiety/arousal;

b. the association between one individual's observed behavior or emotional expression and the partner's subsequent anxiety/arousal;

c. the association between one individual's anxiety/arousal and his
    or her own subsequent observed behavior or emotional expres-
    sion; and
d. the association between one individual's observed behavior or
    emotional expression and the partner's observed behavior or
    emotional expression.

Time-series were created from the physiological data. The observational codes already formed time-series, because of the time-interval
sampling method used by the CCS, the coding system developed for
this study. All data streams had trend removed before bivariate time-
series analysis was conducted on them. Bivariate time-series analysis was then used to quantify, in the form of a z-score, the extent to
which one time-series was able to account for a second time-series after
controlling for the second time-series' own past (Williams & Gottman,
1981). It was decided to limit the number of lags to three, which corresponds to 30 seconds of the interaction. Thus a particular emotion or
behavior would be considered as predictable from an emotion or behavior if it tended to occur in the 30 seconds following that emotion or
behavior.

Emotional Linkage

For this dependent variable, three measures of the extent to which the
female partner's anxiety/arousal could be predicted from the male partner's anxiety/arousal were created, one each for interbeat interval, skin
conductance level, and self-reported anxiety ratings. Likewise, three
measures of the extent to which the male partner's anxiety/arousal
could be predicted from the female partner's anxiety/arousal were created. The three measures of predictability of female anxiety/arousal
were averaged into a single measure (the emotional linkage score
for females), as were the three measures of predictability of male
anxiety/arousal (the emotional linkage score for males). The final variable reflects emotional linkage between partners as measured by a combination of their self-reported anxiety and their physiological reactivity.
For this reason, the measure is better referred to as emotional linkage
rather than physiological linkage (cf., Levenson & Gottman, 1983).

A mixed-design analysis of variance was conducted to determine
whether emotional linkage differed for couples in violent and nonviolent relationships during couple interaction. The between-subjects

variables were violence and satisfaction, whilst gender and topic served as within-subjects variables. No significant effects involving violence were obtained. Hence, we did not find evidence of greater emotional linkage for couples in violent than in nonviolent relationships.

The finding that violence was not related to the level of emotional linkage couples displayed in the present study was contrary to our expectations. We were especially surprised because, in a similar study of couples in dating relationships, it was found that higher levels of emotional linkage during conflict interaction occurred for those in violent relationships than for those in nonviolent relationships (Roberts, 1998). If individuals in violent relationships rely on negative responses when they experience heightened levels of anxiety/arousal during conflict interaction, and if they respond to the partner's negativity with heightened anxiety/arousal, then higher levels of emotional linkage should have been displayed by couples in violent relationships in the present sample. It is important to note, however, that although emotional linkage was not related to couple violence, it was associated with relationship satisfaction, with unhappy couples displaying higher levels of emotional linkage, as found by Gottman and Levenson (Gottman, 1994; Gottman & Levenson, 1985; Levenson & Gottman, 1983).

Partner Behavior/Affective Display and Anxiety/Arousal

This set of dependent variables reflected the extent to which an individual's anxiety/arousal could be predicted from the partner's preceding behavior or emotional expression. The three measures of predictability of female anxiety/arousal from the partner's behavior or emotional expression were averaged into a single measure, as were the three measures of predictability of male anxiety/arousal from the partner's behavior or emotional expression. Thus, for example, the predictability of female anxiety/arousal from male withdrawal (the female withdrawal-arousal score) was the average of the predictability of female skin conductance level from male withdrawal, the predictability of female interbeat interval from male withdrawal, and the predictability of female anxiety ratings from male withdrawal. The averaging of these measures served to decrease the skew in the data, and reduce the number of analyses required.

Four mixed-design analyses of variance were conducted to determine whether the extent to which individuals' anxiety/arousal was driven by their partners' behaviors or emotional expressions was greater for those in violent compared to nonviolent relationships. The between-subjects variables were violence and relationship satisfaction, whilst gender and topic served as the within-subjects variables. Separate analyses were conducted for the different temporal associations under investigation: invalidation → anxiety/arousal, withdrawal → anxiety/arousal, hostility → anxiety/arousal, and despair → anxiety/arousal.

Invalidation → Anxiety/Arousal

For the analysis of variance conducted on the invalidation → anxiety/arousal association, there was a significant main effect of violence, F (1, 42) = 3.87, p = .05. This result indicates that there was a tendency for the anxiety/arousal of individuals in violent relationships to be more linked to the use of invalidation by a partner over the preceding 30 seconds than was the anxiety/arousal of individuals in nonviolent relationships. Thus it seems likely that those in violent relationships are more reactive to their partner's criticisms and put-downs and general lack of sensitivity than are those in nonviolent relationships.

Withdrawal → Anxiety/Arousal

In the analysis of variance conducted on the withdrawal → anxiety/arousal linkage, a three-way interaction between violence, satisfaction, and gender was obtained, F (1, 42) = 8.25, p < .01. This interaction is depicted in Figure 13.1. Follow-up analyses revealed the presence of

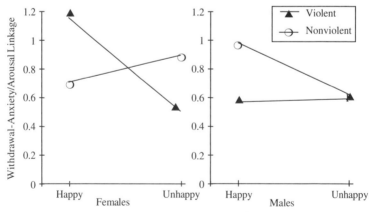

Figure 13.1. Interaction between violence, satisfaction, and gender for the temporal link between one partner's withdrawal and the other partner's subsequent anxiety/arousal.

an interaction between violence and satisfaction for females, F (1, 42) = 8.04, p < .01, but not for males. As can be seen from the figure, the anxiety/arousal of females in violent but happy relationships was more linked to the withdrawal of the partner than was the anxiety/arousal of females in nonviolent happy relationships, F (1, 42) = 5.03, p < .05. This finding suggests that female anxiety in violent relationships is driven, at least in part, by the withdrawal of the partner.

Hostility → Anxiety/Arousal

For the analysis of variance conducted on the hostility → anxiety/arousal association, there was a main effect of topic, F (1, 42) = 6.35, p < .05, indicating that there was greater linkage between individuals' anxiety/arousal and the partner's preceding displays of hostility during discussion of the male's issue of disagreement than during the female's issue of disagreement. There was also a three-way interaction between violence, satisfaction, and gender, F (1, 42) = 9.12, p < .01. This three-way interaction is depicted in Figure 13.2. Follow-up tests revealed a two-way interaction between violence and satisfaction for males only, F (1, 42) = 5.01, p < .05.

The anxiety/arousal of males in violent happy relationships was more linked to the hostility of the partner than was the anxiety/arousal

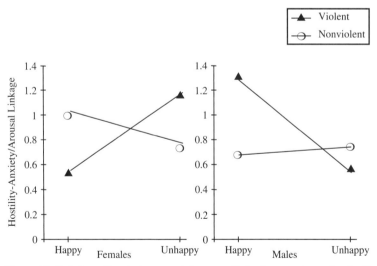

Figure 13.2. Interaction between violence, satisfaction, and gender for the temporal linkage between one partner's expression of hostility and the other partner's subsequent anxiety/arousal.

of those males in nonviolent happy relationships. For unhappy males, there was no difference in the linkage scores for those who were in violent compared with nonviolent relationships. In contrast, the effect of violence for happy males reached significance, $F (1, 42) = 5.28, p < .05$. Thus, it seems that males in violent but happy relationships are highly reactive to their partner's hostility, and may well become more anxious in response to that hostility than those in nonviolent but happy relationships. Perhaps what keeps these relationships happy is that the female partner recognizes that the violence is linked to her displays of hostility, and she tends to take the blame.

Despair → Anxiety/Arousal

For the analysis of variance conducted on the despair → anxiety/arousal linkage, there was a main effect of gender, $F (1, 42) = 12.52$, $p < .001$, indicating that males' anxiety/arousal was more linked to the partner's display of despair during the preceding 30 seconds than was females' anxiety/arousal. There was also a two-way interaction between violence and topic, $F (1, 42) = 5.61, p < .05$. This two-way interaction is presented in Table 13.1.

It appears that, during the male topic of disagreement, the anxiety/arousal of individuals in violent relationships was more strongly linked to the displays of despair (a combination of sadness and shame) of the partner than were the arousal levels of individuals in nonviolent relationships; however, no such difference occurred during the female issue of disagreement. Analyses of simple effects confirmed this interpretation. There was a significant effect of violence during the male issue of disagreement, $F (1, 42) = 3.94, p = .05$, but not during the female issue of disagreement. It seems likely then that, during the male's issue of disagreement, partners in violent relationships are more reactive to

Table 13.1. Interaction of Violence and Topic for the Temporal Linkage between One Partner's Expression of Despair and the Other Partner's Anxiety/Arousal

Topic	Violent	Nonviolent
Male's issue	0.88	0.50
Female's issue	0.56	0.74

their partner's displays of despair, and may well become more anxious in response.

Understanding the Linkage between Partner Behavior and Anxiety/Arousal

As was predicted, the temporal associations between one individual's behavior or emotional displays and the partner's subsequent anxiety/ arousal was stronger in violent compared with nonviolent relationships. Firstly, those in violent relationships tended to be more reactive to the partner's invalidation. That is, the internal emotional reactions of individuals in violent relationships tended to be more tied to the partner's criticisms, put-downs, and general lack of sensitivity, than were the emotional reactions of those in nonviolent relationships. Secondly, females in violent but happy relationships were more reactive to the partner's withdrawal than were females in nonviolent happy relationships. Thirdly, males in violent but happy relationships were more reactive to the partner's displays of hostility than were males in nonviolent happy relationships. Fourthly, individuals in violent relationships were more reactive to the partner's expression of despair during discussion of the male issue of disagreement than were individuals in nonviolent relationships.

All of these findings are consistent with Lloyd's (1990) suggestion that individuals in violent relationships may be hypersensitive to the partner's negativity. More than for individuals in nonviolent relationships, the internal emotional reactions of those in violent relationships appear to be predictable from the preceding observable behavior of the partner. Consequently, the emotional reactions of those individuals in violent relationships appear to be driven by the partner's behavior, more so than are the emotional reactions of those in nonviolent relationships. In addition, it seems that those in happy but violent relationships may be particularly sensitive to their partner's behavior. This hypersensitivity to the partner's negative affect suggests that these individuals may be carefully attending to the behavior of the partner, scrutinizing this behavior for aversive responses.

Overall, these findings are consistent with individuals in violent relationships (in comparison with those in nonviolent relationships) experiencing greater increases in feelings of anxiety and greater physiological arousal when a partner expresses increasing levels of negativity. To this extent, these findings lend support to the hypotheses being tested in the present study. Of course, we need to bear in mind that the anxiety/arousal of these individuals may be *decreasing* in response to the negativity of their partners, although this possibility seems unlikely.

Anxiety/Arousal and Own Behavior/Affective Display

This set of dependent variables consisted of measures of the extent to which individuals' levels of anxiety/arousal were able to predict their own subsequent behaviors or emotional expressions. Again, for all individuals, there were three z-scores reflecting the degree to which their anxiety/arousal could predict their own subsequent behavior or emotional expression. The three measures of the temporal linkage between individuals' anxiety/arousal and their own behavior/emotional expression were averaged, and this procedure successfully served to lessen the severe positive skew present in the data.

Three mixed-design analyses of variance were conducted to determine whether the extent to which individuals' behaviors or affective displays were driven by their own preceding levels of anxiety/arousal was related to the occurrence of violence. The between-subjects variables were violence and relationship satisfaction, whilst gender and topic served as the within-subjects variables. Separate analyses were conducted for the different temporal associations under investigation: anxiety/arousal → invalidation, anxiety/arousal → withdrawal, and anxiety/arousal → hostility. There were no significant effects for the anxiety/arousal-invalidation linkage.

Anxiety/Arousal → Withdrawal

The analysis of variance for the degree of linkage between individuals' anxiety/arousal and their own subsequent use of withdrawal revealed a significant two-way interaction between violence and gender, $F(1, 42) = 4.66, p < .05$. The nature of this interaction is best understood through inspection of Figure 13.3. From the figure it can be seen that there is a trend for the degree to which a man's anxiety/arousal predicted his later use of withdrawal to be larger for males in violent relationships than for males in nonviolent relationships. The degree of anxiety/arousal → withdrawal linkage was marginally higher for males in violent relationships compared to males in nonviolent relationships, $F(1, 42) = 3.68$, $p = .062$. Thus there seems to be a tendency for these males to respond to their own anxiety/arousal by withdrawing from the interaction, supporting earlier claims by Gottman and Levenson (1988).

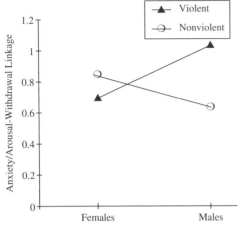

Figure 13.3. Interaction between violence and gender for the temporal linkage between one partner's anxiety/arousal and their own subsequent use of withdrawal.

Anxiety/Arousal → Hostility

The analysis of variance on the level of linkage between an individual's anxiety/arousal and his or her later expression of hostility revealed the presence of a three-way interaction between violence, satisfaction, and topic, F (1, 42) = 12.75, p < .001. Analyses of simple effects revealed that there was an interaction between violence and satisfaction during the female's issue of disagreement, F (1, 42) = 7.38, p < .01 (see Figure 13.4). Within the female's issue of disagreement, there was a significant effect of violence on the linkage between a person's anxiety/arousal and their subsequent expression of hostility for happy couples, F (1, 42) = 7.81, p < .01, but not for unhappy couples. During the female's issue, the anxiety/arousal → hostility linkage was stronger for individuals in *nonviolent happy* relationships than for those in *violent happy* relationships.

Understanding the Links between Individuals' Anxiety/Arousal and their own Subsequent Behavior

These findings provide some support for our predictions with regard to the temporal associations between individuals' anxiety/arousal and their own subsequent behavior or emotional expressions. Specifically, the anxiety/arousal of violent males was more linked to their subsequent withdrawal from the interaction than was the anxiety/arousal of nonviolent males. This finding is consistent with men in violent

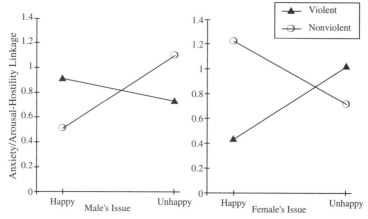

Figure 13.4. Interaction between violence, satisfaction, and issue for the temporal linkage between one partner's anxiety/arousal and his or her own expression
of hostility.

relationships increasing their use of withdrawal when they become
highly aroused. Gottman and Levenson (1988) suggested that males,
more than females, may use withdrawal as a response to the unpleasant levels of anxiety and physiological arousal they experience
during conflict. The current findings suggest that this gender difference occurs mainly in violent relationships. In nonviolent relationships,
women's withdrawal was as much a response to their experience of
anxiety/arousal as was men's withdrawal. However, contrary to predictions, during discussion of the female issue only, individuals in
nonviolent happy relationships showed greater linkage between their
anxiety/arousal and their subsequent expression of hostility than did
individuals in violent happy relationships.

There are two possible interpretations of this last result. Firstly, relative to females in violent relationships, those in nonviolent relationships
may be generally more likely to decrease their expression of hostility
following increases in their feelings of anxiety/arousal (that is, negative temporal association). If the temporal association is negative, then it
may mean that females in nonviolent relationships actively decrease the
level of hostility they display when upset (highly anxious and aroused),
perhaps in order to express these feelings in a more constructive fashion.

The second, and preferred interpretation is that, relative to females
in violent relationships, those in nonviolent relationships may be more
likely to increase their expression of hostility when their feelings of

anxiety/arousal increase (that is, positive temporal association). If the temporal association is positive, it may indicate that the communication of females in nonviolent relationships is more reflective of their actual (internal) feelings. Rather than letting unpleasant feelings build up to destructive levels, the women in nonviolent relationships may express their negative feelings when they experience them.

This finding may indicate that, relative to females in happy nonviolent relationships, women in happy violent relationships *sometimes* suppress their expression of hostility. In an attempt to control hostility, women in violent relationships may attempt to curb their expressions of hostility when overly aroused. The suppression of hostile affect is also consistent with what might be expected of a woman who has experienced couple violence in previous conflict interactions with the partner, and may flow from the desire to avoid the recurrence of a violent episode that occurred in the context of an angry and heated argument. However, according to hydraulic models of emotion, emotion is a type of energy (Cacioppo et al., 1983; Gross & Levenson, 1993), and any blockage to release of that energy through one channel will lead to its release through another. The suppression of this negative affect may have short-term beneficial effects in avoiding an escalation of negative affect and so improving the emotional climate and overall satisfaction with the relationship; however, it may have long-term negative consequences in the form of a violent outburst, as pent-up hostilities are expressed in one explosive incident.

It has to be remembered that couples who experience typical couple violence, as opposed to patriarchal terrorism, experience violence in their relationships relatively infrequently. Thus, although most violent incidents may begin with an argument (Stets & Henderson, 1991; Straus, 1979) most arguments do not result in violence. Rather than focusing solely on the communication patterns that may lead to violence within a single conflict interaction, researchers may need to place a greater emphasis on communication patterns that, over time, foster an atmosphere in which violence is more likely to occur. Although suppression of negative affect may not seem a particularly dangerous tactic within a single argument, over time it may have explosive consequences.

Partner and own Behavior/Affective Display

This final set of dependent variables assessed the extent to which an individual's behavior or emotional expression could be predicted from *the partner's* behavior or emotional expression. The data were positively skewed; however, this time there was only one measure for each of the temporal associations of interest. Therefore, in order to reduce the skew in the data, the measures of temporal linkage from each of the two conflict issues (the male issue of disagreement and the female issue of disagreement) were averaged. Although averaging these measures led to the loss of potentially important information (the effects of whose issue was being discussed could no longer be examined), this disadvantage was offset by the attenuation of the otherwise severe skew in the data.

Thirteen mixed-design analyses of variance were conducted. The between-subjects variables were violence and relationship satisfaction, whilst gender served as the within-subjects variable. Separate analyses were conducted for the different temporal associations under investigation. There were no significant effects for the following linkages: invalidation-withdrawal, withdrawal-hostility, hostility-hostility, hostility-invalidation, and hostility-despair. In addition, there were no effects of violence for invalidation-invalidation, invalidation-hostility or despair-despair. Thus, only five effects will be reported.

Withdrawal → Invalidation

The analysis of variance on the linkage between an individual's use of withdrawal and the partner's subsequent use of invalidation revealed a two-way interaction between violence and gender, $F (1, 43) = 5.73$, $p < .05$. As can be seen from Table 13.2, the use of invalidation by women in nonviolent relationships was more strongly predicted by the partner's use of withdrawal (over the preceding 30 seconds) than was the use of invalidation by women in violent relationships. This interpretation of the two-way interaction was supported by the presence of a significant simple effect of violence for females, $F (1, 43) = 4.35$, $p < .05$, but not for

Table 13.2. Interaction of Violence and Gender for the Temporal Linkage between One Partner's Withdrawal and the Other Partner's Invalidation

Gender	Violent	Nonviolent
Males	0.6	0.26
Females	0.48	1.1

Table 13.3. Interaction of Violence and Satisfaction
for the Temporal Linkage between Partners'
Expression of Fear/Anxiety

Satisfaction Level	Violent	Nonviolent
Happy	0.46	0.78
Unhappy	1.1	0.57

males. Thus, in this case, women in nonviolent relationships seem to be more reactive to the partner's withdrawal than are women in violent relationships, who may even be relieved by the partner's withdrawal.

Withdrawal → Withdrawal
The analysis of variance on the linkage between partners' use of withdrawal revealed a significant main effect of violence, F (1, 43) = 4.97, $p < .05$. Withdrawal by individuals in violent relationships was more closely related to the partner's use of withdrawal than was withdrawal by individuals in nonviolent relationships. In other words, partners in violent relationships tended to reciprocate one another's withdrawal.

Fear/Anxiety → Fear/Anxiety
For the linkage between partners' *expressions* of fear/anxiety, the analysis of variance revealed a significant two-way interaction between violence and satisfaction, F (1, 43) = 5.07, $p < .05$. Analyses of simple effects revealed that there was an effect of violence within unhappy relationships, F (1, 43) = 4.36, $p < .05$, but not within happy relationships. As can be seen from Table 13.3, the predictability of an individual's expression of fear/anxiety from the partner's expression of fear/anxiety (over the preceding 30 seconds) was greater for those in violent unhappy relationships than for those in nonviolent unhappy relationships. Thus partners in these relationships seem to reciprocate each other's expressions of fear-anxiety, and perhaps may fear the escalation of the conflict to the point where violence may occur.

Despair → Hostility
For the temporal association between individuals' expressions of despair and the partner's consequent display of hostility, the analysis of variance revealed a significant three-way interaction between violence,

Table 13.4. Interaction of Violence, Satisfaction, and Gender for the Temporal Linkage between One Partner's Expression of Despair and the Other Partner's Hostility

	Violent		Nonviolent	
Satisfaction level	Males	Females	Males	Females
Happy	1.38	0.39	0.58	1.15
Unhappy	0.50	0.98	0.46	0.75

satisfaction, and gender, $F(1, 43) = 6.63, p < .05$. Follow-up analyses revealed the presence of an interaction between violence and satisfaction for males, $F(1, 43) = 5.67, p < .05$, but not for females.

Further, the expression of hostility by men in violent but happy relationships was more predictable from the partner's expression of despair than was the hostility of men in nonviolent happy relationships, $F(1, 43) = 3.99, p = .05$. (There was no effect of violence for unhappy males; see Table 13.4.) Thus, these men in happy but violent relationships seem to be more reactive than other men to their partner's expression of despair, perhaps because despair does not fit with their concept of a happy relationship.

Hostility → Withdrawal

For the hostility → withdrawal linkage variable, analysis of variance revealed the presence of a significant two-way interaction between violence and gender, $F(1, 43) = 4.44, p < .05$. Analysis of simple effects revealed that there was a simple effect of violence within female participants but not male participants, $F(1, 43) = 4.18, p < .05$. From Figure 13.5, we see that the withdrawal of females in violent relationships was more predictable from the hostility of the partner than was the withdrawal of females in nonviolent relationships.

Understanding the Linkages between Partners' Behaviors and Emotional Displays

Overall, individuals in violent relationships, compared to those in nonviolent relationships, showed more temporal connection between the withdrawal of the partner and their own withdrawal; in other words,

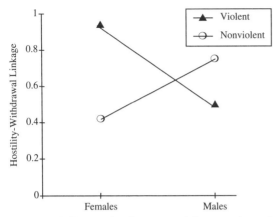

Figure 13.5. Interaction between violence and gender for the temporal linkage between one partner's expression of hostility and the other partner's subsequent use of withdrawal.

partners in violent relationships tended to reciprocate one another's withdrawal. This reciprocation of withdrawal may be their way of avoiding violence, at least in the short term. As we have indicated earlier, however, this strategy may not be the most appropriate one.

Females in violent relationships showed more linkage between their withdrawal and the partner's preceding displays of hostility than did females in nonviolent relationships. This finding suggests that these women may respond to their partners' hostility by withdrawing, perhaps again, to avoid the possibility of violence. Of course, it is also possible that they are *less* likely than women in nonviolent relationships to withdraw in response to the partner's hostility. However, partner hostility was not linked with other negative behaviors such as invalidation or hostility, only with anxiety/arousal and withdrawal. Hence, it seems more likely that the partner's expression of hostility increases the probability that these women will withdraw.

Partners in violent unhappy relationships showed more linkage between one another's expressions of fear/anxiety than did partners in nonviolent unhappy relationships. It seems likely that fear/anxiety may escalate in response to the partner's expression of fear/anxiety, in a process reminiscent of emotional contagion (Hatfield, Cacioppo, & Rapson, 1994).

In addition, the hostility of males in happy violent relationships was more predictable from the partner's expression of despair than was the hostility of individuals in happy nonviolent relationships. There are two possibilities here: One is that these males *increase* their hostility in response to their partner's expression of despair, and the other is that these males *decrease* their hostility in response to their partners' expression of despair. Given the earlier finding that those in violent relationships are highly reactive to their partner's expression of despair, at least when discussing the male issue of disagreement, the former possibility seems more likely than the latter. We will discuss this issue further, later in this chapter.

On the other hand, females in violent relationships also showed less temporal connection between their use of invalidation and the partner's use of withdrawal than did females in nonviolent relationships. Thus, females in nonviolent relationships may be more likely to invalidate the partner in response to their withdrawal than are those in violent relationships. This finding may be another example of women in nonviolent relationships being more willing to react in line with their feelings, as did females in happy nonviolent relationships who responded with hostility when they were feeling anxious and aroused.

GENERAL DISCUSSION

Consistent with predictions, couples in violent relationships were found to differ from those in nonviolent relationships in terms of the temporal linkages between a number of important variables. Although these temporal associations were frequently greater in violent compared to nonviolent relationships, in a small number of cases these linkages were lower in violent relationships. These unexpected findings have important theoretical implications for the association between individuals' *experience* of affect and their *expression* of affect, and how this association may differ across violent and nonviolent relationships.

Conflict Patterns

Three general patterns of observable behavior are theoretically important to the conflict interactions of couples in violent relationships: negative reciprocity, mutual withdrawal, and the demand-withdraw pattern of interaction. Each of these will be considered separately here, in light of previous research, and the results discussed so far.

Negative Reciprocity

Only limited evidence for an association between violence and negative reciprocity was obtained. Firstly, partners in violent unhappy relationships showed more linkage between one another's *expressions* of fear/anxiety than did partners in nonviolent unhappy relationships. This finding is consistent with partners in violent unhappy relationships driving one another's visible displays of fear/anxiety. Perhaps such displays of unrest have been associated with previous incidents of violence and are interpreted as warning signs of impending aggression (physical or verbal). It is interesting to note that partners did not reciprocate each other's expressions of despair, or even hostility.

Secondly, the linkage between men's expression of hostility and the partner's previous expression of despair was greater for men in violent happy relationships than for men in nonviolent happy relationships. It should be recalled that, in the results reported earlier for the links between partner behavior and own anxiety, couples in violent relationships were more reactive to the partner's expression of despair than were couples in nonviolent relationships, albeit only during discussion of the male issue of disagreement. For those in happy violent relationships, this hyper-reactivity to the partner's expression of despair may help explain the greater linkage between their use of hostility and the partner's preceding expression of despair. This finding is consistent with men in happy but violent relationships finding the unhappiness of partners particularly distressing, and this distress may be expressed in the form of a hostile response. It is almost as if women in happy violent relationships are punished by the partner if they express sadness or shame. The expression of unhappiness appears to be prohibited in these relationships. This finding is consistent with men in happy violent relationships finding the partner's unhappiness distressing and responding in an angry blaming manner. Violence may result as an extension of that anger.

Alternatively, Retzinger (Retzinger, 1991a, 1991b; Scheff & Retzinger, 1991) has proposed a model of marital conflict in which threatened bonds result in the emotional reaction of shame, which, if not acknowledged by the partner, leads to rage and violence. The hostile responses of males in happy but violent relationships to the partner's despair may reflect this kind of process, and may place the couple at risk of experiencing a violent incident. Of course, it is also possible that these men reduce their hostility in response to the partner's expression of despair, but this seems unlikely, given that they are likely to be highly aroused.

No support was found for the claim that reciprocation of more hostile forms of negativity (invalidation and hostility) would characterize the interaction patterns of couples in violent relationships. Although individuals in violent relationships (particularly happy violent relationships) were more reactive to the partner's negativity, in that their anxiety/arousal was more predictable from the partner's negativity, these individuals did not necessarily respond in an overtly negative manner. The temporal links between individuals' anxiety/arousal and their own subsequent hostility and invalidation were no higher amongst individuals in violent relationships than amongst those in nonviolent relationships. Indeed, during discussion of the female issue of disagreement, individuals in violent happy relationships showed *less* linkage between their own anxiety/arousal and their own subsequent expression of hostility than did individuals in nonviolent happy relationships. It is this breakdown in the links between anxiety/arousal and behavior that may account for the lack of negative reciprocity in the present study. It appears that, when emotionally aroused, individuals in violent relationships may not characteristically express that affect in a negative fashion any more than do individuals in nonviolent relationships.

The findings of this study run somewhat contrary to the findings of previous researchers. Previous researchers have found that, compared to couples in nonviolent relationships, those in violent relationships tend to display higher levels of negative reciprocity (Burman et al., 1992; 1993; Cordova, Jacobson, Gottman, Rushe, & Coy, 1993; Murphy & O'Farrell, 1997; Vivian & O'Leary, 1987). However, in these studies, significant cross-correlations could have been obtained simply because each individual's behavior was predictable from his or her own past behavior (Gottman, 1981; Heyman, Weiss, & Eddy, 1995). By not taking autocorrelation effects into account, previous researchers may have somewhat overestimated the amount of negative reciprocity shown by couples in violent, as compared with nonviolent, relationships.

Mutual Withdrawal

Although individuals in violent relationships did not always reciprocate one another's negativity more than those in nonviolent relationships, they did show more temporal connection between the withdrawal of the partner and their own withdrawal. Other researchers have found that partners in violent relationships reciprocate one another's withdrawal (for example, Margolin, John, & O'Brien, 1989). Although this pattern of interaction may not appear particularly destructive within a single argument, it may be extremely damaging over time. The avoidance of conflict may actually lead to greater hostility and aggression over time. Certainly, as unresolved conflicts build up, the frustrations and unexpressed hostilities that consequently develop may increase the likelihood of a violent outburst (Burman et al., 1993; Margolin, 1988a; 1988b). With both partners feeding off one another's withdrawal, the level of frustration may well compound, as neither individual is likely to have his or her position understood, or to understand the position of the partner.

The anxiety/arousal of females in violent happy relationships was more predictable from the partner's preceding use of withdrawal than was the anxiety/arousal of females in nonviolent happy relationships. This finding is consistent with women in violent happy relationships finding the withdrawal of the partner particularly anxiety provoking. However, rather than expressing hostility or invalidation in response to this withdrawal, it appears that women in violent relationships (both satisfied and dissatisfied) may respond with withdrawal of their own.

The Demand-Withdraw Pattern of Interaction
The importance of withdrawal is further highlighted by the fact that females in violent relationships showed more linkage between their withdrawal and the partner's preceding displays of hostility than did females in nonviolent relationships. This finding suggests that females in violent relationships are more likely to increase their use of withdrawal in response to a partner's expression of hostility than are women in nonviolent relationships (although it is, of course, possible that they decrease their use of withdrawal in this situation). However, the female-demand/male-withdraw pattern of interaction was not found to characterize the conflict interactions of couples in violent relationships. Babcock et al. (1993) also found that couple violence was related to the male-demand/female-withdraw pattern of interaction, but not the generally more common female-demand/male-withdraw pattern.

However, in the present study, the invalidation of females in violent relationships was less predictable from the partner's withdrawal than was the invalidation of females in nonviolent relationships. This finding was contrary to expectations, and suggests that couples in violent relationships may be less likely to engage in the female-demand/male-withdraw pattern of interaction than couples in nonviolent relationships. This finding complements the finding that females (and males) in violent relationships reciprocate the partner's withdrawal with withdrawal of their own. Rather than punishing the withdrawal of the partner, these women may negatively reinforce the partner's withdrawal by withdrawing from the argument themselves, thus ameliorating the unpleasant subjective feelings of anxiety/arousal that these men experience during conflict interaction. The women's own use of withdrawal may similarly be negatively reinforced.

Effects of Violence and Satisfaction

For the purposes of the current chapter, we have chosen to focus primarily on violence as our major independent variable, and have not reported effects for satisfaction, except where satisfaction interacted with violence. There were many cases where the association between violence and communication processes was moderated by relationship satisfaction. Frequently, differences were identified only when the effects of violence and satisfaction were considered together. In particular, violence and satisfaction tended to interact in such a way that differences were apparent between violent and nonviolent relationships that were happy, but no differences were apparent between violent and nonviolent relationships that were unhappy, or vice versa.

These findings point to the importance of adopting a factorial design in investigating the associations between communication, and both violence and satisfaction. Many previous researchers have compared couples in violent relationships with groups of satisfied and dissatisfied couples, ignoring the fact that many couples in violent relationships are not dissatisfied with their relationships (Lloyd, 1988; 1990).

Comments on the Current Study

Time-Series Analysis

The biggest limitation of the current study is related to the statistical technique that was used to analyze sequence. The interpretative difficulties that this limitation represents have already been dealt with earlier in this chapter. However, the strength of the study also lies in this same statistical technique. It was only because time-series analysis was used that autocorrelation effects were able to be so easily controlled. Furthermore, without the use of time-series analysis, it would not have been possible to examine the associations between ongoing physiological processes and observable behavior as it occurs continuously throughout an interaction.

Topic
In this study, the effect of whose issue of disagreement was being dis-cussed was shown to be important. The association between violence and communication was found to be moderated on several occasions, by whose topic was being discussed, with the effects of violence only be-ing apparent within either the male issue of disagreement or the female issue of disagreement, but not both.

Physiological Measures
Although extremely informative, the psychophysiological component of the present research program is limited, in that there were only two measures of psychophysiological arousal for each partner. The two mea-sures used in the present study (skin conductance level and interbeat interval) may represent, however, the two most useful measures for as-sessing the activity of the autonomic nervous system (Dawson, Schell, & Fillion, 1990), as well as being the best predictors of relationship functioning in Levenson and Gottman's initial research (Gottman & Levenson, 1985; Levenson & Gottman, 1983).

CONCLUSIONS

The present study has clearly demonstrated the potential of psycho-physiological techniques for studying couple interaction. Social psycho-physiology has had a relatively brief history, and this study represents a small advance in the progress of this discipline. To examine the asso-ciations between observable behavior and physiological processes, pre-vious researchers have mainly examined correlations across subjects. In the present study, careful synchronization of physiological mea-sures and outsider ratings of participants' observable behavior have allowed for the assessment of the temporal connection of behav-ior and physiology within subjects. The associations between these physiological (and self-reported anxiety) and observable behaviors have then been compared across couples in violent and nonviolent relationships.

These techniques have allowed for the in-depth investigation of the communication patterns of couples in violent relationships, and the role that anxiety/arousal plays in generating those communication patterns. The expectation that partners' anxiety/arousal and their behavioral re-sponses were related in a temporal manner was supported in a number of important ways.

In closing, it is important to note that many of the differences obtained between violent and nonviolent relationships were moderated
by relationship satisfaction. Future researchers should consider using
a similar factorial design as used in the present study. The distinction
between happy and unhappy violent relationships is an important one,
which has frequently been overlooked by researchers.

REFERENCES

Arias, I., & Beach, S. R. H. (1987). Validity of self-reports of marital violence.
   Journal of Family Violence, 2 (2), 139–149.
Babcock, J. C., Waltz, J., Jacobson, N. S., & Gottman, J. M. (1993). Power and vi-
   olence: The relation between communication patterns, power discrepancies,
   and domestic violence. *Journal of Consulting and Clinical Psychology, 61*, 40–50.
Burman, B., John, R. S., & Margolin, G. (1992). Observed patterns of conflict
   in violent, nonviolent, and nondistressed couples. *Behavioral Assessment, 14*,
   15–37.
Burman, B., Margolin, G., & John, R. S. (1993). America's angriest home videos:
   Behavioral contingencies observed in home reenactments of marital conflict.
   Journal of Consulting and Clinical Psychology, 61, 28–39.
Cacioppo, J. T., Marshall-Goodell, B. S., & Gormezano, I. (1983). Social psy-
   chophysiology: Bioelectrical measurement, experimental control, and analog-
   to-digital data acquisition. In J. T. Cacioppo, & R. E. Petty (Eds.), *Social
   psychophysiology: A sourcebook* (pp. 666–690). New York: Guilford.
Christensen, A., & Heavey, C. L. (1990). Gender and social structure in the de-
   mand/withdraw pattern of marital conflict. *Journal of Personality and Social
   Psychology, 59 (1)*, 73–81.
Cordova, J. V., Jacobson, N. S., Gottman, J. M., Rushe, R., & Cox, G. (1993).
   Negative reciprocity and communication in couples with a violent husband.
   Journal of Abnormal Psychology, 102 (4), 559–564.
Dawson, M. E., Schell, A. M., & Fillion, D. L. (1990). The electrodermal system. In
   J. T. Cacioppo & L. G. Tassinary (Eds.), *Principles of psychophysiology: Physical,
   social, and inferential elements* (pp. 295–324). New York: Cambridge University
   Press.
Gottman, J. M. (1981). *Time-series analysis: A comprehensive introduction for social
   scientists*. Cambridge: Cambridge University Press.
Gottman, J. M. (1994). *What predicts divorce? The relationship between marital
   processes and marital outcomes*. Hillsdale, NJ: Lawrence Erlbaum Associates.
Gottman, J. M., & Levenson, R. W. (1985). A valid procedure for obtaining
   self-report of affect in marital interaction. *Journal of Consulting and Clinical
   Psychology, 53 (2)*, 151–160.
Gottman, J. M., & Levenson, R. W. (1986). Assessing the role of emotion in marriage. *Behavioral Assessment, 8*, 31–48.
Gottman, J. M., & Levenson, R. W. (1988). The social psychophysiology of marriage. In P. Noller, & M.A. Fitzpatrick (Eds.), *Perspectives on marital interaction*
   (pp. 182–200). Clevedon, England: Multilingual Matters.

Griffin, W. A., & Gottman, J. M. (1990). Statistical methods for analyzing family interaction. In G. R. Patterson (Ed.), *Depression and aggression in family interaction* (pp. 131–168). Hillsdale, NJ: Lawrence Erlbaum Associates.

Gross, J. J., & Levenson, R. W. (1993). Emotional suppression: Physiology, self-report, and expressive behavior. *Journal of Personality and Social Psychology, 64 (6),* 970–986.

Hatfield, E., Cacioppo, J. T., & Rapson, R. (1994). *Emotional contagion.* New York and Paris: Cambridge University Press.

Heyman, R. E., Weiss, R. L., & Eddy, J. M. (1995). Marital interaction coding system: Revision and empirical evaluation. *Behavior Research and Therapy, 33 (6),* 737–746.

Hooley, J. M., & Hahlweg, K. (1989). Marital satisfaction and marital communication in German and English couples. *Behavioral Assessment, 11,* 119–133.

Izard, C. E. (1991). *The psychology of emotions.* New York: Plenum Press.

Levenson, R. W., & Gottman, J. M. (1983). Marital interaction: Physiological linkage and affective exchange. *Journal of Personality and Social Psychology, 45,* 587–597.

Levenson, R. W., & Gottman, J. M. (1985). Physiological and affective predictors of change in relationship satisfaction. *Journal of Personality and Social Psychology, 49,* 85–94.

Lloyd, S. (1988). Physical aggression and distress in marriage: The role of everyday marital interaction. Paper presented at the National Council on Family Relations Annual Conference, Philadelphia.

Lloyd, S. (1990). Conflict types and strategies in violent marriages. *Journal of Family Violence, 5,* 269–284.

Margolin, G. (1988a). Interpersonal and intrapersonal factors associated with marital violence. In G. T. Hotaling, D. Finkelhor, J. T. Kirkpatrick, & M.A. Straus (Eds.), *Family abuse and its consequences* (pp. 203–217). Newbury Park, CA: Sage.

Margolin, G. (1988b). Marital conflict is not marital conflict is not marital conflict. In R. D. Peters & R. J. McMahon (Eds.), *Social learning and systems approaches to marriage and the family* (pp. 193–216). New York: Brunner/Mazel.

Margolin, G., John, R. S., & O'Brien, M. (1989). Sequential affective patterns as a function of marital conflict style. *Journal of Social and Clinical Psychology, 56,* 24–33.

Murphy, C. M., & O'Farrell, T. J. (1997). Couple communication patterns of maritally aggressive and nonaggressive male alcoholics. *Journal of Studies on Alcohol, 58,* 83–90.

Norton, R. (1983). Measuring marital quality: A critical look at the dependent variable. *Journal of Marriage and the Family, 45,* 141–151.

Retzinger, S. M. (1991a). Shame, anger, and conflict: Case study of emotional violence. *Journal of Family Violence, 6(1),* 37–60.

Retzinger, S. M. (1991b). *Violent emotions: Shame and rage in marital quarrels.* Newbury Park, CA: Sage.

Roberts, L. J., & Krokoff, L. J. (1990). A time-series analysis of withdrawal, hostility, and displeasure in satisfied and dissatisfied marriages. *Journal of Marriage and the Family, 52,* 95–105.

Roberts, N. D. (1998). Communication in violent relationships: The role of attachment and arousal. Unpublished Ph.D thesis, University of Queensland, Australia.

Rosenbaum, A. (1988). Methodological issues in marital violence research. *Journal of Family Violence, 3(2)*, 91–104.

Sayers, S. L., & Baucom, D. H. (1991). Role of femininity and masculinity in distressed couples' communication. *Journal of Personality and Social Psychology, 61 (4)*, 641–647.

Scheff, T. J., & Retzinger, S. M. (1991). *Emotions and violence.* Lexington, MA: Lexington Books.

Stets, J. E., & Henderson, D. A. (1991). Contextual factors surrounding conflict resolution while dating: Results from a national study. *Family Relations, 40*, 29–36.

Straus, M. A. (1979). Measuring intrafamily conflict and violence: The Conflict Tactics (CT) Scales. *Journal of Marriage and the Family, 41*, 75–86.

Straus, M. A. (1990). Measuring intrafamily conflict and violence: The Conflict Tactics (CT) Scales. In M. A. Straus & R. J. Gelles (Eds.), *Physical violence in American families: Risk factors and adaptations to violence in 8,145 families* (pp. 29–47). New Brunswick, NJ: Transaction Press.

Vivian, D., & O'Leary, K. D. (1987). Communication patterns in physically aggressive engaged couples. Paper presented at the Third National Family Violence Research Conference, Durham, NC.

Wagner, H. L., & Calam, R. M. (1988). Interpersonal psychophysiology and the study of the family. In H. L. Wagner (Ed.), *Social psychophysiology and emotion: Theory and clinical applications* (pp. 211–229). Chichester, England: John Wiley & Sons.

Weiss, R. L. (1989). The circle of voyeurs: Observing the observers of marital and family interactions. *Behavioral Assessment, 11*, 135–147.

Williams, E. A., & Gottman, J. M. (1981). *A user's guide to the Gottman-Williams time-series analysis computer programs for social scientists.* New York: Cambridge University Press.

MARITAL INTERACTION AT IMPORTANT TRANSITION PERIODS

Introduction to Section Five

As conceptualized in this section, transitions are points where partners' roles within the marital relationship change markedly. These transition points are interesting to study because forces internal and external to the relationship can create major changes in relationship roles and shape new interaction patterns. These changes require partners to actively renegotiate aspects of their marriage, and these processes are likely to be critical for the future success of the relationship.

The chapters in this section are concerned with marital interaction following two major transitions: the transition to parenthood and the transition from a relatively equal partnership to one where one partner becomes the caregiver of the other. The chapters explore such key issues as the nature of couple communication, expectations and perceptions of the partner, and changes in individual and couple well-being.

Simpson and his colleagues explore attachment-related issues in the transition to parenthood. First-time parenthood is likely to make attachment issues highly salient, as the marital relationship needs to accommodate a new and highly dependent family member. The demands of caring for a newborn infant can make it difficult for partners to give each other the attention they have been used to, and fulfilling these demands may interfere with opportunities for couple intimacy. Ambivalently attached women, who are highly anxious about their relationship, are likely to find these changes very difficult to cope with, particularly if they see their spouse as unavailable or unsupportive.

The longitudinal study reported by Simpson and his colleagues assessed couples using self-report questionnaires six weeks before the baby was born, and again six months after. These researchers focused on adult attachment and perceptions of spousal support as predictors of changes in marital satisfaction. Consistent with their expectations, the greatest changes in marital quality occurred for highly ambivalent women who perceived low levels of prenatal support from their husbands. These women reported significant declines in marital satisfaction and spousal support across the transition period, and were less likely than other women to seek support from their husbands.

This type of research can help to explain the different trajectories of couple satisfaction following the transition to parenthood. The results also emphasize the couple nature of such transitions, and the way that husbands' attitudes and behaviors can either exacerbate or relieve the wives' concerns. They also point to the necessity for counselors to work on the relationship, rather than the individual level, with couples who are struggling with these changes.

The Feeney and Noller chapter again explores the transition to parenthood, but focuses more specifically on issues related to the division of labor in the family during this period. This focus reflects previous findings suggesting that many new parents feel dissatisfied with the way household and baby-related tasks are shared following the birth of a new baby. In particular, parents often complain about the increasing traditionalization of roles, with men focusing on paid employment and women believing that they are expected to take primary responsibility for infant care and other tasks around the home.

The study reported by Feeney and Noller was based primarily on a diary methodology: About three months after the babies were born, husbands and wives were asked to keep detailed records of their day-to-day involvement in infant care and other household tasks. The diary records enabled the researchers to assess not only the time spent on specific tasks, but also spouses' perceptions of the fairness or unfairness of their partner's contribution. In addition, a comprehensive set of questionnaires assessing individual and couple functioning was administered both in the second trimester of the pregnancy and when the babies were about six months old. In this way, it was possible to explore links between these variables and patterns of household work.

Overall, these data point to the crucial role of perceptions of fairness and unfairness. For example, husbands who reported difficulties in individual or couple functioning during the pregnancy often regarded their wives as "doing too much" around the home after the birth. Further, when one spouse was dissatisfied with the partner's contribution around the home, that partner often became increasingly stressed and insecure. As with the results reported by Simpson, these findings emphasize the importance of looking at the transition to parenthood as a process rather than a single event. Both partners are intimately involved in this process: Difficulties and dissatisfactions experienced by one spouse are likely to have implications for the overall relationship, particularly if spouses have poor coping resources and/or negative communication patterns.

Focusing much later in the life cycle, Edwards and Noller examine marital communication in the context of spousal caregiving among elderly couples where one suffers from a physical disability. This transition is a difficult and stressful one because of the changes in the balance of the relationship, with a partner who has previously been relatively autonomous in functioning becoming dependent on the other for even basic needs. These researchers explore the effects of gender and role (caregiver, carereceiver) on the goals and strategies employed by these couples when dealing with issues in the relationship. The theoretical basis for this work was Communication Accommodation Theory (CAT), which focuses on the ways speakers modify their communication style in order to achieve the desired goals of an interaction. These modifications are seen as being based on the speaker's perceptions of their interaction partner's communicative competence. Although these modifications can be helpful in many contexts, a problem that often arises during communication with elderly people is the tendency for carers to use a patronizing style of communication that may be seen by the carereceiver as showing a lack of respect. Such communication may reinforce negative stereotypes of aging, and may have a detrimental effect on the well-being of carereceivers.

According to Communication Accommodation Theory, there are four major strategies that speakers use to modify their communication when dealing with children or the elderly. Two of these were particularly evident in the communication of the elderly couples in this study: Interpretability involves modifying the complexity of the communication to assist the listener in understanding the message, and interpersonal control involves using such behaviors as holding the floor and initiating topic changes to control the flow of the interaction. Many of the carers' utterances involved the use of these strategies.

Overall, the communication of the elderly spouses was influenced mainly by role rather than by gender. The communication patterns were generally consistent with the carer having the more powerful role and the carereceiver being more passive. This situation is just what would be expected given that one spouse had been officially designated as the carer of the other. Despite the finding that spousal carers used strategies that appeared controlling, their intentions were generally positive, with their main concern being to promote understanding between themselves and their carereceivers. Interestingly, one of the ways that caregivers used their power was by controlling topic changes and avoiding contentious issues. Given that requiring care from one's spouse involves a major transition in the relationship, communication between the couple is critical in affecting levels of stress, and hence the quality of the relationship.

Despite the very different life-cycle stages involved, both the transitions discussed in this section tend to be stressful for both partners. Both transitions change, at least to some extent, the roles that marital partners play, and require them to negotiate new ways of interacting. Spouses who perceive their partner as caring and supportive are likely to cope more effectively and make a smoother transition.

CHAPTER FOURTEEN

Adult Attachment, the Transition to Parenthood, and Marital Well-Being

Jeffry A. Simpson, W. Steven Rholes,
Lorne Campbell, Carol Wilson, and Sisi Tran

The transition to parenthood is one of the most stressful and life-altering events that many people ever face (Belsky & Pensky, 1988). Compared to other life transitions, it is unique in that most people experience it (United States Department of Census, 2000), its onset is typically known and often planned, and it involves a fairly uniform sequence of stages and experiences through which most people pass. For many couples, having a child is associated with declines in marital quality over time (Belsky, 1985; Cowan, Cowan, Core, & Core, 1978). However, variation in marital quality also increases across the transition period (Tucker & Aron, 1993), suggesting that while some couples experience decrements in marital well-being, some show improvements. Which couples fare well and which ones fare poorly, and what is happening in their marriages across the transition period?

In this chapter, we address these questions by applying principles from attachment theory (Bowlby, 1969; 1973; 1980). After reviewing prior research and models of the variables that predict changes in marital well-being across the transition to parenthood, we discuss how attachment theory sheds light on which individuals in which marriages should be more versus less susceptible to experiencing downturns in marriage. We propose that attachment security should serve as an "inner resource" (Mikulincer & Florian, 1998) that allows secure people to cope with the trials and tribulations of new parenthood more effectively, buffering them from downturns in marriage. Conversely, when

The writing of this chapter was supported by National Institute of Mental Health grant MH49599 to Jeffry A. Simpson and W. Steven Rholes. Correspondence should be addressed to either Jeffry A. Simpson or W. Steven Rholes, Department of Psychology, Texas A & M University, College Station TX, 77843-4235; e-mail correspondence jas@psyc.tamu.edu or wsr@psyc.tamu.edu.

faced with the chronic stresses of new parenthood, many insecurely attached individuals – particularly highly ambivalent (preoccupied) ones – should process and interpret interpersonal events in defensive ways that may amplify their worst fears, resulting in precipitous declines in marital quality.

We then present the findings of a longitudinal research project that assessed new parents' (both wives' and their husbands') attachment orientations and perceptions of their spouse, themselves, and their marriage six weeks prior to the birth of their first child and six months after birth. This is one of the first studies to examine how individuals' perceptions of their spouses and marriages systematically forecast pre-to-postbirth *changes* in marital well-being in certain individuals. We conclude by discussing how an attachment perspective extends our understanding of how and why certain people experience serious relationship difficulties across the transition period, and we speculate about what individuals might do to maintain, or possibly enhance, marital well-being across this difficult period.

THE TRANSITION TO PARENTHOOD
AND MARITAL WELL-BEING

For many couples, the birth of a first baby launches a myriad of significant marital changes. Following childbirth, spouses usually spend less time together, engage in fewer joint activities, have more conflict, and report decreased sexual activity (Cowan et al., 1978; Levy-Shiff, 1994). In many marriages, these negative changes merely compound the already stressful and taxing nature of child care. Prospective studies (that is, those assessing marriages both before and after childbirth) have documented modest but significant declines in marital satisfaction in most new parents, particularly for wives (Belsky & Pensky, 1988; Cowan & Cowan, 2000). These declines in satisfaction tend to be associated with heightened marital conflict and increased discrepancies between spouses' respective views of their marriage (Cowan, Cowan, Heming, Coysh, Curtis-Boles, & Boles, 1985), reduced paternal involvement or increased maternal involvement in childcare (Levy-Shiff, 1994), lower prepartum marital satisfaction (Cowan & Cowan, 1988; Wright, Henggeler, & Craig, 1986), violated prepartum role expectations (Cowan & Cowan, 1988; Gottlieb & Pancer, 1988), strongly sex-typed division of labor (Belsky, Lang, & Huston, 1986), deficient affiliative and care-giving behaviors in the marriage after birth (Levy-Shiff, 1994), and deficient social support (Cowan & Cowan, 2000).

Though most studies have found general declines in marital well-being across the transition period, a few have reported no general declines (McHale & Huston, 1985; Ryder, 1973). Some couples, in fact, show significant *improvements* in marital satisfaction and functioning after childbirth (see Belsky & Rovine, 1990; Cowan & Cowan, 1988; 2000). Cowan and Cowan (1988), for instance, report cases of increased sexual activity, enhanced feelings of closeness, and more efficient problem solving for certain spouses in certain marriages. Considered together, these findings indicate that not all new parents experience downturns in marriage following the birth of a first child.

MODELS OF THE TRANSITION TO PARENTHOOD

Several investigators have developed models to explain how the transition to parenthood affects marital quality and functioning in different couples over time. Broadly speaking, these models can be classified in two categories: *ecological/environmental models* that focus on how contemporary environmental conditions impact marriages, and *dispositional models* that address how past relationship experiences affect current marital functioning. The majority of ecological/environmental models are grounded in social-cognitive learning theory and principles. According to these models, changes in the perceived balance of positive versus negative experiences during the transition to parenthood should influence vacillations and long-term changes in marital quality. More specifically, judgments of marital dissatisfaction should be based on the degree to which spouses experience negative moods and blame one another for problems during the transition period. For the most part, ecological/environmental models address perceptions of current environmental and relationship events, and ignore whether systematically biased perceptions of the partner or marriage deriving from prior relationship experiences in childhood and adolescence might affect assessments of marital quality and functioning.

Levy-Shiff (1994), for example, has developed a five-factor ecological model that posits that marital changes across the transition are due to shifts in parent psychological characteristics, child characteristics, family variables, social networks, and cultural/societal norms. For example, societal variables such as the relative importance of work and career goals may be associated with declines in marital adjustment, particularly when spouses disagree about household responsibilities or the division of tasks. However, in families or cultures in which sex roles are more distinct and women's parenting roles are valued, declines in marital adjustment should be less severe. Recently, Levy-Shiff, Dimitrovsky, Shulman, and Har-Even (1998) have proposed that the way in which individuals appraise parenthood (for example, the degree to which they view parenthood as challenging, threatening, stressful, or controllable), the extent to which they use different coping strategies (for example, problem-focused versus emotion-focused coping), and the availability of social support should jointly predict changes in marital well-being across the transition period.

Other researchers have sought to explain the effects of the transition to parenthood by specifying how dispositional variables molded by prior relationship experiences might affect marital functioning. Unlike ecological/environmental models, most dispositional models attempt to delineate how and why experiences in past relationships (for example, with parents) can affect marital interaction and outcomes after a child is born. Cowan and Cowan (1988), for example, have developed a model addressing "family of origin" effects. This model predicts that people who (a) had more positive relationships with their opposite-sex parent during childhood and (b) had parents whose marriages were happier, should experience greater satisfaction in their own marriages following childbirth. Indeed, perceptions of greater conflict in one or both spouses' families of origin do predict postpartum declines in marital satisfaction (Cowan & Cowan, 2000).

Moreover, Antonucci and Mikus (1988) have speculated that major, unresolved issues from an individual's past (for example, issues involving dependence, autonomy, intimacy, deprivation, control, anger, or separateness) should become salient during pregnancy and across the transition period. When these issues resurface, new parents should reexamine and try to resolve old conflicts, instigating changes in self-perceptions and their marital relationships. Supporting this model, Belsky and Isabella (1985) have found that husbands and wives who report being raised in rejecting, emotionally cold households have views of their marriages that become more discrepant from their spouse's views over the transition period. Furthermore, wives who report less rejection and greater acceptance from their own parents experience smaller declines – and sometimes slight improvements – in marital adjustment across the transition.

Most models connecting past relationship experiences with current marital quality and functioning across the transition period have been largely descriptive. Few have been couched within a major theoretical perspective. Recently, however, investigators have utilized attachment theory to more fully explain *why* the transition period has such variable effects on people with different relationship histories. Cowan and Cowan (2000), for example, have begun to explore how internal working models and the security of spouses' own childhood relationships with their parents are related to marital conflict and warmth following childbirth. Mikulincer and Florian (1998) have shown that romantic attachment styles moderate the impact of becoming a new parent on long-term mental health, such that new mothers who are securely attached tend to be more resilient and display better mental health across the transition than do insecure mothers.

Most recently, Alexander, Feeney, Hohaus, and Noller (2001) have examined how romantic attachment styles are related to the use of different coping strategies across the transition, revealing that relations between attachment styles and patterns of coping tend to be partially mediated through appraisals of strain (stress) and coping resources (self-esteem and perceptions of social support). In what follows, we elaborate on how and why internal working models of attachment to romantic partners should predispose certain individuals to view their marriages differently, and to undergo changes in marital satisfaction and functioning during this stressful life event.

ATTACHMENT THEORY

In developing attachment theory, Bowlby (1969; 1973; 1980) wanted to understand why individuals typically respond to prolonged parental separations by displaying the sequence of protest, despair, and detachment, and why people differ in how they regulate and cope with negative emotions. Bowlby began formulating attachment theory after observing the debilitating effects of prolonged maternal deprivation on primates (Bowlby, 1969), juvenile thieves (Bowlby, 1944), and institutionalized children (Bowlby, 1958). On the basis of these observations, he conjectured that care-giving experiences with attachment figures – especially in situations where individuals are distressed and need comfort – have significant and lasting effects on how people view themselves and significant others across the lifespan (Bowlby, 1979). Bowlby claimed that sensitive, responsive care giving tends to encourage the development of secure working models, the basic constituents of which are beliefs that one is worthy of others' love and care, and that attachment figures will generally be available, trustworthy, and caring. Insensitive, unresponsive care giving, in contrast, usually promotes insecure models, which involve views of the self as unworthy and of attachment figures as uncaring, unavailable, and untrustworthy. Although working models can change when new, incongruent, or inconsistent attachment experiences are encountered, Bowlby (1973) believed that working models typically lead individuals to process social information in model-consistent and confirming ways. Accordingly, working models tend to remain fairly stable across time.

Working models are thought to contain multiple beliefs, expectations, and emotions that guide how people process information relevant to relationships and how they behave toward attachment figures (Collins & Allard, 2001; Collins & Read, 1994). Working models that compel people to doubt or question their self-worth in relationships, for instance, can selectively direct attention toward possible signs of abandonment, distort interpretations of recent events that actually increase the perceived likelihood of being left, or bias memories from past relationships that accentuate the perceived likelihood of relationship loss (see Cassidy & Berlin, 1994). Indeed, one of the hallmarks of attachment insecurity is the tendency to process attachment-relevant information in a biased, defensive, and often negative manner (Mikulincer & Florian, 1998). Instead of evaluating or judging their partners according to what they factually say or do, insecurely attached individuals often monitor, encode, interpret, and remember the actions of their partners in ways that verify and sustain their negative working models (cf. Collins & Feeney, 2000).

Securely attached adults have had most of their needs for proximity and comfort met in past attachment relationships (Ainsworth, Blehar, Waters, & Wall, 1978; Hazan & Shaver, 1994). These positive experiences, in turn, lead securely attached persons to turn toward significant others for comfort and support when they are upset (Mikulincer, Florian, & Weller, 1993; Simpson, Rholes, & Nelligan, 1992). Secure people typically are less defensive, evaluate their partners and relationships more benevolently, and routinely use constructive problem-focused and support-seeking modes of coping, especially when they are distressed (Mikulincer & Florian, 1998). Consequently, if their romantic partners offer less-than-desired levels of support, secure individuals should make more benevolent (relationship-enhancing) attributions for their partner's deficient support, and should not let experiences in past relationships unduly taint or color their current relationship assessments (Bowlby, 1973).

These attributes should allow secure individuals to remain optimistic, supportive, and resilient during stressful life events that would overwhelm other people. In essence, security serves as an "inner resource" that helps secure people obtain support from attachment figures when it is needed. At the same time, it permits secure people to appraise stressful life experiences more positively, resolve emergent difficulties with their partners more constructively, and to cope with stressful events – those both internal and external to their relationships – more effectively. These attributes should *buffer* secure people from experiencing declines in relationship satisfaction and functioning during stressful life transitions. Furthermore, if secure people have highly supportive partners, stressful experiences might actually spark *improvements* in relationship quality and functioning, at least in certain situations (see Simpson & Rholes, 1994).

Avoidantly attached individuals, on the other hand, have endured persistent rejections in past relationships (Crittenden & Ainsworth, 1989). To suppress the pain and anger associated with chronic rejection, highly avoidant people learn to be "compulsively self-reliant," especially when they are distressed (Bowlby, 1973; 1979). Two types of avoidant adults have been identified in past research (Bartholomew & Horowitz, 1991): fearful-avoidants (who have negative self-views), and dismissive-avoidants (who have positive self-views); however, all avoidant adults harbor negative and distrusting views of others (Bartholomew, 1990).

In order to keep their attachment systems from being chronically activated, avoidant persons recruit cognitive, emotional, and behavioral defenses that help them to (a) avoid situations that might activate their attachment systems, (b) dampen activation when it occurs, (c) downplay the importance of attachment-related needs and issues, and (d) enact distancing/withdrawal coping strategies to control and mitigate negative affect (Kobak & Sceery, 1988; Main, Kaplan, & Cassidy, 1985). By using these defenses, avoidant persons decrease the likelihood of experiencing further rejections from current attachment figures, ensuring that their attachment systems will remain deactivated (Bartholomew, 1990). Since they have received little support in past relationships, avoidant people should not be bothered by receiving low levels of support (especially emotional support) from their current romantic partners. Indeed, they are less likely than other individuals to seek support from their partners during stressful events (Mikulincer et al., 1993; Simpson et al., 1992).

Ambivalently attached (that is, preoccupied) individuals have received inconsistent or unpredictable care and support in past relationships (Cassidy & Berlin, 1994). As a result, they typically resent attachment figures and continually question their own self-worth. Over time, highly ambivalent people develop negative self-views, and tentatively positive (that is, hopeful yet suspicious and uncertain) views of significant others. Given their negative self-views, highly ambivalent persons remain vigilant to signs or cues of possible abandonment (especially perceived declines in their partners' support or commitment). As a result, highly ambivalent persons vacillate between seeking support from their partners and reacting angrily toward them (Ainsworth et al., 1978; Cassidy & Berlin, 1994), which may explain why they report large emotional swings in their relationships (Tidwell, Reis, & Shaver, 1996). In many situations, their erratic behavior may emanate from beliefs that they have not (or will not) receive sufficient support from their attachment figures in times of real need (Cassidy & Berlin, 1994). Accordingly, highly ambivalent individuals should often perceive deficient support, unless they happen to have unusually supportive partners. These negative perceptions, in turn, should have pernicious effects on the quality and functioning of their relationships, particularly during stressful life events (Ognibene & Collins, 1998).

Three types of stressful situations have been conjectured to activate the attachment system (Kobak & Duemmler, 1994): situations that (1) induce fear, (2) destabilize attachment relationships, and (3) challenge individuals beyond their abilities. Depending on the content of their working models, individuals should also differ in the degree to which specific situations trigger their attachment systems. Highly avoidant persons, for example, should be more likely to experience attachment activation in situations that require giving or receiving emotional support (Mikulincer & Florian, 1998; Simpson et al., 1992). As discussed previously, having to give or receive emotional support should be highly aversive to avoidant people because these situations should elicit negative, painful memories of past rejections. Given their deep-seated concerns about loss and abandonment, highly ambivalent individuals should experience attachment activation in situations that might precipitate the destabilization or eventual demise of their current relationships (Mikulincer & Florian, 1998; Simpson, Rholes, & Phillips, 1996).

ADULT ATTACHMENT AND THE TRANSITION TO PARENTHOOD

According to Bowlby (1988), the transition to parenthood should have powerful effects on highly ambivalent individuals. This should be particularly true for highly ambivalent women, who not only are likely to enter parenthood with reservations about their spouse's supportiveness, but must endure the stresses of giving birth and caring for their new baby.

Anxiety/Ambivalence

Highly ambivalent individuals worry and ruminate about not receiving sufficient support from their attachment figures in times of need (Cassidy & Berlin, 1994), and the chronic stress associated with having a child should amplify these concerns for many ambivalent people. The degree to which these concerns adversely affect marital perceptions and behavior should depend, however, on how much spousal support ambivalent women perceive available prior to childbirth. If highly ambivalent women believe that their husbands are (or will be) available and supportive across the transition period, their working models ought to have relatively weak effects on their marital perceptions and behavior. Conversely, if highly ambivalent women perceive that their husbands are not (or will not be) available and supportive (which may be true for most highly ambivalent women), their working models should be strongly activated and, therefore, have stronger and more pernicious effects on their perceptions and behavior.

Thus, we hypothesized that if highly ambivalent women entered parenthood with lingering doubts about their husbands' supportiveness, they would report significant pre-to-postnatal declines in perceptions of spousal support, marital satisfaction, and efforts to seek support from their husbands, along with significant *increases* in perceptions of anger received from their husbands. Prenatal perceptions of low spousal support, in other words, should moderate the effects of women's ambivalence on pre-to-postpartum changes in marital quality and functioning over the transition period. Given ambivalent women's preoccupation with their partners' availability and supportiveness, the moderation (interaction) effects involving satisfaction, support seeking, and perceptions of anger might be mediated through changes (declines) in perceived spousal support from the prepartum to the postpartum period. That is, we expected mediated moderation effects (see Baron & Kenny, 1986). Our general mediated moderation model is shown in Figure 14.1.

In summary, we expected that highly ambivalent women would report significant pre-to-postpartum declines in perceived spousal support, declines in marital satisfaction, declines in seeking spousal

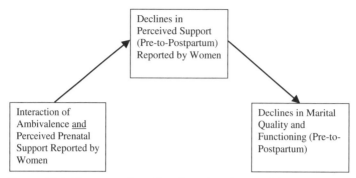

Figure 14.1. The general mediated moderation model.

support, and increases in perceptions of spousal anger (directed at them), especially if they entered parenthood perceiving lower levels of spousal support (Hypothesis 1). In terms of the more proximate psychological processes generating these effects, we reasoned that perceptions of declining spousal support across the transition period might mediate associations between wives' prenatal ambivalence and changes in measures of marital quality over time (Hypothesis 2).

Past research has found that men who date or are married to highly ambivalent women tend to be very dissatisfied with their relationships (Feeney, 1994; 1999; Kirkpatrick & Davis, 1994; Simpson, 1990). This marked dissatisfaction could stem from the belief that they cannot fulfill their female partners' seemingly endless needs for comfort and support (Cassidy & Berlin, 1994). It might also emanate from the realization that their female partners do not give them sufficient "credit" for the support they offer. Accordingly, we expected that men who were married to highly ambivalent women would also report pre-to-postnatal declines in marital satisfaction and increases in anger directed at their wives, particularly if their wives perceived them as less supportive in the prenatal period (which, as discussed earlier, should activate wives' ambivalent working models and prototypic styles of behavior; Hypothesis 3). Furthermore, pre-to-postpartum changes in wives' perceptions of spousal support might also partially mediate relations between wives' prenatal ambivalence and changes in *husbands'* marital quality over the transition period (Hypothesis 4). Finally, if the working models of highly ambivalent women lead them to "underperceive" spousal support, men married to highly ambivalent women should report offering more support than their wives believe is available to them. (Hypothesis 5).

Avoidance

As discussed earlier, highly avoidant persons value independence and self-reliance, dislike situations that involve giving or receiving support, and suppress their emotions and withdraw from others when distressed (Crittenden & Ainsworth, 1989; Simpson et al., 1992). Because they neither seek nor want support – especially emotional forms of support – when distressed, the stress and challenges of caring for a new infant may not have adverse effects on their marriages, at least in the early stages of the transition to parenthood (see Rholes, Simpson, Campbell, & Grich, 2001). The stress and pressures associated with the transition may, of course, create feelings of anxiety or depression in some highly avoidant women. If, however, such women neither want nor expect their husbands to assuage such feelings (preferring to handle their problems self-reliantly), their perceptions of their spouses may not become more negative across time. As a result, the marriages of highly avoidant women may be relatively unaffected by the early stages of the transition, even if they find the transition to be taxing. Thus, our only hypothesis regarding women's avoidance was that more avoidant women would seek less support from their husbands than less avoidant women would (Hypothesis 6).

Security

Current conceptualizations of adult attachment define security as the absence of anxiety and avoidance (see Brennan, Clark, & Shaver, 1998; Griffin & Bartholomew, 1994). Mikulincer and Florian (1998) contend that attachment security serves as an "inner resource" that *buffers* secure people from experiencing personal and relational declines. Past research, however, has noted that some couples actually experience improvements in marital satisfaction and functioning following the birth of their first child (Belsky & Rovine, 1990; Cowan & Cowan, 2000). Simpson and Rholes (1994) have conjectured that if securely attached people work with their partners to overcome the challenges posed by a major stressor, such experiences might strengthen (improve) their relationships. This premise implies that, if securely attached women have (or perceive they have) highly supportive husbands, the combination of high security and high levels of spousal support might predict *accentuation* (improvement) in marital quality over the transition to parenthood.

A STUDY OF THE TRANSITION TO PARENTHOOD

Sample and Procedures

To test these hypotheses, we conducted a study of the transition to parenthood (see Rholes et al., 2001). One hundred and six husbands and their wives completed a battery of self-report measures (privately and without consulting each other) six weeks before the birth of their first child and six months after the birth. The average age of women and men was 28.5 years, and couples had been married for an average of 3.8 years.

During the prenatal and postnatal assessment periods, both spouses completed scales assessing their attachment orientations toward romantic partners *in general* (measured by the Adult Attachment Questionnaire; Simpson et al., 1996) and their marital satisfaction (measured by the Satisfaction Subscale of the Dyadic Adjustment Scale; Spanier, 1976).

Wives also completed scales assessing how available and emotionally supportive they perceived their husbands to be (measured by the Social Provisions Scale; Cutrona, 1984), how often their husbands behaved angrily toward them (measured by the Test of Negative Social Exchange; Finch, Okum, Pool, & Ruehlman, 1999), and the degree to which they sought support from their husbands (measured by the Coping Scale; Moos, Cronkite, Billings, & Finney, 1983). Because this study focused on support provided by husbands to their wives, men completed parallel scales that assessed how available and emotionally supportive they behaved toward their wives, and how often they behaved angrily toward their wives.

Primary Results

Corroborating previous research (see Belsky & Pensky, 1988, for a review), the transition period was difficult for the majority of couples. On average, wives and husbands reported statistically significant pre-to-postnatal declines in marital satisfaction. In addition, wives perceived less support and greater anger from their husbands and reported seeking less support from the prepartum to the postpartum period, while husbands reported providing less support to their wives across this period.

Although mean changes in marital quality and functioning are informative, we were mainly interested in how wives' attachment orientations and their prenatal perceptions of their husbands predicted pre-to-postpartum *changes* in marriage across the transition period. To test for changes in wives' perceptions of their husbands' support, their husbands' level of anger, their own support seeking, and their own marital satisfaction, we partialed out wives' prenatal (Time 1) scores on each measure from their postnatal (Time 2) scores in hierarchical regression analyses (Cohen & Cohen, 1983). We followed similar procedures to test for changes in husbands' marital measures. We also controlled for the modest correlations between wives' and husbands' attachment scores by partialing out the attachment scores of participants' *spouses* in each analysis. This allowed us to isolate the effects of participants' *own* attachment scores (that is, attachment actor effects), independent of their partners' attachment scores (that is, attachment partner effects).

Ambivalence
The most dramatic changes in marital quality occurred for highly ambivalent women. As predicted, a series of interactions involving wives' prenatal ambivalence and their prenatal perceptions of spousal support were found. Supporting Hypothesis 1, more ambivalent wives who perceived less prenatal support from their husbands reported significantly larger declines in spousal support (relative to other women) from the prenatal to the postnatal period. Moreover, wives who were more ambivalent and perceived lower prenatal support sought significantly less support from their husbands and reported significant declines in marital satisfaction. Highly ambivalent women who perceived higher levels of prenatal spousal support, on the other hand, were just as satisfied with their marriages as less ambivalent women. Importantly, all of these effects remained significant when husbands' attachment scores were statistically controlled. Thus, the steep declines in marital well-being reported by highly ambivalent women who entered parenthood with lower expectations of spousal support were *not* attributable to the fact that their husbands were less secure.

As just described, the interaction of wives' ambivalence and perceptions of prenatal spousal support predicted changes in marital satisfaction and support seeking over time. Hypothesis 2 tested whether the relation between changes in marital well-being and the interaction of ambivalence and perceptions of prenatal support was mediated by

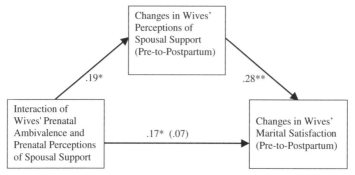

Figure 14.2. The mediated moderation model representing the interaction between wives' prenatal (Time 1) ambivalence and their prenatal (Time 1) perceptions of spousal support predicting pre-to-postpartum changes in marital satisfaction, mediated through pre-to-postpartum changes in wives' perceptions of spousal support. The .17 Beta indicates the direct effect of the interaction term on changes in marital satisfaction; the .07 Beta reflects the effect controlling for changes in perceptions of support. * $p < .05$, ** $p < .01$

declining perceptions of spousal support across the transition period. In other words, we wanted to determine whether more ambivalent women who perceived lower spousal support six weeks prior to childbirth would perceive significantly lower levels of support at six months postpartum, and whether these declines in perceived support would mediate downward changes in marital satisfaction or support seeking. These mediated moderation predictions were tested using procedures recommended by Baron and Kenny (1986). A significant effect emerged only for changes in marital satisfaction. As shown in Figure 14.2, perceptions of declining spousal support across the transition to parenthood may be one of the proximate psychological mechanisms through which certain prenatal variables (that is, the combination of high ambivalence and low perceived spousal support in women) instigate marital changes (that is, declines in marital satisfaction over the transition).

Husbands also reported significant marital changes contingent on their *wives'* prenatal ambivalence and perceptions of spousal support. Corroborating Hypothesis 3, if their wives believed they were less supportive prenatally, men married to more ambivalent women also became significantly *less* satisfied, reported being *less* supportive, and admitted behaving *more* angrily over the transition period, relative to men married to less ambivalent women. Conversely, if wives viewed their husbands as more supportive during the prenatal period, men married to more ambivalent women became slightly *more* satisfied, *less* likely to display anger, and *more* supportive across the transition. Further analyses showed that the association of wives' prebirth ambivalence and perceptions of support with changes in husbands' self-reported support was mediated by declines in wives' perceptions of spousal support. This finding suggests that wives' perceptions of husbands as unsupportive may discourage their husbands from providing support, or may lead them to adopt their wives' views of them as unsupportive.

Contrary to Hypothesis 4, changes in wives' perceptions of support did *not* mediate the relation between the interaction of wives' prenatal ambivalence and perceptions of support and their *husbands'* changes in marital satisfaction. In line with Hypothesis 5, however, highly ambivalent women did report receiving less support than their husbands said they actually provided, even when their husbands' attachment orientations and personality traits (for example, neuroticism, extraversion, and agreeableness) were statistically controlled. This finding is important because it suggests that a portion of the variance underlying highly ambivalent wives' perceptions of deficient spousal support may stem from their working models, rather than being entirely attributable to the characteristics and behavior of their husbands.

Avoidance

As expected, avoidance did not predict significant changes in wives' perceptions of spousal support, their husbands' anger, or their own marital satisfaction. However, confirming Hypothesis 6, women who were more avoidant sought significantly less support from their husbands across the transition compared to less avoidant women.

Security

Greater attachment security has been conjectured to buffer people from negative personal and relational outcomes that commonly follow stressful life events (Mikulincer & Florian, 1998). It is also possible, however, that the optimistic and benevolent working models harbored by highly secure people might lead them to experience significant *improvements* in relationship well-being in certain stressful situations, especially if secure people and their partners work together and successfully overcome major obstacles (Simpson & Rholes, 1994). (Secure individuals tend to score low on both the anxiety and avoidance attachment dimensions; Bartholomew, 1990.) Unfortunately, only a few husbands or wives in this sample reported noteworthy improvements in marital satisfaction over the transition period. Marital satisfaction increased by one-half of a standard deviation or more for only 10% of the wives and 8% of the husbands, whereas it decreased by this amount for 42% of the wives and 33% of the husbands. Therefore, although security may buffer spouses from marital declines during the transition to parenthood, it does not appear to be associated with significant improvements in marital quality (at least at six months postpartum). Whether accentuation effects might be found at later points in the transition (after peak levels of stress, social adjustment, and sleep deprivation have subsided) needs to be addressed in future studies.

IMPLICATIONS AND EXTENSIONS

The present study raises several intriguing questions about the perception and provision of spousal support during the transition to parenthood, especially in marriages where wives are highly ambivalent and enter parenthood perceiving (and most likely expecting) deficient support from their husbands. In what follows, we address eight fundamental questions, most of which center on ambivalent attachment.

Question 1

Regardless of their degree of attachment security, men married to highly ambivalent women reported that they provided less support during the transition period than did men married to less ambivalent women. Nevertheless, these men claimed to provide more support than their ambivalent wives thought they received. These husbands also reported that they behaved more angrily toward their wives during the transition period. What might explain these effects?

One possibility is that highly ambivalent women may choose husbands who are predisposed to view them negatively and treat them badly. This explanation, however, is problematic. In our study, highly ambivalent women (relative to other women) were *not* more likely to be married to more insecurely attached, neurotic, or disagreeable men. In other words, they were no more likely to have husbands who were highly cynical, difficult, demanding, or negative than other women (cf. Karney & Bradbury, 1997). A more plausible explanation may be that husbands *reacted* more negatively to highly ambivalent wives. Moreover, the heightened negativity of such men might have been compounded by the realization that they were not receiving "full credit" for the support they had already given to their highly ambivalent wives.

Question 2

Assuming this conjecture is at least partially valid, what might highly ambivalent women be doing to discourage or undermine spousal support? According to attachment theorists (Bowlby, 1973; Cassidy & Berlin, 1994), highly ambivalent people become anxious and distraught when they perceive that their partners might be withdrawing from them. However, they do not always seek support from their partners in these situations, particularly when they are acutely distressed (Fraley & Shaver, 1998; Simpson et al., 1992).

Husbands of highly ambivalent women, therefore, may have received fewer direct requests to provide support during the transition period, especially considering the high level of distress being experienced by their wives. Highly ambivalent women may have also been uncertain about the type of support they wanted and, as a result, may not have communicated their needs and desires very clearly. Moreover, such women may not have given their husbands sufficient credit for the support their husbands thought they had offered. For example, instead of attributing supportive behaviors to the possible benevolence or good intentions of their husbands (by making positive partner-based attributions), highly ambivalent women might have attributed the support they received to situational factors (by making external or self-based attributions). To compound matters, husbands of highly ambivalent wives may have thought that they had become a target of their wives' frustrations, instead of being viewed as a possible source of comfort and support. Across the transition period, some or all of these factors could have conspired to make the husbands of highly ambivalent women feel incapable of meeting their wives' needs, eliciting both higher levels of anger as well as reduced support.

Question 3

Do highly ambivalent women perceive less spousal support only because their husbands provide less? As noted above, men married to more ambivalent women admitted that they gave less support to their wives than was provided by men married to less ambivalent women.

Since providing lower levels of support during the transition to parenthood ought to be socially undesirable, husbands' reports of lower support probably contain a kernel of truth. However, the fact that more ambivalent women perceived significantly less support than their husbands reported giving, whereas less ambivalent women actually perceived *more* support, insinuates that working models could be systematically distorting perceptions of support in both negative and positive directions. It is conceivable, of course, that men married to highly ambivalent women overstated or overestimated the amount of support they actually gave to their wives. Hence, the fact that highly ambivalent women perceived less support than their husbands reported giving does not provide conclusive evidence of bias among these wives.

Although ambivalent wives' perceptions of spousal support might be veridical, several lines of evidence suggest that other factors may contribute to this effect. First, past research has shown that persons who typically believe that social support is less available are less likely to remember others' helpful actions and more likely to interpret supportive behaviors in negative terms (Lakey & Cassady, 1990). Second, previous studies have shown that working models tend to slant cognitive and perceptual processes in model-confirming and sustaining ways (see Collins & Allard, 2001). Third, the difference in perceptions of support reported by more versus less ambivalent women in the present study remained significant when several potential confounds were statistically controlled (such as husbands' self-reports of support provided, husbands' degree of ambivalence and avoidance, their neuroticism, extraversion, and agreeableness, and both spouses' reports of marital satisfaction). A large portion of the variance in wives' perceptions of spousal support, therefore, is associated with factors other than these potential confounds. Viewed in its entirety, this evidence suggests that the working models of highly ambivalent wives *may* bias their perceptions of spousal support in a negative direction.

Question 4

Why do many highly ambivalent women have such negative perceptions of spousal support? According to attachment theory (Bowlby, 1973), highly ambivalent people crave unconditional and complete love, yearn to be the center of their partners' lives, and want their relationships to last forever. Set against these lofty ideals, many highly ambivalent women should view their husbands' support as deficient or incomplete, particularly when they feel distressed and crave support. Given that they felt unloved or unlovable in earlier relationships, highly ambivalent adults require strong and unequivocal displays of love from their current partners to bolster self-doubts and quell deep-seated worries that their partners might eventually leave them. Consequently, they expect – and sometimes demand – frequent and strong expressions of love from their partners. To facilitate these expressions, highly ambivalent individuals strive to attract and retain their partner's undivided attention, and they hypervigilantly monitor their partner's behavior for signs that their partner may be withdrawing from, or decreasing their commitment to, the relationship (see Cassidy & Berlin, 1994; Simpson, Ickes, & Grich, 1999).

These factors could explain why highly ambivalent women appeared to have negatively biased perceptions of their husbands' support in the present study. Highly ambivalent people enter situations with very high expectations and needs for support. Ironically, it is in situations where highly ambivalent people need support the *most* that their deep-seated doubts and worries about being unsupported or abandoned are triggered, leading them to misinterpret, discount, or discredit *some* of the support their partners may, in fact, have given them (see Collins & Feeney, 2000). Hence, the disparity between their ideal expectations of support and their current perceptions of partner support should be greatest in highly stressful situations, possibly generating even more negative perceptions of support.

Question 5

Are highly ambivalent women certain to experience marital declines during the transition to parenthood? Fortunately, the answer is no. As the present study reveals, if highly ambivalent women enter parenthood with positive views of their husbands' support, neither they nor their husbands experience significant declines in satisfaction. Thus, even though men may report being especially unhappy with ambivalent romantic partners (Feeney, 1999), long-term relationships with highly ambivalent women can be just as rewarding as relationships with more secure women. Other research has shown that highly ambivalent individuals experience more pronounced highs and lows in their relationships over short periods of time (Tidwell et al., 1996), and that they view their partners and relationships in highly idealized ways, especially when events are going well (Hazan & Shaver, 1987). In conjunction with the current study, these findings suggest that the satisfaction and quality of highly ambivalent individuals' relationships are likely to hinge both on how their partners behave toward them, *and* on how they view their partners. The quality of their relationships, therefore, is not exclusively or irrevocably determined by the nature of their working models.

Question 6

Why are highly ambivalent women dependent on emotional support from their husbands? Strong dependence may arise from the fact that highly ambivalent people have fewer internal resources to maintain and protect their rather tenuous and unstable self-esteem. Consequently, such people may learn to rely heavily on the presence and unwavering attention of their partners to support their vulnerable self-concept and to suppress fears of abandonment. Mikulincer (1995) has found that highly ambivalent people tend to have more negative and poorly integrated self-views. Specifically, their self-views contain more negative attributes, are poorly differentiated and poorly integrated, and are riddled with large, unresolved discrepancies. As a result, when they experience threat to one area of their self-structure (for example, questioning their competence as a new parent), it can spread to other, unrelated areas (for example, questioning their general worth as a spouse or a person). This situation should make it difficult for highly ambivalent people to control and quell negative affect once it has been aroused. Particularly when experiencing chronic stress, highly ambivalent individuals should be more inclined to lash out at their partners, sometimes for reasons that may have nothing to do with their partners' current or recent actions.

Question 7

How can the negative marital outcomes experienced by many highly ambivalent women be ameliorated? In particular, what can husbands do to support highly ambivalent women more effectively? How can highly ambivalent women learn to recognize support when it is genuinely available? And how might highly ambivalent women become less dependent on their husbands for support?

Husbands must first learn how to avoid escalating their wives' aversive behaviors, and how to tolerate negativity without becoming angry, withdrawn, or despondent (see Gottman, 1998; Snyder, 1999). To accomplish this task, husbands eventually need to achieve deeper insight into the specific causes and sources of their wives' distress, en route to developing greater empathic understanding. Wives, on the other hand, must reduce their exclusive reliance on their husbands' attention and support to sustain their self-worth. Initially, wives could identify other life domains within which a stronger and broader sense of self-esteem might be built. Ultimately, however, they must revise their dysfunctional working models, moving toward "earned" security.

Bowlby (1973) distinguished between two types of interpersonal anger: the "anger of hope" (in which individuals communicate their needs clearly, and constructively elicit care and attention from their partners), and the "anger of despair" (in which individuals vent their rage and punish or reprimand their partners in a vengeful manner). Bowlby (1973) observed that highly ambivalent individuals frequently display the anger of despair, particularly in distressing situations (see Rholes, Simpson, & Orina, 1999). While this form of anger usually gains partners' attention quickly and induces compliant behavior, its recurrent use alienates partners. Therefore, highly ambivalent women must learn to seek support in ways that communicate and emphasize their needs constructively, rather than resorting to destructive blame and counterattacks. For their part, husbands of highly ambivalent women need to understand why their wives are so distressed, and refrain from making demeaning personal attributions. Furthermore, both spouses should focus greater attention on each other's positive attributes and behaviors. Selective attention to negative aspects of partners and relationships – which is one hallmark of ambivalence – should only amplify the downward spiral of dysfunctional cognitions and affect.

Question 8

How can security be increased in insecure people? According to Main and Goldwyn (1998), persons who are insecure as a result of adverse experiences in past attachment relationships can learn to "set aside" earlier negative experiences. This process can minimize the negative impact of earlier relationships on how people think and feel in their current relationships. With time, insecure persons can develop a sense of "earned security," whereby working models of self and others are recast within a more positive perspective. Greater security can also be achieved through understanding and forgiving the past transgressions of others (Main & Goldwyn, 1998). By doing so, persons with insecure relationship histories may be able to change certain dysfunctional expectations (for example, that all romantic partners, including the current one, can never be trusted) and gradually adopt more benevolent attitudes toward their partners. Through these processes, rigid defensiveness and obsessive preoccupation associated with past relationships can be replaced with a more constructive and benevolent focus on the present.

CONCLUSION

Highly ambivalent people, of course, should not be blamed for having working models that might accentuate or amplify difficulties in their relationships, particularly during stressful life events. After all, the preoccupied, anxious, and ruminating nature of their models is probably a reflection of how they have been treated by attachment figures in previous relationships. Nevertheless, the working models that individuals bring to parenthood can – and apparently do – have powerful and theoretically meaningful effects on perceptions of partners and marriages across the transition to parenthood. Theoretical perspectives that fail to consider how perceptions of *current* relationships might be influenced by events, memories, or interpretations of *past* relationships are likely to paint an incomplete portrait of how and why the transition to parenthood is more difficult for certain people in certain marriages. Greater attachment security appears to operate as an "inner resource" that effectively buffers individuals from experiencing precipitous marital downturns. Greater ambivalence combined with perceptions of deficient spousal support, by contrast, renders individuals vulnerable to declines in marital well-being. Much remains to be learned about the specific psychological and interpersonal processes responsible for these buffering and deteriorating effects.

REFERENCES

Ainsworth, M. D. S., Blehar, M. C., Waters, E., & Wall, S. (1978). *Patterns of attachment: A psychological study of the strange situation.* Hillsdale, NJ: Lawrence Erlbaum Associates.
Alexander, R. P., Feeney, J. A., Hohaus, L., & Noller, P. (2001). Attachment style and coping resources as predictors of coping strategies in the transition to parenthood. *Personal Relationships, 8,* 137–152.

Antonucci, T. C., & Mikus, K. (1988). The power of parenthood: Personality and attitudinal changes during the transition to parenthood. In G. Y Michaels & W. A. Goldberg (Eds.), *The transition to parenthood: Current theory and research* (pp. 62–84). New York: Cambridge University Press.

Baron, R. M., & Kenny, D. A. (1986). The moderator-mediator variable distinction in social psychological research: Conceptual, strategic, and statistical considerations. *Journal of Personality and Social Psychology, 51,* 1173–1182.

Bartholomew, K. (1990). Avoidance of intimacy: An attachment perspective. *Journal of Social and Personal Relationships, 7,* 147–178.

Bartholomew, K., & Horowitz, L. M. (1991). Attachment styles among young adults: A test of a four-category model. *Journal of Personality and Social Psychology, 61,* 226–243.

Belsky, J. (1985). Exploring individual differences in marital change across the transition to parenthood: The role of violated expectations. *Journal of Marriage and the Family, 47,* 1037–1044.

Belsky, J., & Isabella, R. A. (1985). Marital and parent-child relationships in family of origin and marital change following the birth of a baby: A retrospective analysis. *Child Development, 56,* 342–349.

Belsky, J., Lang, M. E., & Huston, T. L. (1986). Sex-typing and division of labor as determinants of marital change across the transition to parenthood. *Journal of Personality and Social Psychology, 50,* 517–522.

Belsky, J., & Pensky, E. (1988). Marital change across the transition to parenthood. *Marriage and Family Review, 13,* 133–156.

Belsky, J., & Rovine, M. (1990). Q-sort security and first-year nonmaternal care. *New Directions for Child Development, 49,* 7–22.

Bowlby, J. (1944). Forty-four juvenile thieves: Their characters and home life. *International Journal of Psychoanalysis, 25,* 19–52, 107–127.

Bowlby, J. (1958). The nature of the child's ties to his mother. *International Journal of Psychoanalysis, 39,* 350–373.

Bowlby, J. (1969). *Attachment and loss: Attachment: vol. 1.* New York: Basic Books.

Bowlby, J. (1973). *Attachment and loss: Separation: vol. 2.* New York: Basic Books.

Bowlby, J. (1979). *The making and breaking of affectional bonds.* London: Tavistock.

Bowlby, J. (1980). *Attachment and loss: Loss: vol. 3.* New York: Basic Books.

Bowlby, J. (1988). *A secure base: Parent-child attachment and healthy human development.* New York: Basic Books.

Brennan, K. A., Clark, C. L., & Shaver, P. R. (1998). Self-report measurement of adult attachment: An integrative overview. In J. A. Simpson & S. W. Rholes (Eds.), *Attachment theory and close relationships* (pp. 46–76). New York: Guilford Press.

Cassidy, J., & Berlin, L. (1994). The insecure/ambivalent pattern of attachment: Theory and research. *Child Development, 65,* 971–991.

Cohen, J., & Cohen, P. (1983). *Applied multiple regression/correlation analysis for the behavioral sciences.* Hillsdale, NJ: Lawrence Erlbaum Associates.

Collins, N. L., & Allard, L. M. (2001). Cognitive representations of attachment: The content and function of working models. In G. J. O. Fletcher & M. S. Clark (Eds.), *Blackwell handbook of social psychology: Interpersonal processes* (pp. 60–85). Oxford: Blackwell.

Collins, N. L., & Feeney, B. C. (2000). Working models of attachment: Implications for the perception of partner behavior. Paper presented at the International Conference on Personal Relationships, Brisbane, Australia.

Collins, N. L., & Read, S. J. (1994). Cognitive representations of attachment: The structure and function of working models. In K. Bartholomew & D. Perlman (Eds.), *Attachment processes in adulthood* (pp. 53–90). London: Kingsley.

Cowan, C. P., & Cowan, P. A. (2000). *When partners become parents: The big life change in couples.* Mahwah, NJ: Lawrence Erlbaum Associates.

Cowan, P. A., & Cowan, C. P. (1988). Changes in marriage during the transition to parenthood: Must we blame the baby? In G. Y. Michaels & W. A. Goldberg (Eds.), *The transition to parenthood: Current theory and research* (pp. 114–156). New York: Cambridge University Press.

Cowan, C., Cowan, P., Core, L., & Core, J. (1978). Becoming a family: The impact of a first child's birth on the couple's relationship. In L. Newman & W. Miller (Eds.), *The first-child and family formation* (pp. 296–326). Chapel Hill, NC: Carolina Population Center.

Cowan, C. P., Cowan, P. A., Heming, G., Coysh, W. S., Curtis-Boles, H., & Boles, A. J. (1985). Transition to parenthood: His, hers, and theirs. *Journal of Family Issues, 6,* 451–481.

Crittenden, P. M., & Ainsworth, M. (1989). Child maltreatment and attachment theory. In D. Cicchetti & V. Carlson (Eds.), *Clinical maltreatment: Theory and research on the causes and consequences of child abuse and neglect* (pp. 432–463). Cambridge: Cambridge University Press.

Cutrona, C. E. (1984). Social support and stress in the transition to parenthood. *Journal of Abnormal Psychology, 93,* 378–390.

Feeney, J. A. (1994). Attachment styles, communication patterns, and satisfaction across the life cycle of marriage. *Personal Relationships, 1,* 333–348.

Feeney, J. A. (1999). Adult romantic attachment and couple relationships. In J. A. Cassidy & P. R. Shaver (Eds.), *Handbook of attachment: Theory, research, and clinical applications* (pp. 355–377). New York: Guilford Press.

Finch, J. F., Okum, M. A., Poole, G. J., & Ruehlman, L. S. (1999). A comparison of the influence of conflictual and supportive social interactions on psychological distress. *Journal of Personality, 67,* 581–622.

Fraley, R. C., & Shaver, P. R. (1998). Airport separations: A naturalistic study of adult attachment dynamics in separating couples. *Journal of Personality and Social Psychology, 75,* 1198–1212.

Gottlieb, B. H., & Pancer, S. M. (1988). Social networks and the transition to parenthood. In G. Y. Michaels & W. A. Goldberg (Eds.), *The transition to parenthood: Current theory and research* (pp. 235–269). New York: Cambridge University Press.

Gottman, J. M. (1998). Psychology and the study of the marital process. *Annual Review of Psychology, 49,* 169–197.

Griffin, D. W., & Bartholomew, K. (1994). Models of the self and others: Fundamental dimensions underlying measures of adult attachment. *Journal of Personality and Social Psychology, 67,* 430–445.

Hazan, C., & Shaver, P. R. (1987). Romantic love conceptualized as an attachment process. *Journal of Personality and Social Psychology, 52,* 511–524.

Hazan, C., & Shaver, P. R. (1994). Attachment as an organizational framework for research on close relationships. *Psychological Inquiry, 5*, 1–22.

Karney, B. R., & Bradbury, T. N. (1997). Neuroticism, marital interaction, and the trajectory of marital satisfaction. *Journal of Personality and Social Psychology, 72*, 1075–1092.

Kirkpatrick, L. A., & Davis, K. E. (1994). Attachment style, gender, and relationship stability: A longitudinal analysis. *Journal of Personality and Social Psychology, 66*, 502–512.

Kobak, R., & Duemmler, S. (1994). Attachment and conversation: Toward a discourse analysis of adolescent and adult security. In K. Bartholomew & D. Perlman (Eds.), *Attachment processes in adulthood* (pp. 121–149). London: Kingsley.

Kobak, R. R., & Sceery, A. (1988). Attachment in late adolescence: Working models, affect regulation, and representations of self and others. *Child Development, 59*, 135–146.

Lakey, B., & Cassady, P. B. (1990). Cognitive processes in perceived support. *Journal of Personality and Social Psychology, 59*, 337–343.

Levy-Shiff, R. (1994). Individual and contextual correlates of marital change across the transition to parenthood. *Developmental Psychology, 30*, 591–601.

Levy-Shiff, R., Dimitrovsky, L., Shulman, S., & Har-Even, D. (1998). Cognitive appraisals, coping strategies, and support resources as correlates of parenting and infant development. *Developmental Psychology, 34*, 1417–1427.

Main, M., & Goldwyn, R. (1998). Adult attachment scoring and classification system. Unpublished manuscript, University of California at Berkeley.

Main, M., Kaplan, N., & Cassidy, J. (1985). Security in infancy, childhood, and adulthood: A move to the level of representation. *Monographs of the Society for Research in Child Development, 50* (1 & 2, Serial No. 209), 66–104.

McHale, S. M., & Huston, T. L. (1985). The effect of the transition to parenthood on the marriage relationship. *Journal of Family Issues, 6*, 409–433.

Mikulincer, M. (1995). Attachment style and the mental representation of the self. *Journal of Personality and Social Psychology, 69*, 1203–1215.

Mikulincer, M., & Florian, V. (1998). The relationship between adult attachment styles and emotional and cognitive reactions to stressful events. In J. A. Simpson & S. W. Rholes (Eds.), *Attachment theory and close relationships* (pp. 143–165). New York: Guilford Press.

Mikulincer, M., Florian, V., & Weller, A. (1993). Attachment styles, coping strategies, and posttraumatic psychological distress: The impact of the Gulf War in Israel. *Journal of Personality and Social Psychology, 64*, 817–826.

Moos, R. H., Cronkite, R. C., Billings, A. G., & Finney, J. W. (1983). Health and Daily Living Form Manual. Unpublished manuscript, Stanford University.

Oakley. A. (1980). *Women confined: Toward a sociology of childbirth*. New York: Schocken Books.

Ognibene, T. C., & Collins, N. L. (1998). Adult attachment styles, perceived social support and coping strategies. *Journal of Social and Personal Relationships, 15*, 323–345.

Rholes, W. S., Simpson, J. A., Campbell, L., & Grich, J. (2001). Adult attachment and the transition to parenthood. *Journal of Personality and Social Psychology, 81*, 421–435.

Rholes, W. S., Simpson, J. A., & Orina, M. (1999). Attachment and anger in an anxiety-provoking situation. *Journal of Personality and Social Psychology, 76*, 940–957.

Ryder, R. G. (1973). Longitudinal data relating marriage satisfaction and having a child. *Journal of Marriage and the Family, 35*, 604–606.

Simpson, J. A. (1990). The influence of attachment styles on romantic relationships. *Journal of Personality and Social Psychology, 59*, 971–980.

Simpson, J. A., Ickes, W., & Grich, J. (1999). When accuracy hurts: Reactions of anxious-ambivalent dating partners to a relationship-threatening situation. *Journal of Personality and Social Psychology, 76*, 754–769.

Simpson, J. A., & Rholes, W. S. (1994). Stress and secure base relationships in adulthood. In K. Bartholomew & D. Perlman (Eds.), *Attachment processes in adulthood* (pp. 181–204). London: Kingsley.

Simpson, J. A., Rholes, W. S., & Nelligan, J. S. (1992). Support seeking and support giving within couples in an anxiety-provoking situation. *Journal of Personality and Social Psychology, 62*, 434–446.

Simpson, J. S., Rholes, W. S., & Phillips, D. (1996). Conflict in close relationships: An attachment perspective. *Journal of Personality and Social Psychology, 71*, 899–914.

Spanier, G. B. (1976). Measuring dyadic adjustment: New scales for assessing the quality of marriages and similar dyads. *Journal of Marriage and the Family, 38*, 15–28.

Snyder, D. K. (1999). Affective reconstruction in the context of a pluralistic approach to couple therapy. *Clinical Psychology-Science and Practice, 6*, 348–365.

Tidwell, M. O., Reis, H. T., & Shaver, P. R. (1996). Attachment, attractiveness, and social interaction : A diary study. *Journal of Personality and Social Psychology, 71*, 729–745.

Tucker, P., & Aron, A. (1993). Passionate love and marital satisfaction at key transition points in the family life cycle. *Journal of Social and Clincial Psychology, 12*, 135–147.

United States Department of the Census (2000). Unpublished data, Washington, DC.

Wright, P. J., Henggeler, S. W., & Craig, L. (1986). Problems in paradise? A longitudinal examination of the transition to parenthood. *Journal of Applied Developmental Psychology, 7*, 277–291.

CHAPTER FIFTEEN

Allocation and Performance of Household Tasks: A Comparison of New Parents and Childless Couples

Judith A. Feeney and Patricia Noller

W: You have to race around and do the housework in between sleeps, and if the baby doesn't sleep during the day – which has happened a lot lately – you get nothing done, and you end up tired and cranky.
H: And then we fight.
W: You take all your frustrations out on each other.
H: Because I work – I work really hard outside. And I come home and I'm just so tired, and she's like 'I've had this terrible day, and I haven't got any housework done, and I need some sleep,' and I'm thinking 'I really don't need this right now.' And I think, 'How hard could it be? Like, you just feed him and put him to sleep and then you go and do your stuff.'

Recent decades have seen marked changes in attitudes toward gender roles and in women's involvement in the labor force. Given these changes, it might seem reasonable to assume that families establish much more equitable patterns of domestic work today than they did in the past. Evidence suggests, however, that this is not the case. With the transition to parenthood, in particular, couples often move toward a traditional division of labor, in which women do the bulk of the child care and other household tasks; further, partners do not necessarily see this situation as "unfair." In fact, perceptions of unfairness are only weakly linked to patterns of task performance, and seem to be shaped by many aspects of individual and couple functioning. The aims of this chapter are to (a) review the literature on division of labor and perceptions of unfairness, particularly in the context of parenthood, and (b) present data from a recent study of first-time parenthood, supporting links among perceptions of unfairness, individual well-being, and the broader relational context.

DESCRIBING COUPLES' PATTERNS OF DOMESTIC LABOR

How equitable are patterns of domestic labor? In considering this question, it is important to note that different research methods paint somewhat different pictures of partners' involvement in domestic work. In particular, "direct-question" measures yield higher estimates of the amount of time spent on domestic tasks than do structured "time diaries." The conclusion drawn from this body of research is that direct-question measures produce overreporting, and that the extent of such overreporting varies according to gender, gender-role attitudes, social class, education, income, family size, and employment status (Press & Townsley, 1998). According to Press and Townsley (1998, p. 188), comparison of findings from direct-question and diary methods casts doubt on the claim that contemporary men do more housework than their predecessors.

In the United States, several large-scale studies of nationally representative samples have explored family work patterns, attitudes, and expectations. For example, Robinson and Milkie (1998) assessed women's attitudes to housework, comparing data from the 1970s and the 1990s. Their results suggested that women still see personal standards for housework (having a neat home, doing the job "right") as very important; in fact, young women surveyed in the 1990s reported putting significantly *more* energy and effort into housework than those surveyed in the 1970s. In short, women report continuing investment in household work, despite their increasing involvement in paid labor.

According to other North American surveys, many respondents consider that housework should be done primarily by the wife, and money earning by the husband; further, although more than half of husbands say that housework should be shared, only one third perform household tasks on a regular basis (Hiller & Philliber, 1986). The prevalence of traditional roles is also supported by the finding that husbands do relatively little domestic labor, unless both they *and* their wives hold egalitarian beliefs about gender and marital roles (Greenstein, 1996). Finally (and rather surprisingly), wives' employment status has little effect on the amount of time that husbands spend on housework (Shelton, 1990). Survey data from other western countries (including Australia and the Netherlands) point to a similar conclusion; namely, that tasks tend to be divided along gender lines (Kluwer, Heesink, & Van de Vliert, 1996; Wolcott, 1997).

DIVISION OF LABOR AND THE TRANSITION
TO PARENTHOOD

The tendency to adopt traditional patterns of labor increases with the transition to parenthood. Moreover, as comments from research participants illustrate (see the extract at the beginning of this chapter), resolving differences about division of labor is an important task at this point in the lifecycle.

Belsky and Kelly (1994) noted that men generally expect their wives to do most of the child care and housework, despite contemporary egalitarian rhetoric. Consistent with this expectation, American studies show that mothers do three to four times as much baby care as fathers, and that women's contribution to household chores also increases substantially with parenthood (Belsky & Kelly, 1994; Huston & Vangelisti, 1995). Again, data from other countries support claims that parents tend to divide chores along gender lines, and that the division of household work is often a source of dissatisfaction and conflict for new parents (Kluwer et al., 1996; Wolcott, 1997). In short, parenthood tends to crystallize a gender-traditional division of labor, largely by reshaping women's daily routines (Sanchez & Thomson, 1997).

It is important to note that this more traditional approach to the division of labor is often neither planned nor expected. In fact, most new mothers report doing much more of the housework and infant care than they had expected (Ruble, Hackel, Fleming, & Stangor, 1988). Equally important, the traditional division of labor tends to apply, regardless of whether the woman returns to the workforce. These findings have been explained in terms of systems theory. According to this perspective, the family is a system consisting of interconnected elements; change in one element affects the other elements, and the system as a whole. Major new events (such as first-time parenthood) act on the internal constraints of the system, causing the system to reorganize itself (Marvin & Stewart, 1990).

Within this broad framework, a number of more specific explanations can be offered for parents' adopting traditional patterns of labor. The sheer number of demands created by new parenthood is an important factor: Parents' resources of time and energy are clearly limited, and traditional patterns of task allocation may seem to be the most efficient. A second factor involves expectations: There tends to be an expectation that the woman should do the lion's share of the housework, especially if she stays at home to care for the child. A third factor relates to issues of earning power and job security. In many couples, the man has greater earning power than his partner, but also enjoys less freedom to fit work schedules around the demands of family life; for these couples, financial considerations can limit men's involvement in parenting (Schwartz, 1994). Yet another factor concerns women's attitudes and behavior in relation to domestic tasks: Women may be critical or "ungrateful" of partners' efforts, discouraging further involvement (Belsky & Kelly, 1994). Finally, traditional patterns of labor can result from wives' tendency to "go along" with husbands' preferences for task allocation: This tendency is more marked if wives' feelings of love for their partners are very strong, suggesting that it represents a deliberate attempt to maintain family harmony (Johnson & Huston, 1998).

EQUALITY VERSUS FAIRNESS

The fact that parents tend to share household tasks unequally raises the question of how they *perceive* their division of labor. As Thompson (1991) pointed out, the rule of "justice" is generally seen as either equality (involving a 50–50 split of tasks), or equity (where fairness is judged in terms of relative contribution or merit). However, in the areas of child care and housework, the picture is not as simple as these rules would suggest. Many couples report that the most important issue about the division of labor is that it should engender a sense of "fairness"; further, this sense of fairness may require neither equality nor strict equity (Wolcott & Glezer, 1995). Consistent with this argument, there is evidence that the majority of couples perceive their division of labor as fair, despite the fact that women do most of the household work, even if they work outside the home (Sanchez & Kane, 1996; Thompson, 1991).

How can we explain couples' tendency to regard their division of labor as "fair play"? The desire to present their relationships favorably may be a contributing factor, but it is also important to recognize the fundamental differences between paid work and domestic work (Ahlander & Bahr, 1995). Paid work is largely individualistic in nature, centering on such incentives as wages, social recognition, opportunities for advancement, and self-fulfillment. In short, the emphasis is on economic outputs. In domestic work, on the other hand, economic outputs are often secondary to matters of association, obligation, and ritual. In other words, much domestic activity involves mutual support and commitment, and the building of collective goals and bonds of affection. From this perspective, strict equity in domestic activity is not only *unnecessary* to a sense of fairness, it may actually *violate the spirit* of the activity (Ahlander & Bahr, 1995).

The claim that domestic work is intertwined with issues of commitment and collective goals is consistent with the work of Major (1987), who argued that three factors contribute to perceptions of fairness (and unfairness): outcome values, comparison referents, and justifications. In other words, when partners assess the fairness of family work, they consider such questions as what they want from the situation or relationship (outcome values), what outcomes they feel they deserve or can realistically imagine receiving (comparison referents), and what circumstances or procedures created the existing outcomes (justifications). As this analysis indicates, couples' perceptions of fairness cannot be understood without considering the characteristics of each partner and their relationship.

To date, studies assessing the predictors of perceived fairness of family work have tended to focus on four sets of factors. First, researchers have addressed the rather obvious question of the link between perceptions of fairness and the actual amount of domestic work performed by each partner. Interestingly, the absolute amount of time that partners spend on domestic tasks generally bears little relation to perceptions of fairness. However, when women spend much more time on traditional female tasks than their partners do, both partners tend to see the division of labor as unfair (Sanchez & Kane, 1996). Similarly, women tend to report dissatisfaction with the division of labor when they spend more time on domestic tasks than they want to, and when their partners spend less time on these tasks than the women think they should (Kluwer et al., 1996).

Second, considerable attention has been paid to the role of demographic variables (sometimes conceptualized as "individual resources"), such as education and income. Findings suggest that level of education is not consistently related to perceptions of fairness. On the other hand, where women's incomes are substantially less than those of their partners, women are more likely to accept their high load of domestic work as "fair" (Dempsey, 1999).

Third, researchers have linked perceptions of fairness with attitudes to gender and family roles, and to the couple relationship. For example, women's perceptions of fairness are generally higher if they regard housework as personally rewarding (Dempsey, 1999), if they endorse traditional gender-role attitudes, and if they perceive that their social and emotional life is better *with* the current relationship than it would be without it (Sanchez & Kane, 1996).

Finally, and consistent with the perspectives of Major (1987) and Ahlander and Bahr (1995), perceptions of fairness have been linked to aspects of couple interaction. When partners spend social time together and achieve a sense of intimacy, both men and women rate the division of labor as more fair, and are more appreciative of each other's instrumental work activities (Sanchez & Kane, 1996). Similarly, research has highlighted the importance of relationship outcomes: Women are more likely to rate work patterns as fair when they see themselves as having companionship and emotional support, when they see their husbands as taking sufficient interest in the children, and when they are satisfied with their marriage overall (Dempsey, 1999).

EXPLORING THE IMPACT OF PERCEPTIONS OF FAIRNESS

We have already seen that perceptions of fairness cannot be defined simply by the amount of time that partners spend on domestic tasks; rather, these perceptions are embedded in a larger context comprising the characteristics of each partner and of their relationship. Similarly, perceptions of fairness have a substantial *impact* on the overall relationship. This point emerges most strongly from studies of the transition to parenthood: At this transition point, couples are confronted by many new tasks and, as already noted, the division of labor often becomes much more traditional. Several longitudinal studies of new parenthood attest to the importance of partners' satisfaction with the division of labor. In fact, this variable has emerged consistently as a key predictor of changes in couple adjustment.

For example, Ruble, Fleming, Hackel, and Stangor (1988) focused on women's experience of the transition to parenthood, exploring the effects on marital satisfaction of violated expectations about child care and other household responsibilities. Overall, women in their samples reported doing more household chores and child care than they had expected. These violated expectations about the division of labor were related to negative feelings about *some* aspects of the marriage; specifically, they predicted feelings about the husband's involvement in child care and about the effect of the child on the marriage, but did not predict feelings of closeness to the spouse. A later study by members of this research group sampled both husbands and wives (Hackel & Ruble, 1992). This study confirmed that *both* spouses saw the women as doing considerably more of the housework and child care than they had expected. Such expectancy violation had a negative impact on women's (but not men's) perceptions of the overall quality of the marriage, with these effects being stronger for women who were more committed to their initial (nontraditional) expectations.

Other studies support the effect of role dissatisfaction on couples' adjustment to parenthood. Terry, McHugh, and Noller (1991) compared levels of marital satisfaction in the last trimester of pregnancy and three months post-birth, arguing that role inequity can account for declines in marital quality. These researchers found interactive effects of time and role satisfaction (satisfied, dissatisfied) on two of the four subscales of Spanier's (1976) Dyadic Adjustment Scale, although these effects were restricted to wives. Specifically, wives who were dissatisfied with their partner's role performance showed a decline in affectional expression (expressions of love and affection), whereas "role-satisfied" wives showed no change. Further, wives who were dissatisfied with their partner's role performance showed no change in consensus (similarity of attitudes and values), whereas "role-satisfied" wives reported *increased* consensus. In short, these findings suggest that when wives see their partners as contributing fairly to domestic chores, prior levels of marital satisfaction may be maintained, or even enhanced.

A more recent study (Huston & Vangelisti, 1995) yielded somewhat different results from those discussed so far, though still supporting the importance of a mutually acceptable division of labor. In this study, declines in wives' satisfaction with division of labor were *not* associated with declines in marital satisfaction or love for husband. In other words, wives in this sample seemed to evaluate the instrumental realm of their marriage separately from its overall quality. In contrast, whereas several researchers have argued that men's dissatisfaction with role performance has only weak and indirect effects on their relationship evaluations, Huston and Vangelisti found that husbands' dissatisfaction with division of labor was related to declines in love for their wives.

THE PRESENT STUDY

In summary, research suggests that the transition to parenthood brings a more traditional division of labor, and that women often find themselves doing more child-care and household tasks than they had expected. Several studies have linked women's dissatisfaction over the division of labor with negative feelings about couple intimacy, or about the overall quality of the marriage. The effect of husbands' dissatisfaction over the division of labor is less clear, but some researchers have argued that such dissatisfaction can have either direct effects on relationship evaluations, or indirect effects that result from changing patterns of marital interaction.

The study reported in the remainder of this chapter was designed to provide a detailed picture of adjustment to parenthood, including the division of labor and partners' perceptions of unfairness. Using longitudinal data, we were interested in assessing both the *predictors* and the *consequences* of perceived unfairness, in terms of individual and relational functioning. The study had several important features. First, we included a group of couples who were not planning to have children in the near future in order to allow comparisons between new parents and childless couples. Second, given the greater validity of diary estimates of domestic work we employed structured time diaries. Third, rather than assessing structural aspects of individual resources (such as education and income), we focused on the underexplored issue of individuals' psychological adjustment (depression, anxiety, and stress). Fourth, rather than defining relational functioning simply in terms of marital satisfaction, we also included measures of attachment security – attachment issues are likely to be highly salient during the transition to parenthood, when partners must reorganize their relationship to accommodate a new and highly dependent individual. Finally, we obtained data from both spouses, and examined how one partner's perceptions of unfairness might be predicted by, and impact on, the other's evaluations of individual and couple functioning.

Overview of the Study

The study was a longitudinal study of marriage that included a group of couples undergoing the transition to parenthood and a comparison group of childless couples. At the beginning of the study, there were 107 couples in the transition group and 100 couples in the comparison group. Both groups of couples were recruited by a variety of methods, including advertisements in the radio and print media, recruitment through the psychology subject pool at the University of Queensland, and use of "snowballing" techniques. In addition, to target transition couples more directly, we approached a number of health services dealing with prenatal care, together with retail outlets specializing in maternity and child-care products.

Couples in the transition group provided major data sets at three points in time: during the second trimester of pregnancy, about six weeks after their babies were born, and when the babies were six months old. Those in the comparison group were assessed at similar time intervals. At each of these times, couples completed a comprehensive set of questionnaires assessing individual and couple adjustment. On the first two occasions, we also conducted interviews focusing on relationship history and reactions to pregnancy and the early weeks of parenthood. In addition, between the second and third assessments, spouses completed structured diaries detailing their involvement in household and baby-related tasks over a four-day period (two weekdays and two weekend days). The data reported in this chapter come from the structured diaries and from a subset of the questionnaires completed at the beginning and the end of the study.

The overall sample of couples varied widely in age, with husbands ranging from 21 to 54 years, and wives from 19 to 47 years. The average age was 30 years for husbands and 29 for wives. Similarly, couples varied widely in terms of the length of their marriages, which ranged from one month to 15 years (with an average of just over three and a half years). The transition and comparison couples did not differ in age, length of marriage, or initial levels of individual or couple adjustment.

Given the longitudinal nature of the study, it is important to consider the question of attrition. The rate of withdrawal from the study was similar for both groups of couples. For example, of the original 107 couples in the transition group, 83 couples completed the diary records and 76 completed all phases of the study. Similarly, of the 100 comparison couples, 76 completed the diary records and 74 completed all phases. This rate of attrition is fairly typical of studies in which couples are mobile geographically and are assessed over relatively long periods of time. There was little evidence of systematic attrition. Of a large number of variables measured at the start of the study, only educational level and relationship satisfaction were related to withdrawal; specifically, respondents with low levels of education and relationship satisfaction were somewhat more likely to withdraw. Given that these findings applied to both groups, they do not threaten the validity of the main analyses.

Measures of Individual and Couple Adjustment

In this chapter, we focus on three of the questionnaires that spouses completed at the beginning and the end of the study.

Relationship Satisfaction
Satisfaction with the marital relationship was assessed using 35 items from Snyder's Marital Satisfaction Inventory (Snyder, 1979). These items were drawn from the scales measuring global distress, affective communication, problem-solving communication, and time together, and were combined to yield an overall measure of relationship satisfaction.

Attachment Security
Researchers generally agree that two main factors underlie individuals' sense of security in their intimate relationships: discomfort with closeness and anxiety over relationships. These two aspects of attachment security were assessed using the Attachment Style Questionnaire (Feeney, Noller, & Hanrahan, 1994), which was factor analyzed to extract the two principal factors.

General Psychological Adjustment
Individual psychological adjustment was assessed in terms of three emotional states: depression, anxiety, and stress. The instrument used was the DASS (Depression, Anxiety, and Stress Scales; Lovibond & Lovibond, 1995), which focuses on the individual's experiences over the *past week*. As a result, the scales are useful for detecting changes in adjustment that may be linked to recent events.

The Diary Measure

Spouses were asked to keep individual diaries over four consecutive days from Friday to Monday, detailing their involvement in specific household and baby-related tasks. They were asked to report how much time they spent performing each task on each day. In addition, they rated each task in terms of whether they thought that the amount of effort that the spouse expended on the task was fair, or should be increased or decreased. All spouses reported on the following eight household tasks, selected from the literature as being central to domestic management (for example, Croghan, 1991; Presland & Antill, 1987):

- cooking meals
- taking care of bills and banking
- washing and hanging out clothes
- doing the grocery shopping

- doing the dishes
- cleaning the house
- doing the gardening
- ironing clothes

In addition, eight baby-related tasks were included in the diary records that were given to spouses in the transition group. (The babies were about three months old at the time these records were completed.) The list of tasks was generated from a pilot study conducted prior to the current research, and the tasks were as follows:

- changing the baby
- feeding the baby
- bathing the baby
- putting the baby to sleep
- preparing bottles, food, and so on for the baby
- general care of the baby (playing, comforting)
- tending to the baby during the night
- tending to baby's medical needs (taking baby to doctor, clinic, or pharmacist)

Using these diary records, we were interested in two broad issues. First, we wanted to chart the amount of time that spouses spent on various household and baby-related tasks, and to assess differences due to gender and group (transition versus comparison). Second, we were interested in spouses' subjective feelings about their partner's effort (perceptions of unfairness), and their predictive relations with measures of individual and relationship functioning.

TIME SPENT ON TASKS

As already noted, the first major purpose of the diaries was to allow us to document the amount of time that couples were spending on household and baby-related tasks. These data help us understand how couples were juggling the various demands on their time.

Total Time Spent on Household Tasks

Within this broad issue, the first question we explored was whether the total amount of time spent on household tasks over the four-day period

Table 15.1. Mean Time Spent on Domestic Tasks
According to Group and Gender

	Husbands	Wives
Household Tasks		
Transition group	6.47	11.39
Comparison group	7.22	7.82
Baby-Related Tasks		
Transition group	12.73	37.95

Notes: Scores are expressed in hours, summed over the four-day period.

differed according to group (transition versus comparison) and gender. (At this stage, because we wanted to compare results across the two groups, we did not include the baby-related tasks.)

Analysis of variance revealed main effects of group and gender, together with a significant interaction effect: New parents spent more time on household tasks than comparison couples, wives spent more time on these tasks than husbands, and new mothers spent a *particularly* large amount of time on these tasks. These findings are shown in the upper section of Table 15.1.

In interpreting these findings, it is important to note that most of the new mothers in this sample were not working outside the home when the diaries were completed. As mentioned earlier, the expectation that women should take primary responsibility for the running of the home is particularly strong when they are caring for their children on a full-time basis. Conversely, husbands' lesser contribution to household tasks may be largely explained by their involvement in paid employment. As Table 15.1 shows, comparison husbands and wives (who were generally both in full-time employment), reported only a small difference in domestic work. The link between husbands' paid and unpaid work contributions is supported by comparison of weekday records with those from the weekends, when men's availability is usually much greater. For the new parents, the difference between men's and women's contributions was much smaller on the weekends (with mean scores of 4.15 and 5.30 hours for husbands and wives, respectively) than on the weekdays (mean scores of 2.32 and 6.09 hours).

Total Time Spent on Baby-Related Tasks

We were also interested in the extent of difference between new mothers and new fathers in the total amount of time spent caring for the baby. Over the four-day period, mothers spent much more time on these tasks than fathers did (see lower section of Table 15.1). This difference was somewhat smaller on the weekends than on weekdays, but was significant in each case.

Overall, then, new mothers in this sample reported spending more than 12 hours per day performing infant care and other household tasks. Given this heavy load of routine domestic work, it is easy to see why many women report missing "down time," when they can relax and turn their attention to pursuits outside the family (Thompson, 1991).

Parenthood and Time on Tasks: Different Approaches?

Despite the gender differences reported so far, it is clear that couples vary widely in their approaches to domestic work. For this reason, we wanted to look more closely at the group of new parents and to identify different types of couples, defined by husbands' and wives' relative contributions to domestic work. To address this question, we conducted a cluster analysis on the diary data provided by the transition couples. Two clustering variables were used, involving the ratio of the number of hours spent by the husband to the number of hours spent by the wife, for each of household and baby-related tasks. This analysis identified three distinct groups of couples.

In the first group (comprising 22 couples), husbands were quite involved in caring for their babies; in fact, their contribution to child care was almost as great as that of their wives. They were slightly less involved in household tasks, but still spent almost two-thirds as much time as their wives did on these tasks. In the second group (comprising 26 couples), husbands were heavily involved with household tasks, and actually spent just as much time as their wives in this arena. In contrast, they had much less involvement in baby-related tasks, spending about one-quarter of the time that their wives did on these tasks. Finally, in the third group (comprising 33 couples), husbands were performing much less work than their wives on both types of domestic tasks (about one-quarter to one-third of the hours spent by wives).

These findings suggest that fathers differ in the *type* of domestic work they prefer to perform, as well as in their general willingness to contribute. For example, the division of labor of the second group of couples suggests that some men, while wanting to support their wives at this challenging time, may not feel very competent or comfortable in the arena of infant care. Of course, the division of labor is also influenced by wives' preferences, and some of the wives may have seen child care as primarily their own domain.

Time Spent on Specific Baby-Related Tasks

For the group of new parents, we were also interested in husbands' and wives' contributions to the various aspects of child care. We found that mothers spent more time than their husbands on all eight baby-related tasks (see Table 15.2, for the total number of hours spent on each task across the four-day period).

Despite this general pattern, the *relative* contributions of fathers and mothers clearly differed across the tasks. The greatest disparities were for time spent feeding the baby and tending to medical needs. This pattern of results is likely to reflect practical considerations, such as which parent is available to meet particular needs: Most mothers in the sample were still breastfeeding their babies at this point in time, and visits to doctors or clinics usually take place at times when fathers are at work. On the other hand, the perceived pleasantness of tasks may also be relevant to fathers' input: The smallest disparities between the contributions of fathers and mothers were for general care (playing and

Table 15.2. Mean Time Spent on Specific Baby-Related Tasks by Wives and Husbands

Task	Wives	Husbands
Changing the baby	2.99	1.17
Feeding the baby	11.38	1.26
Bathing the baby	1.19	0.53
Putting the baby to sleep	3.07	1.33
Preparing bottles and food	1.00	0.26
General (playing, comforting)	16.13	7.57
Tending to the baby during the night	1.93	0.61
Tending to the baby's medical needs	0.26	0.03

Notes: Scores are expressed in hours, summed over the four-day period.

comforting), and bathing the baby, tasks that are likely to be seen as relatively pleasant. This finding supports the claim that involvement in domestic chores is "patterned"; that is, the degree of segregation differs from task to task, and couples' division of labor cannot be understood without considering between-task differences (Twiggs, McQuillan, & Ferree, 1999).

PERCEPTIONS OF UNFAIRNESS

As we discussed earlier in this chapter, many couples report being less concerned by "who does what" around the house, than by the broader issue of "fairness." To explore this issue, we turned to individuals' ratings of their spouses' effort on domestic chores. For each task, ratings could range from −2 to +2, where positive scores indicate a desire for the spouse to increase their effort, scores of zero indicate satisfaction with current spousal effort, and negative scores indicate a desire for decreased effort.

Household and Baby-Related Tasks: Overall Perceptions of Unfairness

These ratings of spousal effort were first used to derive overall measures of perceived unfairness for household and for baby-related tasks. These summary measures focused on the *absolute* difference between partners' current and desired effort, and ratings were averaged across the eight tasks in each set. Hence, scores could range from 0 to 2, where 0 indicates no unfairness and 2 indicates a great deal of unfairness.

Spouses generally perceived each other's effort on household tasks as reasonably fair: The mean unfairness rating was 0.29, and scores on this measure were similar for men and women, and for transition and comparison couples. On average, new parents also rated each other's effort on baby-related tasks as quite fair; the mean score was only 0.19. Again, men and women did not differ in their perceptions.

The Nature of Perceived Unfairness for Baby-Related Tasks

Although new parents were generally reasonably satisfied with their partner's efforts on baby-related tasks, it is important to take a more fine-grained look at this issue. Specifically, we wanted to examine feelings about the performance of infant care on a task-by-task basis, and

to assess whether respondents wanted their partners to increase or decrease their current effort. To address these issues, we next examined the
ratings of spousal effort (from -2 to $+2$) for each baby-related task.

Husbands' and wives' ratings of spousal effort differed for all eight
baby-related tasks. In every case, husbands wanted their partners to
decrease their contribution to infant care, whereas wives wanted their
partners to *increase* their contribution. This gender difference in ratings
of spousal effort was particularly strong for three tasks: tending to the
baby in the night, changing the baby, and putting the baby to sleep. Interestingly, these tasks were *not* the ones for which husbands' relative
contribution was the lowest (refer to Table 15.2). Rather, it seems that
these three tasks may have been seen as the least enjoyable aspects of
infant care; if tasks are seen as tiring or unpleasant, any differences in
spouses' contributions may be highly salient and a source of dissatisfaction and complaint.

Consistently, then, husbands wanted wives to put less effort into
child care, whereas wives wanted husbands to put in more effort. This
finding might seem to suggest an easy solution to any dissatisfaction
with spouses' effort: If husbands became more actively involved in
tending to their infants, their wives could reduce their own effort. In
reality, however, many factors conspire to prevent this "solution" from
being simple or straightforward. For example, competing demands on
men's time affect their availability for doing things around the home,
and traditional role expectations support this division of labor. Moreover, as we suggested earlier, partners may differ in their standards of
orderliness and their perceptions of "appropriate" effort. These differences can inhibit men's involvement, especially if men have less exact-
ing standards for task performance or think that their infants may be
receiving too much attention.

Predicting New Parents' Perceptions of Unfairness

Next, for couples in the transition group, we wanted to examine the predictors of perceived unfairness. Possible predictor variables were defined using the diary-based measures of time spent on tasks, and the
prenatal questionnaire measures of individual and couple functioning.

Time on Tasks and Perceived Unfairness
We started by asking whether perceptions of unfairness were related
to the actual amount of time that new parents devoted to infant care

and other household tasks. As mentioned earlier, this possibility is intuitively appealing, but has received quite limited support from previous studies.

We found no link between perceptions of unfairness and the *absolute* amount of time that spouses spent on domestic tasks. On the other hand, there was some evidence of the importance of spouses' *relative* contributions. In the section on "Time Spent on tasks," we described three groups of couples among the new parents, defined by men's and women's relative contributions to domestic tasks: Some fathers contributed heavily to general household tasks, some contributed primarily to infant care, and others made little contribution to either domain. Spouses in these groups differed in their perceptions of the unfairness of the division of labor, although only for baby-related tasks. When husbands made little contribution to *either* domain, husbands and wives seemed to acknowledge this inequity; in these couples, the mean score for unfairness of infant care was .30, compared with .12 in the other two groups (as noted earlier, scores could range from 0 to 2). That is, both spouses saw husbands' low involvement as somewhat unfair. Unfortunately, we have no data to indicate whether husbands and wives discussed this situation, or whether husbands were prepared to remedy it.

Hence, it did not seem to matter whether husbands contributed to general household chores or to infant care; as long as they were making a substantial effort in *one* arena, spouses accepted the situation as fair. This finding emphasizes that there is no one "right way" for couples to negotiate home duties. In addition, it seems that couples are usually able to evaluate each other's efforts in terms of "the big picture," rather than focusing on shortcomings in one area. It is interesting that group differences in perceived unfairness were limited to infant care, despite the fact that the groups differed in their division of baby-related *and* general chores. It seems that new fathers' efforts in the area of general chores are noted and appreciated, but primarily because they are seen as facilitating the more crucial activities of infant care.

Individual and Couple Adjustment and Perceived Unfairness

Next, we addressed the role of individual and couple adjustment (assessed by questionnaires administered at the beginning of the study) in predicting perceptions of unfairness. Correlational analyses revealed no links between perceptions of unfairness and wives' initial reports of individual adjustment, attachment security, or relationship satisfaction. In contrast, perceptions of unfairness were consistently linked

Table 15.3. Correlations between Husbands' Prenatal Characteristics and Spouses' Perceptions of Division of Labor

	Unfairness in Household Tasks		Unfairness in Child-Care Tasks	
	Husbands' Perception	Wives' Perception	Husbands' Perception	Wives' Perception
Relationship measures				
Relationship satisfaction				
husbands	−.28*	−.26*	−.25*	−.07
wives	−.18	−.17	.06	−.14
Discomfort				
husbands	.04	.03	.06	.12
wives	−.07	−.01	−.10	.16
Relationship anxiety				
husbands	.23*	.17	.16	.01
wives	−.06	−.12	−.06	.01
Psychological adjustment				
Depression				
husbands	.43**	.20	.30**	.24*
wives	.01	.01	−.12	.09
Anxiety				
husbands	.15	.32**	.16	.25*
wives	.01	−.10	−.08	−.09
Stress				
husbands	.18	.09	.14	.12
wives	−.01	.10	−.06	−.06

Notes: $*p < .05$, $**p < .01$.

to *husbands' initial feelings* about themselves and their relationships. Husbands who were depressed, or who were anxious or unhappy about their relationships at the beginning of the study, were more likely to perceive patterns of household *and* baby care as unfair (see Table 15.3). Further, the *wives* of husbands who were depressed, anxious (general anxiety), or dissatisfied with their relationships, were also likely to rate work patterns as unfair.

It is important to note that these associations between husbands' questionnaire ratings and perceptions of unfairness were not reduced in strength when partners' absolute *or* relative contributions to tasks were partialed out. This result suggests that husbands' perceptions of the division of labor can be colored by global mindsets. That is, characteristics such as depressed mood, negative working models of attachment, and "sentiment override" (Weiss, 1980), may cause some new fathers to perceive many aspects of their situation in a negative light.

The finding that their wives shared these negative perceptions of work patterns points to the interdependence between marital partners. In fact, partners may be particularly reactive to each other's thoughts, feelings, and behaviors at major transition points, when new response patterns are being shaped. From the analyses reported earlier, we know that husbands generally wanted wives to reduce their effort on baby-related tasks, whereas wives wanted husbands to increase their effort. (Other analyses not reported here revealed a similar pattern for general household tasks.) Hence, it seems that insecure and unhappy husbands may have been prone to complain about their wives' "over-involvement"; in this difficult situation, wives may have responded by crosscomplaining about husbands' "under-involvement."

The Impact of New Parents' Perceptions of Unfairness

As mentioned earlier, satisfaction with the division of domestic labor is a key predictor of partners' adjustment to parenthood. For this reason, our final research question concerned the link between perceptions of unfairness and measures of individual and couple adjustment, completed at the *end* of the study (when the babies were six months old). We explored this issue using partial correlation; that is, we correlated each respondent's perceptions of unfairness with own and partner's ratings of adjustment, controlling for initial scores on the corresponding measure of adjustment.

Again, we found that the measures of adjustment were related more strongly to *husbands' perceptions of unfairness* than to wives' perceptions. When husbands saw domestic work patterns as unfair, they became more stressed over the course of the study, and their wives became more stressed, depressed, anxious, and more dissatisfied with their relationships. These negative outcomes were associated most strongly with husbands' perceptions of unfairness in the area of baby care (see Table 15.4). Although wives' perceptions of unfairness were less consistently linked to outcome measures, one important finding emerged: When wives saw husbands' involvement in baby care as unfair, those husbands became more anxious about their relationships (that is, more insecure) over the course of the study.

Table 15.4. Partial Correlations between Perceived Unfairness of Division of Labor and Relationship and Individual Outcomes at Final Follow-up

	Unfairness in Household Tasks		Unfairness in Child-Care Tasks	
	Husbands' Perception	Wives' Perception	Husbands' Perception	Wives' Perception
Relationship measures				
Relationship satisfaction				
husbands	−.02	.02	.07	.01
wives	−.12	−.22*	−.27*	−.18
Discomfort				
husbands	.23*	−.11	.12	.06
wives	.14	−.12	.18	−.01
Relationship anxiety				
husbands	−.09	−.02	−.20	.30*
wives	.14	−.11	.19	.19
Psychological adjustment				
Depression				
husbands	.19	−.15	$.21^+$	−.08
wives	.26*	−.08	.31**	.18
Anxiety				
husbands	−.07	−.27*	−.03	−.03
wives	$.21^+$	−.16	.33**	.17
Stress				
husbands	.23*	.14	.25*	.04
wives	.37***	−.17	.39***	−.02

Notes: These correlations control for initial (Time 1) scores on the outcome variable. $+p < .10$, $* p < .05$, $** p < .01$, $*** p < .001$.

These findings support the proposition that the division of labor plays a crucial role in the transition to parenthood. Moreover, they point to the delicate interplay between husbands and wives. Although husbands' perceptions of unfairness were predicted only by their own psychological adjustment and relationship evaluations, wives ended up being deeply affected by these concerns. Similarly, wives' perceptions of unfairness were predicted by their husbands' psychological adjustment and relationship evaluations, and had implications for husbands' later feelings of security. This situation is illustrated schematically in Figure 15.1.

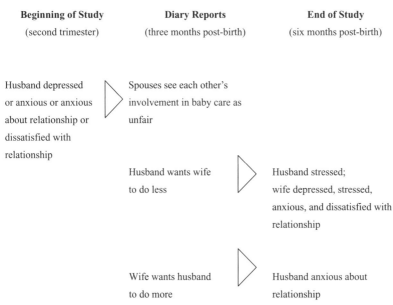

Beginning of Study	Diary Reports	End of Study
(second trimester)	(three months post-birth)	(six months post-birth)

Husband depressed or anxious or anxious about relationship or dissatisfied with relationship ▷ Spouses see each other's involvement in baby care as unfair

Husband wants wife to do less ▷ Husband stressed; wife depressed, stressed, anxious, and dissatisfied with relationship

Wife wants husband to do more ▷ Husband anxious about relationship

Figure 15.1. Representing the process.

Overall, the strongest and most consistent finding regarding the impact of perceived unfairness was the negative effect of *husbands' perceptions of "unfair" patterns of infant care*. This finding raises important questions about what these husbands may have been doing that contributed to their own feelings of stress and to their wives' increasing levels of personal and relational distress. As noted earlier, husbands generally wanted their wives to reduce their effort on baby-related tasks. Husbands who endorsed this view quite strongly may have been feeling "left out" and neglected; that is, they may have been missing the shared couple intimacy that they had before the baby arrived, and may have even seen the baby as threatening their place in their wife's affections. Given that these husbands were already prone to depression and insecurity, they may have responded to the situation negatively, by withdrawing from their wives or complaining about their involvement with the baby. Such behaviors are likely to result in wives' feeling quite vulnerable and unsupported.

On the other hand, we have seen that wives wanted their husbands to increase their effort on baby-related tasks. When wives felt strongly about this issue, husbands reported more relationship anxiety by the end of the study. That is, they felt more anxious about whether their partners really loved them and were fully committed to the relationship. Some researchers have suggested that women interpret their partner's involvement in family tasks in terms of interpersonal issues of love and care. In other words, women value the symbolic meaning of partners' acts of involvement more than the acts themselves (Thompson, 1991). Hence, wives who are unhappy with their spouse's efforts may express their concerns in terms of these key relational issues of love and care, causing husbands to perceive a threat to the relationship. The resultant increase in male insecurity is consistent with attachment theory, which proposes that working models of attachment can be influenced by major relationship events (Rothbard & Shaver, 1994).

GENERAL DISCUSSION AND CONCLUSIONS

Our findings replicate and extend previous research into the allocation and performance of household tasks. The diary records indicated that, overall, women in this sample were doing significantly more domestic work than their partners. This finding is consistent with many other studies conducted in western countries (for example, Bittman, 1991; Greenstein, 1996). However, the gender difference in task input was much more pronounced in the transition group, supporting the claim that parenthood results in a more traditional division of labor (Belsky & Kelly, 1994; Kluwer et al., 1996). Most women in this group were not working outside the home when the diaries were completed; in this situation, particularly, infant care and housework are often seen as a "package deal." As other researchers have noted, the factors influencing new parents' expectations of role performance are complex and interwoven; for example, it is almost impossible to disentangle the effects of mothers' income and their hours of employment (Deutsch, Lussier, & Serris, 1993). Regardless of the precise factors involved, we have seen that these expectations can result in women carrying a very heavy load of family work and having little "down time."

The extent of difference between men's and women's involvement in infant care varied according to the specific task, being greatest for feeding the baby and tending to medical needs, and smallest for general care and bathing the baby. This pattern of effects may reflect both practical constraints (that is, which parent is available to perform certain tasks), and the perceived pleasantness of tasks. Furthermore, our data suggest that issues concerning the fairness of partners' contribution may be particularly salient for the less pleasant tasks of infant care (for example, changing the baby).

Perceptions of unfair division of labor were not linked to the absolute amount of time that partners spent on baby-related or general household tasks. On the other hand, when men's relative contribution to *both* types of tasks was low, partners perceived more unfairness in the division of infant care. Despite this effect of partners' relative contributions, the strongest and most consistent predictors of perceived unfairness were aspects of men's prior adjustment (both individual and relational). Together, these findings suggest that perceptions of unfairness are rather subjective, and can be shaped by psychological characteristics such as depressive mood and negative working models of attachment.

The subjective nature of perceptions of unfairness may also reflect the fact that "fairness" is open to many interpretations. According to Goodnow and Bowes (1994), the word "fair" can be used in at least six different ways in the context of domestic work: (a) no one person should do it all, (b) no one person should do all the disliked jobs, (c) when one partner is working, the other should not sit idly by, (d) one person should not be more privileged than the other, (e) the work of partners should be as equal as possible in terms of time and quality, and (f) people should have some choice in what they do. Hence, the word "fair" may have different meanings for each partner and couples may not necessarily be aware of these differences. In short, resolving issues about household work is difficult when one person's definition of "fair" is not shared by the other (Goodnow & Bowes, 1994).

Both men's and women's perceptions of unfairness had important consequences for the individual and the relationship. Women's dissatisfaction with the division of infant care (wanting husbands to do more) led to increased male insecurity. This finding may reflect women's tendency to see their partners' limited contribution in relational terms: Wives' doubts about partner's love and care may, in turn, cause husbands to perceive a threat to the relationship. On the other hand, men's dissatisfaction with the division of labor (wanting wives to do less) led to increases in their own stress, and in their partners' personal and relational distress. As noted earlier, these men may feel neglected and threatened by their wives' involvement with the baby. If husbands respond to this situation by becoming withdrawn or hostile, their behavior is likely to add substantially to the strain experienced by the new mothers.

In summary, the division of labor is an important relational issue, particularly during the transition to parenthood. Because spouses are highly interdependent, one person's perceptions of unfairness can affect, and be affected by, the psychological characteristics of the partner and the state of the relationship. Over the last few decades, discussions of gender and power have provided useful insights into patterns of domestic work. However, integrating these approaches with perspectives such as attachment theory, which emphasize the link between individual and relational concerns, can enhance our understanding of couples' perceptions of domestic work.

REFERENCES

Ahlander, N. R., & Bahr, K. S. (1995). Beyond drudgery, power, and equity: Toward an expanded discourse on the moral dimensions of housework in families. *Journal of Marriage and the Family, 57*, 54–68.

Belsky, J., & Kelly, J. (1994). *The transition to parenthood: How a first child changes a marriage*. New York: Delacorte Press.

Bittman, M. (1991). *Juggling time: How Australian families use time*. Canberra, Australia: Office of the Status of Women, Department of the Prime Minister and Cabinet.

Croghan, R. (1991). First-time mothers' accounts of inequality in the division of labour. *Feminism and Psychology, 1*, 221–246.

Dempsey, K. C. (1999). Attempting to explain women's perceptions of the fairness of the division of housework. *Journal of Family Studies, 5*, 3–24.

Deutsch, F. M., Lussier, J. B., & Serris, L. J. (1993). Husbands at home: Predictors of paternal participation in childcare and housework. *Journal of Personality and Social Psychology, 65*, 1154–1166.

Feeney, J. A., Noller, P., & Hanrahan, M. (1994). Assessing adult attachment: Developments in the conceptualization of security and insecurity. In M. B. Sperling & W. H. Berman (Eds.), *Attachment in adults: Theory, assessment and treatment* (pp. 128–152). New York: Guilford.

Goodnow, J. J., & Bowes, J. M. (1994). *Men, women, and household work*. Melbourne, Australia: Oxford University Press.

Greenstein, T. N. (1996). Husbands' participation in domestic labor: Interactive effects of wives' and husbands' gender ideologies. *Journal of Marriage and the Family, 58*, 585–595.

Hackel, L. S., & Ruble, D. N. (1992). Changes in the marital relationship after the first baby is born: Predicting the impact of expectancy disconfirmation. *Journal of Personality and Social Psychology, 62*, 944–957.

Hiller, D. V., & Philliber, W. W. (1986). The division of labor in contemporary marriage: Expectations, perceptions, and performance. *Social Problems, 33*, 191–201.

Huston, T. L., & Vangelisti, A. L. (1995). How parenthood affects marriage. In M. A. Fitzpatrick & A. L. Vangelisti (Eds.), *Explaining family interactions* (pp. 147–176). Thousand Oaks, CA: Sage.

Johnson, E. M., & Huston, T. L. (1998). The perils of love, or why wives adapt to husbands during the transition to parenthood. *Journal of Marriage and the Family, 60*, 195–204.

Kluwer, E. S., Heesink, J. A. M., & Van de Vliert, E. (1996). Marital conflict about the division of household labor and paid work. *Journal of Marriage and the Family, 58*, 958–969.

Lovibond, S. H., & Lovibond, P. F. (1995). *Manual for the Depression Anxiety Stress Scales (DASS)* (2nd ed.). Sydney, Australia: Psychology Foundation of Australia.

Major, B. (1987). Gender, justice, and the psychology of entitlement. In P. Shaver & C. Hendrick (Eds.), *Sex and gender* (pp. 124–148). Newbury Park, CA: Sage.

Marvin, R. S., & Stewart, R. B. (1990). A family systems framework for the study of attachment. In M. T. Greenberg, D. Cicchetti, & E. M. Cummings (Eds.), *Attachment in the preschool years: Theory, research, and intervention* (pp. 51–86). Chicago: University of Chicago Press.

Presland, P., & Antill, J. K. (1987). Household division of labour: The impact of hours worked in paid employment. *Australian Journal of Psychology, 39*, 273–291.

Press, J. E., & Townsley, E. (1998). Wives' and husbands' housework reporting: Gender, class, and social desirability. *Gender and Society, 12*, 188–218.

Robinson, J. P., & Milkie, M. A. (1998). Back to the basics: Trends in and role determinants of women's attitudes toward housework. *Journal of Marriage and the Family, 60*, 205–218.

Rothbard, J. C., & Shaver, P. R. (1994). Continuity of attachment across the life span. In M. B. Sperling & W. H. Berman (Eds.), *Attachment in adults: Theory, assessment, and treatment* (pp. 31–71). New York: Guilford.

Ruble, D. N., Hackel, L. S., Fleming, A. S., & Stangor, C. (1988). Changes in the marital relationship during the transition to first time motherhood: Effects of violated expectations concerning division of household labor. *Journal of Personality and Social Psychology, 55*, 78–87.

Sanchez, L., & Kane, E. W. (1996). Women's and men's constructions of perceptions of housework fairness. *Journal of Family Issues, 17*, 358–387.

Sanchez, L., & Thomson, E. (1997). Becoming mothers and fathers: Parenthood, gender, and the division of labor. *Gender and Society, 11*, 747–772.

Schwartz, P. (1994). *Love between equals: How peer marriage really works*. New York: Free Press.

Shelton, B. A. (1990). The distribution of household tasks: Does wife's employment status make a difference? *Journal of Family Issues, 11*, 115–135.

Snyder, D. K. (1979). Multidimensional assessment of marital satisfaction. *Journal of Marriage and the Family, 41*, 813–823.

Spanier, G. B. (1976). Measuring dyadic adjustment: New scales for assessing the quality of marriage and similar dyads. *Journal of Marriage and the Family, 38*, 15–39.

Terry, D. J., McHugh, T. A., and Noller, P. (1991). Role dissatisfaction and the decline in marital quality across the transition to parenthood. *Australian Journal of Psychology, 43*, 129–132.

Thompson, L. (1991). Family work: Women's sense of fairness. *Journal of Family Issues, 12*, 181–196.

Twiggs, J. E., McQuillan, J., & Ferree, M. M. (1999). Meaning and measurement: Reconceptualizing measures of the division of household labor. *Journal of Marriage and the Family, 61*, 712–724.

Weiss, R. L. (1980). Strategic behavioral marital therapy: Toward a model for assessment and intervention. In J. P. Vincent (Ed.), *Advances in family intervention, assessment and theory* (Vol. 1, pp. 229–271). Greenwich, CT: JAI Press.

Wolcott, I. (1997). Work and family. In D. de Vaus & I. Wolcott (Eds.), *Australian family profiles: Social and demographic patterns* (pp. 82–89). Melbourne: Australian Institute of Family Studies.

Wolcott, I., & Glezer, H. (1995). *Work and family life: Achieving integration.* Melbourne: Australian Institute of Family Studies.

CHAPTER SIXTEEN

Care Giving and Its Influence on Marital Interactions between Older Spouses

Helen E. Edwards and Patricia Noller

The following is an extract of a conversation between an elderly man and his wife who was caring for him:

Husband: Well I'd like to talk about the showering.
Wife: Oh we've been over that and over.
Husband: Because I have some problems in the night I might be smelly when people come to visit and I'd like to be fresh and clean for the day.
Wife: Poof – been over – over all this.
Husband: I know you want to clean me up before I go to bed but I'd rather you showered me in the morning.
Wife: Oh, let's talk about the garden. What should we plant this year? Do you think the roses need pruning?
Husband: I want to shower in the morning.
Wife: Enough, enough. (laughs) Come on, let's talk about our beautiful garden.
Husband: Plant what you like.
Wife: Well how about your favorites, zinnias?

As this extract demonstrates, communication is an important, but sometimes difficult, part of care giving. Family care giving for older people has received much attention in the literature, especially from the perspective of the caregiver. Interestingly, only a limited number of studies have examined the interactional processes of care (for example, Phillips, Morrison, Steffl, Chae, Cromwell, & Russell, 1995). Studies that have examined these issues have shown that, in terms of well-being

The study reported in this chapter was supported by Research and Development Grant HS 252 from the Research and Development Advisory Committee, Department of Health, Housing and Community Service, Australia.

and quality of relationships, the outcomes of care giving may be just as "negative" for older care recipients as for their carers; further, communication is an important aspect of these relationships. Studies have examined the relationship between carer and care receiver and found that affection, attachment, intimacy, conflict, reciprocity, and communication are important for the well-being of older people, family relationships, and quality of life (Braithwaite, 1998; Carruth, Tate, Moffett, & Hill, 1997; Edwards, 2001; Edwards & Noller, 1998; Ferris & Bramston, 1994; Neufeld & Harrison, 1998; Whitbeck, Hoyt, & Huck, 1994).

Two areas of research highlight the important role of communication to the well-being of older carereceivers: overly protective care and patronizing communication. The communication of overprotection by carers (for example, offering extensive and unnecessary help) is important, as it has been shown to reduce the physical and psychological health of carereceivers (Thompson & Sobolew-Shubin, 1993; Thompson, Sobolew-Shubin, Graham, & Janigian, 1989). Similarly, Baltes has demonstrated that care provided to older people often encourages dependence, rather than independence, with negative consequences for the well-being of the older person (Baltes, 1996).

Several studies have also shown that communication addressed to older people can convey a lack of support and respect for the older person (for example, Giles, Fox, & Smith, 1993; Ryan, Bourhis, & Knops, 1991). The Communication Predicament of Aging (CPA) model, developed by Ryan, Giles, Bartolucci, and Henwood (1986), outlines how well-intentioned communication addressed toward older people can be perceived to be patronizing and evaluated negatively by them. The selected extract is an example of patronizing communication and is likely to be interpreted by the carereceiving husband as nonsupportive and disrespectful.

The Communication Predicament model draws on the Communication Accommodation Theory (CAT). According to CAT, speakers make certain modifications to their communication style to achieve the desired goals of an interaction. These goals include making the exchange as smooth as possible, seeking social approval, promoting distinctiveness, and exerting control (Coupland, Coupland, Giles, & Henwood, 1988). The modifications are based on the speaker's perceptions of their communication partner and, in particular, of their communicative competence.

There are four major strategies that speakers use to modify their communication: approximation (emphasizing similarities or differences between conversational partners); interpretability (modifying the complexity of communication to assist the listener to understand the message); discourse management (assisting the communication partner to contribute to the conversation); and interpersonal control (controlling the communication by holding the floor, initiating topic changes). The selected extract is an example of the care-giving wife controlling the conversation by ignoring the comments and wishes of her husband. Such strategies are evaluated by the communication partner in terms of whether the speaker is perceived to have accommodated appropriately or inappropriately (for example, over- or underaccommodated).

The communication predicament perspective proposes that, during encounters with older people, conversational partners recognize old age cues that, in turn, stimulate stereotyped expectations about older people being incompetent and dependent. Based on these stereotyped expectations, people commonly modify their communication goals and strategies (for example, speak slowly, loudly, more simply). These modifications are usually unnecessary, reinforce negative age stereotypes, and often limit the older person's opportunities for, and enjoyment of, social interaction. Such communication has been described as "elder speak," "baby talk," or "patronizing" talk, and is considered to be demeaning (Ryan, Hummert, & Boich, 1995).

Paradoxically, communication that is intended to display support often conveys a message of disrespect, and can have negative consequences for older people. Many research studies have confirmed the negative effect of patronizing communication for older people who live in residential care units or in the community (Edwards & Noller, 1993; Giles et al., 1993; Harwood, Giles, Fox, Ryan, & Williams, 1993; Ryan, Hamilton, & Kwong See, 1994; Ryan, Meredith, & Shantz, 1994). Older people who are continually exposed to patronizing communication are likely to experience negative changes to their self-esteem, health, and age identity (Giles & Coupland, 1991).

Given that care giving can be viewed as a communicative process and that communication is the linchpin between social support, psychological well-being, and physical health (Giles, Coupland, & Wiemann, 1990), it is surprising that more attention has not been given to communication processes during family care giving for older people. The research presented in this chapter was undertaken as part of a large study of older people and their family carers, and examines communication processes between spouses where one partner is caring for his/her husband or wife who is frail and can no longer care for themselves.

The purpose of this chapter is to examine marital communication in the care-giving context.

The participants in the study were 53 elderly spousal dyads. Each dyad lived together in the community. To be included in the study, participants had to have adequate sight and hearing (able to see and hear a television set), be able to speak and understand English, and have no diagnosis or history of dementia, confusion, or depression. The care-giving spouses had to be the major provider of care for their spouse. The total sample comprised two groups: 27 wives cared for by husbands, and 26 husbands cared for by wives, and was recruited through community health-care centers and community health-care agencies.

The ages of carereceivers and carers were, respectively, 78 years ($SD = 7.35$) and 74.5 years ($SD = 7.14$). The majority of participants were born in Australia, with the others having been born in the United Kingdom or Europe. The dyads had been married for an average of 51 years ($SD = 14.47$). The carers reported caring for their spouses for an average of 9 years ($SD = 2.68$).

The majority of carers and carereceivers said that the carereceivers suffered from arthritis, muscular-skeletal problems, or cardio-vascular problems. Because carereceivers with a diagnosis of dementia, confusion, or depression had been excluded from the study, the incidence of mental illness in the sample was low, with only one percent reporting that they had experienced a mental health problem in the previous year.

The data were collected by two interviewers who visited the couples in their homes at a mutually convenient time. Responses were obtained using a questionnaire that was administered as a structured interview for both carer and carereceiver. The items in the questionnaire asked the carers and carereceivers to consider the general or usual patterns of communication between them. In addition, to obtain a more objective and in-depth description of communication, a conversation between each spousal dyad was videotaped. The questionnaire was therefore administered before the videotaping segment, to avoid participants' responses about general communication patterns being influenced by a current and salient conversation.

COMMUNICATION GOALS AND STRATEGIES:
HYPOTHESES AND MEASURES

As communication in marital care giving is likely to influence the care-giving experiences, data were collected from the dyads to determine what communication goals and strategies were used by the carers and to what extent these differed by gender of carer. Interactional goals and strategies are the core elements of Communication Accommodation Theory. According to the theory, interaction partners aim to seek approval, promote understanding, promote distance, or exert control (Coupland et al., 1988). Because of the history and the nature of the spousal care-giving relationship, it was hypothesized that carers would report being more concerned about promoting understanding than about seeking approval, exerting control, or promoting distance.

Based on research evidence that females place more emphasis on interpersonal goals (Holmes, 1985), that males are more oriented to task-related goals (Tannen, 1990), and that females have a greater understanding of emotional communication (Noller, 1993), it was hypothesized that female carers would be more concerned about promoting understanding and seeking approval than male carers. In addition, male carers were expected to be more likely to exert control than were female carers.

Most of the theoretical papers on Communication Accommodation Theory have centered on the interactional strategies (briefly defined in the previous section). As the communication partners in spousal care giving are not strangers but share a close, intimate relationship, it was expected that any convergence of the conversational style of the carer toward the carereceiver would occur over time, and would gradually be adopted, unconsciously, as the carer's own style. It was therefore hypothesized that the approximation strategy would be the strategy used least by the carers.

There is extensive evidence in the literature (for example, Kemper, 1994; Montepare, Steinberg, & Rosenberg, 1992) of carers' use of interpretability strategies (for example, simplifying the register, using more repetitions, and talking more slowly). Hence, it was hypothesized that spousal carers would use interpretability strategies more frequently than other strategies. Further, it was expected that care-giving wives would use interpretability strategies more frequently than care-giving husbands.

Conversational partners of older people in institutions and in the community have been found to use discourse management in a negative way, by limiting the range of topics discussed with the older person (Edwards, Moyle, Clinton, Weir, & Eyeson-Annan, 1994; Gibb & O'Brien, 1990; Hummert & Mazloff, 1993 cited in Ryan et al., 1995).

Family carers report using discourse management in this negative way to avoid painful and emotional topics (Wright, 1991), and common techniques include using deflection or active avoidance. Spousal carers were therefore expected to use discourse management in a negative way to avoid discussing painful and difficult issues. Further, as discourse management strategies tend to have a strong interpersonal focus (Gallois, Franklyn-Stokes, Giles, & Coupland, 1988), it was expected that care-giving wives would use these strategies more than care-giving husbands.

Research has shown that interpersonal control strategies are widely used when communicating with older residents in institutions (Caporael, 1981; Edwards et al., 1994; Gibb & O'Brien, 1990; Lanceley, 1985) and in the community (Hummert & Mazloff, 1993 cited in Ryan et al., 1995). Hence, it was hypothesized that the spousal carers in the current study would use interpersonal control strategies more frequently than they used discourse management and approximation strategies. As male carers deal with care giving by managing and directing care (Dwyer & Coward, 1991; Montgomery & Kamo, 1989), it was expected that care-giving husbands would use interpersonal control more than care-giving wives.

The couples in this study were asked questions about the carer's general communication with his or her carereceiver. Questionnaire items represented five interactional goal categories (social approval, attaining communication efficiency, promoting distinctiveness, exerting/confirming control, and meeting emotional needs), and four strategy categories (interpretability, discourse management, interpersonal control, and approximation). Carers were asked to indicate how much they tried to achieve the selected goals in their communication with their carereceivers, and how much they used the selected strategies when conversing with their carereceivers. Carereceivers were asked to indicate how much they believed their carers used the selected strategies when conversing with them.

The items comprising the goal and strategy items were factor analyzed to form scales theoretically consistent with CAT. Three scales – Promoting Understanding, Seeking Approval, and Exerting Control – were formed as measures of carers' goals in communicating with their carereceivers. Four scales – Discourse Management, Interpersonal Control, Interpretability, and Approximation – were formed as measures of strategies used by carers when communicating with their carereceivers.

Table 16.1. Means and Standard Deviations for
Carers' Goals and Strategies

	H-W M (SD)	W-H M (SD)
Goals (Range 1–3)		
Promoting understanding	2.91 (.24)[a]	2.72 (.47)[a]
Seeking approval	2.74 (.29)[a]	2.66 (.49)[a]
Exerting control	2.04 (.56)[b]	2.09 (.62)[b]
Strategies (Range 1–3)		
Reported by Carer		
Discourse management	2.94 (.12)[a]	2.83 (.38)[a]
Interpersonal control	2.06 (.36)[b]	2.02 (.49)[b]
Interpretability	1.84 (.66)[b]	2.01 (.78)[b]
Approximation	1.63 (.48)[c]	1.55 (.50)[c]
Reported by Carereceiver		
Discourse management	2.71 (.43)[a]	2.87 (.21)[a]
Interpersonal control	2.28 (.48)[b]	2.13 (.43)[b]
Interpretability	1.53 (.48)[c]	1.79 (.52)[c]
Approximation	1.51 (.49)[c]	1.51 (.44)[c]

Notes: H-W Husbands caring for wives; W-H Wives caring for
husbands.
For columns within each block, means with different super-
scripts are significantly different from each other at $p = .05$.

Differences in Reported Goals and Strategies

To develop an understanding of how spousal carers communicate with
their carereceivers, the first step was to determine how much carers
wanted to achieve certain goals when communicating with their carereceivers. The dependent variable for this analysis was the carers'
reported desire to achieve the goals. Next, to determine whether carers
tended to use particular strategies, two analyses were undertaken.
In one analysis, the dependent variable was the carers' self-reported
use of the four strategies, and for the other analysis, the dependent variable was the carereceivers' reports of how frequently their carers used
the strategies.

Carers reported wanting to achieve some goals more than others.
Specifically, post-hoc analyses revealed that carers reported wanting to
promote understanding and to seek approval more than they wanted to
exert control (see Table 16.1). The effects of gender and the interaction
of gender and type of goal were not significant.

Carers also used some strategies more than others, as reported both by themselves and by their carereceivers. Specifically, post-hoc analyses revealed that carers reported using Discourse Management more often than any other strategy, Approximation less often than the other strategies, and Interpersonal Control and Interpretability less often than Discourse Management, but more than Approximation (see Table 16.1). Similarly, carereceivers reported that their carers used Discourse Management more often than any other strategy, Interpretability and Approximation less often than the other strategies, and Interpersonal Control less than Discourse Management, but more than Interpretability and Approximation (see Table 16.1). The effects of gender and the interaction of gender and type of strategy were again not significant.

As expected then, the results for desired goals indicated that carers wanted to promote understanding more than they wanted to exert control. Contrary to expectations, however, the gender of carers did not affect their goals.

The hypothesis regarding carers' use of Approximation was confirmed, as this was the least used of all the strategies. As suggested earlier, members of the dyads have probably adapted to each other's styles of communication over time, and consequently convergence was not a salient strategy within the relationship at this time.

Contrary to expectations, Discourse Management, not Interpretability, was reported as the most frequently used strategy in both samples. An explanation for this finding could be that carers tend to address the individual communication needs of their carereceivers, rather than modifying their communication on the basis of stereotyped expectations, as commonly occurs in intergenerational and institutional contexts. Because of the nature of spousal care giving, a carer is more likely to be aware of his or her carereceiver's actual abilities, hence leading to carers' greater reported use of Discourse Management, and less frequent use of Interpretability. The more frequent use of Discourse Management is consistent with the carers' desire to promote understanding, and confirms the tenet of CAT that people select certain strategies to achieve their desired goals. It is also possible that some participants gave socially desirable responses, and reported what they believed *should* happen, rather than what actually did happen.

Carers were predicted to use Discourse Management in a negative way, as research has found that family carers avoid emotional and difficult issues by discouraging discussion of them (Wright, 1991). The behaviors from the Discourse Management scale predominantly reflect the carers' management of the communication *process* (but not the selection of content). The high reported use of positive Discourse Management by carers therefore suggests that carers may try to facilitate carereceivers' contributions to "safe topics" (for example, by head nodding, responding to, and answering carereceivers' questions), but may not facilitate carereceivers' changing of topics. The issues of topic introduction and topic changes are explored further in the next section.

Interpersonal Control was, unexpectedly, used less often than Discourse Management. This unexpected finding reflects a greater use of Discourse Management than expected, rather than a lesser use of Interpersonal Control; although used less frequently than Discourse Management, Interpersonal Control was still used quite frequently by carers. This result is easily understood, as it is reasonable to expect that most spousal carers are very serious about their careprovider role and want to provide the best care they can.

None of the hypotheses about the gender of the carer were confirmed. As many of these hypotheses were based on gender differences identified in noncare-giving contexts, it is likely that, within the context of spousal care giving, the role of being a carer overshadows traditional gender roles. Other care-giving variables (for example, burden, coping) may have a greater effect on carer communication than does gender. Alternatively, husbands who take on the caring role may be similarly oriented to relating and communicating as wives who take on the caring role.

In summary, spousal carers' intentions regarding their communication with their carereceivers were largely positive, as they generally wanted to promote understanding with their carereceivers. To achieve this goal, the carers used predominantly Discourse Management, but also frequently used Interpersonal Control and Interpretability strategies. The pattern of use for goals and strategies was similar for husband and wife carers.

The data presented so far have examined participants' reports ("insider" data) of carers' communication when conversing, in general, with their carereceivers. Such reports of general communication from involved participants are important data. It is equally important, however, to have a complementary and more objective description of how spousal carers and carereceivers actually communicate with one another. In the following section, the content and linguistic features of videotaped conversations between the spousal carers and their carereceivers are described.

CONTENT OF CONVERSATIONS IN SPOUSAL CARE-GIVING COUPLES

No reported studies have specifically examined the content and processes of communication between elderly carereceivers and their spousal carers. In reporting results from care-giving studies, however, comments are often made about the communication of the dyad. For example, in a study on spousal care giving, Wright (1991) noted that tension between spousal dyads was kept low, as a direct result of spouses' avoiding or deflecting discussions about topics likely to give rise to conflict. Some research has examined communication between older people and their professional carers and found that the majority of talk is about physical care, and that deflecting or dismissing concerns raised by older carerecipients is common (Edwards et al., 1994; Gibb & O'Brien, 1990; Grainger, Atkinson, & Coupland, 1990). Based on these findings, it was expected that the content of the couples' conversations would focus on issues related to the care-giving situation, and that the participants would avoid discussing contentious topics, or topics likely to upset their conversational partners.

Briefly, in the study reported here, carers and carereceivers individually selected a "hot" topic (a topic that was a source of tension or disagreement, or was of great concern to them) to discuss with each other. Five minutes of conversation on each participant's topic was videotaped, and the order in which the two topics were discussed was counterbalanced. The recording apparatus was set up in the least intrusive manner possible and the researchers left the room during the videotaping. The videotaping was carried out in the participants' own homes, so that the conversations would be as natural as possible. In an attempt to gauge the "naturalness" of the videotaping segment, participants were asked to complete a questionnaire on their responses to the videotaping. Over 80% of carers and carereceivers reported that the videotaped conversation was "very typical" of the things they usually talked about, and "very typical" of the way they would normally talk to each other. Based on these responses, the videotaped conversations were deemed to provide a realistic sample of how carers and carereceivers talk with one another.

Three aspects of the conversations are described: the content of the issues selected; the topics that were actually discussed during the conversations; and who introduced the topics that were actually discussed. The data were analyzed in terms of the frequency of content

Table 16.2. Percentage of Categories for Issues Selected by Participants According to Role and Gender of Carer

Issue	H-W		W-H	
	Cg	Cr	Cg	Cr
Getting out/doing more	22	18	21	4
Changing partner behavior	13	17	8	18
Aspects of care	13	0	25	4
View on caring situation	13	9	4	9
Alternative living arrangements	9	13	4	4
Wanting to help	4	13	0	4
Major decisions	9	4	8	25
Family events	4	4	14	18
Planning respite/holidays	0	9	4	14
Safety	4	4	8	0
Health services	9	9	4	0
	100%	100%	100%	100%

Notes: H-W Husbands caring for wives; W-H Wives caring for husbands. Cg = Carer; Cr = Carereceiver.

areas. In order to avoid overanalysis of the data, only dominant patterns in the data are discussed.

Content of Issues Selected for Discussion

Prior to the videotaping of the conversations, each member of the dyad was asked to identify an issue that they would like to discuss with their spouse. The most commonly selected issues were getting out/doing more and wanting to change partner's behavior (see Table 16.2). The issue of getting out/doing more was selected quite frequently by both spouses in husband-carer dyads and by care-giving wives, but much less frequently by care-receiving husbands. On the other hand, spouses in the husband-carer dyads and care-receiving husbands selected changing partner behavior much more frequently than did care-giving wives. The frequent selection of these two issues suggests that the majority of participants wanted to improve their situation and wanted to be more active in terms of personal and social interactions.

Such a finding raises doubts about the stereotype that older people are inactive, passive, and prepared to withdraw from society.

Carers, especially care-giving wives, were more interested in discussing aspects of care than were carereceivers. It is understandable that carers would want to discuss care management, and the more frequent selection of this issue by care-giving wives probably reflects the fact that the caring, nurturing role is often seen as more relevant to females.

"Major decisions" was the issue most frequently selected by care-receiving husbands. While of considerable interest to these men, this topic was selected much less frequently by their care-giving wives and by spouses in husband-carer dyads. A similar pattern of selection occurred for the issue "planning respite/holidays." Husbands who are being cared for by their wives may feel in a very dependent situation, in contrast to their precaring situation. In an attempt to exert some control and authority, care-receiving husbands may therefore elect to discuss issues that are of great importance and that require considerable planning. These care-receiving husbands may also be afraid that their point of view will not be taken into account in the discussions with their spouse.

Spouses in wife-carer dyads selected "family events" more frequently than spouses in husband-carer dyads. Dealing with family events (for example, organizing birthdays and outings) is traditionally considered part of the female role, so it is not surprising that issues concerning family events were seen as important in dyads where the wife was the careprovider.

It is interesting to note that two issues, safety and health services, were selected infrequently by members of both types of dyads. In fact, these issues were *never* selected by care-receiving husbands. The infrequent selection of safety as an issue for discussion suggests that the majority of couples do not consider safety to be an area of concern for them, perhaps because they have talked about any potentially unsafe situations. Alternatively, safety may not be an issue that is often discussed, because any risks may be well understood and accepted as part of being older, infirm, and choosing to remain at home.

Content of Topics Actually Discussed

During the conversations that were videotaped, five topics that were not selected as "issues" arose, and formed the major part of the content

Table 16.3. Percentage of Content Categories for Topics Discussed by Participants According to Role and Gender of Carer

	H-W		W-H	
Topic	Cg	Cr	Cg	Cr
Getting out/doing more	12	5	4	2
Changing partner behavior	5	13	7	13
Aspects of care	8	4	14	7
View on caring situation	3	4	1	2
Alternative living arrangements	10	2	4	7
Wanting to help	1	13	0	2
Major decisions	2	7	5	5
Family events	5	7	11	5
Planning respite/holidays	2	9	1	5
Safety	3	0	4	0
Health services	3	5	1	7
Extraneous (for example, sport)	11	15	11	15
The study	8	2	15	11
Hobbies and activities	12	5	7	7
Family and friends	7	7	11	7
Household/personal tasks	8	2	4	5
	100%	100%	100%	100%

Notes: H-W Husbands caring for wives; W-H Wives caring for husbands. Cg = Carer; Cr = Carereceiver.

for the conversations (see lower section of Table 16.3). Nearly 50% of topics discussed by care-giving husbands, care-giving wives, and care-receiving husbands involved these more socially oriented topics (for example, hobbies, family, and friends). For care-receiving wives, these topics accounted for 31% of the topics discussed. While some of this "chit-chat" that took place could be attributed to the demand characteristics of the videotaping task, it could also reflect the tendency of spouses to avoid discussing the real issues. During topic selection, spouses often noted that they would not select an issue for discussion that would "upset their partners." It appears that, even when selecting an issue deemed to be "safe" enough to discuss, spouses may avoid talk that is oriented to solving the problem. Consistent with the emphasis on more socially oriented talk, the most commonly discussed topics (across all spouses) were extraneous things such as the weather and sport.

As noted earlier, the most commonly *selected* issues for the dyads had been getting out/doing more and changing partner behavior. Getting out/doing more was *discussed* frequently by care-giving husbands, while changing behavior was *discussed* frequently by carereceivers of both sexes. These data suggest that many spouses want to be more active and to make changes in their lifestyle. In particular, it appears that care-giving husbands want to be more active and to get out of the home more, while carereceivers appear to want their carers to change some of their own behaviors.

Although some of the issues that had been *selected* frequently for discussion were actually *discussed* during the conversations, many were not. Some spouses, therefore, took the opportunity to discuss issues of concern for them, whereas others did not. As expected, the participants reported wanting to talk about issues related to the care-giving situation. During the conversations, however, they avoided many of these issues and engaged in social chit-chat. This avoidance has been noted previously in spousal caring dyads (Wright, 1991), intergenerational families (Hagestad, 1985), and carers of residents in nursing homes (Edwards et al., 1994; Grainger et al., 1990).

Introduction of Issues Actually Discussed

In husband-carer dyads, husbands' topics were more likely to be introduced by themselves than by their wives. Similarly, in wife-carer dyads, wives' topics were more likely to be introduced by themselves. However, in these dyads, husbands' topics were also more likely to be introduced by their wives. This finding suggests that the care-giving wives were taking a dominant role in the management of the interactions, or that these wives were concerned that, if there was an issue, it should be discussed.

It is interesting to note that, with the exception of those issues raised by care-giving wives, in about a quarter of the conversations in this study, the issue a participant selected was not discussed *at all*. Care-giving wives were, therefore, the participants most likely to have their issues discussed, either by introducing these issues themselves, or by their care-receiving husbands introducing them on their behalf. The care-giving wives in this study appear to be conforming to the general perception that females are better than males at managing conversations, in order to deal with and confront issues (Christensen, 1988; Christensen & Heavey, 1990; Tannen, 1986; 1990).

Summary

Overall, carers introduced their own issues more frequently than did carereceivers. Being the more powerful partner in the conversation, carers probably felt less vulnerable than carereceivers in discussing issues that had the potential to create conflict and unease. The potential power associated with the care-giving role may encourage carers to take a leading and dominant position when communicating with their carereceivers.

The spouses, with the exception of care-giving wives, generally avoided introducing their own or their partners' issues. That is, the spouses actively avoided discussing issues of concern, even the ones they had deemed "safe" enough to discuss. Given that the average length of marriage for couples in this study was 51 years, it is possible that the spouses may have taken it for granted that they were concerned with each other's issues, to the point that these issues were not overtly discussed. From what the spouses told the researchers, however, issues were actively avoided because they were "too upsetting" for their partners. The spouses may have been protecting their partners, or themselves, from displaying their feelings in a situation that was considered threatening. The avoidance of issues in these couples may also be due to a history effect, as issues have probably been discussed many times, and partners may consider that there is no point "going over old ground." Presumably, however, these issues of concern are not yet resolved.

The nature of the issues chosen by the participants suggests that most couples wanted some changes in their situation. The issue of "changing an aspect of their conversational partners' behaviour" was *selected* and *discussed* quite frequently, particularly by the carereceivers. The types of changes the carereceivers reported wanting involved changes to the care-giving routine (for example, bedtime, meal time, bath routines), changes to the partners' communication (for example, talk more, be less bossy or angry), and changes to the partners' activities (for example, less drinking of alcohol, less gambling). These data suggest that carereceivers believe that their carers, and not they themselves, have control over the care-giving routine, reinforcing the dominant role of carers and the submissive role of carereceivers.

In this section, the content of the videotaped conversations between the spousal carers and carereceivers has been discussed. As processes of communication are just as important as content, in the next section a number of communication processes involved in the dyadic conversations are described.

COMMUNICATION PROCESSES DURING THE CONVERSATIONS

These processes were examined in terms of specific communication behaviors, including verbal and nonverbal behaviors, as coded by trained coders. Because a wide range of behaviors can be studied from conversational data, it was necessary to select sets of behaviors that could meaningfully describe communication within the spousal care-giving context.

From the literature, behaviors associated with the four interactional strategies proposed by CAT (discourse management, interpretability, interpersonal control, and approximation) were identified. The communication processes were operationalized as communication behaviors, and the overall patterns of the behaviors were interpreted in terms of the strategies as proposed by CAT.

Verbal processes within the conversations were analyzed in terms of how topics were changed and developed by the dyads, and how turn taking was managed. Two categories of nonverbal behavior were also examined: visual, including touch, gesturing, posture, nodding, and emotional expression; and vocal, including speech rate, pauses, interruptions, and simultaneous speech. A number of hypotheses were posed with regard to the communication behaviors. Briefly, these hypotheses were that: carers would use the various behaviors in a more dominating way than carereceivers; carers would use the behaviors in ways consistent with the CAT strategies; males would use behaviors associated with control and dominance more than females; females would use behaviors associated with affiliation and interpersonal relations more than males; and discussions of carers' issues would be more limited and restricted than discussions of carereceivers' issues.

To examine these hypotheses, the effects of gender, role (carer, carereceiver), and issue (whose issue was being discussed) were examined. A difficulty in examining data from dyads is the potential nonindependence of the data (Kenny, 1995). Because the carers' and carereceivers' communication with one another and their discussions of their own and their partners' issue were unlikely to be independent, role and issue were treated as within-subject variables. For topic management, turn taking, and vocal behaviors (already noted above), the verbatim transcripts of the conversations were used to code the data. For visual behaviors, the videotaped recordings of the conversations were used.

Topic Management

The participants' behaviors that were coded in relation to topic management were : frequency of topic changes; how topics were introduced; how topics were developed (back channelling, partner continuing the topic, topic changing); and whether the spouses shared a common viewpoint or not. Significant effects were obtained for role and gender of carer. Specifically, role had a significant effect on the percentage of "topics changed," "partner continuing," and "partner back channelling," and gender had a significant effect on the two viewpoint variables, "shared" and "not shared."

Carers changed topics more frequently than carereceivers. Carers, in their helping role, may have been trying to help the carereceivers to keep the interaction flowing, or they may have been avoiding certain topics. The carers, nevertheless, tended to control the content of the conversations during discussion of both their own issues and those of their carereceivers.

Partners (that is, those not initiating a topic change) were more likely to provide most of the input into the topic when a carer initiated a topic change than when a carereceiver initiated a topic change. This finding suggests that when a carer changes topics, the carereceiver takes over and provides most of the input for the discussion. As carers change topics more frequently than carereceivers, taking over and dominating the input may be one way in which the carereceivers get to have their say in the interactions.

Partner back channelling was more likely to occur when carers initiated a topic change than when carereceivers initiated a topic change. The data suggest that carereceivers displayed much more interest and encouragement for carers when the carers introduced a topic, than carers provided when carereceivers introduced a topic. As partner back channelling also gives control to the one who initiated the topic change, carereceivers appear to be conforming to the general perceptions about power relations in caring situations: that carers (as the providers of care) hold the power, and that carereceivers are compliant, dependent recipients of care (Dalley, 1993). In addition, the carers may avoid using back channelling in order to discourage their partners from talking, with the result that they maintain control.

As noted earlier, the gender of the carer had an effect on the two viewpoint variables, "shared" and "not shared." Viewpoint was more likely to be shared in husband-carer dyads than in wife-carer dyads. Consistent with this result, there was more "nonshared" viewpoint in wife-carer dyads than in husband-carer dyads. These results suggest that members of husband-carer dyads select topics on which similar viewpoints are generally shared. In contrast, members of wife-carer dyads select topics where a common viewpoint is not shared. Perhaps there is simply more disagreement in dyads where wives care for husbands than in dyads where husbands care for wives. "Safe" topics appear to be selected when the husband is in the more powerful position of carer, while "less safe" topics appear to be discussed when the wife is in the more powerful position of carer. This finding is consistent with research showing that, in marital conflict, wives are more likely to be demanding and to escalate conflict, while husbands tend to withdraw (Christensen & Heavey, 1990).

Turn Taking

Turn-taking behaviors were coded according to five categories: giving suggestions/opinions, giving information, asking for suggestions/opinions, asking for information, and agreeing with the communication partner. There were significant effects for role and for the interaction of role and gender. Role had a main effect on three categories: Carereceivers agreed more than did carers, carers asked for more information than did carereceivers, and carers also asked for more suggestions/opinions than did carereceivers. Together, these results suggest that the carers have more control in the conversation, as they seek disclosure more than carereceivers, but do not offer any more disclosure than carereceivers. The higher rate of agreement from carereceivers also suggests that the carers have an authoritative role. Carers probably believe that, as careproviders, their role is to determine the needs of their carereceivers; hence, they try to make sure that they get the necessary information and suggestions from them.

There was an interaction effect of role and gender of carer on giving suggestions/opinions. Husbands cared for by wives gave fewer suggestions/opinions than their care-giving wives, and fewer than either wives or husbands in husband-carer dyads. Care-receiving husbands' reluctance to give suggestions to their care-giving wives could reflect their possible loss of control. The usual norms for these husbands would be that they should be the provider for the family and consequently hold the more powerful role within the family. In order to deal with the change in power and control, and the ensuing uncertainties, the care-receiving husbands may have adopted the "traditional" or "accepted" role for carereceivers: to be a passive recipient of care (Dalley, 1993).

Vocal Behaviors

Five vocal behaviors were coded: speech rate, short pauses, long pauses, interruptions, and simultaneous speech. Role had a significant main effect on three of these behaviors: speech rate and short and long pauses. No main effects were found for gender or issue.

Carers had a higher speech rate and used more short and long pauses than carereceivers. Using more pauses slows down the overall conversation, and carers may have used this tactic to give the carereceiver time to comprehend what was being said, behavior which is indicative of the interpretability strategy. Although the carers had a higher speech rate than the carereceivers, their speech rate during the conversations could have been lower than their usual speech rate. The higher speech rate and more pausing from carers could also indicate that carers were attempting to hold the floor and, consequently, to dominate the conversations.

Visual Nonverbal Behaviors

Seven visual behaviors were coded: emotional expression (for example, laughing, crying), gesturing, self-touch, fiddling, functional touch, head nodding, and open posture. Role had a main effect on open posture, with carereceivers having more open posture than carers. Perhaps the carereceivers were more relaxed and comfortable during the conversations than were the carers and more open to suggestions and advice from the carers.

Gender of carer had a main effect on functional touch, with more functional touch being observed overall in wife-carer dyads than in husband-carer dyads. The greater use of functional touch in couples where the wife was the carer probably reflects the example set by the care-giving wife. In their roles as wives and carers, these wives were probably used to doing things for their husbands and may have enjoyed this type of activity. The husbands are likely to have reciprocated and started to do some things for themselves or for their wives. Care-giving husbands, in contrast, may not feel very comfortable with their nontraditional role of helper, and consequently may use less functional touch. Further, care-receiving wives may respond to their husbands' low rates of functional touch by reducing their own levels of functional touch.

Whose issue was being discussed had a main effect on self-touch, with more self-touch being observed when the carereceiver's issue was discussed than when the carer's topic was discussed. An explanation for this finding could be that carereceivers' issues are not usually openly discussed between dyad members: Hence, there may be a heightened sense of anxiety or discomfort from both members of the dyad when these issues are discussed, as evidenced by the greater amount of self-touch (Burgoon, Buller, & Woodall, 1989).

Summary

The hypothesis that carers would use communication behaviours in a more dominant way than carereceivers was supported. Carers changed topics more frequently than carereceivers, asked for more information and suggestions than carereceivers, and had higher rates of speech and more long pauses than carereceivers. Additionally, caregiving spouses used more short pauses than their carereceiving spouses. On the other hand, carereceivers agreed more than carers, back-channelled more than carers, and were more likely to continue with topics introduced by their partners than were carers. The posture of the carereceivers was also more open than that of their carers.

IMPLICATIONS OF THE FINDINGS

The data presented in this chapter confirm that the participants' communication was influenced predominantly by their role, with carers dominating and leading the conversations (as seen in the extract at the beginning of the chapter), and carereceivers complying with their carers. In general, although the gender of carer had limited effects on the participants' communication, the direction of the effects observed was consistent with documented gender differences in communication.

The dominant influence of role probably reflects the long-term relationships involved, in which gender issues may be less salient than the frailty of the carereceiver. The communication patterns are consistent with the carer having the more powerful role, and the carereceiver having a more passive and subservient role. These roles can be viewed as legitimate, as the function of a carer is to provide and care for the person who needs assistance. In providing that care, the carer may consider it necessary to ensure that certain issues are talked about, or not talked about, and to help the carereceiver with his or her communication. The carers appear to have adopted a guidance-cooperation style of caring. In this style, the careprovider takes the bulk of responsibility for the care, and although the carereceiver is asked questions (that they are required to answer), the decision making is largely in the hands of the careprovider (Di Matteo, 1991).

As expected, many of the carers' communication behaviors were consistent with the interactional strategies proposed by CAT. Carers made their conversations more comprehensible and suitable for their carereceivers (interpretability) by slowing the conversation down (for example, greater use of short and long pauses), and by avoiding certain topics (through topic changes and deflection). Carers also used their position of power as the careprovider, and maintained control of the conversations (interpersonal control) by holding the floor (for example, increased speech rate, short and long pauses) and directing the content through topic changes and deflection). It could be argued that, by asking for information and by introducing topics to be discussed, the carers were actually helping the carereceivers to contribute to the conversation (discourse management). There is no evidence, however, that the carers facilitated ongoing contributions from the carereceivers (for example, back channelling to carereceiver). While the carers may have intended to facilitate their carereceivers' contributions, the overall pattern of the carers' communication suggests that they directed and dominated the conversations. Interestingly, there did appear to be an attempt from the carereceivers to hold the floor, as carereceivers were more likely to continue with a topic introduced by their carer, than carers were to continue with a topic introduced by their carereceivers. The selected extract demonstrates a care-receiving husband trying to talk to his wife about an aspect of his care that obviously concerns him, but his wife deflects the topic and introduces another topic.

The general pattern of avoidance of certain conversational content between care-giving spouses is consistent with the interpretability and interpersonal control strategies proposed by CAT. When speaking to older persons, people often limit the range of conversational content to topics that they believe the older person can comprehend, or that will not be too cognitively challenging for them (Coupland et al., 1988). Limiting topic choices can also be a way to maintain control of the conversation and to limit the older person's contribution. In short, carers in the current study communicated with their carereceivers in ways suggested by CAT.

The carers' use of many communication behaviors in the current study is consistent with how CAT proposes that people can, inadvertently, communicate inappropriately with older people. Regardless of the classification given to these behaviors, many older people find this style of communication inappropriate and are therefore likely to evaluate it as patronizing, or as conveying disrespect. There is evidence that formal carers of older people use patronizing communication (Ryan et al., 1995), and the current study indicates that patronizing communication is also used by family carers. This communication pattern is likely to have a negative impact on the quality of the relationship, and on the emotional well-being of the carereceivers. For example, if the husband involved in the extract at the beginning of this chapter were to continually have his topic ignored, he could begin to feel very disempowered; in turn, this feeling could negatively affect his relationship with his care-giving wife. Research has shown that overly directive and patronizing communication in family care-giving is related to lowering of positive affect in older carereceivers and high relationship conflict (Edwards & Noller, 1998). Further, in terms of well-being, the negative effect of patronizing communication is likely to be stronger than is the positive effect of supportive communication.

Consistent with results of other care-giving studies, the spousal dyads avoided discussion of issues likely to be contentious. Some researchers suggest that conflict avoidance in intimate relationships may be beneficial (Fitzpatrick, 1988; Raush, Barry, Hertel, & Swain, 1974), especially when confronting conflict does not fit the relational style of those involved. There is, however, evidence that conflict avoidance is not healthy for relationships. Issues cannot be resolved unless they are addressed, and avoidance means that issues are not resolved (Roloff & Cloven, 1990). The person who raises the issue or wishes to discuss it may feel resentful and angry. If spouses are constantly *not* having their issues dealt with, then these negative feelings will increase. When issues *are* finally discussed, therefore, it is not surprising that spouses find it distressing. A self-fulfilling cycle of avoidance and negative affect is likely to develop, and will continue until the spouses are assisted in discussing their issues in a constructive way. Care-giving spouses may therefore benefit from health professionals' guiding and assisting them with problem solving and conflict resolution.

The data presented in this chapter have implications for health practitioners working with husbands and wives where one is caring for the other. It is interesting to note that programs dealing with family relationships have been well accepted by health professionals. Such programs include marriage guidance, parent effectiveness training, and positive parenting instruction. However, programs dealing with relationship issues for older people and their families do not appear to have been a high priority. There is an opportunity for practitioners to develop programs to assist spousal carers and carereceivers with their interpersonal issues. Health professionals working with spousal dyads need to address the power changes within the relationship, and help the dyad to develop a mutual participation mode of care (joint decision making, joint responsibility; Di Matteo, 1991). Practitioners could help couples to discuss the issues that concern them, and work with them toward resolution. In addition, practitioners could work with couples to promote more effective communication patterns, where the carers are less controlling, and carereceivers are less passive.

In this chapter we have examined marital communication within a care-giving context. Little attention has been given to this context in the past and, with the aging profile of our society, these issues should be the focus of more research. The research to date suggests that communication between older care-giving spouses and their carerecipients is influenced more by the roles of carer and carereceiver than by gender. Spousal carers use a style of communication that may reinforce negative stereotypes of aging, be viewed as patronizing, and have a negative effect on the well-being of the carereceivers. The carers are faced with a predicament that often arises in communication with older people: how to show care and concern without conveying disrespect.

Health professionals who work with care-giving dyads need to assist them to develop a more participatory style of care giving, and a communication pattern that promotes well-being. For older couples, care giving and care receiving can be sources of distress, and communication can be the vehicle by which the stresses and strains can be ameliorated. It is therefore crucial that positive and effective communication is maintained between older people and their care-giving spouses.

REFERENCES

Baltes, M. M. (1996). *The many faces of dependency in old age*. New York: Cambridge University Press.

Braithwaite, V. (1998). Institutional respite care: Breaking chores or breaking social bonds. *The Gerontologist, 38(5)*, 610–617.

Burgoon, J. K., Buller, D., & Woodall, W. (1989). *Nonverbal communication: The unspoken dialogue*. New York: Harper & Row.

Caporael, L. R. (1981). The paralanguage of caregiving: Baby talk to the institutionalized aged. *Journal of Personality and Social Psychology, 40*, 876–884.

Carruth, A., Tate, U., Moffett, B., & Hill, K. (1997). Reciprocity, emotional well-being, and family functioning as determinants of satisfaction in caregivers of elderly parents. *Nursing Research, 46(2)*, 93–100.

Christensen, A. (1988). Dysfunctional interaction patterns in couples. In P. Noller & M. A. Fitzpatrick (Eds.), *Perspectives on marital interaction* (pp. 31–52). Avon, England: Multilingual Matters.

Christensen, A., & Heavey, C. L. (1990). Gender and social structure in the demand withdraw pattern of marital conflict. *Journal of Personality and Social Psychology, 59*, 73–81.

Coupland, N., Coupland, J., Giles, H., & Henwood, K. (1988). Accommodating the elderly: Invoking and extending a theory. *Language in Society, 17*, 1–41.

Dalley, G. (1993). The ideological foundations of informal care. In A. Kitson (Ed.), *Nursing: Art and science* (pp. 11–25). London: Chapman & Hall.

Di Matteo, M. R. (1991). *The Psychology of health, illness, and medical care: An individual perspective*. Pacific Grove, CA: Brooks/Cole.

Dwyer, J. W., & Coward, R. T. (1991). A multivariate comparison of the involvement of adult sons versus daughters in the care of impaired parents. *Journal of Gerontology: Psychological Sciences, 46*, 259–269.

Edwards, H. E. (2001). Family caregiving, communication, and the health of care receivers. In M. L. Hummert & J. Nussbaum (Eds.), *Communication, aging and health: Theory and practice* (pp. 203–224). New York: Lawrence Erlbaum Associates.

Edwards, H. E., Moyle, W., Clinton, M., Weir, D., & Eyeson-Annan, M. (1994, May). Nurses' talk in a dementia unit: What is said and what is not. Paper presented to the Second International Conference on Communication, Aging and Health, Hamilton, Canada.

Edwards, H. E., & Noller, P. (1993). Perceptions of overaccommodation used by nurses in communication with the elderly. *Journal of Language and Social Psychology, 12*, 207–223.

Edwards, H. E., & Noller, P. (1998). Factors influencing caregiver-care receiver communication and its impact on the well-being of older care receivers. *Health Communication, 10(4)*, 317–341.

Ferris, C., & Bramston, P. (1994). Quality of life in the elderly: A contribution to its understanding. *Australian Journal on Ageing, 13*, 120–122.

Fitzpatrick, M. A. (1988). *Between husbands and wives*. Newbury Park, CA: Sage.

Gallois, C., Franklyn-Stokes, A., Giles, H., & Coupland, N. (1988). Communication accommodation in intercultural encounters: Intergroup and interpersonal considerations. In Y. Y. Kim & W. B. Gudykunst (Eds.), *Theories in intercultural communication* (pp. 157–185). Newbury Park, CA: Sage.

Gibb, H., & O'Brien, B. (1990). Jokes and reassurances are not enough: Ways in which nurses related through conversation with elderly clients. *Journal of Advanced Nursing, 15*, 1389–1401.

Giles, H., & Coupland, N. (1991). *Language: Context and consequences*. Milton Keynes, England: Open University Press.

Giles, H., Coupland, N., & Wiemann, J. (Eds.). (1990). *Communication, health and the elderly*. Fulbright International Colloquium, 8. Manchester: Manchester University Press.

Giles, H., Fox, W., & Smith, E. (1993). Patronizing the elderly: Intergenerational evaluations. *Research in Language & Social Interactions, 26*, 129–149.

Grainger, K., Atkinson, K., & Coupland, N. (1990). Responding to the elderly: Troubles talk in the caring context. In H. Giles, N. Coupland, & J. Wiemann (Eds.), *Communication, health and the elderly* (pp. 192–212). Manchester: Manchester University Press.

Hagestad, G. O. (1985). Continuity and connectedness. In V. L. Bengston & J. F. Robertson (Eds.), *Grandparenthood* (pp. 31–48). Beverly Hills, CA: Sage.

Harwood, J., Giles, H., Fox, S., Ryan, E. B., & Williams, A. (1993). Patronizing young and elderly adults: Response strategies in a community setting. *Journal of Applied Communication Research, 21*, 211–226.

Holmes, J. (1985). Sex differences and miscommunication: Some data from New Zealand. In J. B. Pride (Ed.), *Cross-cultural encounters: Communication and miscommunication* (pp. 24–43). Melbourne: Riversein.

Kemper, S. (1994). "Elderspeak": Speech accommodation to older adults. *Aging and Cognition, 1*, 17–28.

Kenny, D. A. (1995). The effect of nonindependence on significance testing in dyadic research. *Personal Relationships, 2*, 67–75.

Lanceley, A. (1985). Use of controlling language in the rehabilitation of the elderly. *Journal of Advanced Nursing, 10*, 125–135.

Montepare, J. M., Steinberg, J., & Rosenberg, B. (1992). Characteristics of vocal communication between young adults and their parents and grandparents. *Communication Research, 19*, 479–492.

Montgomery, R. J., & Kamo, Y. (1989). Parent care by sons and daughters. In J. A. Mancini (Ed.), *Aging parents and adult children*. Lexington, MA: Lexington Books.

Neufeld, A., & Harrison, M. (1998). Men as caregivers: Reciprocal relationships or obligation? *Journal of Advance Nursing, 28(5)*, 959–968.

Noller, P. (1993). Communication in marriage: Different cultures or differential social power. *Journal of Language and Social Psychology, 12*, 132–152.

Phillips, L., Morrison, E., Steffl, B., Chae, Y., Cromwell, S., & Russell, C. (1995). Effects of the situational context and interactional process on the quality of family caregiving. *Research in Nursing, 18*, 205–216.

Raush, H. L., Barry, W. A., Hertel, R. K., & Swain, M. E. (1974). *Communication and conflict in marriage*. San Francisco: Jossey-Bass.

Roloff, M., & Cloven, D. H. (1990). The chilling effect in interpersonal relationships: The reluctance to speak one's mind. In D. D. Cahn (Ed.), *Intimates in conflict: A communication perspective* (pp. 49–76). Hillsdale, NJ: Lawrence Erlbaum Associates.

Ryan, E. B., Bourhis, R., & Knops, U. (1991). Evaluative perceptions of patronizing speech addressed to elders. *Psychology and Aging, 6*, 442–450.

Ryan, E. B., Giles, H., Bartolucci, G., & Henwood, K. (1986). Psycholinguistic and social psychological components of communication by and with the elderly. *Language and Communication, 6*, 1–24.

Ryan, E. B., Hamilton, J. M., & Kwong See, S. (1994). Younger and older adult listeners' evaluations of baby talk addressed to institutionalized elders. *International Journal of Aging and Human Development, 39*, 21–32.

Ryan, E. B., Hummert, M. L., & Boich, L. H. (1995). Communication predicaments of aging: Patronizing behavior toward older adults. *Journal of Language and Social Psychology, 14*, 144–166.

Ryan, E. B., Meredith, D. S., & Shantz, G. D. (1994). Changing the way we talk with elders: Promoting health using the communication enhancement model. *International Journal of Ageing and Human Development, 41*, 89–107.

Tannen, D. (1986). *That's not what I meant!: How conversational style makes or breaks relationships*. New York: Ballantine Books.

Tannen, D. (1990). *You just don't understand: Women and men in conversation*. New York: Morrow.

Thompson, S. C., & Sobolew-Shubin, A. (1993). Perceptions of overprotection in ill adults. *Journal of Applied Social Psychology, 23*, 85–97.

Thompson, S. C., Sobolew-Shubin, A., Graham, M. A., & Janigian, A. S. (1989). Psychosocial adjustment following a stroke. *Social Science and Medicine, 28*, 239–247.

Whitbeck, L., Hoyt, D. R., & Huck, S. M. (1994). Early family relationships, intergenerational solidarity and support provided to parents by their adult children. *Journal of Gerontology: Social Sciences, 49*, S85–S84.

Wright, L. K. (1991). The impact of Alzheimer's disease on the marital relationship. *The Gerontologist, 31*, 224–237.

INTERVENTIONS FOR STRENGTHENING RELATIONSHIPS

Introduction to Section Six

We have learned a great deal about marital interaction from the extensive research carried out over the last few decades. However, the findings have not always been readily available to the general population. The results of research studies can only help couple relationships to the extent that they find their way into the popular literature, or are applied in the therapeutic context. The chapters in this section emphasize ways in which couple relationships can be strengthened through appropriate intervention.

Story, Rothman, and Bradbury explore the risk factors for marital dysfunction, using a longitudinal study of the first four years of marriage. Their main focus is on the effects of parental divorce and negativity in the family of origin; that is, on the intergenerational transmission of relationship difficulties. Given that these family of origin factors are not, of themselves, amenable to change, an important issue associated with intergenerational transmission concerns the identification of variables that may mediate the effects of negative family-of-origin experiences on marital functioning. Interpersonal processes are particularly relevant in this context, because these processes can be modified by teaching couples appropriate relationship skills.

Story and her colleagues recruited couples in the first six months of marriage, in order to monitor their progress across the critical early years. They also assessed the couples using multiple measures of marital behavior, including problem solving, physical and psychological aggression, and negative affect (coded from a problem solving interaction). Marital outcome was defined by an assessment of marital adjustment after four years of marriage.

For wives, marital outcome was predicted by parental divorce. For husbands, on the other hand, marital outcome was predicted by negativity in the family of origin (that is, low parental marital satisfaction, poor family functioning, and high levels of family conflict). These links were mediated by spouses' marital behavior. The effect of parental divorce for wives was mediated by their levels of physical and psychological aggression in the first year of marriage, whereas the effect of family-of-origin negativity for husbands was mediated by the level of negative affect observed in the couple's interaction. The authors emphasize the possibility of developing prevention programs tailored to the specific vulnerabilities of young couples whose family backgrounds put them at risk for marital difficulties.

Halford and his colleagues are also concerned with intervention processes. They take the perspective that relationships need to be "worked at," a perspective that is at odds with the widely held perception in western society that love is mysterious, effortless, all-consuming, and an act of fate or destiny.

Halford and colleagues focus on the concept of self-regulation, or partners' ability to modify their own behavior in relationship-enhancing ways. They argue that interventions for couples should emphasize the importance of a broad set of self-regulation skills, rather than specific communication skills. In this way, partners are provided with the flexibility to deal with difficult situations in their relationship in whatever context they arise.

In this chapter, the authors report on the development of a measure of relationship self-regulation, and of an intervention program designed to foster these skills. Their measure, the Self-Regulation for Effective Relationships Scale (SRERS), assesses three aspects of self-regulation: self-regulation strategies, relationship effort, and relationship goals.

The intervention program comes in three different formats, all of which emphasize goal setting, as well as the implementation and evaluation of self-change strategies. The various formats allow the program to be applied in either a clinical or an educational setting, with the latter being based on either face-to-face or flexible delivery. The researchers provide preliminary evidence that self-regulation is associated with relationship satisfaction (both concurrently and longitudinally), and that the principles of self-regulation can be usefully applied both to general samples of couples, and to those experiencing relationship distress.

In both of these chapters, spouse behavior is seen as pivotal to marital outcomes. Hence, whether practitioners are dealing with general samples of couples, or with those whose earlier family experiences may place them at risk for marital distress, an important focus is on interpersonal processes and skills. Skills in controlling the emotional climate of couple interaction, and in defining and evaluating relationship goals, appear to be particularly crucial.

CHAPTER SEVENTEEN

Risk Factors, Risk Processes, and the Longitudinal Course of Newlywed Marriage

Lisa B. Story, Alexia D. Rothman,
and Thomas N. Bradbury

> After all, the rosy love-making and marrying and Epithalamy are no more than the dawn of things, and to follow comes all the spacious interval of white laborious light. Try as we may to stay those delightful moments they fade and pass remorselessly . . . We go on – we grow. At least we age. Our young couple, emerging presently from an atmosphere of dusk and morning stars, found the sky gathering grayly overhead and saw one another for the first time clearly in the light of every day.
> —H. G. Wells, *Love and Mr. Lewisham*, 1900

The heavy emphasis on dyadic process that typified marital research in the past is giving way to studies that examine marital interaction in relation to characteristics of individual spouses. Promising findings are emerging, for example, in studies linking marital processes to attachment (for example, Carnelley, Pietromonaco, & Jaffe, 1996; Collins & Feeney, 2000), personality (for example, Karney & Bradbury, 1997), and divorce in spouses' families of origin (for example, Amato, 1996). However, the interaction between the various intrapersonal and interpersonal factors relevant to marriage is complex, and the specific pathways leading to marital dysfunction remain unclear. In this chapter, we discuss the ways in which an applied emphasis may help to sharpen this focus, and we examine the implications of premarital

This work was supported by National Science Foundation Graduate Fellowships awarded to Lisa Barcelo Story and Alexia Rothman, by the Committee on Research of the UCLA Academic Senate, by the John Templeton Foundation, and by grant R01 MH48674 from the National Institute of Mental Health.

We thank Benjamin Karney, Catherine Cohan, Matthew Johnson, Kieran Sullivan, Erika Lawrence, Rebecca Cobb, Ron Rogge, and Tyler Story for their helpful comments on this chapter and assistance in the data collection.

Address correspondence to Lisa Story, UCLA Department of Psychology, Box 951563, Los Angeles, CA 90095-1563. E-mail: lbarcelo@ucla.edu.

interventions for basic research. We then review previous work that explores the mechanisms by which premarital risk factors may affect marital outcome, and we present new data that highlight the advantages of this perspective for integrating premarital risk factors, interpersonal behaviors, and marital outcome.

AN EMPHASIS ON CHANGE

Framing research questions in terms of their potential for altering the course of marriage can focus research on the most critical aspects of marital functioning. Rather than exploring possible relationships among a vast number of possible predictors, this approach leads us to study the factors presumed to be most important for generating change in marital functioning. This emphasis also underscores the value of stringent methodological standards such as representative samples, longitudinal methods, and multiple methods of measurement for the key variables of interest. Such methods rise in importance when findings must generalize to community populations and when the correlates of dysfunction must be disentangled from the causal factors to be targeted in intervention.

More specifically, an applied approach focuses our work on two critical questions: "Who" is our population of interest? and "what" should we attempt to change? It has been argued elsewhere that answering these questions has far greater relevance to the goals of preventive intervention than to marital therapy (Bradbury, 2000; Bradbury, Rogge, & Lawrence, 2001). Therapists encounter clients with a variety of unique histories and manifestations of distress, and they may gain little from mean comparisons between distressed and nondistressed couples. Such interventions may be better informed by case studies and by experimental research assessing the value of particular treatment strategies.

Prevention programs, in contrast, can teach newlyweds critical skills without direct reference to each couple's unique issues, concerns, and history. Preventive interventions are also appealing in that they may intervene to remedy maladaptive behaviors early when it is still relatively easy for couples to learn new patterns of interaction. Marital therapy may be likened to a visit to the dentist for a sore tooth. Each patient requires an assessment of his or her relatively unique personal ailment and medical history to determine the most appropriate procedure. In contrast, premarital prevention programs may be likened to educating people about the benefits of daily brushing and flossing. It is relatively simple to disseminate this information to many people, and all are expected to benefit from the same preventive resource. This simple and relatively uniform intervention has potential to reduce the likelihood that those who receive the intervention will have to endure potentially unpleasant and complicated procedures in the future. Whether our interventions for couples can become even more effortless – the equivalent of fluoridated water in the drinking supply, perhaps – remains to be seen.

Implications of Prevention for Basic Research

There are three basic approaches to preventing marital difficulties, each of which would have different implications for whom to target and what to change (Heller & Monahan, 1977). Primary prevention is available to all couples and provides them with resources that may prevent difficulties from developing. Such programs are well-informed by research that identifies the general predictors of marital outcome for all couples. In contrast, secondary prevention aims to reduce the severity of marital difficulties among high-risk populations. These programs would benefit from identifying which couples are at elevated risk for dysfunction, and on the mechanisms by which risk factors affect marital outcome. Finally, tertiary prevention is undertaken to reduce the recurrence of problems in couples who are already exhibiting marital dysfunction. Marital therapy employs tertiary prevention strategies and may not be best informed by basic research, as previously discussed. Thus, our options are to intervene before some adverse situation arises (primary prevention), before it gets worse (secondary prevention), and before it is too late (tertiary prevention).

Primary and secondary prevention strategies each confer unique advantages and disadvantages. Primary prevention programs, which comprise the majority of prevention programs available to newlywed couples today, typically focus on effective conflict management by providing couples with basic communication tools (Bradbury & Fincham, 1990; see Sayers, Kohn, & Heavy, 1998 for a recent review). Conflict and negative communication appear to be appropriate targets for change, given their association with marital distress (see Weiss & Heyman, 1997; cf. Bradbury et al., 2001). This approach is also quite efficient, as participation is available to all couples and there is no need to recruit high-risk couples for participation. Markman, Floyd, and Dickson-Markman (1982) argue that primary prevention programs are preferable to secondary prevention due to inaccuracies in the prediction of risk, and to possible ethical considerations that arise in sharing that information during recruitment. These are important, but not insurmountable obstacles, given that risk algorithms can be improved (for example, Rogge & Bradbury, 1999) and that simple risk indicators (for example, parental divorce) could be used to heighten awareness of risk without undue stigma.

The concern can be raised, however, that primary prevention programs have not been reaching couples at greatest risk for adverse marital outcomes. The couples who have been most likely to seek premarital counseling appear to be those who are least likely to encounter marital difficulties (Sullivan & Bradbury, 1997). The cost associated with recruitment of high-risk couples for secondary prevention may be worthwhile, if it improves the likelihood of reaching the couples most in need with an effective intervention.

Can we assume that programs devised for primary prevention of marital distress are effective for at-risk couples? At present, the efficacy of traditional primary prevention programs in general, and with high-risk populations in particular, is an empirical question still open to discussion (for example, see Bradbury, Cohan, & Karney, 1998). To refer back to our earlier analogy, simple education about brushing and flossing may not suffice for those dental patients who are predisposed to cavities or who report eating sweets excessively. Those at elevated risk may require unique preventive strategies. Likewise, couples who are at elevated risk for marital dysfunction may benefit from interventions that recognize and address this fact.

Two recent studies have applied the basic communication-focused preventive approach to high-risk couples. Van Widenfelt, Hosman, Schaap, and van der Staak (1996) examined the effectiveness of a communication skills based prevention program with married and dating couples in the Netherlands. Couples were classified as high-risk if either partner had experienced parental divorce. At the nine-month follow-up, the only significant difference between the treatment and control conditions was an increase in reported intensity of marital problems in the treatment condition. This finding, taken in conjunction with the increase in problem intensity among high-risk couples in both the treatment and control conditions, suggests that such preventive programs should be modified in order to be effective with higher risk populations. However, the possible inefficacy of the intervention could also explain this pattern of results, as the increase in problem intensity among high-risk couples would also be expected under conditions in which they receive no treatment.

More recently, Halford, Sanders, and Behrens (2001) examined the effectiveness of a communication-based prevention program for high- and low-risk couples in Australia. Couples were classified as high-risk if the wife reported parental divorce and/or the husband reported parental domestic violence (also see Halford, Sanders, & Behrens, 2000; Sanders, Halford, & Behrens, 1999; Skuja & Halford, 2000). In light of the Hahlweg, Markman, Thurmaier, Engl, and Eckert (1998) findings that a preventive program improved observed but not self-reported behaviors, observational data were collected before and after treatment. At the one-year follow-up, high-risk couples demonstrated improved marital satisfaction and observed communication in the treatment condition, but not in the control condition. Although these findings contradict the Van Widenfelt et al. (1996) conclusion that prevention programs are not well-suited to high-risk couples, the inclusion of behavioral data and the apparent treatment efficacy lend credence to these findings. The low-risk couples in the treatment and control conditions demonstrated similar communication patterns, raising concerns about the appropriateness of such programs for this population. Despite the possibility of a ceiling effect for positive functioning among these couples, these results highlight the importance of evaluating the efficacy of preventive programs for high- and low-risk populations in future research.

There are clear advantages to both primary prevention and secondary prevention. Primary prevention is available to all couples, avoiding the costs and complexities associated with recruiting high-risk couples; secondary prevention focuses resources where they are most needed, and can address the unique deficits of specific populations. In view of the relative paucity of information pertaining to secondary prevention and the likelihood that at-risk couples will not participate routinely in premarital intervention programs, we have chosen to emphasize the goals inherent in secondary prevention in this chapter. Our discussion focuses on the two key considerations raised earlier: Who is at risk for marital dysfunction and what are the mechanisms by which risk factors affect outcome.

RISK FACTORS AND MECHANISMS

Prior to reviewing previous research on risk factors for marital dysfunction, it is useful to clarify the meanings of basic risk terminology. Variables that can be altered through intervention will be referred to as *variable risk factors*, whereas those that cannot be manipulated, such as year of birth or race, will be referred to as *fixed markers*. Although many fixed markers may have been open to change at some point in the couple's history, we will treat as fixed any marker variable that is not open to change by the time of marriage. An important subset of those variables that are open to manipulation can be demonstrated to affect outcome, and are known as *causal risk factors* (Kraemer, Kazdin, Offord, & Kessler, 1997).

Fixed markers and causal risk factors are of interest to marital researchers. Even though fixed markers cannot be altered, they may help to identify high-risk couples. For example, people who experienced parental divorce as children are at an elevated risk for marital dysfunction and divorce (Amato, 1996). By the time couples marry, this event is not open to change. (The meaning of the event may be open to modification, of course, but the fact that the event occurred cannot be changed.) However, once high-risk couples are identified using fixed markers, putative causal risk factors such as interpersonal negativity may be targeted for change. Fixed markers are particularly useful for recruitment when causal risk factors would require significantly greater screening resources, as might be the case with interpersonal negativity. Once the associations between fixed markers and causal risk factors have been clarified, interventions can begin to target the risk mechanisms among these populations.

Fixed Markers

In this section we review the effects of fixed markers such as parental divorce, premarital cohabitation, and age at marriage on marital quality and divorce. We then discuss interpersonal risk factors and examine the associations between fixed markers, behavioral mechanisms, and marital outcome.

The increased probability that children of divorce eventually will divorce themselves (for example, Amato, 1996; Glenn & Kramer, 1987) and report lower marital quality than those from intact families (for example, Amato & Booth, 1997; Feng, Giarusso, Bengston, & Frye, 1999; Kulka & Weingarten, 1979; McLeod, 1991) has been replicated across studies. Bumpass, Martin, and Sweet (1991) estimated that parental divorce increases the odds of marital dissolution within the first five years of marriage by 70%. Likewise, parents' marital quality has been shown to predict offspring marital quality and likelihood of divorce (Amato & Booth, 1997; Feng et al., 1999).

Premarital cohabitation also appears to increase the likelihood of divorce and marital dissatisfaction (Bennett, Blanc, & Bloom, 1988; Newcomb, 1986; Watson, 1983; Watson & DeMeo, 1987), although the underlying mechanism of this effect is still open to debate. The effect appears to be stronger among females and African Americans than among males and Caucasians (Crohan & Veroff, 1989; DeMaris & Leslie, 1984; Newcomb, 1986). There is also some evidence that this association may be due, in part, to a weaker commitment to the relationship (Kurdek & Schmitt, 1986). When Booth and Johnson (1988) controlled for commitment to marriage, parental pressure, personality problems, and difficulties with unemployment, the law, or money, the association between cohabitation and marital disagreement became nonsignificant. These findings suggest that the apparent effect of cohabitation on marital outcome may stem in part from less traditional attitudes and lifestyles among some cohabiting couples.

Finally, demographic factors such as level of education or age at marriage are associated with marital outcome. Couples of lower socioeconomic status are more likely to experience high levels of marital dissatisfaction (Conger, Cui, Bryant, & Elder, 2000; Voydanoff, 1991) and divorce (White, 1991; U.S. Bureau of the Census, 1992). The age at which couples marry is also predictive of divorce (Bumpass et al., 1991; White, 1991), perhaps due to the inadequate preparation for marital roles, and the lack of economic resources available to young couples. South (1995) also concluded that some of this effect could be attributed to lower levels of education in younger couples.

Interpersonal Processes

In addition to the vulnerabilities that each partner brings to marriage, the nature of their dyadic interaction may increase further the likelihood of marital dysfunction. Interpersonal processes in marriage may operate independently of partners' individual vulnerabilities, or they may serve as the mechanisms by which fixed risk factors affect marital outcome. There is consistent evidence that behaviors displayed during marital problem-solving discussions, such as criticism, withdrawal, and negative reciprocity, are associated with marital quality (see Weiss & Heyman, 1997). In a recent review of marital interaction research, Heyman (2001) concluded that distressed couples are more likely to engage in pursuit-withdrawal patterns of interaction, demonstrate lower levels of positive behavior and higher levels of hostility, and reciprocate partner hostility. In fact, even when dissatisfied couples are asked to "fake good" or pretend that they are maritally satisfied, they can be distinguished from satisfied couples by their negative affect (Vincent, Friedman, Nugent, & Messerly, 1979).

Whereas the cross-sectional literature on interaction and satisfaction is reasonably coherent, the longitudinal findings do not yet tell a simple story. On one hand, a number of studies have shown that adverse marital outcomes are predicted by physical aggression (Heyman, O'Leary, & Jouriles, 1995; O'Leary, Barling, Arias, & Rosenbaum, 1989; Quigley & Leonard, 1996) and by negative behavior in marital interaction (for a review see Karney & Bradbury, 1995). On the other hand, contradictory findings have led to some dispute about the nature and magnitude of the association between interpersonal behaviors and changes in marital functioning over time (see Fincham & Beach, 1999 and Bradbury et al., 2001 for discussion). Review of this debate is beyond the scope of this chapter, though it does appear that resolution of this matter awaits (a) refined methods for quantifying change in marital functioning and (b) identification of variables that moderate the effect of specific behaviors on marital outcome (see Krokoff, 1991).

Heyman (2001) raises an interesting question regarding the malleability of couples' communication patterns. If these behaviors are relatively stable, then they should be treated as fixed markers, rather than causal risk factors that can be targeted for change. In two recent studies that have addressed this issue, Gottman and Levenson (1997) found that couples' observed affect during conflict discussions remained relatively stable over a period of four years, whereas Lord (1999) found low levels of behavioral consistency over the first five years of marriage. Because the Lord (1999) couples were still newlyweds, whereas the Gottman and Levenson (1999) couples had been married for five years, these conflicting findings introduce the possibility that marital behaviors become more stable over time (but see high stability figures over the first three years of marriage obtained by Kiecolt-Glaser, personal communication, 1999, reported in Bradbury et al., 2001). The early malleability of couple communication has received further support through the repeated success of premarital prevention programs in altering marital communication styles (Hahlweg, Markman, Thurmaier, Eckert, Engl, & Markman, 1998; Halford, Sanders, & Behrens, 2001).

To this point we have provided a brief overview of current thinking on the primary demographic, interpersonal, and family of origin risk factors for marital dysfunction. For further discussion of these and other vulnerabilities that predispose couples to marital dysfunction, we refer readers to a recent review by Karney and Bradbury (1995). We now turn to an integration of fixed markers, causal mechanisms, and marital outcome.

Integrating Fixed Markers, Interpersonal Processes, and Outcome

Once fixed markers and causal risk factors have been identified, the relationship between risk factors and causal mechanisms may be explored. For example, family of origin experiences appear to be linked closely to demographic risk factors and to interpersonal behaviors that predict marital outcome. Adults who have experienced parental divorce are more likely to cohabit before marriage (Amato, 1996; Booth & Edwards, 1989; Bumpass et al., 1994), marry at a younger age (Amato, 1996; Mueller & Pope, 1977), and obtain fewer years of education (Mueller & Pope, 1977; Zill, Morrison, & Coiro, 1993). Adults who experienced parental divorce also tend to report higher levels of conflict and maladaptive interpersonal patterns (Amato, 1996; Booth & Edwards, 1989; Silvestri, 1992; Tallman, Gray, Kullberg, & Henderson, 1999; Webster, Orbuch, & House, 1995). In a recent study, Sanders, Halford, and Behrens (1999) videotaped couples during a conflict discussion and found that, when wives had experienced parental divorce, couples demonstrated higher levels of negative communication patterns such as withdrawal and invalidation, as well as lower levels of positive discussion. The couples were then asked to watch their taped interaction and report their cognitions regarding the discussion. Again, the couples in which wives had experienced parental divorce reported more negative and fewer positive cognitions.

These findings are consistent with the view that demographic variables and interpersonal processes mediate the link between experiences in the family of origin and subsequent marital outcomes. Unfortunately, much of this research focuses upon the correlates of parental divorce in adulthood, without extending findings to a formal mediation model. That is, in the absence of direct tests of mediation, it is not clear whether such demographic and interpersonal risk factors are the mechanisms by which family of origin risk factors affect marital outcome. For example, marital hostility may be correlated spuriously with parental divorce, without mediating the path between parental divorce and outcome. In this case, altering the level of hostility may do little to reduce the risk associated with parental divorce. Only by identifying the associated risk mechanisms can the effects of such fixed markers be reduced by targeting those causal risk factors for change.

In one notable test of mediation, Amato (1996) followed a sample of 1,387 married couples for 12 years in an attempt to compare the interpersonal behaviors of partners from intact and divorced families of origin. Upon examination of a variety of demographic risk factors, attitudes, and reported interpersonal problems, Amato concluded that maladaptive interpersonal behaviors accounted for the largest portion of the association between parental divorce and offspring divorce; demographic risk factors mediated a smaller portion of the association. Discrete-time hazard models were used to estimate the odds of couple divorce, and the association between parental divorce and couple divorce became nonsignificant when interpersonal behaviors and demographic risk variables were introduced into the model.

Following this work, Feng et al. (1999) attempted to identify the variables mediating the effects of parental marital functioning, in addition to the effect of parental divorce. The intergenerational transmission of divorce was stronger for wives, whereas the transmission of marital quality was stronger between husbands and their fathers. Age at marriage mediated the transmission of divorce but not the transmission of marital quality. In other words, when age at marriage was taken into account, the association between parental and couple divorce became nonsignificant. However, the comparative strength of interpersonal mediators was not examined. Bumpass, Martin, and Sweet (1991) also concluded that demographic risk factors mediated the effects of parental divorce on couple divorce. However, their findings are somewhat ambiguous because the hierarchical models used to test this hypothesis were not included in their results.

Finally, Conger et al. (2000) examined the effects, on romantic relationships eight years later, of family interactions among 193 families, assessed when children were in the seventh grade. The quality of the young adults' relationships was higher to the extent that the parents had been nurturing, involved, and supportive during the family interactions. This association appeared to be mediated by the quality of the offspring's affective behaviors toward their partners. These findings are particularly noteworthy because all participating families remained intact until they had a child in the seventh grade. Thus, the level of marital dissatisfaction in the population was probably undersampled, providing a fairly stringent test of these effects (see Bradbury, Johnson, & Story, 2001 for further discussion of this study).

Limitations of Previous Work

The three studies discussed in the previous section raise interesting questions regarding the importance of interpersonal and demographic risk factors for couples from high conflict or divorced families of origin. As a group, they suggest that the effect of parental divorce on marital outcome is mediated by interpersonal behavior, and to a lesser degree by demographic risk. The quality of family functioning appears to be mediated solely by interpersonal behavior. However, there are several limitations to this body of work. First, the level of marital distress common to these samples is fairly low. Participants in the Conger et al. (2000) study reported relatively high levels of marital satisfaction and commitment (with mean scores of 8.22 and 8.97, respectively, on scales ranging from 1 to 10), and only 12% of the couples included in the Amato (1996) main analyses actually divorced. The pitfalls associated with sampling high functioning couples are highlighted in Feng et al. (1999), in which couples' low endorsement of physical aggression precluded a test of interpersonal mediators in their analyses. Even when low-risk samples do not result in such extreme consequences, they may limit the extent to which main predictors can be generalized to lower functioning couples.

The heterogeneity of the relationship lengths within these samples is also of concern. For example, the Conger et al. (2000) study included married, dating, and cohabiting relationships. The couples included in the Feng et al. (1999) and Amato (1996) analyses could have been married for any length of time, and the couples in the Feng et al. (1999) study were not required to be in their first marriage. As the majority of divorces occur within the first four years of marriage (Bumpass, Sweet, & Martin, 1990; London & Wilson, 1988), samples composed of older relationships will miss a significant portion of couples in the same population cohort that have already divorced. In a reanalysis including only those participants in the first four years of marriage, Amato (1996) found that the effect of parental divorce was stronger, and that demographic variables no longer mediated the path between parental divorce and marital outcome. Interpersonal behavior was the only remaining mediator of the association. Such inconsistent findings demonstrate that risk mechanisms apply to specific populations; therefore, clear identification of these populations is paramount.

Measuring maladaptive behaviors several years into marriage may also obscure the differences between factors that *predict* marital outcome, and those that are merely symptomatic of the marital dissatisfaction that has already developed. This problem becomes even greater when interpersonal behaviors and marital outcome are measured at the same point in time, as in the Conger et al. (2000) paper. Although their test of mediation rested on the assumption that interpersonal processes predict relationship quality, the direction of the effects remains unclear. Due to the concurrent assessment of behavior and outcome, it is also plausible that relationship quality was predicting the interpersonal behaviors. In order to clarify causal relationships between potential mediators and marital outcome, it becomes critical to conduct longitudinal studies in which the potential mediators are measured at an earlier point in time, and are shown to predict subsequent outcome.

Finally, future research may improve the precision with which key variables are assessed. The inclusion of behavioral observation in the Conger et al. (2000) study is a noteworthy contribution to this end, particularly in light of the known discrepancies between partners' reports of relationship events and actual behaviors (for example, Floyd & Markman, 1983; Jacobson & Moore, 1981). In contrast, Amato (1996) relied upon a brief checklist of interpersonal mediators and Feng et al. (1999) did not include interpersonal behavior in their analyses. The main advantage afforded by the Amato (1996) behavioral checklist was the statistical power of a sample containing over 1,500 couples, compared to the 193 families studied by Conger et al. (2000). Observational methods provide very valuable information about the behaviors that might be targeted in intervention programs, but they often lead to studies with smaller samples, thereby reducing the number of variables that may be included in the analysis. In other words, what is gained in precision and specificity with observational data is often sacrificed in the power and in the breadth of behavioral measurement. However, once early exploratory work has identified the key behaviors of interest, subsequent research may refine the assessment of these variables in smaller samples.

In this section we have reviewed previous work that points to the ways we might integrate the effects of family of origin, demographic risk, and interpersonal mechanisms on marital outcome. However, few of these studies included formal tests of mediation, and there is suggestive evidence that those that did were limited by the restricted range of couple functioning, inadequate behavioral measurement, or the concurrent measurement of mediators and outcome. We now turn to a presentation of a study we conducted in an attempt to address these issues.

THE PRESENT STUDY

We examined behavioral and demographic risk factors as the potential mechanisms linking family of origin risk to marital outcome in a study involving 60 newlywed couples. Our study sought to build upon previous work by including multiple measures of marital behavior, recruiting couples at greater risk for marital dysfunction, and following newlywed couples over the first four years of marriage, a critical period for marital dissolution. For a complete description of this study, see Story, Karney, Lawrence, and Bradbury (2001).

We tested five hypotheses. First, parental divorce and negativity in the family of origin were hypothesized to predict outcome in the fourth year of marriage, thus replicating the intergenerational transmission of marital dysfunction effect. Second, the association between parental divorce and marital outcome was predicted to be greater for wives than for husbands (Amato, 1996; Booth & Edwards, 1989; Feng et al., 1999; Glenn & Kramer, 1987; Sanders et al., 1999). In contrast, no gender effects were hypothesized for negativity in the family of origin, because the link between more subjective indices of family functioning and marital outcome has not consistently been shown to vary by gender. Third, interpersonal behavior and demographic risk were hypothesized to mediate the effect of parental divorce on marital outcome in Year 4, although comparatively weaker effects were hypothesized for demographic risk, consistent with the Amato (1996) findings. Fourth, interpersonal behavior but not demographic risk was hypothesized to mediate the effect of family of origin negativity, in light of the Feng et al. (1999) and Conger et al. (2000) findings. Finally, marital satisfaction in the first year of marriage was examined as an alternative mediator of marital outcome four years later, due to the possibility that the early maladaptive behaviors thought to mediate the effects of family of origin risk are merely reflecting lower levels of marital satisfaction.

Newspaper advertisements were used to recruit 60 newlywed couples for a larger project on newlywed marriage. Couples were eligible for participation if they were in the first six months of marriage, had not been married previously, had no children, and were currently living together. The initial lab session was scheduled within six months of their wedding.

An aggregate measure of family of origin negativity was created by combining normalized measures of parental satisfaction (Semantic Differential measure of parental marital satisfaction), family conflict (Family Conflict subscale of the Family Environment Scale; Moos, 1974;

Waldron, Sabatelli, & Anderson, 1990), and overall family functioning (Family of Origin index of the Marital Satisfaction Inventory; Snyder, 1979). These three variables correlated significantly among husbands and among wives ($p < .001$, 1-tailed).

Couples reported, via questionnaire and individual interviews, basic demographic information such as income, premarital cohabitation, parental divorce, and level of education. Reported interpersonal behaviors were measured using the Constructive Communication subscale of the Communication Patterns Questionnaire (CPQ-CC: Heavey, Larson, Zumtobel, & Christensen, 1996) to assess problem-solving strategies, and the Conflict Tactics Scale (Straus, 1979) to assess physical and psychological aggression (see Murphy & O'Leary, 1989).

Audiotaped 15-minute problem-solving discussions were coded for affective behavior using the Specific Affect Coding System (SPAFF; see Gottman, 1994).[1] The codes of anger, contempt, and humor had the highest interrater reliabilities,[2] were most frequently coded, and provided the least skewed distributions. For these reasons, and to limit the number of variables included in the analysis, anger and contempt codes were combined for husbands and wives to create an observed negativity composite score (cf. Burman, Margolin, & John, 1993); at the couple level, anger and contempt were significantly correlated, $p < .01$.

Because we were interested in the prevention of adverse marital outcomes generally, and because the sample size was relatively small, we created a dichotomous outcome variable to distinguish between the 35 couples with poor marital outcomes in Year 4 (19 divorced and 16 in which one partner scored below 100 on the MAT (Locke & Wallace, 1959) and the 22 couples with satisfactory marital outcomes, in which both spouses scored above 100 on the MAT. Three couples were lost to attrition.[3]

---

[1] The coders classified each 5-s interval according to whether it contained anger, contempt, whining, sadness, anxiety, humor, affection, interest, or neutral affect. When coding for each emotion, the coders were instructed to consider voice tone, volume, and verbal content. Each specific instance of affect was coded once within each 5-s interval. Each tape was coded independently by two coders. The data from one of the coders were randomly selected for analysis, as their coding was considered to be interchangeable.

[2] Interrater correlations indicated that six of the eight emotions were coded reliably, including humor (husbands, $r = .83$; wives, $r = .92$), affection (husbands $r = .55$; wives, $r = .56$), anger (husbands, $r = .72$; wives, $r = .88$), contempt (husbands $r = .81$; wives, $r = .99$), whining (husbands $r = .69$; wives, $r = .81$), and sadness (husbands $r = .95$; wives, $r = .61$).

[3] Previous papers on this sample (for example, Cohan & Bradbury, 1994; Karney & Bradbury, 1997; Pasch & Bradbury, 1998) included only 56 couples in the analyses,

Baron and Kenny (1986) identify three main requirements for mediation, using multiple regression analyses. First, the original predictor (family of origin) must predict outcome (marital outcome). Second, this predictor (family of origin) must also be associated with the mediating variable (interpersonal or demographic risk). Third, the original predictor and the mediating variable are simultaneously entered into a regression equation predicting outcome: In this final step, outcome must be associated with the mediator, but may no longer be associated with the original predictor. These requirements were examined in the following tests of mediation.

Family of Origin and Marital Outcome

Husbands and wives from divorced families had higher family of origin negativity scores than those from intact families, $p < .05$. In the following analyses, parental divorce and family negativity were examined individually to clarify their relative contributions to marital outcome. In our first hypothesis, family of origin risk was hypothesized to predict marital outcome. This association was significant for wives' parental divorce and husbands' family of origin negativity, $p < .05$, but not for husbands' parental divorce or wives' family of origin negativity.

Second, gender effects were hypothesized for parental divorce, but not for family of origin negativity. As predicted, the effect size for parental divorce was significantly greater for wives than for husbands, $p < .05$. The effect sizes for family negativity did not vary significantly by gender. Wives' parental divorce and husbands' family of origin negativity were the only variables shown to significantly predict marital outcome (the first requirement of mediation), so these were the only family of origin variables included in the following analyses.

Mediating the Effect of Parental Divorce
Interpersonal and demographic risk were hypothesized to mediate the effect of parental divorce on marital outcome, with comparatively weaker effects hypothesized for demographic risk. Chi square and

because four couples originally dropped from the study. In 1999, three of those couples were recontacted to determine whether they had divorced within the original study period and one couple had done so. As the other two couples had remained intact, but had not reported marital satisfaction in Year 4, they were not included in further analyses. When a measure was missing data for an individual item, the item score was imputed from the mean of the existing items in that composite for that participant. When a measure was missing data for all items, the sample mean for that composite was imputed.

t-tests were conducted to identify the interpersonal and demographic risk variables that were associated with parental divorce (that is, the second requirement for mediation). As predicted, wives who had experienced parental divorce were significantly more likely to have cohabited with their husband, to report higher levels of physical and psychological aggression, and to have partners who reported higher levels of psychological aggression, all $p < .05$. Contrary to predictions, these couples were not significantly more likely to display negative affect during the conflict discussion, or to report maladaptive conflict resolution patterns on the CPQ-CC (Heavey et al., 1996). Wives' physical and psychological aggression each met the third requirement for mediation, thereby mediating the path between parental divorce and marital outcome (see Figure 17.1, top left and top right). Again, these findings are consistent with the Amato (1996) study, in which interpersonal behavior was the primary mediator of the association between parental divorce and marital outcome among newlyweds.

Mediating the Effect of Family of Origin Negativity

Interpersonal behavior but not demographic risk was hypothesized to mediate the effect of family of origin negativity. T-tests and correlations were conducted to identify the interpersonal and demographic risk variables that were significantly associated with husbands' family negativity. Consistent with Levy, Wambolt, and Fiese (1997), family negativity significantly predicted couples' observed negativity during the problem-solving discussion, $p < .05$. Contrary to our predictions, however, it did not predict reported interpersonal behaviors. The quality of family of origin functioning was not significantly associated with demographic risk, consistent with Feng et al. (1999). Finally, the third requirement for mediation was examined, and observed couple negativity was found to mediate the path between family negativity and marital outcome (see Figure 17.1, bottom center).

Initial Marital Satisfaction as a Potential Mediator

Due to the possibility that marital satisfaction is driving the behavioral mediation effects, Time 1 satisfaction was also examined as a possible mediator. However, wives' parental divorce and husbands' family negativity were not found to differ by initial marital satisfaction. This finding suggests that the effects of family of origin are not merely a function of global judgments of relationship functioning. Instead, it appears that

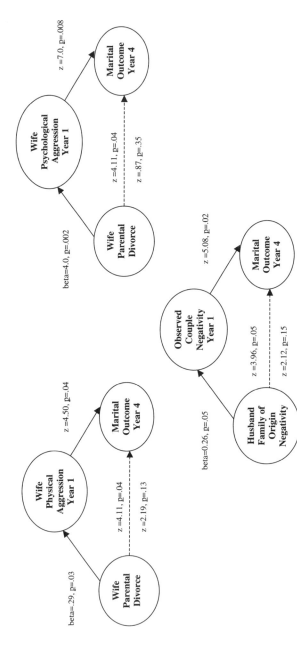

Figure 17.1. Marital behavior mediates family of origin effects. (*Note*: N = 57. Linear and logistic regression coefficients are reported for continuous and dichotomous dependent variables, respectively. Significance levels reported above and below the dotted path reflect the prediction of outcome from parental divorce/family of origin negativity in unmediated and mediated forms, respectively.)

these partners bring to their marriages specific behavioral patterns, which are associated with poor marital outcomes.

Implications for Future Research

These findings address important limitations in previous work, yet they corroborate and extend prior studies by showing that spouses' experiences in their families of origin predict maladaptive interpersonal behaviors, which in turn predict adverse marital outcomes. Nevertheless, the sample size limited our ability to draw strong conclusions from nonsignificant findings, and limited the extent to which the mediated pathways could be refined; future replication of these findings is therefore warranted. For example, future researchers may wish to examine specific aspects of family of origin negativity or apply our mediated pathways to various marital outcomes. Likewise, researchers could explore the impact of factors that may buffer the effects of family of origin risk on these pathways.

We have argued throughout this chapter that framing questions in terms of their potential applications for marital change results in improved methodology and more informative hypotheses. Previous longitudinal studies of spouses' families of origin have been limited by high levels of marital functioning, heterogeneous relationship lengths, inadequate behavioral measurement, and the concurrent assessment of mediators and outcome. Our applied focus highlighted the importance of a generalizable sample and the refined assessment of mediators, thus helping to overcome several of the previous limitations. Other researchers may find this applied approach to be a useful tool that focuses research questions and methods on the most critical factors associated with changes in marital functioning.

Finally, future research should examine the mechanisms by which other fixed markers, such as demographic risk or personality characteristics, affect marital outcome. Significant advances have been made in the exploration of such fixed markers, and of the causal processes associated with marital dysfunction. However, an integration of these fixed markers and causal risk factors is only beginning. It may be useful to examine not only the causal processes associated with a fixed marker, but also to begin with a causal risk factor, such as interpersonal negativity, and identify the associated markers. Whereas the first approach helps target the behavioral mechanisms operating among specific high-risk populations, the second may aid in the recruitment of couples with poor interpersonal functioning. The importance of formal tests of mediation cannot be overstated, as these tests clarify the extent to which behavioral processes are mechanisms by which premarital risk factors affect marital outcome, or are merely spurious correlates.

Implications for Applying these Findings

This study helps to clarify the behavioral mechanisms that mediate the effects of family of origin risk on subsequent marital outcome. Whereas the effect of wives' parental divorce on outcome was mediated by their physical and psychological aggression during conflict, the effect of husbands' family negativity was mediated by observed couple negativity during a problem discussion. It is possible that the experience of a parental divorce (and the marital interaction that precedes it) sets the stage for aggressive conflict behaviors, whereas family of origin negativity predisposes offspring to recreate emotional negativity in their intimate relationships. If this pattern of results is replicated, interventions may begin to target the specific vulnerabilities brought to marriage by couples at high-risk for poor marital functioning.

On a broader level, these findings draw attention to the value of working with young at-risk couples to modify expressions of strong negative affect. Couples most frequently receive premarital counseling through church-related settings, which traditionally focus on religious values and compatibility (Markman et al., 1982; Sullivan & Bradbury, 1997). Such programs are rarely validated empirically and many do not include training in communication skills. In contrast, empirically based programs such as the Prevention and Relationship Enhancement Program (PREP; Markman, Floyd, Stanley, & Storaasli, 1988) typically focus on building communication and problem-solving skills. Although the high rates at which couples decline treatment may artificially inflate the success rate of PREP, this program appears to increase marital satisfaction in comparison to a control group up to five years later (Hahlweg et al., 1998; Markman et al., 1988). Such communication-based programs appear to help couples regulate negative affect (Hahlweg et al., 1998; Halford et al., 2001), and may effectively modify negative communication patterns among couples reporting high family of origin risk (Halford et al., 2001; cf. Van Widenfelt et al., 1996). The elevated rates of physical and psychological aggression among wives from divorced families in our sample also suggest that it may be appropriate to offer

SAVE (Stop Anger and Violence Escalation) to these couples, a prevention program that focuses on alternatives to physical and emotional aggression (Holtzworth-Munroe, Markman, O'Leary, & Neidig, 1995).

Although behaviorally based programs such as PREP and SAVE may be appropriate for couples reporting family of origin risk, the Halford et al. (2000) study suggests that they may be less effective for lower-risk populations. If this is the case, then such programs could be offered at the level of secondary prevention, but would not be appropriate as a form of primary prevention. Before such questions can be addressed, however, future outcome studies must clarify the efficacy of such programs for high- and low-risk populations.

CONCLUSION

This chapter has illustrated the ways in which applied research goals can help focus hypotheses upon the key questions of importance. Specifically, we have discussed the implications of a secondary prevention agenda for "who" is our population of interest and "what" should be the target of change. Once the associations between fixed markers and causal risk factors have been clarified, mediation analyses should examine the extent to which the causal risk factors are the mechanisms by which premarital markers affect marital outcome.

Our recent study clarifies the behavioral mechanisms by which parental divorce and family of origin functioning impact marital outcome. This work builds upon previous research by including multiple measures of marital behavior, recruiting couples at greater risk for marital dysfunction, and following newlywed couples over the first four years of marriage, a critical period for marital dissolution. As the nuances of family of origin vulnerabilities are further specified, early interventions may begin to target the behavioral mechanisms by which they affect outcome in this high-risk population.

REFERENCES

Amato, P. R. (1996). Explaining the intergenerational transmission of divorce. *Journal of Marriage and the Family, 58*, 628–640.
Amato, P. R., & Booth, A. (1997). *A generation at risk: Growing up in an era of family upheaval*. Cambridge, MA: Harvard University Press.
Baron, R. M., & Kenny, D. A. (1986). The moderator-mediator variable distinction in social psychological research: Conceptual, strategic, and statistical considerations. *Journal of Personality and Social Psychology, 51*, 1173–1182.

Bennett, N. G., Blanc, A. K., & Bloom, D. E. (1988). Commitment and the modern union: Assessing the link between premarital cohabitation and subsequent marital stability. *American Sociological Review, 53,* 127–138.

Booth, A., & Edwards, J. N. (1989). Transmission of marital and family quality over the generations: The effect of parental divorce and unhappiness. *Journal of Divorce, 13,* 41–58.

Booth, A., & Johnson, D. R. (1988). Premarital cohabitation and marital success. *Journal of Family Issues, 9,* 225–272.

Bradbury, T. N. (2000). Research on relationships as a prelude to action. Manuscript submitted for publication. University of California, Los Angeles.

Bradbury, T. N., Cohan, C. L., & Karney, B. R. (1998). Optimizing longitudinal research for understanding and preventing marital dysfunction. In T. N. Bradbury (Ed.), *The developmental course of marital dysfunction* (pp. 279–311). New York: Cambridge University Press.

Bradbury, T. N., & Fincham, F. D. (1990). Preventing marital dysfunction: Review and analysis. In F. D. Fincham & T. N. Bradbury (Eds.), *The psychology of marriage: Basic issues and applications* (pp. 375–401). New York: Guilford Press.

Bradbury, T. N., Johnson, M., & Story, L. B. (2001). Extrapolating from basic research to preventive interventions with couples and families. *Prevention and Treatment, 4.*

Bradbury, N., Rogge, R., & Lawrence, E. (2001). Reconsidering the role of conflict in marriage. In A. Booth, N. Crouter, & M. Clements (Eds.), *Couples in Conflict* (pp. 13–41). Hillsdale, NJ: Lawrence Erlbaum Associates.

Bumpass, L. L., Martin, T. C., & Sweet, J. A. (1991). The impact of family background and early marital factors on marital disruption. *Journal of Family Issues, 12,* 22–42.

Bumpass, L., Sweet, J., and Martin, T. C. (1990). Changing patterns of remarriage. *Journal of Marriage and Family, 52,* 747–756.

Burman, B., Margolin, G., & John, R. S. (1993). America's angriest home videos: Behavioral contingencies observed in home reenactments of marital conflict. *Journal of Consulting and Clinical Psychology, 61,* 28–39.

Carnelley, K., Pietromonaco, P., & Jaffe, K. (1996). Attachment, caregiving, and relationship functioning in couples: Effects of self and partner. *Personal Relationships, 3,* 257–278.

Cohan, C. L., & Bradbury, T. N. (1994). Assessing responses to recurring problems in marriage: Evaluation of the marital coping inventory. *Psychological Assessment, 6,* 191–200.

Collins, N. L., & Feeney, B. C. (2000). A safe haven: An attachment theory perspective on support seeking and caregiving in intimate relationships. *Journal of Personality and Social Psychology, 78(6),* 1053–1073.

Conger, R. D., Cui, M., Bryant, C. M., & Elder, G. H., Jr. (2000). Competence in early adult romantic relationships: A developmental perspective on family influences. *Journal of Personality & Social Psychology, 79,* 224–237.

Crohan, S. E., & Veroff, J. (1989). Dimensions of marital well-being among white and black newlyweds. *Journal of Marriage and the Family, 51,* 373–383.

DeMaris, A., & Leslie, G. R. (1984). Cohabitation with the future spouse: Its influence upon marital satisfaction and communication. *Journal of Marriage and the Family, 46,* 77–84.

Feng, D., Giarusso, R., Bengston, V., & Frye, N. (1999). Intergenerational transmission of marital quality and marital instability. *Journal of Marriage and the Family, 61,* 451–463.

Fincham, F. D., & Beach, S. R. H. (1999). Conflict in marriage: Implications for working with couples. *Annual Review of Psychology, 50,* 47–77.

Floyd, F. J., & Markman, H. J. (1983). Observational biases in spouse observation: Toward a cognitive/behavioral model of marriage. *Journal of Consulting and Clinical Psychology, 51,* 450–457.

Glenn, N. D., & Kramer, K. B. (1987). The marriages and divorces of the children of divorce. *Journal of Marriage and the Family, 49,* 811–825.

Gottman, J. M. (1994). *What predicts divorce? The relationship between marital processes and marital outcomes.* Hillsdale, NJ: Lawrence Erlbaum Associates.

Gottman, J. M., & Levenson, R. W. (1999). How stable is marital interaction over time? *Family Process, 38,* 159–165.

Hahlweg, K., Markman, H. J., Thurmaier, F., Engl, J., & Eckert, V. (1998). Prevention of marital distress: Results of a German prospective longitudinal study. *Journal of Family Psychology, 12,* 543–556.

Halford, K., Sanders, M., & Behrens, B. (2001). Can skills training prevent relationship problems in at-risk couples? Four-year effects of a behavioral relationship education program. Manuscript submitted for publication. Griffith University, Brisbane, Australia.

Halford, W. K., Sanders, M. R., & Behrens, B. C. (2000). Repeating the errors of our parents? Family of origin spouse violence and observed conflict management in engaged couples. *Family Process, 39,* 219–235.

Heavey, C. L., Larson, B. M., Zumtobel, D. C., & Christensen, A. (1996). The communication patterns questionnaire: The reliability and validity of a constructive communication subscale. *Journal of Marriage and the Family, 58,* 796–800.

Heller, K., & Monahan, J. (1977). *Psychology and community change.* Homewood, IL: Dorsey.

Heyman, R. (2001). Observation of couple conflicts: Clinical assessment, applications, stubborn truths, and shaky foundations. *Psychological Assessment, 13,* 5–35.

Heyman, R. E., O'Leary, K. D., & Jouriles, E. N. (1995). Alcohol and aggressive personality styles: Potentiators of serious physical aggression against wives? *Journal of Family Psychology, 9,* 44–57.

Holtzworth-Munroe, A., Markman, H., O'Leary, K. D., & Neidig, P. (1995). The need for marital violence prevention efforts: A behavioral-cognitive secondary prevention program for engaged and newly married couples. *Applied & Preventive Psychology, 4,* 77–88.

Jacobson, N. S., & Moore, D. (1981). Spouses as observers of the events in their relationship. *Journal of Consulting & Clinical Psychology, 49,* 269–277.

Karney, B. R., & Bradbury, T. N. (1995). The longitudinal course of marital quality and stability: A review of theory, methods, and research. *Psychological Bulletin, 118,* 3–34.

Karney, B. R., & Bradbury, T. N. (1997). Neuroticism, marital interaction, and the trajectory of marital satisfaction. *Journal of Personality and Social Psychology, 72*, 1075–1092.

Kraemer, H. C., Kazdin, A. E., Offord, D. R., & Kessler, R. C. (1997). Coming to terms with the terms of risk. *Archives of General Psychiatry, 54*, 337–343.

Krokoff, L. J. (1991). Communication orientation as a moderator between strong negative affect and marital satisfaction. *Behavioral Assessment, 13*, 51–65.

Kulka, R. A., & Weingarten, H. (1979). The long-term effects of parental divorce in childhood on adult adjustment. *Journal of Social Issues, 35*, 50–78.

Kurdek, L. A., & Schmitt, J. P. (1986). Relationship quality of partners in heterosexual married, heterosexual cohabiting, and gay and lesbian relationships. *Journal of Personality and Social Psychology, 51*, 627–636.

Levy, S. Y., Wambolt, F. S., & Fiese, B. H. (1997). Family-of-origin experiences and conflict resolution behaviors of young adult dating couples. *Family Process, 36*, 297–310.

Locke, H. J., & Wallace, K. M. (1959). Short Marital-Adjustment and Prediction Tests: Their reliability and validity. *Marriage and Family Living, 21*, 251–255.

London, K. A., & Wilson, B. F. (1988). Divorce. *American Demographics, 10*, 22–26.

Lord, C. (1999). Stability and change on interactional behavior in early marriage. Unpublished doctoral dissertation, Stony Brook, NY, State University of New York.

Markman, H. J., Floyd, F., & Dickson-Markman, F. (1982). Toward a model for the prediction and prevention of marital and family distress and dissolution. In S. Duck (Ed.), *Personal relationships: 4. Dissolving personal relationships* (pp. 173–195). New York: Guilford Press.

Markman, H. J., Floyd, F. J., Stanley, S. M., & Storaasli, R. D. (1988). Prevention of marital distress: A longitudinal investigation. *Journal of Consulting and Clinical Psychology, 56*, 266–289.

McLeod, J. D. (1991). Childhood parental loss and adult depression. *Journal of Health and Social Behavior, 32*, 266–289.

Moos, R. (1974). *Combined preliminary manual for the family, work, and group environment scales.* Palo Alto, CA: Consulting Psychologist Press.

Mueller, C. W., & Pope, H. (1977). Marital instability: A study of its transmission between generations. *Journal of Marriage and the Family, 39*, 83–93.

Murphy, C. M., & O'Leary, K. D. (1989). Psychological aggression predicts physical aggression in early marriage. *Journal of Consulting and Clinical Psychology, 57*, 579–582.

Newcomb, M. (1986). Cohabitation, marriage and divorce among adolescents and young adults. *Journal of Social and Personal Relationships, 3*, 473–494.

O'Leary, K. D., Barling, J., Arias, I., & Rosenbaum, A. (1989). Prevalence and stability of physical aggression between spouses: A longitudinal analysis. *Journal of Consulting and Clinical Psychology, 57*, 263–268.

Pasch, L. A., & Bradbury, T. N. (1998). Social support, conflict, and the development of marital dysfunction. *Journal of Consulting and Clinical Psychology, 66*, 219–230.

Quigley, B. M., & Leonard, K. E. (1996). Desistance of husband aggression in the early years of marriage. *Violence & Victims, 11*, 355–370.

Rogge, D. R., & Bradbury, T. N. (1999). Till violence does us part: The differing roles of communication and aggression in predicting adverse marital outcomes. *Journal of Consulting and Clinical Psychology, 67*, 340–351.

Sanders, M. R., Halford, W. K., & Behrens, B. C. (1999). Parental divorce and premarital couple communication. *Journal of Family Psychology, 13*, 60–74.

Sayers, S. L., Kohn, C. S., & Heavey, C. (1998). Prevention of marital dysfunction: Behavioral approaches and beyond. *Clinical Psychology Review, 18*, 713–744.

Silvestri, S. (1992). Marital instability in men from intact and divorced families: Interpersonal behavior, cognitions and intimacy. *Journal of Divorce and Remarriage, 18*, 79–108.

Skuja, K., & Halford, W. K. (2000). Repeating the errors of our parents? II: Parental spouse abuse in men's family of origin and conflict management in dating couples. Manuscript submitted for publication. Griffith University, Brisbane, Australia.

Snyder, D. K. (1979). Multidimensional assessment of marital satisfaction. *Journal of Marriage and the Family, 41*, 813–823.

South, S. J. (1995). Do you need to shop around? Age at marriage, spousal alternatives, and marital dissolution. *Journal of Family Issues, 4*, 432–449.

Story, L., Karney, B., Lawrence, E., & Bradbury, T. (2001). Interpersonal mediators in the intergenerational transmission of marital dysfunction. Unpublished manuscript. University of California, Los Angeles.

Straus, M. A. (1979). Measuring intrafamily conflict and violence: The conflict tactics (CT) scales. *Journal of Marriage and the Family, 41*, 75–88.

Sullivan, K. T., & Bradbury, T. N. (1997). Are premarital prevention programs reaching couples at risk for marital dysfunction? *Journal of Consulting and Clinical Psychology, 65*, 24–30.

Tallman, I., Gray, L. N., Kullberg, V., & Henderson, D. (1999). The intergenerational transmission of marital conflict: Testing a process model. *Social Psychology Quarterly, 62*, 219–239.

U.S. Bureau of the Census. (1992). *Studies in household and family formation.* (Current Population Reports, Series P23, No. 179). Washington, DC: U.S. Government Printing Office.

van Widenfelt, B., Hosman, C., Schaap, C., & van der Staak, C. (1996). The prevention of relationship distress for couples at risk: A controlled evaluation with nine-month and two-year follow-ups. *Family Relations: Journal of Applied Family & Child Studies, 45*, 156–165.

Vincent, J. P., Friedman, L. C., Nugent, J., & Messerly, L. (1979). Demand characteristics in observations of marital interaction. *Journal of Consulting and Clinical Psychology, 47*, 557–566.

Voydanoff, P. (1991). Economic distress and family relations: A review of the eighties. In A. Booth (Ed.), *Contemporary families: Looking forward, looking back* (pp. 429–445). Minneapolis, MN: National Council on Family Relations.

Waldron, R. J., Sabatelli, R. M., & Anderson, S. A. (1990). An examination of the factor structure of the family environment scale. *American Journal of Family Therapy, 18*, 257–272.

Watson, R. E. (1983). Premarital cohabitation vs. traditional courtship: Their effects on subsequent marital adjustment. *Family Relations: Journal of Applied Family and Child Studies, 32*, 139–147.

Watson, R. E., & DeMeo, P. W. (1987). Premarital cohabitation vs. traditional courtship and subsequent marital adjustment: A replication and follow-up. *Family Relations: Journal of Applied Family and Child Studies, 36*, 193–197.

Webster, P. S., Orbuch, T. L., & House, J. S. (1995). Effects of childhood family background on adult marital quality and perceived stability. *American Journal of Sociology, 101*, 404–432.

Weiss, R. L., & Heyman, R. E. (1977). A clinical-research overview of couples interactions. In W. K. Halford & H. Markman (Eds.), *Clinical handbook of marriage and couples interventions* (pp. 13–41). New York: John Wiley & Sons.

Wells, H. G. (1900). *Love and Mr. Lewisham.* New York: Harper & Brothers.

White, L. K. (1991). Determinants of divorce: A review of research in the eighties. In A. Booth (Ed.), *Contemporary families: Looking forward, looking back* (pp. 141–149). Minneapolis, MN: National Council on Family Relations.

Zill, N., Morrison, D. R., & Coiro, M. J. (1993). Long-term effects of parental divorce on parent-child relationships, adjustment, and achievement in young adulthood. *Journal of Family Psychology, 7*, 91–103.

CHAPTER EIGHTEEN

Does Working at a Relationship Work? Relationship Self-Regulation and Relationship Outcomes

*W. Kim Halford, Keithia L. Wilson,
Alf Lizzio, and Elizabeth Moore*

Good marriages don't just happen – they take a lot of love and a lot of work.

—Tipper Gore, *Life*, February 1999

Life happens and where does the magic go? Can it be revived? Yes, but it takes more than magic. It takes work; it takes time.

—Arp & Arp, 2001, p. 118

The idea of making marriage work may seem to conflict with how relationships should be – magical and romantic. . . . But, if couples can learn how to make the magic themselves, then they will be able to keep their relationship's promise – the creation of a better life together.

—Lucas, 1997, p. 11

Happiness in marriage is entirely a matter of chance.

—Jane Austen, *Pride and Prejudice*, p. 1

It is a commonly held belief in western cultures that successful marriage requires work by the partners. In the first quote above, a prominent member of the American community proffers the view that partners need to work at their relationships. In the next two quotes, some authors of widely read popular books on marriage express a similar idea. However, as the final quote from one of the world's best-known romantic writers demonstrates, the view that work is a major determinant of marital satisfaction is not universally endorsed.

The preparation of this chapter was supported by the Australian Research Council Grant entitled *Effects of a flexible delivery relationship education program on relationship skills, satisfaction, and stability in high risk couples* to W. Kim Halford and Keithia Wilson, and by the Australian Research Council Grant entitled *Relationship self-regulation in the prediction of relationship satisfaction and stability in the early years of marriage* to W. Kim Halford, Keithia Wilson, and Alf Lizzio.

In this chapter, we describe a program of research evaluating the proposition that the work or effort that partners put into their relationship determines, in part, whether couples sustain relationship satisfaction. When beginning this program of research, we reflected on how best to conceptualize and measure the commonsense notion of relationship work. The construct of relationship self-regulation seemed best to capture the phenomenon of interest, so our research and this chapter are focused upon this construct. We first outline the dependent variable of interest: the trajectory of relationship satisfaction over time in married couples. Next is a brief critique of previous attempts to predict the trajectory of relationship satisfaction, which leads to an argument for how we think the concept of relationship self-regulation may add to existing knowledge. Then we describe the construct of relationship self-regulation, as well as our development of measures of that construct. This description is followed by an overview of preliminary evidence on the extent to which relationship self-regulation predicts relationship satisfaction. Finally, we outline some research on the effects of teaching relationship self-regulation to couples.

PRIOR RESEARCH ON SATISFYING MARRIAGE AND ITS DETERMINANTS

The Trajectory of Relationship Satisfaction

Relationship satisfaction in couples is almost universally high at the time of marriage, but average satisfaction levels decrease markedly across the course of marriage, at least for the first 10 years of marriage (Bradbury, Cohan, & Karney, 1998; Glenn, 1998; Huston, McHale, & Crouter, 1986; Karney & Bradbury, 1997; Kurdek, 1998; Veroff, Douvan, Orbuch, & Acitelli, 1998). Decreased satisfaction is associated with high risk of separation (Gottman, 1993), particularly if there is physical aggression between the partners (Rogge & Bradbury, 1999). About 42% of Australian marriages, 55% of American marriages, 42% of English marriages, and 37% of German marriages end in divorce (De Guibert-Lantoine & Monnier, 1992; McDonald, 1995). About half of these divorces occur in the first seven years of marriage (McDonald, 1995).

Notwithstanding the average trend for relationship satisfaction to decrease over time, there is great variability among couples with respect to the trajectory of relationship satisfaction. Many couples sustain high relationship satisfaction, while other couples develop distressed relationships (Karney & Bradbury, 1995). The key issue we are addressing in our research is what determines the different trajectories of relationships. In pursuing this issue we focus on the factors influencing couple relationships that may be modifiable, as our long-term goal is to develop interventions that assist couples to have more satisfying relationships.

Prediction of Relationship Satisfaction and Stability

There are over 120 published studies assessing the association between psychological variables and the longitudinal course of couple relationship satisfaction and stability (Halford, 1999; Karney & Bradbury, 1995). There are also numerous studies that have examined social and demographic variables as predictors of relationship satisfaction and stability (Glenn, 1998; Larson & Holman, 1994). Building upon the work of Bradbury (1995), Halford (1999; 2001) proposed a model that provides a useful heuristic device to summarize the extensive literature on prediction of relationship satisfaction and stability.

Halford (2001) suggested that four broad classes of variables impact upon the trajectory of relationship satisfaction and stability: (1) Contextual variables are the broader cultural and social circumstances within which couple relationships exist. Factors such as the support of the relationship by family and friends, religiosity, and the country in which the couple live, predict relationship satisfaction (Larson & Holman, 1994). (2) Life events include both socially normative transitions, such as the birth of a child, a change of job, or minor illness in the family, and major stressful events such as death or severe illness in the family. Both normative and major stressful life events predict relationship satisfaction (Karney & Bradbury, 1995). (3) Individual characteristics are relatively stable individual differences that partners bring to the relationship, such as the family-of-origin experiences of the partners, partner similarity on education and religion, individual partner psychological disorder, and certain personality variables. Each of these individual characteristics predicts relationship satisfaction (Bradbury, 1998; Fowers & Olson, 1986; Karney & Bradbury, 1995; Larson & Holman, 1994). (4) Finally, couple adaptive processes refer to the patterns of interaction between the partners, and partners' thoughts and feelings during interaction. Couple communication, relationship expectations, gender role flexibility, and mutual partner support are examples of adaptive couple processes that predict relationship satisfaction and stability (Bradbury, 1998; Fowers & Olson, 1986; Karney & Bradbury, 1995; Larson & Holman, 1994).

Considering that a wide range of variables predicts the trajectory of relationships, there are two major implications for studying the effects of people working on their relationships. First, the variance accounted for by working on a relationship is likely to be limited by the effects of some individual characteristics. For example, violence by men has major deleterious effects on their spouse and the relationship (Cascardi, Langhinrichsen, & Vivian, 1992; McLaughlin, Leonard, & Senchak, 1992; O'Leary, Malone, & Tyree, 1994; Straus & Gelles, 1986). For a substantial proportion of men who engage in severe violence toward their spouse, this violence reflects a broad antisocial, aggressive interpersonal style (Holtzworth-Munroe, Smutzler, Bates, & Sandin, 1997). The female partner's behavior has little influence on the level of aggression in such relationships (Cordova, Jacobson, Gottman, Rushe, & Cox, 1993; Jacobson, Gottman, Waltz, Rushe, Babcock, & Holzworth-Munroe, 1994). Consequently, any work the woman does to improve the relationship may make little difference.

A second implication of the wide range of variables that predict relationship outcomes is that work on the relationship may interact with these other variables. In particular, certain contexts or life events might make working at the relationship more important at some times than others. For example, the transition to parenthood is often associated with increased demands on both partners' time, the need to renegotiate relationship roles (Sanders, Nicholson, & Floyd, 1997), and declines in couple relationship satisfaction (Belsky & Pensky, 1988; Cowan & Cowan, 1992; Shapiro, Gottman, & Carerre, 2000). Working on the relationship might have greater impact on relationship satisfaction or stability during these times of change than at other times.

Skills Training to Promote Better Relationships

Across the United States, Western Europe, and Australia, relationship education programs are widely available to marrying couples (Halford, 1999; Simons, Harris, & Willis, 1994; Van Widenfelt, Markman, Guerney, Behrens, & Hosman, 1997). These programs are intended to assist couples to sustain satisfying marriages and so reduce divorce rates (Van Widenfelt et al., 1997). Most relationship education programs are offered by religious and community groups, the content of these programs is often not documented, and the effects of most of these programs have not been evaluated (Halford, 1999; Van Widenfelt et al., 1997). Relationship education programs that have been evaluated empirically have a substantial focus on training couple communication skills (Halford, 1999). For example, the Minnesota Couples Communication Project (Wampler & Sprenkle, 1980), the Guerney Relationship Enhancement Program (Avery, Ridley, Leslie, & Milholland, 1980; Ridley, Jorgensen, Morgan, & Avery, 1982), and the Prevention and Relationship Enhancement Program (PREP; Markman, Stanley, & Blumberg, 1994) all place emphasis upon training couples in communication skills.

The focus on couple communication in relationship education probably reflects a number of factors. For instance, couple communication is seen as a dynamic variable that can be changed (Silliman, Stanley, Coffin, Markman, & Jordan, in press). In addition, communication is perceived by most couples as central to a good relationship (Halford, 2001). Furthermore, it has been claimed that poor couple communication predicts deterioration in relationship satisfaction in the first few years of marriage (for example, Gottman, Coan, Carrere, & Swanson, 1998; Kurdek, 1998; Markman, 1981).

However, the existing literature on the prediction of relationship satisfaction by communication skills has a number of significant limitations. It is true that in several studies, observed deficits in partners' communication during conflict discussions predicted relationship satisfaction (for example, Gottman et al., 1998; Kurdeck, 1998; Markman, 1981). Similarly, observed communication deficits when partners were offering each other social support have also predicted relationship satisfaction (Pasch & Bradbury, 1998). However, in other studies, certain couple communication skills were predicted *by* relationship satisfaction, rather than the reverse (for example, Noller & Feeney, 1994). Among the researchers who found that communication deficits predicted deterioration in relationship satisfaction, the exact communication problems predicting deterioration were inconsistent, and there is controversy over which communication behaviors (if any) may promote sustained relationship satisfaction (Gottman et al., 1998; Stanley, Bradbury, & Markman, 2000).

The mixed findings on the association between communication and changes in relationship satisfaction could reflect a complex interplay of communication with other influences on relationship satisfaction. This complexity makes it difficult to specify communication behaviors that are universally adaptive for couples. For example, the particular communication behaviors associated with relationship satisfaction vary by culture (Halford, Hahlweg, & Dunne, 1990). Moreover, deficits in supportive couple communication predict deterioration of relationship satisfaction primarily in couples who experience high rates of stressful life events (Pasch & Bradbury, 1998). Thus, the extent to which particular couple communication behaviors predict relationship satisfaction varies, depending on the culture in which couples live and the life events they experience.

Relationship education programs that emphasize skills training do not focus exclusively on couple communication; most programs include other content, such as promoting mutual partner support, expressing affection, and having fun (for example, Markman, Stanley, & Blumberg, 1994; Miller, Nunnally, & Wackman, 1975). In the same way that variations in context and life events make it difficult to define generally adaptive communication behaviors, we doubt that it will be possible to define specific, relationship-enhancing behaviors that are generally adaptive for all couples. If we accept that it is difficult to specify particular behaviors that enhance relationships for all couples, then the prediction and promotion of relationship satisfaction and stability need to be focused on a broader concept of what is adaptive for promoting satisfying and stable relationships. We suggest that a useful focus to consider is how effectively people work at their relationship, rather than whether they use specific behaviors.

SELF-REGULATION AND RELATIONSHIP OUTCOMES

The idea of working at a relationship invokes notions of partners attending to the relationship and the influences on that relationship, and engaging in effective action to promote relationship satisfaction. Halford, Sanders, and Behrens (1994) first proposed that relationship self-regulation is a useful means of conceptualizing partners working toward successful couple relationships. The notion of self-regulation has a long history in psychology, and focuses specifically on how people influence their own behavior. There have been several comprehensive formulations of self-control phenomena, and of the role of self-generated events in the regulation of human behavior (Bandura, 1977; 1986; Catania, 1975; Karoly, 1993; Mahoney & Thoreson, 1974; Skinner, 1953). Although several self-control theorists acknowledge the interdependent nature of self-generated and externally imposed influences on behavior, the assumption that individuals can regulate their own behavior remains central to the overall conceptualization of self-regulatory processes. From an intervention perspective, self-regulation is a process whereby individuals are taught skills to modify their own behavior.

Karoly, a pioneer in the field of self-regulation, offers the most comprehensive definition (1993, p. 25) of self-regulation:

Self-regulation refers to those processes, internal and/or transactional, that enable an individual to guide his/her goal-directed activities over time and across changing circumstances (contexts). Regulation implies modulation of thought, affect, behavior, or attention via deliberate or automated use of specific mechanisms and supportive meta-skills. The processes of self-regulation are initiated when routine activity is impeded, or when goal directedness is otherwise made salient (e.g., the appearance of a challenge, the failure of habitual action patterns, etc.).

In this definition, self-regulatory processes are embedded in a social context that not only provides opportunities and limitations for individual self-directedness, but also implies a dynamic reciprocal interchange between the internal and external determinants of human motivation.

Halford et al. (1994) proposed that self-regulation of couple relationships consists of four key metacompetencies: self-appraisal, self-directed goal setting, self-implementation of change, and self-evaluation of change efforts. Self-appraisal of relationship functioning involves being able to describe current relationship functioning, and the major influences on that functioning, in a manner that facilitates relationship maintenance and enhancement. In practice, this means being able to analyze the couple adaptive processes operating in one's relationship, in terms of one's helpful and unhelpful cognitions, affect, and behavior. It also means being able to identify life events, personal characteristics, and contextual variables that influence couple adaptive processes. Examples of poor relationship self-appraisal are the common patterns evident in the interactions of distressed couples, wherein partners ignore the impact of contextual factors and life events on couple adaptive processes, ignore their own behavior within the relationship, and focus on partner-blaming attributions for relationship problems (Bradbury & Fincham, 1990).

The second metacompetency, self-directed goal setting, involves defining specific, actionable goals for change in one's own behavior, based on the self-appraisal of relationship functioning. Self-implementation of change is the process whereby each partner takes active steps to implement their self-defined goals, with the aim of changing future adaptive processes. Finally, self-evaluation is the process by which the individual appraises the extent to which desired behavior changes were achieved, and the extent to which those changes produced the desired relationship changes.

Halford et al. (1994) suggested that interventions to promote successful relationships need to teach people relationship self-regulation, rather than prescribing specific forms of relationships to which couples should conform. Thus, the key distinction between the self-regulation approach to understanding couple relationships and previous models is the emphasis upon satisfied couples having a dynamic changing pattern of interaction produced through self-directed relationship change, rather than engaging in particular relationship behaviors (Halford, 1998).

The first preliminary testing of the relationship self-regulation model was by Osgarby and Halford (1997), who asked individuals to rate their capacity to identify and carry out specific personal behavior changes to correct problems in their relationship. As predicted, partners in distressed relationships reported lower confidence in their ability to identify or change relationship-enhancing behaviors than did partners in nondistressed relationships. However, a major limitation of this study was that measures of self-regulation that had no established psychometric properties were used. Hence, an important step in investigating relationship self-regulation was to develop adequate measures of the construct.

MEASURING RELATIONSHIP SELF-REGULATION

There are several existing measures of self-regulation. In some of these measures, self-regulation is conceptualized as a broad life metacompetency (for example, Rosenbaum, 1980). That is, it is assumed that self-regulation is a general trait, and that the level of self-regulation demonstrated by an individual in one domain (for example, work) is strongly related to self-regulation in other domains (for example, education). However, in several other measures of self-regulation, the focus is on specific domains such as adult learning (Gredler & Schwartz, 1997), or control of addictive behaviors (Werch & Gorman, 1988). These domain-specific measures of self-regulation often have better predictive validity than generic measures of self-regulation (Gredler & Schwartz, 1997). Within the domain of couple relationships, there seem to be some distinctive challenges to the exercising of self-regulation, such as the strength of emotional arousal elicited by one's relationship with a spouse, and the need to appraise the long-term impact of one's behavior on relationship interaction. Consequently, there was a need to develop a measure of relationship self-regulation. We expected that such a measure would show only a modest association with a generic measure of self-regulation.

Development of the Self-Regulation for Effective Relationships Scale (SRERS)

Seven psychologists with extensive experience in couple relationship research and relationship education developed an initial pool of 39 items to reflect Kanfer's (1970) self-regulation framework, as articulated in the context of couples' relationships by Halford et al. (1994). The items were developed to reflect the four key relationship self-regulation metacompetencies: (1) self-appraisal of relationship behavior and influences on the relationship ("I can identify aspects of my behavior in our relationship which could be improved."); (2) setting relationship self-change goals ("I tend to fall back on what is comfortable for me in relationships rather than trying new ways of relating."); (3) implementation of and persistence with change efforts ("I persist with my plans for personal change efforts even in the face of difficulties."); and (4) monitoring and evaluation of change outcomes ("If the way I am approaching change doesn't work, I can usually think of something different to try.").

Collectively, these items are proposed as a measure of relationship self-regulation. For each item, participants rated the extent to which the statement was true of their behavior in their relationship on a 5-point scale from 1 "not true at all" to 5 "very true." Two forms of the Self-Regulation for Effective Relationships Scale (SRERS) were developed (Wilson, Halford, Lizzio, Kimlin, Islen, & Morre, 2001): one for self-assessment (SRERS-Self), and one for partner assessment (SRERS-Partner).

Approximately 200 newly married couples were recruited via a mail-out from the Register of Marriages to couples married in April 1999 in the state of Queensland, Australia. Couples represented a wide range of socioeconomic circumstances and were living in both country and city locations. The couples agreed to participate in a longitudinal study (The Griffith Newlywed Project) of the trajectory of relationship satisfaction over the first five years of marriage. The findings reported here primarily derive from data collected from this cohort in the first two months after marriage and again 12 months later. These and additional findings are described in more detail in Wilson et al. (2001).

The initial pool of 39 items was reduced to 27 items on the basis of pilot testing. We conducted factor analyses separately on the SRERS-Self and SRERS-Partner, using principal axis factoring followed by oblique rotation. Initially this analysis was performed for the male and female responses separately, but the factor structures for the genders were almost identical, so we report the men's and women's responses analyzed together. The factor structures found for the SRERS-Self and SRERS-Partner were nearly identical, with each analysis yielding three factors with exactly the same items loading on those factors. In each case a total of 19 items loaded onto one of the three factors, each of which was internally consistent and theoretically meaningful. The three factors accounted for 46% of the variance in the SRERS-Self and 52% in the SRERS-Partner.

The first factor of the SRERS had 10 items loading onto it, and those items focus on the change strategies used in the relationship. These strategies include goal setting ("I try to apply ideas about effective relationships to improving our relationship."), planning ("I work out practical ways or strategies to achieve the goals I set myself."), implementation of change ("I actually put my intentions or plans for personal change into practice."), responsiveness to partner feedback ("I adjust my goals or strategies for personal change in the light of feedback from my partner."), self-monitoring ("If the way I am approaching change doesn't work, I can usually think of something different to try."), and persistence ("I persist with my plans for personal change efforts even in the face of difficulties."). This factor clearly describes the strategies of self-regulation in couple relationships identified by Halford et al. (1994), and is labeled *self-regulation strategies*.

The second factor had six items loading onto it. These items focused on lack of change effort ("I tend to fall back on what is comfortable for me in relationships rather than trying new ways of relating." and "I tend to put off doing anything about problems in our relationship in the hope that things will get better by themselves."), and lack of persistence in change efforts ("If my partner doesn't appreciate the change efforts I am making, I tend to give up."). This factor was labeled *relationship effort*.

The third factor had three items loading onto it, all of which related to the extent to which partners were clear about the type of relationship they wanted (for example, "I am clear about the type of relationship I want to have with my partner."). This factor was labeled *relationship goals*. The three factors of the SRERS, relationship strategies, effort, and goals, showed low to moderate correlations with each other (*r*s from .28 to .58).

Psychometric Properties of the Self-Regulation for Effective Relationships Scale

The SRERS-Self and SRERS-Partner both show adequate reliability. The Cronbach's alpha was high for each of the individual factors (range of .75 to .86, and .71 to .88, for the self and partner scales respectively), and for the whole scale (.88 and .89 for the self and partner scales respectively). Test-retest reliability of the total score on the SRERS-Self, assessed across a 12-month period on our sample of newlywed couples, was moderate to high for both men ($r = .66$) and women ($r = .67$). Test-retest reliability was somewhat lower for some factor scores, but at least moderate for all factors for both men and women (*r*s from .48 to .65). Given that the first year of marriage is a time of great change in relationships (Noller & Feeney, 1994), finding even moderate stability in relationship self-regulation across this time period is striking. The SRERS-Self and SRERS-Partner showed moderate agreement. Reports of women's self-regulation on the female SRERS-Self and on the male SRERS-Partner were correlated at $r = .54$ ($p < .01$), and men's self-regulation on the male SRERS-Self and on the female SRERS-Partner correlated at $r = .50$ ($p < .01$).

When developing a measure of a new construct like relationship self-regulation, it is important to establish that the construct is actually new, and is not simply an existing construct with a new label. One common criticism of self-report measures is that scores are greatly influenced by mood. Specifically, people with negative mood tend to report less positive self-evaluations regardless of the specific aspect of self that is being asked about. In our sample of newlyweds, depression was assessed on the Depression Anxiety Stress Scale (DASS) (Lovibond & Lovibond, 1995), and showed significant but low negative correlations ($r < .3$) with the SRERS total and with each of the factor scores for both men and women. Thus, the SRERS is not just reflecting mood.

In order to further evaluate the divergent validity of the SRERS from established individual difference measures, we recruited a sample of 73 individuals in committed relationships (Wilson et al., 2001). We assessed these participants on the SRERS-Self, the BL Advanced Test (Australian Council for Educational Research, 1982), which is a widely used brief measure of intelligence, and the NEO Five-Factor Inventory (NEO-FFI: Costa & McCrae, 1992), which is a widely used measure of personality. The SRERS showed no significant association with intelligence, and low association ($r < .35$) with all five personality factors from the NEO-FFI. Thus, self-regulation is clearly different from traditional constructs of intelligence and personality.

There were two constructs that we expected should show a moderate positive association with relationship self-regulation: general self-regulation and emotional intelligence. We had our 73 participants complete the Self-Control Schedule (SCS; Rosenbaum, 1980), which is a measure of generic self-regulation in the solution of behavioral problems. The concept of emotional intelligence, as proposed by Salovey and Mayer (1990), involves the use of emotion-focused information processing in solving problems, and includes effective appraisal of emotion in others, regulation of emotion in self and others, and utilization of emotions in solving interpersonal problems. Given the strong emotions evident in couple relationships, we expected these abilities to show a moderate association with relationship self-regulation. Participants completed the Emotional Intelligence Scale (EIS; Schutte, Malouff, Hall, Heggerty, Cooper, Golden, & Dorheim, 1998), which is based on the model of Salovey and Mayer (1990). As predicted, there were significant, moderate correlations between relationship self-regulation on the SRERS and general self-regulation on the SCS, $r = .51$, $p < .001$, and between the SRERS and emotional intelligence on the EIS, $r = .64$, $p < .001$. Thus, relationship self-regulation shows convergent validity with the related constructs of generic self-regulation and emotional intelligence.

SELF-REGULATION AND RELATIONSHIP SATISFACTION

The key prediction we wanted to test is that relationship self-regulation leads to more satisfying couple relationships. In order to evaluate that prediction, we are following the cohort of newlywed couples in the Griffith Newlywed Project for the first five years of marriage, and are predicting that high relationship self-regulation will predict a stable, high level of relationship satisfaction. As a preliminary test of the association between relationship self-regulation and relationship satisfaction, we examined the concurrent correlation between self-regulation on the SRERS and relationship satisfaction as assessed by the Dyadic

Adjustment Scale (DAS; Spanier, 1976). We did this for data collected at the time of recruitment of the couples, which was just a few months after marriage. We conducted a multiple regression analysis using the three factor scores of the SRERS-Self as predictor variables, and relationship satisfaction as the criterion variable. The equation was significant, accounting for 36% of variance, with all three SRERS factors significantly predicting relationship satisfaction ($p < .001$). We also examined the SRERS as a predictor of change in DAS across the first year of marriage. There was a small mean decrease on the DAS in the first year of marriage for women from 125.5 (SD = 11.5) to 116.4 (SD = 11.5), and for men from 124.6 (SD = 12.8) to 117.2 (SD = 10.5). The extent of change on the DAS was predicted significantly by the SRERS for both men and women, though it only accounted for about 10% of the variance in both genders (Wilson et al., 2001).

As already noted, the concurrent prediction of DAS from the SRERS in the newlywed sample was substantial, accounting for over one third of the variance, but the proportion of variance accounted for in the longitudinal prediction was modest (about 10% of the total variance). However, given the high satisfaction reported in our newlywed sample at the time of marriage, and the modest changes across the first year of marriage, the variance accounted for is probably limited by the restricted range of scores. The crucial test is whether relationship self-regulation predicts the trajectory of relationship satisfaction over a longer period of time, when the satisfaction of the sample can be expected to become more variable.

TEACHING RELATIONSHIP SELF-REGULATION

Assuming relationship self-regulation is a significant influence on relationship outcomes, teaching self-regulation may enhance relationships. This does not mean that all couples would necessarily benefit from education about relationship self-regulation. Many couples have lifelong, mutually satisfying relationships without any formal relationship education. Perhaps some couples learn effective ways to work on their relationship during their individual development, such as through modeling in the family of origin. Alternatively, other couples may have low need for self-regulation because of the influence of other factors on their relationship. For example, if a couple has high social support for their relationship from their extended family and their community, and faces few major life challenges, then there may be limited need for training in how to work on their relationship.

Couples who seem most likely to benefit from enhancement of their relationship self-regulation are those who are at high risk of developing relationship problems in the future, and those who currently have relationship problems. For example, couples in which the woman's parents were divorced, or the man's parents were violent toward each other, have high relationship satisfaction at the time of marriage but are known to have a significantly higher chance than other couples of developing relationship problems later (Halford, Sanders, & Behrens, 2000; Sanders, Halford, & Behrens, 1999). Relationship education with a focus on self-regulation might assist such couples.

Couples who currently have relationship problems may benefit from enhanced relationship self-regulation for at least two reasons. First, most distressed partners inaccurately attribute most, or all, of their relationship problems to their spouse's negative behavior (Bradbury & Fincham, 1990; Fincham & Bradbury, 1992). As they have no direct control over their spouse's behavior, they often feel powerless to produce any change in a distressed relationship (Vanzetti, Notarius, & NeeSmith, 1992). A focus on self-regulation might empower the partners to do something constructive about their relationship. Second, the focus on self-regulation promotes metacompetencies that allow the partners not only to change current problems, but also to produce self-change that enhances the relationship in the future.

Relationship Education

We have developed two different relationship education programs that have a self-regulation focus. In one program, referred to as the Self-Regulation Positive Relationship Education Program (Self-PREP), education is provided in face-to-face groups. Self-PREP was evaluated in a controlled trial (Halford, Sanders, & Behrens, in press). In a second version, known as the Couple Commitment And Relationship Enhancement program (Couple CARE), similar content is covered, but is delivered as a flexible, self-directed learning program. This program involves the couple watching a videotape and undertaking exercises from a guidebook with the assistance of a telephone-based education service. Couple CARE is currently the subject of a controlled trial evaluation.

The content of Self-PREP and Couple CARE falls into six units that are described in detail in Halford (in press) and Halford and Moore (in press), and are summarized in Table 18.1. The initial session is focused on relationship goal setting. To that end, couples develop a shared

Table 18.1. Content of Couple CARE, a Six-Session Relationship Education Program

Module	Detail of Content
1	**Introduction and Goal Setting** Introduction of leader(s) and couple(s); overview of program; rationale for skills-training focus of program; identification of key behavioral domains promoting relationship intimacy; review of relationship expectations, development of relationship goals; intimacy enhancement through self-directed goal setting.
2	**Communication** Review of key communication skills; guided self-evaluation of current communication skills; self-directed selection of communication enhancement goals and practice of implementation of those skills; self-directed goal setting and definition of homework task to enhance communication.
3	**Intimacy** Review of communication homework tasks, self-directed further goal selection and definition of further homework tasks; review of factors promoting intimacy; assessing partner support, expressions of caring, reviewing individual and joint activities; self-directed change plan.
4	**Conflict Management** Review intimacy enhancement tasks; introduction to the concepts of conflict patterns and effective conflict management; negotiation with partner about relationship rules for managing conflict; self-directed goal setting for effective management of conflict; introduction to the concept of flexible gender roles, couple review of current gender roles, self-directed goal setting for future gender role flexibility.
5	**Sexuality** Review of communication homework task; review of the role of sexuality in relationship intimacy; couple discussion and goal setting to enhance sexual intimacy; introduction to the concept of partner support, self-directed goal setting to enhance partner support; self-directed definition of homework tasks to implement selected goals in areas of sexuality or partner support.
6	**Managing Change** Review of homework tasks; self-directed selection of any further goals to enhance relationship functioning; introduction of issue of maintenance of relationship functioning; self-directed identification of future life events impacting upon relationship; planning to promote relationship adaptation to predictable life events. Closure.

relationship goal statement, which we refer to as their "relationship vision." Development of this vision involves having couples discuss a number of dimensions of expectations about relationships, such as the desired degree of closeness versus autonomy in the relationship, gender roles, power and control, and styles of communication. Their vision becomes a basis for developing self-change goals to achieve that vision.

An important element of all skills-based relationship education programs is communication skills training. In our programs, individuals self-select goals for enhancing their own communication from an array of available skills, and evaluate their own, rather than their partner's, communication. In a similar manner, partners are focused upon processes that develop and maintain intimacy in a relationship, such as mutual support, expressions of affection, and shared positive activities, and they develop self-change strategies to enhance intimacy. Conflict management is another important element of relationship education. Once couples have a reasonable level of communication skills, they can use these skills to handle conflict more effectively. As part of the session on conflict management, partners are assisted to identify their usual conflict patterns and to self-select goals that will help them avoid destructive conflict. Sexuality also is a focus of Couple CARE, with partners reviewing their communication about sex, their expectations, and developing self-guided change to enhance sexual expression.

In order to maintain relationship satisfaction over time, couples need to adapt their relationship to changes produced by major life transitions. In Couple CARE, couples rate the likelihood of various life events occurring in the next year, and the likely effect of those changes on their relationship. Couples discuss these effects, and self-select goals to promote relationship-enhancing ways to adapt to these life transitions. For example, a number of couples have identified that they may have reduced time together as a couple once they have children. They then set individual goals, such as ensuring the availability of child minding or cultivating activities they can do at home, that will increase their chance of sharing enjoyable couple activities.

In summary, Self-PREP and Couple CARE focus on developing relationship self-regulation. In common with the original PREP, information is provided about influences on relationships, and relationship skills are trained. In Self-PREP and Couple CARE, couples are also assisted to set relationship goals, to monitor their individual contributions to the relationship, to set self-change goals, and to implement and evaluate self-change.

Turning now to the evidence regarding the effectiveness of relationship education with a focus on self-regulation, Halford et al. (in press) stratified engaged couples into high- and low-risk for relationship distress based on negative family-of-origin experiences, and randomly assigned couples to either Self-PREP or a discussion and information control condition. There was evidence of differential effects of Self-PREP on high- versus low-risk couples. High relationship satisfaction was sustained significantly better in the high-risk couples receiving the Self-PREP than high-risk couples in the control condition, but in the low-risk couples there was no evidence of benefits from Self-PREP on relationship satisfaction. A significant limitation of this study was that self-regulation was not directly assessed. Therefore it was not possible to determine whether the intervention produced changes in self-regulation, or whether such changes mediated the effects of Self-PREP on relationship satisfaction in the high-risk couples.

In ongoing work, we are evaluating the effects of Couple CARE on self-regulation and relationship satisfaction. In a preliminary evaluation of Couple CARE, 34 currently satisfied couples in the early stages of a committed relationship (married or living together for less than three years), completed the Couple CARE program. They were assessed on relationship self-regulation using the SRERS before and after the program. Both self- and partner-reported self-regulation increased across the course of the program, for both male and female participants. In an ongoing randomized controlled trial, we have found that self-regulation increased significantly more in the Couple Care group than in a waitlist control group, and we are currently evaluating whether these increases in self-regulation are associated with sustained relationship satisfaction.

Couple Therapy

Self-Regulatory Couple Therapy (SRCT) is the application of relationship self-regulation theory to relationship problems (Halford, 2001). The emphasis in SRCT is on helping each partner in a distressed relationship to learn metacompetencies to change problematic patterns of behavior, cognition, and affect, and thereby to enhance their relationship. Specifically, the focus is on helping partners develop a number of separate but interconnected metaskills, including relationship appraisal, goal setting, self-change implementation, and evaluation of self-change attempts.

The central concept of SRCT is that partners, not therapists, produce long-term change in couple relationships. Couple therapy is successful to the extent that it engages partners in self-regulated change processes. Self-regulation begins by helping each partner to appraise their relationship, and based on this appraisal, to self-select personal goals for change. This process involves the use of structured assessment, and discussion of assessment results, to help each partner define personal change goals intended to enhance the relationship. For some couples, once the partners are able to define specific personal change goals, they are able to successfully implement these goals. In other words, one implication of the self-regulated approach is that brief couple therapy, usually consisting of assessment and goal setting, can be sufficient to achieve relationship improvement for some couples.

A brief form of self-regulatory couple therapy (SRCT) has been evaluated in two published studies. The authors did not label the first study as involving SRCT, but Worthington, McCullough, Shortz, Mindes, Sandage, & Chartrand (1995) did evaluate the effects of assessment and goal setting on enhancement of couples' relationship functioning. In a randomized controlled trial, they found that assessment, feedback, and goal setting produced significantly greater increases in relationship satisfaction than assessment alone. Couples in the study were only mildly distressed relative to couples in some other couple therapy studies, but the study showed that couples can self-direct improvements in relationship satisfaction.

The second study was a quasiexperimental evaluation of brief SRCT with severely distressed couples (Halford, Osgarby, & Kelly, 1996). In a brief therapy condition, couples undertook a systematic assessment of their relationship across three sessions, which culminated in feedback and goal setting. In the feedback, partners were encouraged to identify specific actions each could take to enhance the relationship. All couples also engaged in some guided reading on how to achieve these goals.

Three months after the assessment and goal-setting sessions, there was a significant increase in relationship satisfaction relative to pretreatment. The increase was of a comparable magnitude to the change in relationship satisfaction reported by couples who had been through a full course of 15 sessions of traditional Behavioral Couple Therapy (Halford, Osgarby, & Kelly, 1996). This study had some significant limitations, notably that couples were not randomly assigned to conditions. However, it was striking that only three sessions of assessment, feedback, and goal setting achieved substantial increases in relationship satisfaction in severely distressed couples.

CONCLUSIONS AND FUTURE DIRECTIONS FOR RESEARCH

In this chapter, we have described a program of research attempting to test the commonsense notion that working on your marriage will improve the quality of that relationship. We used the concept of self-regulation to operationalize in psychological terms what "working on the relationship" means. An initial step in our research was developing a measure of relationship self-regulation: the Self-Regulation for Effective Relationships Scale (SRERS). The SRERS shows good psychometric properties in terms of its theory-consistent factor structure, test-retest reliability, inter-partner agreement, and divergent and convergent validity. As predicted, relationship self-regulation was associated with relationship satisfaction in newlywed couples, and the variance explained was substantial. A modest association was shown with longitudinal change in relationship satisfaction across the first year of marriage. A crucial hypothesis currently being tested is that relationship self-regulation will predict the trajectory of relationship satisfaction in couples over time.

Relationship education that focuses on teaching relationship self-regulation increases relationship self-regulation, and enhances the maintenance of relationship satisfaction in high-risk couples. Brief couple therapy, based on a self-regulation model, produces positive change in distressed couples. However, a major limitation of these intervention studies is a failure to assess whether changes in relationship self-regulation mediate long-term benefits. This question is being tested in ongoing research.

There are several issues about the impact of working on a relationship that merit mention. First, working on a relationship is not a panacea that will guarantee all couples life-long, mutually satisfying relationships. As noted earlier, there are multiple influences on relationship satisfaction and stability, and working on the relationship is only one of these. However, working on the relationship may shift the relationship toward satisfaction for enough couples to make relationship self-regulation a useful construct.

Second, a potential misunderstanding about relationship self-regulation is the misconception that relationships necessitate work *all the time*. As stated in Karoly's (1993) definition, self-regulation is initiated when routine activity is impeded or when goal-directedness is otherwise made salient. In other words, as we argued earlier, times of change and adaptation may necessitate work on a relationship. At other times the relationship may be in a balance that is satisfying for both partners, with little need for self-regulation.

Third, Karoly's definition (1993, p. 25) of self-regulation emphasizes that self-regulation involves both "*deliberate* or *automated* use of specific mechanisms and supportive metaskills." The SRERS is a self-report measure, which implicitly assumes that people are able to report accurately on their use of relationship self-regulation. Perhaps some important relationship self-regulation processes are automatic, and these might not be accurately assessed by self-report. Hence, we have been developing a behavioral measure of relationship self-regulation. In this assessment procedure, we interview partners individually about their relationship over the past six months and what they would like to happen in the next six months. We then rate the frequency of use of self-regulation competencies such as appraisal of the relationship, goal setting, implementation of change, and evaluation of change efforts. In this methodology we sample the frequency with which partners use these self-regulation competencies, rather than asking for ratings of the typical use of the competencies. In ongoing research, we are looking at the convergence between this behavioral measure and the SRERS, and at the prediction of relationship satisfaction by this behavioral measure.

Finally, the concept of relationship self-regulation is focused on the processes by which an individual works on their relationship. That is, the steps of relationship appraisal, goal setting, implementing self-directed change, and evaluating self-change are emphasized. The concept of relationship self-regulation does not address the specific behavior changes that a partner makes through implementation of these steps. While we have argued that it is difficult to define specific behaviors that are generally adaptive in couple relationships, we do not mean to argue that the behavior of partners is irrelevant to sustaining a satisfying relationship.

It is possible that simply working at the relationship will lead to relationship-enhancing behavior change in most couples. Committed couple relationships exist universally across cultures (Buss, 1994), and perhaps most partners have adequate understanding of what broad classes of behavior are required for a good relationship. If this is true, then what is crucial is simply that the partners work at the relationship. Alternatively, there may be considerable individual differences with respect to people's knowledge of what constitutes relationship-enhancing behavior, which we refer to as "relationship wisdom." In a related program of research, the first author, (WKH), is working with a colleague, Jill Smythe, in an attempt to measure relationship wisdom and its association with relationship satisfaction. Perhaps relationship satisfaction is best achieved by a combination of process (working at the relationship, as reflected in relationship self-regulation), and knowledge of what is needed to enhance relationships at crucial times (relationship wisdom).

So, let us return to the original question posed in the title of the chapter. Does working at a relationship work? We have preliminary evidence to suggest that working at a relationship does help, at least for some of the people some of the time. We can reliably measure the extent to which people are working at their relationship. We have found that level of work correlates with relationship satisfaction, and that interventions aimed at increasing the extent of work enhance relationship satisfaction. We hope that the data now being collected will provide more definitive information about the effects of working at a relationship.

REFERENCES

Arp, A., & Arp, D. (2001). The magic of older love: Stoking your marital fires through the years. In J. R. Levine & H. J. Markman (Eds.), *Why do fools fall in love?* (pp. 117–122). San Francisco: Jossey Bass.

Australian Council for Educational Research advanced tests manual. (1982). Hawthorn, Australia: Australian Council for Educational Research.

Avery, A., Ridley, C., Leslie, L., & Milholland, T. (1980). Relationship enhancement with premarital dyads: A six month follow-up. *American Journal of Family Therapy, 8*, 23–30.

Bandura, A. (1977). *Social learning theory.* Englewood Cliffs, NJ: Prentice-Hall.

Bandura, A. (1986). *Social foundations of thought and action: A social cognitive theory.* Englewood Cliffs, NJ: Prentice-Hall.

Belsky, J., & Pensky, E. (1988). Marital change across the transition to parenthood. *Marital and Family Review, 12*, 133–156.

Bradbury, T. N. (1995). Assessing the four fundamental domains of marriage. *Family Relations, 44*, 459–468.

Bradbury, T. N. (Ed.) (1998). *The developmental course of marital dysfunction.* New York: Cambridge University Press.

Bradbury, T. N., Cohan, C. L., & Karney, B. R. (1998). Optimizing longitudinal research for understanding and preventing marital dysfunction. In T. N. Bradbury (Ed.), *The developmental course of marital dysfunction* (pp. 279–311). New York: Cambridge University Press.

Bradbury, T. N., & Fincham, F. D. (1990). Attributions in marriage: Review and critique. *Psychological Bulletin, 107,* 3–33.

Buss, D. M. (1994). *The evolution of desire: Strategies of human mating.* New York: Basic Books.

Cascardi, M., Langhinrichsen, J., & Vivian, D. (1992). Marital aggression: Impact, injury, and health correlates of husbands and wives. *Archives of Internal Medicine, 152,* 1178–1184.

Catania, A. C. (1975). The myth of self-reinforcement. *Behaviorism, 3,* 192–199.

Cordova, J. V., Jacobson, N. S., Gottman, J. M., Rushe, R., & Cox, C. L. (1993). Negative reciprocity and communication in couples with a violent husband. *Journal of Abnormal Psychology, 102,* 559–564.

Costa, P. T., & McCrae, R. R. (1992). *NEO Personality Inventory Professional Manual.* Florida: Psychological Assessment Resources.

Cowan, C. P., & Cowan, P. A. (1992). *When partners become parents.* New York: Basic Books.

De Guilbert-Lantoine, C., & Monnier, A. (1992). La conjoncture demognishique: L'Europe et les pays developpes d'Outre-Mer. *Population, July-August.*

Fincham, F. D., & Bradbury, T. N. (1992). Assessing attributions in marriage: The relationship attribution measure. *Journal of Personality and Social Psychology, 62,* 457–468.

Fowers, B. J., & Olson, D. H. (1986). Predicting marital success with PREPARE: A predictive validity study. *Journal of Marital and Family Therapy, 12,* 403–413.

Glenn, N. D. (1998). The course of marital success and failure in five American 10-year cohorts. *Journal of Marriage and the Family, 60,* 569–576.

Gottman, J. M. (1993). A theory of marital dissolution and stability. Special Section: Families in transition. *Journal of Family Psychology, 7,* 57–75.

Gottman, J. M., Coan, J., Carrere, S., & Swanson, C. (1998). Predicting marital happiness and stability from newlywed interactions. *Journal of Marriage and the Family, 60,* 5–22.

Gredler, M. E., & Schwartz, L. S. (1997). Factorial structure of the self-efficacy for self-regulated learning scale. *Psychological Reports, 81,* 51–57.

Halford, W. K. (1998). The ongoing evolution of behavioral couples therapy: Retrospect and prospect. *Clinical Psychology Review, 18,* 613–633.

Halford, W. K. (1999). *Australian couples in millennium three: A research development agenda for marriage and relationship education.* Canberra: Department of Family and Community Services.

Halford, W. K. (2001). *Brief couple therapy: Helping partners help themselves.* New York: Guilford.

Halford, W. K. (in press). Relationship education in groups: A skills training approach. In T. Patterson (Ed.), *Comprehensive handbook of psychotherapy, volume 2: Cognitive-behavioral-functional approaches.* New York: Wiley.

Halford, W. K., Hahlweg, K., & Dunne, M. (1990). The cross-cultural consistency of marital communication associated with marital distress. *Journal of Marriage and the Family, 52,* 109–122.

Halford, W. K., & Moore, E. M. (in press). Relationship education and the prevention of couple relationship problems. In A. S. Gurman (Ed.), *Clinical handbook of couple therapy (3rd ed.)* New York: Guilford.

Halford, W. K., Osgarby, S. M., & Kelly, A. (1996). Brief behavioural couples therapy: A preliminary evaluation. *Behavioural and Cognitive Psychotherapy, 24,* 263–273.

Halford, W. K., Sanders, M. R., & Behrens, B. C. (1994). Self-regulation in behavioral couples therapy. *Behavior Therapy, 25,* 431–452.

Halford, W. K., Sanders, M. R., & Behrens, B. C. (2000). Repeating the errors of our parents? Family of origin spouse violence and observed conflict management in engaged couples. *Family Process, 39,* 219–235.

Halford, W. K., Sanders, M. R., & Behrens, B. C. (in press). Can skills training prevent relationship problems in at-risk couples? Four-year effects of a behavioral relationship education program. *Journal of Family Psychology.*

Holtzworth-Munroe, A., Smutzler, N., Bates, L., & Sandin, E. (1997). Husband violence: Basic facts and clinical implications. In W. K. Halford & H. J. Markman (Eds.), *Clinical handbook of marriage and couple interventions* (pp. 129–156). Chichester, England: Wiley.

Huston, T. L., McHale, S., & Crouter, A. (1986). When the honeymoon's over: Changes in the marital relationship over the first year. In R. L. Gilmour & S. W. Duck (Eds.), *The emerging field of personal relationships* (pp. 109–132). Hillsdale, NJ: Lawrence Erlbaum Associates.

Jacobson, N. S., Gottman, J. M., Waltz, J., Rushe, R., Babcock, J., & Holzworth-Munroe, A. (1994). Affect, verbal content, and psychophysiology in couples with a violent husband. *Journal of Consulting and Clinical Psychology, 62,* 982–988.

Kanfer, F. H. (1970). Self-regulation: Research, issues and speculations. In C. Neurum & J. L. Michael (Eds.), *Behavior modification in clinical psychology* (pp. 37–62). New York: Appleton Century-Croft.

Karney, B. R., & Bradbury, T. N. (1995). The longitudinal course of marital quality and stability: A review of theory, method and research. *Psychological Bulletin, 118,* 3–34.

Karney, B. R., & Bradbury, T. N. (1997). Neuroticism, marital interaction, and the trajectory of marital satisfaction. *Journal of Personality and Social Psychology, 66,* 413–424.

Karoly, P. (1993). Mechanisms of self-regulation: A systems view. *Annual Review of Psychology, 44,* 23–52.

Kurdeck, L. A. (1998). The nature and predictors of the trajectory of change in marital quality over the first 4 years of marriage for first-married husbands and wives. *Journal of Family Psychology, 12,* 494–510.

Larson, J. H., & Holman, T. B. (1994). Premarital predictors of marital quality and stability. *Family Relations, 43,* 228–237.

Lovibond, S. H., & Lovibond, P. F. (1995). *Manual for the Depression Anxiety Stress Scales.* Sydney: The Psychology Foundation of Australia.

Lucas, J. C. (1997). *Conscious marriage.* Sydney: Simon and Schuster.

Mahoney, M. J., & Thoreson, C. E. (1974). *Power to the person.* Pacific Grove, CA: Brooks/Cole.

Markman, H. J. (1981). The prediction of marital distress: A five-year follow-up. *Journal of Consulting and Clinical Psychology, 49,* 760–762.

Markman, H. J., Stanley, S., & Blumberg, S. L. (1994). *Fighting for your marriage: Positive steps for preventing divorce and preserving a lasting love.* San Francisco: Jossey Bass.

McDonald, P. (1995). *Families in Australia: A socio-demographic perspective.* Melbourne, Australia: Australian Institute of Family Studies.

McLaughlin, I. G., Leonard, K. E., & Senchak, M. (1992). Prevalence and distribution of premarital aggression among couples applying for a marriage license. *Journal of Family Violence, 7,* 309–319.

Miller, S., Nunnally, E., & Wackman, D. (1975). Minnesota Couples Communication Program (MCCP): Premarital and marital groups. In D. Olsen (Ed.), *Treating relationships* (pp. 21–40). Lake Mills, IN: Graphic.

Noller, P., & Feeney, J. A. (1994). Relationship satisfaction, attachment, and nonverbal accuracy in early marriage. *Journal of Nonverbal Behavior, 18,* 199–221.

O'Leary, K. D., Malone, J., & Tyree, A. (1994). Physical aggression in early marriage: Prerelationship and relationship effects. *Journal of Consulting and Clinical Psychology, 6,* 594–602.

Osgarby, S. M., & Halford, W. K. (1997) Rated relationship self-regulation and relationship satisfaction. Unpublished data, Griffith University.

Pasch, L. A., & Bradbury, T. N. (1998). Social support, conflict, and the development of marital dysfunction. *Journal of Consulting and Clinical Psychology, 66,* 219–230.

Ridley, C. A., Jorgensen, S. R., Morgan, A. C., & Avery, A. W. (1982). Relationship enhancement with premarital couples: An assessment of effects on relationship quality. *American Journal of Family Therapy, 10,* 41–48.

Rogge, R. D., & Bradbury, T. N. (1999). Till violence does us part: The differing roles of communication and aggression in predicting adverse marital outcomes. *Journal of Consulting and Clinical Psychology, 67,* 340–351.

Rosenbaum, M. (1980). A schedule for assessing self-control behaviors: Preliminary findings. *Behavior Therapy, 11,* 109–121.

Salovey, P., & Mayer, J. D. (1990). Emotional intelligence. *Imagination, Cognition and Personality, 9,* 185–211.

Sanders, M. R., Halford, W. K., & Behrens, B. C. (1999). Parental divorce and premarital couple communication. *Journal of Family Psychology, 13,* 60–74.

Sanders, M. R., Nicholson, J. M., & Floyd, F. (1997). Couples relationships and children. In W. K. Halford & H. J. Markman (Eds.), *Clinical handbook of marriage and couples interventions* (pp. 225–254). Chichester, England: Wiley.

Schutte, N. S., Malouff, J. M., Hall, L. E., Haggerty, D. J., Cooper, J. T., Golden, C. J., & Dorheim, L. (1998). Development and validation of a measure of emotional intelligence. *Personality and Individual Differences, 25,* 167–177.

Shapiro, A. F., Gottman, J. M., & Carerre, S. (2000). The baby and the marriage: Identifying factors that buffer against decline in marital satisfaction after the first baby arrives. *Journal of Family Psychology, 14,* 59–70.

Silliman, B., Stanley, S. M., Coffin, W., Markman, H. J., & Jordan, P. L. (in press). Preventive interventions for couples. In H. Liddle, D. Santisteban, R. Levant, & J. Bray (Eds.), *Family psychology intervention science.* Washington, DC: APA Publications.

Simons, M., Harris, R., & Willis, P. (1994). *Pathways to marriage: Learning for married life in Australia.* Adelaide, Australia: Centre for Research in Education and Work, University of South Australia.

Skinner, B. F. (1953). *Science and human behavior.* New York: Macmillan.

Spanier, G. B. (1976). Measuring dyadic adjustment: New scales for assessing the quality of marriage and similar dyads. *Journal of Marriage and the Family, 37,* 63–275.

Stanley, S. M., Bradbury, T. N., & Markman, H. J. (2000). Structural flaws in the bridge from basic research on marriage to interventions for couples: Illustrations from Gottman, Coan, Carrere, and Swanson (1998). *Journal of Marriage and the Family, 62,* 256–264.

Straus, M. A., & Gelles, R. (1986). Societal change and change in family violence from 1975 to 1985 as revealed by two national surveys. *Journal of Marriage and the Family, 48,* 465–479.

Van Widenfelt, B., Markman, H. J., Guerney, B., Behrens, B., & Hosman, C. (1997). Prevention of relationship problems. In W. K. Halford & H. J. Markman (Eds.), *Clinical handbook of marriage and couples interventions* (pp. 651–678). Chichester, England: Wiley.

Vanzetti, N. A., Notarius, C. I., & NeeSmith, D. (1992). Specific and generalized expectancies in marital interaction. *Journal of Family Psychology, 6,* 171–183.

Veroff, J., Douvan, E., Orbuch, T. L., & Acitelli, L. K. (1998). Happiness in stable marriages: The early years. In T. N. Bradbury (Ed.), *The developmental course of marital dysfunction* (pp. 152–179). New York: Cambridge University Press.

Wampler, K. S, & Sprenkle, D. (1980). The Minnesota couple communication program: A follow-up study. *Journal of Marriage and the Family, 42,* 577–585.

Werch, C. E., & Gorman, D. R. (1988). Relationship between self-control and alcohol consumption patterns and problems of college students. *Journal of Studies on Alcohol, 49,* 1, 30–37.

Wilson, K. L., Halford, W. K., Lizzio, A., Kimlin, S., Islen, G., & Morre, E. M. (2001). Measuring how couples work at their relationship: The Self-Regulation for Effective Relationships Scale. Paper submitted for publication. Griffith University, Brisbane, Australia.

Worthington, E. L., McCullough, M. E., Shortz, J. L., Mindes, E. J., Sandage, S. J., & Chartrand, J. M. (1995). Can couples assessment and feedback improve relationships? Assessment as a brief relationship enrichment procedure. *Journal of Counseling Psychology, 42,* 466–475.

CONCLUSIONS

Conclusions

Like fingerprints, all marriages are different.

—G. B. Shaw

The study of marriage has advanced significantly over the last two decades, with new theories and methodologies coming to the fore. In this book, we have assembled some of the most innovative and creative work in this area, and the studies represent a broad sample of the latest research. The contributions shed new light on the characteristics of couples' day-to-day interactions, together with their attempts to negotiate major problems and transitions.

THEORETICAL PERSPECTIVES

The studies of marriage presented in this book come from a range of theoretical perspectives. This theoretical underpinning is a major strength, allowing researchers and clinicians to develop and test specific predictions about the nature of interaction processes and their effects on marital outcomes.

Attachment Theory

Attachment theory provides a guiding framework for the research by Simpson and his colleagues, and is also discussed in a number of other chapters. This theory highlights the importance of the bond between marital partners and the implications of earlier relationship experiences for the success of their couple relationships. This focus on intimate relationships as attachment relationships comes from the work of Hazan and Shaver (1987), who explored the relevance of attachment history and attachment security to adult romantic love. According to this perspective, attachment behavior is a normal part of romantic involvements, and these relationships play a central role in meeting partners' needs for comfort and security.

As Simpson and his colleagues note, attachment issues are likely to be particularly salient at the transition to parenthood, as the couple relationship needs to accommodate a new and highly dependent family member. Where either partner has basic insecurities about the relationship, dealing with the many tasks and changes that arise as a result of the birth of a child is likely to be difficult. The data presented by Simpson support this contention, and point particularly to the difficulties experienced by new mothers who are anxious about their couple relationship and who perceive their partner as providing insufficient support.

Other researchers explore attachment security as one of several factors likely to affect relationship processes. For example, Feeney and Noller argue that attachment security is important to the successful negotiation of the division of household labor during the transition to parenthood. Results of their study indicate that husbands' insecurity was associated with dissatisfaction with wives' involvement in household tasks. On the other hand, when wives were dissatisfied with husbands' involvement in household tasks, husbands became more insecure across the transition period. This latter finding is important because it illustrates how working models of attachment can be influenced by relationship experiences, particularly during major transitions. Similarly, Clark and her colleagues point to attachment insecurity as one factor that may affect a couple's risk for abandoning a communal norm in favor of alternative norms such as equity, exchange, or self-interest. Given that the communal norm seems the most effective in terms of maintaining a sense of mutual caring, attachment security is likely to play a key role in shaping successful relationships.

Rather than focusing on individual differences in attachment security, L. J. Roberts and Greenberg discuss the four functions of attachment behavior: proximity-seeking, safe haven, separation protest, and secure base. Their work shows that, when spouses are asked to talk about love or other positive feelings they have for one another, their disclosures clearly reflect these four functions. In other words, the marital relationship has the potential to provide a sense of comfort and security that promotes effective involvement not only in the relationship, but also in other activities.

The work of Story and her colleagues focuses on the intergenerational transmission of relationship difficulties, a perspective that acknowledges the important role of attachment processes. Both divorce and destructive patterns of conflict in the family of origin have been implicated as risk factors for relationship breakdown. Although these factors are not amenable to change, Story et al. explore aspects of couple interaction that mediate the negative effects of family-of-origin experiences.

Theories of the Self in Relationships

A range of other theoretical perspectives are also examined in this book. Several of these perspectives emphasize perceptions of the self, and how these are shaped by relationship experiences. Neff and Karney, for example, discuss perceptions of the self in terms of the motives for self-enhancement and self-verification. They argue that, although these motives are often seen as being in opposition to each other, both motives may operate simultaneously in close relationships such as marriage. In particular, the relative importance of each motive is likely to depend on whether the partner's feedback is being given at a global (overall worth) or specific (strengths and weaknesses) level.

Another theoretical perspective that focuses on the self is Self Evaluation Maintenance, which explores the link between perceptions of the self and perceptions of the partner, particularly in terms of areas of expertise involved in the relationship. Beach and his colleagues suggest that, by openly exploring each other's strengths and weaknesses, relationship partners can define areas in which they take leadership roles, support roles, or shared roles. Rather than couples relying on gender stereotypes, this process is likely to help them make the best use of partners' individual skills and abilities, and minimize destructive forms of competition.

Taking a totally different perspective on the self, Aron and his colleagues argue that the excitement associated with falling in love is due, in large part, to the "expansion of the self" created by incorporating aspects of the partner into the self concept. In other words, discovering novel aspects of the partner enables the individual to increase his or her own resources and perspectives. This self-expansion process is at its peak in the early stages of a relationship when everything is new, but is prone to habituation over the long term. These researchers claim that by engaging in novel and challenging activities together, couples can minimize the decline of passion in their relationship.

Theories of Interaction Processes

Several chapters focus on theories that particularly emphasize the nature of couple interaction processes. The work of Rusbult and her colleagues is based on interdependence theory, which describes the ways in which relationship partners manage the complex interactions central to their ongoing relationship. For example, their work addresses such issues as accommodation to the partner's negative behavior, and willingness to sacrifice when partners' interests conflict. These issues are particularly important in the context of norm violation and betrayal. Although high levels of interdependence are present throughout the lifecycle of marriage, the ability to negotiate roles and accommodate to partner behavior is particularly crucial for elderly couples where one spouse is totally dependent on the other. Edwards and Noller use Communication Accommodation Theory to explore the ways in which these couples deal with issues of conflict. L. J. Roberts and her colleagues note the tendency for researchers to concentrate on the study of negative marital processes, and these researchers redress this imbalance by documenting spouses' attempts at increasing their intimacy and expressing positive feelings.

MULTIPLE MEASURES AND METHODS

As we noted at the beginning of this chapter, the theoretical underpinnings evident throughout this book generate a variety of frameworks for testing predictions about marital processes. One of the highlights of the research presented in this book is the multimethod approach adopted by many of the research groups. The use of multiple methods enables the inevitable weaknesses of any one method to be offset by the strengths of another, and generally provides a more complete understanding of the phenomena of interest.

For example, Feeney and Noller used questionnaires to tap a range of general perceptions of individual and couple functioning, together with structured diary records that provided detailed accounts of partners' day-to-day involvement in household tasks. Diaries can be very useful for collecting data about marital behaviors as they occur, rather than having participants try to "average" the frequencies of these behaviors across a longer period of time. Aron and his colleagues combined surveys with laboratory and field experiments: The field experiment functions to deal with the problems of ecological validity inherent in laboratory experiments, while retaining the emphasis on establishing causal direction. Noller and N. D. Roberts collected physiological measures as couples engaged in a videotaped interaction, as well as having the interactions evaluated both by the participants and by trained coders. They then used time-series analysis to assess the temporal associations between anxiety/arousal and specific emotions and behaviors.

Coding Interaction

In terms of methodological advances, a number of the researchers have developed specific schemes for coding the particular aspects of marital interaction that are the focus of their research. Sillars and his colleagues developed the Interaction Cognition Coding Scheme to analyze partners' thoughts during discussions of areas of disagreement in the marriage. In the study reported in this chapter, partners were required to watch a video replay of their interaction and to report on their thoughts every 20 seconds. These thoughts were then coded according to the emphasis on own or partner's emotion, appraisal of issues being discussed, attributions and personal evaluations, and aspects of the communication process. One of the strengths of this coding scheme is that it can highlight "punctuation differences" in interaction, whereby each partner may have a different attentional focus and draw different conclusions about the nature of the interaction.

L. J. Roberts and her colleagues developed the Intimate Interaction Coding System to describe the process of vulnerable disclosure and responsive caregiving. Although these researchers are still in the process of developing a microanalytic coding system for this purpose, the current chapter presents a thematic analysis that highlights the great variety in partners' approaches to intimate interactions. For example, responses to a partner's expressions of positive feeling can range from care and validation to intrusive advice and behaviors that undermine the partner's status or worth.

Vangelisti and Alexander developed a system for coding the strategies that partners use to cope with instances of disappointment in the relationship. This coding system was drawn from an inductive analysis of face-to-face interviews with adults involved in long-term couple relationships. The resulting coping strategies emphasize both behaviors and the expression of emotions, and again illustrate the wide variety in relationship behavior. For example, three of the strategies explicitly deal with psychological hurt, but vary in terms of the focus on either the individual's own hurt or anguish, intentional attempts to hurt or punish the partner, or attempts to punish a third party who is seen as responsible for the disappointment.

Each of these three groups of researchers provides a detailed description of their coding schemes. These coding schemes are likely to act as a springboard for further research, and to increase our understanding of the complexity and variety of marital processes.

Methodologies from Other Fields

Another interesting feature of some of the research presented in this book is the use of methodologies that have traditionally been applied in vastly different areas of study. For example, Schweinle and Ickes use a signal detection paradigm to assess the level of bias of violent men toward inferring criticism and rejection from women. Signal detection methods have been widely used in cognitive psychology and have the important advantage of distinguishing between bias and poor discrimination. In their study of power in marriage, Gottman and his colleagues provide a novel definition of power, based on mathematical modeling of marital interaction. In this approach, power is defined as the ability of one partner's affect to influence the other's subsequent affect. Mathematical modeling has been used widely in the biological sciences and, when applied to marital interaction, provides an analysis of what happens as each partner begins influencing the other in particular ways. Again, these creative approaches to methodology are likely to act as an impetus for further research in these areas.

IMPORTANT THEMES

Several important themes emerge from the work reported in this book. Specifically, the chapters highlight the inextricable links between cognition, emotion and behavior, the need to examine systematic differences in spouses' perceptions of their marital interaction, the importance of studying relationships during times of transition, and the significance of maintaining and supporting healthy couple relationships.

Links between Cognition, Emotion, and Behavior

One important theme that runs through the chapters concerns the strong links among cognition, emotion, and behavior. In other words, relationship behavior can not be studied in isolation because it is affected so strongly by the way that events are interpreted and by the associated emotions.

For example, Noller and N. D. Roberts focus on the temporal link between own and partner's emotion and behavior, demonstrating the role of emotion in generating communication behavior, particularly in violent relationships. Similarly, a key feature of the work of Gottman and his colleagues is the exploration of the relative effects of positive and negative affect on couple interaction, highlighting particularly the strong link between affect and behavior when couples are involved in power struggles. In contrast to these two chapters, L. J. Roberts and Greenberg focus on the role of positive interactions in maintaining relationship satisfaction. In this work, the strong link between affect and behavior is further indicated in the coding of spouses' attempts at intimacy: Codes such as validation, vulnerable, and contempt are regarded as "behavior codes," but are heavily affect laden.

Other researchers have designed studies that integrate all three aspects of relating: cognition, emotion, and behavior. For example, Manusov explores spouses' attributions for their partner's nonverbal behavior and the impact of these attributions on their own emotional reactions and nonverbal behavior. Vangelisti and Alexander explore spouses' emotional and behavioral responses to instances of violated standards and expectations, illustrating the complexity of coping strategies and their links with both previous and future relationship experiences. Similarly, Rusbult and her colleagues emphasize the central role of cognitive processes in spouses' responses to betrayal and rejection; when spouses reframe these events more positively, they tend to feel less anger and hurt, and are less likely to engage in retaliatory behavior. A different integrative approach is taken by Sillars and his colleagues; in this study, behaviors occurring during videotaped couple interactions were used as stimuli to elicit spouses' thoughts and feelings. Again, this work highlights the importance of studying both observable behavior and underlying cognitions and emotions.

Spouses' Perceptions of Marital Interaction: Understanding the Differences

Earlier literature on marital interaction tended to adopt one of two extreme positions with regard to similarities and differences between the perceptions of the two relationship partners. On the one hand, many researchers tended to assume that either partner could provide the information they were seeking, and that, because a single relationship was involved, each partner would provide a similar perspective. Consequently, these researchers would generally focus on only one spouse; for example, early studies of the transition to parenthood tended to obtain reports from women only. If researchers from this tradition did sample both spouses, they tended to assume that any differences in their reports reflected "error," and were of no intrinsic interest.

On the other hand, some researchers adopted a very different position, arguing that every marriage involves two fundamentally divergent perspectives: "his" and "hers." These researchers have taken the view that, because of biological and environmental factors, men and women have very different expectations of relationships and different perceptions of relationship events. One of the disadvantages of this position is that differences between the sexes are seen as inevitable and immutable.

The research presented in this book suggests the importance of moving beyond both of these extreme positions. It is increasingly clear that researchers and practitioners need to understand both partners' differing perspectives as representing equally valid sources of information about the relationship. Further, these differing perspectives cannot be understood simply in terms of gender differences; several studies reported in this volume suggest that other types of roles are equally, if not more, important than gender per se.

Sillars and his colleagues, for example, illustrate the very different perspectives that each spouse can adopt on the same conflict interaction. That is, on the surface they can appear to be talking about the same issue, but one may be thinking about the issue itself, whereas the other may be appreciating the partner's validation and support or, alternatively, focusing on a negative aspect of the partner's behavior or personality. Similarly, in their discussion of spouses' reactions to betrayal and rejection, Rusbult et al. note that "victims" and "perpetrators" tend to perceive these events in very different, and largely self-serving, ways. These role-related differences can, themselves, create further conflict and misunderstanding. The chapter by Eldridge and Christensen focuses on conflict patterns in marriage and also demonstrates the value of integrating gender differences and role differences (conceptualized in terms of which partner is seeking change on an issue). If the husband's issues are generally solved more effectively, gender-linked patterns of demand and withdraw (involving wife demand and husband withdrawal) are likely to become more marked over the course of the relationship.

As other authors point out, differences in spousal perspectives are not confined to conflict situations. With regard to spousal care giving, Edwards and Noller's work shows that, although caregivers' intentions are generally positive, they can give rise to behaviors that those in the role of carereceiver perceive as patronizing or frustrating. For example, caregivers' attempts to avoid distressing their spouse may be seen as reflecting on the carereceiver's competence. Moreover, as L. J. Roberts and Greenberg illustrate, marital partners can respond very differently, even in situations that focus explicitly on intimacy and supportive exchanges.

The Importance of Relationship Transitions

Several of the chapters in this volume deal with important transitions in marriage. Because of the extent of change that often occurs in relationships at these times, studying these transitions can provide a window on how couples negotiate new stages and issues in their relationships. The research presented in these chapters examines the relationship processes involved in this negotiation, and explores factors that predict differences in relationship outcomes.

Both Simpson et al. and Feeney and Noller take the view that the transition to parenthood is likely to make attachment issues highly salient. Further, because attachment security is closely linked to patterns of support, care giving, and communication in relationships, there is likely to be a complex interplay between these variables. The results reported by these researchers support this proposition, showing that attachment insecurity is linked with negative perceptions of partners' practical and emotional support, and with a more difficult transition. Their data also highlight the need to consider the transition to parenthood as a process in which both partners are intimately involved, and to recognize the implications that the difficulties experienced by one spouse have for the adjustment of the other, and for the couple relationship. The crucial nature of the transition to parenthood is also acknowledged by other researchers, who point to this period as a time of increasing traditionalization of roles (Vangelisti and Alexander), and a time when couples may be at risk of departing from a communal norm (Clark et al.).

At a much later stage in marriage, issues of providing care for an ill or disabled spouse may arise. This transition represents the ultimate dependence of one spouse on the other, and can involve a complete loss of autonomy. Edwards and Noller's data suggest that communication is a key factor in the successful negotiation of this transition, and that attempts by caregivers to avoid contentious issues in order to protect the partner can interfere with the goal of promoting understanding between themselves and their spouses.

Maintaining and Supporting Healthy Relationships

Given the high rates of separation and divorce in western societies, the task of maintaining and supporting healthy relationships is clearly an important one for couples themselves, and for clinicians trying to help couples deal with their issues. Conflict is inevitable in close relationships, and we have already seen that spouses may hold quite different perceptions of their interactions and may also become involved in protracted power struggles. Moreover, these effects can be exacerbated by the high levels of emotionality that often characterize disagreements between spouses.

All of these issues underline the importance of spouses developing and maintaining effective relationship skills. One broad group of skills that emerges from several chapters involves the ability to perceive one's own and one's partner's communication in relationship-enhancing ways. In particular, negative distortions of partners' intentions can contribute to the escalation of conflict and have very negative implications for relationships.

For example, Schweinle and Ickes explore the issue of whether abusive men over attribute criticism and rejection to women's thoughts and feelings. Their results suggest that the tendency to be overly sensitive to rejection can cloud spouses' perceptions of their partner's intentions, and drive responses that lead to conflict and violence. Similarly, the data reported by Sillars et al. point to spouses' frequent lack of awareness of the complexity and potential ambiguity of their communication. When discussing conflict issues, spouses tend to focus on their own perspective and to engage in minimal relationship-level thinking. These tendencies seem to be exacerbated when spouses have been drinking, presumably because alcohol interferes with the ability to make complex judgments. The importance of decoding ability is also illustrated by the work of Manusov, who explores how spouses' perceptions of their partner's nonverbal behavior affect their own expressive displays. Attributions that reflect a positive view of the relationship tend to lead to positive behaviors and emotional expressions.

Another broad set of skills (not unrelated to those already mentioned) centers on the constructive resolution of conflict. Several of the chapters (Eldridge and Christensen; Gottman et al.; Noller and N. D. Roberts; Story et al.) point to the importance of spouses' being able to prevent conflict from escalating. Although the main focus of Story et al.'s chapter is on the effects of negativity and divorce in the family of origin, they explore potential mediators between these factors and marital outcomes. Their results highlight the negative effects of physical aggression, psychological aggression, and couple negativity on later stability and satisfaction. As Gottman's work on the study of power and violence illustrates, it is important that spouses try to maintain a positive emotional climate even when discussing conflict issues, rather than being caught up in a cycle of negative reciprocity.

Similarly, in their study of temporal linkage, Noller and N. D. Roberts focus on the different responses of violent and nonviolent couples to their own anxiety/arousal and to their partner's behavior. Their findings highlight the need for spouses, particularly those prone to violence, to avoid becoming "hooked" into each other's negativity; to this end, the use of withdrawal may be judicious in some contexts. On the other hand, Eldridge and Christensen's work on the demand-withdraw pattern shows that in general, relationships benefit when spouses are prepared to discuss conflict issues as they arise, and respond to each other's requests for change. Collectively, the findings from these research projects emphasize the importance of several skills related to conflict management: making clear requests for change when needed, choosing the appropriate time for dealing with conflict, maintaining a positive relational climate, and using assertive (rather than aggressive or defensive) behavior.

A variety of other relationship skills are discussed by contributors to this book. Halford and his colleagues discuss the construct of self-regulation, which they define as the ability to modify one's own behavior in relationship-enhancing ways. This construct includes such skills as setting relationship goals, self-evaluating and improving communication patterns, promoting expressions of intimacy and caring, and negotiating rules for conflict management. Beach's analysis of relationship identities suggests that another important skill is that of defining each partner's roles and abilities, and working out ways to use this expertise to the benefit of the relationship. They refer to this process as "niche-building," and see it as highly adaptive for individuals and their relationships. Neff and Karney discuss the type of feedback that shows both respect and understanding of the partner, and enhances relationship quality. Specifically, they showed the benefits of spouses affirming one another at the global level, while being aware of one another's specific strengths and weaknesses. The studies reported by Aron et al. suggest a very different approach to relationship skills, highlighting the benefit of couples learning the value of participating in self-expanding activities. These activities allow couples to share novel and challenging experiences that increase their positive feelings about each other and about their relationship.

The work presented in this book also highlights characteristics that are crucial to the success of long-term relationships, such as trust and commitment. For example, Clark focuses on trust as a necessary prerequisite to partners adhering to a communal norm; trust is essential in this context, because adopting a communal norm requires that couples take a long-term perspective on the reciprocity of benefits provided by the relationship. Rusbult et al. also focus on relationship norms, but in terms of the *violation* of norms and relationship rules. These researchers note that high levels of trust are likely to promote more benign interpretations of these relationship events, and more constructive approaches to reconciliation and forgiveness. Similarly, commitment to the relationship encourages spouses to reframe their understandings of acts of betrayal in terms of long-term relationship goals, and hence to respond more constructively to situations that might otherwise lead to relationship breakdown.

The chapters also have implications for practitioners working with couples, in terms of suggesting areas where intervention can be useful. As we have already noted, Story et al. discuss the risk factors of negativity and divorce in the family of origin, together with factors that mediate the effects of these experiences on marital outcomes. Although it is not possible to change individuals' family-of-origin experiences, Story et al. note the possibility of developing programs specifically designed to help young couples whose family backgrounds increase their vulnerability to marital distress. In particular, they emphasize the need to reduce partners' displays of aggression, anger, and contempt during couple interaction.

As we noted earlier, Halford and his colleagues also discuss intervention processes, particularly emphasizing the need to teach spouses "self-regulation." In fact, they argue that these skills are more important than specific communication skills because they provide spouses with the ability to set relationship goals and develop strategies that will help them meet these goals. In their chapter, they report on the development of a measure of self-regulation, as well as intervention programs designed to help couples work at their relationship in effective ways.

CONCLUDING REMARKS

The studies outlined in this book represent a range of theoretical perspectives and are based on sophisticated, and often innovative, methodologies. Although the findings highlight the complexity of marital interaction, they also extend our understanding of the factors and processes that promote satisfying and stable marriages. As such, we anticipate that the findings will stimulate new and exciting research directions, as well as guide the development of programs of education and intervention.

REFERENCE

Hazan, C., & Shaver, P. R. (1987). Romantic love conceptualized as an attachment process. *Journal of Personality and Social Psychology, 52,* 511–524.

Index

abstraction
  enhancement at higher levels of, 45
  levels of, 91
  negative criticism at lower levels of, 53
  self-perceptions (views) and, 33–34, 42–43, 49
abusive men, 286
  anger evoked by, 243–44, 245, 246
  anxious/fearful attachment in, 234, 242, 244
  clinical intervention for, 246, 247
  content accuracy of, 240t, 241–42
  discrimination of, 238
  emotional trigger of abuse in, 243–44
  empathic accuracy (decoding) by, 231–35
  empathic accuracy, inaccuracy, bias and, 232–33, 235, 238–39, 240t, 246–47
  enhanced accuracy for actual criticism/rejection of, 233–35
  future research implications for, 243–47
  insensitivity of, 232
  lack of intimacy in relationships of, 232
  nonviolent *vs.*, 237, 299–301, 531
  overattribution bias/effect of, 235, 239, 240t, 241, 242, 243, 244, 245, 246–47

perceptions of partners of, 230
power lack compensated by aggression in, 300
rejection and negative reactions by, 198–99, 229, 232–33, 241, 242, 244, 245, 247
research, empathic accuracy and, 235–42
self-reporting of, 237
sensitivity/vigilance of, 233–34, 244, 245
social skill deficits in, 231–35, 246, 247
types of, 244–46, 301, 326
verbal *vs.* physical abuse by, 237, 246
wife and, 198–99, 229, 232–33, 234, 241, 242
accommodation, 253, 272, 273
accuracy
  content, 240t, 242, 247
  empathic, 161, 235–42, 240t, 246–47
  selective, 230, 235
  thematic, 235, 237–42, 240t, 247
Acitelli, L., 93, 121, 296, 499
active listening, 138
active understanding, 132, 133t, 135, 137, 138
Adams, S. H., 204, 291
admiration, 139, 140, 144, 145
Adult Attachment Questionnaire, 396